THE HOME HANDYMAN'S HELPFUL HINTS

READER'S DIGEST

THE HOME HANDYMAN'S HELPFUL HINTS

READER'S DIGEST • AUCKLAND, CAPE TOWN, LONDON, NEW YORK, SYDNEY

THE HOME HANDYMAN'S HELPFUL HINTS

CONTRIBUTORS

Designers
Virginia Wells Blaker
Joan Gramatte
Marta Strait

Art Production Coordinator
Jessica Mitchell

Copy Editor
Katherine G. Ness

Associate Editor
Tracy O'Shea

Indexer
Sidney Wolfe Cohen

Writers
Thomas Christopher
Mark Feirer
Wade A. Hoyt
Laura Tringali

Researcher
Willard Lubka

Artists
Sylvia Bokor
Ron Chamberlain
Tracey Cox
Mario Ferro
Tony Kentuck
Don Mannes
Robert Steimle

Proofreader
Ron Buck

Consultants

Charles Avoles
Roy Barnhart
Steven Beatty
Don Bunting
Bob Buteyn
Phil Englander
Dora Galitzki
Warwick Geering
Allan R. Hildenbrand
Thor Johanneson
Jim McCann
Tim McCreight
Dieter Mylius
Americo Napolitano
Ian Neeson
Kathleen Poer
Evan Powell
Meryl Prichard-O'Rourke
Dee Quigley
John Ronk
Mark Russo
Stanley H. Smith, Ph.D.
Jay Stein
Peter de Waart
Paul Weissler
Brian Woodward
Tom Zera

First edition
Published by Reader's Digest (Australia) Pty Ltd
26–32 Waterloo Street, Surry Hills, NSW 2010
Copyright © 1996 Reader's Digest (Australia) Pty Ltd
Copyright © 1996 Reader's Digest (New Zealand) Ltd
Copyright © 1996 Reader's Digest Association
Far East Ltd
Philippine Copyright 1996 Reader's Digest Association
Far East Ltd

Printed and bound by Toppan Printing Company (S)
Private Ltd, Singapore

**National Library of Australia
cataloguing-in-publication data:**

The home handyman's helpful hints : quick and easy
solutions, time-saving tips, tricks of the trade.

   1st ed.
   Includes index.
   ISBN 0 86449 007 0

1. Dwellings–Maintenance and repair–Amateurs' manuals.
2. Repairing–Amateurs' manuals–Do-it-yourself work.
I. Reader's Digest (Australia).
643.7

> **Warning**
> All do-it-yourself activities involve a degree
> of risk. Skills, materials, tools and site condi-
> tions vary widely. Although the editors have
> made every effort to ensure accuracy, the
> reader remains responsible for the selection
> and use of tools, materials and methods.
> Always obey local codes and laws, follow
> manufacturers' operating instructions, and
> observe safety precautions.

ABOUT THIS BOOK

This is a do-it-yourself guide with a difference. Unlike most how-to manuals, it doesn't set out to show you how to carry out complex projects. Rather, it has something different to offer. Within its pages are thousands of nuggets of information that make up a treasure trove of hints, tips and tricks of the trade. These priceless gems will make your do-it-yourself jobs easier and quicker, and will save you time, money and effort. And what's more, they'll help you not once but over and over again.

The inspiration for this book came from our readers. Over the years, hundreds of enthusiastic do-it-yourselfers have sent in clever solutions to the many vexing problems they encountered in carrying out projects around the house and in the workshop, garden and garage. More than half of the 2000 lively hints and tips described in the following pages are based on ideas that readers submitted. In preparing this book we, the editors, sorted through the suggestions, weighing each in turn. We were on the lookout for ideas that are truly ingenious and practical, ideas that save time and work, ideas that are likely to cause you to exclaim, 'Why didn't I think of that!' And applying these same criteria, we have rounded out the ideas selected with hints and tips from other sources to produce a genuinely helpful combination of quick and easy solutions, tricks of the trade and timesaving tips.

THE HOME HANDYMAN'S HELPFUL HINTS contains 11 chapters. The first three cover the fundamentals: Basic Tools and Equipment, Workshop Organisation and Workshop Skills. The next five chapters concentrate on tips that help you upgrade your home and make it a better place to live in: Household Storage, Home Improvements, Paint and Wallcoverings, Home Systems (electricity, plumbing, heating and cooling) and Household Repairs. Then there's a chapter on Backyard and Garden and one on Car and Garage. The final chapter, More Hints, is a miscellany of tips and tricks on a variety of subjects, a bonanza of ingenious suggestions that were just too good to leave out.

In addition to the hints and tips, you'll find dozens of special boxes that will help you work more safely, keep your home healthy and select the best tools for a job. Longer features show you, step by step, the best way to perform basic do-it-yourself tasks, such as repairing a window screen or mending a fence. The Recycling Directory at the back of the book is especially helpful in these days of environmental awareness. It lists alphabetically the items that we often throw out or tuck away, and it leads you to hints that show you how to reuse these items instead of just consigning them to a tip.

We hope you will enjoy reading and using this book as much as we enjoyed gathering this collection of remarkable hints and tips for you.

— The Editors

CONTENTS

CHAPTER 1

BASIC TOOLS AND EQUIPMENT

DRILLS AND DRILL BITS

Drilling basics

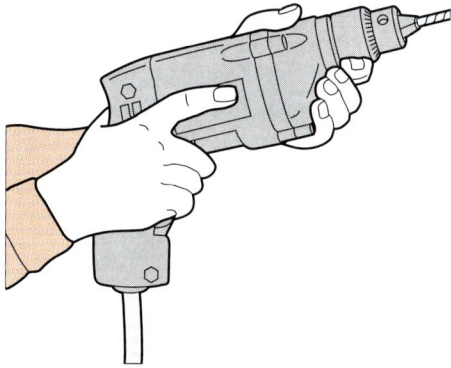

Hold it right ▲

To drill a straighter hole and avoid breaking a bit, hold the drill so that the force you exert helps push the bit straight into the wall. Place the palm of your hand in line with the chuck, extending your index finger along the drill body. Pull the trigger with your second finger.

Keep it level

Newer power drills often have one or two built-in levels to help you drill straight perpendicular holes. To upgrade an older drill, cut the hooks off a bricklayer's line level and attach it to the top of the drill with tape. ▼

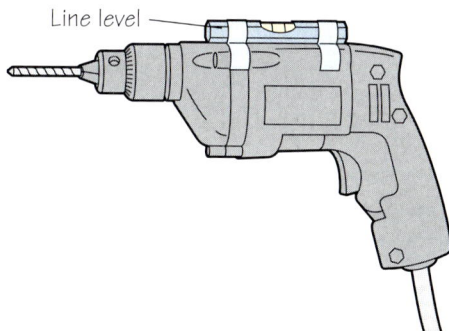

Line level

Hole starters

To keep the bit from skating around when you are starting a hole in wood and most materials (except masonry and tile), draw cross marks where you want to drill. Then use a centre punch to dimple the cross marks. Use a star drill for masonry. For ceramic tile, scratch an X with a carbide masonry bit. ▼

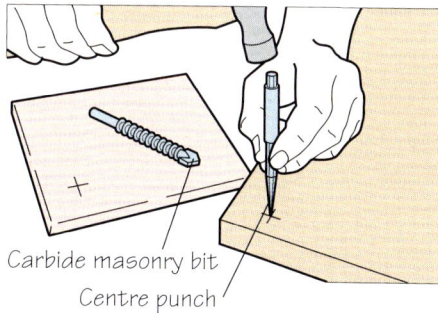

Carbide masonry bit
Centre punch

How deep?

When drilling to a precise depth, mark the depth on the bit with a piece of masking tape. Cut the piece a little long and stick the overlapping ends together to make a flag. When the right depth is reached, the flag will brush away the debris.

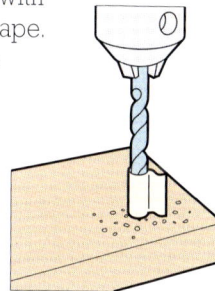

The right-sized bit

Suppose you need to drill a clearance hole for a bolt or screw, but you don't have a drill gauge at hand. Use the fastener itself and the drill's chuck to gauge the right bit diameter. Chuck the fastener lightly into the drill; then remove it without changing the chuck setting. Try shanks of various bits until one fits snugly.

Replacing a drill chuck

If you find that the chuck jaws of your trusty old electric drill don't hold bits tightly enough, replace the old chuck with a new one. You can buy one that requires a key or one that needs no key. In either case, you'll have to remove the old chuck first. Apply some penetrating oil inside the chuck, place the drill on your workbench, and insert the key so that it is parallel with the bench top. Next, follow the steps shown below. To mount a keyless chuck, follow the directions on the package. Finally, lightly lubricate the new chuck's jaws and work it back and forth until it operates smoothly. ▼

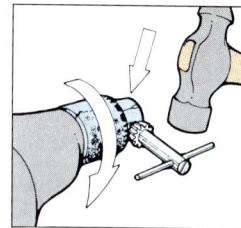

Use a ball-pein hammer to strike the key with a solid blow so that the key will turn in an anticlockwise direction.

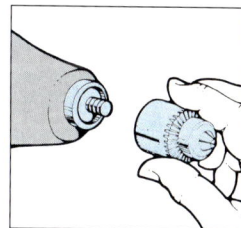

Next, unscrew the old chuck, using pliers (vice grip or multigrip) if necessary. Screw the new chuck on.

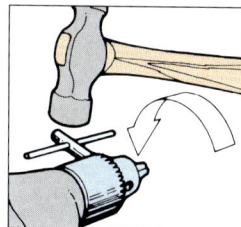

To lock a new keyed chuck in place, insert the chuck key and tap the key lightly in a clockwise direction.

DRILLS AND DRILL BITS

More basics

Straight bits

A bent bit is likely to break and damage your work. Because bits bend easily (especially the thinner ones), test them for straightness before use and discard any bent ones. To test a bit, roll it slowly with your fingertips on a flat surface. If the bit wobbles, it's bent. Or place the bit against a straightedge and look for gaps between the two surfaces. ▼

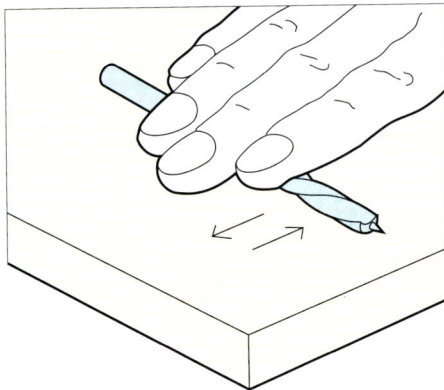

Pointed bits

Brad point

When drilling wood, use a brad-point bit instead of a common twist bit. The little spur on the tip of a brad-point bit cuts cleanly into the wood and keeps the bit from skating around when you start the hole, or from drifting if the bit hits a knot.

Spade bit

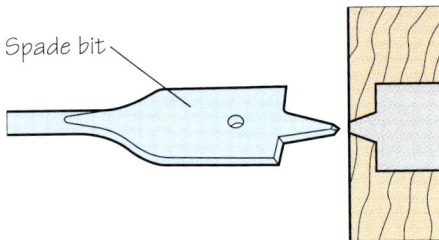

Splinter-free drilling ▲

Drilling a hole completely through timber leaves a rough, splintery edge where it exits. To make a clean hole, look (don't feel) for the point of the bit as it pierces the back side of the work. Pull out the bit, and using the little hole as a centring guide, drill from the back. This method works with spade, auger, Forstner, and brad-point bits.

Metal tips

Use a high-speed steel (HSS) bit for drilling metal. To protect the bit and keep the drill and the bit from over-heating, lubricate the surface with plenty of light machine oil. If you need to drill a large-diameter hole (13 mm or larger) in thick metal, work up to the desired diameter in stages: first 6 mm, then 10 mm, and so on.

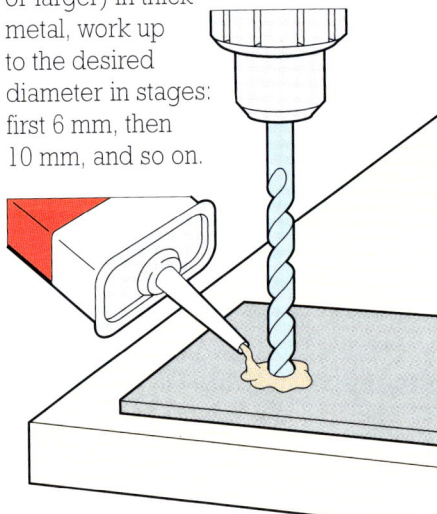

The hard stuff

For drilling tile, concrete, and masonry, use a masonry bit with a carbide tip. When drilling into concrete, start with a small hole, then enlarge it. If you have to drill many holes in concrete, rent or buy a hammer drill to use with the carbide tip bits. By actually banging the spinning bit into the surface, a hammer drill makes your work much easier.

Wall hang-ups

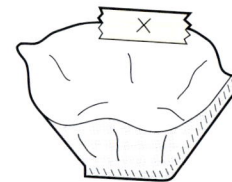

Drilling into a plaster wall often damages the wall's surface and leaves a mess on the floor. To avoid both problems, tape an open paper bag or envelope under the location of the new hole, with the tape covering the spot you intend to drill into. When you've finished drilling, peel off the tape and empty and reuse the dust catcher.

Another dust catcher

Here's how to keep the dust from falling all over the floor or into your eyes when you drill into a ceiling. Simply drill through the centre of a plastic coffee can lid, leave the lid on the drill bit, and drill the hole. Any size lid will do; clear plastic ones allow you to see the bit as you drill.

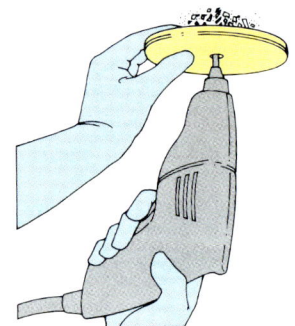

Neat and clean

Here's the pitch

Used on resinous wood, a bit becomes coated with wood pitch. If allowed to build up, the pitch dulls the bit. To clean a bit, lay it on newspaper and spray it with oven cleaner. (Or to contain the fumes, you can put the bit inside a plastic bag and then spray.) Let the bit soak for about 20 minutes, and then wipe it clean with a rag.

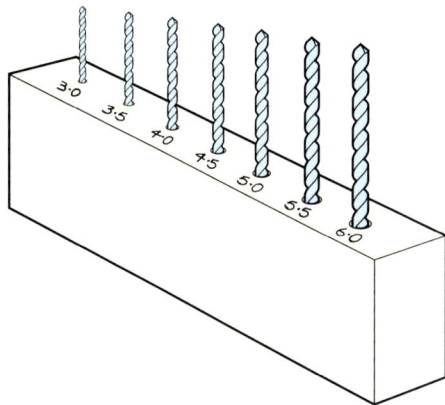

Bit holder ▲

To keep drill bits from bumping against other tools or against each other, and thereby losing their cutting edge, don't store them loose. You can either a buy bit holder for a few dollars at a hardware store or improvise your own with a compartment or niche for each bit. To make the holder shown here, drill different-size holes in a block of wood and label each hole with the size of the bit it will hold. If you always keep the bits in their proper places in the holder, they will stay sharp and be easy to find.

Put a cork on it

Protect the business end of expensive bits such as brad-point, spade, and Forstner bits by screwing a piece of cork onto the end of each bit. The cork, which should have a diameter slightly larger than the bit, will protect the bit's lead-in point and the cutting spurs.

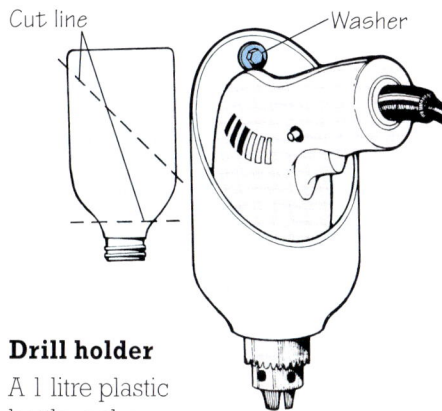

Cut line — Washer

Drill holder

A 1 litre plastic bottle makes a handy holder for your drill. Cut off the bottom and the top of the bottle as shown, and attach it to the wall with wall anchors or screws. You can also make a power tool holder out of a 200 mm length of 100 mm diameter PVC pipe.Cut a notch into the top rim to accommodate the tool's handle.

Another hang-up

To hang your drill on a pegboard hook, insert a screw eye into the chuck and tighten it.

BUYING A DRILL

A good basic electric drill has a 10 mm chuck and a variable-speed reversing (VSR) capability. Such a drill accepts bits with shanks up to 10 mm and lets you control how fast you drill. Buy the best, most powerful model you can afford. Be sure that the drill fits comfortably in your hand. A built-in level is a handy feature.

Cordless drills are very convenient, but they are usually slower and less powerful than the plug-in type and of course require recharging (from 15 minutes to several hours). As a result, you may opt to use a plug-in drill and a cordless one as a team.

Cordless drills come in three categories: screwdrivers, light drills, and full-size drill/drivers. The first type lives up to its name, and not much more. The second kind is more powerful and is easy to handle overhead. However, a charge powers only about 10 minutes of drilling time and the built-in recharger is slow. Full-size drill/drivers have more features than the light drills, usually have a detachable battery, and are powerful enough to handle most drilling jobs yet are good at driving screws. If you buy a second battery pack, you can use one while the other is recharging, and drill as long as you wish.

SCREWS AND SCREWDRIVERS

Treat it right

By using a screwdriver for a job it was not designed for, you risk damaging the tool and injuring yourself. Try not to use a screwdriver as a crowbar, chisel, hole punch, scraper, or paint stirrer. If you must use a screwdriver for one of these tasks, choose an old one that's already damaged.

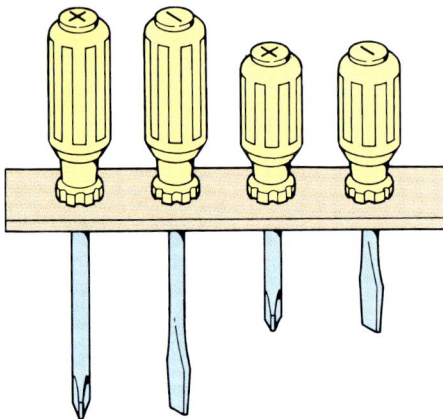

This end up ▲

To protect your screwdrivers and make it easy to find the size you're looking for, store them with their handles up. If your screwdrivers are not colour-coded, you can make identification even easier by marking the tops of the handles with a minus sign for slot screwdrivers or with a plus sign for Phillips and Pozidriv screwdrivers. Either write the sign with indelible ink on a piece of tape and attach it to the top of the handle, or burn the sign into the handle with a soldering gun.

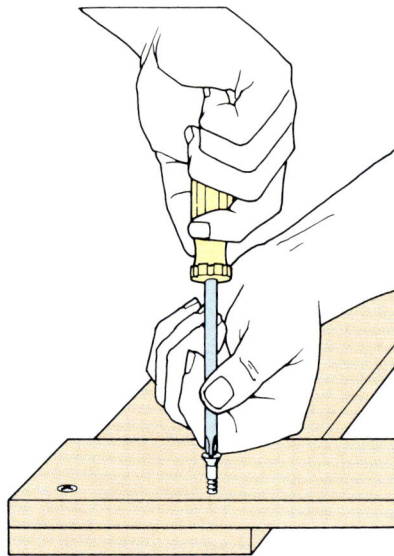

Avoiding slips ▲

▷When driving a screw, always hold the screwdriver blade in the screw slot. If you hold the work as you drive the screw, the blade can easily slip out of the slot and injure your hand.
▷In selecting a screwdriver, be sure that the tip fits the slot perfectly. If the tip is too big or too small, the blade will slip out of the slot.
▷A screwdriver with a damaged (rounded) tip or edges can slip and in-jure you or damage the work. Similarly, a screwdriver that has a split or broken handle can cause injury.
▷Keep screwdriver handles clean. A greasy handle can easily slip out of your hand.
▷Never use a screwdriver near live wires or for electrical testing.
▷Don't use pliers to increase the torque (turning power) of a screwdriver. Use a spanner for this purpose, and only with square-shank screwdrivers.

Smoother driving

Holding power

Before driving a screw, dip the tip of the screwdriver blade into a small mound of scouring powder or dig it into a cone of carpenter's chalk. The coating of chalk or cleanser will help the tool stay firmly in the screw slot.

Magnetic tip

To start screws in tight places, use a magnetised screwdriver. You can either buy a factory-magnetised screwdriver or magnetise one yourself by dragging its blade over a magnet several times in one direction. To prevent the charge from draining out of a magnetised screwdriver, keep it away from other metal objects. A home-magnetised screwdriver should hold its charge for about a week. To demagne-tise the tool, just drag the blade over the magnet in the opposite direction.

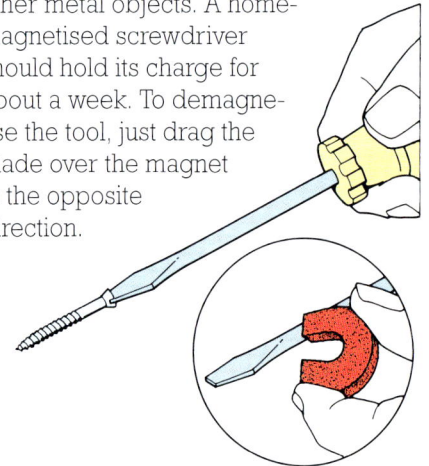

Wax job

You'll have an easier time driving a screw if you first pull its threads across a bar of soap, beeswax, furniture wax, or lip balm. Dipping a screw in linseed oil before driving not only eases the job, it also protects the screw from rust.

Getting a grip

Another way to start screws in difficult places is to push the screw through the sticky side of a piece of adhesive tape, insert the screwdriver into the slot, and wrap the tape around the blade of the screwdriver. Or try dabbing a little rubber cement on the screw head.

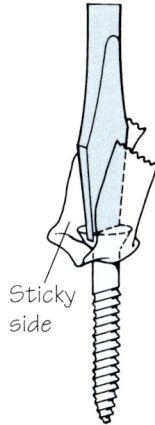

Sticky side

Hammer time

Despite the rule that says you should never hit a screw with a hammer, a few light taps when a screw is almost in place causes the wood fibres to compress and slant downwards against the screw threads. As the screw is given its final tightening, it will get a better bite.

Brass screws

Brass screws make attractive but fragile fasteners. Because the metal is soft, a screwdriver can damage the slot or break the screw. To avoid this problem, drill a pilot hole, pick a steel screw the same size as the brass one, and drive it into the hole. Then remove the steel screw, lubricate the threads of the brass one with soap, and drive it into place.

Set in shellac

To keep a screw from being loosened by vibrations, dab shellac underneath the screw head. If it's necessary to remove the screw later on, you can break the shellac film by pressing firmly on the screwdriver as you turn it. (When working with shellac, follow the maker's safety instructions.)

SCREWDRIVERS

Having the right screwdriver in hand makes most jobs a lot easier. A basic screwdriver set includes four standard slot-tip and four cross-tip (Phillips) drivers in various shaft lengths and blade sizes. Larger sets are also available. There is a second type of cross-headed screw in common use, called a Pozidriv. This has small extra indentations between the main slots, giving the head a star-shaped appearance and improved grip. Buy a special Pozidriv screwdriver to use with this screw type. If you plan to work with many different screw types and sizes, consider buying a set of tips that fit just one handle.

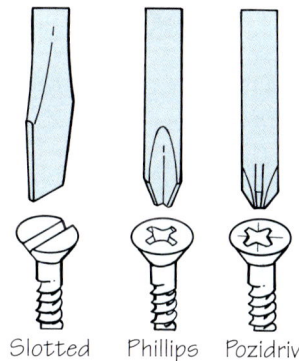

Slotted   Phillips   Pozidriv

Buyer's guide. Buy only the best screwdrivers, never the cheap kind. The best tools have handles made of wood or a strong plastic and strong steel blades that are rough-finished or ridged to resist slippage. Cheap screwdrivers are likely to be made of steel that is softer than many fasteners. Choose screwdrivers that feel comfortable in your hand. You may find that a triangular handle or one that has deep ridges is easiest to grip and turn. As you shop, keep in mind that the larger the handle, the more torque (turning power) you can bring to bear on the screw.

Power drivers.

The proliferation of power screwdrivers coincides with the use of hardened plasterboard screws instead of wood screws. (The screw has a deeply cut Phillips or Pozidriv head that is ideal for power driving.) The most basic type of power driver is the pocket-sized cordless screwdriver which, although slow, is convenient for driving any type of small screw. A drill/driver is essentially a drill, typically cordless, that has a variable-speed trigger to adjust the drill's torque, or a low-speed setting for screwdriving.

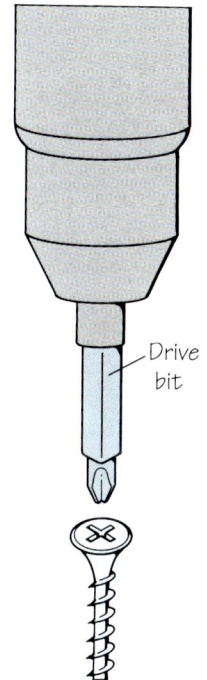

Drive bit

Power driver and plasterboard screw

SCREWS AND SCREWDRIVERS

Reusing and adapting

Renew-a-screw

Removing and reseating a slotted or Phillips-head screw often results in a damaged slot, especially if the blade of your screwdriver didn't fit the slot in the first place. If you don't have a replacement screw on hand, try restoring the old screw by running a hacksaw along the slot (or slots in the case of a Phillips-head screw) to deepen it. If you're repairing a screw out of its hole, don't hold the screw in your fingers. Put it in a vice between two wood off cuts. This way you'll avoid injury and protect the threads. ▼

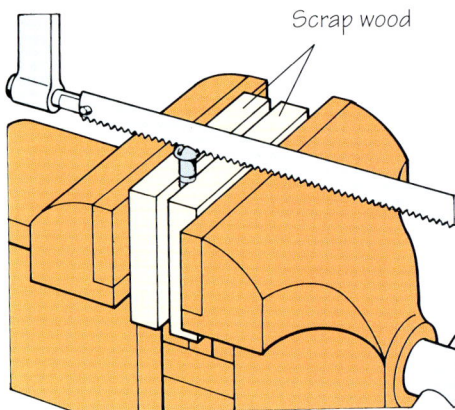

Scrap wood

Converting Phillips-head screws

Suppose you need to seat or remove a Phillips-head screw and you have only a slotted screwdriver on hand. Use a hacksaw to extend one of the slots in the screw head so that it goes all the way across the screw. Again, if the screw is out of its hole, make sure you hold it in a vice, not in your fingers.

Unclog it

To remove a screw whose slot is clogged with paint, first use a sharp point to dig out the paint from the slot.

Keeping track

When disassembling a piece that needs to be repaired or moved, thread the screws into the edge of a strip of corrugated cardboard. Then tape the strip to one of the larger parts. To make reassembly easier, write notes about the screws' positions on the strip of cardboard.

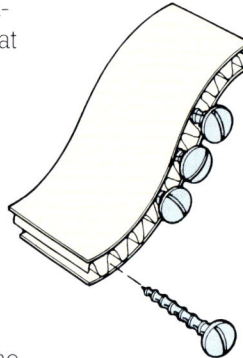

Golf tee trick

To restore a worn or stripped screw hole, plug it with several glue-covered toothpicks, a piece of dowel, or a wooden golf tee. Fill the hole with glue and insert the plug. When the glue has set, cut off the excess plug. You'll then be ready to drill the pilot hole and drive the screw back into place. ▼

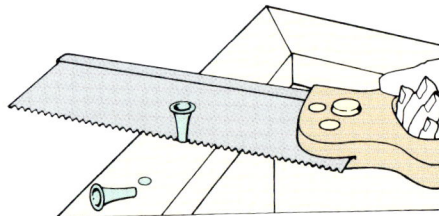

Stuck screws

Break it up

Winning the war against stuck screws usually depends on breaking up the layer of corrosion (grime and rust) that develops around the head. Before you try to force the offending screw, spray it with a suitable lubricant, such as penetrating oil. If you don't have a lubricant on hand, try using a little vinegar, lemon juice, or cola drink (the carbonate fizz does the work). Allow some time for the lubricant to do its job; then help break the bond by tapping a hammer on the area surrounding the screw.

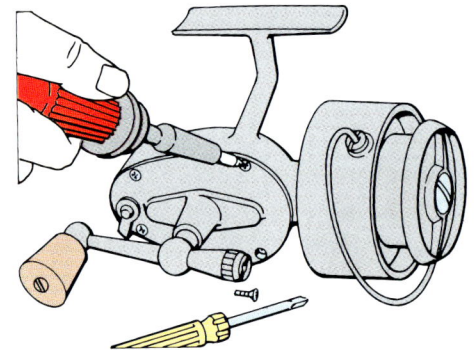

Hot metal ▲

If you still can't get that screw out of a metal object, lubricate the screw as described above and then heat it with a soldering iron or a propane torch. (An iron works well on the thin metal of home appliances; you'll need a propane torch if the screws are large and the metal thicker.) The heat makes the lubricant thinner, so it can seep into the threads. While the screw is still hot, gently tap the area around the screw with a hammer.

HAMMERS AND NAILS

Basic tips

Swing time

Everyone bends a nail now and then. To reduce your chances of doing so, try to drive a nail home with the fewest possible hammer blows—no more than three or four. Hold the hammer at its end, not in the middle, and swing your arm like a clock pendulum, keeping your wrist stiff during the swing. Always wear eye protection.

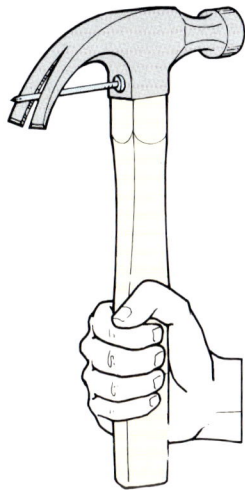

One-handed start ▲

Starting a nail with one hand allows you to hold on to the work or to the side of a ladder with your free hand; it also makes it much easier to drive a nail in a hard-to-reach place. One way to do this is to wedge the nail tightly in the claw of your hammer, with the nail head against the base of the hammer head. Swing the hammer, claw side first, to start the nail; then lift the hammer off the nail and drive it in the usual way.

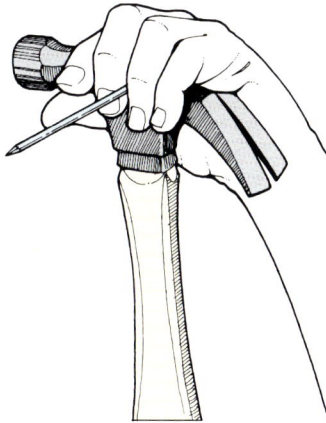

Another nail starter ▲

Grasp the hammer head in your fist as shown, and hold the nail firmly between your fingers and against the side, or *cheek,* of the hammer. To start the nail, rap the nail point against the work.

No more smashed fingers

Holding a small nail when you start it can often result in pain. To keep your fingertips out of harm's way, stick the nail through one end of a folded sheet of stiff paper. Using the paper as a holder, drive in the nail. Before finally seating the nail, tear the paper away. The teeth of a comb, tweezers, or long-nose pliers can also serve as nail holders. ▼

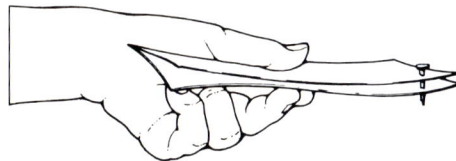

Protective cover

Here's a way to shield a work surface from an accidental hammer blow when you're driving finishing nails. Simply drive the nail through a hole in a scrap of pegboard with 6 mm holes. As you near the surface, lift off the pegboard and use a nail set to sink the nail. ▼

Cushion the blow

Need to tap a joint together without marring the wood? Convert your hammer into a mallet by slipping a rubber furniture leg tip over the hammer's striking face. Or cut an X in an old tennis ball and slip the ball over the hammer's face.

Directory assistance

When hammering indoors, use a pair of old thick telephone books as a work surface. The books will not only protect the surface but also deaden the sound. (And if you're working on a messy project, you can tear out the pages of the book and use them to catch spills.)

HAMMERS AND NAILS

Easy driving

Pilot holes

Driving a nail into hardwood is easier if you drill a pilot hole first, just as you would for a screw. If you don't have the right drill bit, nip off the head of a nail that is the same size as the nail you are going to drive, and chuck it tightly in the drill. ▼

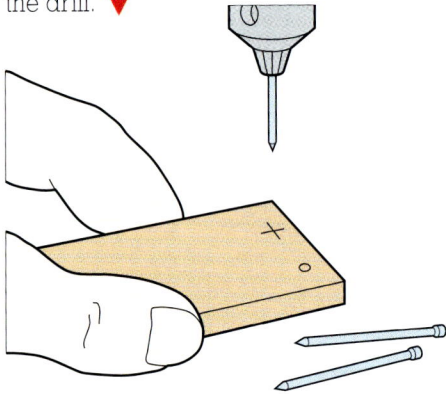

Fast driver

Another strategy for easing nails into hardwood is to lubricate the nails. Beeswax, lubricating (household) oil, even lip balm, all work well. If your hammer has a wooden handle, you can drill a hole in the handle end and fill it with beeswax or lip balm. ▼

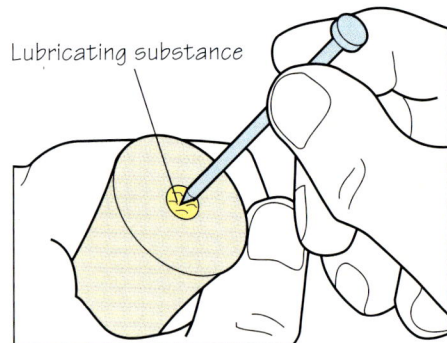

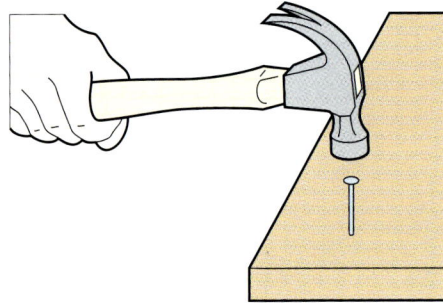

Lubricating substance

No more split wood ▲

To keep wood from splitting when you drive a nail into it, blunt the point of the nail slightly. Turn the nail so that the point faces up, and tap it gently with a hammer. Then try to drive the nail into the soft lighter areas of the wood, not the darker grain lines.

Nail attractor

Glue a small magnet to the end of your hammer handle. When you want to pick up a few nails, just stick the handle into your nail container or apron pocket.

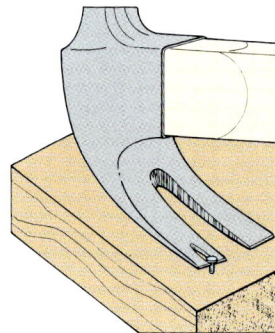

Mini-claw ▲

To pull nails too small for the claw of your hammer to grip, create a miniature nail puller by filing a V-shaped notch into one claw tip. A triangular-shaped needle file will do the job nicely.

Versatile nail-pulling wedge

To get just the right leverage under the hammer head when you're pulling a nail, make a nail-puller block like the one shown below from a scrap piece of 100 × 100 mm timber. Cutting the piece at about a 35° angle will give you a great deal of flexibility. ▼

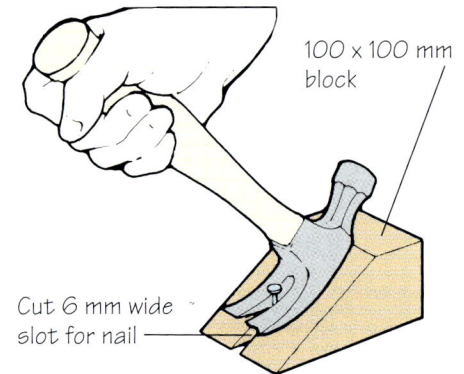

100 × 100 mm block

Cut 6 mm wide slot for nail

Care and handling

Put on a smooth face

A good-quality hammer will perform well for years. But with use—and abuse—its face will become nicked and gouged. When that happens, you can restore the hammer's face by lightly filing it smooth. Make sure the outer edge of the face remains bevelled so that it is less likely to leave hammer marks on the work.

Sharp claws

The claw, that handy nail puller and crowbar, may need restoration too. When the claw becomes damaged, restore the ends and the inside edges of the V with a flat metal file. Deepen the point of the V with a triangular file.

Clean face

When you are fastening a project with cement-coated nails, you may find that you are bending more than your share of nails. That's a signal that the hammer head has become coated with cement. To clean the head, rub it with a scrap of sandpaper or a bit of steel wool.

Handle remedies

If your wood hammer handle is loose, put it in a jar of linseed oil for an hour. The wood fibres swell in the oil, making for a snugger fit. If a handle cracks or breaks, replace it or discard the hammer. To attach a new handle, first shape it to fit. Then coat the handle tip with five-minute epoxy, insert it in the hammer head, drive in the end wedges, and let the epoxy cure for 24 hours.

Hammer hold

Make your nail apron do double duty as a convenient holder for your hammer. Just drill two holes in a 40 mm PVC pipe coupling and thread one of the apron strings through the holes. ▼

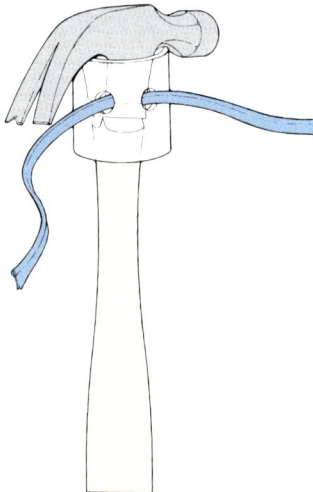

HAMMERS

Most types of hammers come in a variety of head weights and handle lengths. Handles made of ash, hickory, tubular steel (with a rubber grip), or fibreglass absorb shock well, are comfortable to hold, and provide a good grip. The head should be cleanly forged (not cast) of quality steel. The face of a hammer intended for general use should be smooth and have slightly bevelled edges. A textured face clings to nails and is best for long nailing sessions. However, it will mar the work surface. A smooth face, found on pein hammers, mallets and sledgehammers, is designed to strike either a work surface or other tools, such as a cold chisel or a punch.

Curved-claw hammer

Claw hammers. The basic everyday household hammer is a 450 g curved-claw hammer. For rough construction work, choose a 680 g straight claw hammer, sometimes called a *ripping* hammer; for finished carpentry, use a light 350 g hammer.

Ball-pein hammer

Cross-pein hammer

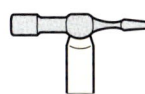

Pein hammers. Instead of a claw, these hammers have a second striking surface, called a pein. The rounded ball pein is used to bend and shape soft metal. The hammer used by cabinet-makers has a long, thin cross pein to start a panel pin, and a flat face to drive a nail. A bricklayer's hammer has a flat end to settle masonry into place and a long chisel-like face to score bricks.

Bricklayer's hammer

Carpenter's mallet

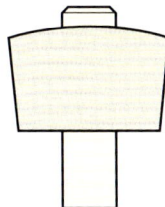

Rubber mallet

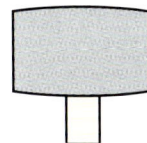

Mallets and sledgehammers. To strike woodworking chisels and assemble wooden parts, use a carpenter's mallet. Assemble other projects and pound out dents in metal with a rubber mallet. Sledgehammers (not shown) have solid steel heads weighing from 1 to 15 kg. Long-handled heavy sledgehammers are used for demolition work, such as breaking up concrete. The short-handled, lighter type is used to drive stakes into place.

STAPLERS

Staple gun operation

Quick screen fix

A staple gun makes short work of small household repairs. For example, to repair a screen that has pulled out of its wood frame, staple the screen to the frame, folding a hem as you go. Doubling over the screen makes the fastening stronger and reduces the chance that the wires will unravel and work loose again. ▼

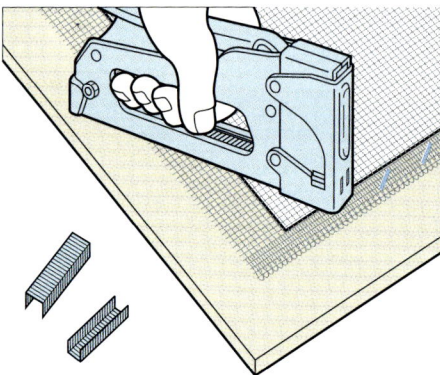

A better angle

When stapling fabric or screen mesh to a surface, place the staples at an angle to the weave or mesh. This way the staple has more material to grip, making the attachment more secure. ▼

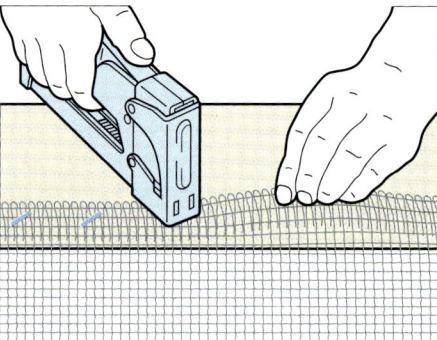

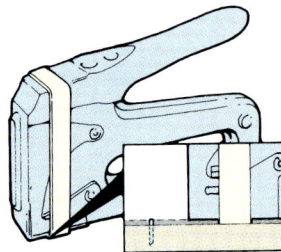

Temporary stapling ▲

Some fastening jobs, such as stapling plastic sheets over a window, are meant to be temporary. Here's a way to make staple removal hassle-free. Slip a heavy-duty rubber band around the staple gun as shown. The rubber band acts as a spacer, leaving the staples sticking up slightly so that they are easy to remove with a staple remover. This method also keeps the staples from cutting through very thin materials.

Specialised staplers

For stereo and phone wire

A quick, neat way to run phone and stereo wire is to staple it in place with a special wiring tacker (which you may have to order in). This tool shoots staples that bridge wire without damaging it. Wire tackers shoot various-sized staples, so measure your wire to determine which tacker to buy. You may also be able to buy a general-purpose stapler with a wire tacker attachment.

Hammer tacker

This handy tool is great for attaching a vapour barrier, insulation, and roofing and builder's felt. A hammer tacker is useful for any job that does not require great accuracy of placement. The tacker also makes it easier to work overhead and is kinder to arm muscles and hands than a regular stapler. To set a staple, just strike the tacker. If you do a lot of stapling, a power stapler may be a worthwhile investment. ▼

COMMON STAPLES

SIZE	USE
6 mm leg	Light upholstering, such as pelmets and blinds
8 mm leg	Heavy upholstering, curtains, insulation foil
10 mm leg	Light insulation, weather-stripping, roofing papers, wire mesh
13 mm leg	Carpet underlay, canvas, felt stripping
15 mm leg	Insulation board, bituminous roofing felt

SPANNERS AND PLIERS

Spanner techniques

Pliers or spanner?

Always turn a nut with a spanner. Using pliers for this purpose will round the edges of the nut and make it even harder to remove later on. If necessary hold the bolt with pliers, but turn the nut with a spanner.

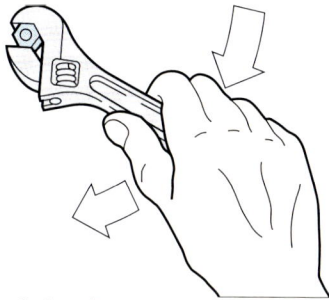

Turn it right ▲

When using an adjustable spanner, pull on the handle so that the stronger fixed side of the jaw is applying pressure rather than the weaker adjustable side. Before you turn the spanner, be sure that the jaws are holding the nut tightly.

Padded jaws

If you're using a pair of pliers on an easily scratched surface, such as chrome, brass, or plastic, be sure to pad the jaws. Either wrap them with adhesive tape, or snip the fingers off an old leather glove and slip these 'sleeves' over the jaws.

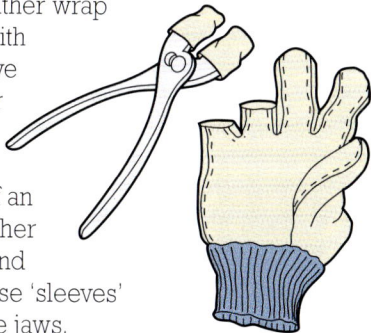

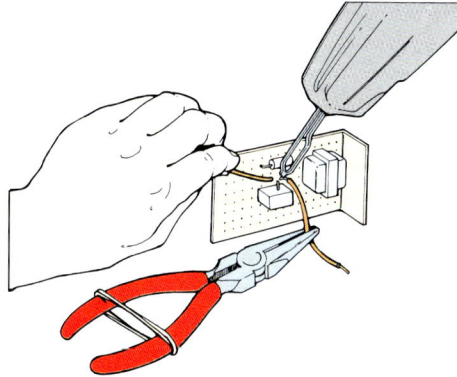

A third hand ▲

Locking pliers act as a third hand that can grip small objects while you assemble, solder, or clamp them. You can convert a pair of ordinary pliers into a mini-vice by slipping a rubber band over the handles. The rubber band will keep the pliers' jaws clamped closed while you work.

Working with bolts

Small nut

Positioning a small nut in a tight place often involves a certain amount of fumbling. To make the task easier, wrap a strip of double-sided carpet tape around the end of your finger. Use the tape to pick up the nut and hold it in place on the end of the bolt. Then turn the bolt to secure the nut.

Hard to reach, easy to fit ▲

Threading a washer and nut onto a bolt in a blind spot can be awkward. The job will be much easier if you glue the washer and nut together. Apply a drop of a suitable glue where the washer and nut meet (be sure to keep the glue well clear of the threads). When the glue has set, thread the nut.

Another nut trick

Say you need to remove a nut with an open-ended spanner that's too large for it. Simply insert an appropriately sized coin or washer between the spanner and the nut. The coin or washer (you'll have to experiment to determine which best fills the gap) will serve as a wedge, making it possible to turn the nut. ▼

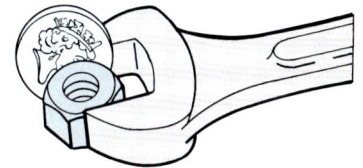

Home-made lock washer

If you don't have a lock washer to secure a nut, wrap a rubber band or a layer of plastic film around the threaded end of the bolt and tighten the nut. As the nut tightens, the material will run into the threads, locking the nut in place.

CUTTING AND SHAPING TOOLS

Files and rasps

Get into shaping

Single-cut

Double-cut

Rasp

A *single-cut* file has parallel rows of ridged teeth that smooth and sharpen metal. A *double-cut* file has a second, crossing, set of parallel ridges; it removes metal and wood excess rapidly. A *rasp* has individual teeth rather than ridges and gives a rough cut on wood and soft metals; the bigger the teeth, the coarser the finish. You can use a *bastard* file for a coarse finish, a *second-cut* file for a medium to coarse finish, and a *smooth* file for a fine finish. Generally the bigger the job, the longer the file. A large file removes a lot of material quickly; a small file removes less material but gives you more control. Most jobs require an all-purpose flat file. But if you are enlarging a round or contoured shape, use a round or half-round file. If you're working on rectangular holes or corners, use a square file, and for acute internal angles, a triangular file. ▼

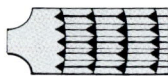

Bastard   **Second cut**   **Smooth**

File shapes

Get a handle on it

For safety and better control, make sure a file has a handle on its tang before you use it. Some handles screw onto the tang. Others are held by friction. In the latter case, insert the tang into the handle, hold it vertically, and rap the handle on a firm surface to seat the file. Don't strike the file or the handle with a hammer.

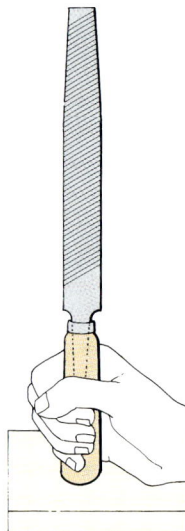

One-way stroke

Files cut only on the push stroke, never on the return. To avoid dulling the teeth, lift the tool off the work surface at the end of the push stroke.

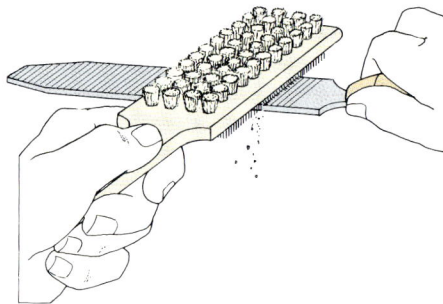

Card sharp ▲

If your file glides over the work without cutting the surface, clean the file teeth with a special wire brush called a file card. To use the card, run the wire bristles over the file, parallel to the grooves of the file teeth.

Chisels and planes

Easy glider

To make a plane glide across a surface, rub the sole-plate with paste wax or a bit of candle. Buff well to spread a thin, even coating. Warming the sole with a hair dryer first will make the job easier.

Tray organiser

Nothing dulls chisel blades faster than bumping into other tools. Either store them individually in a kitchen utensil tray, or if you wish to put more than one chisel in a compartment, add a layer of cotton or bubble packing between tools.

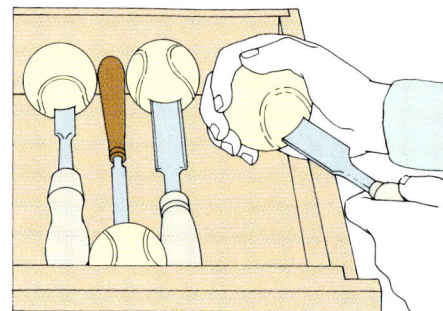

Guard duty ▲

Another way to keep chisels away from other tools is to protect the ends with inexpensive plastic chisel covers. You can also make your own chisel protectors out of slit tennis balls or hollowed-out pieces of cork.

Plane rest

To protect the cutting edge of a plane when it is not in use, set it down on its side or rest it on a block of polystyrene, such as Styrofoam. To store the plane, secure a block of polystyrene to the tool with a couple of sturdy rubber bands.

HANDSAWS

Sharp ideas

The right way to hold a saw

Instead of gripping the handle with all four fingers around it, extend your index finger and place it against the handle as though you were pointing along the saw blade. You'll have better control and cut a straighter, truer line. ▼

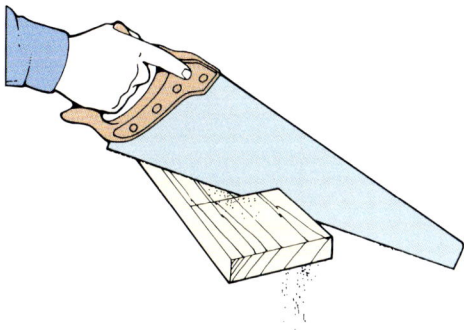

Don't gum it up

Sawing resinous softwoods such as pine clogs saw teeth with a gummy build-up that soon makes the saw seem dull. To remove the resin, apply oven cleaner (see p. 27). To keep the sticky stuff from adhering in the first place, spray silicone on the teeth. Or try polishing them often with hard paste wax or running a bar of soap across them. *Note:* Saws treated this way should be used only for construction work, not for finished pieces.

Keeping your (hacksaw) teeth clean

If you cut soft metals with a hacksaw, the saw's teeth will soon clog. You can avoid this problem by using a blade with bigger teeth, slowing down your strokes (so the metal doesn't melt), and pushing down more gently on the saw.

THE RIGHT SAW

For most 'around-the-house' jobs you can probably get away with owning just two handsaws: a hacksaw for metal and a general-purpose, or panel saw that will make cross-grain and ripping (with the grain) cuts in wood. For home improvement jobs that require cutting holes in plasterboard, choose a plasterboard saw. If you plan to make joints in wood, you'll want a tenon saw and, for complicated joints, a smaller dovetail saw. These saws make finer cuts because they have more teeth per 25 mm than a panel saw, ripsaw, or crosscut saw. (The more teeth, the smoother—and slower—the saw cuts.) In addition, the teeth of a tenon saw and dovetail saw are set to make a narrow kerf and so are essential for making neat, tightly fitting joints in cabinet making.

Japanese saws. Unlike Western saws, which cut on the push stroke, Japanese saws cut on the pull stroke. General-purpose standard saws are made of heavy steel to keep them from bowing as they cut. But because the pulling action doesn't bow the blade, Japanese blades can be extremely thin. These saws cut a very fine kerf that allows work to be very precise. The most common one, the Ryoba saw, has teeth on both sides of the blade: the coarser ones for ripping, and the others for crosscutting.

How dull

How can you tell if a saw is dull *before* you use it? Check the teeth closely to see if the points are rounded and the cutting edges show wear. (Use a magnifying glass to inspect fine-tooth saws.) If the saw appears dull, take it to an expert for resharpening. ▼

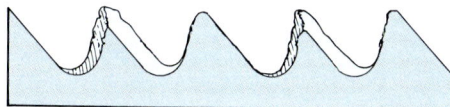

Dull saw blade

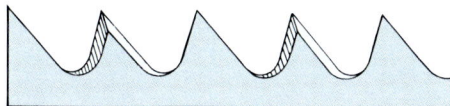

Sharp saw blade

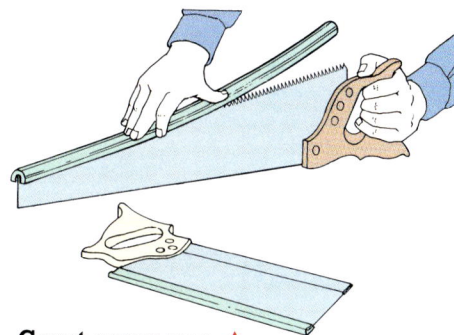

Great cover-ups ▲

When you store handsaws, be sure to cover the cutting teeth. In lieu of a store-bought saw case, cover the teeth with a section of old garden hose that has been slit along its length. You can also use a section of rigid foam or a couple of slip-on spines from a plastic report cover.

KEEPING TOOLS SHARP

On edge

Dull tools are dangerous and inefficient. Save time and money by learning how to sharpen the blades of simple hand tools like chisels, planes, knives, and shears (see facing page; for tips on sharpening large garden tools, see p. 273). However, let a professional sharpen tools that have complex or contoured cutting edges, such as router and drill bits, handsaws, and circular saw blades. Similarly, leave tools with hardened (carbide-tip and diamond-coated) surfaces to the professionals.

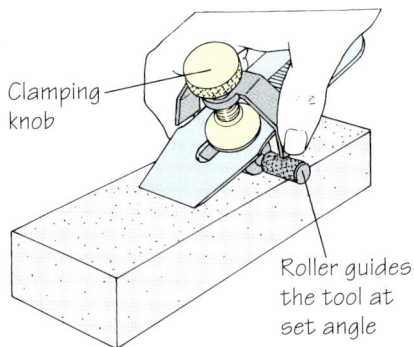

Clamping knob

Roller guides the tool at set angle

Honing guide ▲

This handy device holds the tool you are sharpening at the correct angle. Insert the tool into the guide, squaring the blade to the stone; then adjust the angle setting (the method varies from guide to guide) and tighten the clamp.

Home-made strop

Need a honing strop to give a fine finish to the edges of newly sharpened tools? You can recycle an old leather belt. Just cut off a 150 mm length and glue it to some wood. If necessary, add a little oil.

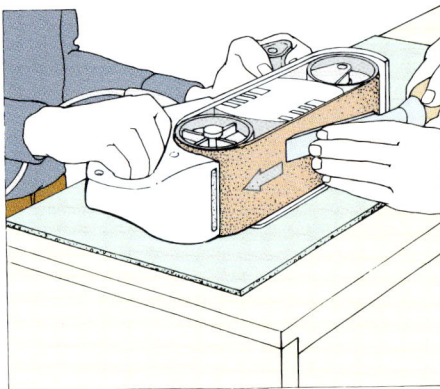

Substitute bench grinder ▲

You can use a belt sander, fitted with a worn 100-grit aluminium oxide belt, to rough-grind a tool. Have a helper hold the sander on its side on a mat of foam carpet padding, angling it if necessary so the belt will turn freely. Put on safety goggles. Hold the tool against the belt, pointing it in the direction of the belt's movement. Otherwise, the tool will catch dangerously on the belt.

Abrasive block

You can make a honing tool by gluing a piece of silicon carbide paper to a wood block. Clamp the block in a vice, and draw the blade along it a few times to give the final touch to a sharpened tool or to touch up a cutting edge. ▼

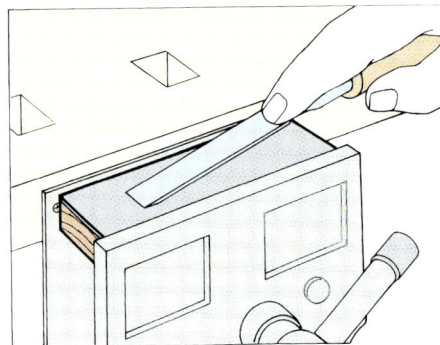

HOW TO SHARPEN

To restore the original bevel, or angle, of a tool, a flat stone or a honing rod (for long blades) will suffice. To remove a nick and to do rough grinding, you'll need a bench grinder. To detect nicks—and to check your progress in restoring the edge—examine both sides of the tool under a magnifying glass.

Chisel and plane angles range between 15° and 30°. Some tools have a narrow secondary bevel at the tip that is 5° greater than the primary one. This secondary bevel slows the dulling of the blade and makes sharpening easier. (Its width varies from 2 mm to a micro-bevel.)

Using a bench grinder. Before mounting a wheel, test it for cracks. Insert an old screwdriver into the wheel's centre hole. Hold the wheel in the air and tap it in several places with the handle of another screw-driver. If it rings, the wheel is intact; if it thuds or rattles, discard it.

The grinding technique shown at right is for rough sharpening or removing nicks. In either case, be sure that the tool doesn't overheat and lose its temper.

Caution: Wear safety goggles and use the wheel guard and eye shield. Never grind on the side of a wheel unless it is designed to be used that way. Keep the tool rest 2 mm from the wheel. For more on power tool safety, see p. 24.

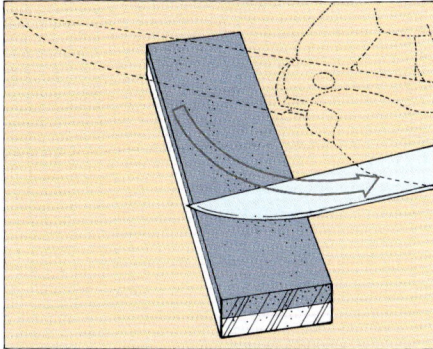

Sharpen a dull knife on a coarse stone first; then finish on a fine stone. Move the blade to the right as you pivot and pull it. Repeat on the other side of the blade, pushing it away as you pivot. Stroke alternate faces the same number of times. Keep the angle and pressure consistent.

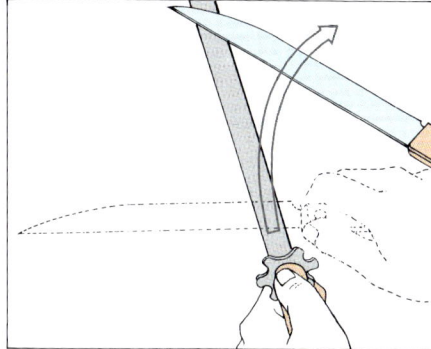

Use a honing rod for long-bladed knives. Holding the rod motionless, begin with the heel of the blade near the rod handle. Move the length of the blade along the rod in an arcing motion. Stroke each side equally. Keep the blade angle and the pressure constant.

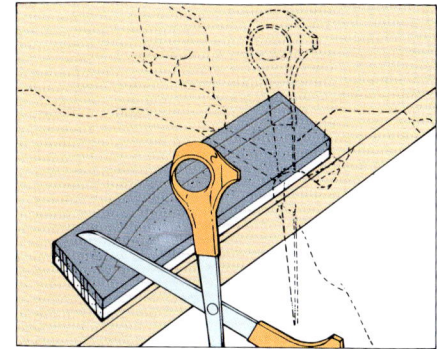

Scissor blades have a secondary bevel that can be sharpened. Place the bevel on the stone, and pull the blade toward you and slightly to the right. Use a pulling motion only.

When sharpening a chisel or a plane iron, use the stone's coarse side first. Rub the primary bevel back and forth a few times (moving across the stone to even up the wear). To create a secondary bevel, raise the tool slightly and rub again on the fine side. To remove the raised burr, turn the tool over and gently rub the flat side, with the blade held flat on the stone.

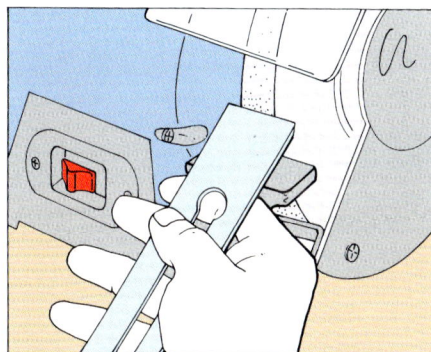

To sharpen a chisel or a plane iron on a bench grinder, set the tool rest so it supports the tool at the correct angle. Hold the tool, bevel side down and square to the wheel, with your forefinger against the tool rest. Keep the metal cool by repeatedly dipping it in water. Use a medium-grit wheel; then finish on a stone.

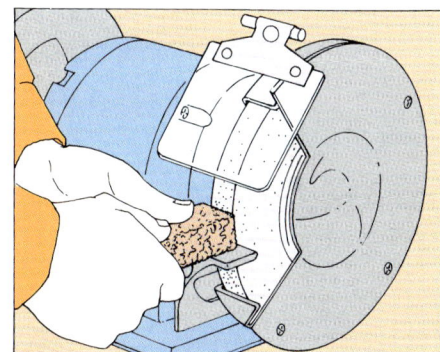

When the wheel of a bench grinder becomes clogged with foreign material or gouged from use, it needs to be cleaned, or dressed. One way to do this is to run a silicon carbide stick over the face of the wheel; the stick will clean and flatten the face, exposing new grit.

POWER TOOL SAFETY

Plugging in

Join the professionals

Some of the major power tool manufacturers sell two lines of tools: one that is for professional use and another for the do-it-yourselfer. Professional tools are usually more powerful, heavier, and more costly. But they are also safer for an experienced do-it-yourselfer—and are usually worth the money, especially if they will be used a lot.

Amps of power

When you are comparison shopping for a power tool, don't rely on the boldly promoted kilowatt (kW) rating as an indicator of the tool's power. Such ratings are less than accurate. Instead, compare how many amperes each tool's motor draws—the more amperes, the more powerful the tool. If the amperage isn't listed on the tool's packaging, check the nameplate on the tool itself. For more on power tools and ampere measures, see p. 43.

Go ahead and blow it

Sawdust is the enemy of all power tool motors. It accumulates inside the motor, around the motor housing, and in the motor vents. Vacuum the stuff from the housing and from the vents every month or so. Or blow it out with compressed air, using either an air compressor or canned air, available at photography supply stores. (Be sure to wear eye protection.) If you fail to keep the vents open and the housing free of sawdust, your tools will probably overheat.

AVOIDING ACCIDENTS

Whenever you use a power tool, make safety your main concern. The following are general power tool safety rules; for more tool-specific tips, see pp. 22, 26, and 31.

Read, understand, and follow the directions in the owner's manual. Use a tool only for the jobs for which it was designed. Don't force a tool or otherwise cause its motor to overheat.

Analyse the job environment. Never operate a tool in a damp, wet, or fume-filled atmosphere. Keep your workspace well-lit, well-ventilated, and free of clutter.

Dress safely. Don't wear jewellery or loose clothing. Keep long hair tied back. Wear the appropriate safety equipment (p. 65).

Evaluate your mood. If you are out of sorts, ill, or taking a medication that could affect your alertness or judgment, postpone the job.

Think before you act. Know the consequences of every move you make. This will slow you down at first, but after a while knowing what's safe—and what's not—will become second nature to you.

Concentrate on the job. Don't talk to anyone while you work, and keep children and pets away. Focus on what you are doing at the moment, not on the next step.

Take your time. Hurrying and taking short cuts are major causes of workshop accidents.

Maintain your balance. Wear nonslip footwear, and make sure your footing is secure. Grip a portable tool firmly. Don't reach too far with a tool or work with it held over your head; stand on a sturdy stepladder instead.

Listen to the sound of the motor. If a tool makes an unfamiliar noise or vibration, turn it off and unplug it.

A plug for safety ▶

You should unplug a power tool whenever you're adjusting or cleaning it, or not using it. To keep a young child from plugging in a power tool, insert a key ring through the hole in a plug prong. If there isn't a hole already, drill one yourself. (Older children will be able to figure out how to unthread the key ring.)

POWER SANDERS

Sanding alternatives

Make a stand

Sanding small pieces with a portable sander is awkward, if not impossible. The stand shown here is designed to hold a sander upside down so that you can press a workpiece against it. To create the cut out for the sander, make a wire template that fits around the sander body, outline it on the timber, and cut the hole with a jig saw. Go over the edges with a rasp until the sander fits snugly. Make the frame deep enough so that the sander doesn't touch the work-bench. To reduce vibration, attach strips of foam insulation on the bottom of the frame and the edges of the opening. ▼

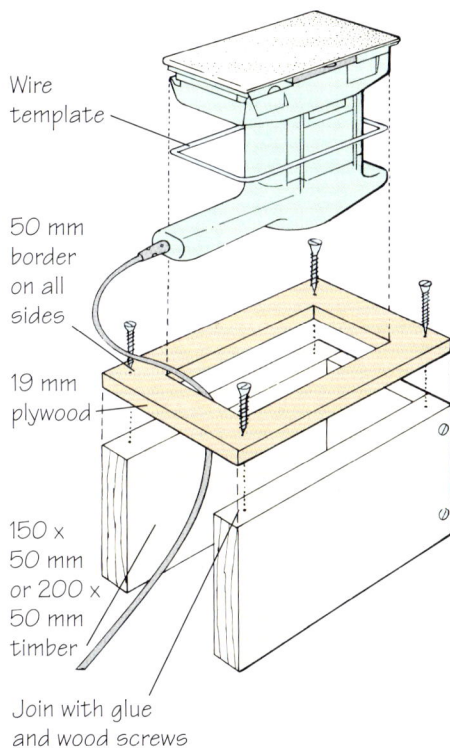

Wire template

50 mm border on all sides

19 mm plywood

150 × 50 mm or 200 × 50 mm timber

Join with glue and wood screws

Random orbiter

Next time you're in the market for a power sander, take a look at a random-orbit sander. Like its cousin the orbital sander, the random orbiter moves the abrasive in tight little circles—but the circles in this case are random, moving first one way, then another, then another. As a result, the sander removes wood faster and doesn't leave those telltale little circles on your finished piece.

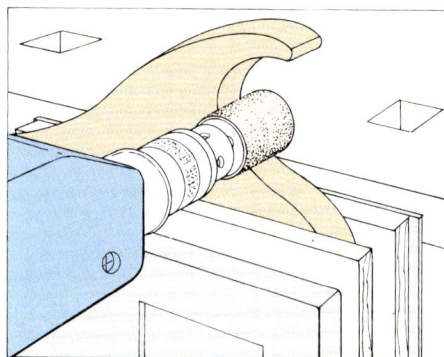

Sanding drill ▲

Tired of hand-sanding curved edges and other tight or hard-to-reach spots? Try a sanding drum attachment on your drill. Some models take special self-adhesive abrasive paper, others a custom cylindrical sanding sleeve. As you sand, hold the drill so that the drum smooths the surface uniformly.

Abrasive advice

Put it on tape

To strengthen sandpaper and sanding belts and keep them from tearing, apply duct or masking tape to the back. Write the grit on the tape; on a sanding belt, mark the direction of rotation as well.

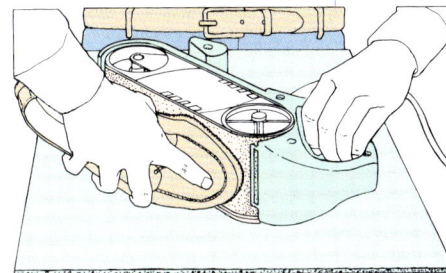

Prolonged life ▲

Sanding belts are expensive and quickly clog up. To remove build up, place the sander on its side, angling it slightly if necessary so the belt turns freely. Hold the bottom of an old crepe-soled shoe or a belt-cleaning stick against the moving belt near the rear wheel. You can use a wire suede brush instead, but only on aluminium oxide belts (the brush would tear garnet or other natural crystalline belts). To use the brush, run it from side to side over the moving belt. Place the sander on a piece of foam carpet padding to help hold the tool.

Put it away

To store sheet abrasives, stick them on a clipboard and hang it on a hook. To help a sanding belt keep its shape and prevent unwanted creases, hang it on a pegboard hook covered with an old paint roller or a length of PVC pipe.

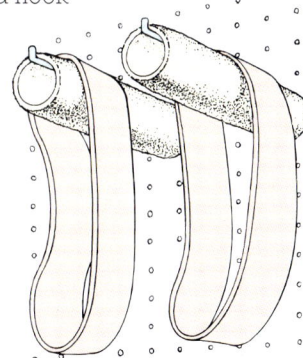

ROUTERS AND ROUTER BITS

Setting up

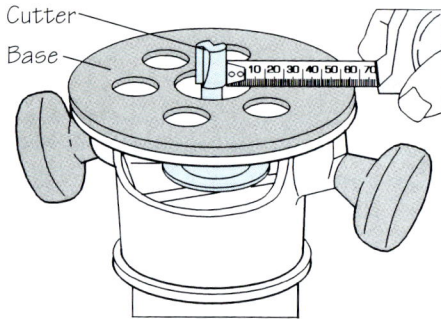

Cutter
Base

Measure for straightedge guide ▲

A straightedge clamped in place on the work serves as a guide for cutting housings, channels or grooves and for trimming or squaring imperfect edges. The trick to setting the guide accurately is to measure from the edge of the cutter to the outside edge of the router base. Measure the same distance on your workpiece; clamp the straightedge tightly in place.

Get a grip

When you insert a bit into the collet, push it in all the way. Then before you tighten the collet, withdraw the bit slightly, about 3 mm. This enables the collet to get a good grip on the bit and makes it easier to remove the bit.

Plan a path

Before turning on the router, make sure its path is clear, with no small fasteners or nails lying around. To avoid tripping when working on a large piece, check that the area where you will walk is unobstructed.

Router tables

Table talk

A router becomes more versatile and easier to use when installed on a router table. Look for a bench-top model that will accept nearly all routers, has a smooth-working adjustable fence, and has a see-through blade guard.

Router table switch

Even though a router table is very useful, reaching the switch under the table can sometimes be awkward. You can solve the problem by having an electrician install an approved foot-control switch from a sewing machine on your router. That way both hands are free to handle the workpiece.

Home-made mount

Instead of buying a router table, you can make one from a piece of 19 mm plywood and clamp it to your workbench.

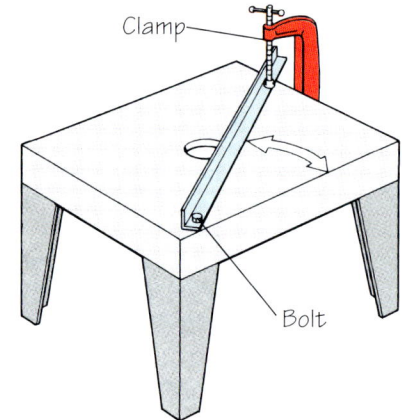

1. Rout a 12 mm deep recess in one side of the plywood, using the router baseplate as a template. Then cut a hole for the bit in the middle of the recess. Next, unscrew the baseplate, place the router in the recess, and attach it to the plywood base with several countersunk screws.

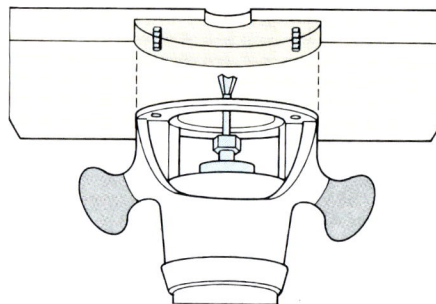

Clamp

Bolt

Quick guide ▲

Here's an easy-to-adjust fence for all routing jobs (except edge routing). Loosely bolt an aluminium angle to one corner of the table. Clamp the other end to the table at the desired position. To adjust the fence, pivot it and reclamp.

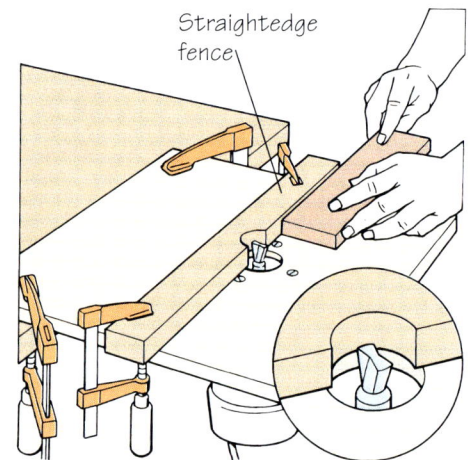

Straightedge fence

2. Clamp the plywood firmly to the workbench. Make a straightedge fence for the table, cutting an opening to accept the bit (inset). On narrow work, use a push stick to move the work safely past the bit. To make workpieces slide more smoothly, glue a piece of hardboard on top of the plywood.

Putting things away

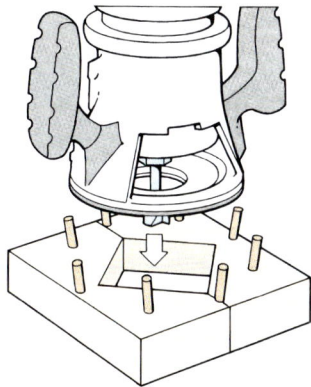

Router rest ▲

After you switch off a router, it takes a while for the bit to stop turning. If placed on its side, a router can roll around. A better idea is to build this stand so you can rest the router upright. Cut V-shapes into two 100 × 50 mm pieces of timber to make an opening for the bit; then glue the pieces together. Draw the outline of the baseplate on the stand and insert 50 mm long dowels at an angle around the circumference line.

Toothbrush tip ▲

To remove resin buildup on a bit, spray it with oven cleaner, scrub it as needed with a toothbrush, and rinse it in water. Wear gloves and safety goggles.

BUYER'S GUIDE

A router with a 1 to 1.5 kW motor can do most jobs and will last a lifetime. Try handling some models in the store. Look for one that can be switched on and off while both hands hold the tool. Check for balance and weight by running it along the edge of a surface.

Router bits. Consider investing in the more expensive carbide-tipped bits. Carbide-tipped bits can rout hard- and softwoods, plastic and manufactured wood panels; they stay sharp for hundreds of uses. Cheap machined-steel bits can't be used on manufactured wood panels and require frequent resharpening.

Basic shapers. Shown here are the most commonly used router bits. A rebating or other edge-shaping bit usually comes with a guide, called a *pilot*. The pilot of a machined-steel bit spins as fast as the bit and tends to burn the work. A carbide-tipped bit has a ball-bearing pilot that rotates much more slowly and will not harm the work. Bits that make an inner groove (straight, V-shaped, corebox and dovetail) have no pilots.

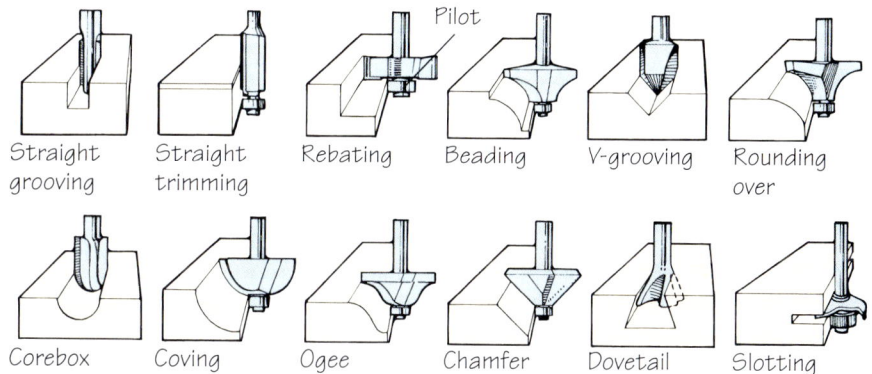

Straight grooving · Straight trimming · Rebating · Beading · V-grooving · Rounding over · Corebox · Coving · Ogee · Chamfer · Dovetail · Slotting

Protect those bits ▶

To protect router bits from bumping into other tools and each other—and to store them so they are easy to find—line a small cardboard box or workbench drawer with rigid foam or foam rubber. Cut out recesses in the liner to create a resting place for each bit.

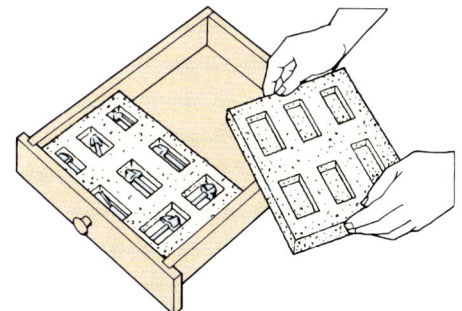

PORTABLE SAWS

Circular saws

The right blade

Two kinds of circular saw blades will see you through just about any job. The first should be a general-purpose combination blade with 20 to 24 teeth; the other should be a fine cutting blade with about 40 teeth. Both blades should be carbide-tipped.

Cutting metal

If you plan to cut metal, use a special metal-cutting blade—and brace yourself for a shower of sparks. To ensure safety, wear hearing protectors and goggles or a full-face mask and work far away—say 15 m—from sawdust, flammable liquids, and anything else that is likely to catch fire. Don't try to saw metal unless your saw has a metal blade guard; a plastic guard will melt.

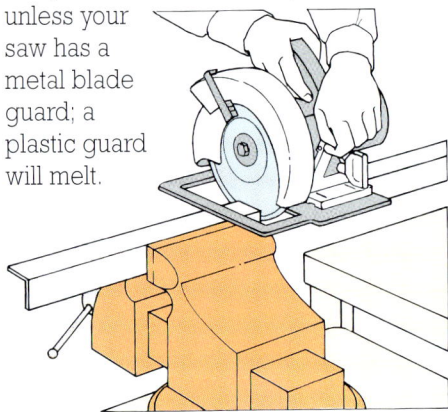

Permanent marker

The cuts you make with a circular saw will be more accurate if you mark the cutting line on the front of the saw's baseplate. Do it with paint or an indelible felt-tip marker.

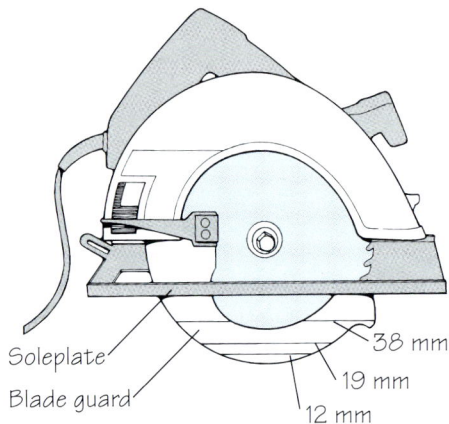

Soleplate
Blade guard
38 mm
19 mm
12 mm

Measuring circular saw cuts ▲

Here's an easy way to measure and set your circular saw's cutting depth without having to pull out a measuring tape every time. Mark 12 mm, 19 mm and 38 mm blade depth measurements on the saw's blade guard with a fine-point permanent marker. Then just line up the bottom of the saw's soleplate with the appropriate mark.

Cord drape

To keep the saw cord out of your way—especially on long cuts—drape it like a cape across your shoulders. It will then move with you and be less likely to snag on something.

Wax works

Want your saw to glide as it cuts? Rub a block of paraffin wax on the underside of the saw's baseplate. If you first heat the surface slightly with a hair dryer, the wax will coat the area more completely.

Jig saws

Cutting curves

Need to cut a curve with a small radius? Choose a 5 mm wide blade rather than a 10 mm one. But be careful—the thinner the blade, the easier it is to break.

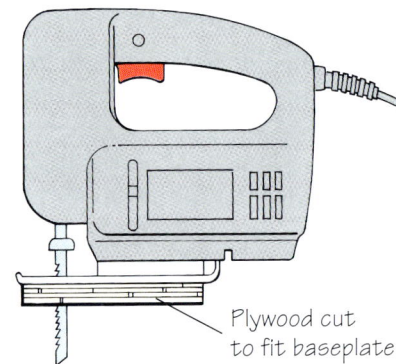

Plywood cut to fit baseplate

Put more teeth into it ▲

As a jig saw blade makes its 'sewing machine' up-and-down motion, only a few of the teeth do the actual cutting. With use, these teeth become dull and the blade useless. You can extend the life of a blade by adding a piece of plywood to the baseplate. This auxiliary baseplate should be at least as thick as the length of the saw stroke. Use your jig saw to cut a notch in the plywood to accept the blade. Then outline and cut the plywood to fit the metal baseplate. Sand, finish, and wax the plywood to make it as smooth as the original metal plate. (It will also guide the blade and keep it from wandering as much.) Mount the plywood base with double-sided tape or hot glue. When the blade wears in the new spot, remove the base and change the blade.

Cleaning and storing

Oven cleaner

Sawing a lot of pine causes pitch and resin to build up on saw blades, making even sharp teeth seem dull. To clean a blade, spray it with oven cleaner. For easy application, suspend a circular blade on a dowel and hang it inside a cardboard box. Because oven cleaner fumes are toxic, close the flaps of the box for the 10 to 20 minutes it takes to loosen the gunk. Then wash the blade off with soap and warm water, dry it, and spray it with a lubricant to protect it from corrosion.

Soaking pan

To clean saw blades by soaking in acetone or mineral turpentine, you'll need a shallow pan with a lid to contain the fumes, rubber gloves, and a stick or other lever for handling the blade. You can recycle an old oven pan and cover it with aluminum foil. Or cut off the bottom from a plastic 20 litre bucket with a knife and use it as your soaking tray (the lid can serve as a cover).

Capping saw teeth

When you are finished for the day, store your unmounted circular saw blades (and table and radial arm saw blades) so that the teeth stay sharp and won't injure anyone. You can buy a carrier made for the purpose or make your own saw cover by slitting a length of garden hose or old plastic tubing. Other possibilities include stacking saw blades in a round plastic pie or cake container (put some cardboard spacers between the blades). Or slip them into old record album covers (one blade in each sleeve). If you use album covers, be sure to reinforce the covers' edges with strong tape because the teeth will soon cut through the cardboard.

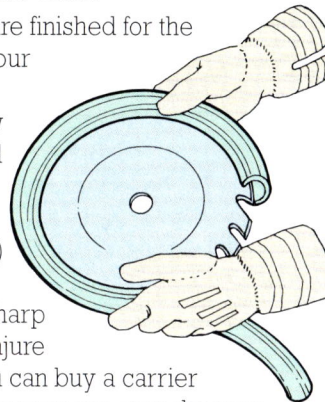

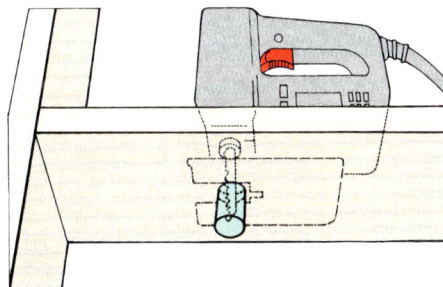

Shelf insert ▲

To store a jig saw upright on a shelf, cut a hole through the shelf to accept the blade. Cover the blade by gluing a length of tubing to the underside of the shelf. Then just rest the saw on the shelf.

JIG SAWS

If you would like to have a great jig saw, try one with an orbital action rather than one with only a simple up-and-down movement. The orbital action, which pushes the teeth into the work on the cutting stroke and away from it on the return stroke, cuts amazingly fast and cleanly.

To make the most of a jig saw, you need to buy the right blades. Here's a sample of what's available: (A) a hollow-ground blade for fine cuts; (B) a double-sided blade that can back out of tight spots; (C) a flush-cutting blade that makes straight cuts flush to a wall or other obstruction (it's too wide to cut a curve); (D) a knife-edge for leather and carpeting; (E) a carbide-grit abrasive blade for cutting hard materials such as ceramic tile; and (F) a metal-cutting blade that will work on aluminium, steel, and pipe with 3 mm thick walls.

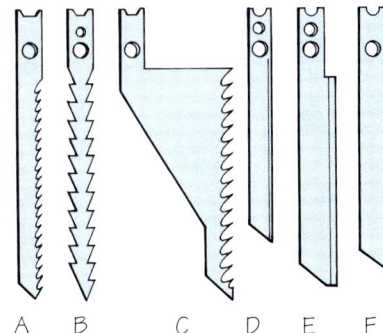

A   B   C   D   E   F

TABLE SAWS

Tips and tricks

Room to work

Setting up your table saw? If you'll be working with 2.4 × 1.2 m sheets of wood panelling, allow enough free room for them around the saw. For ripping, you'll need at least 3 m at the front of the saw and 2.5 m at the rear. For crosscutting, leave 2.5 m on each side of the blade.

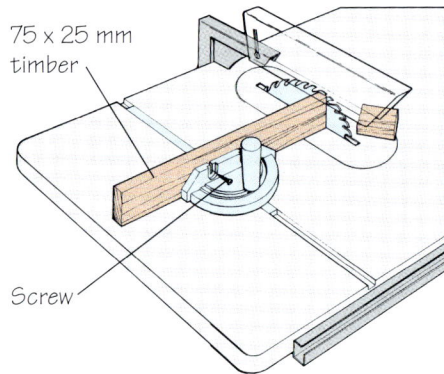

75 × 25 mm timber

Screw

Mitre gauge guide ▲

When you're crosscutting, a mitre gauge places the work at the proper angle to the blade. However, the gauge doesn't show you exactly where the blade is going to cut, nor does it provide enough support to cut long pieces. To make a cut-off guide that will provide added support, attach a 75 × 25 mm piece of timber to your mitre gauge so that it extends from the edge of the saw to just beyond the path of the blade. Make a pass to cut off the excess. The cut end will mark the exact cut-off point of your saw. To keep the work from shifting as it comes in contact with the blade, glue sandpaper to the face of the guide.

Parallel and square ▶

To ensure a proper rip cut and avoid kickback, align your table saw blade so it is parallel to the fence and square to the table. Here's a way to check that the blade is aligned properly. Measure the distance between the blade and the fence at both the front and the back. The measurements should be the same. Adjust the fence if necessary. Set the blade and the mitre gauge to 0° and test-cut a piece of scrap timber. Turn one piece upside down and place the cut ends together. If the pieces match perfectly, the blade is aligned correctly.

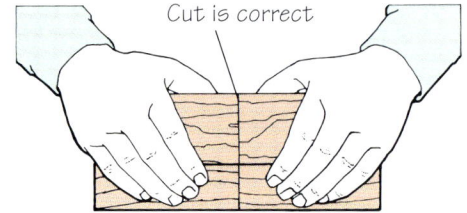

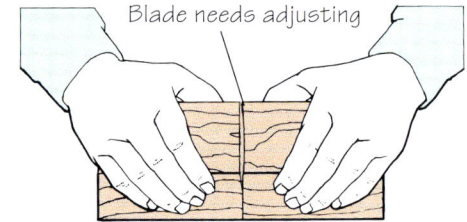

Make a height gauge

Here's a jig that will help you adjust the height of your saw blade quickly and precisely. Take a scrap piece of plywood and cut accurate notches at a series of commonly used measurement steps, alternating sides as you cut. Mark the measurements on the jig. To set the blade, simply place the gauge over it and raise it until it just touches the appropriate notch in the gauge.
Caution: Don't forget to unplug the saw when you're adjusting the blade.

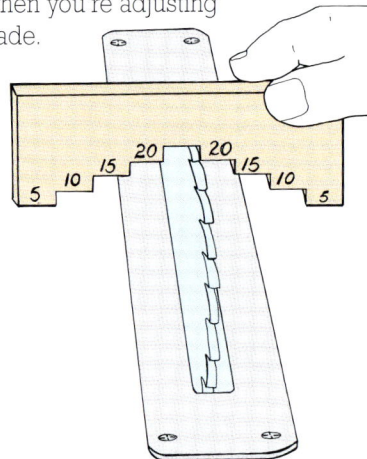

Cut is correct

Blade needs adjusting

Improvements

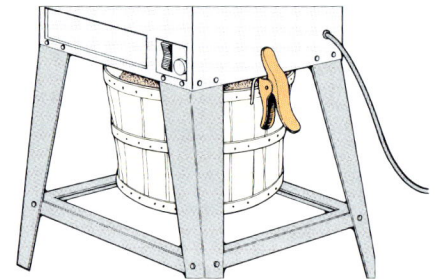

Collecting dust ▲

Ripping wood on a table saw generates a great deal of sawdust. Here are two ways to collect most of the larger sawdust particles as they fall. Attach a large plastic garbage bag to the underside of the table saw with clothes pegs or duct tape. Or mount a large basket inside the saw apron, holding it in place with two spring clamps through the handles. These dust catchers are easy to empty and remount, but play safe by unplugging the saw before doing so.

Wax your table

To keep the metal surface of your table saw free from rust—and help the work move smoothly as you cut—rub the surface with paste floor wax.

Bumpers for fence guides

Don't leave those metal fence guides that protrude beyond the saw base unprotected. Slit a pair of tennis balls and fit them over the ends. You'll save yourself many a bruise and avoid causing a head or eye injury to a child. ▼

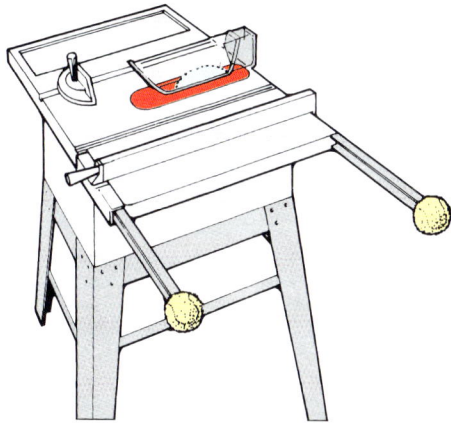

Seeing red ▲

As a graphic reminder to keep your fingers and hands away from the blade of your table saw (and any other stationary power saw, for that matter), paint the area around the blade a bright red. First make a new table insert and paint it red. Then spray paint 100 mm in front of and behind the blade. Be sure to mask the fence and any other areas you don't want painted.

Hang the accessories

As you accumulate accessories for your table saw, you'll appreciate having them all within easy reach. One way to organise accessories is to hang them on a piece of 6 mm pegboard attached to two side legs of the table saw. Drill holes in the legs and mount the pegboard with machine screws and nuts.

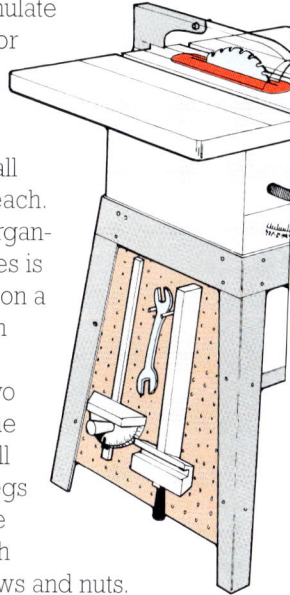

Push sticks and feather boards

When you're ripping timber, you need to guide the piece accurately while keeping your fingers from coming too close to the blade. Using a push stick on small pieces keeps fingers at a safe distance (at least 75 mm away). To brace the work, clamp a feather board to the saw table so that it is in front of the blade (side pressure next to the blade would cause it to bind in the cut). Adjust the splitter to keep the cut open.

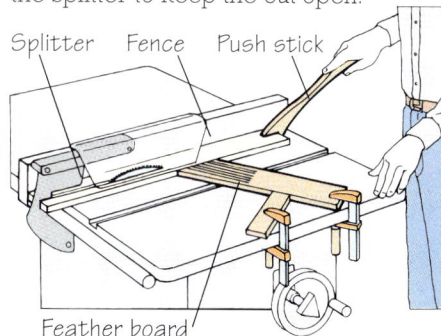

Splitter   Fence   Push stick

Feather board

POWER SAWS

▷ Always let the saw reach its full speed before you do any cutting.
▷ Keep all levers and clamps tight.
▷ Support both the work and the waste when cutting.
▷ Keep your fingers away from the saw blade.
▷ Always wear protective gear for your eyes and ears.
▷ Feed the work against the rotation of a stationary saw's blade.

Table saws

▷ Never remove the blade guard.
▷ Never reach behind a moving saw blade.
▷ Set the blade so that it protrudes just 3–6 mm above the work.
▷ Use push sticks, as shown at left.
▷ Hold the widest portion of the board you are ripping against the fence. Feed the work until it is completely clear of the blade.
▷ Never cut freehand.
▷ Use either the fence or the mitre gauge—never both at once.

Radial arm saws

▷ Stay out of the path of the blade.
▷ When ripping, use a push stick and the antikickback mechanism.

Band saws

▷ Follow the manual's guidelines on the proper speed, rate of feed, and turning radius for each blade.
▷ Keep the blade guide 3–6 mm above the work.

For more on power tool safety, see p. 24.

MEASURING TOOLS

Home rules

One for the money

If you are ever at a loss for a ruler don't despair. There is almost certain to be something close at hand that can be pressed into service in an emergency. How about the contents of your wallet for example? Laid out flat a $5 note measures 130 × 65 mm (135 × 66 mm in New Zealand), a $10 note 139 × 65 mm (140 × 68 in New Zealand) and a $20 note 145 × 65 mm (145 × 70 mm in New Zealand). By folding, adding and subdividing the edges of notes you should be able to reach a close approximation of almost any measurement you need. If you're short of cash then you'll just have to look elsewhere. How about the paper drawer? A sheet of A4 paper— the common size used for letters and photocopies— measures 297 × 220 mm, while the next size up, A3, measures 420 × 297 mm.

Painted numbers

Have you noticed that the numbers and graduation marks etched in metal measuring tools become hard to read after a while? You don't need to replace the tools when that happens. Instead, paint them white and wipe off the excess paint while it is wet. The numbers and marks will be easy to read again. On aluminium tools, use black paint.

For good measure

Rather than discard an old tape measure, snip off a 150 mm section and keep it in your wallet. This portable ruler is handy for checking the size of small items in hardware stores.

Oversize ruler ▶

Cutting timber to size is much easier if you have an oversize ruler painted on your workshop floor and wall. Scribe the lines at convenient intervals, depending on the sorts of measurements you are most often likely to need, and then label them. When you're ready to measure, butt the timber against the wall. If you need to find intermediate lengths, use a 300 mm ruler. To protect the marks from foot traffic, coat them with a clear sealer.

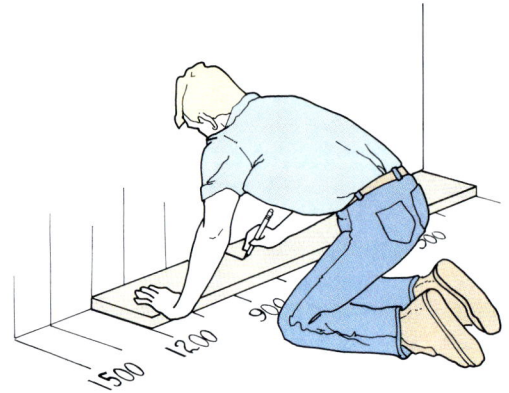

BE YOUR OWN RULER

If you need a tape measure or a ruler and there's none to be had, take a cue from our ancestors and use your body to estimate distances from less than 25 mm to as much as 2100 mm. The illustrations below give some approximate measurements and their traditional names. To achieve more exact guidelines, measure your own fingers, hands, limbs etc. (Be sure you are fully extended when you do so.) Memorise the results and you're ready to go.

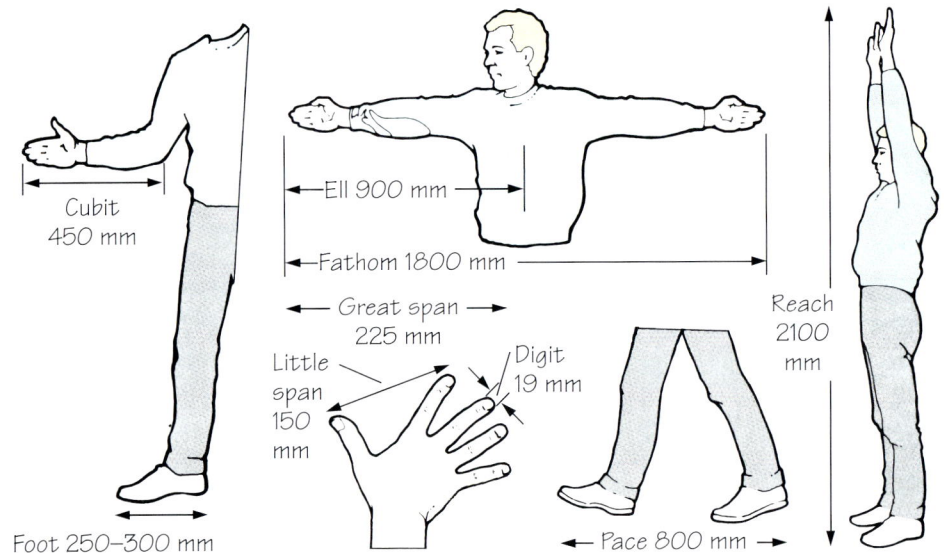

Cubit 450 mm

Foot 250–300 mm

Ell 900 mm

Fathom 1800 mm

Great span 225 mm

Little span 150 mm

Digit 19 mm

Pace 800 mm

Reach 2100 mm

Mounted rule

For quick and easy measuring, tack a metre-long stick or glue a metal rule to your workbench. If you glue a smaller rule to your tool box, you'll find that measuring on the run is easy.

Make a transfer

Because an incorrect measurement can ruin a project, transferring it accurately is critical. If you don't have the right measuring tool handy, slip a thin rubber band around a straight stick. This way, you'll have a sliding marker that will preserve your last measurement. For best results, don't use a rubber band that is so large you have to double it over to make it snug.

Magnetic measurer

You can also use a scrap piece of steel to transfer a measurement. Mark the place with a small rectangular or square magnet. It will clamp onto the metal and stay there as long as needed.

Tape

Sliding track ▲

If you don't have the right tools to measure an inside dimension, press a sliding curtain track into service. Cut off the elbows of the track, stretch it to fit the space, wrap tape around the point where the sections of the track overlap to keep them from sliding out of position, then remove the track and measure it. To measure smaller dimensions, cut the track down.

Dip straw

Would you like a simple, accurate, and spill-proof way to measure out a small amount of stain or other liquids? Dip one end of a plastic straw in the liquid just deep enough to get the amount needed. Then place a finger on the other end to hold the liquid in the straw. Keep your finger on the straw while you take it to its new destination. For greater accuracy, mark often-used measures on the straw.

Hammer gauge

If one hand holds the hammer and the second hand holds the nail, how do you gauge the distance between nails without using a third hand to measure? Let your hammer be a measuring tool. Large hammers are longer than 400 mm, the most common distance between studs in Australia (600 mm in New Zealand). Wrap tape of one colour 400 mm from the head of the hammer; use different colours to mark 300 mm and other often-used lengths.

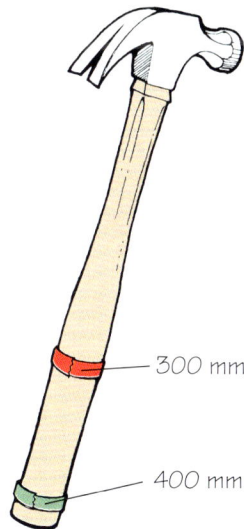

300 mm

400 mm

Wax tape

Professionals use a steel tape because it gives an accurate measurement and retracts at the touch of a button. To protect the numbers and keep the action smooth, coat the tape with a little wax; then buff it thoroughly with a cloth. ▼

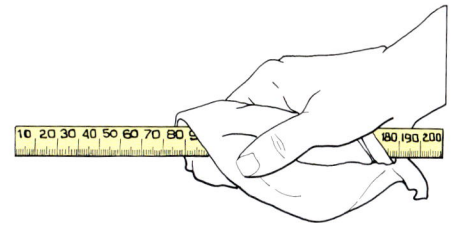

Taking notes

You'll always have a place to jot down measurements if you stick a self-adhesive label to the side of your tape measure. Either replace the label when you're done or erase the marks and reuse it.

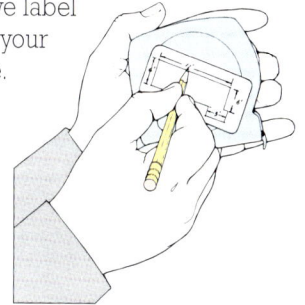

Easy subtraction

The hook of a metal tape—so handy when measuring from one edge—gets in the way of a measurement that starts in the middle of a surface. To obtain an accurate measurement in this case, begin your measurement at the 100 mm mark. Just remember to subtract the amount later on.

MARKING TOOLS

Sharp and snappy

Sandpaper sharpener

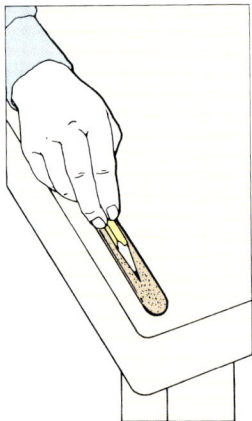

A sharp pencil is indispensable for making precise layouts. One way to keep your pencils sharp at all times is to tape or glue a strip of medium-grit sandpaper or an emery board to your workbench or a nearby wall. To sharpen a pencil, just rub the pencil point back and forth a few times against the abrasive surface. To achieve the chisel-shaped point that's best for marking wood, rub only the opposite sides of the point.

Another one-handed sharpener

You can also glue a small plastic pencil sharpener to the underside of your workbench. To catch shavings, position the sharpener over a rubbish bin.

Chalk talk

The coloured chalk used for snapping lines is highly visible, but it can be hard to remove from porous surfaces such as brick and unfinished wood. To make cleaning up easier in such cases, carry in your tool kit an extra chalk box filled with talcum powder. The white powder is almost as visible as the traditional chalks on dark-coloured surfaces and is easy to remove. On lighter surfaces, however, the white can be hard to see.

Snap line holder

When snapping a chalk line, both ends of the line must be anchored while the line is snapped. On wood, tie the line around a nail driven into one end of the plank or panel. Or cut a narrow saw kerf and hook the string in the kerf.

Mechanical compass

To avoid having to resharpen and reposition the little pencil in a compass over and over again, substitute a mechanical pencil for the wooden one. You'll have a durable marking tool that needs no sharpening and little adjusting. All you have to do to get a fresh point is push down on (or twist) the end.

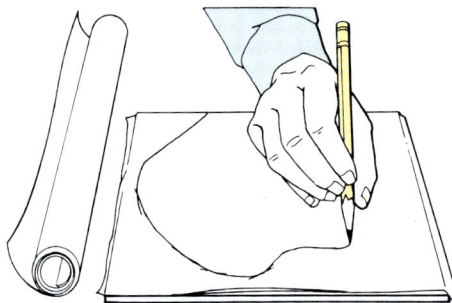

Draw anywhere ▲

Ceramic tiles, glass, and metal are hard to mark. One solution is to cover the area to be marked with a tape that's easy to peel off, such as artist's tape, or with a sheet of contact adhesive paper. This way you'll be able to draw (and see) your pencil marks. Leave the tape or contact paper in place until you've finished cutting. Then remove it.

Unconventional tools

Circle chain

Use a length of flat-link chain to draw various-size circles. Drive the tip of a nail through one of the links and into the centre of your circle. Use this nail as a pivot point, and insert the point of a pencil at the desired radius. To make your circle accurate, keep the chain taut and the pencil perpendicular to the work surface. ▼

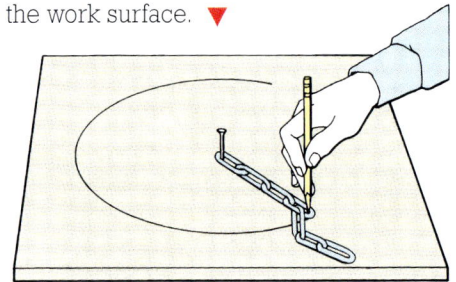

Pegboard circle

A 50 mm wide strip of pegboard makes a great substitute trammel—a tool used to mark large circles—because the pegboard's holes offer a variety of radii. To use your pegboard trammel, first locate the pivot point by fastening one end of the pegboard to the workpiece with a screw. Use a screw that fits the hole, but leave it a little loose so that the pegboard can pivot freely. Place a pencil in the appropriate hole and rotate the pegboard to draw an arc or circle. ▼

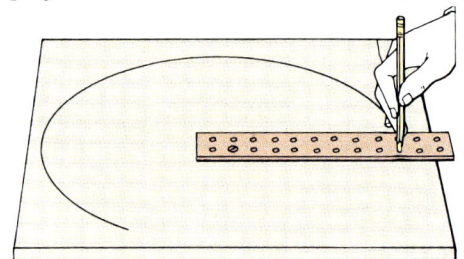

LAYOUT TOOLS

Improvisations

Marble-ous level

If you don't have a level, you can still check your work. Place a marble at the midpoint of the work and at various positions along the work surface. If it doesn't immediately roll off in any direction, your work is level.

Here's the pitch

If you want an easy way to align your work to a specific angle or pitch, try this. Place the level at the desired angle; then mark the positions of the bubbles by placing tape on the glass vial at the ends of each bubble. To duplicate this pitch, angle the level in a new location, centring the bubbles between the pieces of tape. When the job is done, remove the tape.

Plumb bob impostor

If you don't have a plumb bob handy, try using a chalk line box as a substitute. Secure the hook end of the chalk line and extend the string; then mark the spot, using the tapered bottom end of the chalk box as a reference. ▼

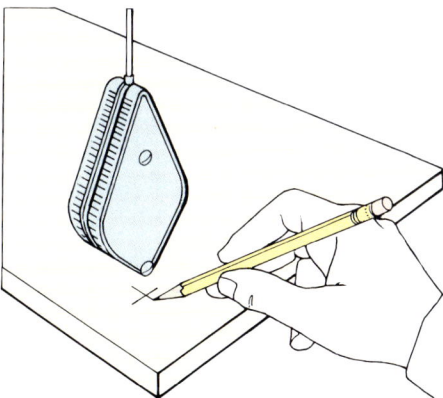

Checking up

Second line matches first

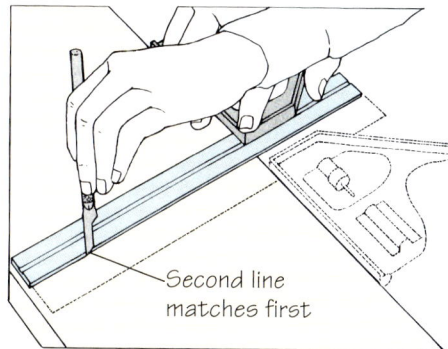

Test for square ▲

Every so often, it's a good idea to test your combination square to see if it is true. Place the tool on a straight plank and draw a line along the square's blade. Then turn the square over, place the blade at the line, and draw a line; if the lines match, the square is true.

Protect your tools

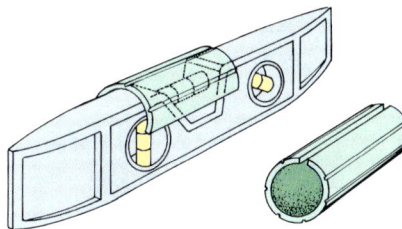

Bubble cover ▲

It's easy to break one of those little glass vials in a level inadvertently. To protect the glass, cut 75 mm lengths of garden hose and slit them lengthwise. Between jobs slip the covers over the vials.

On the level

Always check a level before you buy it, and test it periodically afterwards. To make the test, place the level on the floor or on a table, mark where you've placed it, and note the bubble positions on the vials. Then rotate the level, end for end, align it on the same spot, and note the reading. Finally, turn the level over top to bottom, and make a final reading. All three readings should be the same. If your level has tiny screws, you can adjust them to true the level. If there are no screws and the level isn't true, you'll have to buy another level. ▼

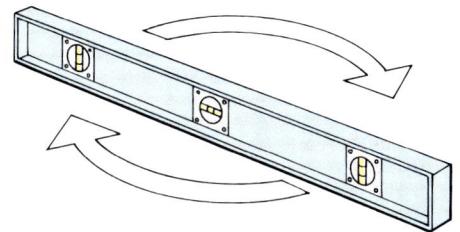

Hanging square

The best way to ensure the accuracy of a square year after year is to take good care it. Try not to drop it accidentally, and always hang it on the wall when you're not using it. To hang your square, take a piece of 75 × 25 mm timber and either bevel one edge at a 45° angle or cut a thin groove to accept the square. Nail or screw the strip to the wall. ▼

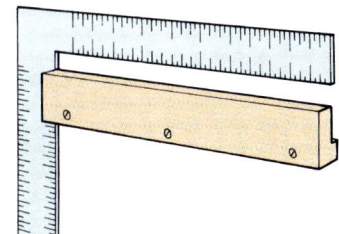

CLAMPS AND VICES

Clamp improvements

Recycled film caps

A tight G-clamp can mar a work surface. To protect your projects, glue the caps from plastic 35 mm film containers to the G-clamp jaws. When you no longer need the caps, just pop them off.

Magnetic pads

Ever wish you had a third hand when fitting protective wood blocks between a workpiece and steel pipe-clamp jaws? Magnets fitted into the blocks can make the job easier. Cut recesses in the blocks so the magnets will be flush with the surface; then glue the magnets into place with epoxy.

Red flag

The ends of long bar and pipe clamps often stick out during a clamping job. To avoid bumping into them, drape a brightly coloured rag over the end of each clamp. That way you won't hurt yourself or tear your clothing. ▼

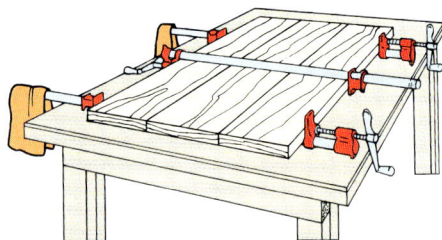

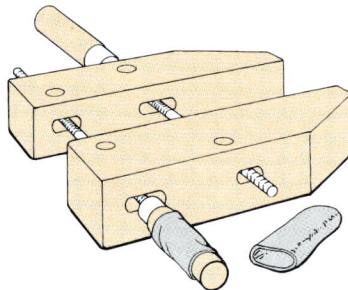

Turning point ▲

If you have trouble getting enough torque (turning pressure) on the smooth handles of a hand-screw clamp, stretch a length of a bicycle tube over the handle. The tube will go on easily if you dust the inside with talcum powder.

Vice advice

Vice cushions

To keep a vice from marring wood or other soft material, make two wooden cushions the same size as the jaws of the vice. To hold the cushions in place on the vice, attach magnetic strips to them with construction adhesive.

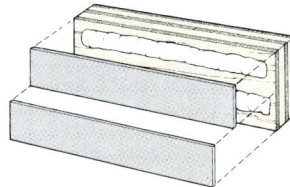

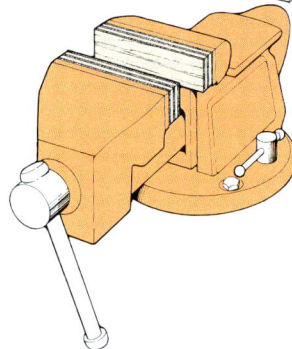

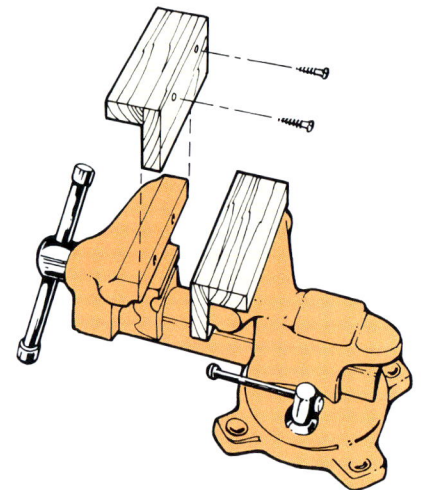

Squeeze-out protection

To keep your clamps free from rust and dried glue, rub them with paraffin- or paste-wax. The coating adds moisture resistance and allows you to easily chip off any accidental gobs of glue. ▼

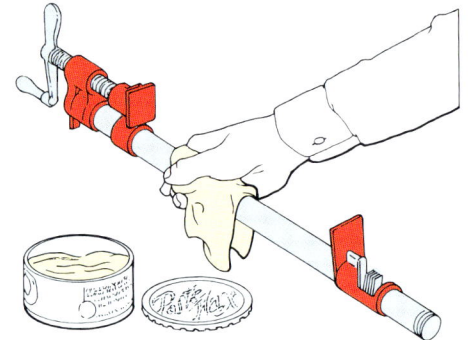

Shield a vice ▲

Another way to protect a work surface from the jaws of a bench vice is with a pair of wooden shields. The ones shown here are easy to make out of four pieces of scrap wood glued and screwed together to form L-joints.

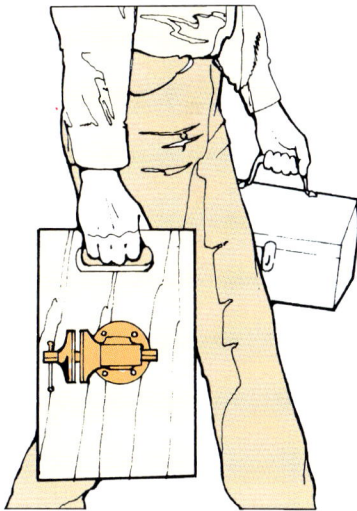

You *can* take it with you ▲

Have you ever been away from your workshop and needed a vice? Here are two ways to take the vice to the job. Bolt a 75 mm vice to a 400 mm long, 300 × 50 mm plank with a cut-out handle. This size plank is heavy enough to remain steady. Or bolt a 50 × 50 mm block of wood to the end of your tool box. Then when you need to support a workpiece on a small job, clamp a 75 mm vice onto the wood block. ▼

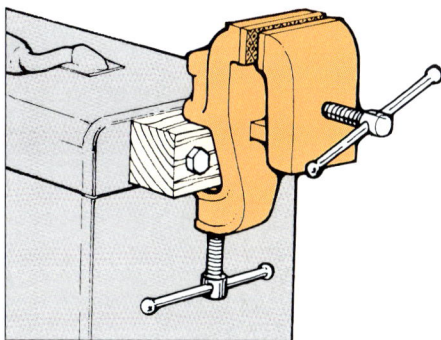

USER-FRIENDLY CLAMPS

Clamps make great assistants. Many home workshops are stocked with G-clamps, spring clamps, pipe clamps and hand screws, but there are other types for just about any job. Some of the handiest are shown below.

Bar clamps

Quick-Grip bar clamp

A *Quick-Grip bar clamp* can be set one-handed. To slide the jaw into place, pull the trigger. To add pressure, squeeze the grip. Removable rubber pads protect the work.

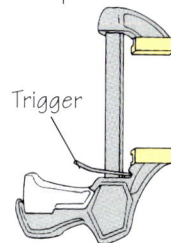

Trigger

Aluminium bar clamp

Lightweight aluminium bar clamps work as well as, or even better than, steel bar clamps. The lighter weight makes a large glue-up easier to move, and the aluminium won't leave glue stains.

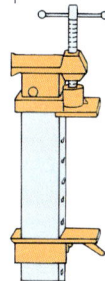

Cam-action bar clamp

Try a *cam-action bar clamp* for light-duty jobs. To set one, slide the movable jaw to the work; lock it in place by turning the cam lever so that it is perpendicular to the bar of the clamp.

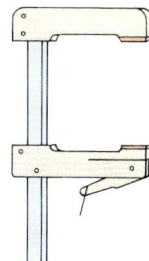

Specialty clamps

Web clamp

Choose a *web clamp* when you need to hold irregularly shaped pieces together, and when you are working with interlocking joints (such as those in a chair).

Deep-throat G-clamp

Use *deep-throat G-clamps* to apply pressure to the centre of wide pieces. These clamps come in a variety of sizes, and they are fairly inexpensive.

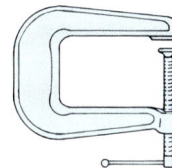

Edge clamp

When you need to hold an edging, such as trim, moulding or laminate, in place, use an *edge clamp*. As you set it, make sure that all the screws are applying equal pressure.

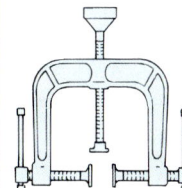

SUPPLIES AND EQUIPMENT

Glues

Economical refills

If you use a lot of woodworking or other glue, buy it in large quantities. You'll save money and avoid the hassle of running out of glue in the middle of a job. To dispense the glue, use old sauce or mustard squeeze bottles with twist-seal nozzles or flip-top caps. Be sure to remove the labels and clearly mark the bottle with its new contents.

Slick tip

Have you ever struggled to get a stuck cap off a tube of glue? If so, here's an easy solution. Rub a little petroleum jelly onto the tip before replacing the cap; the jelly will keep the glue from sticking.

The right glue

Always choose the right adhesive for the job on hand. Here are the most common adhesives used around the home.
▷ PVA adhesive: suitable for indoor woodwork; dries clear within 30 minutes; fills gaps.
▷ Urea formaldehyde: for protected exterior use; good gap-filling properties.
▷ Resorcinol formaldehyde: exterior use; waterproof; very durable.
▷ Epoxy resin: two-part adhesive; bonds most materials (not plastics).
▷ Construction adhesive: applied with a glue gun; for protected exterior use; excellent gap-filler.
▷ Contact adhesive: bonds most materials, including porous ones; little resistance to stress.
▷ Cyanoacrylates (Supa Glue): suitable for non-porous materials; grabs instantly; not for stressed joints.

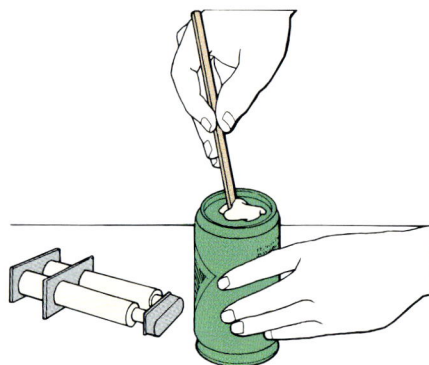

Cool it ▲

To keep epoxy from setting too quickly in warm weather or in a heated workshop, turn over a cold unopened can of soft drink and mix the ingredients in the recessed bottom of the can (dry it first). The cold aluminum will slow the setting process, and the recess in the can makes a fine mixing bowl.

Other adhesives

Cement can collar

When applying contact cement, keep the rim of the cement can clean by covering it with an aluminum foil collar. The foil will catch the drips and prevent gummy buildup. Once the job is done, discard the foil; the lid will fit tightly in place. ▼

Removable adhesive

Inexpensive wall adhesive, also known as Blue-tack, has many uses around the workshop. Use it to secure a screw on the tip of a screwdriver, to hold nuts and washers together, and to post assembly instructions and notes to yourself. In many situations it's a good substitute for tape or staples.

Carpet scrap applicator

Cleaning brushes that have been used to apply contact cement is an impossible job. Instead of throwing away brush after brush, make a reusable applicator out of scrap wood; then just staple a fresh scrap of carpet to the block for each new job.

Storing adhesives

An upside-down trick

Storing glue bottles and tubes upside down keeps the contents ready to pour. To make a holder for your glue bottles, drill holes through an existing shelf in your workshop. Otherwise drill holes through a scrap of timber and attach it to the wall.

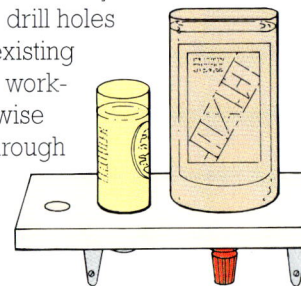

Hang tubing

Here's a clever solution to a common workshop storage problem. Since plastic squeeze tubes of contact cement and caulking don't lie flat and can't be stacked, try hanging them up. Cut a piece of tape about 50 mm long and trim it to fit the width of the tube. Stick one end of the tape on the bottom of the tube; then fold the tape in half over the tube, pinching the sticky sides together. Punch a hole through the tape and hang it on a nail or on a pegboard hook.

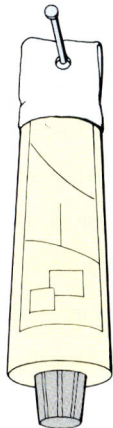

Glue gun holder

The hot dripping tip of a glue gun can be a safety hazard. To keep it out of harm's way, park it in this handy holder made by mounting a spring-metal broom clip on a small piece of scrap timber. To catch the drips, screw a small jar lid to the holder. ▼

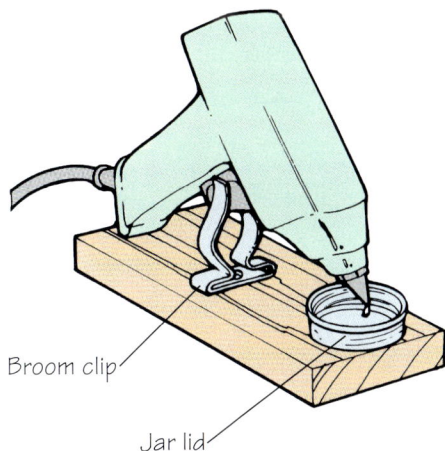

Broom clip

Jar lid

DISPOSING OF HAZARDOUS WASTE

Products containing solvents or other ingredients that carry cautionary warning labels (such as *flammable, reactive* and *corrosive*) are likely to be classified as hazardous waste. Before you buy such a product, try to find a safer (water-based) substitute. If none is available, buy only as much as you can use. If you are unsure of how to dispose of a material, contact your local waste disposal service/centre, environmental protection agenc, or health department (Occupational Safety and Health Service in New Zealand). The table below outlines some general guidelines for workshop materials.

TYPE OF WASTE	●	◆	▼	▲
Contact cement, solvent-based*		◆		▲
Contact cement, water-based		◆		
Degreasing chemicals				▲
Glue, adhesive and sealants, solvent-based				▲
Glue, adhesive and sealants, water-based		◆		
Kerosene			▼	
Paint, water-based		◆		
Paint and varnish stripper	●			
Paintbrush cleaner, phosphate	●			
Paintbrush cleaner, solvent				▲
Paint remover or thinner (residue)				▲
Paints, oil (alkyd) and rust-inhibiting				▲
Polish, furniture (solvent-based)				▲
Rust remover, phosphoric acid	●			
Wood finishes (polyurethane, oil, varnish)				▲
Wood preservative				▲

● Dilute *small* amount with plenty of water and pour down the drain. For *large* amount or if you have a septic tank, recycle or treat as hazardous waste.

◆ Let evaporate, away from people and pets, or solidify with absorbent material, such as cat litter. Double-wrap in plastic; discard with rubbish going to landfill or incinerator.

▼ Recycle at special centre set up for the purpose, or treat as hazardous waste.

▲ Do not discard this hazardous waste. Save for special collection day or contact your local waste disposal service/centre, environmental protection agency, or health department (Occupational Safety and Health Service in New Zealand) for instructions.

*Wrap and discard applicators when dry. Any unused cement is hazardous waste.

SUPPLIES AND EQUIPMENT

Putty and filler

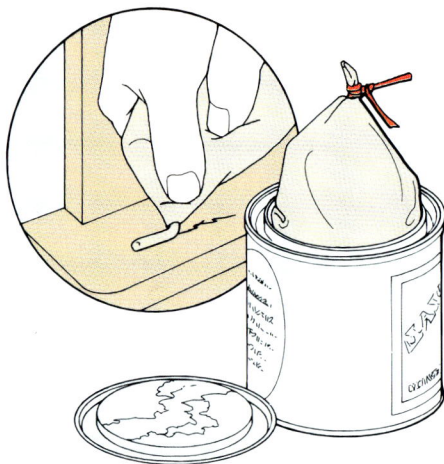

Airless container ▲

Filler and putty dry out quickly when exposed to the air. To slow the drying, use a putty knife to transfer the material to a small sealable plastic bag. Seal the bag, then cut a small hole in one corner. To dispense the material, just squeeze the bag as if you were decorating a cake. When the job is done, twist the corner closed and secure it with a twist tie. Store the closed bag in the original container when it's not in use.

Reviving Plastic Wood

Acetone-base cellulose fibre-filler, known as Plastic Wood, also dries out quickly. To restore Plastic Wood that has begun to harden, mix in a little acetone-based nail polish remover. As long as you don't add too much remover, the Plastic Wood will be as good as new. If, however, the material has dried out thoroughly, there's no rescuing it.

Steel wool and brushes

Magnetic attraction

Small particles of steel wool can collect on a work-piece and even become airborne as metal dust. To contain metal particles and avoid breathing metal dust, wrap a small or medium-size magnet in the wad of steel wool. As you work, periodically wipe off the magnet. When the job is done, run the magnet over the work to remove any remaining metal particles. Always wear a dust mask when working with steel wool.

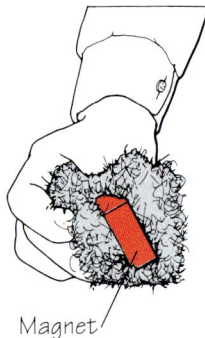

Magnet

For tight spots

How can you rub steel wool effectively in a tight corner or a groove? Cut off the end of a plastic or rubber bicycle handlebar grip. Then stuff a piece of steel wool tightly into the opening, leaving a knot of the stuff protruding. The handle lets you apply pressure—and at the same time protects your hands. ▼

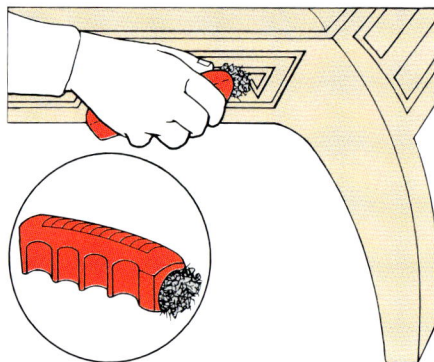

Adjust a brush

Here's a way to convert an ordinary paintbrush into a small scrubbing brush. Simply wrap the bristles securely with masking tape. The closer the tape is to the tips of the bristles, the stiffer the brush will be.

Wire brush renewal

The front section of a wire brush always wears out before the rest. To rejuvenate a worn brush, clamp it upside down in a vice and saw about 25 mm off the brush along with the worn bristles. Another option is to snip off bent or damaged edges with a wire cutter. Cut them diagonally so the ends will be sharp. Wear eye protection when cutting.

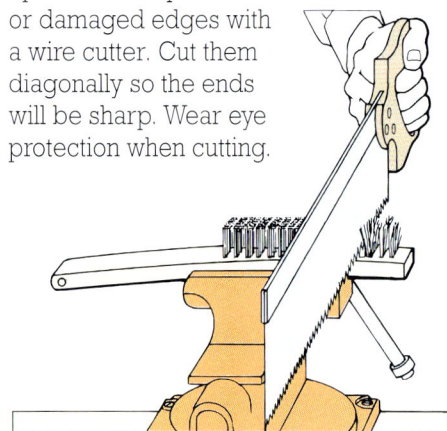

Oil

About spouts

To reduce the flow of oil from a spout, you need to make the opening smaller. One way to do this is to dab a little fingernail polish over the tip. When the polish is dry, reopen the spout by poking it with a pin.

Straw applicator

You can extend the reach of an oil can by holding a straw from a broom next to the spout. Or if holding the straw is awkward, you can tape it to the spout. In either case, the drops of oil will follow the broom straw to its end.

Knives in the workshop

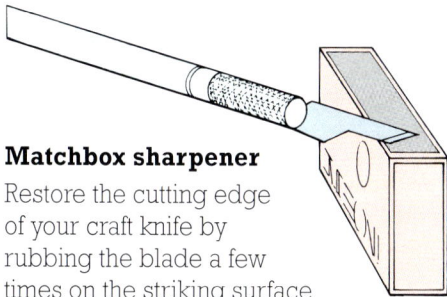

Matchbox sharpener

Restore the cutting edge of your craft knife by rubbing the blade a few times on the striking surface of a matchbox. Sharpen both sides of the cutting edge, holding the blade at the correct angle (pp. 22–23).

Quick-change artist

Ever wished there was an easier way to change the blade in your utility knife? Take a look in hardware stores and home centres for knives that will do so with the push of a button and a twist of the wrist. No more messing around with a screwdriver and then trying to line up the halves of the knife so that it works properly again.

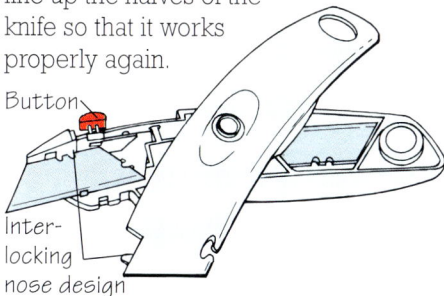

Button

Interlocking nose design

Sharp storage ideas

If you need to take a razor blade to a job, tear the matches out of a book of matches, insert the blade, and close the cover. Back in your workshop, you can store your razor blades in slots cut into a small scrap piece of rigid foam packing material.

Plans and instructions

Write your own

If you are tackling a job that doesn't come with its own instructions, take a few minutes to write your own *before* you begin. It also helps to make your notes on an oversize pad of paper, such as the flip charts you see in conference and meeting rooms. Available at office supply stores, flip charts provide all the room you need to write down instructions and to draw plans and diagrams. For easy viewing, mount the pad on a nail in a workshop wall.

Blow it up

Ever strained to see the fine print and small details of assembly instructions? A trip to a photocopier that can enlarge your original is in order. By enlarging hard-to-read instructions, you can work without reading glasses or eyestrain.

Sheer protection

Protect plans, drawings, and instructions with a piece of clear self-sticking plastic. The papers stay clean and dry, won't tear with use, and are easy to roll up. If needed, you can make notes on the plastic with a Chinagraph pencil. To erase the marks, just rub with a cloth.

Hang 'em high

Instead of leaving instruction sheets on your workbench, where they can get lost, torn or badly soiled, separate the pages and tape them at eye level to the wall just above your work area.

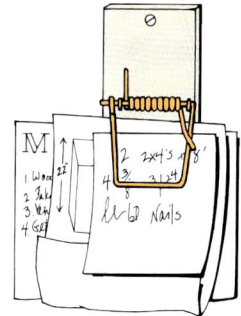

Mousetrapping ▲

Mount a spring-type mousetrap to your workshop wall with screws and you'll have a sturdy holder for your plans. Before you mount the trap, however, prise the bait holder off.

Handy manuals

Can't find your owner's manual when you need it? Keep the manuals for all your power tools in one place. Punch holes in them and store them in a three-ring binder, or keep them in a magazine storage file. Or make your own file by cutting off one end of a large detergent box as shown. Make it a habit to put the manual for a new tool in your special storage place as soon as you finish reading it.

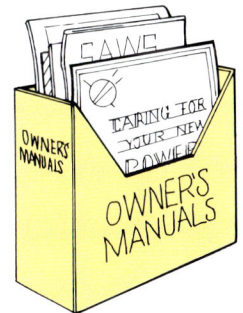

SUPPLIES AND EQUIPMENT

Buckets

Recycled plastic buckets

Twenty-litre plastic buckets have a multitude of uses, from storing extension cords to mixing paint or plaster. Food preparation stores, which buy many ingredients by the bucket, are good sources of free or cheap buckets. If you have small children, be sure to empty a bucket after each use and store it where a child can't get at it. It's not unheard of for a child to crawl into a bucket, become stuck, and drown or suffocate.

Heavy load

When you are carrying a heavy load in a bucket, the container's thin handle can cut painfully into your hand. Make the task easier by fitting an open-ended spanner around the handle as shown. The spanner is kinder to your hand and stabilises the load.

Leaky buckets

To find the exact location of a bucket leak, turn on a small table lamp, remove the shade, and place the bucket upside down over it. The light will shine through the hole.

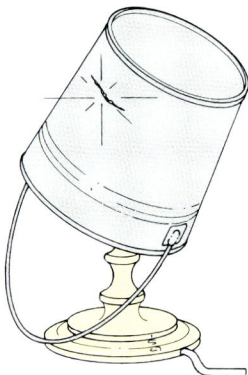

Hole repairs

To make a temporary patch over a small hole in a plastic bucket, fill the hole from both sides with silicone sealant. (The sealant layers stick to each other better than to plastic.) Or drip candle wax over the hole. The wax plug will stay intact, however, only if the bucket is filled with cold water—hot water will melt the wax.

Ropes

Rope saver

To keep a rope from fraying where it rubs against something, slip a length of rubber hose over the rope at the stressed spot. Hold the hose in place with knots tied on either side of it.

No more unravelling

The ends of a length of rope will not unravel if you dab them with either silicone sealant, liquid (air-drying) rubber, or vinyl coating.

Untangle that mess

Don't struggle with a snarled string, rope or cord. Begin untangling by gently pulling outward all around the edges of the snarl. As the tangled mass becomes bigger and looser, the loops will untangle themselves, and you will be left with fewer knots to undo.

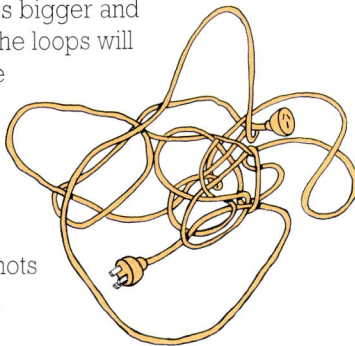

Extension cords

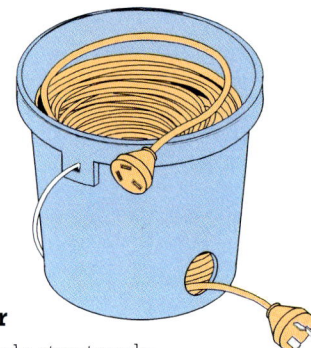

Cord keeper

Extension cords stay tangle-free when kept inside a 20 litre bucket. Near the bottom of the bucket, cut or drill a hole large enough so that the cord's pronged end can pass through it. Then coil the rest of the cord into the bucket. The cord will come out easily when pulled. Plug the ends of the cord together when it's not in use. You can use the space in the centre of the coil to carry tools to a work site.

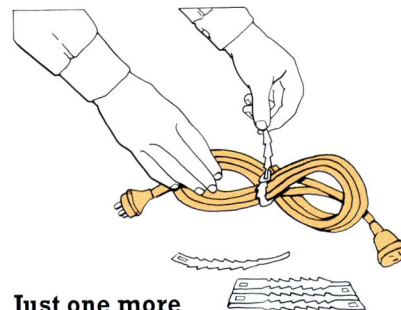

Just one more

If you want to store your cords flat—and keep them organised—coil or loop the cord as shown above. Bind the centre of the cord tightly with one of the plastic 'key lock' ties that come with large polyethylene garbage or garden bags. To hold very long cords, join two or more plastic ties.

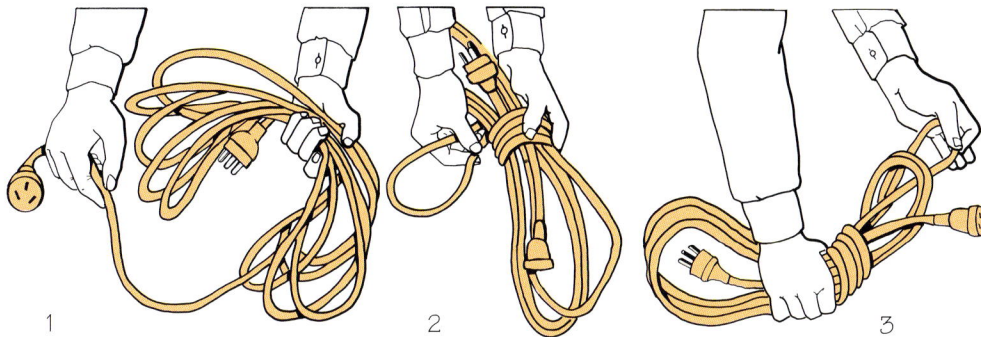

1 2 3

Coil and hang ▲

Here are three quick steps to coiling and hanging a long extension cord. Hold the end of the cord in one hand. With the other hand, loop it back and forth in figure 8s (1). When the cord is coiled, take a single loop and wrap it twice around one end of the coil (2). Finally, insert that same loop through the centre of the smaller coil opening and pull it tight (3). To store the cord, hang this loop on a large nail or peg.

Preventing a sudden disconnect ▶

Does the plug of your power tool tend to pull out of the extension cord socket when you are working overhead or are moving around a lot? To keep this from happening with any portable power tool, tie the ends of the two cords together loosely in a simple knot.

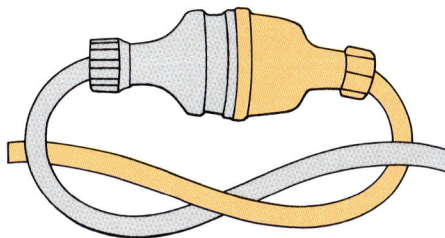

THE RIGHT EXTENSION CORD FOR THE TOOL

The wire gauge of an extension cord determines how much current it can safely carry. (The larger the wire diameter the greater its current-carrying capacity.) Other measures of current are *amperage* and *wattage*. Look for these ratings on the cord's packaging, and on the tool's specifications plate. The cord ratings should be equal to or greater than those shown on the tool. *Note:* If a cord seems to get hot when it is in use, or if it is over 15 m long, choose the next amp rating up.

AMP RATING	WATT RATING	TYPICAL USE
10	2400	Light industrial or handyman: small drill, belt sander, reciprocating saw, router, circular saw
15	3600	Heavier power use, building site: small and large table saws, radial ram saw, band saw, caravans and mobile homes

Torches

In tight places

To drive a screw in a dark corner, attach a little pen-light to the shaft of your screwdriver. You'll be able to see the screw-head easily.

A point of light

Create a mini light for small jobs in tight places by plugging a night-light into a household extension cord. You'll

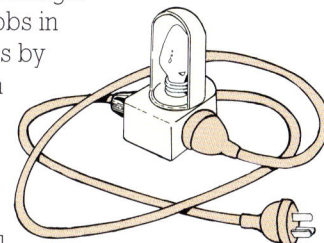

be able to move this little light as far as the cord will reach. When finished, you can disassemble the pieces in a flash.

Prop it up

Turn a pair of pliers into a handy torch stand. Prop the torch at the needed angle in the jaws of the pliers. To hold the jaws firmly around the torch body, stretch a rubber band to link the handles of the pliers.

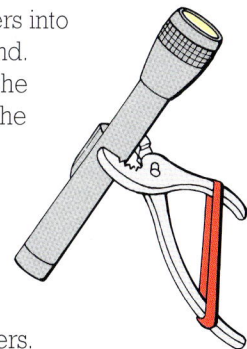

LADDERS

Extension ladders

Hand over hand

To raise an extension ladder, place its feet at the base of the wall. Starting at the top, walk the ladder up, hand over hand, until it is vertical. Then pull its feet out from the wall, extend the ladder to the height you want, lock the extension, and set the feet of the ladder at a 75° angle—you should be able to stand with your toes against the feet of the ladder, your arms and back straight and your hands on the rungs at shoulder height (below). To move a ladder, lower it, hand over hand, and carry it parallel to the ground. ▼

Ground support

If you've ever tried to use a ladder on soft ground, you know that the ladder's feet will sink as soon as you start to climb. To keep the legs from sinking, set them on a piece of 19 mm plywood or particleboard that is at least 150 mm longer and wider than the ladder. The board acts like a snowshoe, distributing the load over a greater area.

Padded ends

The best ladders have padded ends that protect the surfaces they lean against. If your ladder lacks pads, buy rubber ones or make your own by wrapping rags around the ends and tying them with elastic cord. Still another option is to cover the ends with thick socks or heavy-duty work gloves.

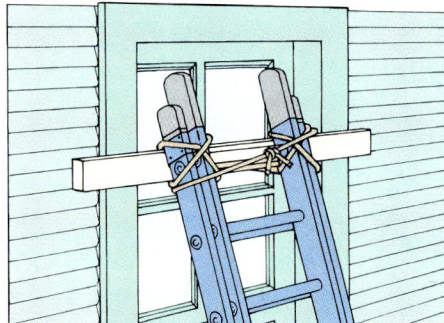

Window treatment ▲

When a job calls for you to rest the top of your ladder in the centre of a window opening, you run the risk of damaging the sill or breaking the glass. One way to avoid problems is to attach a store bought stabiliser bar, which widens the top of the ladder. Or tie a piece of 100 × 50 mm timber to the top rung so that it spans the opening and rests on the window frame or cladding on both sides.

Tie one on

When using a ladder as a way to get up and down from the roof, tie it to a stack or vent pipe with an elastic strap or rope. (Try not to rest the ladder on the gutter.) A gust of wind can knock over an unsecured ladder, damaging things in its path and leaving you stranded.

Customising ladders

Tools at hand ▲

Tired of climbing up and down a step-ladder to retrieve fallen tools? Just drill a minimum of holes in the top step of the ladder to hold your most-used tools.

Basket case

To turn your ladder's shelf into a handy tool and equipment holder, use an elastic strap to fasten a plastic household basket to the shelf.

Bucket holder ▲

Keep a paint can or small bucket within easy reach on an extension ladder by hanging it on a length of broom handle or plastic water pipe extending from one of the ladder's hollow rungs. The pole should be about 600 mm longer than the width of the ladder; notch it at both ends to keep the bucket in place.

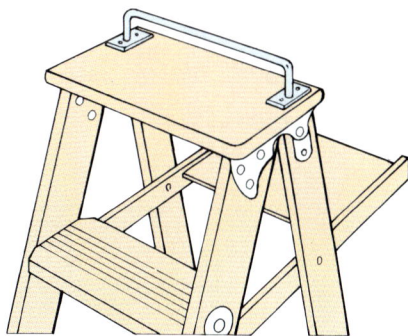

Rail steady ▲

Keeping your balance while standing on a ladder is of utmost importance. A metal towel rail fastened to the top step of the ladder makes a convenient handrail for steadying yourself.

Shoe cleaner

Clean shoes mean surer footing on a ladder. Staple or glue a strip of scrap carpet to the bottom rung of your ladder, and use it to wipe the soles of your shoes each time you climb the ladder.

More on treads

To improve the traction on ladder steps, glue narrow strips of abrasive paper to the treads. Another way to slip-proof the treads is to paint them with clear varnish and then sprinkle a layer of sand onto the wet coating. When the coating dries, you'll have a gritty surface to step on.

Storage

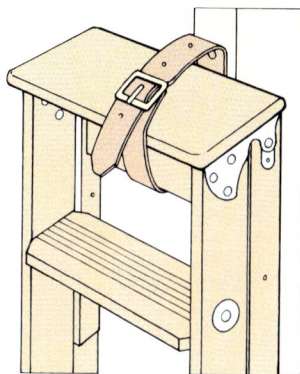

Buckle up ▲

When it's time to store a ladder, don't just lean it against the wall—it can easily fall over. A better way is to attach an old leather belt to the wall and wrap it around the ladder's top step. Or mount a stepladder vertically on a pair of pegs securely fastened to the wall. Hang an extension ladder horizontally on pegs spaced no more than 1800 mm apart.

Keep it closed

A simple hook-and-eye fastener will keep a wooden stepladder closed while you're carrying or storing it. Screw the hook into one leg and the eye in the other leg, directly across from the hook. If you have a metal stepladder, hold the legs together with a belt or strap.

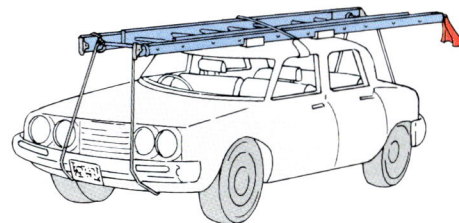

Car carrier ▲

How do you get a hired extension ladder home if you don't have a roof rack? Place the ladder on dense foam pads laid on the car's roof, and then tie the ladder through the windows, and the ends to the front and rear bumpers with stout rope. Tie on a couple of red caution flags and be sure the ladder is secure before you drive away.

Theft protection

Never store a ladder outside or in an unlocked garage. A burglar may use it to reach a window that would otherwise be out of reach. If you have to leave a ladder out, chain it securely to a tree.

Compact ladder

If you don't have room to store an extension ladder, consider buying a multipurpose articulated ladder, which unfolds to make a 3 m extension ladder. An articulated ladder is fairly expensive, but it can double as a stepladder and as a support for scaffolding planks.

TOOL CARE AND STORAGE

Better boxes

Tool box organiser

Use magnets to hold your favourite flat tools, such as spanners and pliers, against the inside lid of your tool box. Purchase magnets of various sizes and of sufficient strength to hold the tools, and glue the magnets firmly onto the inside lid of the box.

Handy storage

A bread box or old lunch box will comfortably hold all the tools you need for small jobs around the house. Such containers are also good for keeping a duplicate set of your favourite and most-used hand tools in a place other than your workshop. Having the right tools close at hand may keep you from putting off needed repairs.

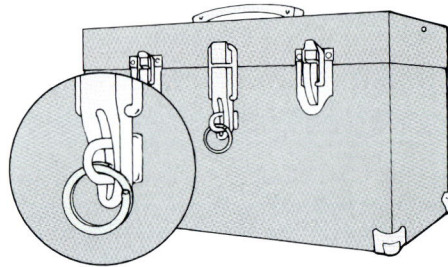

Keyless lockup ▲

To keep curious small children out of your tool box, secure its lock hasp with a spring-steel key ring rather than with a lock. This way, you can childproof the tool box (little hands are not strong enough to remove the key ring) without having to carry around another key.

Tool cushion

Line the bottom of your tool box with felt or scrap carpeting. The padding will protect the tools and help reduce noise when you handle them.

Tool carrying tips

Pick some pockets

A jacket or vest with lots of pockets, like those worn by professional photographers and sport fishermen, can help you organise and hold small tools, fasteners, and other items you regularly need on a job.

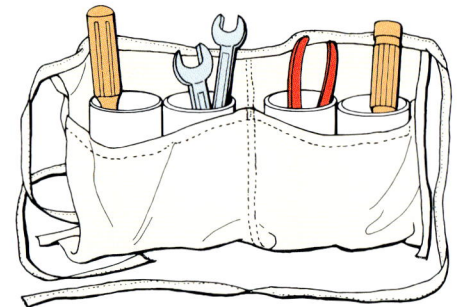

Pockets for tools ▲

Use empty tin cans of various sizes, or short lengths of 50 mm plastic pipe to transform the deep, wide pockets of a nail pouch into a convenient carrier for spanners, pliers and screwdrivers. If you use cans, remove their tops and bottoms. Glue or tape the cylinders together to keep them from shifting around, and slip them into the pouches to create dividers.

Tool roll-up

A handy way to store drill bits, chisels and files is to roll them up in one of those segmented silverware pouches. If you don't have one, make your own by sewing parallel seams in a nail pouch.

Multipurpose box ▶

This simple plywood tool box doubles as a step for reaching high places or as a portable mini workbench/sawhorse. Make the box 370 mm high, 650–750 mm wide, and just deep enough to accommodate a sturdy plastic cutlery tray. (Use the tray for storing small tools, bits and assorted fasteners.) Using a jig saw, make cut outs for carrying the unit.

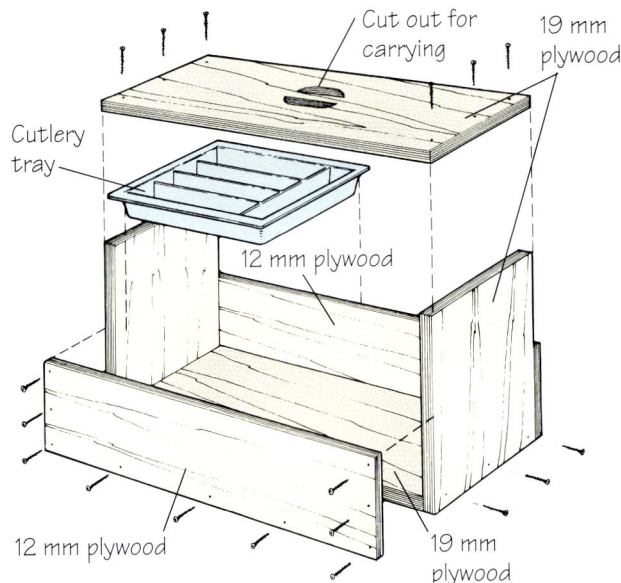

Cut out for carrying

19 mm plywood

Cutlery tray

12 mm plywood

12 mm plywood

19 mm plywood

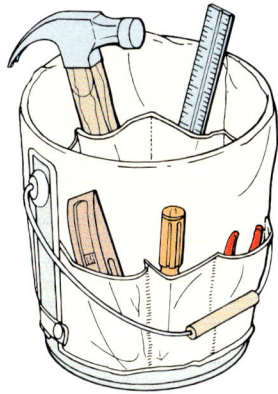

Bucket belts ▲

Turn an empty 20 litre plastic bucket into a handy tool carrier by fitting it with a sturdy tool 'belt'. Make the belt from a a couple of lengths of stout canvas or nylon and sew in as many pockets as you need. Work out which tools are to go where, and plan accordingly. Even when filled, the belt will still leave plenty of room in the bucket for storing larger tools, such as saws, levels, extension cords and small power tools.

Keeping track

Tag time

Before lending a tool, write your name on a stick-on label and affix it to the handle. The label will serve as a reminder to the borrower to return the tool when the job is done.

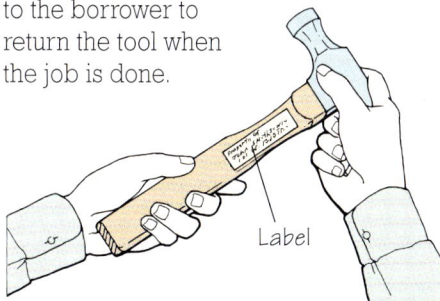

Label

Permanent ID

Another way to identify your tools permanently (and discourage thieves in the process) is to inscribe your name on them with an electric engraver.

Show your colours

If you are working with a partner on a job and are using similar tools, code them with coloured tape so there'll be no mix-ups at the end of the day. Using reflective tape provides an added advantage. A mislaid tool is easier to spot by day and, with a torch, by night.

Rust busting

A measure of prevention

Moisture in the air invites rust, and if moist air gets into a tool box, it corrodes the tools. One way to keep the air in your tool box dry is to drop in some packets of silica gel, sold at craft shops, or sometimes available free in the packing of new products. Once the silica gel becomes saturated you can renew its effectiveness by placing it near a lit 60 watt light bulb for 15 minutes.

Two more measures of prevention

Other effective moisture absorbers that will keep the contents of your tool box rust-free are a handful of mothballs and a 50 g cube of camphor (sold at local pharmacies). Because camphor loses its effectiveness after about six months, you'll have to replace the cube twice a year.

The brush-off

If your tools do become corroded, you'll find that a wire brush is useful for scrubbing off the rust. To make your own sturdy brush, all you need is a strip of bronze window screening and a screw cap from a bottle of laundry detergent. First, make a fringe of wire 'bristles' at one edge of the screening by cutting three rows of horizontal wire strands. Then roll up the screening tightly, secure it with wire, and wedge it firmly in the cap.

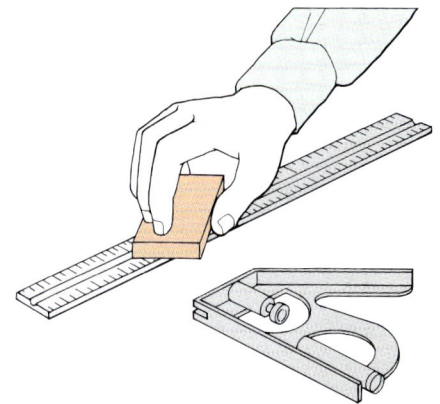

Wonderful bar ▲

A moulded rubber and silicon carbide bar works like an eraser to clean and polish metal that's become dirty and corroded. To clean a tool, just rub the bar over the surface and wipe off the dust. You can use it dry or wet (with water, oil or detergent). These light-weight flexible bars are sold through major tool and woodworking outlets.

WORKSHOP ORGANISATION

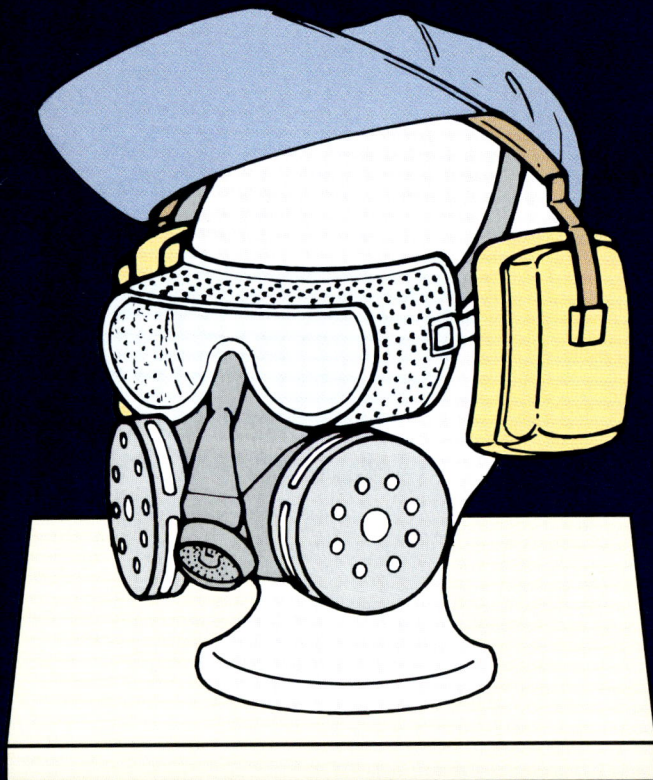

WORKSHOP BASICS

Creature comforts

Foot ease

Here's relief from tired feet and legs: cover the floor in front of your workbench with a scrap of low-pile carpet. Besides providing cushioning, it prevents a major cause of leg discomfort—the transfer of body heat from legs and feet to cold concrete. And it's easily cleaned with a vacuum cleaner. You can also reduce strain on leg and back muscles by standing on a rubber antifatigue mat, available from home centres and floor-covering stores.

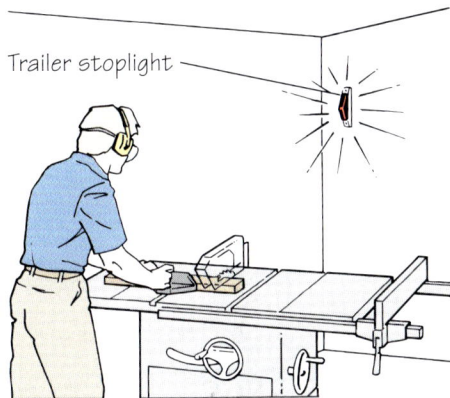

Trailer stoplight

Home alone ▲

Can't hear the doorbell in your workshop? Buy a trailer stoplight (check the voltage first) at a car parts store and connect it to the doorbell wiring at the point where the wires run closest to your workshop. Install it at eye level so that it will catch your attention whenever someone rings the bell. To amplify your workshop phone, electronics stores carry an extension bell.

Attention getter

Family members can also call you to come to dinner or to the phone by 'ringing' the trailer stoplight (see below, left). Just hook it to a separate doorbell transformer and to a doorbell button inside the house. It's a lot safer than getting an unexpected tap on your shoulder while you're running a machine.

It's not the heat

If your workshop is damp, install a dehumidifier. In addition to making life less muggy for you, it will keep tools from rusting, prevent timber from swelling and rotting, and speed up the drying of glue, paint and other finishes.

Clearing the air

To rid your workshop of fine dust particles and noxious fumes, it's essential to have good cross-ventilation. If your workshop has two facing windows, open one and place a fan in the other so that it blows out. If there is only one window, consider installing an exhaust fan in the wall opposite, or in the ceiling.

Chilly workshop?

Give it a quick warm-up by installing an infrared heat lamp over your workbench. It will warm your hands and tools so that you can work comfortably on cold days. Use a heat lamp that screws into a standard ceramic screw light fitting. Heat lamps typically draw 250 watts, so check that the wiring can handle the lamp plus whatever other equipment you use on that circuit.

Extended work season

Is your workshop inside an unfinished garage? For the cost of insulation, you can use the space for a greater part of the year and increase your comfort in extreme weather. Give priority to the roof, where most heat is lost or gained. Staple fibreglass batts, vapour barrier down (if there is one), between the joists, or install a ceiling of plasterboard and lay insulation between the joists. ▼

Save steps

Take a cue from kitchen designers. Arrange your workshop in an efficient triangle that puts the workbench, tool storage and assembly areas all within easy reach of one another. Set up your timber storage and wood-cutting and wood-shaping tools in similar fashion. ▼

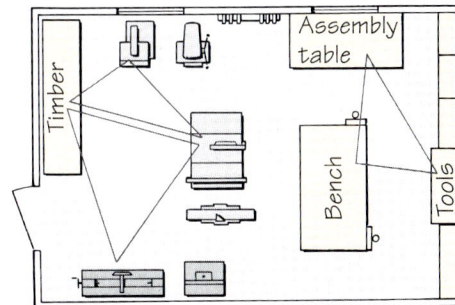

WORKSHOP BASICS

Noise control

Workshop door sealants

Keep both noise and dirt out of the rest of the house by sealing the gaps around your workshop door. Tack spring-metal or tubular-gasket weatherstripping along the edges of the frame and mount another strip along the door bottom. If yours is a hollow-core door, glue or staple acoustic tiles onto its workshop side or replace it with a solid-core door.

Sound barrier

Contain loud workshop noises by soundproofing the walls between your workshop and living areas. If a wall is unfinished, install batts of rockwool or noise control blanket between the studs, and cover them with wallboard. Cover a finished wall (or ceiling) with acoustic tiles, or even better, apply a sound-deadening board, such as Sonoboard, followed by a second layer of wallboard.

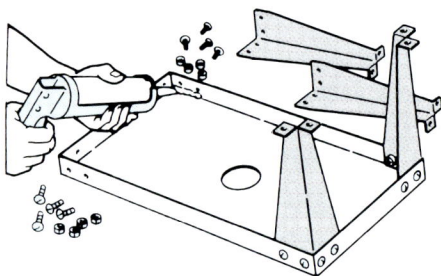

Glue rattling parts together ▲

To silence a freestanding piece of workshop equipment, take apart its base, stand or cabinet. As you reassemble the piece, apply a bead of silicone sealant wherever metal parts join. This will bond the parts and keep them from vibrating against one another.

Clamp down on vibrations

Reduce the noisy vibrations of a bench top power tool by putting a rubber pad or carpet scrap under each tool leg and clamping the tool to the bench.

Shedding light

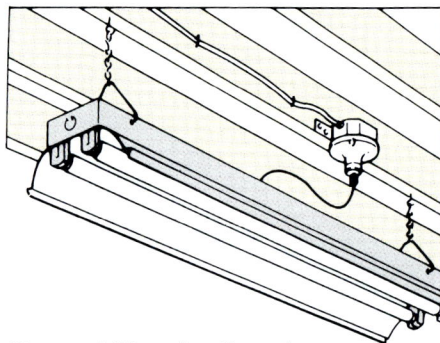

General illumination ▲

Replace overhead incandescent bulbs with fluorescent fixtures, which are cheaper to operate, last longer, and give an even, diffused light. Suspend two-tube units over major work areas. Choose 1200 mm units and, for a large workshop, double the number of tubes. Plug each unit directly into a ceiling light outlet. If that's not possible, have an electrician install permanently wired units. Fluorescent tubes are available in a variety of light 'types', so that you can have ordinary tubes or 'daylight' units, which emit a light that more closely mimics daylight conditions outdoors.

Reflected glory

To improve general visibility in your workshop, paint wall and ceiling areas white or a light colour (the lighter the colour, the better it will reflect both natural and artificial light).

Workbench lighting

A folding-arm lamp is perfect for close work. But having it clamped on the workbench edge can limit its usefulness. To put the lamp wherever you need it, remove the lamp bracket and drill holes at various points in the bench top for the lamp to fit into. Make each hole the same diameter as the hole in the lamp bracket.

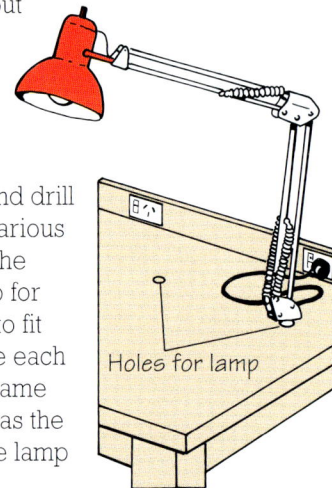

Holes for lamp

Mobile light

Clip-on lamps with reflectors also provide a flexible source of light for close work. If you don't have a shelf that you can attach them to, mount a 50 × 25 mm timber strip onto the wall, 600 mm or so above the workbench. This will allow you to light your work from many angles, or from two angles at once. ▼

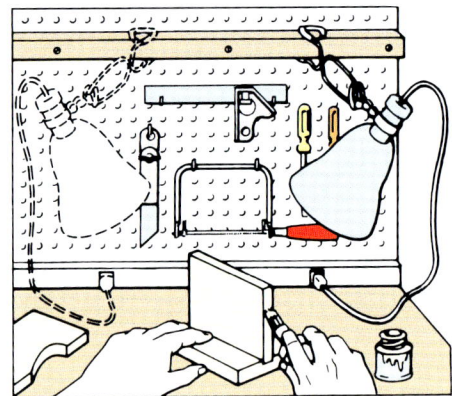

Prevent popping lights

Flying debris produced by power tools can shatter a hot light bulb. Use shatterproof bulbs or tape window screening over the front of the lamp reflector.

Power supply

Dust off

Keep your workshop's electrical outlets from becoming sawdust-clogged fire hazards. Cap unused outlets with plug-in 'childproof' plastic covers. Or install outdoor weatherproof covers that face down and do not trap dust.

Cord hangers

Use clothes pegs to keep power cords out of your way. Screw or glue them to overhead joists or other strategic spots. Or, for a hanger that lets a cord move without chafing it, slit a short length of old garden hose diagonally. Open the slit to tack the hanger in place and to insert or remove the cord. ▼

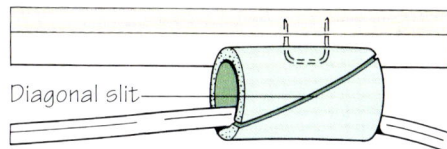

Diagonal slit

Convenient outlets

A multi-outlet power strip installed under the front edge of your workbench provides a handy place to plug in power tools while keeping cords out of your way. Use a properly earthed power strip with a fuse or circuit breaker and a reset button to prevent overloads. Also make sure it is rated to handle the maximum total amperage that you will use on it.

Power from above

For easy access to electricity, hang a retractable (reel-type) extension cord from a hook screwed into an overhead joist. Or mount a multi-outlet power strip on a drop-down board bolted to a joist, as shown. Plug your new overhead power source into an existing power point. If you have to run an extension cord to it, secure the cord loosely with slit-hose hangers, like the one shown below, left. Permanently attaching an extension may violate electrical codes. ▼

Turn button to hold board up

Board swings up when not in use

Rewiring?

Make sure you have enough circuits and a safety switch installed in your main meter box. Have your electrician install a sub-board near the workshop to control all workshop circuits. This way, you can easily turn off all power to the workshop and lock the sub-board to prevent unapproved use of your power tools. Check with your electrician to see if separate circuit breakers can be installed on your sub-board so that you won't have far to go when a breaker trips, or if an emergency requires you to turn the power off immediately.

AVOID SHOCK

SAFETY FIRST

Here are some simple ways to cut electrical risks in your workshop:

Safety switches. Have an electrician install a safety switch on the main meter board for your house, to protect all power circuits. You can also buy power points with safety switches, as well as in-line units for use with extension cords.

Cords and plugs. Replace frayed or cracked electrical cords and plugs. Damaged cords are extremely dangerous and should be replaced immediately. Never try to fix a cord with electrical tape. Keep cords from being trampled underfoot and away from the work area as much as possible. Pay particular attention when using power cutting tools, such as saws and grinders. Always use heavy-duty cords rated to handle more current than your tools will draw (see chart, p. 43). Avoid tangles and fully retract coiled cords when using high-wattage tools or heaters.

Earthing. If you have a metal workbench, have it earthed to reduce the chances of a shock from shorted equipment. An electrician can earth it by running a wire from the bench to an electrical sub-board, or to a metallic electrical conduit.

THE WORKBENCH

AN ALL-PURPOSE BENCH

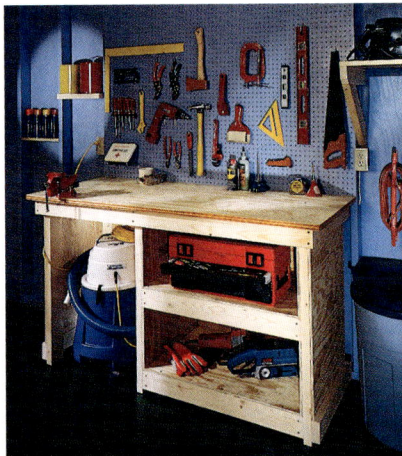

No workbench is ideal for everyone, but this design will fit many needs. It has two shelves for power tools, and room for a vacuum cleaner underneath. It measures 1676 mm long, 600 mm deep and 914 mm high.

Materials: You will need to buy five 3600 mm lengths of dressed 100 × 50 mm timber, two 2440 × 1220 mm sheets of 12 mm, A-bond plywood (or alternatively Customwood), some 70 and 45 mm woodscrews, 38 mm nails and white wood glue.

Assembly: First, screw together the frames for the top and the two shelves, and screw the legs to them. Then screw on the side and back bottom frame pieces, the shelf ends and shelves, and the side and back panels. Tack one top piece to the frame, spread wood glue on it, and screw the other sheet to it and the frame. Predrill holes for all screws.

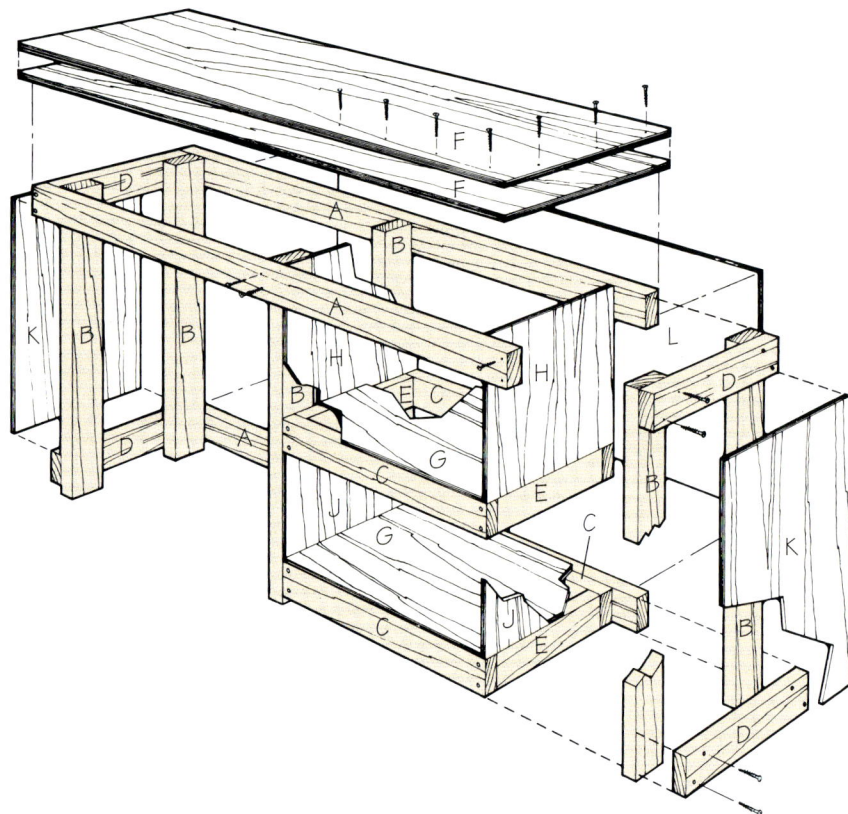

Cutting guides

Plywood (2440 x 1220 mm sheets)

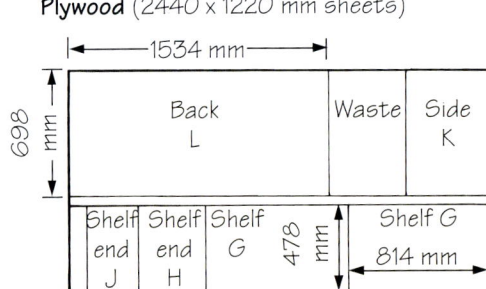

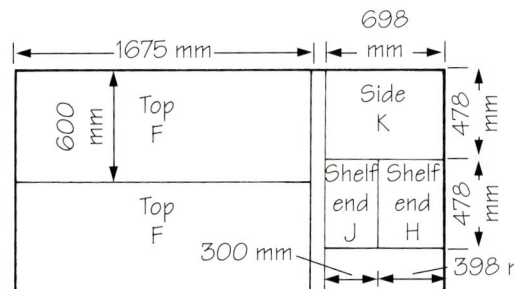

Back L (1534 mm, 698 mm)	Waste / Side K (698 mm)
Shelf end J / Shelf end H / Shelf G / 478 mm	Shelf G 814 mm

Top F (600 mm, 1675 mm)	Side K (698 mm, 478 mm)
Top F	Shelf end J / Shelf end H (478 mm)
	300 mm / 398 r

Side view

600 mm

568 mm

32 mm

523 mm

Front view

1676 mm

38 mm

814 mm

838 mm

38 mm

1600 mm

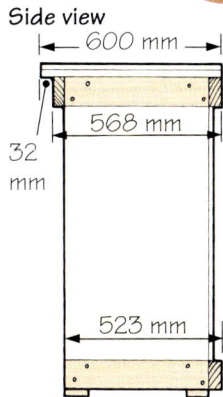

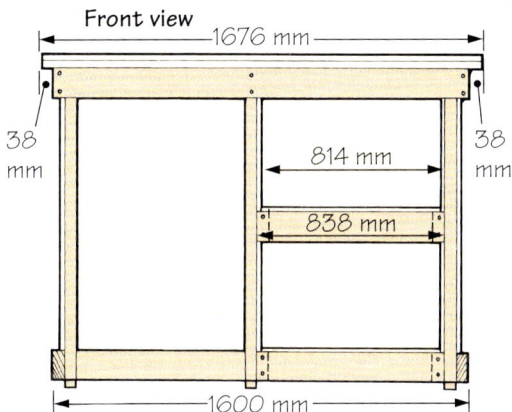

100 x 50 mm (1800 mm lengths)

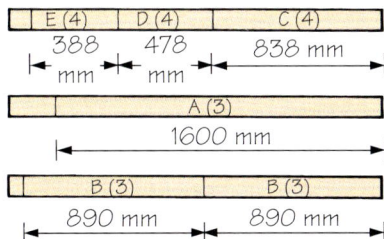

E (4)	D (4)	C (4)
388 mm	478 mm	838 mm

A (3)
1600 mm

B (3)	B (3)
890 mm	890 mm

Bench amenities

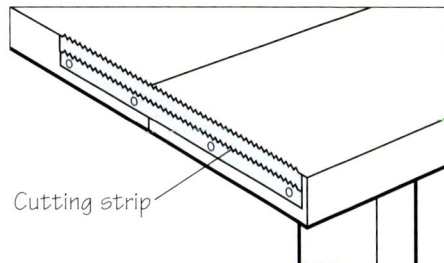

Cutting strip

Handy cutter ▲

Tack a cutting strip from a foil or plastic wrap box to your workbench and use it to cut tape and cords. An old hacksaw blade will also work. Mount the cutter on an edge that's easily accessible but where you're unlikely to brush against it.

Hooked in place

If your bench tends to move when you are working on it, attach each end to a wall stud with a hook and eye.

Sprout a leaf

12 mm steel rod

Add extra length to your work-bench when you need it with a removable extension leaf. Cut a piece of 300 × 50 mm timber to fit along the edge. Drill matching 12 mm holes, 150 mm deep, in the leaf and the bench edge. Then fit 12 mm steel rods, 300 mm long, into the holes.

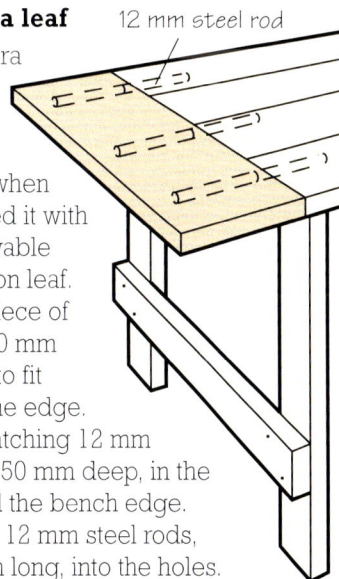

Solid bench top

Want a bench top with the durability of a hardwood butcher block without the cost? Get a solid-core exterior flush door from your timber yard.

Bench top savers

Roll-on protection

To avoid staining your bench top with paint, mount an old window blind on one end. When you're ready to paint, just pull out the blind and hook it to the other end. Let it dry before rerolling. ▼

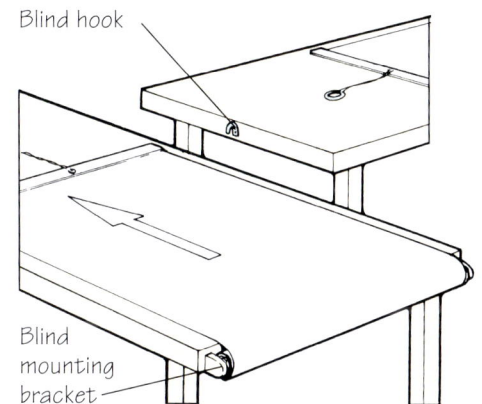

Blind hook

Blind mounting bracket

Cheap resurfacing

For a smooth surface that can take a lot of punishment, tack 6 mm hardboard over your bench top and seal it with pure tung oil. When it becomes pitted, just replace it. Also use a scrap of 300 × 50 mm timber as a cutting board to absorb drill holes and saw and knife cuts.

Mat top

Don't mar your project on a rough, battered bench top. Cover the work area with a rubber bath mat or carpet scrap.

OTHER WORKSHOP FURNITURE

Sawhorses

Soft saddle

The battered, saw-chewed top rails of most sawhorses can scratch finished wood or furniture. To provide a non-marring surface, cover 300 mm or so at one end of the rails with some lengths of scrap carpeting. Even better, make a timber cap for each sawhorse as shown, and cover its top with carpet. Then you can slip the caps on the sawhorses whenever you need them. ▼

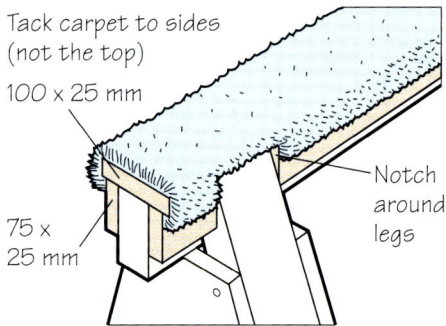

Tack carpet to sides
(not the top)

100 x 25 mm

75 x 25 mm

Notch around legs

Tools at your fingertips

Add a tool tray between the legs of your sawhorse. Make a shallow box—a 100 x 25 mm frame with a plywood bottom—and attach it to cross braces running between each pair of legs. Put the tray on just one sawhorse so the pair will still stack.

Instant measure

Nail, screw or glue an old steel tape measure blade to the side of your sawhorse's top rail. You'll find it invaluable every time you need to make a cut. Don't use a wooden rule because it will soon become damaged and illegible.

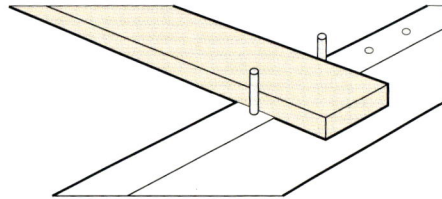

Sawhorse dogs ▲

To hold your work in place on sawhorses, drill a series of holes along each top rail, then put nails or pegs in the holes. Measuring from a hole near the rail's centre, make the distance to each hole correspond to a standard timber dimension—38, 50, 75, 100, 125, 150, 200, 250 and 300 mm (see chart, p. 67). At most, you'll need to apply light hand pressure to steady a piece.

Knock-down horses

Here's a way to quickly set up and take apart sawhorses made with metal sawhorse brackets and 100 x 50 mm timbers. Screw the brackets to the legs, but not to the top rail. On each pair of legs, hinge a brace on one leg and cut a slot for it on the other leg. When you force the brace between the legs, the bracket teeth bite into the top rail and forms a sturdy sawhorse. When you release the brace, the rail lifts out and the legs fold.

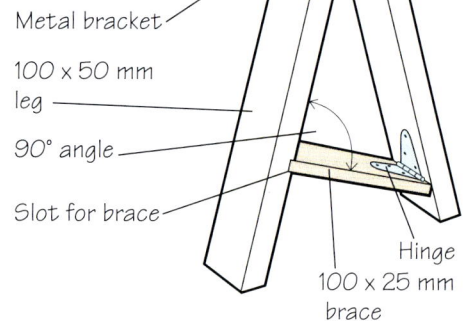

Metal bracket

100 x 50 mm leg

90° angle

Slot for brace

Hinge

100 x 25 mm brace

Build your own ▶

Here is a design for a strong sawhorse with the load bearing directly on the legs. There are no nails in the top rails to damage your saw blade, and the slot between the rails serves as a built-in handle for easy carrying. The sawhorse is made entirely from 100 x 50 mm timber, and all ends are either cut square or at a 17.5° angle.

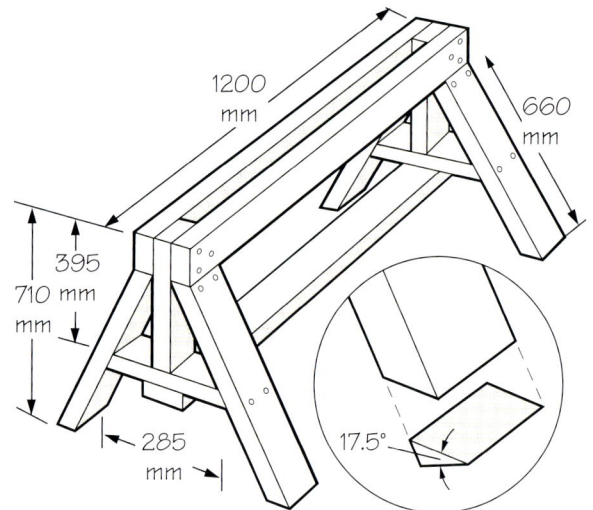

1200 mm

660 mm

395 mm

710 mm

285 mm

17.5°

Sawhorse substitute

No sawhorse? Your stepladder can sometimes provide instant support for sawing, sanding, planing or painting timber. Simply lay the ladder on its side, open its legs, and support the timber as shown.

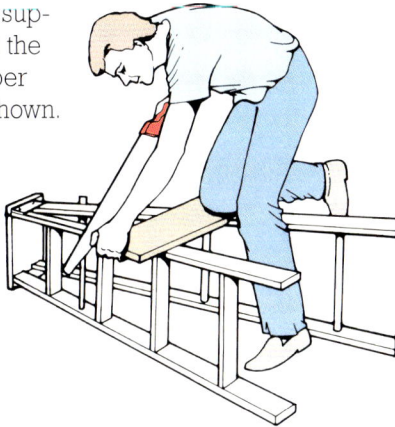

Relieve your aching back

When oversize projects force you out onto the patio, don't keep stooping to retrieve drills, saws, tapes, pencils and other items from the ground. Instead, take along this fold-up tool table. Made of 19 mm particleboard or plywood, the table is bench height when set up, but only 100 mm deep when collapsed. ▼

600 mm square top with 19 mm moulding around upper edges

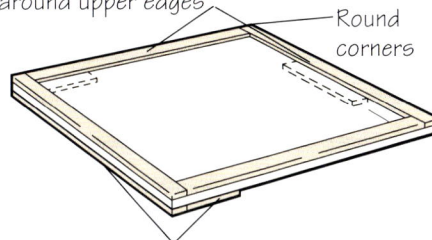

Round corners

Nail moulding under top to position base

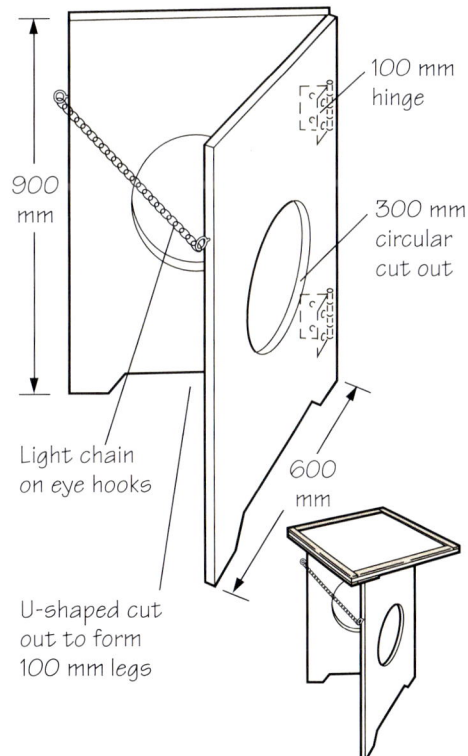

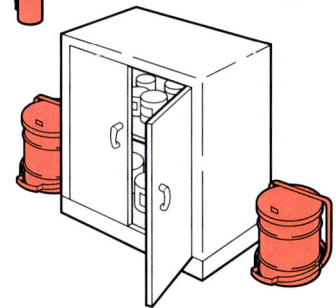

Versatile pieces

Extra reach

Need to hold a wider piece in your portable workbench? Make four extension pieces from 50 × 25 mm timber. At one end of each piece, drill a hole and glue in a dowel that fits in the bench dog hole on the bench. At the other ends drill holes that will accept the bench dogs.

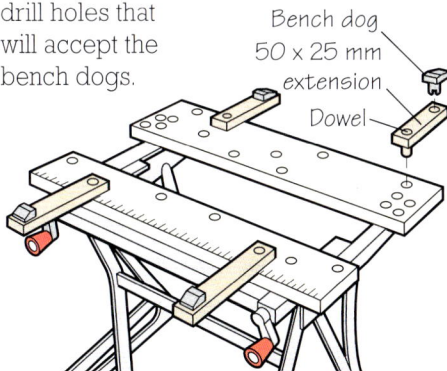

Bench dog

50 x 25 mm extension

Dowel

900 mm

Light chain on eye hooks

100 mm hinge

300 mm circular cut out

600 mm

U-shaped cut out to form 100 mm legs

SAFETY FIRST

FIGHTING FIRE

In a home workshop, a fire extinguisher is more essential than any piece of furniture. Get one rated AB(E), indicating that it can handle most common types of fires: wood and paper, flammable liquid and electrical. Locate it in a highly visible, easily accessible place away from volatile substances, preferably near an exit. Check periodically to make sure it's fully charged. Install a smoke detector as well. Keep flammable paints and solvents in sealed containers in a locked metal cabinet. Don't store them near any flame source or in a living area, basement or confined space with little airflow. Also get two metal rubbish bins with lids—one for sawdust and wood chips and the other for oily and solvent-soiled rags. Empty both of them frequently. (For more on the disposal of hazardous workshop waste materials, see p. 39.)

WORKSHOP STORAGE

Free organisers

Instant order

Get your workshop shipshape quickly by storing everything you can in same-sized cardboard boxes. Cut off the tops, label the boxes by general categories, such as 'brackets' or 'sandpaper', and arrange them alphabetically on shelves. Identical boxes measuring 300 mm or so in height, width and depth work well. Storage firms and office supply stores are good box sources.

Recycled dish rack

Turn that old vinyl-coated wire dish rack into storage racks. Use bolt cutters and pliers to cut and bend the rack into the sizes and shapes you need. The long sides of a dish rack make convenient wall racks for hanging tools and supplies. Turn the bottom and ends into a portable table rack by bending the cut ends at the bottom and fitting them into holes in wooden dowels as shown. ▼

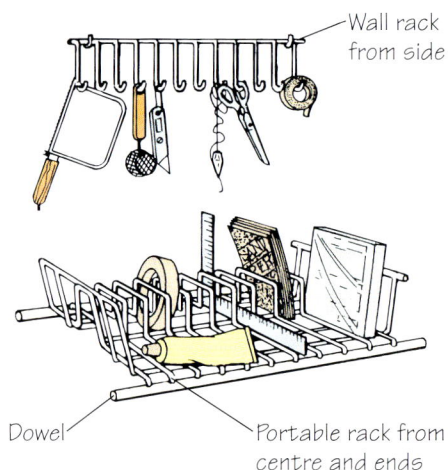

Wall rack from side

Dowel

Portable rack from centre and ends

Serving up hardware

Turn discarded baking trays (or other items with a projecting top lip, such as cake or cafeteria trays) into handy, ready-made pull-out shelves for tools or fasteners. Mount the trays in a box made from plywood or particleboard, with grooves routed in the sides so that the trays can slide in and out of the box. ▼

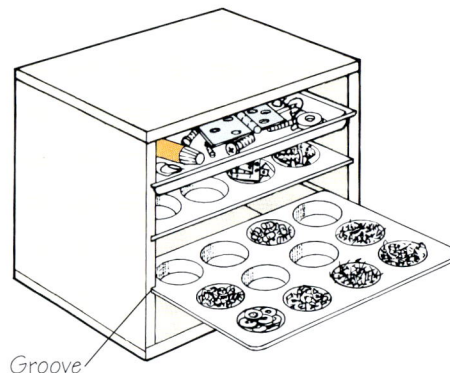

Groove

Pegboard lore

Put it everywhere

Don't limit your use of perforated hardboard, otherwise known as pegboard, to workshop walls. Mount it on the inside of cupboard doors and on the sides of your workbench and cupboards. Pegboard is fine for hand tools; as well as for heavier items. (To install pegboard, see p. 127.)

Hook security

Keep a pegboard hook from coming loose by putting a dab of glue on the ends that hook into the board. If you need to move the hook, a light tug will usually free it. Otherwise, you should be able to soften the glue with a heat gun.

Outline reminder

You'll always return tools to their proper places on pegboard if you outline each tool with a wide permanent marker. Or put up tool silhouettes cut from the adhesive plastic used for shelf lining.

Drawer magic

Protect your toes

To avoid pulling a heavy drawer out too far and spilling its contents, paint lines on the drawer edges to indicate how far it can be safely pulled out. Also attach a wood block on the back that will catch on the frame. Pivot the block and make one end longer than the other. That way it will hang vertically but you can turn it aside to take out the drawer. ▼

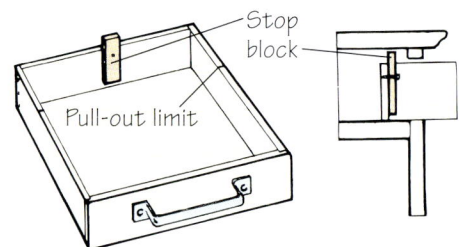

Stop block

Pull-out limit

Stronger pull

Does the handle on a tool-laden drawer keep pulling off? Replace it with a garage door handle, or similar, secured with bolts going through the drawer front. Put flat and lock washers onto each bolt before screwing on the nut. ▼

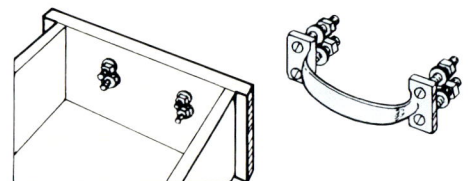

Garage shelves

Open stud wall?

Narrow 50 × 25 mm shelves installed between open studs in a garage workshop are ideal for storing 1 litre cans of paint, jars of fasteners and car needs. Secure the shelves with 75 mm woodscrews going through predrilled holes in the studs into the shelf ends; stagger the shelves in adjacent spaces. ▼

Deeper shelves on studs ▲

To store larger items in the space between studs, install 19 mm particleboard shelves supported by 100 × 50 mm brackets. When making a bracket, cut the diagonal support's ends at a 45° angle; attach both pieces to the stud and to each other with 75 mm woodscrews. Mount a bracket on every other stud for a moderate load, on every stud for heavier loads. Notch the shelves to fit around the studs and attach them to the brackets with 38 mm woodscrews.

UTILITY SHELVING

Great for workshops with no exposed studs to hold shelves, this four-shelf, 285 mm deep storage unit can be up to 2.4 m high and 900 mm wide. To make it, you need five 2.4 m lengths of 50 × 50 mm DAR timber, two 1.8 m lengths of 300 × 25 mm shelving, one 2.4 m long 100 × 25 mm brace and two 2.4 m long 50 × 25 mm braces. Multiple units can be screwed together.

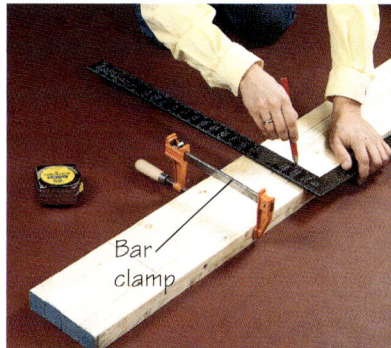

1 Clamp four of the 50 x 50 mm timbers together. With a square and pencil, mark across all four pieces the length you want the legs, and the position of each cleat. Cut the legs to size.

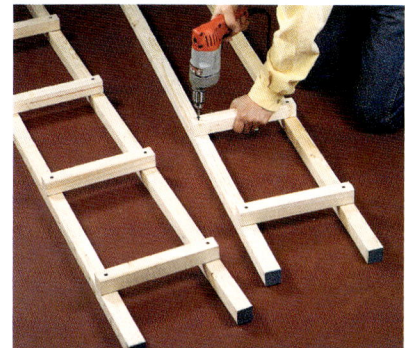

2 From the remaining 50 x 50 mm timbers, cut cleats that are the same length as the shelves' depth. Then align each cleat on a marked line and attach it with 75 mm woodscrews.

3 Cut the shelves to the length you want. With the end frames on edge, secure the shelves to the cleats with 38 mm woodscrews. Stand the unit up and check that it's level and square.

4 Mark and cut a 100 x 25 mm brace to run diagonally across the back from the top to bottom shelf. Attach with 38 mm woodscrews. Add 50 x 25 mm braces to both sides in the same way.

WORKSHOP STORAGE

Handy hand tools

Easy-reach holder

Make a tool holder out of scrap wire mesh. Form the mesh into the shape shown below by bending it over the edge of a board, and attach it to the wall with screws and washers. A 12 mm square mesh holds a variety of tools, especially screwdrivers. ▼

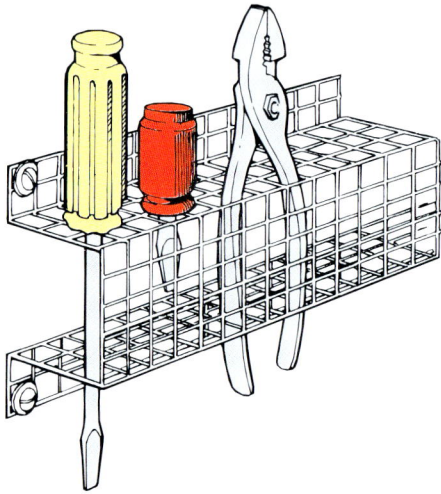

Holding power

For a convenient spot to store chuck keys, scissors, punches and other small hand tools, screw a magnetic knife-holder strip to the underside of a shelf over your workbench. Available in kitchenware stores, these powerful magnets can also hold larger hardware items, such as spanners and screwdrivers. They work equally well when mounted on the sides of the stands for table saws and other large tools.

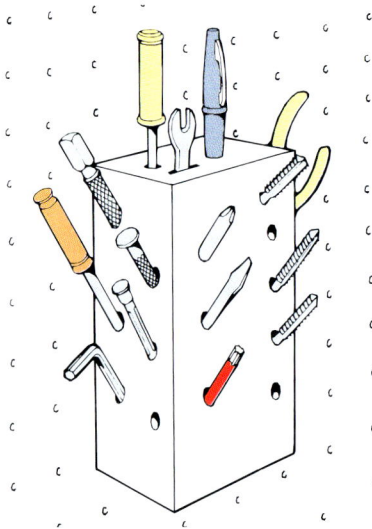

Small tool organiser ▲

Mount a small block of polystyrene foam above your workbench and press punches, bits, knives, screwdrivers and other such tools into it to keep them handy. Buy the foam plastic from a home centre or craft store, or recycle foam used as packing material.

Tool belt

Tack an old leather or strong canvas belt along the edge of a shelf to hold tools. As you nail it, leave small loops in the belt for tools to slip into. ▼

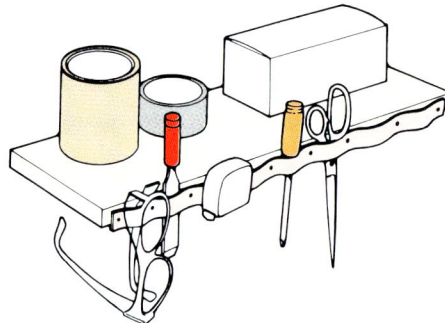

Handle holder

Chest handles—available in a variety of sizes from any large hardware store—are great for hanging heavy tools, such as hammers and hand axes, up out of the way. Mount the handles directly on a convenient wall over a stud, or alternatively on a plywood backing, putting them upside-down so that the handles stick out from the wall.

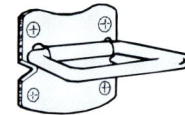

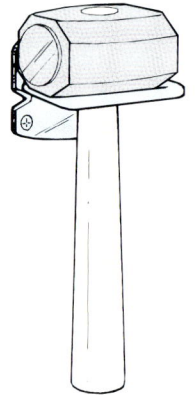

Orderly power tools

Power tower

To keep power tools handy, build a tall, narrow box out of 300 × 25 mm strips of plywood. Then staple carpet scraps between the sides to form soft cradles for your tools.

Concentrated power

Put your most frequently used power tools on a shelf mounted over your workbench. Cut slots along the back for your circular and jig saws, and bore 25 mm holes along the front for your drill, electric screwdriver and router. ▼

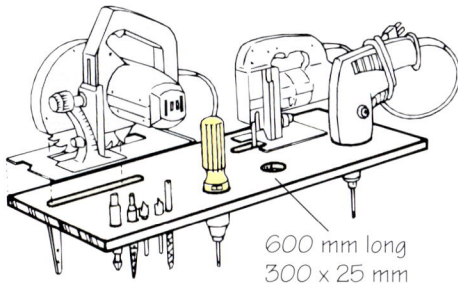

600 mm long
300 × 25 mm

In the wall

Another way to keep tools close at hand yet out of the way is to store them on shelves built between exposed studs. Make the shelves out of 100 × 25 mm timber and cut notches into them so that the tools seat firmly. Nail 50 × 25 mm cleats to the studs, angling them downward toward the wall to keep the tools from falling. Then glue the shelves to the cleats with construction adhesive. ▼

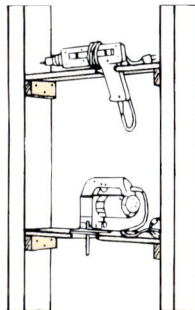

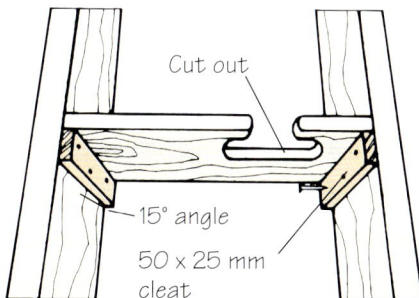

Cut out

15° angle

50 × 25 mm cleat

Ready supplies

String out

Make a dispenser for string by cutting off the bottom half of a 2 litre plastic bottle. Then mount the top half upside-down on the wall with the string coming out of the bottle neck.

All-in-one tape dispenser

A toilet paper holder mounted on a workshop wall or on a workbench makes a great dispenser for as many as five or six rolls of masking, friction, duct and other types of tape. For easy cutting, tie scissors to the dispenser with a length of string.

Quick wipes ▲

Facial tissues are great for quickly cleaning up water, oil and glue and for wiping your hands when the phone rings. To make a holder for a box of tissues, bend a wire coat hanger as shown and hang it on a hook or a nail.

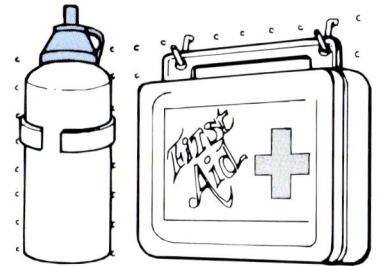

FIRST-AID KITS

An inexpensive and essential safety item for any workshop is a well-stocked first-aid kit. Buy one at a local chemist, and mount it where it is easy to see and reach. A standard kit will include antiseptic, bandages, gauze, elastic and adhesive tape, cotton swabs, eye drops, tweezers and scissors. Latex gloves and an instant cold pack are also useful. Make sure the container closes tightly to keep out dirt and dust.

When working with paint, solvents, strippers or any chemical with an eye hazard warning, keep a squeeze bottle of eyewash solution handy. If any chemical gets into your eyes, use the solution immediately. If a chemical irritates your skin, wash it off with water. *A first-aid kit is for minor injuries only. Get prompt medical attention for a serious injury such as a deep cut or puncture or a head blow. Also see a doctor if eye irritation persists after washing.*

WORKSHOP STORAGE

Nuts and nails

Self-identification

Here's an easy way to label boxes of nails, screws and other fasteners: just attach a sample of each item to the outside of its box with some glue. You'll be able to see at a glance what you have in stock and where it is.

Recycled labels

If you store screws or other fasteners in small glass jars, cut the label from the package the item was purchased in and push the label inside the jar before filling it. Hold the label face out against the inside of the jar as you pour in the fasteners. The label will remain visible through the glass.

Great cheap parts bins

Use clean plastic oil containers to make bins for screws, bolts, nuts and many other small hardware items. Cut each container as shown with scissors or a utility knife; make a simple wooden frame to hold the bins. ▼

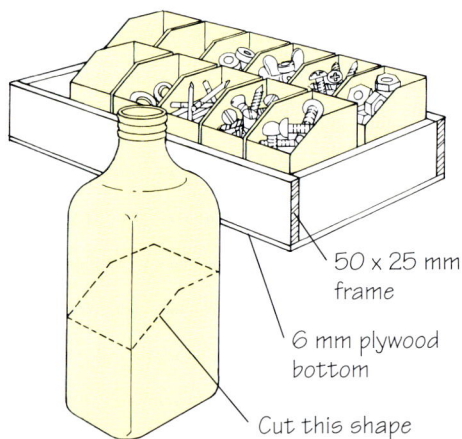

50 x 25 mm frame

6 mm plywood bottom

Cut this shape

Spill preventer

Put a magnet in a container of small items such as screws or panel pins. This way, the metal pieces will bind together in a ball around the magnet and won't spill out if you accidentally knock over the container. If a few items do scatter, use the magnet to pick them up. For inexpensive magnets, buy a roll of magnetic edging at a hardware store and cut it into whatever lengths you need.

Nut rings

Store nuts and washers on metal shower curtain rings hung from pegboard hooks. (The ring's pear shape and latching action allow for secure storage.) Hang nuts and washers of similar size on their own ring, so that you can find the right size quickly. ▼

Ready-made storage modules

Plastic electrical boxes, either single or double size, are just right for storing small items like fasteners. The boxes are inexpensive, and they stack or fit neatly side by side. Just make sure to remove any flanges or 'wings' meant for attaching the boxes to studs.

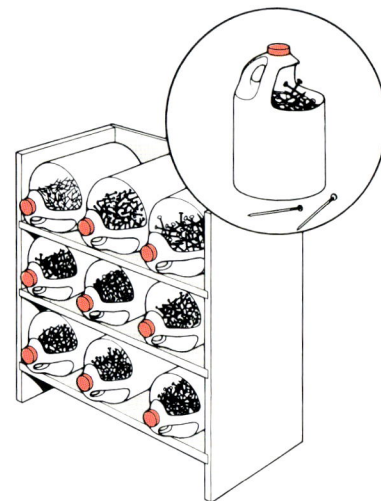

Neat nail organisers ▲

Four litre plastic bottles with a section of their tops cut out make great nail bins. When the bottles are stored on their sides, the weight of the nails keeps them from rolling. Off the shelves, the bottles can stand upright, and their handles make for easy carrying to a job site.

Workbench catchall

Don't let nuts, bolts and other leftovers clutter your workbench. Bolt a cake tin or baking tray under a shelf. Swing it out and drop your odds and ends into it as you work. Occasionally pick over the pan's contents to separate the useful from the useless. ▼

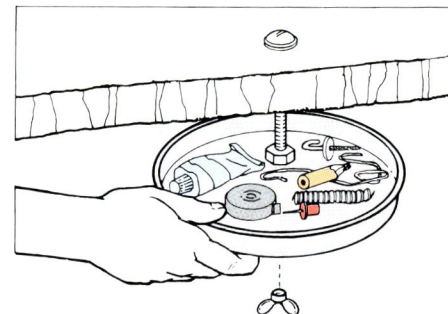

Under-shelf storage

Make the most of your workshop shelf space by storing nails, nuts and other fasteners in jars attached to the underside of a shelf. To mount the jars, simply screw their lids to the bottom of the shelf (place a washer under each screw head for better security). ▼

Timber and long items

Gutter shelving

Inexpensive vinyl gutters provide convenient, surprisingly strong storage for mouldings, lightweight timber, pipes and other long thin items. To install them, just screw the mounting brackets to studs and snap in the gutters. Use the brackets alone as hooks for garden hoses, extension cords and wire coils. ▼

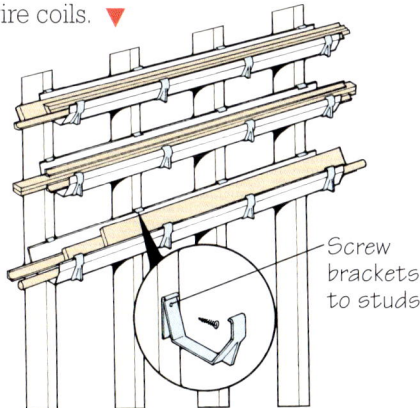

Screw brackets to studs

Stand-up storage

Fill a sturdy cardboard box with sawn-off mailing tubes (or scraps of large-diameter PVC pipe) and use it to organise all those short pieces of moulding, pipe and dowels.

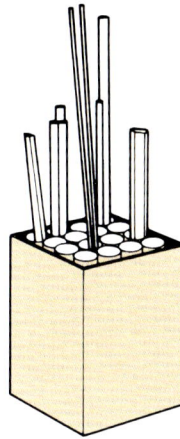

Retreads

Tie a series of old car tyres to overhead joists and use them to hold long pieces of timber and pipe. You can also lay old tyres flat on the floor or ground to provide a pallet that will keep timber and plywood sheets high and dry.

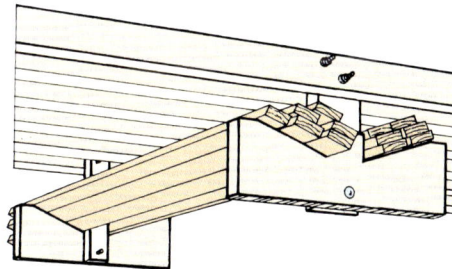

Timber overhead ▲

Keep timber out of the way yet handy with these 'inverted T' racks. Bolt two to the bottom of your garage roof trusses; spaced about 1500 mm apart to support 2400 mm lengths of timber. To avoid straining the trusses, limit stored pieces to the equivalent of twenty 50 × 25 mm timbers and distribute the load evenly.

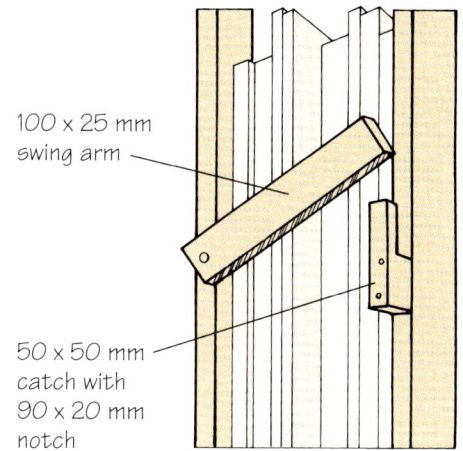

100 × 25 mm swing arm

50 × 50 mm catch with 90 × 20 mm notch

Easy-reach timber ▲

Store timber vertically between studs. Hold it in place with a 100 × 25 mm swing arm, fastened to one stud with a 50 mm woodscrew. Make a catch with a piece of 50 × 50 mm timber, notched and attached with 75 mm woodscrews.

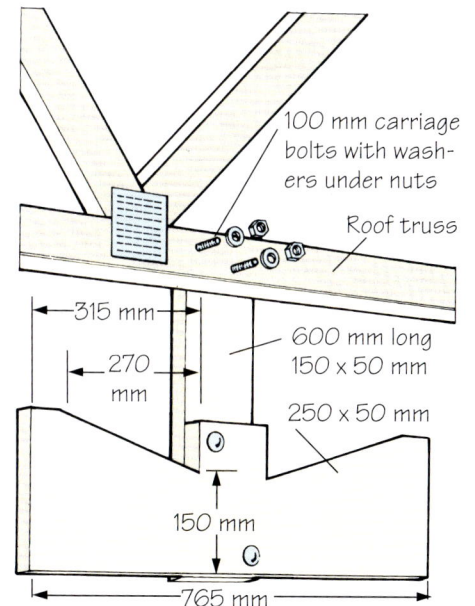

100 mm carriage bolts with washers under nuts

Roof truss

315 mm

270 mm

600 mm long 150 × 50 mm

250 × 50 mm

150 mm

765 mm

WORKSHOP CLEAN UP

Picking up small items

Nuts and bolts scoop

Get small fasteners back into their boxes quickly with a scoop made from a square-shaped plastic milk, or other container that has a handle. Use a utility knife to cut off the bottom half of the container at an angle as shown. ▼

Magnetic bagger

Here's an easy way to pick up spilled washers, nuts or nails. Drop a bar magnet into a plastic sandwich bag. The spilled items will stick to the magnet through the plastic. Then turn the bag inside out and pour the items back into their container. Similarly, to clean up small metallic filings, put plastic wrap around a magnet, sweep it over the work area, then fold the wrap over the filings and discard it.

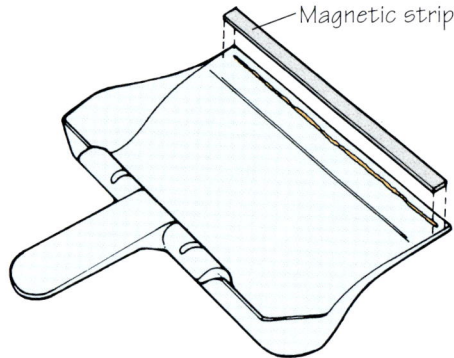

Magnetic strip

Magnetic sweep ▲

Separate out screws, nails and other reusable small iron and steel items while sweeping up. Use contact cement to glue a flexible magnetic strip onto the edge of a dustpan. The items will cling to the strip when you empty the pan.

Dust busting

Brush it off

No vacuum cleaner readily at hand? Trim the frayed bristles from an old paintbrush and use it to sweep fine sawdust or filings from your bench top, or to clean out blind corners on a drill press or lathe. Also, keep a child's broom handy for sweeping around stationary tools, bench legs and other tight spots you can't reach with a regular broom.

Blow it away

If you have a spare hair dryer, use it to blow away dust, dirt and shavings in the workshop; to dry sweaty hands before handling new timber; and to speed the drying of paint touch-ups.

Enclose it

Before undertaking a large messy sanding or sawing job, tape or staple plastic sheets around the work area to contain the dust. If your home's heating or cooling ducts serve your workshop, turn off the system while doing heavy sanding; otherwise it will spread fine particles all over the house.

Trap it

To capture fine airborne dust when sawing or sanding, mount an air conditioner filter on the air-intake side of a box fan, using adhesive tape, wire or an elastic stretch cord. Put the fan next to your work area, blowing away from you. Vacuum the filter when it becomes filled with dust. ▼

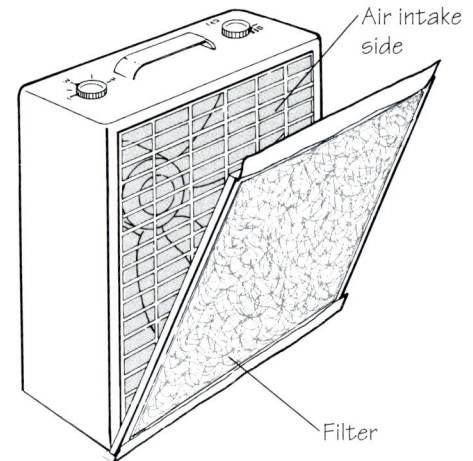

Air intake side

Filter

Recycle it

Save the sawdust from your workshop projects. It will come in handy for soaking up grease, oil, paint or other spills. You can also use it to rub glue off your hands or mix it with carpenter's glue to make a wood filler.

Vacuuming

Thrifty timesaver

You can extend the life of some workshop vacuum cleaner filters, and so avoid having to clean them so frequently. Cut the legs from an old pair of panty hose, tie the cut ends as shown, and then stretch the waistband top over the filter. The suction won't be affected, and you can clean the panty hose by just rinsing it.

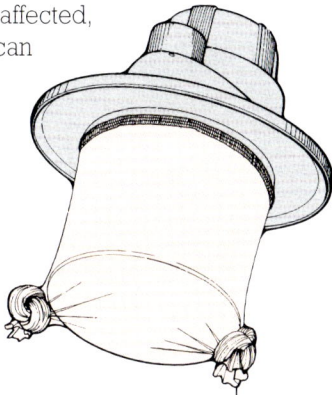

Easy-empty cleaner

To avoid the mess of emptying a workshop vacuum cleaner, line the canister with a plastic garbage bag (fold the bag over the canister rim so the top holds the bag in place). To empty the cleaner, all you need to do is take the bag out.

Long reach

If the crevice tool on your vacuum cleaner isn't long enough to reach the accumulated sawdust behind your workshop cabinets, make your own extra-long crevice attachment using the cardboard tube from a roll of wrapping paper. Fit one end of the tube into the hose nozzle and secure it with cloth tape. Then flatten the rest of the tube.

A WORKSHOP CLEANER

A wet/dry workshop vacuum cleaner is an invaluable aid that gobbles up sawdust, chips and nails as well as large and small spills. You can also hook one to a sander or other tool to remove dust as you work (but a vacuum cleaner is no substitute for a proper dust collector if you do a lot of sawing and sanding).

Power and performance. Determining a vacuum cleaner's power is not an easy matter. Neither a high wattage nor a gee-whiz demonstration of lifting power is a reliable indicator of a unit's capabilities. Luckily, most brand-name units sold in home centres and department stores are adequate for a home workshop. However, if you do want to compare units, multiply the cleaner's 'sealed pressure' (measured in millibars) by its 'airflow' (measured in cubic decilitres per second). The resulting figure should be at least 7000; the higher the number, the better. If the information is not available at the store, the manufacturers may be able to send facts sheets on request.

Tank body. Plastic is the most common material and is fine for most workshops. It has the advantages of being lightweight, rustproof, and dent-resistant. Steel, used on some higher-end models, is durable and less prone to damage from heat and solvents. A 45 to 70 litre capacity is adequate for most home workshops.

Filter type. If you vacuum mostly dry debris, a pleated paper cartridge filter provides more surface area for dust, reducing the number of filter cleanings. But the pleats are hard to clean when the dust is wet or caked on. If you do a lot of wet vacuuming, a flat paper (or foam) filter is better. Some units accept both filter types.

Attachments. Large- and small-diameter hoses (typically 65 and 30 mm) are available. A large-diameter hose is handy for picking up sawdust and chips, a small one for picking up nails and heavy particles. Many large-hose units have adaptors to accept small hoses. Extension wands, a floor nozzle and a crevice tool are essential.

PERSONAL SAFETY AND PROTECTION

Work clothes

Take it off

Never wear a watch, ring, neck chain or other piece of jewellery when working with a power tool. Mount a bright-coloured hook over your workbench to hold these items. The hook will remind you to take them off when you come into the workshop, and you'll always know where you put them.

Extended life

Reinforce knees, elbows, pocket bottoms and other heavy-wear areas on work clothes by putting iron-on patches on their undersides. Coat the edges of pockets with clear fingernail polish to prevent fraying.

Rubber gloves hanger

Can't ever find your rubber (or work) gloves when you need them? Use a binder clip (available from office supply shops) to hang them on a pegboard hook in full view. ▼

Binder clip

Coming to grips

Rub clear silicone sealant onto the palms of your work gloves. Once the sealant cures you'll be able to get a much firmer grip with the gloves.

Safety gloves

Fine sawdust can make your fingers slip when you are working with a power tool. To avoid this, wear household latex gloves with nonslip palms. Put talcum powder inside the gloves to ensure easy removal. To cut down on the likelihood of your slipping on a dust-strewn floor, wear rubber-soled shoes.

Trim off bottom

Instant aprons ▲

Keep some plastic garbage bags in your workshop to use as aprons for messy jobs; buy ones with built-in handles if possible. Trim 20 mm from the bottom of a bag, then pull it over your head, slipping your arms through the handles.

Easy-on, easy-off apron

Tired of fumbling to tie your workshop apron behind your back? Replace the strings with a single piece of 12 mm twill tape (a standard sewing item). Sew the tape to one side of the apron; then attach it snugly and neatly to the other side of the apron with Velcro fasteners.

Eyewear

No more broken glasses

Do your reading glasses keep falling out of your shirt pocket when you bend over? Attach a removable metal clip from a ballpoint pen to one of your glasses' side arms. Position the clip so that it catches in your pocket, and use pliers to gently squeeze it on. ▼

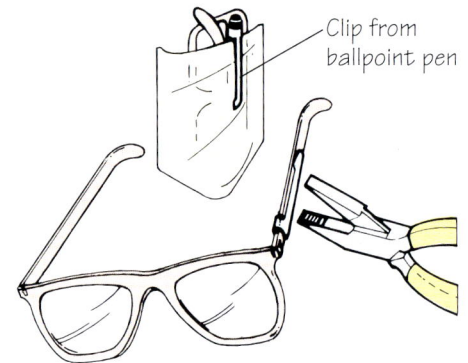

Clip from ballpoint pen

A clearer view

Fine sawdust tends to stick to safety glasses because of the static electricity that builds up in dry workshop air. To cut static and remove dust, wipe the surface of your safety eyewear with a sheet of fabric softener—one already used in the dryer so that it won't scratch or smear the surface of the glasses.

Face-shield wrap

To keep your plastic face shield clean and scratch-free, cover the front with clear plastic wrap. It won't affect your vision, and when it gets dirty you can just peel it off and replace it. ▼

Plastic wrap

Quick spray and wipe

Keeping your safety goggles crystal clear takes only a matter of seconds if you simply equip your workbench with a small bottle of window cleaner and a roll of paper towels.

PROTECTIVE EQUIPMENT

Store your safety goggles, ear protectors and respirator on a foam head made for displaying hats and wigs (a shop that sells hats or wigs may be willing to give you an old foam head or at least the name of a supplier). Put the head in a prominent place in your work shop, and it will serve as a constant reminder to use your safety equipment. Here are some tips on selecting safety equipment.

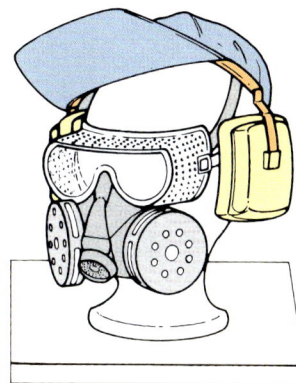

Eye protectors. Don't rely on ordinary spectacles to guard your eyes. Wear special protective safety glasses with side shields, or safety goggles, which can be worn over your normal glasses. For full face protection, wear a face shield.

Ear protectors. Earmuffs are easier to take off and put on than earplugs and harder to misplace. But both protect equally well if their noise reduction rating is the same. Look for an SLC number of between 25 and 32.

Respiratory protectors. Look for a respirator with changeable dual cartridges colour-coded to filter-out specific types of toxic dust and fumes. For ordinary dust, use disposable dust masks, labelled as meeting Australian Standard or WorkCover Authority specifications. They are thicker than cheaper masks. Don't buy a mask that doesn't have a rating guide on it.

Keeping clean

Skin protection

Before beginning a messy job, give your exposed skin a light coat of petroleum jelly or barrier cream. It keeps paint or grease from getting into pores and washes off with soap. Rubbing undiluted liquid soap on your hands and letting it dry will also repel grease. To keep dirt from collecting under your fingernails, scrape your nails over a bar of soap.

Safe and effective cleaner ▶

Clean your greasy or paint-stained hands with vegetable oil. It's inexpensive and works well. More important, it won't irritate your skin or be absorbed through it like solvents. Put the vegetable oil into a plastic spray bottle; that way, you can just spray it on your hands and it won't spill. Laundry prewash and shampoo for oily hair are also good grease removers.

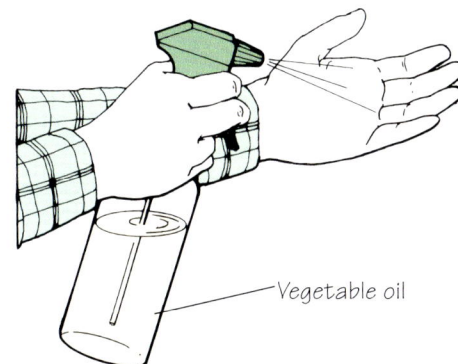

Vegetable oil

WORKSHOP SKILLS

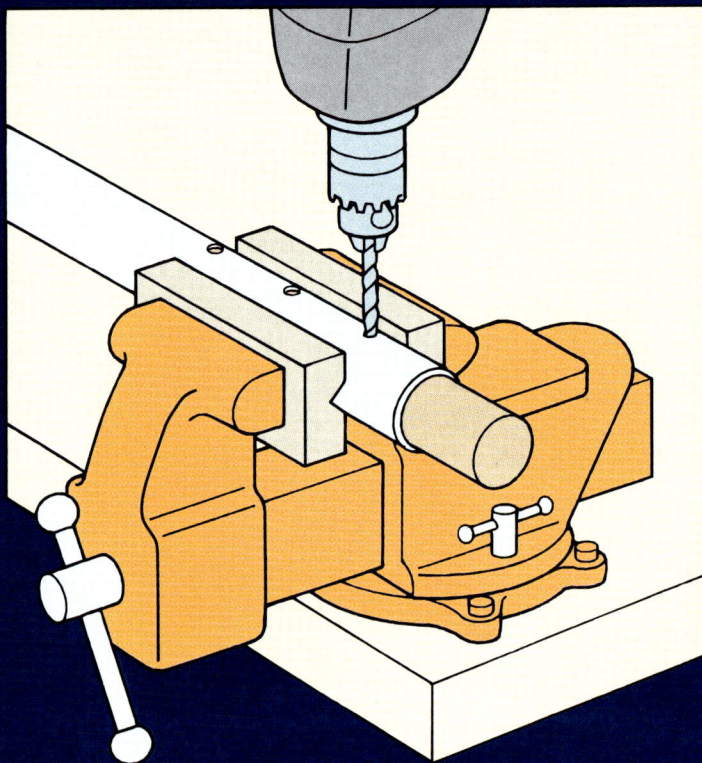

WOOD BASICS

Buying wood

Numbers game

When buying a piece of dressed timber, you'll find that its actual dimensions are a bit smaller than those specified. That's because timber is sold by 'nominal size'—the size it is when it's cut at the sawmill. After planing and shrinkage, the actual size is a bit smaller. To remind you of timber's real dimensions, make a chart and tack it to a workshop wall.

Nominal size	Real size (approx.)
150 x 25 mm	140 x 19 mm
200 x 25 mm	180 x 19 mm
250 x 25 mm	230 x 19 mm
300 x 25 mm	280 x 19 mm
50 x 50 mm	45 x 45 mm
100 x 50 mm	90 x 45 mm
200 x 50 mm	180 x 45 mm
300 x 50 mm	280 x 45 mm
100 x 100 mm	90 x 90 mm

By the length

Timber is usually sold in standard lengths, which range from 1.8 m to 7.2 m, in increments of 300 mm. When large quantities of timber are ordered—say for flooring—it is generally supplied in random lengths which add up to the total number of metres ordered. Timber can be bought cut to length, but you will be charged for the piece it was cut from—a piece measuring 2145 mm will cost the same as the standard 2400 mm length. The price of timber is usually quoted in lineal metres, at so many dollars and cents per metre, according to dimensions. Timber is also sold in cubic metres, but it is unlikely that any domestic job will call for such a large quantity.

Resuscitating old timber

Before you throw any old timber away, consider reusing it. First remove any nails (a magnetic stud finder will find nails covered by plugs). Fill the nail holes with wooden toothpicks or matchsticks dipped in wood glue. If a knot falls out, glue it back in with wood glue.

Warped

Is it straight?

As timber dries, the outside part of the original log tends to dry faster, and the timber will cup. To detect any warping, sight along the length of the plank. Some slight cupping is common, but reject any plank that has very pronounced warping. Also check timber for cracks, stains and other signs of damage.

Stacking it up

To ensure air circulation and minimise warping, store timber off the ground and separate the layers with strips of 25 x 25 mm timber. Position the strips at each end of the stack and at 400 mm intervals along the length of the planks.

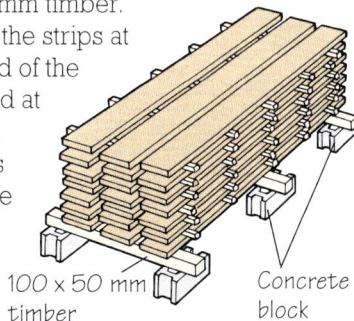

100 x 50 mm timber

Concrete block

Get rid of that warping

Place a warped board, concave side down, on wet grass on a sunny day. The ground moisture on the concave side of the board and the sun's heat on the convex side may straighten it in time. If one end is more warped than the other, weight it down with a heavy rock. Wait before using to see if it will warp again.

Getting a handle on it

Hammer carrier

Carrying a full sheet of plywood (or other wood sheets) can be awkward at best. A claw hammer can help. Hook the claw under the bottom edge of the material, somewhere near the centre of the sheet. The hammer handle makes a convenient carrying grip. Use your free hand to steady the load.

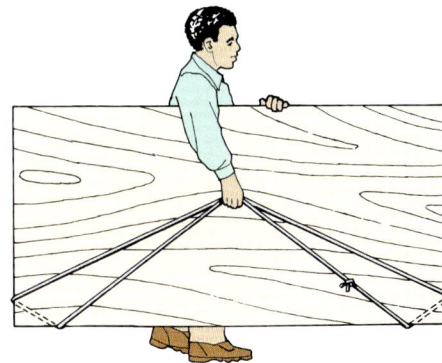

All tied up ▲

Another way to carry a large, awkward sheet is with an 6 m long rope tied into a loop. Slip the loop over the two bottom corners of the sheet. Grasp the middle sections of the loop with one hand; steady the sheet with the other.

MEASURING

Boxed in

If you don't have a folding rule with a metal extension bar, you can still accurately measure inside a drawer or similar workpiece by using a retractable tape measure and a combination square. Place the square against one corner. Starting at the opposite corner, measure the remaining distance with the tape measure. Add the two measurements for the total width. ▼

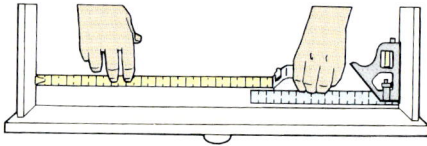

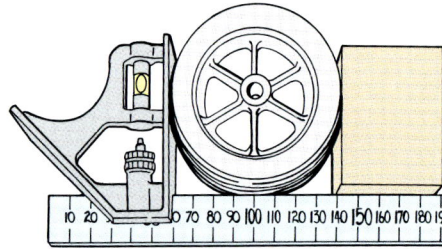

Too round for rules? ▲

Finding the exact diameter of a round object isn't that tricky. Place the object against a straightedge rule and between two blocks or other items with true straight edges. Then just read the diameter on the rule (the distance between the blocks). You can create variations of this gauge with a mix of try squares, framing squares and combination squares.

Gauging depth

Stopped hole

Improvise a depth gauge for stopped holes or recesses with a bolt and two nuts. With the nuts on the bolt, place the bolt in the hole. Twist the nuts down to the surface of the work. To hold the measure in place, tighten the top nut to the bottom one.

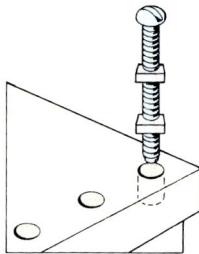

Rubber gauge

A car mechanic's gauge for measuring the depth of tyre treads is also a handy gadget for the woodworker. Use the gauge (which measures in increments down to 0.5 mm) to check the depth of stopped holes and shallow recesses.

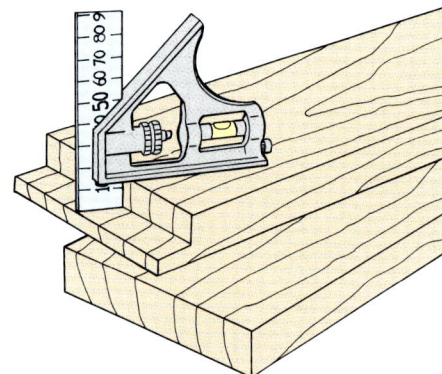

Deep down

Use a combination square to determine the depth of a recess. Making sure the blade is free to slide, rest the square on a flat edge of the work. Adjust the blade to the depth of the recess, then lock the blade in place using the thumbscrew. Besides measuring the recess, you can use the square to transfer the depth dimension to other workpieces. ▼

Squared straight

Bright idea

If you're not sure that an edge is straight, place it against a known straightedge and hold the two pieces up to a light. If the light shines through, the edge isn't straight. To straighten it, shave off the high spots with a file, sander or plane.

Get it square

When making a rectangular object, such as a drawer, check that it is actually square. Here's how. First measure across the workpiece diagonally from corner to corner. Then measure along the opposite diagonal. If the two measurements match, the workpiece is square.

Another angle

To make sure that a right angle is true, use the 3:4:5 method of triangulation. For example, to check a corner for squareness, measure three units along one wall and four units along the other. If the distance between the two end points is five units, the corner is square. To create a right angle, tack two strings where you want the right angle to be. Measure two legs of a triangle; one 300 mm and the other 400 mm. Position the two legs so that the distance between their end points is 500 mm. You can also figure in metres, or in multiples of 3, 4, and 5 if you use the same multiple for all three.

MARKING

Chalk it up

Back to school

To identify parts when assembling a project, use white or yellow blackboard chalk. It's easy to sand off, and chalk doesn't leave a hard-to-remove impression the way a pen or pencil can.

Snappy line

When marking building material with a chalk line, first remove excess chalk from the line by snapping it on the ground or floor or against studs or joists. Then you'll be ready to stretch the line over the material and snap it as usual. The result will be a crisp line.

Plumb bobbing

A windy day can make it difficult to use a plumb bob. To keep the bob from bobbing around, sink the weighted end in a bucket of water. (The bob shouldn't touch the side or the bottom of the bucket.) Since you can't align the work directly against the plumb bob string, measure the distance between the work and the string at the top and bottom. If they are aligned, the measurements will be the same.

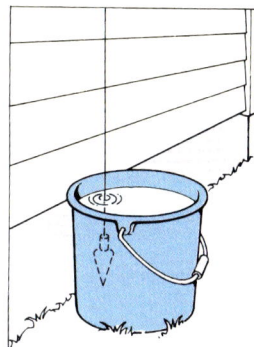

Dividing rules

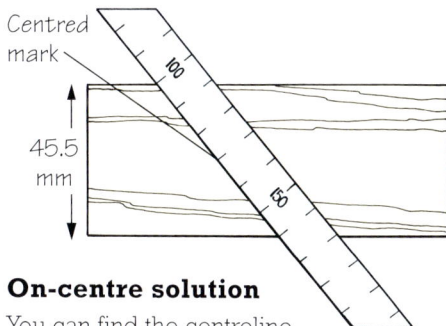

On-centre solution

You can find the centreline of an odd-size board without having to divide awkward numbers. Place a rule or measuring tape diagonally across the board with an even-numbered mm or 10 mm mark on each of the board's two edges. Subtract one figure from the other and halve it to locate the centre of the board.

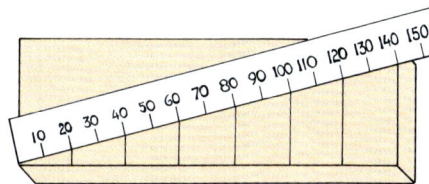

Equal time ▲

To mark equal segments, angle a ruler across the work. Place the beginning of the ruler on one edge of the work, and adjust the angle so that a 10 mm mark divisible by the number of segments needed lies at the other end of the work. For example, to divide the work into 7 segments, let the ruler measure 140 mm; then mark every 20 mm.

Walk this way

Another way to mark equal segments is with dividers or a compass. Set the points at the desired distance; then walk the dividers along a straightedge by swinging one point in front of the other.

In the round

Centre finder

To find the centre of a circle, clamp a combination square to a framing or try square. The combination square should be set against the framing square so that its rule intersects the inside corner of the framing square at 45°. Slide the contraption over the work until both sides of the framing square rest against it. Using the rule of the combination square as a guide, draw a pencil line on the work; rotate the work and draw a second line. The intersection of the lines marks the centre. You can also make a plywood jig. Cut out a right angle in the plywood; then attach a straightedge to it with screws, creating a 45° angle. Use the jig in the same way as the one above.

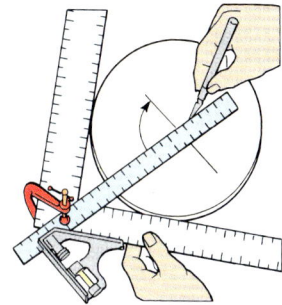

Cylindrical trick

To mark equal distances around a cylinder, measure the circumference with a strip of paper; then lay the paper flat and mark off equal segments with a compass (see left). Wrap the paper around the cylinder, tape down the end, and transfer the marks.

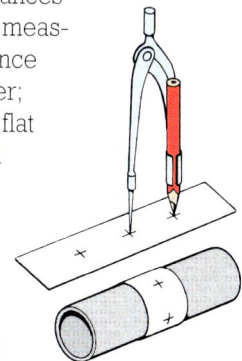

LAYING OUT

Got it straight?

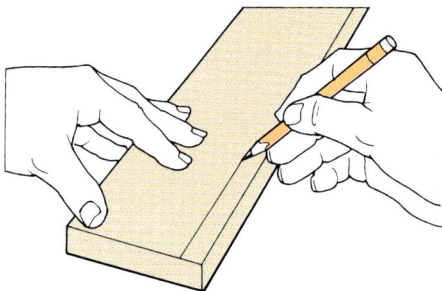

Let your finger do the work ▲

When scribing a straight line near the edge of a board, use your finger as a guide (but only if the edge of the board is straight). Hold the pencil between your thumb and first finger, and rest the tip of your middle finger on the edge of the board. Slide your hand along the board by adjusting your arm at the elbow and shoulder and keeping the wrist steady. With just a little practice your finger will soon be gauging straight lines.

Clothes peg on the line

Here's how to turn an old clothes peg or similar object into a handy gauge. Cut off one prong at a right angle. Then drill holes at measured intervals along the length of the intact prong; making the holes large enough to take a pencil point. Butt the head of the peg against the work, and slide it along to mark the line.

That versatile square

A combination square is an accurate aid for marking straight lines. Adjust the blade to the desired length, and position the square along the edge of the wood. Set the pencil at the end of the blade and pull the two toward you in a smooth motion. If you have problems keeping the pencil steady, you can file a notch into the end of the blade; the notch should be just wide enough to accommodate the pencil point. ▼

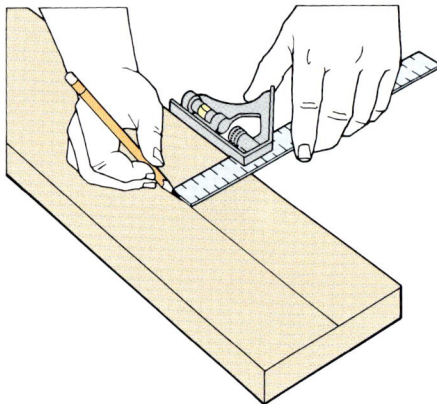

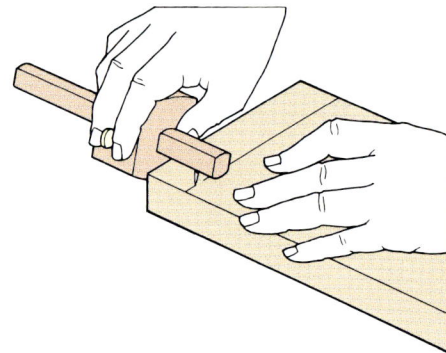

Down the centre

Use this jig to mark the centre of your work without first measuring. You'll need four 6 mm dowels and a block of wood at least 50 mm wide and 200 mm long (longer if you're working with material more than 150 mm wide). Mark centre lines (p. 69) down the length and across the width of the block on both faces. Drill a hole wide enough for a pencil through the centre of the block. On one face drill two dowel holes on the longer centre line, 25 mm in from each end; on the other face drill two holes on the same line, centred 25 mm on either side of the pencil hole. Glue dowels into the holes. To use the jig, insert a pencil and place the jig over the work, with the dowels pressed tightly against the edges of the work.

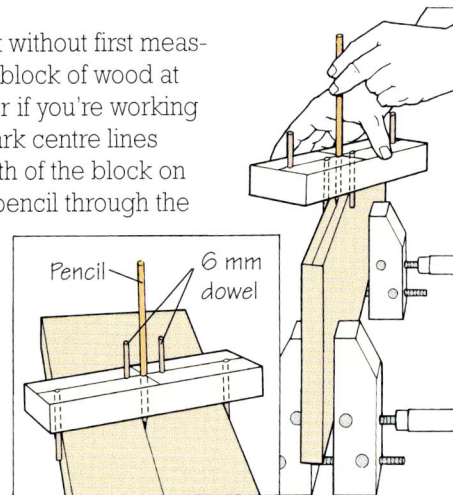

No more bumpy lines ▲

When you're using a marking gauge it's not unusual for the scribe to be a little wavy near the edge of the wood. (The reason is that as the body of the gauge passes the edge of the wood, the pin may jump.) Instead of pulling or pushing the gauge all the way to the end of the work, stop just short of it—say about 10 mm. Reposition the gauge so that the pin is at the end of the wood; then push or pull it until the two scribed lines meet.

Pencil   6 mm dowel

Going round in circles

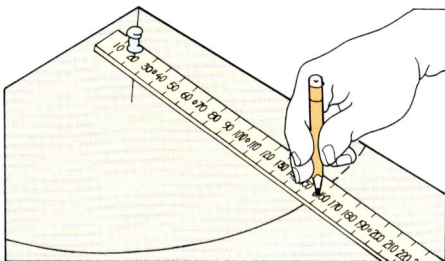

Double-duty rule ▲

If your compass isn't large enough to make the circle or arc you need, try using a cheap wooden rule. Drill a hole large enough for a thumb tack at the 20 mm mark. Then drill holes for a pencil point at the distances you need along the rule. When you're ready to use this home-made compass, insert a tack through the hole at the 20 mm mark and into the work. The rule will pivot at the tack. (Because the pivot is set at the 20 mm mark, make sure you add 20 mm to your measurements.)

Adjustable rod

An adjustable curtain rod is ideal for creating a large adjustable compass. Tape a 75 mm nail securely to one end of the rod as a pivot; then tape a pencil to the opposite end. Slide the curtain rod sections to the desired radius, and clamp them together with a G-clamp. You're ready to scribe a circle.

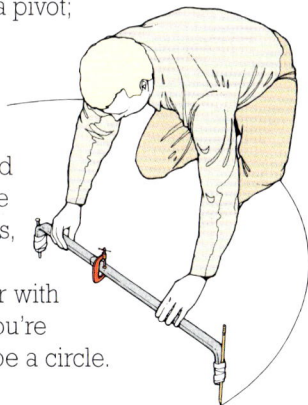

Irregularities

For the perfect fit

To fit together two objects, one of which is irregularly shaped (for instance, a lipped cabinet against a wall with a moulding), use a compass. Set the compass point on the wall and the pencil point on the cabinet. With a steady motion and without varying the distance between the compass legs, follow the original contour with the point. The pencil will trace out the shape.

The two points should always be at the same height

Lipped edge

Chair rail

Shape it with solder

Malleable wire solder can become the perfect contour gauge, especially when you're making duplicates of odd shapes. Place the solder against the irregular object and push it in to fit the contour. Then position the bent solder on the workpiece and trace the contour onto it.

Dressmaker's trick

To transfer patterns—especially curved ones—to wood, slip a sheet of dressmaker's tracing paper between the work and the pattern. Then use a tracing wheel to copy the pattern onto the work. The radiating points on the wheel will pierce the pattern and press against the tracing paper, leaving a dotted ink line on the work that's easy to follow.

Save your pattern

Often-used woodworking patterns soon become frayed and worn. To preserve your patterns, use the originals to make longer-lasting templates. Suitable materials include cardboard, which is easy to cut with a utility knife, thin plywood, hardboard and acrylic plastic sheet, which is easy to shape with most woodworking tools. An extra advantage to the clear acrylic template is that you'll be able to see the work under the template and know exactly where the pattern will fall—which means you can avoid knots and select sections of timber that have better-looking grain.

Make it larger (or smaller)

A three-sided drafter's rule is the tool you need to reduce or enlarge objects or patterns. To make your own version of a drafter's rule, make photocopies of a 300 mm ruler, scaled to various percentages (ratios) such as 50 (1:2), 75 (1:1.3), 100 (1:1), 150 (1.5:1), and 175 (1.75:1). Cut out and glue the rules to two four-sided sticks—one with decreasing ratios, the other with increasing ratios. Use the 100 per cent rule to measure the object or pattern that you wish to copy; then look for the final measurement you want on the rule with the desired ratio.

DRILLING

Bull's eye

Making the curve

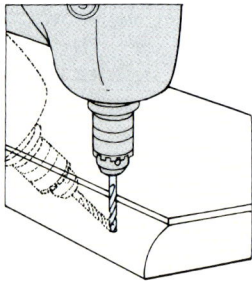

Drilling a hole on a curved surface, such as moulding, can be tricky because the bit has a tendency to wander. To keep the bit centred, first use an awl or nail to punch a hole where you plan to drill. Then start drilling the hole with the bit perpendicular to the surface; once the bit takes, swing it gradually to the proper angle.

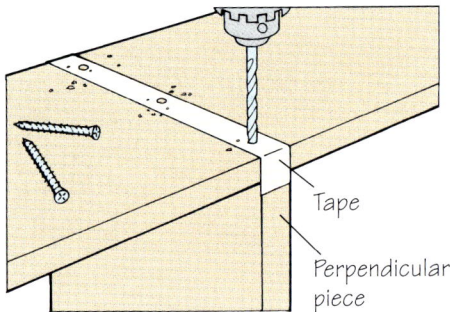

Tape

Perpendicular piece

At the joint ▲

Masking tape is an ideal guide for drilling into housed and butt joints. The tape should be the same width as the end of the workpiece (for example, a shelf or a partition in a stereo cabinet) that butts against the face of the other workpiece. Lay the tape across the work with the ends overhanging and lining up with the perpendicular piece. Mark the hole locations on the tape and begin drilling. When you remove the masking tape, you'll find that the wood will be less chipped than usual.

Groovy jig ▶

Here's how to make a handy two-in-one jig for guiding drill bits. Cut a V-groove in each end of a scrap block of wood. One groove should be at a 90° angle for drilling perpendicular holes; the other one at another commonly used angle, such as 45°. Use the jig to start the drill bit at the desired angle; then remove it to continue drilling.

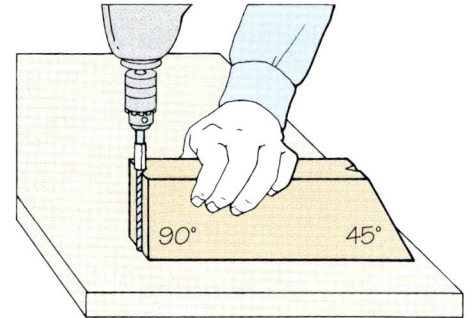

90°   45°

Shelf help

Drilling holes for shelf pins is easy with this handy hole-spacing template. Cut a strip of pegboard three to five holes wide and long enough to cover the height of the work. To avoid drilling too many holes, cover every other row of holes with tape. Because the lowest shelf normally starts 200 mm from the bottom, you can also cover the bottom 200 mm of holes with tape. Label the top end of the template so you don't accidentally position it the wrong way around. Secure the template flush to the edge of the work with spring clamps. Then start drilling through the centre strip of holes.

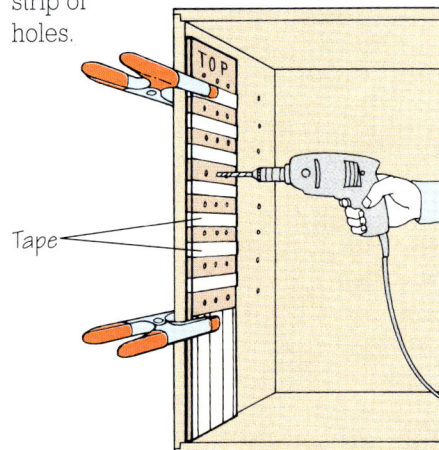

Tape

Hole truth

A bit of a trick

When drilling through some timbers and all plywood, the bit may chew up the exit hole unless you drill the hole partway from both sides. A faster and neater method is to firmly back up the work with a piece of scrap wood. The bit will chew up the scrap, not the work.

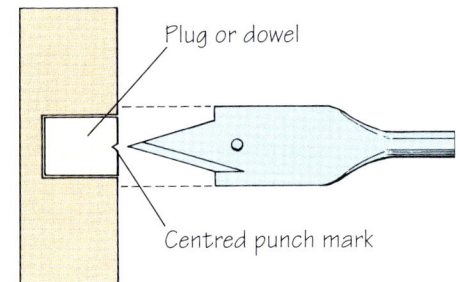

Plug or dowel

Centred punch mark

Hole in a hole ▲

Centring a drill bit can be difficult when you're enlarging an existing hole. The solution is to first fill the hole with a same-size dowel or plug (which you can make with a hole saw). Punch the centre of the dowel or plug with an awl or nail; then use the punch mark to centre the spade bit for the larger hole.

CHISELLING AND PLANING

Chisel it away

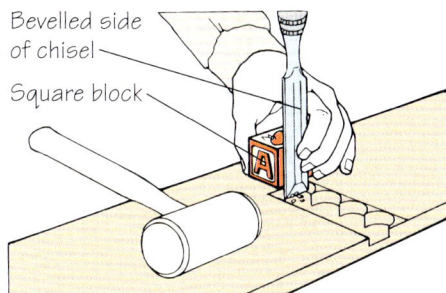

Bevelled side of chisel

Square block

Hold it straight ▲

To create a neat cut when making a stopped housing, mortise or dovetail joint, the chisel must be held precisely perpendicular to the wood. One way to guide the chisel is to hold a square block tight up against the blade. Or try clamping a board with a straight edge along the chisel line.

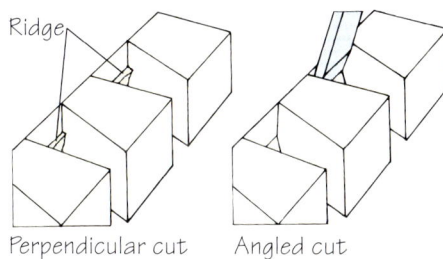

Ridge

Perpendicular cut   Angled cut

Another angle ▲

Perpendicular chisel cuts to remove waste in dovetail joints rarely line up at the halfway point where the cuts meet from the two opposite sides. Ridges that jut out at the halfway point require a separate removal step. To avoid this extra step, after making the first initial cuts along the marking lines with the chisel perpendicular to the work, continue the remaining cuts with the blade angled away from the waste slightly.

Plane sense

It's just scribble

It's hard to know if you've missed a spot after planing a large surface. Here's one way to be sure. Before you start planing, scribble on the surface with a pencil. As you plane, the scribbling will disappear. Repeat this step for additional passes.

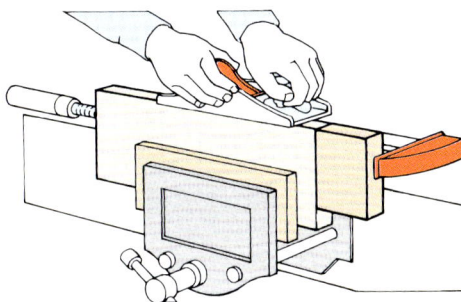

No more splinters ▲

To keep the end of a workpiece from splintering as it's being planed, clamp a block of scrap wood to the end. The height of the scrap should be the same as the height of the work.

Knotty solution

If there's a knot close to an edge that you want to plane, try holding the plane at an angle. The slicing action you get from an angled blade will yield a better cut than a standard pass.

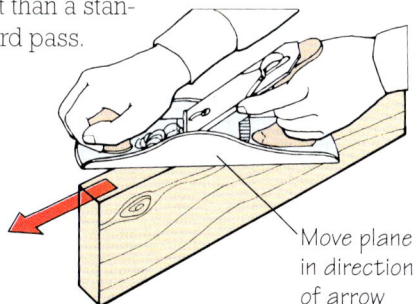

Move plane in direction of arrow

Holding block

When planing a long board, you may find that the clamps interfere with the plane. To avoid having to reposition the clamps, make two V-shaped holding blocks, and clamp the blocks rather than the workpiece. With the clamps out of the way, you can plane the work without encountering any interference.

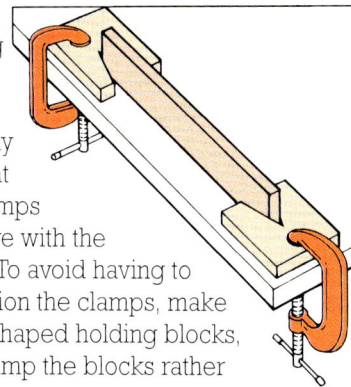

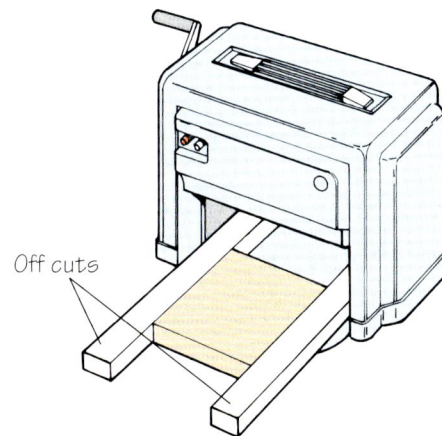

Off cuts

Too small for a planer? ▲

Here's how to plane short pieces of timber in a thickness planer. Glue an off cut of wood to each side of the work, with the bottom faces of all three pieces flush. After planing, tap the off cuts to break them from the work. To plane wood under 13 mm thick, use cloth-backed, double-sided carpet tape to attach the wood to a wider piece of waste timber at least 25 mm longer than the work. (The waste must be of a uniform thickness and free of warps.)

SAWING

Avoiding splinters

Here's the bad side

Cutting plywood across the grain can create a splintered edge on one side of the board. This won't matter as long as you have a good side and a bad side on the workpiece. The trick is to cut on the correct side. Here are the rules: good side facing up for a handsaw, table saw and radial arm saw; good side facing down for a circular saw and jig saw.

Haven't got a bad side?

If both faces of a panel are intended as good sides, you have two options. One is to first make a deep score line with a sharp knife on both faces of the wood. This will ensure a cleaner saw cut and prevent the saw from leaving a ragged edge. The other option (which doesn't always work) is to apply a strip of masking tape to both faces of the board where you intend to cut. Mark your cut line on the tape. After you make the cut, peel off the two strips of tape.

Circular saw

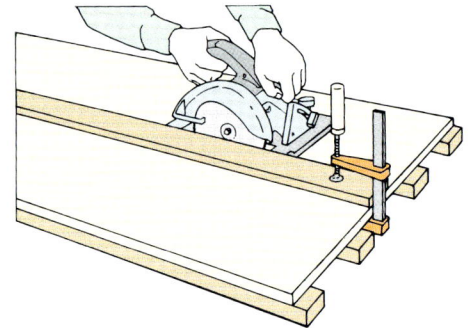

Ground level ▲

Forget about struggling with sheets of plywood on sawhorses. Here are three ways to cut plywood on the floor:
▷ Support the plywood on two or more lengths of 100 × 50 mm timber.
▷ Put another piece of plywood under the one you're cutting, and set your saw depth so that the blade barely grazes the lower sheet (which will be marked).
▷ Set your saw so that the blade doesn't go all the way through; then break the two pieces apart and clean up the cut edges with a plane and sandpaper.

Handsaw

Guidance ▶

To ensure a straight cut, use a guide to keep the saw vertically straight, and make frequent visual checks of the blade. A block of 50 × 50 mm wood cut straight and square will suffice as a guide for short cuts. For long cuts in thin plywood, clamp a length of 50 × 50 mm wood alongside the cutting line.

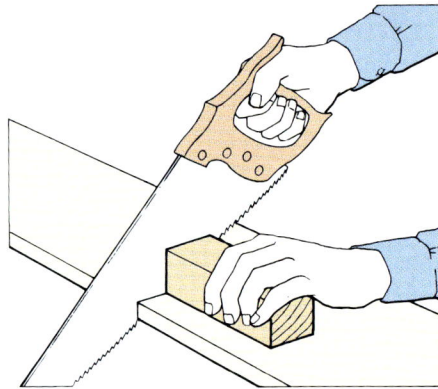

Deep thoughts

This depth gauge will help you cut saw kerfs to a specific depth. First measure the desired depth from the tips of the saw teeth up on both sides of the saw blade; then draw lines parallel to the teeth, again on both sides of the blade. Position strips of wood with a straight edge along the guidelines, straight edges facing down. Secure the strips to the blade with a pair of spring clamps. Make the cut until the edges of the depth gauge meet the work surface.

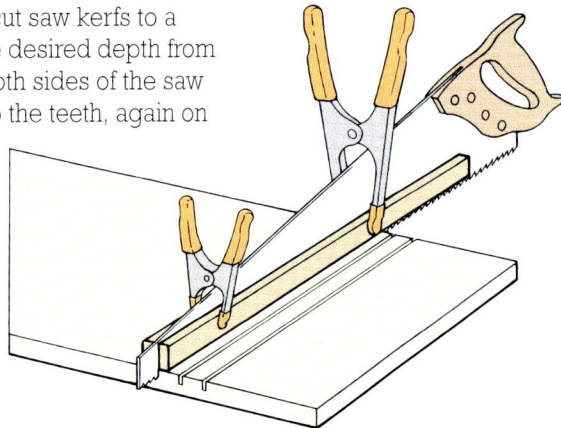

Binding kerf

A circular saw blade tends to catch the work when the kerf behind it closes up. Keep the kerf from binding the blade by inserting a wood shim or other small object into the kerf. When making longer cuts, slide the shim closer (but not too close) to the blade as you gradually progress.

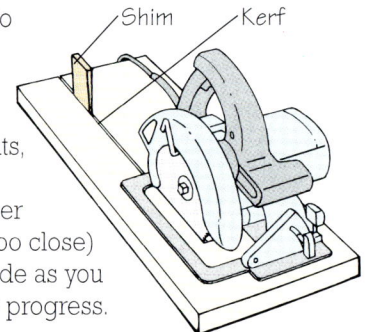

Easy measuring

For those of you who have to cut several boards to the same length, here's a way to speed up the job. Cut one end of each board square; butt those ends against a straightedge nailed to your bench. On one board, measure and mark the desired length minus the distance between the saw blade and the end of the base; clamp a straightedge at this mark, extending it across all the boards. Now you can make one pass. ▼

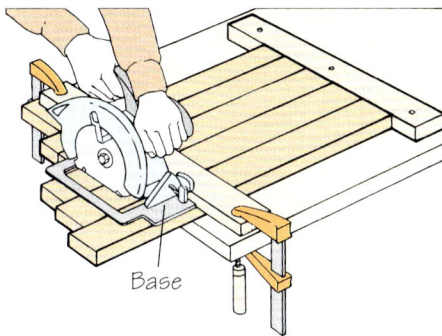

Base

Kerf bender

Bending wood is as easy as making a series of straight kerfs with your circular saw, using a square to guide the cuts. There's no rule of thumb about how far apart or how deep to cut the kerfs. Practice on scrap first. For tighter bends, space the kerfs more closely, but don't make them too deep or they will be visible from the opposite side. Before bending the wood, briefly soak it in hot water.

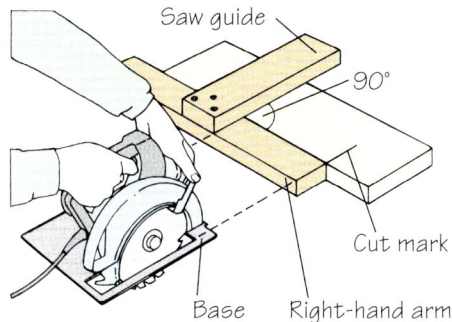

Saw guide

90°

Cut mark

Base   Right-hand arm

Seeking guidance ▲

If you plan to cut a lot of wood to the same length, give this jig a try. Use any scrap pieces of wood with straight and squared edges. Attach the two pieces with glue and screws, making sure they are set at an exact right angle. Make the right-hand arm of the guide slightly longer than the distance from the circular saw blade to the left edge of the saw's base. Your first pass with the guide will cut off the arm's extra length. When you're ready to use the guide, line up the right end of the guide with the cut mark on the wood.

Jig saw

Take an iron to it

It takes more than a pencilled line and good intentions to cut a straight line with a jig saw. For long cuts, use a length of 25 mm angle iron as a straightedge guide. Clamped parallel to the cutting line, the angle iron will guide the blade along the desired path, as well as helping to keep the blade perpendicular.

Supporting role

To support the work while using a jig saw, clamp it to your workbench so that the area you are cutting juts past the edge of the bench. Or support the work on blocks made from scrap wood that is thicker than the length of your blade. As you reach the end of a cut, the work can collapse toward the cut and bind the blade. To prevent this from happening, slide additional blocks under the work after you cut halfway through it. Make sure the path for the saw blade avoids both the bench and the blocks.

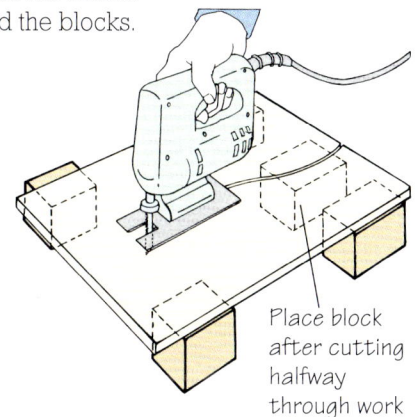

Place block after cutting halfway through work

Taking the plunge

To start a cut in the centre of the wood —not at an edge—without drilling a hole first, tilt the saw, resting the front of its base on the work; then, with the saw on medium speed, slowly and firmly lower the blade into the wood.

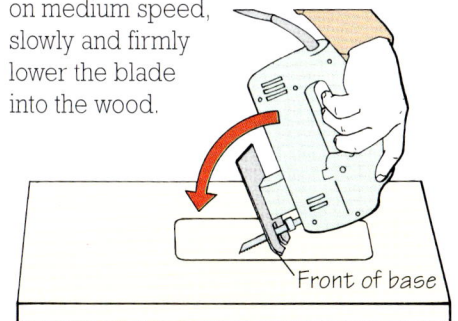

Front of base

SAWING

Mitre saw

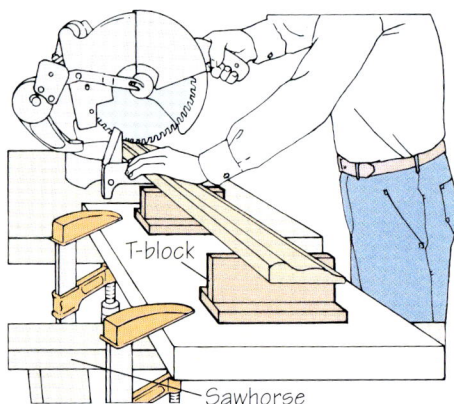

T-block

Sawhorse

Supporting role ▲

If you don't have a helper around to support long pieces of wood, make a couple of T-blocks. They'll support the work whether you're working on a table or on the floor. If your mitre saw is set up in a permanent area, you can nail or screw the T-blocks in place.

Ending repetition

If you have to cut a series of workpieces to the same length, try avoiding repetitive measuring and marking by using a stop block. To raise the stop block to the correct height, nail it to another block of the same thickness as the bed of the mitre saw. Clamp the block in place.

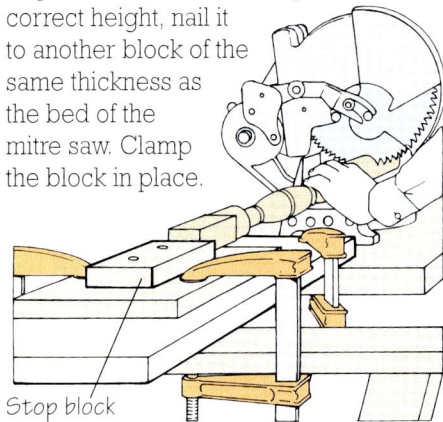

Stop block

On the wide side

Here's how to trick your mitre saw into making a wider cut. Slide a piece of 19 mm scrap wood under the workpiece. This raises the work so that a wider part of the blade will reach it.

Table saw

Ripping fun

To rip an uneven board straight when neither edge is true, nail a straight board on top of it. Use the straight board as a guide to run against the rip fence; the newly cut edge of the uneven board will then be true.

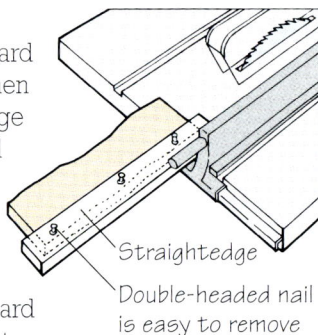

Straightedge

Double-headed nail is easy to remove

Narrow escape

To safely cut a narrow board, fasten a wider board to its edge with contact adhesive. After the cut is complete, pull the boards apart; there'll be no damage.

Tall order ▶

To create a raised panel for a door, make a tenon, or cut a slot into the end of a board, use this jig to make a smoother, more controlled cut. The jig is designed to straddle the rip fence of a table saw. Make the jig out of scrap wood and plywood, and size it to fit your needs—the jig's face can be smaller or larger, depending on the project. The jig should slide snugly and smoothly on the fence. Secure the work to the jig with G-clamps or other small clamps.

Mighty mitre jig

With this jig on your table saw, you'll cut perfect mitre angles every time. To guide the jig, fit two strips of hardwood into the mitre gauge grooves in the saw's table; then glue a 15 mm or 17 mm plywood base to the top of the strips and square the base to the table. Cut a slot for the blade partway through the base. Mark a 45° angle from both sides of the blade slot; screw two wood blocks with straight edges along these lines. Glue sandpaper strips to the outside edges of the wood blocks to keep the work from slipping. ▼

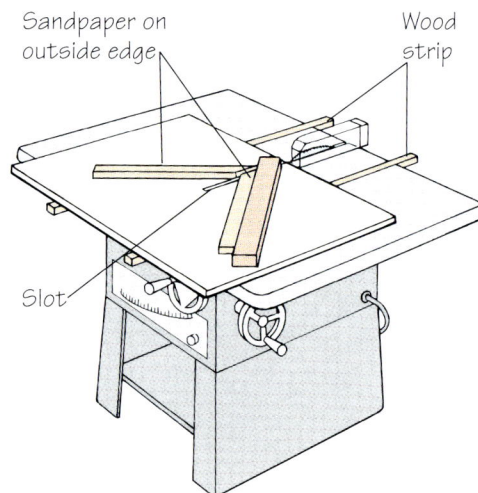

Sandpaper on outside edge

Wood strip

Slot

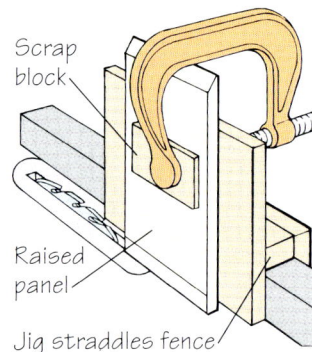

Scrap block

Raised panel

Jig straddles fence

Radial arm saw

Stop action

Controlling the depth of the blade cut is easy with this depth stop. Lower the blade to the desired height, measure the distance between the column castings, and cut a piece of scrap wood to that measurement. Place the wood between the castings and hold it in place with a hose clamp. ▼

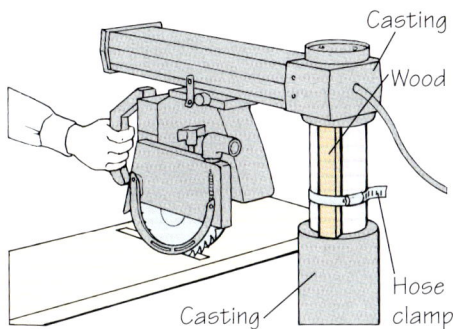

Casting
Wood
Casting
Hose clamp

Narrow rip

To rip a thin strip of wood or avoid getting your fingers too close to the blade, clamp a straightedge guide to the wood. The guide should slide along the front edge of the saw's table. With this setup the blade won't hang far out on the arm, which reduces cutting accuracy. ▼

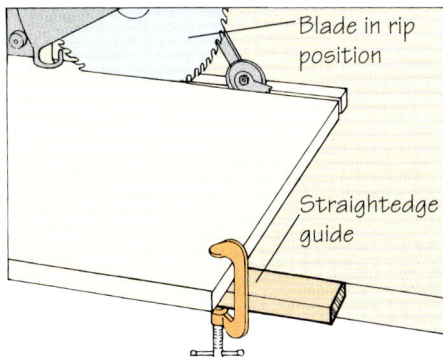

Blade in rip position
Straightedge guide

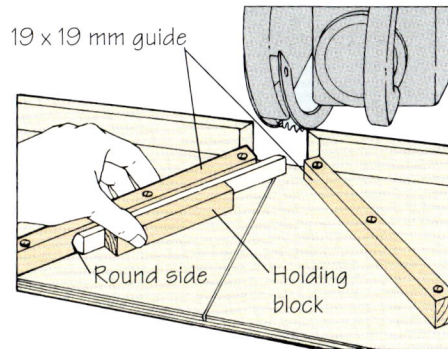

19 x 19 mm guide
Round side
Holding block

Mind over mitre ▲

This jig allows you to cut accurate mitres on rounded stock or mouldings. Screw two guides to a plywood base at opposite 45° angles to the saw blade. Place the rounded stock against the guide that will give you the desired mitre angle. Press a square holding block against the stock, and make the cut. The holding block will keep the piece upright and will also prevent it from creeping out of place while it's being cut.

Band and scroll saws

Blade aid

If the band saw blade slips off the wheel when you try to replace it, use masking tape to hold it in place temporarily. Tape the blade to the top wheel; then slip the blade around the lower wheel and tighten it in place. Remove the tape.

Super duping

When cutting duplicate parts on a band or scroll saw, stack the parts together, using double-sided tape between the pieces to hold them in place. The whole stack can then be cut without any worry about the pieces moving.

Veneer

To make clean band or scroll saw cuts in thin sheets of veneer or metal, layer the work between two pieces of plywood. To indicate the position of the work, set the work on the bottom layer; then mark and drill holes through the plywood at each corner of the work. Dab some glue along each edge of the work, and place the second piece of plywood on top. (Or tape the plywood layers together.) Flip the assembly over; using the holes as a guide to the corners of the work, mark the cutting lines or glue a cutting pattern to the plywood.

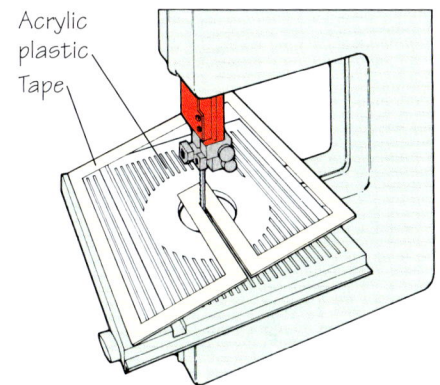

Acrylic plastic
Tape

Work jam ▲

Small pieces can drop into the band saw table slot and jam against the blade. To keep this from happening, cut a sheet of 3 mm acrylic plastic the same dimensions as the saw table. Drill a 6 mm hole in the plastic where the blade will be located; then cut a slot from the back edge of the plastic to the hole. Anchor the plastic to the saw's table with strips of double-sided tape down the centre and around all four edges. Besides reducing the clearance around the blade, it also provides a smooth work surface. For a larger blade, drill a larger hole.

ROUTING

Router rules

Which way to go?

When it comes to moving a router, the basic rule is: left to right as you face the cut. When making an interior cut, move the router clockwise. For perimeters, move it anticlockwise. If you're using a router table (in which case the router is mounted upside down), move the work from right to left. ▼

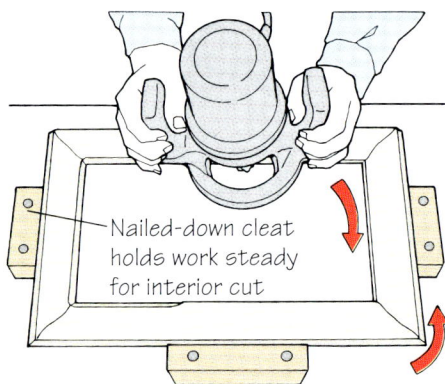

Nailed-down cleat holds work steady for interior cut

Four easy solutions

Here are simple solutions to common router problems:
▷Burned edges: move the router faster; check for a dull bit.
▷Chatter marks: move the router slower over the wood; check for a dull bit.
▷Corner tearouts: rout the end grain first, then remove splinters by routing the sides; instead of one pass, make your cut in two or three passes.
▷Uneven depth of cut: tighten the router's depth adjustment and collet; replace the collet if it is worn.

Shaping the work

Look! No clamps

This friction board may solve the problem of clamps in your router's path. Attach a block of wood to one end of a length of plywood. Spread wood glue on the plywood, lay medium-grit sandpaper on it, and leave the board upside down until the glue dries. Then hook the block over the edge of the worktable or hold it in a vice. The friction from the sandpaper will hold your work in place.

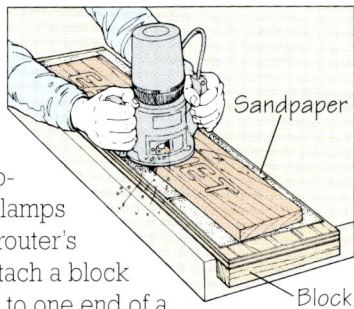

Sandpaper

Block

Housing jig

Make a T-square by screwing together two pieces of straight wood at a right angle. Clamp the jig to a piece of scrap, and rout with the bit you plan to use. The jig will then have a housing in it. To use the jig, mark the work where you want a housing, and clamp the jig in place so that the housing in the jig is lined up with the mark. Use this jig only with the same router and the same size bit.

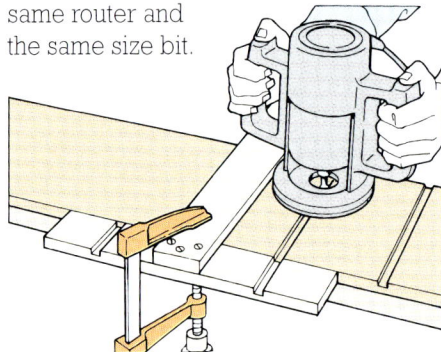

Tipping over the edge

When routing along a narrow edge, the router base can tip and create an uneven profile. For more control, clamp or glue a straight board along the edge of the work.

Straight board

Again and again

If you are making a number of duplicate shapes with a router, you can simplify the job by using the original pattern to make a template out of 6 mm thick hardboard. Cut the workpiece to about 1 mm outside the layout line. Then nail the template to the bottom side of the workpiece, and rout off the excess with a ball-bearing bit designed for trimming plastic laminate.

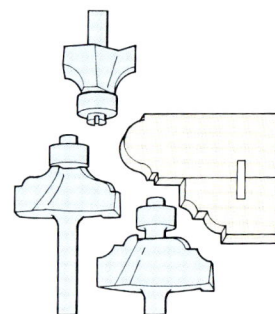

Combining bits ▲

Even if you own a complete set of bits, you don't have to settle for predesigned shapes. To increase the variety and style of the edges you make, try combining two or more bits.

JOINING WOOD

Edge, mitre and tenon

An edgy solution

The table saw is the best tool for cutting straight gluing edges. If a table saw isn't available, first glue together the sections to be joined. When the glue has completely dried, cut the pieces apart with a circular saw, making sure the blade runs down the centre of the glued seam. The blade will remove a bit of the wood from each edge; even if the cut wavers, the edges will vary the same amount and will butt together perfectly.

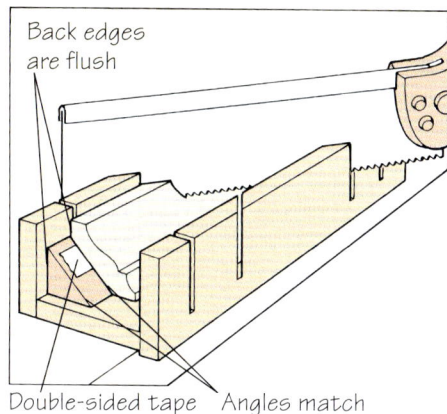
Back edges are flush
Double-sided tape   Angles match

Mitring moulding ▲

Here's an aid to stop cornice moulding from slipping in a mitre box. Cut one edge of a 100 × 50 mm scrap block at an angle that matches that of the moulding. Apply double-sided tape to the cut edge, or glue sandpaper to it. Trim the block so that its back edge is flush with the back edge of the moulding. Set the moulding on the angled edge of the block. Hold the moulding and the block against the mitre box as you saw. The tape or sandpaper will grip the moulding. To clamp the moulding, see p. 84.

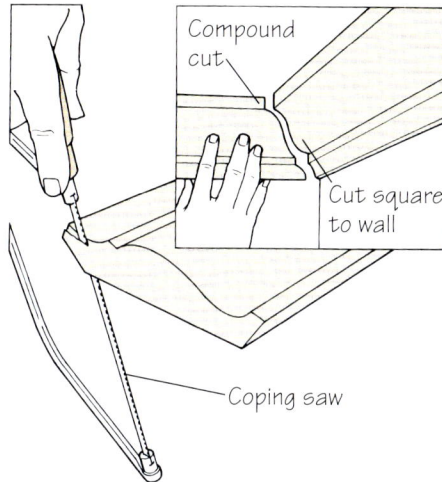
Compound cut
Cut square to wall
Coping saw

Coping a joint ▲

To install cornice moulding at an inside corner, you will have to make a compound cut. First cut one piece to butt against the wall. Then make a 45° inside mitre cut on the end of the other piece. With a coping saw, cut along this profile at the face of the trim, undercutting the edge about 30°. With practice, you'll get it to fit, creating a neat coped joint.

Binding tenon

To find out where a tenon is binding in a mortise, tape a piece of carbon paper over the tenon and drive it into the mortise until it binds. When you remove the tenon, you'll find a smudge on it that indicates where the joint is binding.

Joining with dowels

To the point

Mount an old pencil sharpener on your workshop wall and use it not only to sharpen pencils but also to chamfer dowels for joining wooden workpieces.

Just a flute

A fluted dowel holds better in wood because it allows more glue to surround it. Make your own flutes on plain dowels by crimping the dowels with the serrated jaws of a pair of pliers.

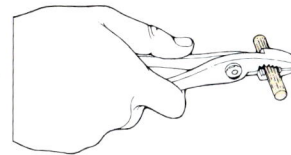

It goes in but won't come out

When test-fitting a dowel joint, the fit may be so snug that you can't pull the joint apart. To prevent this, use test dowels. Make them by cutting a slot into each end at right angles (use a dovetail or small backsaw). After the test fit, use regular dowels to assemble the joint.

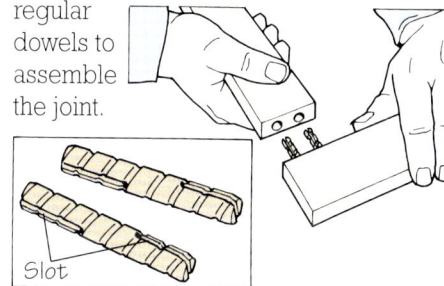
Slot

A better butt

Increase the holding power at a butt joint by driving the screw through a dowel. Drill a hole for a 12 mm dowel so that it cuts across the path of the screw that will be driven into the end grain of one of the workpieces. Put wood glue in the hole and insert the dowel. When the glue has dried, drive in the screw and sand or cut the dowel flush to the surface.

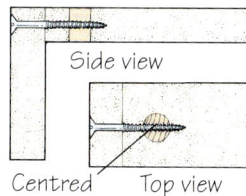
Side view
Centred   Top view

SANDING

Handling the paper

Curling clues

Abrasive paper will curl up and crack if it's left lying around. To keep the paper from curling, place a weight on it. Or store the paper in the freezer so that heat and humidity won't affect the adhesive holding the abrasive to the paper.

Flexing paper

Abrasive paper is usually stiff and brittle, making it tough to fold and likely to leave scuff marks on the work surface. To make the paper more flexible, pull it, with the grit side up, back and forth over the edge of a table or workbench.

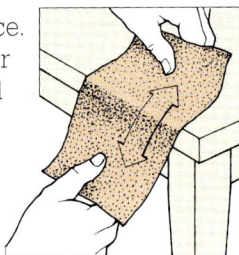

Hack it up

If you cut a lot of abrasive paper, here's one way to save time and effort. Screw a hacksaw blade to the edge of a piece of plywood; the teeth should point up and jut above the plywood. For a fence, glue or screw a straightedge or ruler along one side of the plywood. Draw lines at often-used intervals for easy measuring.

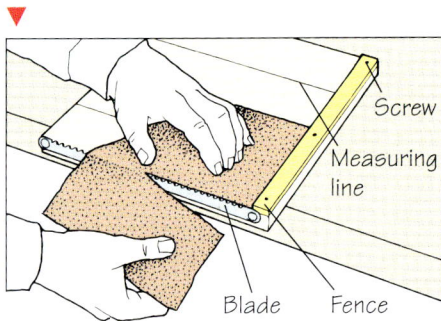

TYPES OF ABRASIVE PAPER

Abrasive paper (commonly called sandpaper) is available in a bewildering number of types. Here are the main choices and the jobs that they're best suited for.

SANDPAPER	CHARACTERISTICS	USES
Aluminium oxide	Familiar light grey paper with tough, durable synthetic grains.	Best general-purpose paper, but more expensive.
Sand	Inexpensive, but cuts slowly and dulls quickly. Sometimes has different grit size classification system to other papers.	Small jobs and sticky surfaces that clog any paper quickly. Otherwise best to avoid.
Garnet	Reddish in colour. Garnet grains fracture during use, exposing fresh, sharp cutting edges; cuts quickly but wears quickly too.	Good all-purpose abrasive, particularly for hand-sanding of timber.
Silicon carbide	Black wet-and-dry paper; has hardest grit and removes material very quickly. Can be wet with water or oil to keep it from gumming up. Available only in fine grits.	Ideal for very fine sanding, such as between coats of varnish and other finishes. Hard enough to abrade metal.
Stearate coated	An aluminium oxide paper coated with a zinc or calcium compound and a lower density abrasive distribution to prevent clogging. Fast-cutting and long-lasting. Generally expensive.	Extremely good for woodworking, especially on softwoods, which can gum up ordinary papers. Also good for removing loose paint and contaminants.

GRADES OF ABRASIVE PAPER

Abrasive paper is classified by a number reflecting the size of the grit particles on it. Higher numbers indicate smaller grains for finer finishing. Here are the common grades of abrasive paper with their grit numbers and uses.

GRADE	TEXTURE	USE
P40–60	Coarse	Rough sanding and shaping; removing paint. Leaves scratches that can be difficult to remove.
P80–150	Medium	Intermediate sanding after rough sanding; sanding on previously painted surfaces.
P180–320	Fine	Final sanding before applying finish. Smoothing paint.
P400–1200	Extra fine	Smoothing between coats of paint. Finer grades for finishing surfaces when spray painting over metal.

Screw

Measuring line

Blade   Fence

HAND-SANDING

Sanding can make or break a wood project's appearance. Even perfect-looking factory-planed timber needs hand-sanding to open the grain and promote even staining. A final hand-sanding is also essential to remove the tiny swirl marks left by orbital power sanders. For professional-looking results, follow these tips:

Use the right grit size. First assess the smoothness of the surface. Start with 60-grit paper for timber that is very rough, although with most wood that has been planed or machined you can start with a finer grade. Progress through finer grits, such as 80, 100 and 120, without skipping any steps. Your first, coarsest sanding should flatten high spots. Subsequent sandings should replace larger scratches with finer ones. Where to stop depends on the work. In general, sand surfaces to be painted to 120 grit, fine objects to be stained and varnished to about 180. An ultra-smooth oiled finish may require even finer grits and a longer progression, such as 120, 180 and 280, finishing with 400 wet-and-dry paper and oil.

Sand with the grain. Sanding at an angle to the grain leaves scratches that are difficult to remove. Overlap sanding strokes and apply equal pressure on both forward and backward strokes. Sand across the grain only when you want to remove a large amount of wood; then follow up by thoroughly sanding with the grain.

Use a sanding block. With a flat backing, abrasive paper can remove bumps and span low spots. Buy a sanding block, or fit a half sheet of paper around a 115 × 115 × 19 mm wood block. Don't use your fingers on flat surfaces—the abrasive paper will follow any irregularities in the wood, leaving a wavy surface.

Don't sand out gouges and dents. You'll get wide, shallow, very noticeable craters. Instead, fill any deep scratches with wood filler; try raising dents with a steam iron (p. 229).

Use a sanding block to ensure flat sanding, but take care not to let the block go more than halfway off the end of the workpiece, or it'll round the edge.

Sand first

Sand last

Avoid cross-grain scratches on pieces that butt at an angle by first sanding the piece with its ends set to the adjacent pieces, then the pieces with free ends.

A sanding sponge is a good alternative for sanding rounded or irregularly shaped pieces. You can also use a sponge for sanding wet surfaces.

Wet-sand between coats of varnish to produce an ultrasmooth finish. Use 400- or 600-grit wet-and-dry silicon carbide paper on a block with water or oil.

SANDING

Odd shapes and sizes

Mopping about

For sanding walls and ceilings before painting or for smoothing wallboard joints, you can buy a pole sander—or you can make one from your sponge mop. Remove the sponge, wrap a sheet of abrasive paper around a block of wood the same size as the sponge, and screw or clamp the block to the mop. The frame will hold the paper in place.

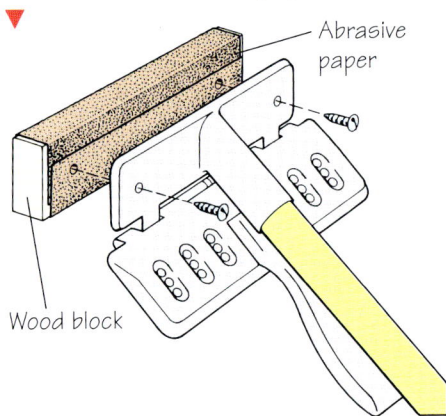

Abrasive paper

Wood block

Shapely paper

When sanding a flat surface, you need to use abrasive paper with a supportive backing. The same is not true, however, when you're sanding curved shapes. You can shape abrasive paper with your fingers or the palm of your hand to match the contour of an irregularly shaped surface. To sand a long turning, such as a chair leg, wrap the paper around the wood (making sure the ends overlap) and slide the paper up and down. For shorter sections on a turning, hold a strip of fine abrasive paper at both ends and run it back and forth over the area as if you were shining a shoe.

A crooked pack

If a sanding sponge isn't handy when you need to smooth a curved surface, improvise one with a pack of playing cards. Wrap abrasive paper around the pack, hold it on edge, and press it firmly against the surface. The cards will conform to the shape of the work and sand it evenly.

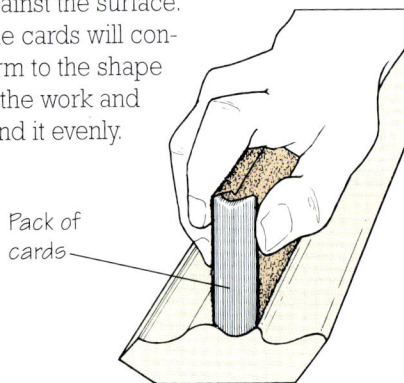

Pack of cards

Matching curves

To smooth curved indentations, cut a short piece of old garden hose and make a slit down the length of it. Wrap abrasive paper, grit side out, around the hose and tuck the ends into the slit. (You can also glue or tape the paper in place.) For smaller grooves, wrap the paper around a wooden dowel. Or fold the abrasive paper and fit the crease into the groove; apply pressure alternately on each side of the groove. For larger surfaces, wrap the paper around a cylindrical plastic container.

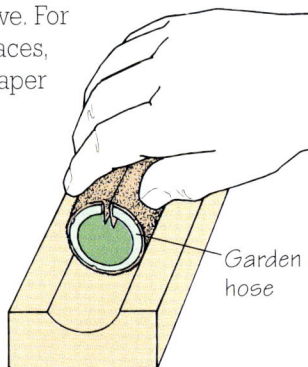

Garden hose

Not just a nail file ▲

Intricate cuts and small, hard-to-reach places can be easy to sand if you use emery boards; these file-like sanders are easy to handle and provide two sanding grits. For a greater range of grits, glue different grades of abrasive paper to ice cream or ice block sticks.

Sticky fingers

Another way to sand hard-to-reach areas is to attach self-adhesive abrasive paper to your fingertip. You'll have a good feel for the surface you're sanding and greater control over the work. To sand into a corner, apply the paper to the blade of a stiff putty knife. As the paper wears, pull it off the blade, move it up, and tear off the used portion.

Holding the work

Padded workbench

To keep the bottom of a workpiece from being scratched while you're sanding the top, use a rubber-backed carpet scrap as a pad for your bench. When you've finished, clean the carpet with your workshop vacuum cleaner.

Against the grit I

When sanding small parts, it's easier to rub the part against the abrasive paper than to rub the paper against the part. To make the job even easier, set the paper on plywood or sturdy cardboard and hold it in place with spring clips.

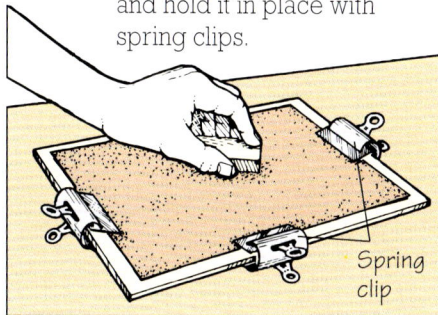

Against the grit II

To rub pieces against abrasive paper, you can cover a block of wood with paper, securing the edges with a rubber band; then hold the block in a vice.

On a stick

Another way to sand small work is to dab hot glue on the back of the piece and stick it on the end of a dowel. Hold the work by the dowel while sanding. To unstick the piece, pop the assembly into the freezer for a few minutes. The cold will quickly free the workpiece.

Power-sanding

Snagging stockings

A problem with power sanders is they don't tell you when the job is done. To test for smoothness, slip an old stocking over your hand and pass it lightly over the work in the direction of the grain. Rough spots will snag the stocking.

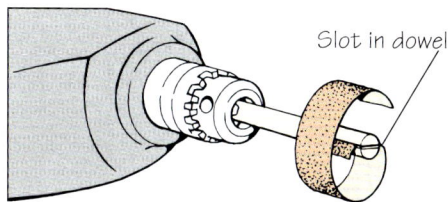

Creating a flap ▲

To sand the inside of a hole that is too small for a drum sander, make a flap sander with a 150 mm length of 10 mm dowel. Using a thin blade in a saw, cut a slot in one end of the dowel. Chuck the opposite end of the dowel into a drill, and slip a strip cut from a sanding belt into the slot. With the slotted end of the dowel facing you, wrap the strip clockwise around the dowel. The grit side of the strip should now be on the outside; if it is, glue the strip in the dowel.

Take a belt to it

Here's a way to keep the edges of a project from being rounded off by your belt sander. Take some timber off cuts the same thickness as the work and secure them to both ends of the work, flush to its surface. Tack the off cuts into place with nails, or clamp them on, making sure the clamps won't interfere with the sander. The sander will then round off the off cuts and not the work.

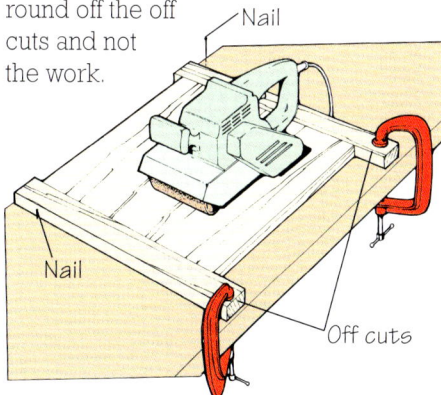

Recycling discs

When sanding a painted surface, sanding discs become clogged and glazed long before they wear out. To get more life out of a disc, apply a coat of semi-paste water soluble paint remover to the encrusted area. Let the remover stand on the disc until the paint has softened; then wash it off.

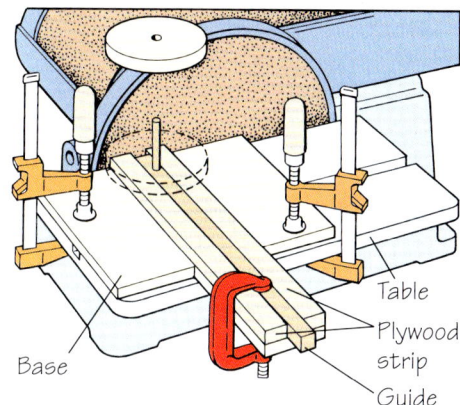

Sanding circles ▲

Sanding wheels and other circular objects is easy with this custom-made disc sander jig. First, make a T-shaped base using a piece of 19 mm plywood. Cut a piece of hardwood to be used as a guide, and drill a hole in one end to hold a dowel. Centre the guide on the base; then nail or glue 19 mm plywood strips along each side of the guide, creating a channel. The guide should be held firmly in place yet be able to slide smoothly in the channel. Glue a dowel into the hole in the guide. In order to use the jig, clamp the base to your disc sander table. After you place the work on the dowel, adjust the guide so the work sits snugly at the disc; clamp it in place. Make sure the work sits on the left side of the disc.

CLAMPING

The basics

Dos and don'ts

Here are some pointers to keep in mind when you're clamping:

▷ Don't rely on clamps to pull together a poorly fitting joint. Glue and pressure may hold things together for a while, but in the long run the joint will fail. Plane or sand the pieces until they fit properly.

▷ Before applying glue, test-fit the parts. Preadjust the clamps so they're ready to apply pressure with just a few twists.

▷ Never force a clamp or use a spanner to tighten it. If the clamp isn't strong enough, use a bigger one or add another clamp next to it.

▷ Too much clamping pressure can squeeze all the glue out of the joint and compress the wood fibres. Too little pressure can result in a glue line that is too thick and therefore weak. An even ridge of glue between clamped parts, at the top and the bottom, indicates proper pressure.

▷ Leave the clamps on for the recommended length of time. Most glues specify a minimum clamping time.

Spreading pressure

Clamp heads exert a cone-shaped area of force. To distribute pressure over a wider area (and to protect the work from damage), place wood off cuts or angle irons between the work and the clamp heads.

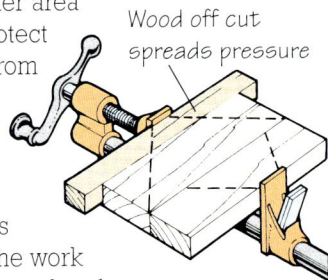

Wood off cut spreads pressure

G-clamp

Strip
Shoe
Trim
Wood block
Throat

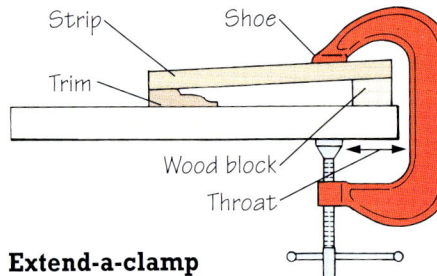

Extend-a-clamp

Suppose you are gluing wood trim to a flat workpiece and your G-clamp can't reach the joint because it has a shallow throat. Here's a way to increase the clamp's reach using only a strip of hardwood and a block of wood that's thicker than the trim. Place the block near the edge of the workpiece, position the strip under the clamp shoe so that it spans the gap between the block and the trim, and clamp down. The strip will transfer pressure to the joint.

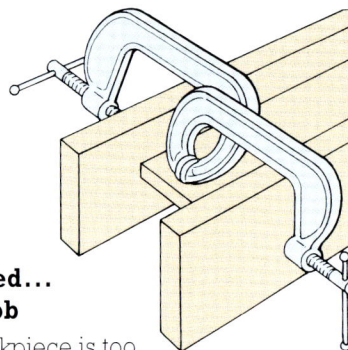

Coupled... for a job

If a workpiece is too wide for one G-clamp to span it and you have no suitable substitute, combine two G-clamps as shown. This trick will work well in situations that require only light clamping pressure. Don't try it if you need to apply heavy pressure.

No more bouncing ball

It isn't easy to hold a curved, irregular piece tightly in a mitre box. An ordinary soft rubber ball can provide a good way around this problem. Cut off a piece of the ball to create a flat area, and glue a film canister cap to the opposite side. Place the cut side of the ball against the workpiece and the clamp head in the cap. Clamp the ball and workpiece in place securely . The ball will conform to fit any shape and won't scratch the work.

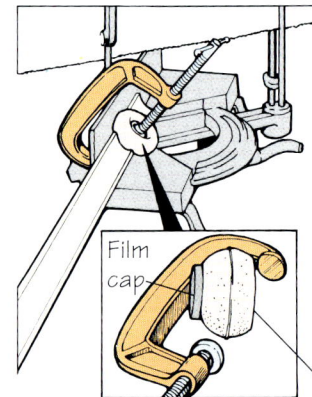

Film cap

Flat face cut on ball

On edge

If you don't have an edge clamp and tape isn't suitable for the job, use shims with a G-clamp. Drive wedge-shaped shims between the edge piece and the back of the clamp until they fit snugly. ▼

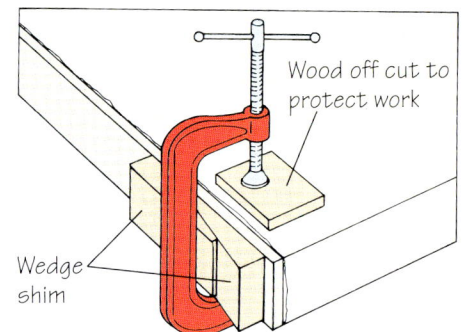

Wood off cut to protect work

Wedge shim

Hand screw

Jaw line-up

Mark the handles on your hand screw to quickly set the jaws parallel. With the jaws closed and parallel, apply a narrow paint line or other mark down the centre of each hand grip. No matter how wide apart the jaws are set, if you keep the lines in the same relationship to each other, the jaws will be parallel. Keep in mind that the jaws can also be set at an angle if the job calls for it.

Working together

Use pairs of hand screws to hold oddly placed pieces together, as shown at right. If you don't have a wood-worker's vice, use a combination of hand screws, bar clamps and G-clamps to hold a work-piece for planing, sanding, chiselling or shaping. A setup like the one below will allow you to work without interference from the clamps. ▼

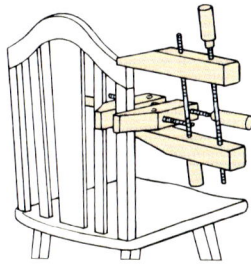

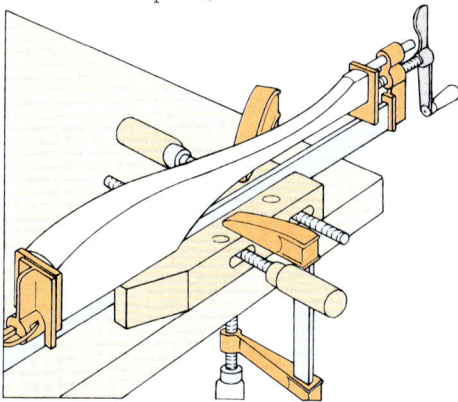

Pipe clamp

Spacer block

Wood dowel

Alternating growth rings

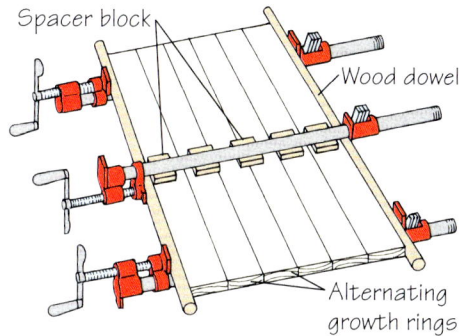

No warpage here ▲

Here are a few tricks for gluing strips edge to edge. When you glue up boards that will form an overhanging surface, such as a table top on a pedestal, set the boards with the growth rings alternating up and down. To hold any glue-up, stagger pipe clamps above and below the workpiece, adding spacer blocks to keep the clamp pres-sure in line with the boards. If the clamp jaws are longer than the thickness of the work, angle them so that they contact more of the work. Or place a wood dowel lengthwise on each side of the work to redirect the clamping force.

Clamping a trapezoid

To clamp shapes with unequal parallel sides, such as a chair seat frame, you'll have to create right-angle clamping surfaces. Place wood off cuts against the two parallel edges as shown; this allows the clamps to seat properly and to apply pressure at the proper angle.

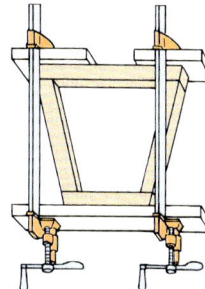

Custom-made block

Round or elliptical edge pieces, which are common on table tops, can be clamped together with the help of a block that fits snugly around the work-piece. You can also make blocks to match other unusual shapes. If you have trouble steadying the block while applying the clamp, contact glue it into place; then pull it off afterwards. ▼

Make block to match shape of work

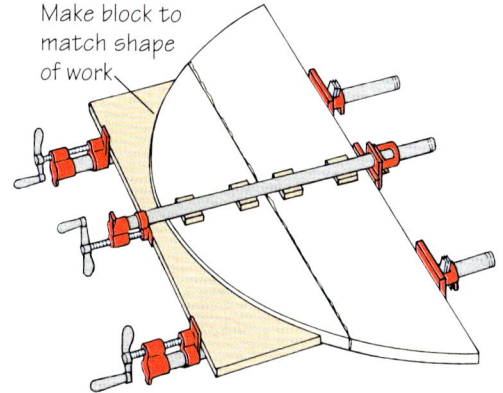

Hold the door

Secure a door in a vertical position for planing or mortising by using pipe clamps or hand screws. Stagger the pipe clamps, alternating left and right, along the bottom edge of the door. ▼

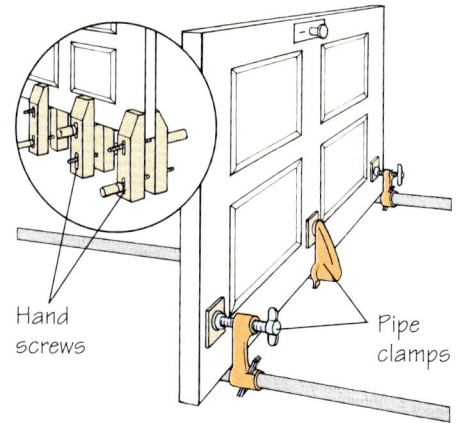

Hand screws

Pipe clamps

CLAMPING

Makeshift clamps

Spring clamp look-alikes

Here are two substitutes for a spring clamp: large battery clips from old damaged jumper leads will accept work up to about 40 mm thick, and the spring clip on the end of a pants or skirt hanger will hold a small work-piece. The jaws of some hanger clips are padded with felt strips that will protect your work from marring.

Mousetrap technology

You can turn a mousetrap into a strong, versatile wide-grip clamp. Prise off the bait holder and cut off the hold-down side of the base before applying the other half to the work.

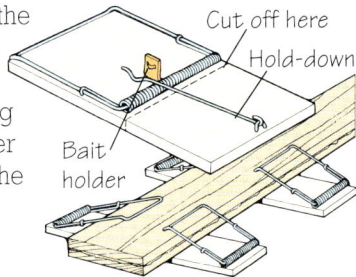

Cut off here

Hold-down

Bait holder

Gun clamp

A caulking gun is ideal for applying light pressure to small pieces. Place the work between timber off cuts, and then position the assembly between the jaws of the gun. The off cuts protect the work and provide a flat surface for even pressure. To apply pressure to the work, squeeze the trigger.

Off cut

Rubber-band clamps

Sometimes clamps just don't work well for gluing small or irregularly shaped objects. To hold such pieces together, keep a variety of large rubber bands in your workshop.

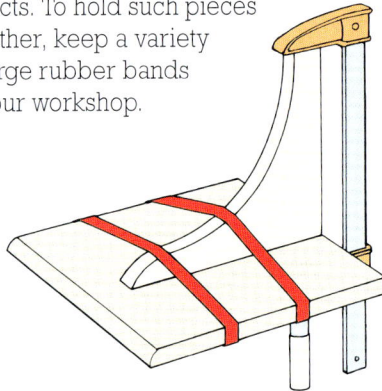

You don't have to jump for the cords

Elastic cords are an ideal substitute for web clamps. Because the cords are not adjustable, keep a variety of sizes in stock. You can combine short cords to make longer ones; wrap long cords around small pieces several times or in a figure of eight.

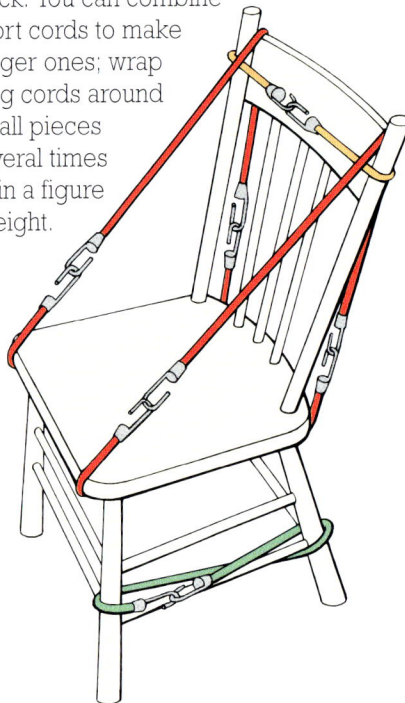

Cloth

From the garage

An ordinary hose clamp, like those found on car radiator hoses, is just right for clamping a cracked or split wooden leg or spindle. This clamp is inexpensive, comes in a variety of sizes and provides good uniform pressure when tightened. Slip a piece of cloth or vinyl under the band to prevent marring.

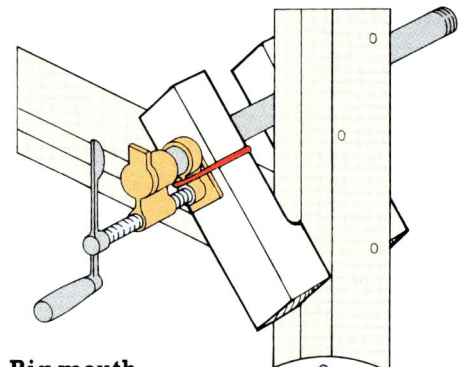

Big mouth

For a longer reach, you can extend the jaws on a pipe clamp. In two wood blocks, drill holes large enough for the pipe to fit through; then carve out jaws to concentrate the pressure. Use stout rubber bands to secure the blocks to the clamp heads as shown, and slip the assemblies onto the pipe.

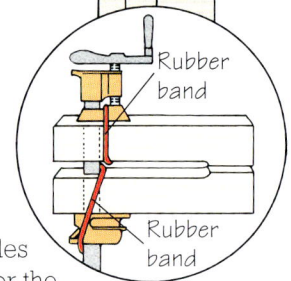

Rubber band

Rubber band

Home-made clamps

Bag it ▲

When you need to join irregular shapes, hold them together with a sandbag. For small fragile items, use a small plastic bag filled with sand. Use larger sand-filled bags for big items. For outdoor projects, try plastic bags or containers filled with water from a hose.

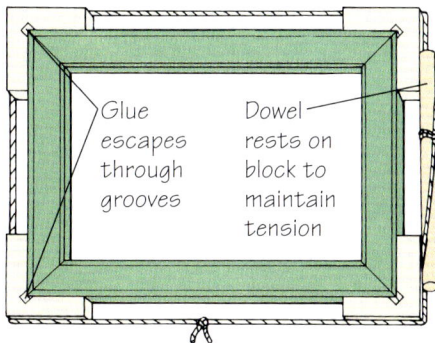

Glue escapes through grooves

Dowel rests on block to maintain tension

Tourniquet a frame ▲

Holding mitred corner pieces together is simple with this tourniquet clamp. Make four L-shaped corner blocks. Rout or chisel grooves on the outer edges to guide the string, and make vertical grooves at the inside corners to allow excess glue to escape. Place the blocks in position and run string around the perimeter. To tighten the string, wrap a dowel or stick in the string and twist it.

Holding a scarf

Here's an easy way to spread pressure evenly along a scarf joint. When you cut off the ends of the work, save the triangular off cuts. When you're ready to clamp, place the off cuts between the work and the clamp as shown. ▼

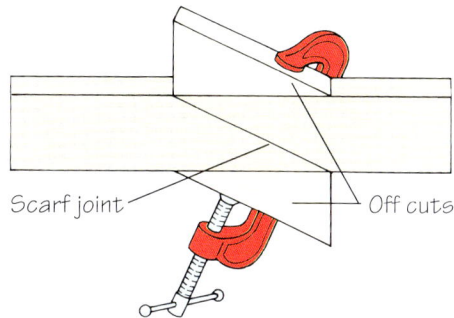

Scarf joint

Off cuts

Edgy situation

If you run out of clamps in the middle of a project, you can make your own out of timber off cuts. Screw one block to each end of a length of board that's slightly longer than the workpiece. Attach each block with only one screw so that it will pivot into alignment. Cut two wedge-shaped pieces of wood, and drive them between one of the blocks and the project for a tight hold. ▼

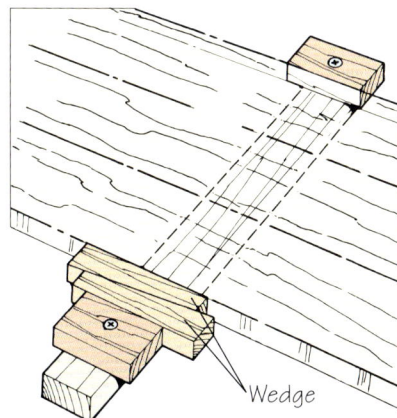

Wedge

H-frame ▲

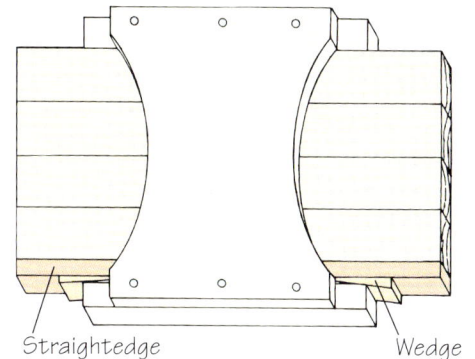

Straightedge

Wedge

This H-frame jig is ideal for edge-gluing two or more boards (the long legs of the frame will apply equal pressure along the boards). The jig is easy to make out of scrap timber and 19 mm plywood; to reduce the weight of the frame, cut the plywood as shown. Create clamping pressure by driving a pair of wedges between the straightedge and the jig.

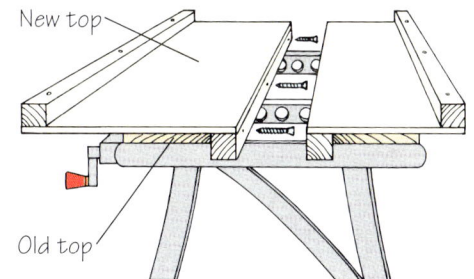

New top

Old top

Extending the top ▲

By building a larger top for your portable workbench, you can use it to clamp large objects. Make the new top out of 19 mm plywood and four pieces of 50 × 50 mm timber. One side of the new top should be slightly wider than the underlying side of the old top; the other side should be about twice as wide. Attach both sides of the new top to the original top with screws, as shown.

GLUING

Applying glue

Which wood glue?

There's more than one way to glue two pieces of wood together. Ordinary white PVA wood glue is perfectly all right for most indoor jobs, but in situations where the joint is likely to be exposed to damp, or might even get wet, you will need to use resorcinol formaldehyde or urea formaldehyde adhesive. Also don't overlook construction adhesive, which is ideal for rough exterior joints.

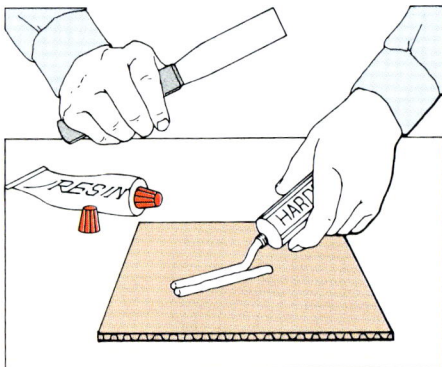

Epoxy mix-up ▲

For a strong epoxy bond, you must mix resin and hardener in equal parts. An easy way to gauge the proportions is to squeeze out the resin and hardener in parallel lines of equal width and length.

Dry run

Here's a good way to tell when glue has dried. At the same time as you apply glue to your work, glue together two scrap pieces of the same material as the work. Test the scraps to determine when the work is dry. If the label on the glue specifies a drying time, you can jot it down on the wood as a reference.

Make it hot

When applying hot glue to a large area, you may find that the glue is cooling and drying too fast. To slow down the drying time, try warming the work with a heat gun. Or put the work out in the sun on a hot day. After the glue dries, you can scrape off any excess with a utility knife.

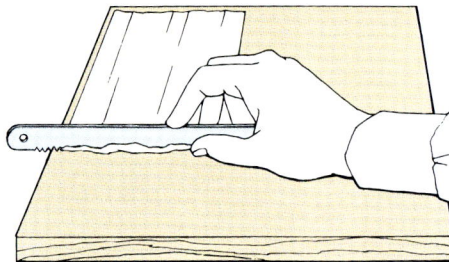

Spreading the glue ▲

A broken hacksaw blade spreads glue quickly over a large, flat area. The teeth let the glue flow easily and keep it to a smooth, even overall depth.

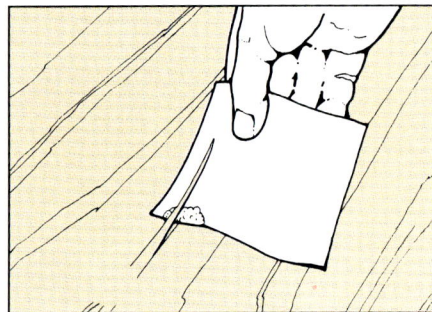

Slivery move ▲

To glue down a wood sliver, dab a spot of wood glue on one side of a piece of paper. Slip the paper under the sliver; then pull the paper out, making sure that the glue contacts the sliver. Tape or clamp the sliver in place until the glue dries; then sand the area.

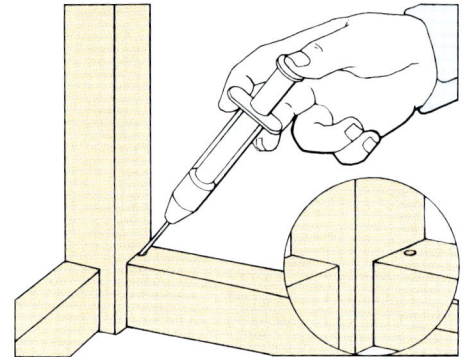

Sure-shot injector ▲

A simple plastic syringe, found in many hobby shops or in woodworking stores or catalogues, is ideal for injecting glue into narrow places, such as in a hole made to reach a loose tenon. After filling the syringe barrel, insert the plunger and hold it upwards while you depress it. This will expel air bubbles and prevent the glue from drying. To store glue in the syringe, insert a nail into its tip.

A tight squeeze

As any model maker knows, toothpicks are perfect for applying glue in tight areas with precise control. ▼

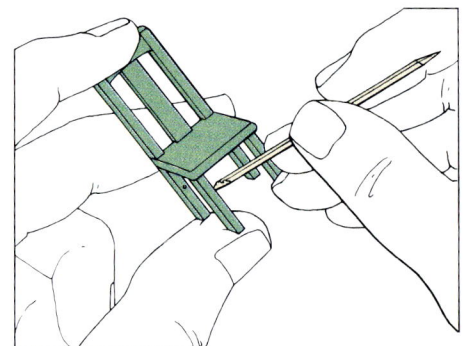

Excess glue

Oozing cure

If you can keep squeezed-out glue off the edges of the wood you're clamping, you'll avoid the bother of removing excess glue later. Here's a trick that will save you time and effort. Before gluing the pieces, clamp them together and apply transparent tape over the joint. Slit the tape along the joint with a utility knife; then remove the clamps. Apply the glue and reclamp the pieces. This way the glue will ooze onto the tape rather than the wood. Once the glue has set, peel off the tape. ▼

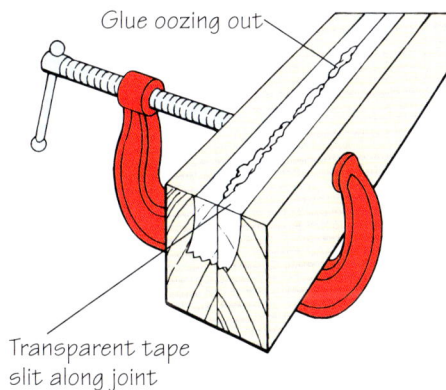

Glue oozing out

Transparent tape
slit along joint

Give it some room

As you make a mortise-and-tenon or a dowel joint, leave extra space at the bottom of the recess. Excess glue will drain there instead of squeezing out of the joint. Chamfer the top edges of the holes for the same effect.

No sticky clamps here

To avoid getting glue on your clamps, place two layers of wax paper strips between the clamp and the work. You can create convenient-sized strips by sawing a roll of wax paper into 100 mm sections; then, when you need the paper, rip off the appropriate lengths. If you run out of wax paper, cut a plastic bag into strips instead. ▼

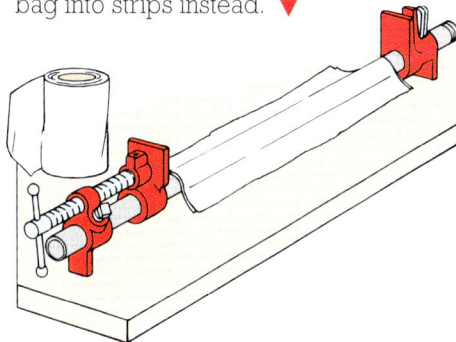

Cleaning up

Sip it up

A drinking straw is a handy instrument for removing excess glue from an inside corner. Slightly crease one end of the straw so that it fits into the corner. The glue will move up the straw as you push it along the joint at a shallow angle. ▼

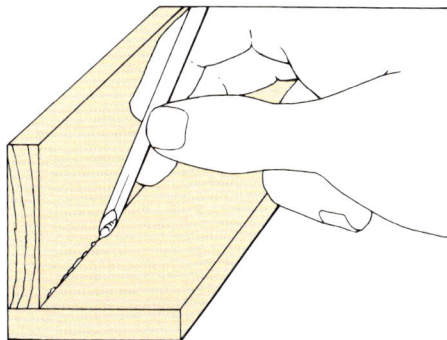

Take it off

Because dried glue won't take stain, it's important to remove any excess before it dries. Use a wet rag to wipe off water-based glues. To avoid leaving behind a film of glue, rinse out the rag periodically and make the final wipe with a well-rinsed rag. (To remove non-water-based glues, use the appropriate solvent.) Sanding will take care of whatever glue residue may remain.

Too late for wiping

If squeezed-out glue has dried to a semi-hard state, use a putty knife to scrape it off. If the glue has dried completely, use a paint scraper to remove it. After scraping, sand the area to eliminate all remaining traces of glue. ▼

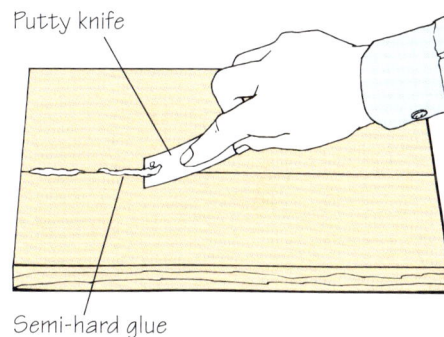

Putty knife

Semi-hard glue

Splotchy job

Before applying a finish, make sure you really have removed all the glue. By wetting the surface with mineral turpentine or acetone you can reveal any remaining glue patches. (The patches will remain light-coloured while the rest of the area darkens.) Remove the glue thoroughly from those spots so that they won't mar your finish.

FINISHING WOOD

Filler

For all those guitarists

Save your old plastic guitar plectrums. Their flexibility makes them ideal for applying putty to nail holes and small nicks in woodwork. ▼

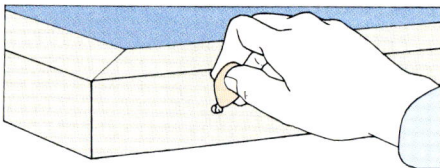

Knotty putty

To fill nail holes in knotty pine, mix raw sienna–coloured acrylic or dry powder paint with wood putty. Make about four mixtures, varying in shades from very light to dark brown. Apply the shades to match the knotty wood. For nail holes in regular unknotted wood, make your own filler by mixing sawdust from the wood with PVA wood glue.

Open pores

If you want a high-gloss smooth finish on an open-grained wood like Tasmanian oak or maple, fill the pores with paste filler. (For a satin or more natural finish, the filler isn't needed.) For a light stain, apply a mixture of the stain and filler. For a dark stain, apply coats of the stain until it's a shade or two lighter than desired; apply the filler mixture as a final coat. Use a plastic card to spread the filler mixture; hold the card with a long side flexed on the wood. Spread the filler diagonally across the grain in each direction, then back and forth with the grain. Scrape off any excess filler with the card. Let the filler dry; then sand it.

From the container

Pour away

Here's how to avoid making a mess when pouring finish, thinner or any other liquid from an oblong container. Just make sure you hold the can so that the opening is at the top. The liquid will leave the can in a steady stream.

Nutty stain mixer

When you open a can of wood stain, drop two medium-sized steel nuts into it. Then each time you use the stain, shake the can to thoroughly stir the contents. (Never do this in a glass jar.) You'll be able to hear when the pigments are no longer sitting at the bottom of the can. Don't try this trick with varnish. Shaking or stirring varnish can create air bubbles that can ruin the finish.

A different filter

Have you run out of paint filters for removing impurities from thinners and light finishing oils, and you don't want to make a special trip to the shop? Instead of a filter, use a clean disposable paper dust mask—it's a perfect substitute.

Out of the kitchen

These two kitchen tools are ideal for removing a small amount of liquid from a large container. A gravy ladle is handy for scooping up stain. A baster is ideal for transferring mineral turpentine and other solvents. (But if the baster has a plastic tube, first test it to make sure the solvent doesn't soften the tube.)

Applying the finish

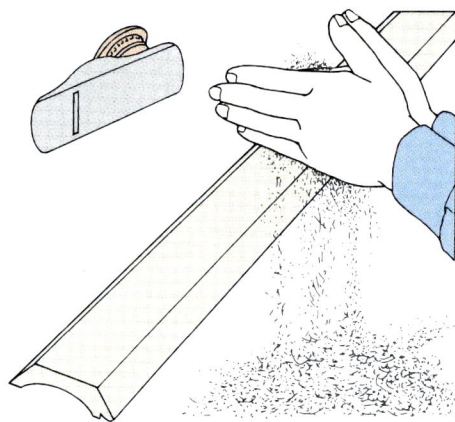

Oily hands ▲

Your hands secrete natural oils that can mark unfinished wood. To protect the work, rub sawdust between your hands before handling the wood. The sawdust will draw out and absorb the excess oil.

Versatile meths

Before finishing a workpiece, remove pencil marks, dirt smudges, grease and oil spots—and wood dust—by wiping (not soaking) the work with methylated spirits. Meths is an effective cleanser and will not raise the grain. Because meths can be absorbed through your skin, wear rubber gloves.

Layer by layer

For professional results, follow this work sequence when staining and varnishing. Before starting the job, use timber off cuts to test how the stain and varnish will colour the wood. When you're ready to begin the sequence, apply the stain; then follow with the sealer and the coats of varnish. Sand the workpiece after sealing it and between coats of varnish. To prevent warpage, make sure you finish every side—even bottoms and backs. This helps keep moisture from entering the wood.

Pour it in

Fitting a brush or rag into a deep recess can be difficult at best. To make the job easier, thin the finish to one-half or one-third of its strength; then pour it into the recess. The thinned finish is less likely to drip. Swirl the finish around to cover the bottom and sides, then pour the excess back into the container. For complete coverage, repeat the process.

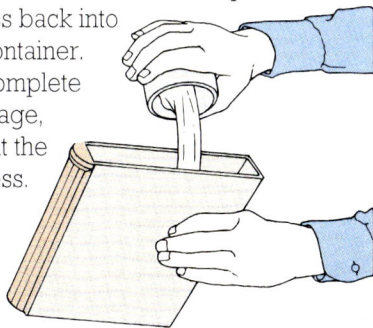

The dark end

When finishing a new wood project, treat the end grain last to keep it from staining darker than the rest of the work. Brush a coat of mineral turpentine or paint thinner onto the end grain just before applying the stain.

Safe finish

To finish salad bowls, butcher blocks, toys, and other wood projects that will hold food or are likely to be chewed on by young children, use mineral oil, salad oil (walnut oil is best), or a brand-name 'salad oil finish'.

Bright idea ▲

After applying a finish to wood, you'll want to know if you've missed any spots. Here's the best way to check. Examine the work at a 45° angle while shining a bright light on it. The wet finish will reflect the light; missed spots will show up as dull areas.

SAFETY FIRST

ABOUT FINISHES

▷ Buy flammable liquids, such as tung oil, varnish and thinners, in quantities that are just enough to do the job on hand.
▷ Because their vapours can ignite, store flammable liquids in tightly sealed containers, away from heaters and naked flames, and out of the reach of children.
▷ Keep a fire extinguisher in your work area. Never smoke in this area or near flammable liquids.
▷ Solvent-base liquids are a skin irritant; wear chemical-resistant rubber gloves when using them.
▷ Items soaked in natural oil-base finishes (tung oil, linseed oil, gel stains and wipe-on finishes) can ignite or explode if exposed to air and then confined. Before disposing of brushes, rags and other materials exposed to one of these finishes, hang them from a line outside, away from children and pets, until they are dry.
▷ To dispose of leftover finishes properly, see p. 39.

FINISHING WOOD

Equipment

Make it tacky

Use a tack rag to remove dust from a workpiece before applying the first coat of stain or finish, and between coats. You can make your own tack rag out of cheesecloth, an old cotton nappy or any other lint-free cotton cloth. Dip the cloth in turpentine and wring it out. Then drizzle a small amount of varnish or polyurethane from a stirring stick onto the cloth, and knead the cloth to distribute the finish. The cloth should be able to pick up dust without leaving any finish. To avoid spontaneous combustion, store the rag in a tightly sealed can.

Absorbent stockings

A rag used to apply a stain may leave lint particles all over the work. To avoid this problem, use discarded nylon stockings or panty hose as an applicator. The material leaves a lint-free finish and also absorbs less stain than some other cloth applicators. ▼

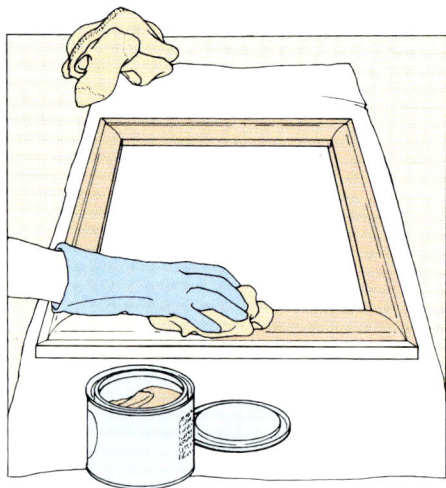

Canned rags

Don't let your stain rags dry out in the middle of a project. When you have finished for the day, store them in an empty stain can. Be sure the lid covers the can tightly, both to keep the rags from drying out and to prevent spontaneous combustion. The rags can be used for a quick touch-up without having to be dipped in the stain again.

Off the cuff

Tired of having stain or finish drip down your arm as you apply it overhead? Wear a long rubber glove on your working hand. Turn up the cuff a few centimetres and stuff it with toilet paper. Besides catching the drips, the paper will absorb them, so you won't have to worry about spills when you lower your arm.

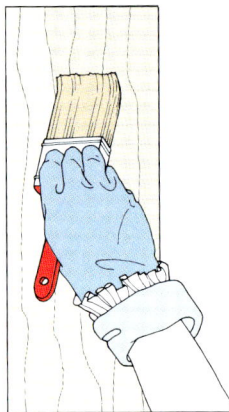

Loose bristles

All brushes lose bristles when first used. Before using a brush for the first time, soak it in the finish for 30 minutes; then clean the brush and let it sit overnight. The dried finish in the ferrule will bond the bristles. To remove any bristles that do come loose, wait for the finish to dry; then pick them out with a knife.

Miniature brush

To apply finishes in hard-to-reach areas, such as crevices on mouldings, recycle an old soft-bristle toothbrush.

Split-end bristle

CHOOSING THE RIGHT BRUSH

One key to a successful finishing job is picking the right brush—or more to the point, the right bristle—for the type of finish you'll be applying.

For oil varnish and polyurethane, use a brush with natural China bristles (black or white hog hairs). Look for long supple bristles, either with split ends or tapered, and a chiselled profile.

For water-based finishes, use synthetic-bristle brushes. (Natural bristles lose their shape in water.) Avoid split-end bristles; they can make the finish foam.

Always look for the best brush. A good-quality brush is worth its price. Select one with a stainless steel ferrule, if available; it won't leave rust marks.

Before dipping a brush in finish, soak it in the appropriate solvent; then squeeze it out. Be sure to clean the brush and reshape the bristles as soon as you have applied the finish.

Neatness counts

Bring out the Yellow Pages

Open up an old telephone book or catalogue and use it as a work surface for small finishing jobs. As the pages get mucky, just rip them out and toss them away—it will take quite some time to use up all those pages.

Knob work

Finishing drawer knobs can be a messy proposition. Here's a way to keep your fingers free of finish by using the screw that secures the knob to the drawer. Fit the screw to the knob; then hold the screw with a clothes peg while you apply the finish. When the job is done, balance the assembly in an upright position on a flat surface until the finish dries.

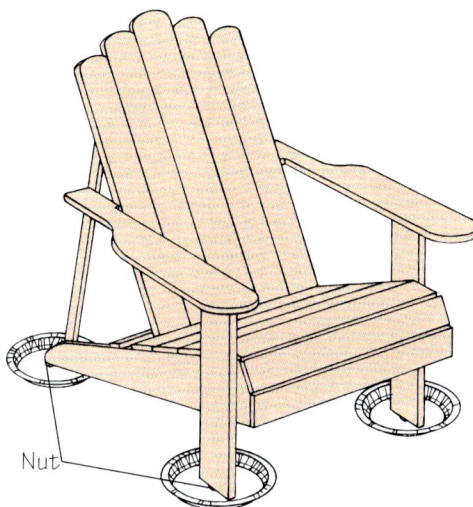

Leg rests ▲

For rot-resistant legs on outdoor chairs, soak the bottom of the legs in a wood preservative. To let the preservative get in, stand the legs in disposable pie trays with a nut under each. Pour preservative into the trays and let the legs soak overnight. (The nuts raise the legs just enough for the preservative to soak in.)

Nut

Suspended on nails

Here's a way to cut drying time when you're finishing (or painting) a door. Drive 75 mm nails into the top and bottom of the door, and then rest the nails on sawhorses. After you apply the finish on one side, flip the door over (use the nails as handles with a helper at the other end) and apply the finish to the other side. Both sides will dry at the same time. If you're working in a dusty area, use this method to suspend the work with one finished side facing down until it dries.

Give it a lift

When applying finish to table or chair legs, keep the legs from sticking to the work surface by slipping washers under them. The diameter of the washers must be smaller than the diameter of the legs.

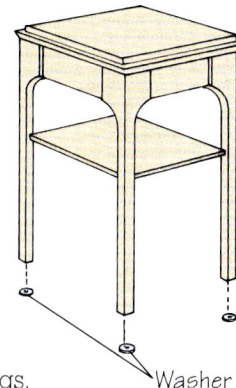

Washer

It's a hold-up

This contraption will allow you to elevate a small project off the work surface while you finish it. Cut 6 mm dowels into 100 mm lengths, and sharpen both ends in a pencil sharpener. Push the dowels into a base made of foam insulation or packing board. Rest the workpiece on the pointed dowels. Make sure you use enough dowels so that the work doesn't tip over. ▼

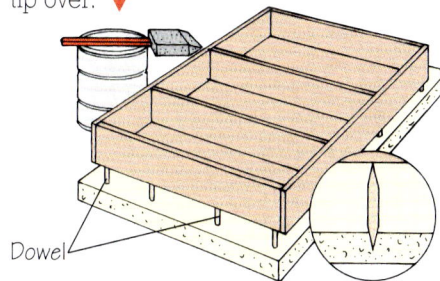

Dowel

For those forgetful people

Prepare for future touch-ups or refinishing jobs by keeping a record of your work. Before applying the finish, stick a label or glue a bit of paper to an inconspicuous area of the project. Record the type of wood, stain and finish you used and the date. The finish you apply over the paper will hold it in place.

METALWORKING

Clean holes

Sandwich time

To avoid rough or bent edges when you're drilling a hole in sheet metal, clamp the metal between two pieces of wood and drill through the assembly. This trick will produce clean holes whether you use a portable drill or a drill press. It will also produce clean lines when you're cutting sheet metal with a hacksaw or jig saw.

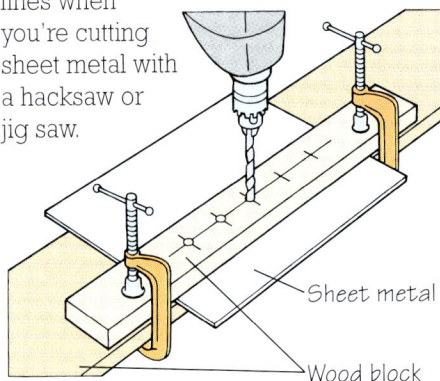

Sheet metal

Wood block

Removing burrs

Even if you've drilled a hole in sheet metal without sandwiching it between wood, you can still get a clean hole. Just twirl a countersink bit in the hole a few times to remove the burrs. ▼

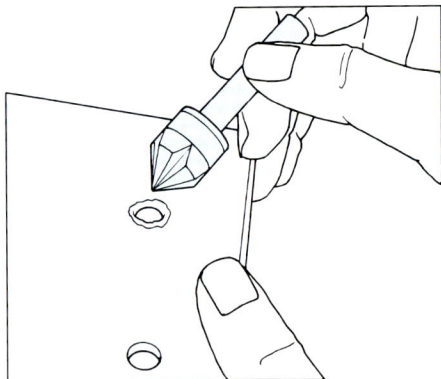

No more wandering bit

When drilling in metal, as in other materials (p. 9), you can keep the drill bit from wandering off centre by dimpling the surface with a centre punch. Don't forget to add some light oil to the hole to keep the bit from overheating (p. 10). Lubrication will also speed cutting time and keep the bit from becoming dull.

Drilling deep

A good way to keep the bit lubricated when drilling in thick metal is to form a wall out of modelling clay around the area to be drilled, thus creating a circular dam. Fill the dam with light machine oil. Keep extra oil on hand in an oil can to replenish the dam as needed.

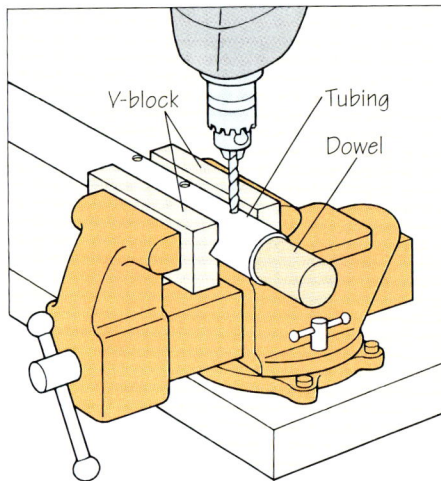

V-block   Tubing

Dowel

Straight through ▲

To drill holes in tubing, secure the tubing in V-blocks held by a vice. Insert a dowel inside the tubing to reinforce the thin walls and to guide the bit straight through to the other side. Be sure the drill bit can leave the bottom end freely.

On file

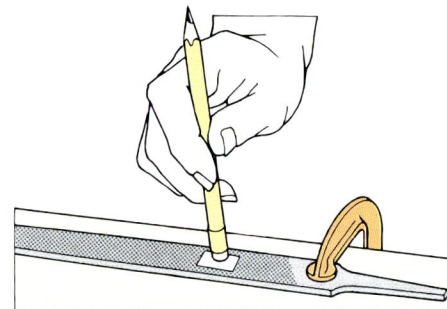

Too small for vices ▲

Sometimes you may want to file a piece of metal that is too small to grip in a vice or to hold with your fingers. The solution is to move the piece against the file with a rubber-tipped pencil. Clamp or hold the file securely to a work surface.

Cover up

While you are using a file, the unused side can mar your work. To protect the work from scratches, cover the file's unused side with adhesive or cloth tape.

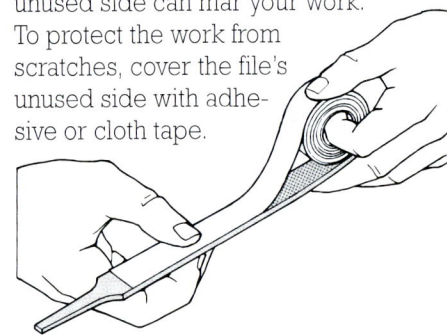

Chalky filler

Soft metals, such as aluminium, copper and brass, clog the teeth of some files. To reduce clogging, first rub talcum powder or a piece of chalk across the file teeth. The powder keeps the metal from caking up and allows the chips to be cleaned out easily with a file card.

Clean up

Never blow on a file to remove metal particles. They might end up in your eyes and cause serious damage. If you don't have a file card, remove the particles from the file by pressing putty or masking tape onto the cutting surface. When you pull the putty or tape off the file, the particles will come up too.

Saw power

Nick a notch

Before making a hacksaw cut, create a starting notch for the blade by nicking the workpiece at the cut line with a file. The notch will act as a guide, preventing the blade from slipping. (On a round piece of metal, use a triangular file to cut a V-shaped notch.)

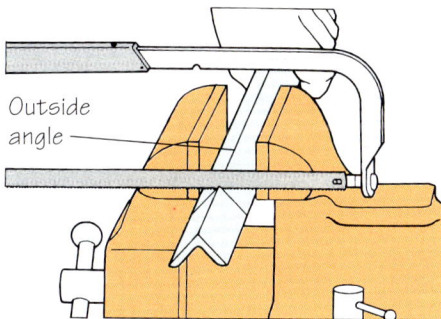

A new angle ▲

When cutting angle iron with a hacksaw, secure it in a vice with the outside angle uppermost. This way, the hacksaw will cut both sides of the angle at the same time. And because more saw teeth are in contact with the work, the resulting cut will be smoother and more accurate.

Stop that annoying chatter

When cutting steel, aluminium or brass sheet in a bench vice, the free end lets out a noisy chatter or screech with every stroke of a hacksaw. To stop the racket, wrap the free end of the workpiece in a wet towel or rag. This will dampen the offending vibrations and calm your nerves too.

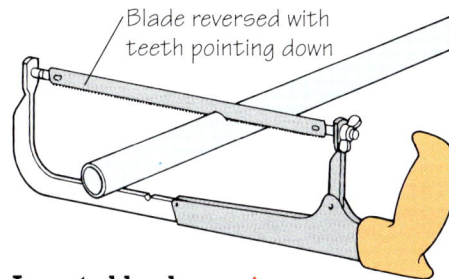

Inverted hacksaw ▲

If you have a hacksaw job to do but no room to use the saw, here's a way around your problem. Simply remove the saw blade and reinsert it upside down. This trick is especially handy for cutting an overhead pipe.

Oily cut ▶

Aluminium and other soft metals are best cut with a jig saw that is equipped with a fine-tooth blade. To keep the teeth on the blade from clogging, apply light machine oil along the cut line. The oil will also keep the blade cooler and sharper.

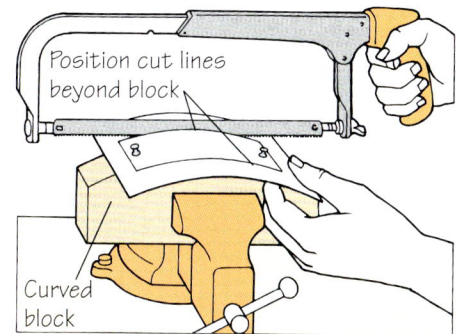

A rectangular hole ▲

It's possible to make a rectangular inside cut in flat sheet metal with a hacksaw without cutting in from the edge. First saw a curve in a block of scrap wood. Clamp the wood, curved edge up, in a vice. Mark cut lines on the sheet metal, and drive two double-headed nails through the waste area to hold the work to the wood. The sheet will bend, with its centre bulging up. Make the two cuts along the length of the block. Then remove and reposition the work to make the last two saw cuts.

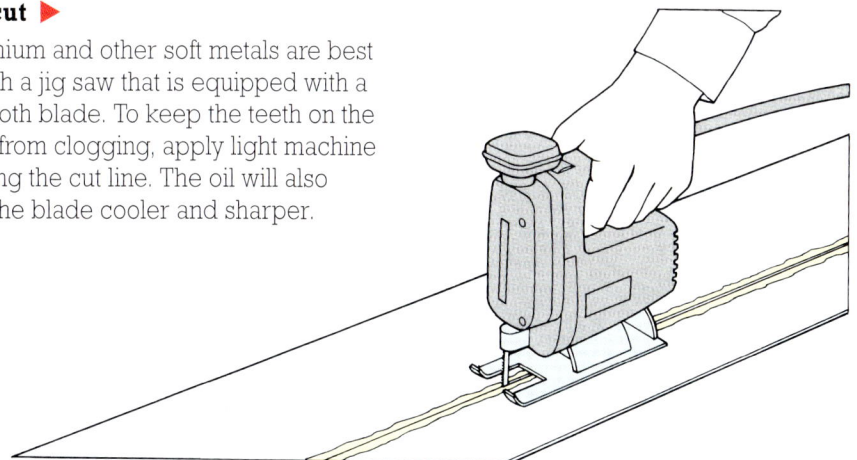

METALWORKING

Fastener facts

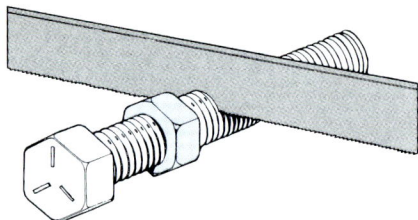

Customised bolt ▲

If a bolt is too long for the intended job, you can cut it to size with a hacksaw; but first twist a nut onto the bolt past the cut mark. Unscrewing the nut after the saw cut is made cleans the threads and removes any burrs at the cut end. To make the newly cut bolt even easier to thread, bevel the end with a grinder or file.

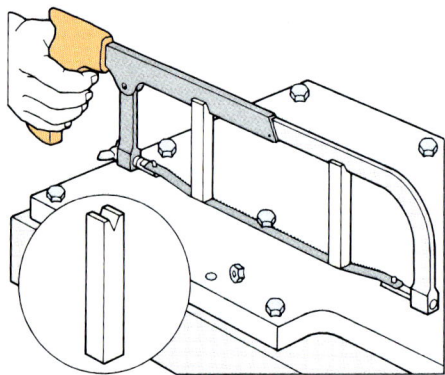

Flush cut ▲

With slight adaptations to a hacksaw, you can cut a bolt or screw flush to the work. Notch one end of two 90 mm long timber off cuts. Loosen the saw blade and rotate it until the teeth are pointing sideways. Place the wood pieces between the saw frame and the turned blade, and tighten the blade. The wood will push the blade down slightly below the saw frame, letting you make the cut.

Rusted nut and bolt

One way to remove a rusted nut and bolt is to apply penetrating oil (p. 14). To keep the oil where it will do the most good, build a circular dam around the nut with wood putty, plumber's putty or modelling clay. The dam not only holds the oil, it lets you soak the whole nut.

Take a hack at it

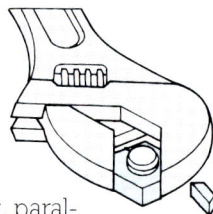

Here's how to remove a rusted nut without damaging the threads of the bolt. Use a hacksaw to make a starting cut in the nut, parallel to one of its faces; then split the nut with a cold chisel. (Make sure you wear safety glasses for this.) Finally, unscrew the nut with an adjustable spanner.

Too loose for comfort?

To keep nuts and bolts from coming loose, apply a small dab of locking solution (from a car parts shop) to the bolt threads before you tighten the nut. For added insurance, smear some locking solution over any exposed threads. Once it's dry, the fasteners won't be able to work loose; but if you have to remove them, the solution will peel off easily.

Sheet metal

Make it clear

Before marking metal with a scriber or awl, run a dark-coloured, wide-tipped felt marker over the area to be scribed. The scribe marks will show up more clearly against the dark background.

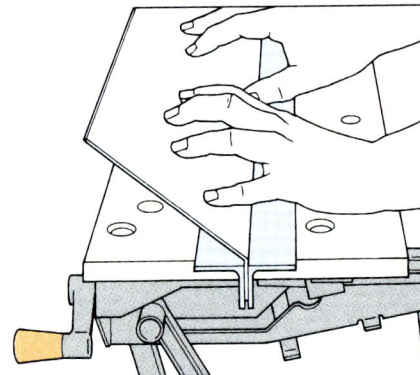

Home made jig ▲

Turn your portable workbench and two pieces of metal angle into a home made bending jig. The metal angles should have sharp 90° edges so that the sheet metal creases evenly. Place the angles in the workbench as shown. Start the fold by hand; then finish it by hammering the metal with a hardwood block and mallet for a sharp crease. If you don't have a portable workbench, use G-clamps to hold the angles together.

Get the dents out

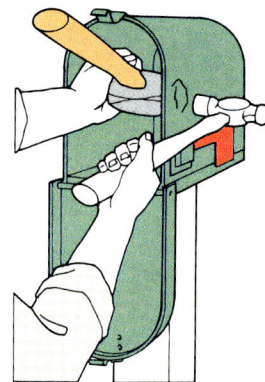

Here are two ways to remove dents from metal objects. Hold the object against a sandbag and gently flatten out the raised side of the dent with a mallet. Or hold the face of a sledgehammer or a dolly block (available at car accessory outlets) against the dent; strike the raised side of the dent with the flat face of a ball-pein or panel-beating hammer.

Soldering

Spool control

Chasing a runaway spool of solder can be a nuisance, especially if it rolls off the table and onto your foot first. To keep the solder from rolling about, try bending out one rim of the spool. ▼

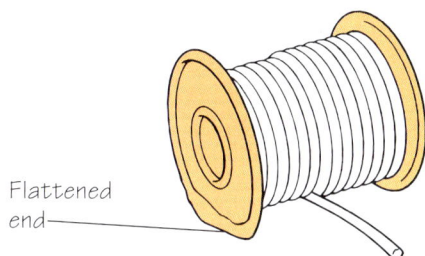

Flattened end

Dispensing solder

Clear plastic pill containers make excellent dispensers for thin wire solder. Just slip a coil of the solder into the container, pierce a hole in the cap, feed the solder through the hole, and snap the cap into place. Now all you have to do is pull out the solder as you need it. A plastic tape dispenser can also hold wire solder. Wind the wire around the empty spool, place it in the dispenser, and feed it through a hole drilled just below the serrated edge. (Break off the serrated edge to avoid cutting yourself on the teeth.)

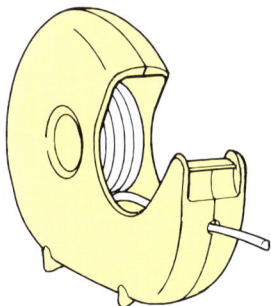

Cut to size

Join small parts more neatly with wire solder by first flattening it with a hammer and then cutting the solder with tin snips into three or more fine strands. ▼

Close quarters

If you have to solder two joints right next to each other, clamp a wet sponge over the first joint before soldering the second one. This will prevent heat from the soldering iron from reaching and loosening the first joint.

Resting place

Finding a place to put a hot soldering iron so it won't roll away or damage something can be tricky. One solution is to make a stand for the soldering iron out of a sturdy metal coat hanger by bending it as shown below. ▼

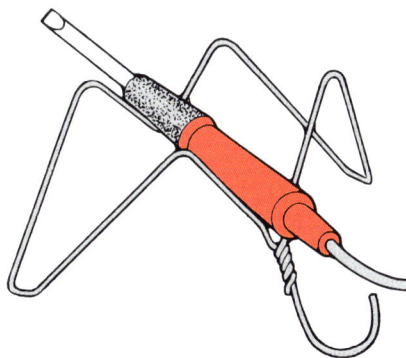

A clean tip

To ensure proper performance, it's important to keep the tip of your soldering gun or iron clean and bright at all times. Here's how to improvise your own tip cleaner. Stuff a pad of fine steel wool inside a shallow metal tin, such as a tuna fish or cat food tin, and crimp the edges of the tin. The crimped edges hold the steel wool in place, and they can also serve as an iron rest. ▼

Clean tip by rubbing it against steel wool

Soldering iron

A chilling problem

When you're soldering outdoors on a very cold day, the solder will get cold and draw heat away from the soldering iron. To remedy this problem, hammer the solder into a thin ribbon. It will melt almost instantly.

Wet cloth philosophy

When soldering copper plumbing pipes and fittings, keep a wet cloth handy to wipe the joint clean. After soldering the joint, wrap the cloth around it and turn the cloth with a twist of the wrist. This will not only result in a neater joint by removing excess solder; it will also fill any tiny holes in the solder, resulting in a more leakproof joint. While wiping the joint, be careful not to touch the hot pipe with your hand.

WORKING WITH GLASS

The equipment

Tape it down

To keep a metal straightedge from slipping when you cut glass, run a strip of thin double-sided tape along the cut line. Then lay the straightedge on the tape and make the cut with the glass cutter. The tape will keep the straight-edge stationary.

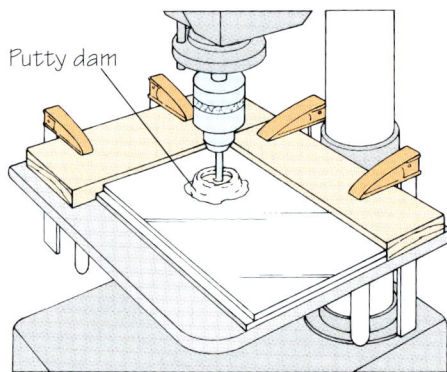

Putty dam

Here's a special bit ▲

Before installing handles, hinges, and other hardware on glass, you may have to drill a hole in the glass. For holes up to 12 mm in diameter, use a special spade-shaped glass bit in a drill press or hand drill. Surround the spot where you'll be drilling with a dam made out of putty. Fill the dam with some mineral turpentine, and run the drill slowly. For larger holes, use a circle cutter or have the job done by a glass merchant. Drill no closer than 25 mm to the edge of the glass. As always when handling glass, make sure you wear goggles and heavy gloves while you work.

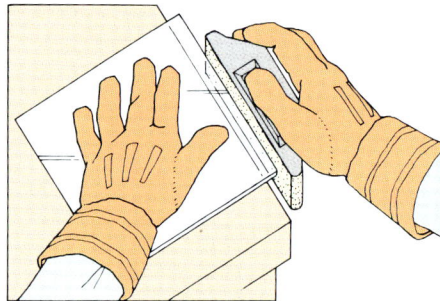

Smooth finish ▲

Rough edges can be smoothed with a silicone carbide stone or silicone carbide abrasive paper supported with a block (p. 81). Lubricate the edge with mineral turpentine and stroke the stone or block along it in one direction.

Supportive putty

Repairing a broken glass object, such as a champagne glass, is easier if you support the pieces with putty while the glue sets. Because the putty will have to be positioned in several spots, test-fit the glass pieces on the putty before applying the glue. Use a clear setting epoxy adhesive specified for glass. ▼

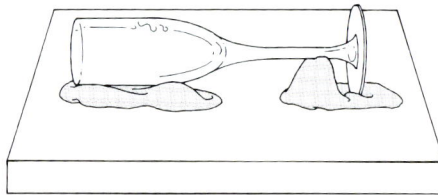

Wheel protection

A traveller's plastic toothbrush holder is the perfect storage container for a glass cutter. To cushion the wheel and retard rust, place a wad of oil-moistened cotton wool in the bottom of the holder.

Safety glass

Plastic and glass sandwich

Laminated glass consists of a layer of plastic sandwiched between two layers of glass. To cut it, score and run both faces of the glass, using a length of wire instead of a larger round object under the glass (see facing page). Heat the exposed plastic along the score with a hair dryer until it is pliable, then pull the glass far enough apart to insert a razor blade and cut the plastic.

Wired glass

To cut safety glass that has wire mesh embedded in it, place the glass on a workbench with the wire mesh closer to the bench top (the mesh is closer to one face of the glass than the other). Score this type of glass in the same way as you would regular glass (facing page); then snap the glass down over the round object until the wires are severed. If any wires poke out, just snip them off.

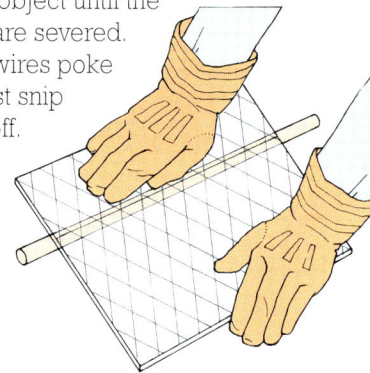

Tempered glass warning

While ordinary glass is easy to work, tempered glass (which you may find in a door, for instance) is a much stronger glass. Do not attempt to cut, drill or smooth the edges of this type of glass.

CUTTING GLASS

Thicknesses and types of glass vary, so ask a retailer which glass is best for your application. Because large pieces are difficult to cut, work with smaller pieces at first.

Getting ready. Work on a flat surface, preferably a workbench or piece of plywood. Clean the glass before you start. Lay out the cut with a marking crayon, glass-marking pencil or Chinagraph marker. To make the cut, you'll need a straightedge and a glass cutter. Use a sharp cutter; one with a carbide wheel or diamond will stay sharp longer. Lubricate the cutter and the cut line with mineral turpentine or with equal parts of light machine oil and kerosene.

Score, then run. Cutting glass isn't cutting at all; it's really controlled breaking. The process has two parts: scoring a line with the glass cutter, and running the cut along the score. Score curved shapes around a wooden pattern. Break a slight curve as you would a straight line. For a sharp curve, score extra radial lines and remove one piece at a time. Smooth all sharp edges by rubbing them with a sharpening stone held at an angle.

Caution: When handling glass, wear goggles and heavy gloves. Dispose of the shards in a closed container or wrap them in paper; then discard.

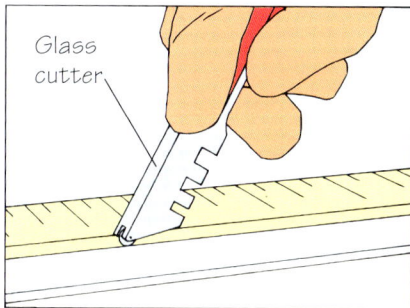

Glass cutter

Draw cutter with a rapid single stroke. A hissing, crackling sound means correct pressure; white flakes, too much.

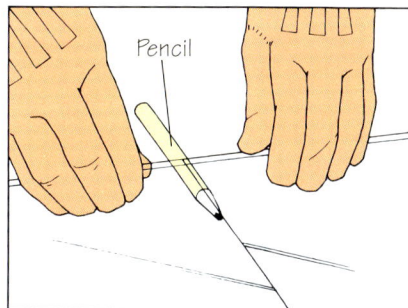

Pencil

Start the cut by placing a round object at the edge of the glass under the score. Exert slight downward pressure.

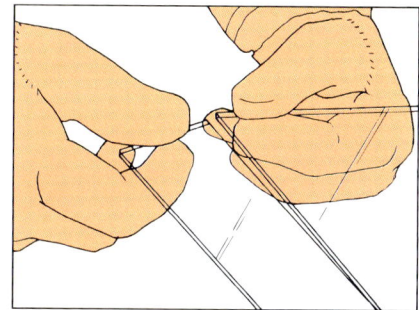

Small pieces and strips can be broken by holding the glass on both sides of the score line and bending down.

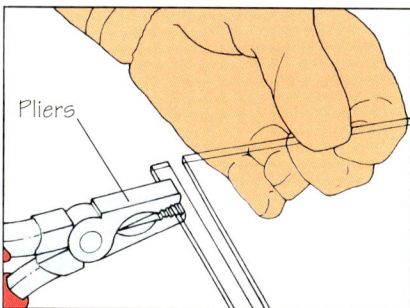

Pliers

Narrow strips should be handled with pliers with flat jaws. Bend the strip down to break it along the score line.

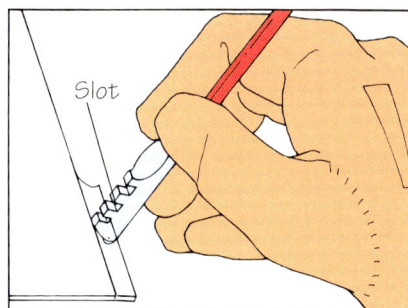

Slot

Nibble away at small pieces that don't break cleanly on the line. Use a pair of pliers or the slots on the cutter.

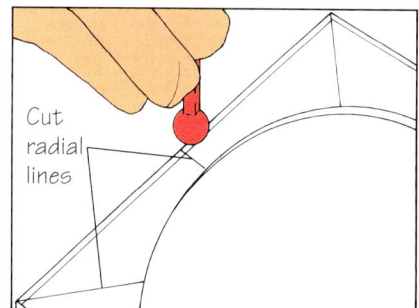

Cut radial lines

Curved cuts are started by turning the piece upside down and tapping with a cutter, or pushing with a gloved thumb.

WORKING WITH PLASTICS

Special tools

Drill bit tip

Plastic laminate and acrylic tend to chip and crack when drilled with standard twist bits. To avoid this problem, buy a specially ground bit from a plastics supplier, or try rounding the tip of a standard twist bit and slowly blunting its two cutting edges on a grinder. Before drilling, make sure you clamp the plastic in place with a timber backing.

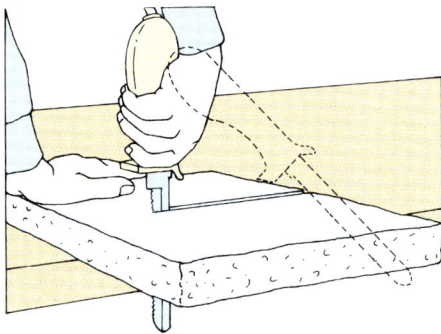

From the kitchen ▲

A kitchen electric carving knife is just the tool you need to make clean cuts in foam rubber or in rigid foam insulation. If you want to make a straight cut, mark the cutting line with a straightedge and marking pen. Place the material on a firm work surface, with the cutting line overhanging the edge of the surface by about 25 mm or more. Begin the cut as you would a cut with a handsaw, starting with the knife at a 45° angle. Draw the knife about 50 mm into the foam; then straighten it until the blade is perpendicular to the work. For round or shaped cuts, hold the material on edge in a vice. With the cutting line facing you, make the cut with the blade facing down. Rotate the work as you go.

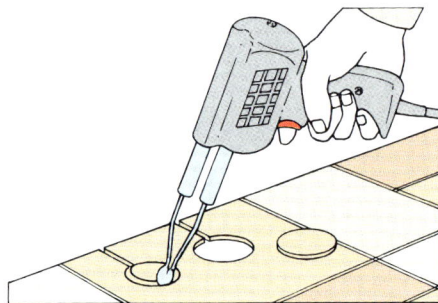

Some like it hot ▲

Some soldering guns come with a cutting tip that lets you cut plastics such as acrylic, vinyl and expanded polystyrene. They're handy for cutting floor tiles to fit around water and heating pipes and door thresholds. To determine how fast to move the tip and how much pressure to apply, first practise cutting on scrap material.

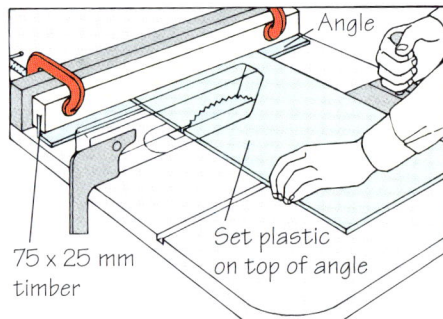

Angle

Set plastic on top of angle

75 x 25 mm timber

Under the fence ▲

Thin material, such as plastic laminate, can easily slip underneath the rip fence of a table saw. The next time you need to rip thin materials, clamp this device to the fence. Cut a piece of 75 x 25 mm timber to the length of your fence; make a groove down the centre of one edge of the piece. Then glue a 19 x 19 x 3 mm aluminium angle into the groove, using epoxy adhesive. Use G-clamps to hold the guide in place while sawing.

Give it a lift

You can cut plastic tubing even if you don't have a pipe cutter. Instead use a mitre box and a hacksaw with a 24-teeth-per-25-mm blade. To raise a piece of small-diameter tubing high enough for the saw to cut through it, place a block of wood under it. Clamp the wood to the work surface to hold it and the mitre box firmly in place. ▼

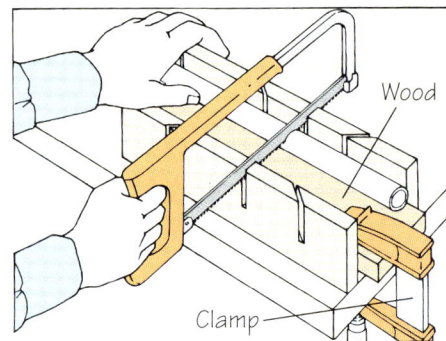

Wood

Clamp

Acrylic

A cushioning point

It's possible to lay out circles on acrylic with a compass or dividers without leaving point marks in the work. At the centre of the circle build up a cushioned area with layers of masking tape. When you position the compass or dividers, make sure the point doesn't go through all the layers of tape and into the acrylic.

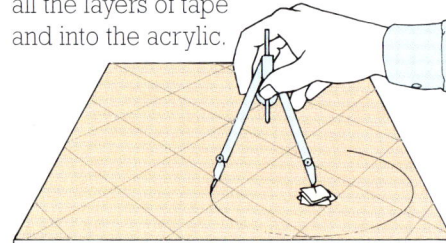

Clear cutting

To make the cutting line more visible on acrylic, apply a strip of masking tape along the area of the cut and mark the cutting line on the tape. Not only will the line stand out, but chipped edges will be kept to a minimum.

Old stuck paper

If you store acrylic for a long time with the protective paper still on it, the adhesive may dry out and make it difficult to take the paper off. To make removal easier, soak the paper in isopropyl alcohol or kerosene. After peeling off the paper, remove any remaining adhesive with alcohol or kerosene on a soft cloth.

Gritty toothpaste

Because toothpaste is a mild abrasive, it's ideal for removing scratches in acrylic plastic. After removing the scratch, buff the area with a clean cloth.

Sheet laminate

Orderly fashion

When laminating a splash back, there's an order that makes the job easier. First laminate and trim the ends, then the front, and finally the top. Don't trim the top piece, however, until the splash back has been mounted; the back edge may have to be shaped to fit the wall (p. 71).

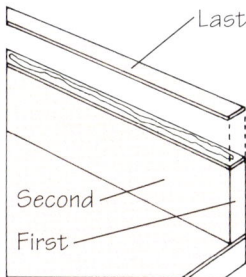

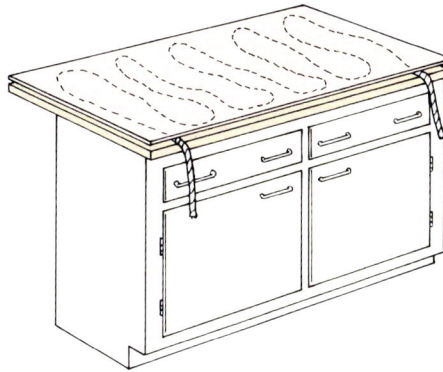

Placement aides ▲

To position sheet laminate on a substrate, you'll need spacers to keep the adhesive-covered surfaces apart until the two materials are properly aligned. You can use wooden dowels or cardboard strips, or you can snake a piece of rope or an extension cord down the length of the work. When the laminate is in the right position, start at one end and pull out one dowel at a time, or gradually remove the rope, as you press the laminate into place.

The other side

Here's a time-saving way to apply plastic laminate to both sides of a door, shelf, or other workpiece at almost the same time. Drive four finishing nails partway into your workbench; place the nails so the work can rest on them. Then spread the contact cement on the work, turn it over, rest it on the nails, and coat the opposite side. Once the cement reaches the correct tackiness, laminate the top side; then turn the work over and laminate the other side. Make sure, however, you work steadily so that you do not take too much time laminating one side.

Exposed edges

If moisture penetrates the unsealed edges of a bench top, the laminate will separate from the particleboard base. To prevent moisture penetration, seal the exposed surfaces of the bench top (especially at the front edge) with a coat of clear polyurethane.

Solid-surface material

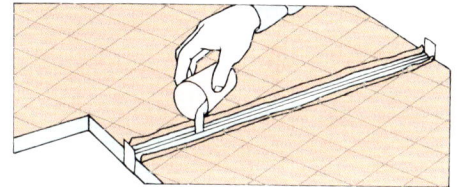

At the seam ▲

When joining pieces for bench tops and other surfaces, set them 3 mm apart (offset the seam from the corner to avoid placing stress on it). To keep the adhesive from running, apply masking tape under the seam and up the ends.

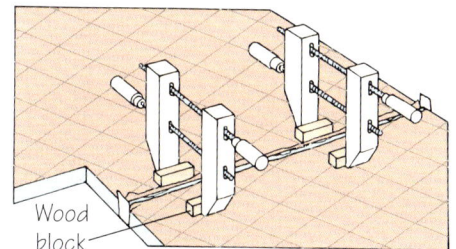

Gripping blocks ▲

If you don't have clamps long enough to hold the pieces while the adhesive dries, attach temporary blocks on each side of the seam with glue. Clamp as shown, but not too tight. After the adhesive dries, tap off the blocks.

HOUSEHOLD STORAGE

HALL AND ENTRY WAY

Hall walls

Overhead shelving

The long walls of a hallway are an often overlooked source of storage space. Extra-wide halls can accommodate floor-to-ceiling shelving, but be sure to leave at least 900 mm of floor space clear so as not to impede the traffic flow. In a narrower hall, install a single open shelf about 300 mm below the ceiling and use it to store seldom used items or to display decorative ones.

Not for kitchens only

If your hallway is wide enough, kitchen wall cabinets—set on the floor and covered with a shallow countertop and/or hung on the wall—are a practical alternative to floor-to-ceiling hallway shelves.

Hall cupboard ideas

Moisture control

This shoe rack allows air to circulate around wet shoes and boots, while the underlying pan makes clean up easy. The rack is a 75 × 25 mm pine frame fitted with 10 mm dowels. Make the frame large enough so that it fits over the aluminium or plastic pan. (Coated wire shelving is a simpler, if homelier, substitute for the wooden rack.) ▼

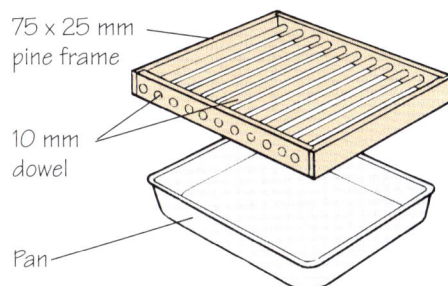

75 x 25 mm pine frame

10 mm dowel

Pan

Winter wear storage

Stow away gloves and hats on this wire rack installed on the back of a hall cupboard door. Straighten a wire coat hanger and feed it through three screw eyes mounted on the door. Once the wire is past the middle eye, start sliding clothes pegs onto it. To secure the rack, bend the wire around the screw eyes at each end.

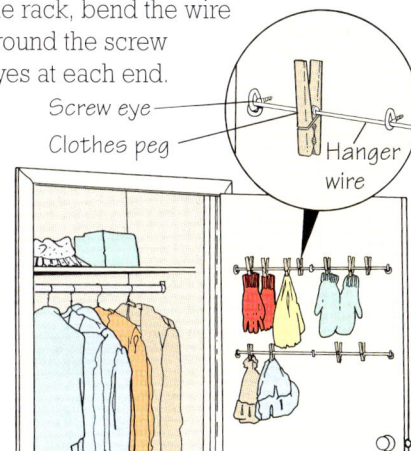

Screw eye

Clothes peg

Hanger wire

Clean-up room

Heavy-duty entrance ▶

An entry room where family members can leave wet or dirty clothes is a great asset. When planning a clean-up room:
▷ Locate it near the busiest entrance, where family members are most likely to pass through it.
▷ Consider enlarging a back-door laundry or partitioning a veranda or garage.
▷ If possible, put a door at each end to make the room an energy-saving, dirt-blocking air lock.
▷ Design the room to meet the needs and activities of all family members.

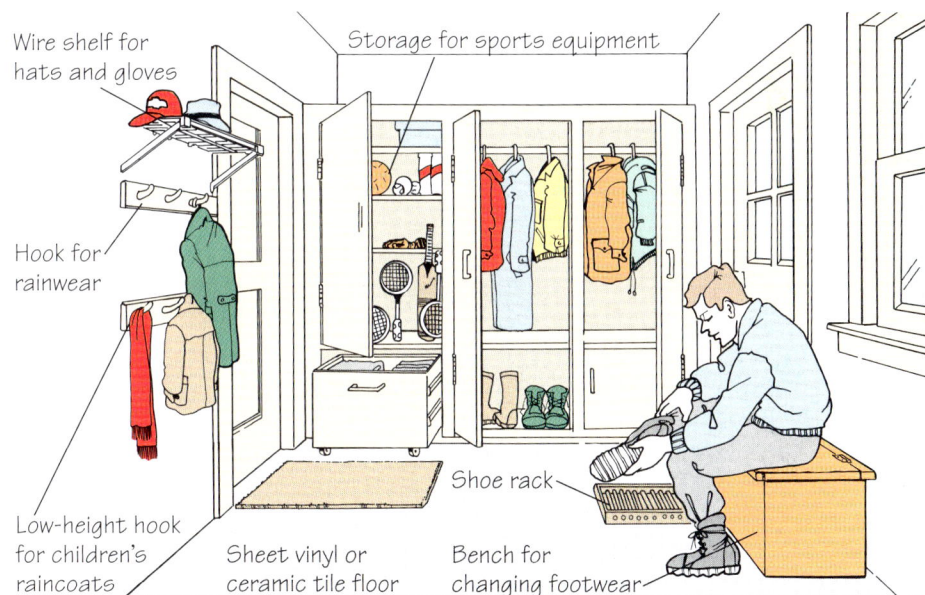

Wire shelf for hats and gloves

Storage for sports equipment

Hook for rainwear

Low-height hook for children's raincoats

Sheet vinyl or ceramic tile floor

Shoe rack

Bench for changing footwear

Out of sight

Space saver

A hideaway wall bed not only saves space, it turns an ordinary bedroom into a multi-use room. A horizontal alternative to the traditional vertical wall bed offers even greater space savings. Available in several sizes from suppliers of wall bed systems and some furniture dealers, a side bed when closed looks like a dining room cabinet or buffet. Opened, the bed takes up remarkably little floor space (the twin-size model, for example, may project as little as half the distance a vertical wall bed would extend). A side bed is usually easy to assemble and install; only a few screws are needed to secure the unit to wall studs. ▼

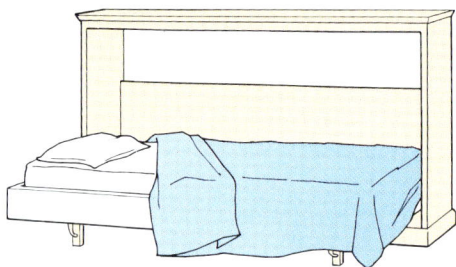

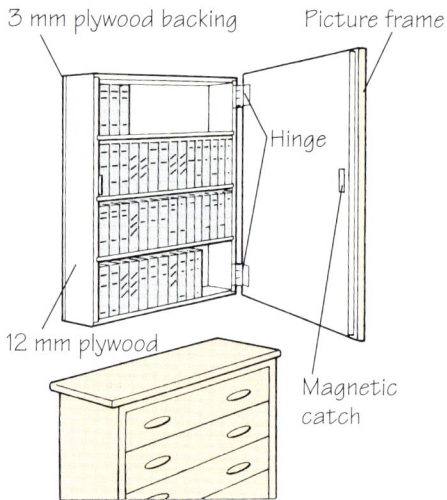

3 mm plywood backing   Picture frame

Hinge

12 mm plywood

Magnetic catch

Hidden tapes ▲

A wall-hung cabinet, securely fastened to wall studs and concealed by a favourite painting or print, is great for storing video- or music cassettes. Make the cabinet frame and the shelves out of 12 mm plywood or particleboard. Match the width and length of the cabinet to the dimensions of the picture frame; the cabinet's depth depends on the items being stored. Use 3 mm plywood for the cabinet back. The picture frame is hinged to the cabinet on one side and held shut by a magnetic catch.

Secret shelves

Between-stud shelving needn't be limited to places where studs are exposed, like an unfinished garage or workshop (p. 57). You can create space for recessed shelves in a finished inside, or partition, wall by cutting into the plasterboard with a keyhole saw. (For more information on locating studs and cutting plasterboard, see pp. 135 and 137.) Nail cleats to the studs to support shelves made of 100×25 mm pine boards. If desired, conceal the storage area behind a painting hinged to the wall. Do not try to create between-stud shelving in exterior walls or in walls with plumbing, ductwork or electrical lines running through them.

Back-of-door hideaway

The back of cupboard and other interior doors is an untapped storage resource just waiting to be used. You can hang a full-length mirror on the back of a door, cover it with clothes hooks, or use it to mount shelves or a tall, slender cabinet for the odd little items that don't fit elsewhere. (For more back-of-door storage ideas, see pp. 103, 111 and 112.) Some of these space savers, however, can add a good deal of weight to the door. In such cases, interior doors, which are sometimes hung with only two 75 mm hinges, may need some added support. If you plan to add substantially to the load on a door's hinges, it's a good idea to install a third (middle) hinge to ensure that the door will operate properly and not sag.

Window seat ▶

Create extra seating and storage space along a window wall by lining the wall beneath the window with sturdy low cabinets. Install a particleboard platform over the cabinets, and top it off with cushions. Edge the platform with a timber moulding for a finished look.

Bedtime storage

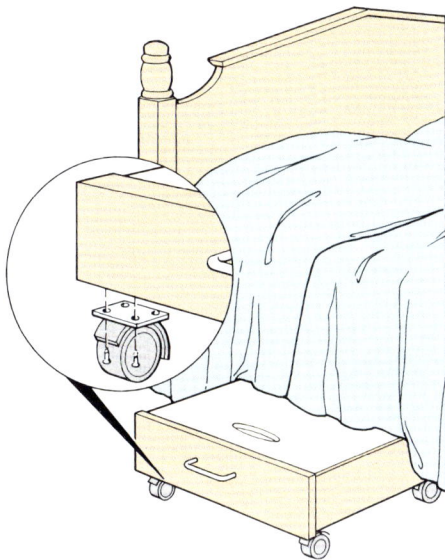

Recycled drawers ▲

Give new life to old dresser drawers as under-the-bed storage bins. Fasten four small casters to the bottoms of the drawers and slide them under the bed to store seasonal clothes, extra blankets and much more. To keep out dust, add a snug-fitting hinged 6 or 7.5 mm plywood top to the drawers. If you don't have any recyclable dresser drawers on hand, look in home centres or storage catalogues for inexpensive, easy-to-assemble under-bed drawer systems.

Head room

When buying a new bed, look for a headboard with shelves or shallow cabinets built into it. This type of bed not only provides convenient storage space, it makes efficient use of available bedroom floor space by eliminating the need for night tables.

Bed box ▶

If you're thinking about building a platform bed, consider one that rests not on drawers but on a deep hollow box built of 19 mm veneered particleboard. Even though you have to remove the mattress and lift off the top of the box to get at it, the space under the bed is ideal for storing cumbersome, seldom used items, family heirlooms and other belongings that you want hidden.

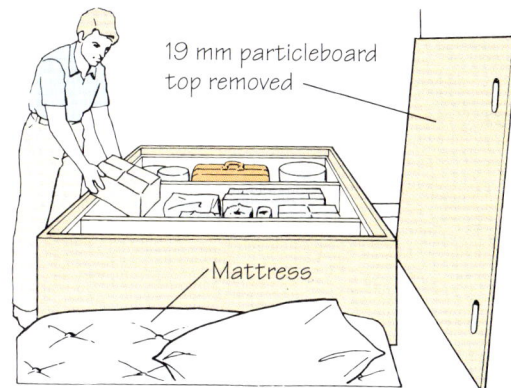

19 mm particleboard top removed

Mattress

Drawer organisers

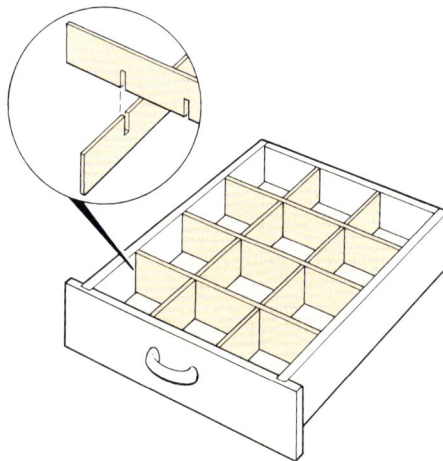

Divide and conquer ▲

Create compartments in a shallow drawer by notching and joining strips of wood lattice (available at timberyards and home centres). Clamp the cross-pieces together and cut the notches all at once so they'll align exactly.

See-through dividers

Drawer dividers may also be made from 6 mm sheet acrylic (have the retailer cut the pieces to size, or cut them yourself using a very fine blade in a table or radial arm saw). Butt the pieces together in whatever arrangement you desire; then bond the joints with acrylic solvent. (For more on working with acrylic, see pp. 100–101.)

Sliding tray

Here's a way to increase a deep drawer's usable space. Make a box of 12 mm MDF and support it on hardwood runners glued to the sides of the drawer. The tray should be half the drawer's width or length so that you can slide it aside for easy access to the bottom of the drawer. Or make the tray full length and add handles so it can be lifted out.

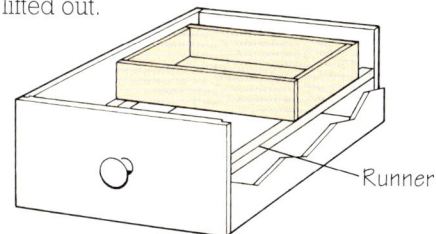

Runner

KITCHEN

Built-ins

Looking up ▶

The space between the tops of kitchen cabinets and the ceiling is ideal for storing pots, pans and serving dishes or for displaying baskets, plants and ornamental pieces. To make the most of this space, install simple storage boxes made out of 19 mm veneered particleboard. Build as many boxes as necessary to fill the space, butt them together, and cover the joints with strips of moulding if necessary; cover any exposed edges with iron-on veneer tape.

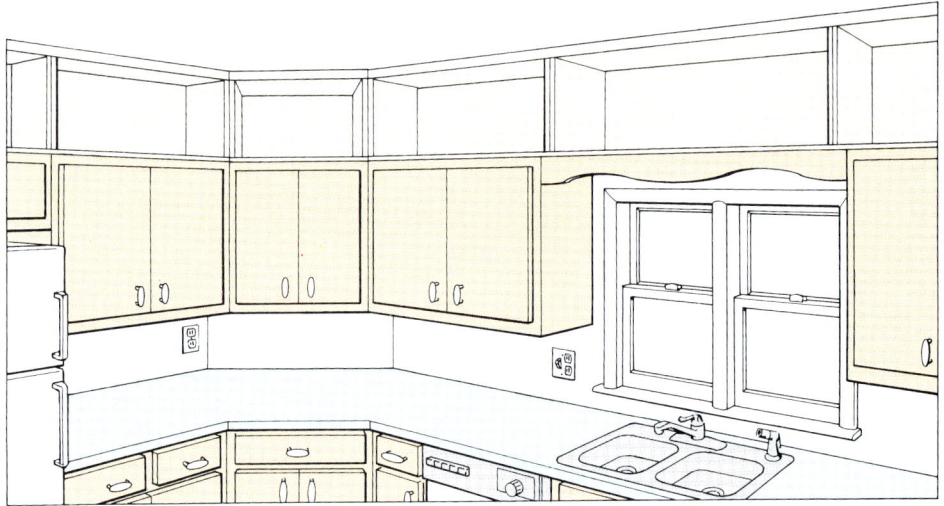

Wall store

One way to increase kitchen storage space is to install a shallow pantry in the cavity between wall studs. Pick an inside wall where there are no pipes or electrical outlets or switches. Use a stud finder to locate the studs (p. 135); then cut through the plasterboard with a plasterboard or panel saw. Line the back of the cavity with 19 mm particleboard. Frame the pantry flush with the wall or extending several centimetres beyond it; then add shelving and doors.

Recycling centre

If you have plenty of room in your kitchen, consider installing a custom-built cabinet with tilt-out bins to sort recyclables. Another alternative is to keep recyclables in a hinged-top bench with internal dividers. Install the bench either in the kitchen or near the back door.

Cupboards to spare? ▲

If you have an underused cupboard in or near the kitchen, why not turn it into a playroom? Simply decorate the walls with bright colours, install shelves and a desk, add a stool, toy bin and wastebasket, and hook the door open. Your children can play close by, but not underfoot, while you work in the kitchen.

Trial run

Before equipping your kitchen with an island or any permanent cabinet, mark its location on the floor with masking tape or place a large box in the area to see how the installation will affect traffic flow. Rethink the layout if you continually overstep the lines or bump into the box.

Hideaway tables

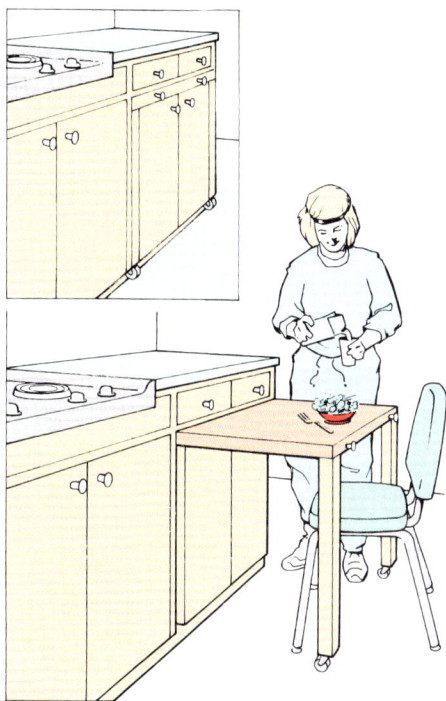

Disappearing act ▲

Even a tiny kitchen can accommodate this custom-made, pull-out table. When not in use, the butcher-block or laminated top and two legs (on casters) slide into slots cut into the base cabinet. The legs and front edge of the table are finished to match the cabinets.

Table in a drawer

Are you short of kitchen bench space? Would you be willing to give up a drawer in exchange for a large extra work surface that can double as a table? If so, here's the hardware you need to create a hideaway work surface/table. Available through suppliers of kitchen cabinet hardware and equipment, this pair of massive metal drawer slides (rated to support about 80 kg) holds a two-part tabletop. Since one part of the top slides out from under the other automatically as the drawer is opened, you get an 800 mm deep table sliding out of an ordinary 600 mm deep drawer. Make the tabletop pieces out of laminated particleboard or other material that is 19 mm thick or less; use the existing drawer front to cap the new tabletop. ▼

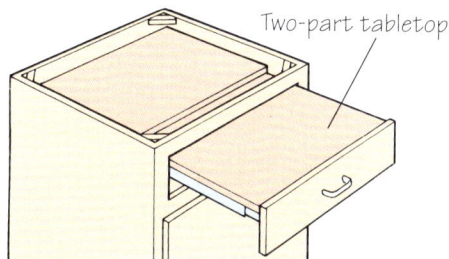

Two-part tabletop

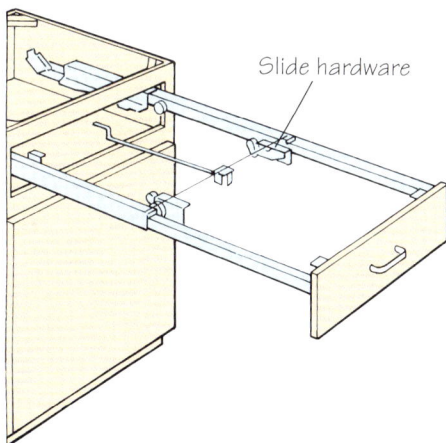

Slide hardware

Counters and shelves

Inset cutting board

Make better use of your bench space by setting a cutting board into it. Buy a ready-to-fit cutting board, and keep the board flush with the bench top. For quick clean up, cut a slot in the cutting board and place a waste bin below. ▼

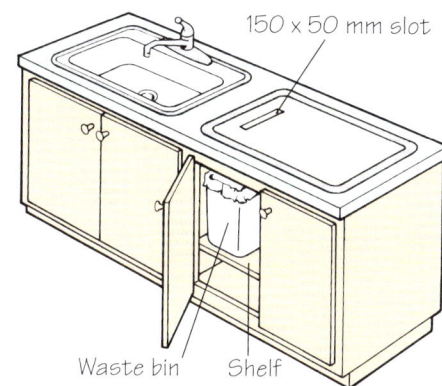

150 x 50 mm slot

Waste bin   Shelf

Add-a-shelf

A slide-in shelf made from 16 mm melamine-faced particleboard is a good way to organise the space below a sink. Determine the height of the shelf and cut two side supports to that height. Cut the shelf 5 mm shorter than the inside width of the cabinet. Attach the shelf to the side supports with 25 mm nails and slide the unit into place. ▼

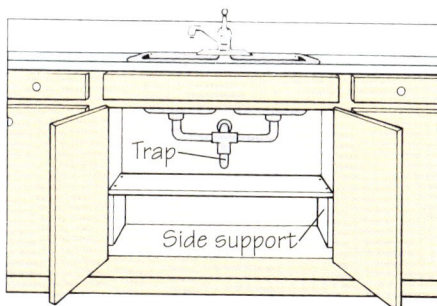

Trap

Side support

KITCHEN

Racks and dispensers

Lid holder

Keep pot lids handy with these simple wooden racks. The ends are made of 75 × 25 mm pine boards, the cross-pieces of 19 mm square moulding. ▼

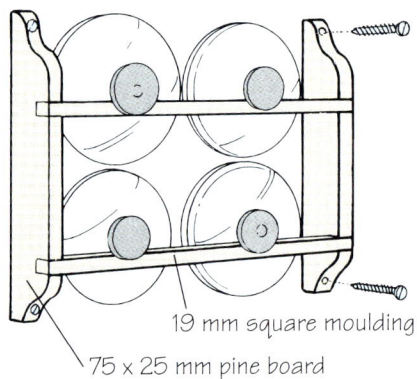

19 mm square moulding

75 × 25 mm pine board

Suspended stemware

Protect fragile wine glasses by hanging them from this under-the-cabinet plywood rack. Cut the openings with a plunge router or jig saw. The same idea can be adapted to make a storage rack for food processor blades. Screw-on wire racks are also available from storage shops.

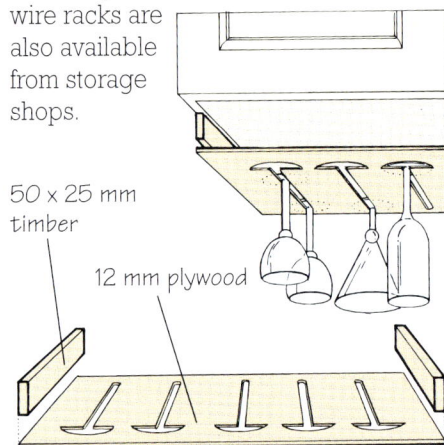

50 × 25 mm timber

12 mm plywood

Organisers

Stow-aways

Shops that specialise in storage systems and supplies, as well as ordinary home centres and hardware stores, offer a wide variety of space-saving cabinet accessories that put every corner of your kitchen cabinets to work. Most of these organisers can be installed in a few minutes and are relatively inexpensive. Among the most useful are two- or three-tier storage racks that roll out on metal slides, roll-out garbage bins, and even entire pull-out pantry systems. Shown at right are a spice rack that folds flat under a wall cabinet and a food processor or mixer shelf that swings up and out of a base cabinet (the cabinet opening must be at least 300 mm wide and about 570 mm deep).

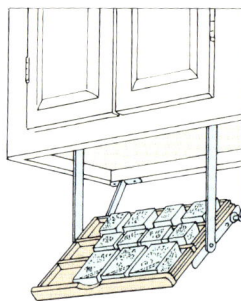

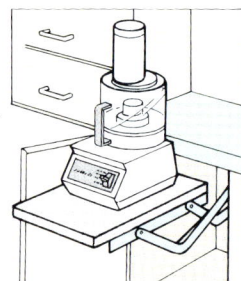

Sink front tray ▶

Trays mounted behind sink front or cooktop panels turn this often wasted space into a convenient storage area for cleaning supplies and small utensils. Secure the panels at the bottom with spring-loaded hinges. Similar trays are available at home centres and hardware stores.

Stair-step shelves

To bring order to a messy cupboard shelf, stagger its contents on stair-step shelves so you can easily see items at the back. Make the steps by gluing together some 100 × 50 mm timber off cuts and then cover them with easy-to-clean contact paper.

100 × 50 mm off cuts

Bulletin board ▲

Use roughly same-size recycled wine corks to create a message centre by gluing them onto plywood. Glue the corks lengthwise to the wood; start in a corner and position two corks vertically, then two horizontally. Continue the pattern until the plywood is covered; frame the board with strips of moulding.

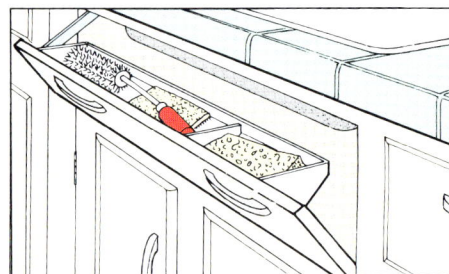

A different slant

If you buy tinned food or drinks in bulk, here's a handy shelving idea that automatically feeds tins towards the front each time you remove one. Using self-anchoring nylon clips and angled brackets (see pp.120–121), mount vinyl-coated wire shelving upside down and at an angle so that the lip sticks up in front to hold the cans in place. ▼

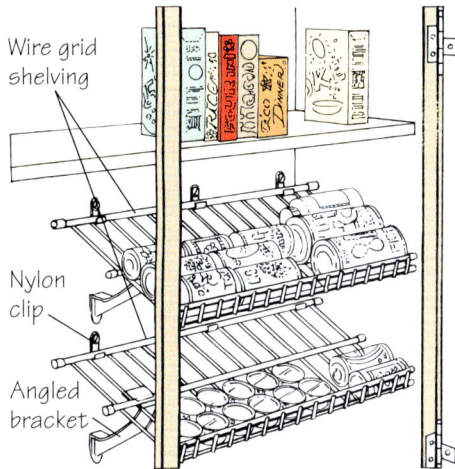

Wire grid shelving

Nylon clip

Angled bracket

More kitchen organisers

▷ A pull-down cookery book rack that mounts on the bottom of a standard wall cabinet, similar to the spice rack shown on the facing page.
▷ A full-circle lazy susan for mounting in a base or wall corner cabinet.
▷ Wire racks installed on the insides of cabinet doors for keeping small items within easy reach.
▷ A pegboard or wire grid wall organiser (see p. 127).
▷ A heavy-duty rack for hanging pots and pans from the ceiling or wall.

ISLAND LIFE

Create a practical kitchen storage and eating area by mounting an inexpensive bench top on prefinished base cabinets. The island shown here uses two cabinets, but you can group together any number. Choose cabinets to fit your needs. If you want a sink in the island, use a base sink cabinet; build an L-shaped island around a corner cabinet fitted with a lazy susan.

To anchor the cabinets, screw 50 × 50 mm cleats to the floor around the cabinets' interior perimeter line. Place the cabinets over the 50 × 50 mm cleats and level the cabinets as needed by wedging wooden shims under their bottom edges. Then drive screws through the cabinet bottoms into

the cleats. Use wood or vinyl base trim to hide the screw holes.

Before building the bench top, work out the optimum overhang. If you're using ceramic tiles, size the top to accept an even number. (Remember to allow space for the grout.) Attach the bench top to the cabinets with screws coming up through the base cabinets' top rails.

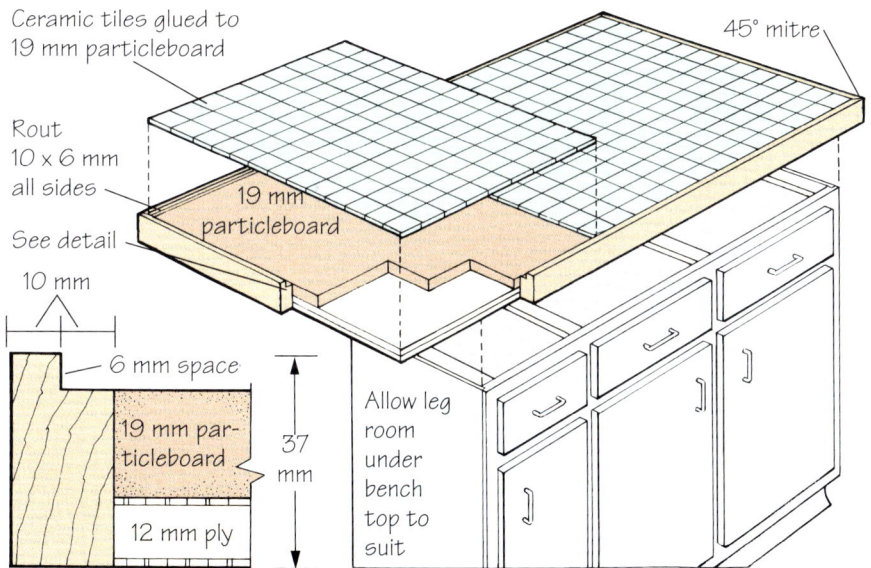

Ceramic tiles glued to 19 mm particleboard

45° mitre

Rout 10 × 6 mm all sides

See detail

19 mm particleboard

10 mm

6 mm space

19 mm particleboard

37 mm

12 mm ply

Allow leg room under bench top to suit

BATHROOM

Shelves and racks

Out of the linen cupboard

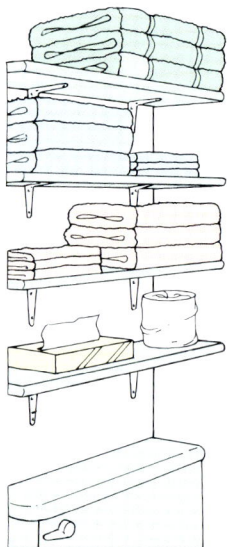

For a colourful decorative touch, store towels on open shelving in the bathroom. The wall over the toilet is also a good place, if the toilet is well ventilated. You can also use the space to store rolls of toilet paper or other bathroom supplies.

Easy-reach towel

If you're installing a new bathroom cabinet or redoing an old one, consider creating a recess that will keep a towel just where you need it most, below the sink. Make the niche about 65 mm deep, line it to match the surrounding cupboards, and fit it with a towel rail. Set the rail 12 mm back from the front of the cabinet. ▼

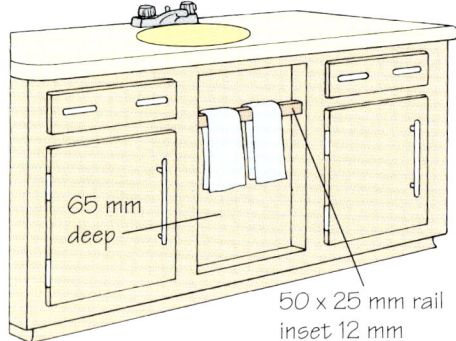

65 mm deep

50 x 25 mm rail inset 12 mm

Park your dryer here ▲

An appliance garage installed within easy reach of the basin is as useful in a bathroom as in the kitchen. In the example shown here, a roll-down door covers a cabinet built into the space between wall studs. (For more information on between-stud shelving and cabinets, see pp. 104 and 106.)

Private library

A plastic magazine file, sold at office supply shops, makes a handy holder for bathroom reading materials. Just mount the file on the wall next to the toilet, and your private reading room is ready.

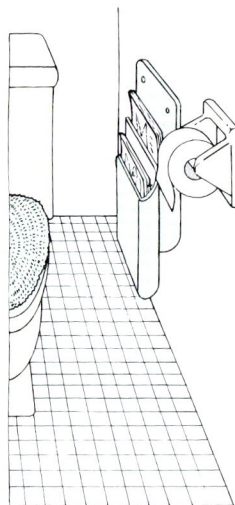

Over your head

The area above bathroom windows and doors is often wasted. Put the space to work by installing a decorative shelf or vinyl-coated wire shelving. Use these out-of-the-way shelves to store extra towels or items you wish to keep out of the reach of children.

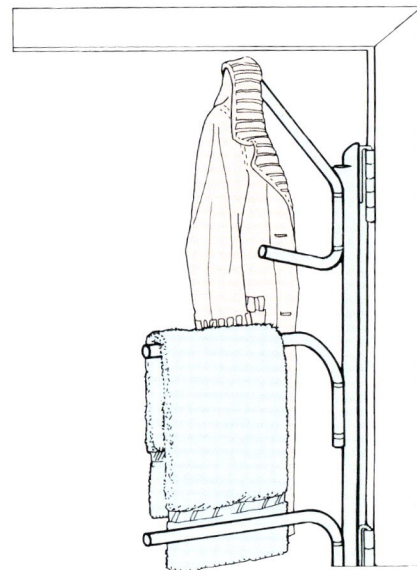

Hinge hanger ▲

Take full advantage of every bit of bathroom space with a door-hinge-mounted towel and dressing gown rack. Available at some hardware stores and home centres, this hinge hanger comes in different sizes, materials and finishes and is easy to install. Simply remove the door hinge pins, position the rack and reinstall the pins. There are no holes to drill (or repair), and if you move, you can take the rack with you.

For small fry ▲

To encourage children to hang up their towels, make sure rails are accessible to them. If you have the wall space, mount one or more towel rails below an existing rail. Or build a towel ladder out of 100 × 25 mm rails and 25 mm dowels; attach the ladder to brackets screwed to wall studs. If wall space is limited, fasten an expandable wooden mug rack to the back of the bathroom door at a level your children can reach.

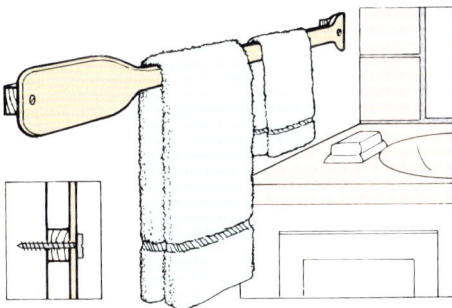

Paddle bar ▲

Make an eye-catching towel rail from an old wooden canoe paddle varnished with clear polyurethane. Mount the paddle to the wall studs with screws through 50 × 50 mm spacer blocks.

Organisers

Shower tower

Tall shower units containing multiple shelves and racks are easy to install in the corner of a bath or shower and provide a place for everything. They're available at most home centres and hardware shops.

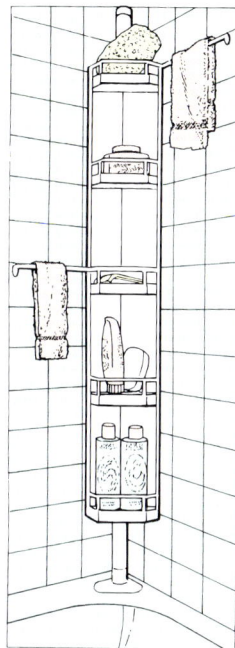

Soap, shampoo, conditioner

Organise your bath products (and avoid spills) with a wall-mounted push-button plastic dispenser, available with one, two or four compartments. ▼

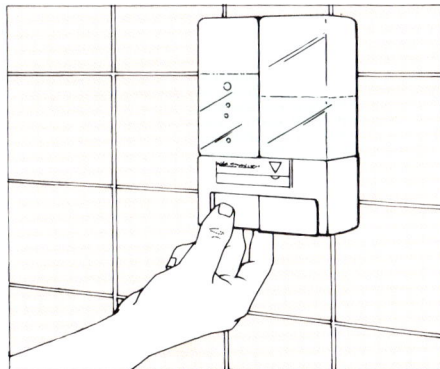

Not for kitchens only

Many of the space-saving cabinet accessories designed for kitchens (p. 108) can also help bring order to your bathroom cabinets. A case in point is this lazy susan, available in single and two-tiered models from home centres and kitchen supply stores. Before buying one of these hardworking organisers, measure the space inside the cabinet carefully, making allowances for drainpipe clearance if necessary. ▼

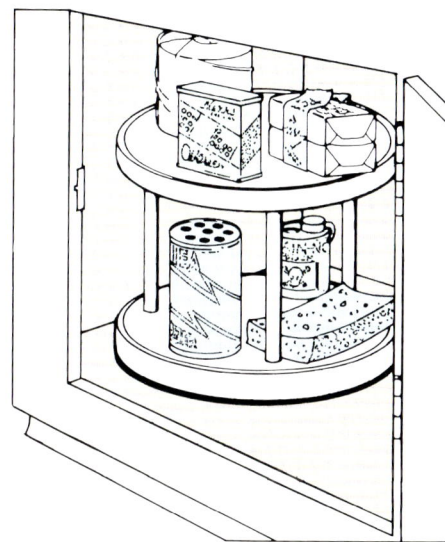

Under a pedestal

One way to increase storage space in a bathroom equipped with a pedestal basin is to hang a skirt on the basin and use the newly created space to house paper goods and cleaning products. You may be able to buy such skirts ready-made, or make your own out of a heavy washable fabric. Sew a Velcro strip to the top inside edge of the skirt, and glue another strip to the basin rim with contact adhesive.

LAUNDRY AREA

Hidden boards

Now you see it...

As they do for
the kitchen
(p. 108), home
centres, hard-
ware shops,
and suppliers
of storage
systems offer
many different
space-saving
laundry items,
three of which
are shown on this page. The ironing-
board-in-a-drawer pulls out and unfolds
in seconds. The drawer opening must
be at least 550 mm deep by 360 mm
wide by 85 mm high. Unfolded, the
board measures about 990 mm long.
There should be at least 450 mm
clearance beyond the end of the board.

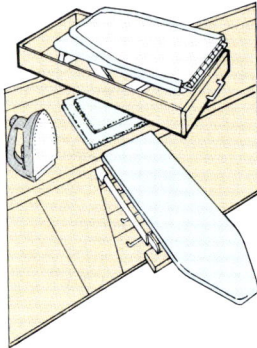

...Now you don't

The door-back ironing board hooks
securely to the top edge of a cupboard
door and
folds down
for use. A
separate
installation
kit enables
you to
mount the
board per-
manently
to a door,
wallboard
or studs.

Bins and racks

Ironing organiser

This rack is specially designed to hold
an iron, a freestanding ironing board
and other ironing paraphernalia.
Mount the rack on a laundry room
wall or in a cupboard near where you
do your ironing. ▼

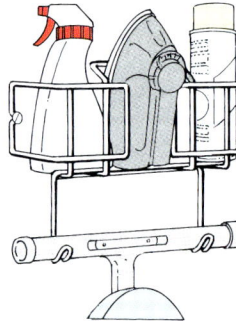

Wood
cleat

19 or 21 mm plywood

Order out of chaos ▲

Sorting bins are essential for any laundry room. Home centres offer a variety
of sorting systems, such as the slide-out
bins shown here, or you can make your
own. Build a frame out of 19 or 21 mm
plywood, and attach pairs of wood cleats
to the side walls to support pull-out
plastic bins. You'll need at least three
bins: for whites, colours and permanent
press; if you can fit a fourth bin, use it
for towels and work clothes.

Laundry rack

This simple
washer/dryer
shelf rack is
especially
useful for an
old, brick-built
laundry, where
the solid walls
make it diffi-
cult to hang
shelves. The
unit is made
out of 19 or
21 mm plywood and assembled with 50 mm
wood screws. To avoid having to disconnect
the washer's hoses, slide the shelf rack in
place before screwing the bottom brace to the
sides. On one side add a rack on which to
hang clothes as you take them out of the dryer.

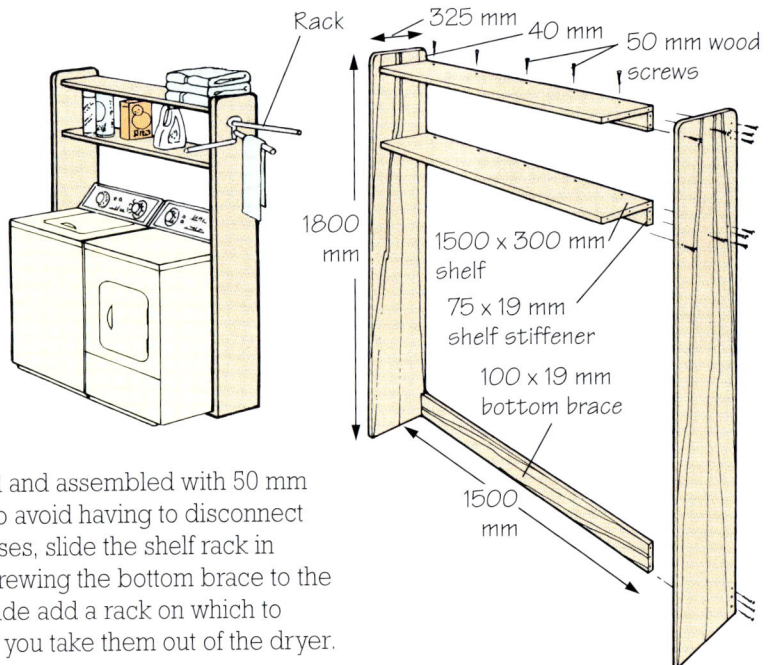

Rack

325 mm
40 mm
50 mm wood
screws

1800
mm

1500 x 300 mm
shelf

75 x 19 mm
shelf stiffener

100 x 19 mm
bottom brace

1500
mm

HOME OFFICE

Found spaces

Guest room office

Most home offices borrow space from an existing room. Here a small guest room does double duty as a home office thanks to the addition of a compact wall unit equipped with shelves, drawers, desk, a computer centre and a variety of slide-out and pull-down work surfaces. ▼

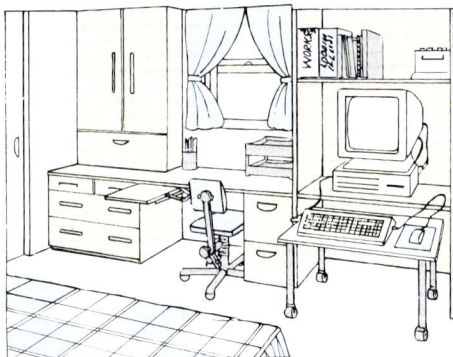

Under the stairs

If you can fit shelves in the area under a stairway (see p. 126), the chances are it can also serve as a small work station. You can leave an under-the-stairway office exposed or conceal it behind doors when not in use. In the example shown here, a bifold door serves as a screen, providing a bit of extra privacy while you work.

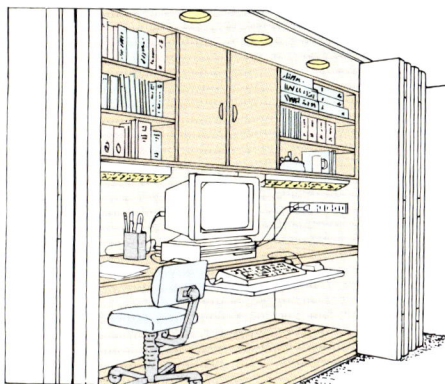

Cupboard hideaway ▲

An important feature of a good home office is a sense of separation from other household activities—which is exactly what this converted cupboard provides. Good lighting and electrical outlets have been added, and books and equipment are within easy reach. Folding doors hide the clutter at day's end.

In the attic

The awkward space under eaves is ideal for storing boxes of seldom used files or other household items. A solid-back bookcase mounted on casters and extending up to the sloped ceiling not only conceals the stored boxes (while allowing access to them), it also serves as a convenient backdrop for an attic office. ▼

Cook's corner

Don't overlook the kitchen as a possible location for a home office. Here are two suggestions for getting more use out of an underutilised kitchen nook.
In a pinch, even a tight galley (top) can do double duty as a makeshift office. Here, the swing-out food processor holder described on page 108 serves as a stand for a laptop computer. In the larger kitchen shown at bottom, an area once devoted to cabinets has been turned into a work centre. ▼

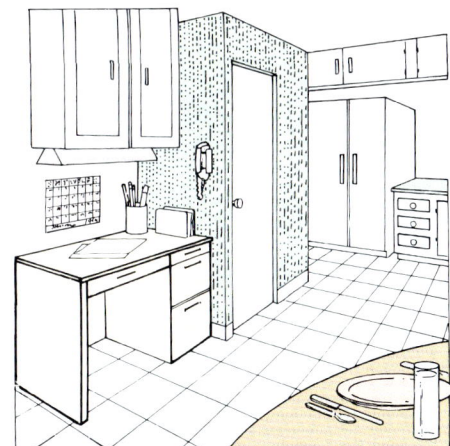

SHELVES

Open shelving

Shelves to go

These notched, knock-down shelves are ready to move any time you are. Make the posts from 100 × 50 mm timber and the shelves from 19 or 21 mm plywood. Cut the notches with a jig saw, spacing them about 300 mm apart on the posts and at least 600 mm on the shelves. Keep all notches at least 50 mm from end of piece. ▼

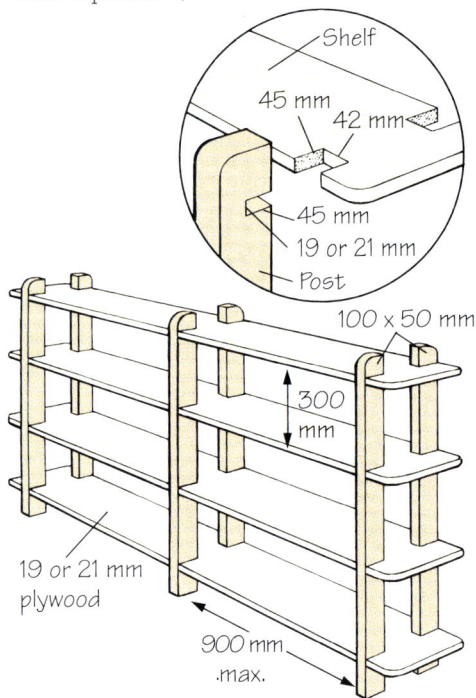

Shelf
45 mm
42 mm
45 mm
19 or 21 mm
Post
100 × 50 mm
300 mm
19 or 21 mm plywood
900 mm .max.

Swinging upright

To install a metal shelf upright without a level, mount it loosely to the wall through the top screw hole. Then lift it to one side and let it swing it like a pendulum. The upright will be vertical when it comes to a stop.

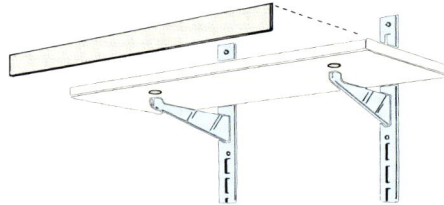

Out of sight ▲

Shelf brackets will be a lot less noticeable if you buy them 25 mm or so shorter than the shelf depth. Drill holes partway into the shelf bottom to accommodate the bracket tips. Attaching moulding along the edges of the shelf and painting the uprights and brackets the same colour as the wall also help camouflage shelf hardware.

Let the sun shine in

Always trying to squeeze another plant onto the windowsill? Turn your window into a miniature greenhouse with glass shelves. Attach metal shelving uprights to each side of the window, insert shelf brackets, and add toughened safety glass shelves. (Don't use standard glass; it might break and injure someone.) ▼

BUILT-IN SHELVING

A built-in shelving unit can bring a bleak wall to life. Available space and the type of items stored will determine a unit's dimensions. For 250–300 mm deep shelves bearing heavy loads, space vertical supports no more than 750 mm apart.

Materials. Use either nominal 25 mm solid timber or 19 mm veneered particleboard. For a clear finish, maple or rimu veneer is a good choice. For a painted finish, consider medium density fibreboard (MDF). Finish edges with matching hardwood edging or iron-on veneer tape, shown at right.

Assembly. Line up the sides and vertical partitions, and install one of the two types of adjustable shelf supports shown at right. Then glue and screw the full-length top and bottom pieces to the sides. Attach the mounting cleat and vertical partitions. Assemble the base, level it with shims and set the case on it. Screw the cleat to the wall. Cover gaps along wall and ceiling edges with a 50 × 25 mm frame scribed to fit, or use 19 mm square moulding as a set-back reveal along edges.

Assembly

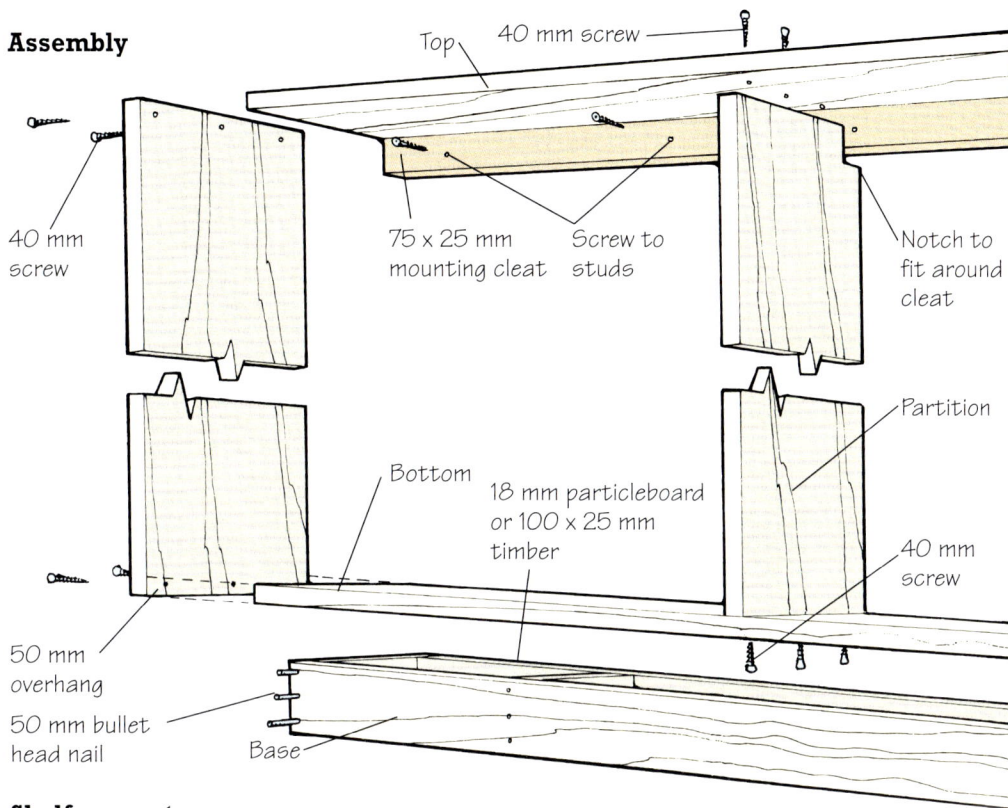

40 mm screw

Top

40 mm screw

75 x 25 mm mounting cleat

Screw to studs

Notch to fit around cleat

Partition

Bottom

18 mm particleboard or 100 x 25 mm timber

40 mm screw

50 mm overhang

50 mm bullet head nail

Base

Shelf supports

Recessed upright

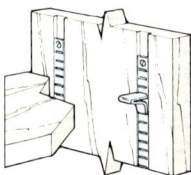

Surface-mounted upright

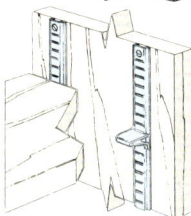

Uprights with snap-in clips look best when set into grooves routed in the vertical supports (top) because the shelves fit snugly against the supports. But surface mounting (bottom) is easier.

Spade pin

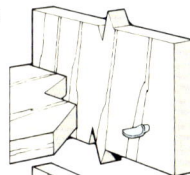

Angle pin

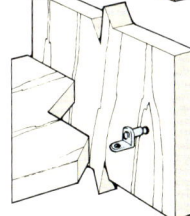

Plug-in pins require two rows of regularly spaced holes on each vertical support (for drilling tips, see p. 72). A shelf rests flat on straight spade pins (top). Angle pins (bottom) offer a little more support.

Edgings

6 mm edge moulding

Bullnose moulding

Scotia moulding

Shelf edging options include 19 x 6 mm hardwood edge moulding, 19 mm half-round bullnose moulding and 19 mm scotia moulding. All three types of moulding can be mounted with glue and panel pins.

Iron-on tape

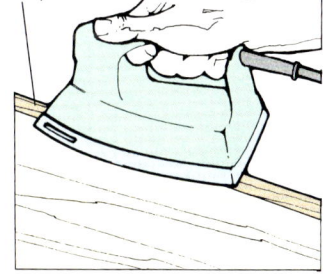

Iron-on tape, sold in rolls by most timber outlets, is another edging alternative. Heat the tape in place, trim it with a utility knife and finish with fine garnet paper.

SHELVES

Bookends

A weighty trick

Do bookends keep sliding off your desk or shelves? Replace the felt on their bottoms with a piece that is long enough to extend under the books for several centimetres. The weight of the books will keep the bookends stationary.

Dowel fence ▶

To keep books from falling from open-ended shelves, install two cup hooks on each shelf end and run dowels through them. Stain the dowels to match the shelves. Pinch the hooks on the bottom shelf to grip the dowels; the other hooks should allow the dowels to slide. If necessary, join dowel lengths with sleeves made of clear plastic tubing.

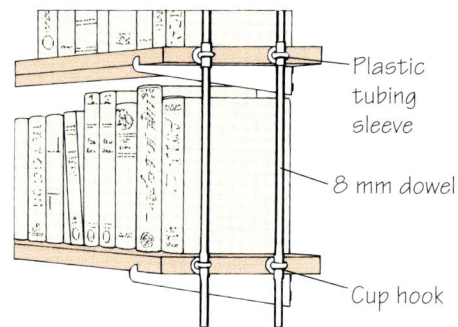

Plastic tubing sleeve

8 mm dowel

Cup hook

Cabinets

The eyes have it

Want to add another shelf to a cabinet to hold lightweight items? Insert two or more small screw eyes in each side of the cabinet and rest the shelf on them. Make the shelf out of a piece of timber sized and finished to suit the cabinet.

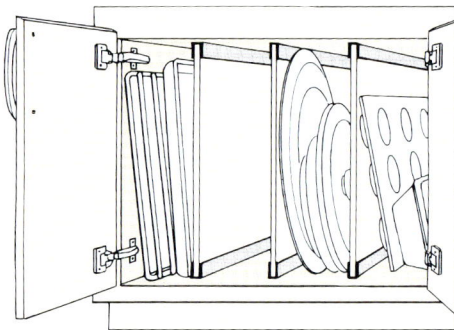

Long division ▲

Vertical dividers in a cabinet make it much easier to store items such as trays, baking pans and magazines. To make the dividers, use 6 or 7.5 mm plywood, or 6 mm acrylic; install U-shaped plastic or metal channels to hold them in place.

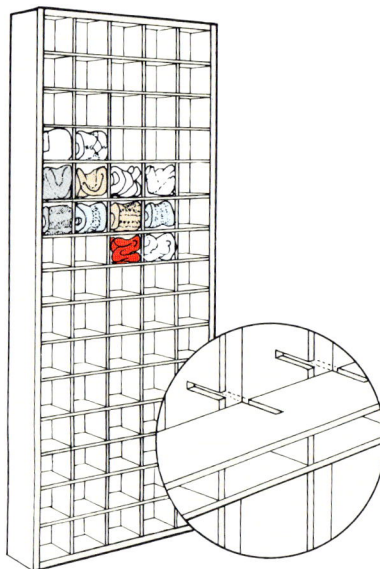

Storage grid ▲

This wall-mounted cubbyhole cabinet holds a variety of small items and protrudes only about 100 mm from the wall. The unit consists of a 100 × 25 mm frame securely fastened to wall studs and a grid made out of 85 mm wide slats of 6 or 7.5 mm plywood. The slats are notched halfway through at 85 mm intervals, then interlocked in cross-halving joints. Scale the cabinet and vary the cubicle size to suit your needs.

On display

Create a china cabinet or collectibles display case by adding sliding glass doors to a shelving unit—either a built-in (see pp. 114–115) or a ready-made bookcase. Buy sliding-door tracks and glides from a major glass merchant, and have them cut to fit. The same store will also cut glass for the doors. To allow room for the doors, trim the middle shelves so that they are set back from the front. ▼

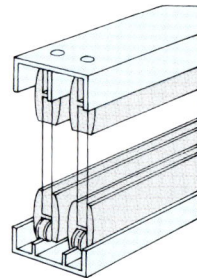

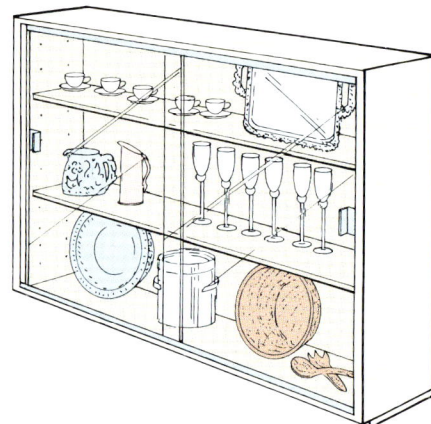

TYPES OF WALL FASTENERS

Whenever possible, attach heavy items directly to wall studs (p. 135) or to a board secured to studs. Use one of the special fasteners below when you want to secure a light to moderate load to plasterboard or plaster, or when you need to attach an object to a masonry wall. For a hollow wall, use a fastener which has a shank length that matches the wall's thickness. On brick or block walls, it's best to attach to mortar joints rather than to bricks or blocks. (To drill into masonry, see p. 10.)

FASTENER	USE	HOW TO INSTALL
Plastic anchor	Very light load on plaster or masonry	Drill hole slightly smaller than anchor, and push in anchor. Attach object with sheet-metal (self-tapping) screw.
Hollow-wall anchor	Moderate load on plaster-board or fibrous plaster	Drill hole same diameter as anchor. Insert anchor, and tighten bolt to collapse sleeve against wall. Remove bolt and use to attach object.
Spring toggle bolt	Moderate load on wall-board or plaster; heavy load on hollow-core concrete block. Also available as gravity toggle	Drill hole large enough to let bolt's folded wings (or gravity toggle) to pass through. Attach object to bolt, then insert in hole. Tighten bolt to pull wings against interior.
Plastic toggle	Moderate load on plasterboard	Drill hole same diameter as anchor. Squeeze wings together and insert in hole. Push nail through screw hole to pop open wings. Attach object with screw.
Metal drive-in anchor	Moderate load on wall-board or plaster	Hammer into wallboard. Predrill 3 mm starter hole in plaster or thin panelling.
Screw-in anchor	Light load on plasterboard. Speeds installation of many fasteners	Screw anchor directly into wall with screwdriver or variable-speed drill. Attach object with screw.
Plastic nail anchor	Moderate load on masonry	Drill hole same diameter as anchor, and insert anchor. Attach object with supplied drive-in/screw-out nail.
Lead anchor	Moderate to heavy load on masonry	Drill hole same diameter as sleeve and insert sleeve. Attach object with coach bolt.
Expansion bolt	Heavy load on masonry	Drill hole same diameter as sleeve. With object attached, insert sleeve in hole and tighten bolt to draw wedge into sleeve.

WARDROBES

Space savers

Quick sorts

You don't need to revamp your entire wardrobe to gain more space. A three-tiered wire basket hung from the wardrobe ceiling makes a great receptacle for socks, balls of wool and other small items; use a cardboard drum or a tall plastic wastebasket to hold umbrellas, canes or sports equipment. ▼

Basket drawer

Add a drawer or two for socks and underwear by mounting a small plastic basket on U-shaped aluminium channels underneath a wardrobe shelf. ▼

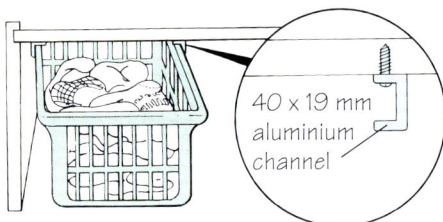

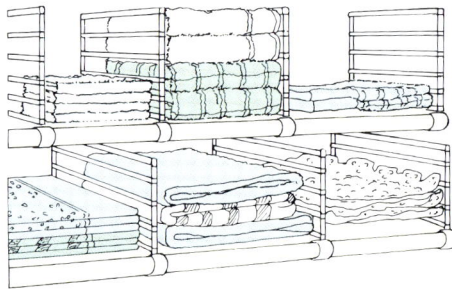

40 x 19 mm aluminium channel

Wire divide ▲

Clamp-on dividers, available at homeware and storage shops, keep piles of jumpers or jeans from toppling over on a wardrobe shelf. In a linen cupboard, use the dividers to separate tablecloths, placemats and pillowcases.

Inner space

When installing a wardrobe system, keep these basic guidelines in mind:
▷ A standard wardrobe is 600 mm deep, with the hanging rail placed 300 mm from the back wall; each hanger requires 25 mm of rail space (bulky winter clothes require 50–75 mm).
▷ Allow 1650 mm from the floor for full-length clothes; 2100 mm for double hanging space (place the bottom rail 1015 mm above the floor, the top rail 2070 mm above the floor).
▷ For standard storage, use 300 mm deep shelves, spaced 325 mm apart; use 400–500 mm deep shelves for bulky items.
▷ Don't plan on using the floor space underneath double-hanging garments. The above guidelines allow for 50 mm between the garments and the floor for easy cleaning.

Central tower

This organiser divides the one and two-rail sides of the wardrobe. Make the shelf tower out of 300 × 25 mm timber or 300 mm wide lengths of 19 mm particleboard, cut to fit between ceiling and floor, or between a shelf and the floor. Install the rails 1650 mm from the wardrobe floor on one side, and 1015 and 2030 mm on the other side. ▼

In the shade

Roller blinds used instead of doors on this built-in wardrobe not only save space but add colour to the room when they are pulled down. You can build the wardrobe frame from 19 mm melamine-faced particleboard, much like a built-in bookcase (pp. 114–115). Make the unit 600 mm deep, and use the dimensions on the facing page as a guide for positioning clothes rails and shelves. ▼

Hangers and rails

Muscle rod

Is your wooden wardrobe hanging rail giving way under the burden? Create a sag-free rail from a length of 12 mm diameter galvanised steel pipe. For a more finished look, insert the pipe into an equal length of 19 mm diameter PVC pipe. Remove any lettering on the plastic pipe with lacquer thinner.

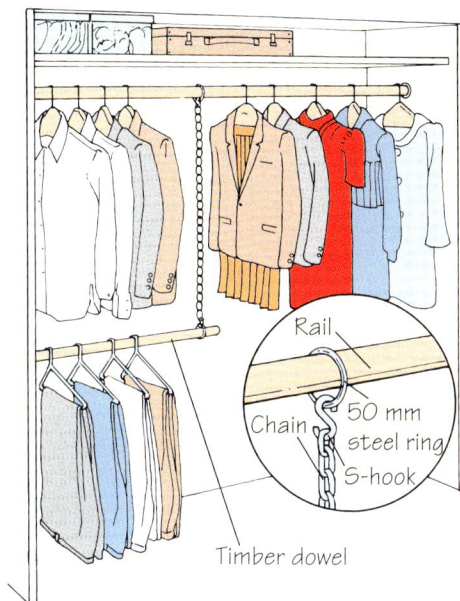

Rail

Chain

50 mm steel ring

S-hook

Timber dowel

Trapeze bar ▲

A wardrobe with a single hanging rail wastes space. An easy way to convert a wardrobe to multilevel storage is to suspend a second rail from the first using steel rings, S-hooks and chain.

Put 'em in chains

Yet another way to increase wardrobe storage is to secure a chain to the clothes rail. Then just hook clothes hangers onto the chain links.

A stronger hanger

Weak wire hangers can support winter coats and other heavy clothes if you tightly bind two (or more) together with masking or cloth tape.

Belt organiser

To turn a wooden hanger into a handy belt rack, simply screw cup hooks into the bottom bar of the hanger and hang your belts from the hooks.

A new angle

If your wardrobe is at least 915 mm deep, expand its usable space by installing two clothes rails in the space now occupied by one. Cut shallow notches in the rails as shown, so that the hangers are held at a 45° angle. Place the clothes you wear most frequently at the front; other garments at the rear. ▼

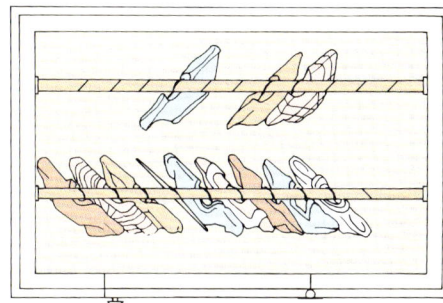

Shoe storage

Shoe-in

When designing shoe storage, plan to use 300–325 mm deep shelves. Allow at least 160 mm between shelves for ordinary shoes, more for boots. Allow 225 mm of shelf width for each pair of women's shoes, 250 mm for men's.

Hang-ups

Doorstops screwed into the back of a hinged wardrobe door make a convenient shoe storage system.

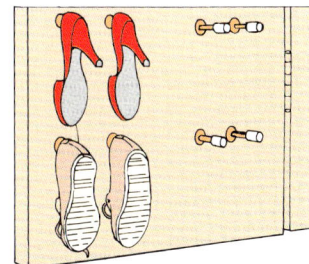

WARDROBES

On the inside

A cedar lining

To repel moths without chemicals, line a wardrobe with 10 mm thick tongue-and-groove Western red cedar strips, available prepackaged from specialist suppliers and timberyards. To install the lining, first remove the shelves, rails and trim from the wardrobe interior; then find and mark the centres of the studs and joists (p. 135). Cut cedar strips to fit across the back wall, about 6 mm shorter than the actual width of the wall. Levelling the lowest strip with a shim if necessary, install the strips (groove side down) with construction adhesive, nailing to the studs as needed. Check the level every 500 mm or so. Cover the back wall first, then the side and front walls, ceiling and door back, butting all edges tightly. Use 38 mm wide strips as trim to cover any gaps. ▼

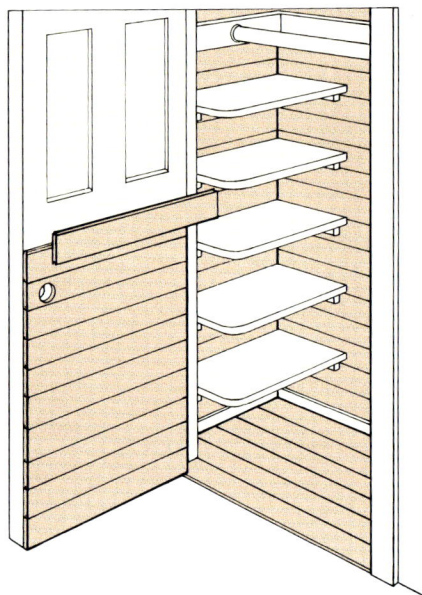

Sheet cedar ▲

Here's an alternative to cedar strips. Fasten Western red cedar plywood sheets directly to smooth walls with panelling nails (on masonry or uneven walls, install furring strips first). For easy installation, cut the sheets 12 mm shorter than the floor-to-ceiling height, use a shim to hold the sheet against the ceiling as you nail, and cover the resulting gap at the bottom with a skirting.

Leftover lining

Don't throw away any scraps of cedar left over from lining a wardrobe. Piece them together to line a drawer.

Cedar hang-up

If you can't line your wardrobe with cedar, and can't stand the smell of mothballs, check home centres or storage shops to see if you can find a garment bag treated with cedar fragrance. If not, you could make one yourself.

Lighten up

Chase away gloom in a dark wardrobe by painting the walls and shelves with gloss or semigloss white enamel paint.

INSTALLING A WIRE

If wardrobe clutter is driving you to distraction, a vinyl-coated wire storage system may be the answer. Not only are these systems efficient organisers, they keep clothes fresher by allowing air to circulate. Most ready-to-assemble wardrobe systems rely on just three basic components: wire baskets in a free-standing frame; a shelf designed for clothes hangers and shelved items; and a linen rack that can double as a shoe rack (just turn it over so that the lip points upward, and attach it with a special bracket that holds it at an angle). The three basic components can be arranged in a wide

WARDROBE SYSTEM

variety of configurations, depending on your storage needs. Before buying a wardrobe system, measure the height, width and depth of your wardrobe; then sketch your plan so you can visualise what the system will look like. Experiment with layouts until you find one that works for you. (For more on wardrobe design, see p. 118.)

Illustrated at right are step-by-step instructions for mounting a typical wardrobe shelf or linen rack. In addition to components and fasteners, you'll need a level, an electric drill, a Phillips screwdriver or a cordless power driver, a measuring tape, a pencil, a hacksaw and a stepladder.

Each system manufacturer has its own recommended hardware and fasteners; be sure to follow kit directions carefully. Some systems include special expanding plastic clips that make shelf installation especially quick and easy. When attached directly to plasterboard, the clip's 'wings' spread inside the wall, holding the clip more securely than a plastic wall anchor. If you hit a stud, trim the clip's shaft to match your plasterboard's thickness; then screw the clip to the stud.

To avoid marring the wardrobe's side walls, cut full-length shelves a minimum of 12 mm shorter than the distance from wall to wall (use a hacksaw or bolt cutters to cut the shelves). Cover the exposed cut ends with rubber caps, which either come with the components or are sold separately.

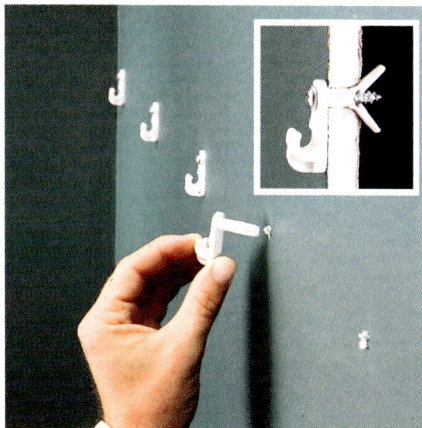

1 Mark a level line for the length of the shelf at the desired shelf height. Drill a 6 mm hole every 225–275 mm, and insert an expanding plastic clip into each hole. Insert and tighten the screw, while holding the clip to keep it from spinning.

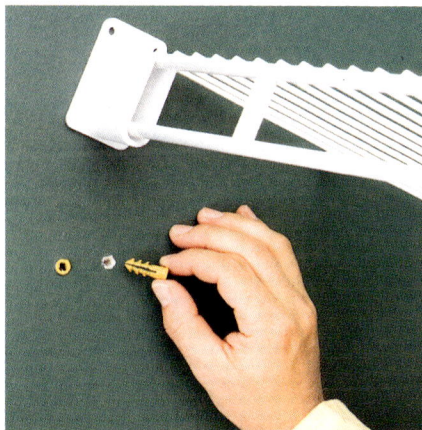

2 Slip an end-mounting bracket over the shelf lip next to the wall. Set the shelf in the clips and hold the end bracket against the wall. Make sure that the shelf is level front to back and side to side, and then mark the screw locations on the wall.

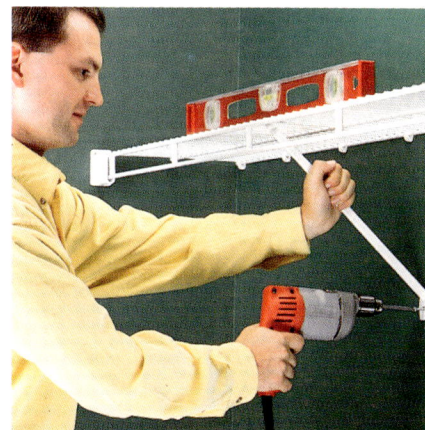

3 Drill 6 mm holes for the end bracket and insert the anchors. Then screw the end bracket to the wall. If the shelf runs from wall to wall, attach an end bracket at the other end of the shelf in the same way.

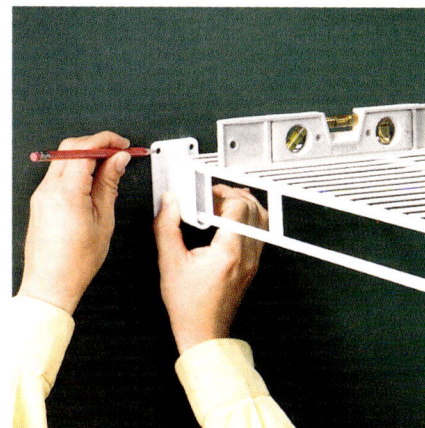

4 Attach a support brace at least every 900 mm along the length of the shelf. Secure the top end of the brace to the shelf; fasten the bottom end to the wall, using a plastic anchor and screw.

CHILDREN'S ROOMS

Toy storage

Stacking bins

Toy clean up is simple with this set of five interlocking bins made from 12 mm pine veneered plywood. Cut all parts as shown. Using the dimensions given below, you can cut all five bins from one 2440 × 1220 mm sheet of plywood. Sand the edges; then assemble the bins with glue and 36 mm nails. Attach casters to one or more bins. For durability, paint the bins with an oil-based primer and top coat. ▼

Assemble with glue and 36 mm bullet head nails

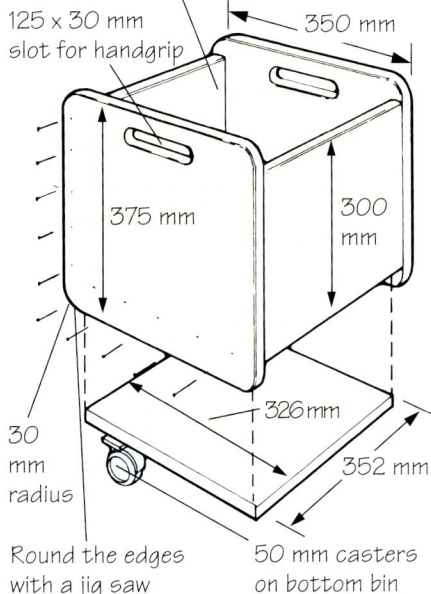

125 x 30 mm slot for handgrip

350 mm

375 mm

300 mm

326 mm

352 mm

30 mm radius

Round the edges with a jig saw

50 mm casters on bottom bin

Chain gang

Keep stuffed animals clean and out of the way with a length of decorative chain. Simply drape the chain (it comes in several colours) near the ceiling from wall to wall. Stitch a loop of bias binding to each stuffed animal, and suspend the animals from the chain with S-hooks. ▼

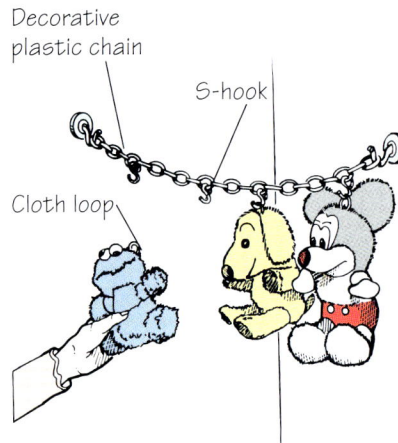

Decorative plastic chain

S-hook

Cloth loop

A tisket, a tasket

Instead of a traditional toy box, sort toys into brightly coloured laundry baskets—the open weave allows children to see what's inside, minimising the need to pull everything out. Another option is to sort toys into cake containers. Tape a representative toy to the front of the container for nonreaders; older children can create their own labels.

Toys to go

A good way to get children to round up toys that stray from their rooms is to keep a bright red wagon on hand. Wheel out the wagon and watch your children race to clean up; afterward, it's easy for even the smallest to pull the whole load back to where it belongs.

Clever combinations

A bed and more

With the right furniture, two children can share even a small room comfortably. A bunk bed is one way to free up floor space. An alternative is to buy (or build) platform beds that rest on drawers, like the one shown here. ▼

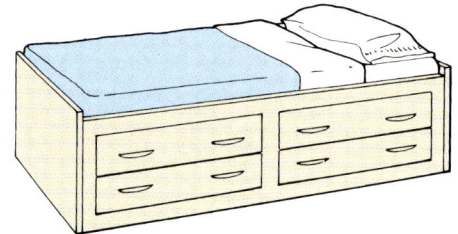

Double-duty desk

When the toy bins are rolled out, this storage chest doubles as a desk. Use 19 mm melamine-faced particleboard to build the sides, back, top and lid; 10 mm particleboard for the bottom of the divided tray; and 100 × 25 mm pine for the tray frame. Assemble with glue and wood screws; then finish timber with colourful enamel. Make roll-out bins as shown at left or buy them. ▼

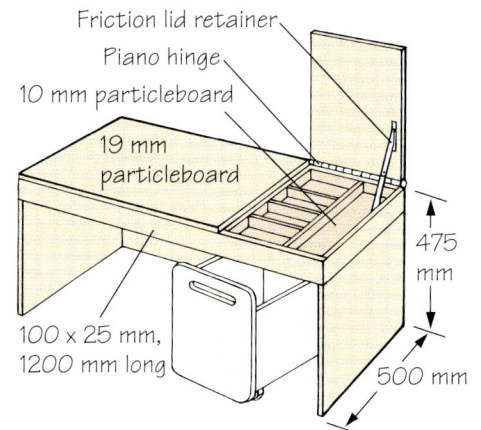

Friction lid retainer

Piano hinge

10 mm particleboard

19 mm particleboard

100 x 25 mm, 1200 mm long

475 mm

500 mm

SPORTS EQUIPMENT

Bicycles

A real hang-up

To eliminate clutter and save floor space in the garage, hang family bicycles from large plastic-coated hooks that are screwed into ceiling joists or wall studs. Bicycle hooks are available at hardware stores and cycling shops. ▼

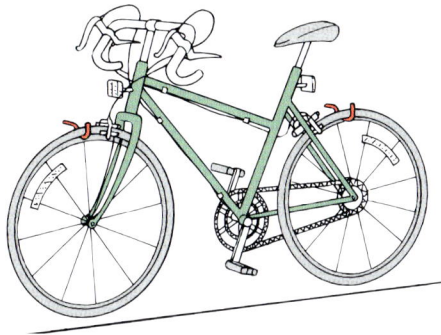

A better bike rack

Tired of seeing bicycles strewn all over your driveway? Here's a convenient two-bike rack that's easy to make out of preservative treated pine. Three stakes anchor the rack to the ground. To hold the thicker wheels of mountain bikes or the thinner ones of racing bikes, use spacers to alter the width of the slots. Fix the bikes to the rack with U-shaped bike locks to prevent theft. ▼

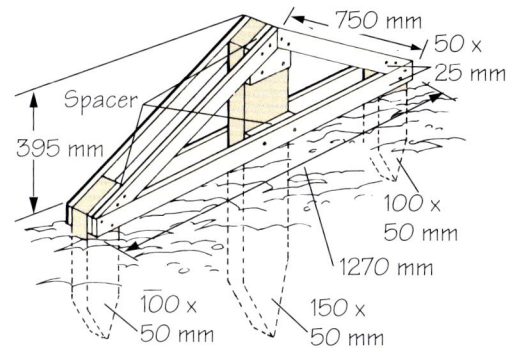

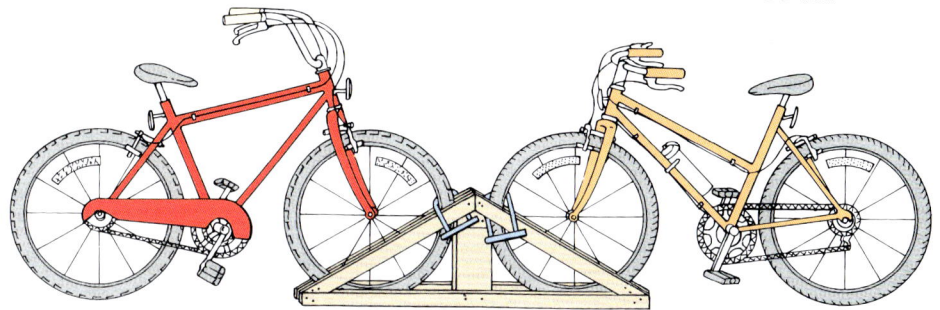

Other equipment

Golf rack ▶

This handy wire organiser, available at specialty storage and sports stores, keeps golf shoes and bags neat and organised. Mount it on a garage wall or in a convenient cupboard.

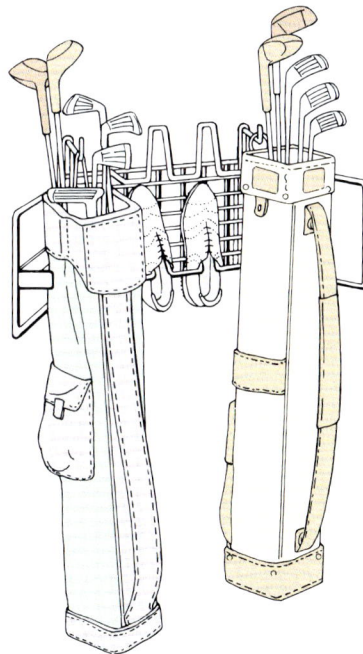

Unfinished business

The space between the exposed floor joists of an elevated house, or ceiling joists of a garage, is often wasted. Put it to work by nailing timber off cuts across any two joists at 900 mm intervals. The resulting storage area is ideal for stowing away fishing rods and other long lightweight items. For a sturdier ceiling rack designed to hold timber, see p. 61.

Batter up

Store softball and T-ball equipment in this corner organiser. Cut a triangle from 19 or 21 mm plywood with the dimensions shown. Bore 30 mm diameter holes for the balls; cut the bat slots with a coping saw. Nail the platform to 50 × 19 mm cleats fastened to studs.

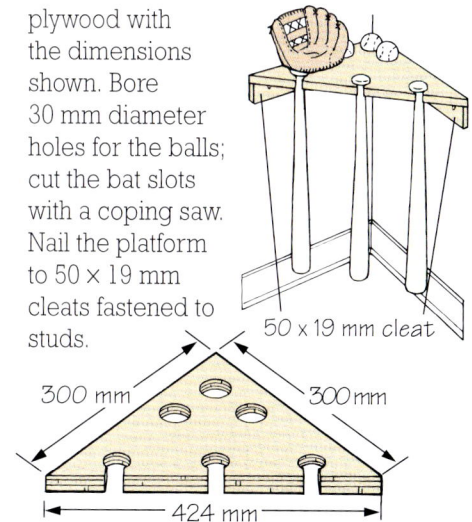

Overhead storage

Over-the-car-bonnet rack

This garage rack hangs over the bonnet of your car, taking up no floor space. Use 75 × 50 mm timber to build the two end supports and the shelf cleats; make the shelving from 19 or 21 mm plywood. The depth and spacing of the shelves can vary depending on your needs. Use 65 mm wood screws to assemble the frame; attach the frame to overhead beams with 65 mm coach bolts. ▼

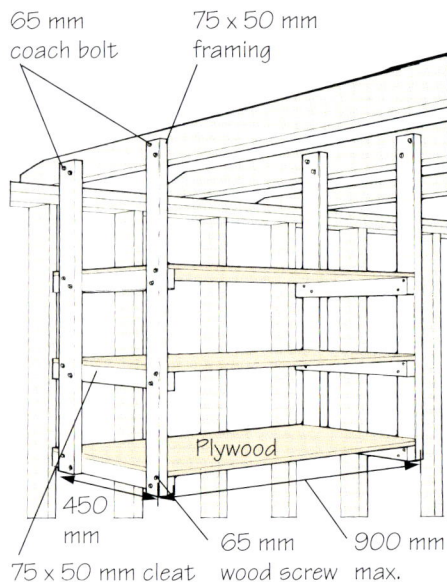

65 mm coach bolt
75 × 50 mm framing
Plywood
450 mm
65 mm wood screw
900 mm max.
75 × 50 mm cleat

Flying carpet

Store a rolled-up rug by suspending it from two old belts attached to the attic or garage rafters. To deter insects from nesting inside, wrap the ends with large plastic bags and tape.

Reel 'em in ▶

To avoid the yearly untangling of Christmas lights, store them on empty electrical wire spools (ask your hardware store to save some for you). For easy access, slide several spools onto a length of 25 mm diameter PVC pipe, then mount the pipe between the joists in your garage or workshop.

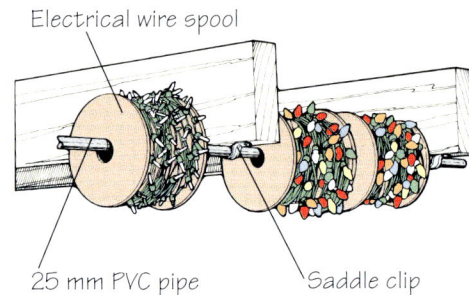

Electrical wire spool
25 mm PVC pipe
Saddle clip

Overhead bins

Overhead storage bins are a great way to put wasted space to work. Construct them from 19 or 21 mm plywood or boards, and assemble them with 38 and 50 mm wood screws. Make sure that one side of each bin extends to attach to a ceiling joist; fasten the other end to the adjacent bin. Mount the doors with butt hinges; provide a hook and eye to hold them in the open position. ▼

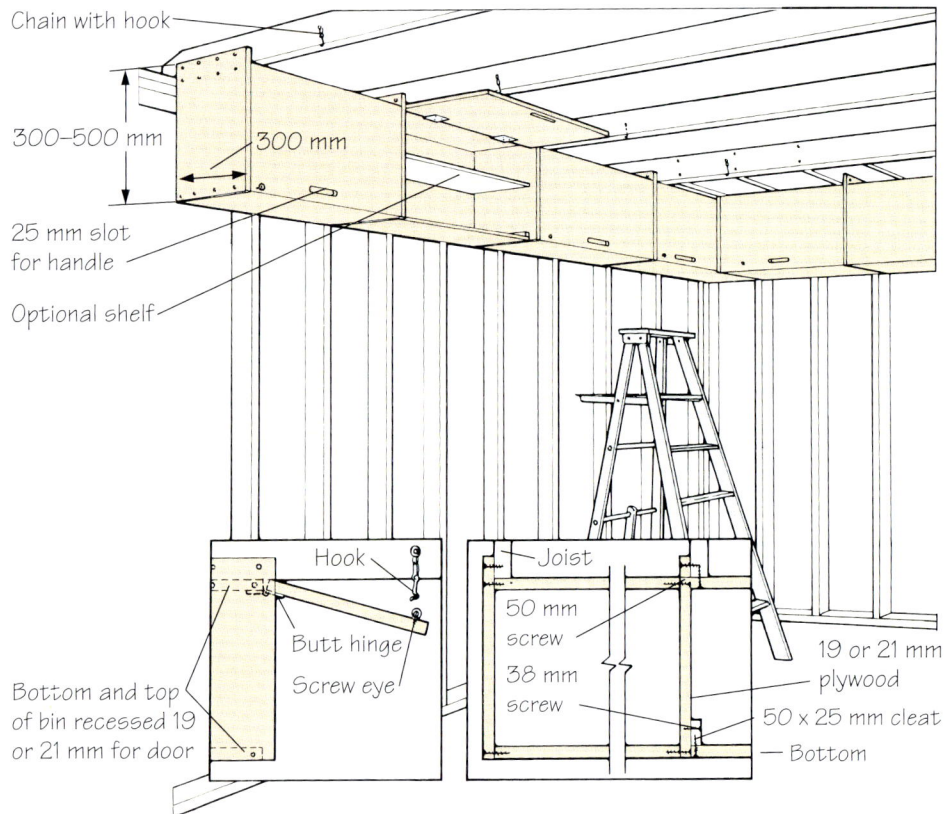

Chain with hook
300–500 mm
300 mm
25 mm slot for handle
Optional shelf
Hook
Butt hinge
Screw eye
Bottom and top of bin recessed 19 or 21 mm for door
Joist
50 mm screw
38 mm screw
19 or 21 mm plywood
50 × 25 mm cleat
Bottom

Hanging around

Here's another way to put the space over your car to work. String a hammock from screw eyes fastened to exposed joists and use it to store sport balls, exercise mats and other light bulky items. ▼

Screw eye

Storage loft ▶

Store patio and pool furniture on this over-the-car-bonnet loft. Use 100 × 50 mm timber for the frame, 100 × 100 mm posts to support the front of the loft, and 17 mm plywood for the top. Bolt the rear ledger to wall studs. Assemble the frame with framing anchors (joist hangers at joist-header connections; universal connectors at post-frame connections). For greater security, anchor the posts to the floor with post bases.

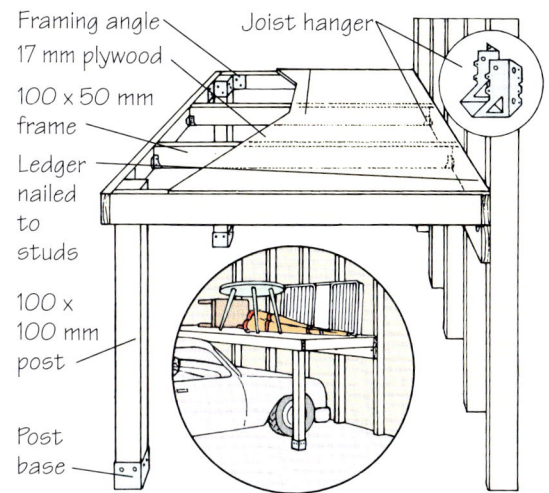

Framing angle
Joist hanger
17 mm plywood
100 × 50 mm frame
Ledger nailed to studs
100 × 100 mm post
Post base

More racks

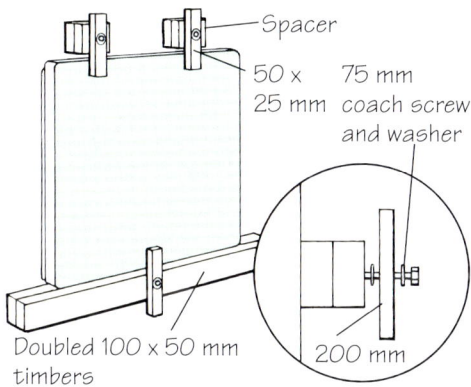

Spacer
50 × 25 mm
75 mm coach screw and washer
200 mm
Doubled 100 × 50 mm timbers

Card table rack ▲

Need to store a games table? Try this easy-to-make rack. Mark parallel lines across wall studs far enough apart to accommodate the width of the table, plus at least 6 mm extra. Fasten doubled 100 × 50 mm timbers along the bottom line and two block spacers on the upper line. The table is held in place by pivoting 200 mm lengths of 50 × 25 mm battens mounted with 75 mm coach screws and washers.

Cushion station

This handy wall-mounted rack is great for storing unwieldy patio furniture cushions indoors. By keeping the cushions off the ground, the rack also helps prevent mildew. Above a 150 × 25 mm shelf, bolt a 75 × 25 mm pine frame to the wall studs. Keep the bolt and washer just loose so that the frame will pivot. ▼

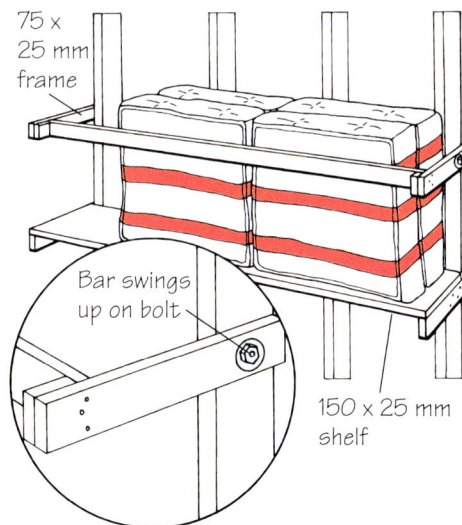

75 × 25 mm frame
Bar swings up on bolt
150 × 25 mm shelf

Furniture racks

Keep garage, attic or workshop clutter under control with this simple space saver. Just fasten ordinary shelf brackets or L-braces to wall studs and use them to hang folding chairs, recliners and other lightweight outdoor furniture. If you don't have any L-brackets, you can make supports out of oversize nails (carpenter's spikes), vinyl gutter brackets or wood dowels fitted into predrilled holes in the studs. Arrange the supports in pairs to fit the items to be stored.

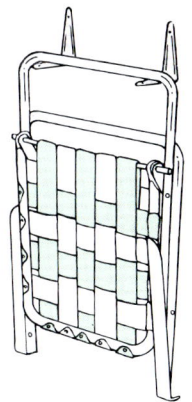

ATTIC, WORKSHOP AND GARAGE

Utility shelves

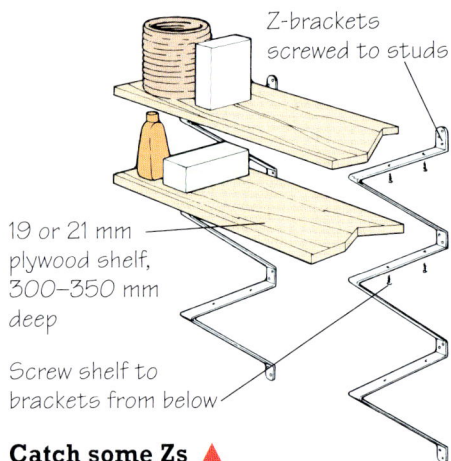

Z-brackets
screwed to studs

19 or 21 mm
plywood shelf,
300–350 mm
deep

Screw shelf to
brackets from below

Catch some Zs ▲

Inexpensive and easy to install,
Z-brackets can support light to medium
loads on shelves up to 350 mm deep.
Z-brackets come in three-shelf units and
can be cut or combined as needed.
They're sold in many hardware shops.

60 mm nails

285
mm

250
mm

50 × 50 mm
spacer for
dampness

300 × 25 mm
board or plywood

600 mm

Under the roof

Turn wasted space under the roof into a
convenient storage area with this handy
shelving system. Screw 50 × 50 mm
uprights and 50 × 25 mm cleats to the
rafters; use 40 mm nails to attach 19 or
21 mm plywood shelves to cleats. ▼

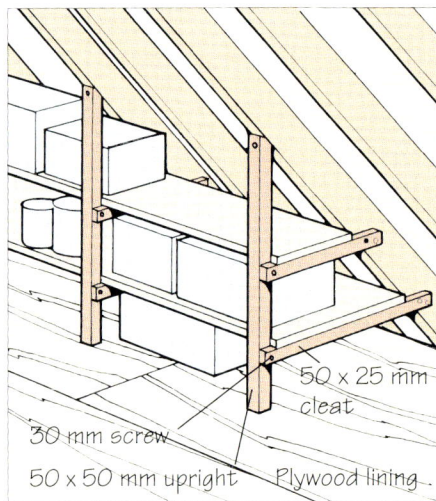

50 × 25 mm
cleat

30 mm screw

50 × 50 mm upright   Plywood lining

◀ Stacking cases

These modules allow you
to change or add to your
storage unit as needed—
they are especially useful
when stacked against a
gable attic wall. The boxes
are made of 300 × 25 mm
boards or 12 mm ply-
wood. Since there is no
stress on the joints, case
parts may be glued and
nailed together rather than
screwed. Double 50 ×
50 mm timbers provide a
base for the assembly.

Double-duty stairs

Roll it away

This roll-out bin is designed to make
the most of the wasted space under the
lower end of a stairway. Use it to store
awkward items ranging from cleaning
supplies to boots and sports equipment. The bin is a simple box made
of 19 or 21 mm plywood, assembled
with screws and glue and mounted on
casters. The corners are reinforced with
19 mm square or quad moulding as
shown. To cut the front, back and filler
pieces at the correct angle, trace the
slope of the stairs on a piece of cardboard and use it as a template for marking the plywood. Allowing for casters,
the bin's front and back should clear the
stairs by 6 mm; the filler panel fits flush.
For easy access, install a handle on the
front of the bin. ▼

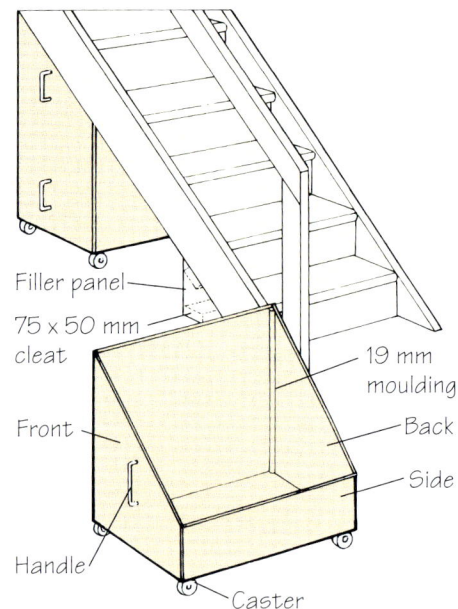

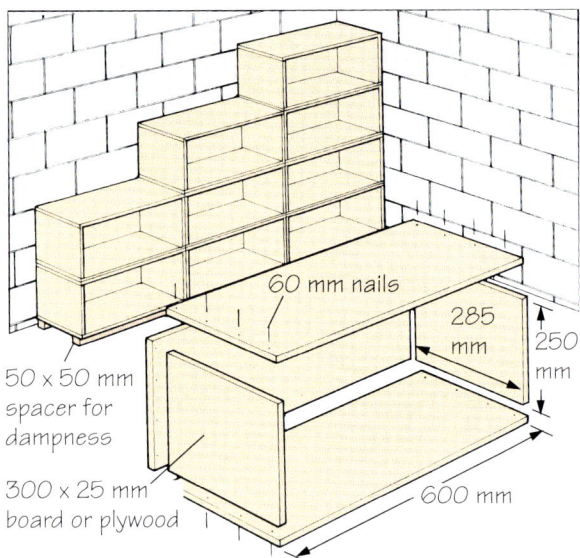

Filler panel

75 × 50 mm
cleat

Front

Handle

Caster

19 mm
moulding

Back

Side

INSTALLING PEGBOARD

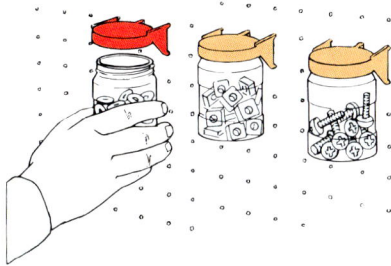

Pegboard—also called perforated hardboard—is an excellent solution to a wide variety of storage problems, both in and out of the workshop and garage. Brightly painted and edged with a decorative moulding, it makes a great kitchen wall organiser. In addition to the standard S-hooks and hangers that can be bought from any hardware shop, a variety of shelves and containers designed to attach to pegboard allow you to customise the storage system to your particular requirements.

Available at home centres and timberyards, pegboard panels are easy to install. In areas with unfinished walls, screw the panels directly to exposed studs. (To keep screw heads from sinking all the way through the pegboard use a washer.) Attach pegboard to plasterboard by driving wood screws through the panel, then through a rubber or plastic spacer and directly into a stud (see right). The spacers, usually included in pegboard kits, hold the panel away from the wall, allowing clearance for the hooks. Mount pegboard on masonry walls with furring strips or grounds, as shown below.

On plasterboard

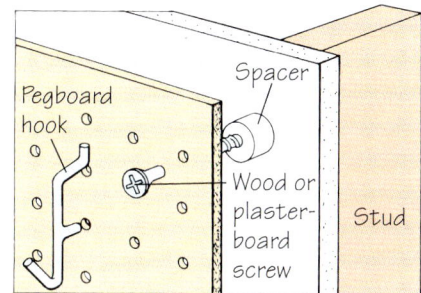

To mount a pegboard panel onto a plasterboard wall, first use a stud finder to locate the wall studs (p. 135). After positioning the panel as desired, drive 50 mm wood or plasterboard screws through the flush surface of the panel, then through a spacer and into a stud. Drive screws at 300 mm intervals vertically and at every stud along the top and bottom of the panel.

On masonry

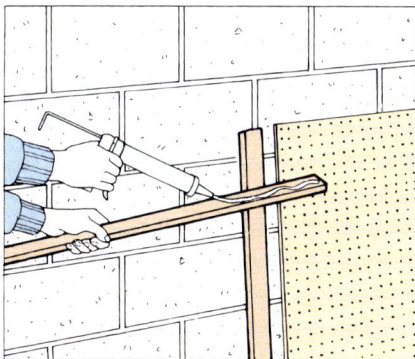

To install pegboard on a masonry wall, cut lengths of 50 x 25 mm furring strips equal to the height of the pegboard panel. Then apply construction adhesive to one side of each strip.

Fasten the furring strips to the wall with 50 mm masonry nails. To make sure the pegboard panels are solidly supported, place the furring strips no more than 1200 mm apart.

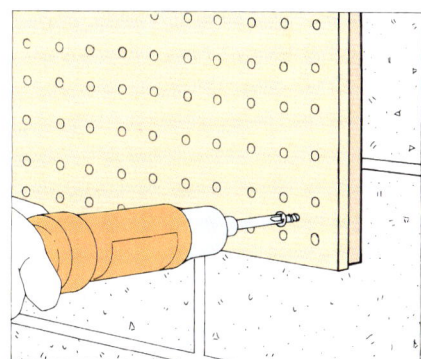

Position the panel, and drive 25 mm screws through the panel's flush surface into a strip. Drive screw at every strip along the top and bottom of the panel and at 300 mm intervals vertically.

HOME IMPROVEMENTS

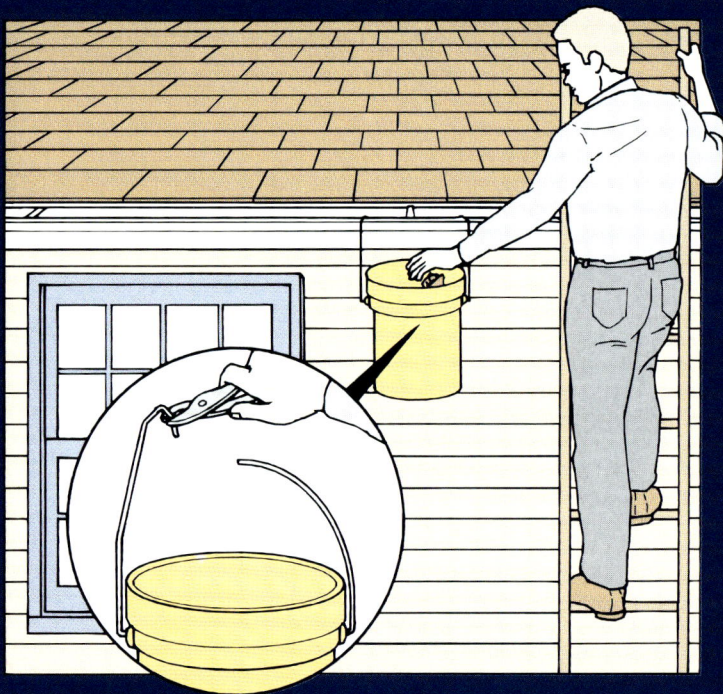

WALL REPAIR

Caulking gaps

Annoyed by gaps between a wall and its trim or between a wall and masonry? Fill them with a paintable sealant. Apply the sealant with a caulking gun; smooth and seal the newly sealed joint using one of the techniques described on page 150. Use sealant that matches the wall colour, or paint it to match.

Popped nail

Flatten a popped nail ▲

Usually caused by shrinking framing, popped nails are the curse of plasterboard interiors. To fix one, drive a plasterboard screw into the stud 20 mm or so below the popped nail, sinking the head just below the surface (p. 132). Then scrape away the loose paint and old filler from around the popped nail, and drive it back into place. Finish with three layers of jointing cement.

Anchors away

To remove a plastic wall anchor from plasterboard or plaster, just insert a tight-fitting screw and wiggle it out.

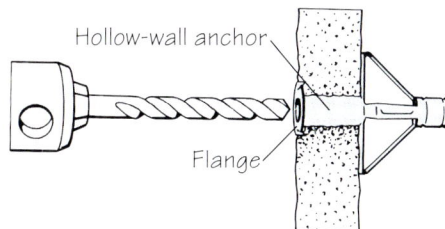

Hollow-wall anchor

Flange

Anchors aweigh ▲

To remove a hollow-wall anchor (p. 117), you have to drive it into the wall cavity. The resulting hole will be much smaller if you use a drill bit slightly larger than the screw hole and drill just enough to cut off the flange. Then push the remainder of the anchor into the wall.

Quick standard patch

To fix a small hole in plasterboard—say up to 40 mm in diameter— use jointing cement and a small piece of scrim cloth. Cut away some of the sound plaster around the hole to form a broad border about 6 mm deep. Cut the scrim cloth to fit into the enlarged hole: two pieces may be necessary if the hole is big. Wet the bared plaster and dab on some small dollops of jointing cement. Press the scrim into the cement and apply a thin coat of plaster. Apply further coats as the plaster dries, gradually building up the surface. When the final coat is nearly dry, run a metal float over it to provide a glassy-smooth finish. ▼

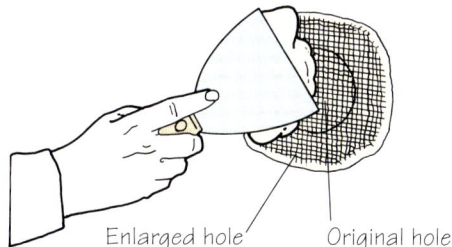

Enlarged hole   Original hole

It's in the mix

For other minor wall repairs, the best choice is cellulose filling compound. It's easier to use than dry-mix patching compound, and it dries faster and shrinks less than jointing cement. However, jointing cement is easier to spread, and therefore better for large areas, such as plasterboard joints.

Smooth ruler

When patching a hole that's wider than your putty knife, don't use the putty knife to smooth and remove compound. You'll just gouge it. Instead use a wide broadknife, or if you don't have one, a metal ruler. Hold the ruler on edge, at an angle, and wipe it across the area.

Blow dry

On damp days, fillers or jointing cement can take forever to dry. To speed the process up a bit, use a hair dryer. Set it on a low temperature and keep moving it back and forth over the area so that the cement doesn't dry out too quickly and begin to crack.

Invisible wall patching

Even on a flat untextured wall, patches can stand out as smooth spots after you paint. To mimic the texture of the surrounding wall, let the patch dry; then before painting the wall, lightly spray the patch with water and brush the surface gently in a circular motion with a small scrubbing brush. After it's painted, the patch won't show as much.

WALL REPAIR

Patching plasterboard

No support

To avoid having to fix a backing sheet behind a small hole before it can be patched, try this simple technique. Thread some string through a piece of light card or ply and pass it through the hole. Tie the string tightly to a length of dowel or thin wood so the temporary backing is held firmly in place. Part fill the hole with jointing cement and when dry, trim the string and fill until flush. ▼

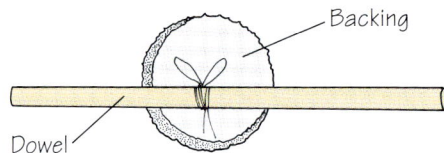

Backing

Dowel

Still no support

Here's how to fix a hole up to 200 mm wide without backing the patch. Square the hole with a utility knife. Cut a plasterboard patch 25 mm larger on all sides than the hole. Score and break it along the back to the hole size. Peel off the backing and gypsum along the edges, leaving a flap of facing paper all around. Lightly sand the flap's back to feather the edges. Then apply cornice cement, set the patch in place, and finish the joint using the flap as tape. ▼

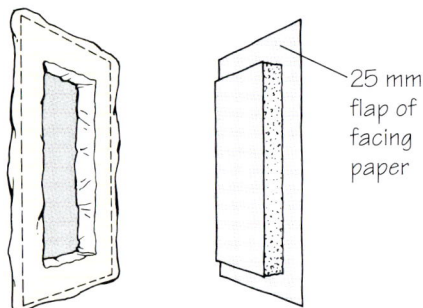

25 mm flap of facing paper

Patching a corner

To patch a badly chipped outside wall corner, use a long flat trowel as formwork. Holding it even with the edge on one side of the corner, fill in the area on the other side with cornice cement or plaster. Then slide the trowel to one side, being careful not to lift it until it is away from the patched area.

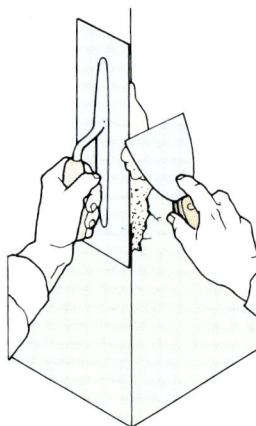

Plaster repair secrets

Give it a thump

When you repair a plaster wall, always remove the plaster down to its soundest layer before attempting a repair. Sound plaster makes a solid, snappy noise when you thump it; loose plaster produces a hollow, dull sound.

Heads up

When patching plaster with exposed laths, drive screws into the wood, leaving the heads sticking up. This gives the new plaster something to hold on to.

No hitting

Hard blows loosen plaster. When repairing it, or the underlying lath or framing, use plasterboard screws instead of nails. To remove damaged plaster, prise it off or lightly chip it with a cold chisel.

No-sag plastering

To fix a large hole in plaster use patching plaster; it's less likely to sag than jointing cement. In order to get the plaster to adhere properly, dampen the old surface well or apply a PVA bonding agent. Apply the plaster in layers no more than 10 mm thick. Crosshatch each layer with the corner of a putty knife as it starts to set. Let it dry; then wet it before applying the next layer.

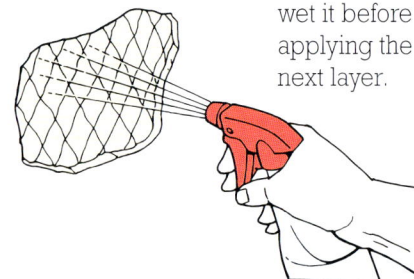

Glue it back up

Here's a way to secure plaster coming loose from laths. Every 300 mm or so, drill a hole and inject construction adhesive through it onto the laths. Then press the plaster against the laths by putting a board over the plaster and forcing a brace against it. Leave the brace until the adhesive sets. If the backs of the laths are accessible, inject the adhesive through the spaces between laths. ▼

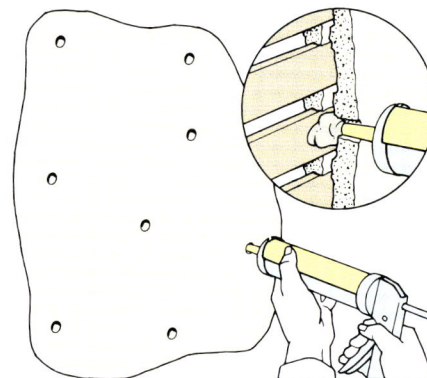

FIXING DAMAGED PLASTERBOARD

Whether it's a hole or dent caused by a doorknob, some careless furniture movers or a teenager's foot, or peeling tape resulting from humidity or the house settling, damaged plasterboard is easy to repair. If you encounter a stud when you are removing a damaged section, cut the plasterboard back to the centre of the stud and secure one edge of your patch to the stud. If the damage to a wall is too extensive for repair, cut out the whole section to accommodate a new sheet of plasterboard.

When finishing a patch or a joint, apply thin coats of jointing cement; let each coat dry and then sand it lightly with fine-grit paper. Each time you apply jointing cement, broaden the area covered with the cement until the patch blends imperceptibly with the surrounding wall.

Retaping a joint

1 Remove all loose tape, including tape that is only partially loose; don't try to salvage old tape. Sand away loose tape remnants and rough edges.

2 Apply a coat of jointing cement and embed new paper tape in it. Then apply two thin coats over the tape, feathering the edges. Sand smooth.

Patching a hole

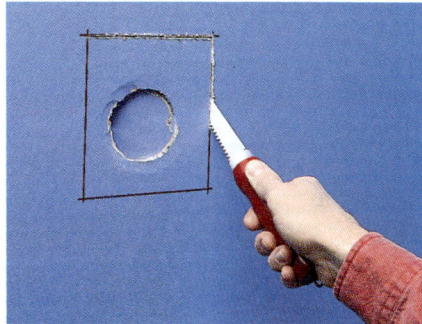

1 Cut out the damaged section, using a small, fine-toothed saw (or a utility knife). Square up and enlarge the area you cut out to make it easier to repair.

2 Cut two 75 x 25 mm battens about 100 mm longer than the hole. Slip them into the hole at top and bottom, and secure with 30 mm plasterboard screws.

3 Cut a plasterboard patch 3 mm smaller on all sides than the hole. Insert the patch into the hole and secure it to the battens with plasterboard screws.

4 Cover seams with self-adhesive fibre-glass plasterboard tape. Then apply three thin coats of jointing cement, sanding the cement smooth after each coat.

PLASTERBOARD INSTALLATION

Installing plasterboard

X-ray walls

Before putting up new plasterboard, take photos of the wall construction, including plumbing and electrical lines. Later, when you need to know what's in there, you'll have a record. Shoot the picture as straight on as possible, and include a stretched-out tape measure.

Take it all off

Even with the most careful finishing, it's hard to hide crushed edges and corners and nail head tears on plasterboard. Instead of trying to salvage the damaged boards, you'll get a much better finish if you simply tear them off and replace them with new ones.

Cutting edge

When cutting plasterboard, a utility knife blade can become clogged and dull. To prevent this, keep a small piece of very fine abrasive paper handy and periodically rub the blade with it to remove the plaster build up.

Across, not up and down

In a room with a standard 2400 mm ceiling, install plasterboard horizontally, using sheets with lengths of 3000 or 3600 mm. Horizontal seams are easier to tape, and the long sheets will reduce the number of vertical joints; often they can reach from wall to wall. Start at the bottom of the wall (put a couple of plasterboard off cuts under the sheet for temporary support), and work across. When installing the upper sheets, make sure any vertical seams are staggered; start with a half sheet if necessary. ▼

Making a point

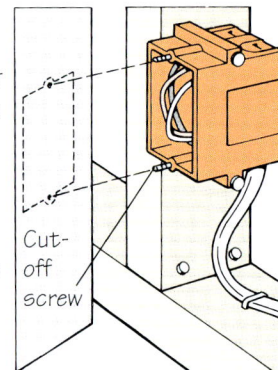

To mark the position of a power point or light switch on plasterboard, insert screws whose heads have been cut off in the holes of the fixing bracket. Then position the plasterboard panel and press it against the screws. To outline the shape on the plasterboard, just place a spare power point over the holes made by the screws. If a switch or power point is wired, be sure to get an electrician to temporarily disconnect the supply.

Kiss and tell

Another, quicker way to mark an electrical outlet's position on plasterboard is to coat the edges of the bracket with lipstick and press the plasterboard into place. Then remove the panel and cut along the 'kiss marks' on the back.

Fold for carrying ▶

Getting plasterboard around stairway turns (or other obstacles) isn't easy. Instead of cutting the sheets up, score the back of each panel at the stud location, fold it as shown, and carefully carry it up the stairs. To install the sheet, simply unfold it and mount it, double-nailing at the scored seam.

A useful warp ▶

When installing predecorated plasterboard, avoid unsightly fasteners along vertical joins by prebowing the sheets. Stack the sheets face up overnight, with the centres on the floor and the ends on 100×50 mm timbers. To attach a sheet, apply adhesive to the studs and fasten the sheet at top and bottom. The bow in the sheet presses its centre against the adhesive.

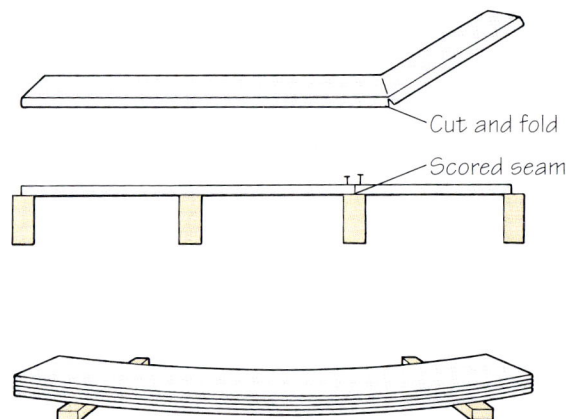

Cut and fold

Scored seam

Don't rip it out

Need to take down a plasterboard panel you just installed? If you haven't finished the joints yet, you may be able to reuse it. Sharpen one end of a short length of 19 mm copper tubing with a file. Place the tube over each nail head, and strike it sharply with a hammer to cut through the plasterboard. Then lift off the panel. To replace the piece, simply fit it back on the studs, placing the holes over the old nails. Renail the plasterboard 20 mm or so from each old nail. ▼

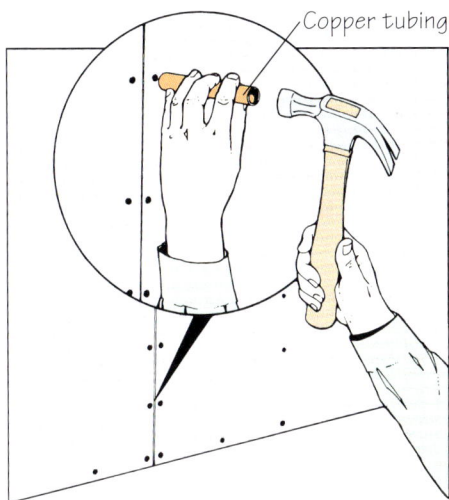

Copper tubing

Dust-free smoothing

Sanding plasterboard patches and joints can stir up a lot of dust. Instead of sanding, try using a damp sponge to remove excess jointing cement after it dries. Select a large, fine-textured sponge, and rinse it regularly in a bucket of water. With practice, you can get perfectly smooth joints that may need a light sanding at most. You can also keep the dust down by using an abrasive-surfaced sanding sponge.

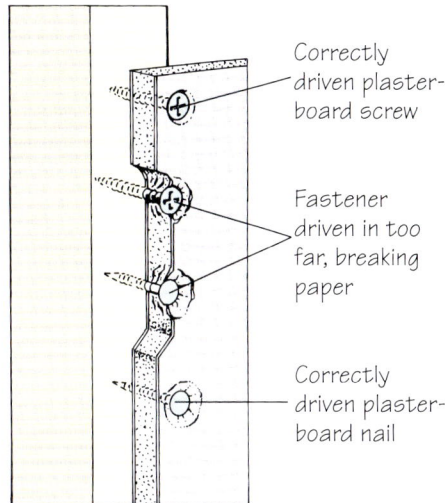

Correctly driven plasterboard screw

Fastener driven in too far, breaking paper

Correctly driven plasterboard nail

Gentle touch ▲

When driving nails or screws into plasterboard, the trick is to set the fastener just below the surface so that it can be hidden with jointing cement. If you drive it too deep, so that it breaks the paper or crushes the plasterboard, you compromise the fastener's holding power.

Jointing cement tricks

Saving leftovers

Do you buy jointing cement in a large economy container, use some, and a few weeks later find that the rest has turned lumpy? Here's how to prevent this. Before it dries, scrape all the excess compound off the inside surfaces of the container and wipe the surfaces clean. Level the cement, and pour half a cup of water over it. Rinse and replace the plastic that was over the cement when you opened the container; then put the lid on tightly.

Stick 'em up

If you put up plasterboard with wall-board adhesive, you'll eliminate about half the fasteners—which means fewer fasteners to hide and fewer potential popped nails later. Apply adhesive to each stud in walnut-sized dollops. Then press the plasterboard into place and secure it with plasterboard nails or screws around the edges and once in the centre. Adhesive must not coincide with nail or screw locations. ▼

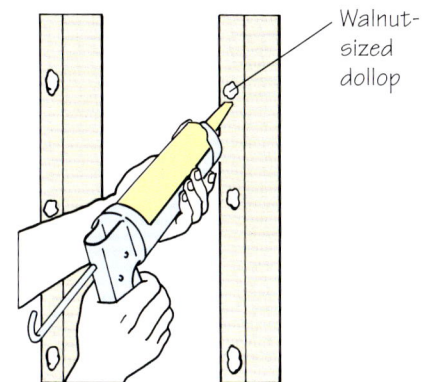

Walnut-sized dollop

Give it a stir

To mix or thin jointing cement, use a paint mixer attachment on a 10 mm variable-speed drill, running at a slow speed. To avoid making a mess, use an old lid with a cut out for the mixer.

Easy clean up

When working with dry jointing cement, mix it in a flexible plastic container. When the job is done, let the leftover jointing cement harden. Then flex the container gently with your hands. The material will break away cleanly. Simply throw it out and wash the container.

WALL TRIM

Moulding

Tells the tale

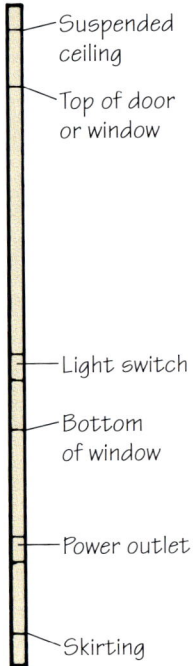

- Suspended ceiling
- Top of door or window
- Light switch
- Bottom of window
- Power outlet
- Skirting

If you're planning a lot of building or remodelling, use any light, rigid length of wood to make yourself a storey rod. This handy tool—a timber batten with frequently used measurements marked on it— cuts the time you spend measuring and helps ensure that you put trim and other items in the same place around the room or from one room to another.

Easy-off moulding

To remove quad moulding without damaging it or the skirting board, slip a putty knife between the moulding and the skirting board and place a thin timber off cut behind the putty knife. Then use a crowbar positioned between the off cut and the putty knife to carefully force the moulding off.

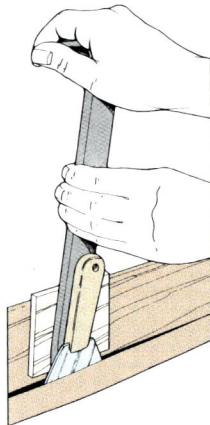

No one will ever know

Can't find a match for old moulding? Look in your built-in wardrobe; it may have the same moulding as your walls. Just remove and use it. Install a matching standard moulding in the wardrobe.

Trim saver

It's possible to reuse trim as long as you remove the old nails from the back rather than the front of the trim. Grip each nail tightly with locking pliers, and pull its small head through the wood. Done carefully, this won't mar the finish or splinter the top surface, and it will even leave the filler in the nail hole. Reinstall as you would new trim.

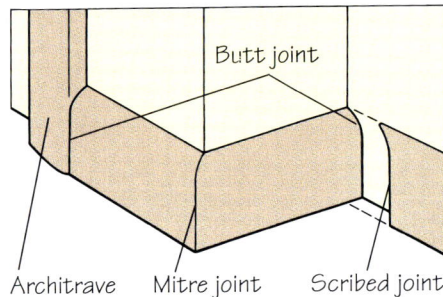

Architrave   Mitre joint   Scribed joint
Butt joint

Corner ins and outs ▲

Here are some rules for installing skirting boards and other wall edge trim.
▷ Fit outside corners first, joining the pieces in a mitre joint.
▷ On an inside corner, butt one piece against the wall and cut the other to fit around it, making a scribed joint (p. 79).
▷ When trim runs into a door architrave, make a butt joint.

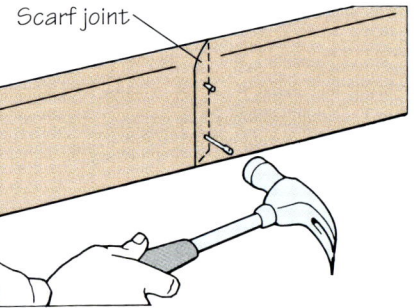

Scarf joint

Joining on the angle ▲

When joining straight lengths of moulding, cut the end of each piece at a 45° angle and splice the pieces together. A scarf joint, as this is known, is less noticeable than a butt joint even if shrinkage occurs. Make sure the splice falls directly over a stud, and nail through both ends into the stud.

Cornice cunning

Installing timber cornice moulding is simpler if you make a template that duplicates the moulding's bearing points. Place the moulding on a framing square and measure its bearing points. Make a template by nailing two timber blocks together. Use it every metre or so to mark the moulding position on the wall and ceiling.

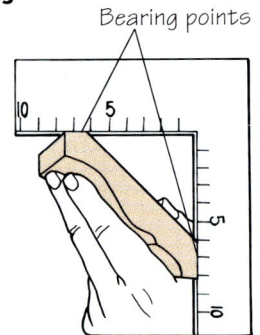

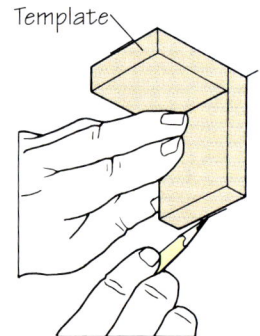

Bearing points

Template

WALL FRAMING

Wall studs

New angle

When installing wall studs, accurate skew nailing—driving nails at an angle to join a stud to the plate—is essential. To keep a stud from shifting as you hammer, place the head of a large flat head nail against the opposite side of the stud and tap it into the plate. If you are installing several studs, cut a 100 × 50 mm spacer to fit between the studs and use it to hold each stud in place as you nail. It also helps to bend the end of the nail slightly so that it curves as it goes into the wood. ▼

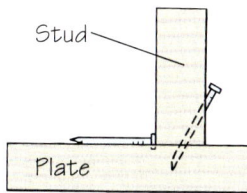

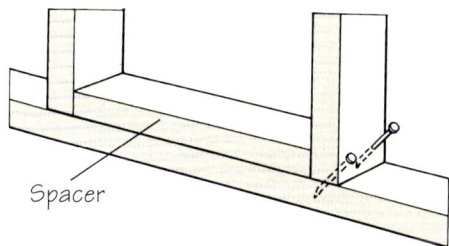

Amicable separation

Need to separate two studs that are nailed together? It's easy with two crowbars. Insert the flat ends as shown, and push the angled ends toward the centre. Start near one end of the studs and work towards the other end.

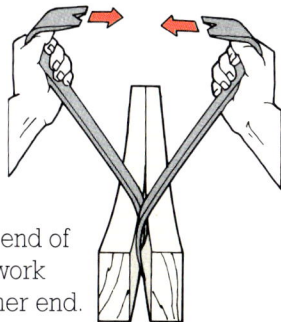

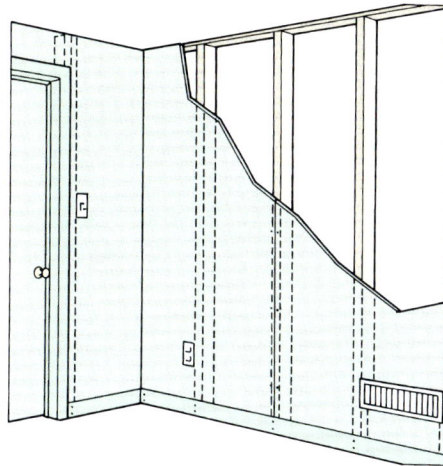

Detective work ▲

Trying to find wall studs can be a frustrating business. Here are a couple of clues to look for: nails on the upper edge of skirting boards go into studs; power points attach to studs and air conditioning ducts run between studs. Also look for plasterboard joints and nail heads (which you may see better at night when you can angle a bright light across the wall surface). Once you've found one stud, you should be able to find the others at 450 or 600 mm intervals, measuring from the centre of one stud to the centre of the next.

Sensitive stud

When nailing, drilling or screwing into a stud, don't use a drill or fastener that penetrates more than 25 mm into the timber. Water pipes and electrical wiring are sometimes routed through the centre of a stud, and any damage will be difficult to repair. Always try to locate the stud's centre. If you're too far off centre, the fastener may go through the side and lose holding power.

TOOLS OF THE TRADE

STUD FINDERS

An electronic stud finder is a handy battery-powered device with a sensor that detects differences in wall density. To use it, you press a button and pass the finder over the wall. A light goes on when the finder reaches the edge of a stud and goes out when it passes over the other edge. Some electronic stud finders are self-calibrating; others have to be calibrated to a wall's density before you can use them.

The simpler magnetic stud finder contains a magnet that swivels like a compass needle when it passes over nails in a stud. Magnetic stud finders work best when used just below the ceiling or just above the floor, where the studs are nailed to top and bottom plates.

Both types of stud finders can be misled by pipes, metal cables, foil-backed insulation and other framing members. And neither works well on plaster walls.

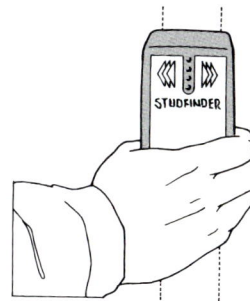

TIMBER WALL PANELLING

Installing panelling

Period of adjustment

Panelling tends to shrink or expand with changes in humidity in the first few days after you get the panels home. To minimise problems after installation, let the panels adjust to their new home first. Separate the panels after delivery, and stand each one up in the area where you plan to install it. Over the course of a couple of days the panels will adjust to the room's humidity; then you can install them without fear of movement.

The perfect panel

The key to perfect panelling is getting the first panel straight—the rest should follow suit. Align the first panel against a corner, and tack it in place with a single nail centred in the top. Use a level to make sure the panel is straight and plumb. If the plumbed panel doesn't fit snugly against the adjoining wall, use a pair of compasses to scribe the panel edge next to the wall (p. 71), copying the profile of the wall onto the panel. Remove the panel, trim to fit, then nail or glue into place.

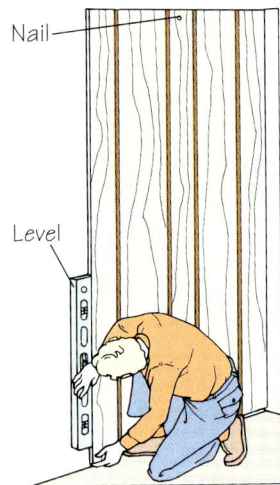

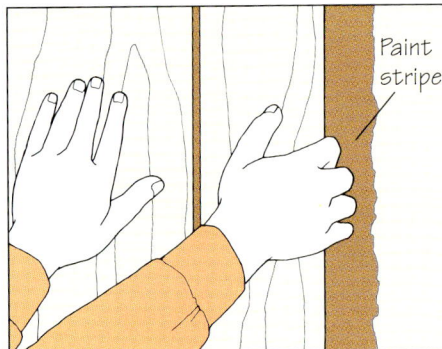

Nail

Level

Paint stripe

Concealing gaps ▲

When you're putting up timber planks as panelling, it's almost inevitable that there will be some space visible between adjoining panels. This can be a real problem when you're installing some dark panelling over a light-coloured wall, because the wall will peek through the open joints. To avoid this, brush a 75 or 100 mm stripe of paint—the same colour as the panel joints—on the wall behind each seam before installing the panels. Use a small roller or can of spray paint to speed the work up. Alternatively, use planks with a shiplap or tongue-and-groove profile.

Warped panels

Even fresh-from-the-factory panelling may be warped. As long as the problem isn't too severe, and the warped panels aren't more than 10 mm thick, you can mount them successfully using both panel adhesive and panelling nails. (Panel adhesive is made specifically for installing panelling and wallboard.) If the panelling is thick or badly warped, however, you'll be better off returning it.

For a firm, clean job

Before mounting panelling over bare framing, or furring strips on masonry walls, make sure that the framing or battens are aligned both down and along the wall. Small shims may be needed between some battens and the wall to correctly align them if they are out of place. If the framing has members that project beyond the rest then they will have to be planed back. If a stud or noggin is hollow, pack it up.

Nail disguise

To camouflage nails in panelling, place them in the grooves milled in the timber, and finish with a nail punch. Some panels allow for 'secret' nailing, where subsequent sheets cover the nail heads.

Finish now, fill later

Fill nail holes after you stain and varnish your panelling. This allows you to match the putty colour to the finished look of the wood. If you fill the nail holes before staining, the putty will absorb the stain differently than the wood, causing the holes to stand out. ▼

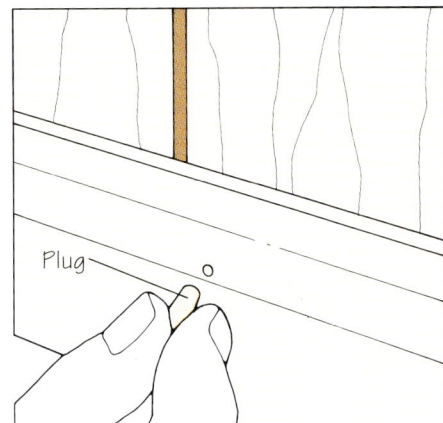

Plug

CEILINGS

Ceiling tiles

An appealing ceiling

To keep ceiling tiles clean while you're installing them, dip your fingers in cornstarch before handling each tile—the powder will shield the tiles from smudges. A little extra powder in one pocket of your tool apron will save you lots of trips up and down the ladder.

Half tile

Tongue tapped ▲

Tongue-and-groove ceiling tiles often don't fit together snugly when installed. To ensure a good fit, cut one tile in half and use it as a striker panel to coax the other tiles into place. Butt the tongue of the cut panel into the groove of the tile being fitted; a light hammer tap on the cut tile will nudge the full tile into place without damaging it. When the striker panel becomes worn, throw it away and use another half tile.

Graceful grid ▶

You can't eliminate the metal grid supporting a suspended ceiling, but you can soften its look. Mount decorative cornice or scotia moulding around the edge of the room to give the ceiling a more elegant, finished look.

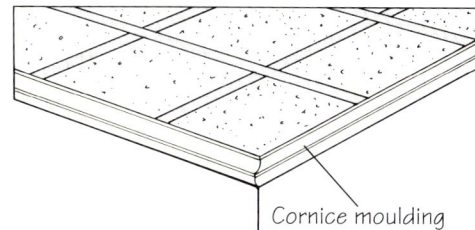
Cornice moulding

Patching plasterboard

The cardboard butler

If you have to cut into a plasterboard ceiling, do it from the roof space if possible. You'll avoid the risk of cutting unseen wires (and keep dust out of your face). Reduce mess by putting a box on the floor below to catch debris.

Corkscrew

Corkscrew handle ▲

If you can only cut into a plasterboard ceiling from below, twist a corkscrew into the centre of the waste area first; then use it as a handle to keep the piece from landing on your head. For smooth, easy-to-patch edges, cut with a utility knife. Always turn off the power to any ceiling lights at the meter box before making a blind cut into the ceiling.

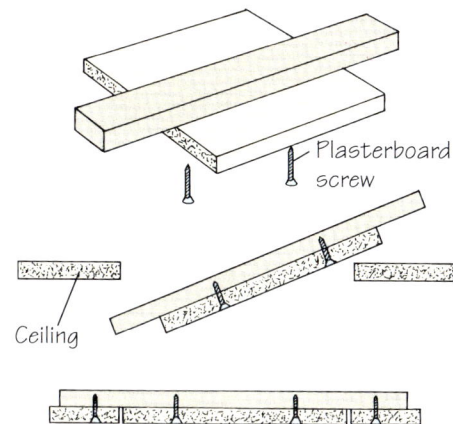
Plasterboard screw
Ceiling

Hole fixes ▲

To patch a moderate-sized hole in a plasterboard ceiling, trim and square up the damaged area, and cut out a plasterboard patch that's slightly smaller than the opening. Then screw (or glue) a timber cleat, such as a furring strip, to the back of the patch. Make the cleat about 150 mm longer than the patch so that it extends about 75 mm on each side. Tilt and drop the patch into position, and screw the cleat to the ceiling. Finish the joints with tape and jointing cement. For a large hole, trim the opening to the centre of the ceiling joists on either side and secure the patch to the joists. Repair a small hole with tape and jointing cement (p. 129).

FLOORS

Squeaking solutions

Shim to the rescue

Squeaking is one of the most exasperating floor problems. The cause is usually wood rubbing against wood or a nail. To stop a squeak caused by the movement of the flooring against a joist, tap a wooden shim between the joist and the floorboard in the vicinity of the squeak. Don't force it in too far, though, or you'll cause more problems than you solve. Dab a little construction adhesive on the shim before installation. ▼

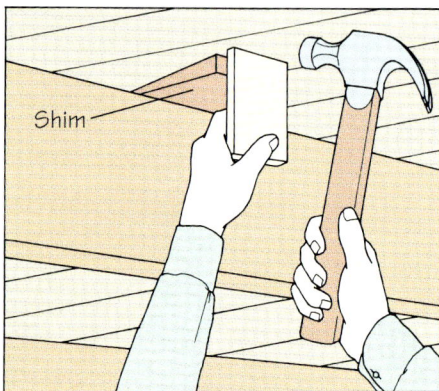

Shim

Squeak end work

Carpet replacement time offers a great opportunity to track down and eliminate squeaks in an unfinished floor that's otherwise always covered. After the carpet is up, walk over the entire area to find the squeaks. Wherever there's a problem, run 50 mm countersunk wood screws through the floorboards into the joist below. A line of existing nails is the best clue to the location of a joist.

Construction adhesive

Glue a squeak ▲

Sometimes you fix a squeak in one place only to find that it has moved to another spot. One squeak-stopper you can quickly apply to large areas of a floor is construction adhesive. Put a tube in a caulking gun and run a bead of the adhesive along both sides of a joist, right where it supports the floorboards. The squeaks should be gone for good.

Sneaky squeak stoppers

The best fix for a squeaky floor is to eliminate the most common culprit: the rubbing of wood against wood. But if this isn't possible, try lubricating the squeak. Any number of lubricants have been known to work, including talcum powder, furniture wax, lubricant spray, graphite and liquid soap. Sometimes linseed oil or teak oil dribbled into the cracks between floorboards will expand the wood enough to tighten the flooring.

Better yet, get home earlier

Squeaky stairs? Screw metal shelf brackets to the underside of the stair to silence them. The brackets needn't be large, but make sure the screws don't poke through to the tread or riser.

Braced for action

Squeaky floors are often caused by floor blocking that has worked loose over the years, allowing the joists to move a bit when the floor above them is walked on. The solution is easy: just reattach the blocking with 50 mm nails. ▼

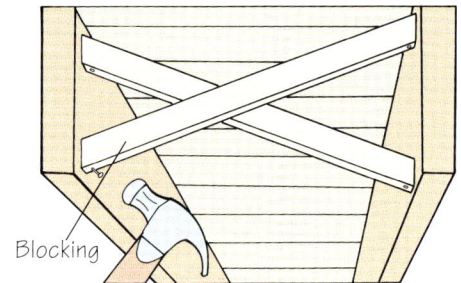

Blocking

Repairing strip flooring

A fix from below

Sometimes you can stop squeaking in strip flooring by screwing a 50 × 50 mm timber batten to the underside of the floor, about halfway between, and parallel to the floor joists. Use an ample layer of construction adhesive to make the cure even more effective. ▼

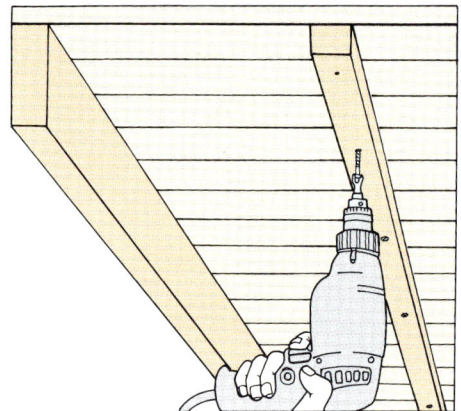

Wayward board

Before you go to the effort of replacing a warped floorboard, try this solution. Strip the finish from the offending board and cover it with a damp cloth for a couple of days. If the moisture temporarily solves the problem, secure the board with countersunk wood screws before it dries and springs back.

Removing a damaged board

Taking out a damaged portion of a floorboard calls for some care and precision. Whenever possible, remove an entire board or at least a length equal to the distance between three joists. If you have to make a crosscut, use a carpenter's square as a guide to mark the cut line. Then drill several overlapping holes just inside the line. Split the board with a chisel, and prise out the pieces carefully, centre piece first. Finally use a sharp wide chisel to square off the opening, using the cut line as a guide.

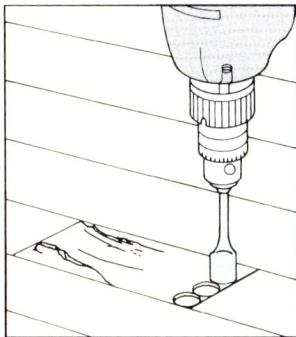

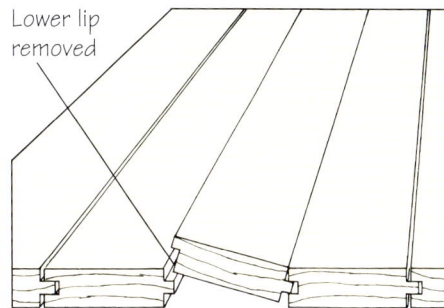

Lower lip removed

Replacing damaged boards ▲

Once you've removed boards from a strip floor, replacing them is simply a matter of lining up the tongues and grooves and nailing the boards into place. Simple, that is, until you get to the last board. The trick to fitting it is to chisel off the lower lip on the board's groove side. With the lip gone, and the tongue rounded off a little, the board can be tapped into place. You'll have to nail through the surface of the board to secure it, but putty over the countersunk nails should conceal your work.

Nailing tip

Whenever you use nails to secure strip flooring, drive them into the floor at an angle. An angled nail is less likely to work itself loose later on.

Save your knees

A large block of rigid polystyrene plastic foam from a discarded appliance carton makes a great kneeling pad when you're working on the floor. It is easy on the knees and it won't scratch the floor finish.

Too much spring

If your floor is bouncing excessively, it is often simply a matter of checking under the floor to see whether the floor bearers are properly supported on their piers (piles). If one or two of the piers have sunk slightly over the years, place some rot-proof packing—such as pieces of fibrous cement—between the bearers and the piers to take up any slight movement. Slight jacking may be necessary to get the packing into place. If the pier has moved noticeably, or tilted, it will need to be rebuilt to the correct height.

Floor stiffeners

The bounce of an old floor may be due to tired or undersized floor joists. If the joists are accessible from below, here's an inexpensive solution. Attach lengths of 12 mm plywood—at least 250 mm wide—to one side of each joist, securing it with construction adhesive and two rows of 50 mm nails spaced about 150 mm apart. Adding these plywood braces to the centre of each joist should stiffen the floor noticeably. ▼

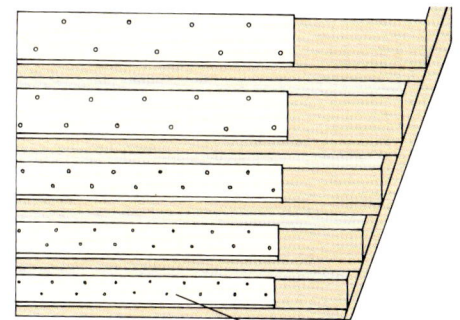

Plywood brace

FLOOR COVERINGS

Carpeting tricks

Pile plugs

To patch small burns or stains in a carpet that has been glued down, file the end of a short length of copper pipe into a sharp cutting edge. Put the sharpened pipe over the carpet and hit it with a mallet to remove a circular plug around the damage. Repeat the procedure on a matching carpet scrap or hidden section of carpeting to create a replacement plug. Dab adhesive on the plug, align its fibres with the surrounding carpet, and set it in place.

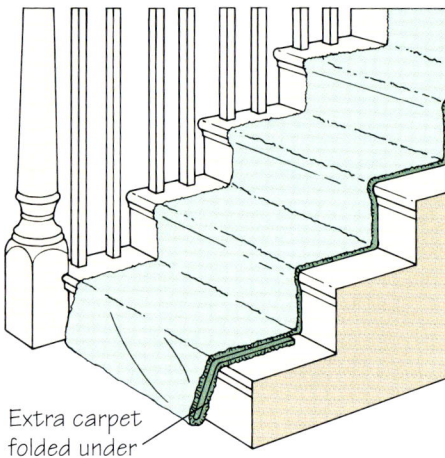

Extra carpet folded under

Carpet retreads ▲

If you're replacing the runner on the stairs, buy an extra 500 mm. When you install the carpet, fold under the extra length at the bottom of the stairs. When the carpet begins to wear—usually along the projecting nose of each tread—just untack the runner, shift it up 50 mm or so and reattach it. You should be able to do this at least two or three times over the life of the carpet.

Good brews for removing glue

Here's a mixture you can use to remove dried carpet adhesive from a floor. Mix one part vinegar with three parts water, and apply the mixture to the floor. Let it stand for 30 minutes or so, and then scrape up the adhesive with a wide, stiff putty knife or paint scraper. Sometimes you can get away with using just hot water instead: the heat alone may be able to soften the dried adhesive enough for you to remove it.

Carpeting at the threshold

Fastening carpet at the threshold between two rooms can be tricky. If the finished floor in one room is more than 12 mm higher than the floor to be carpeted in the other room, use a cover strip to hold the carpet down near the threshold, just as in the rest of the room. But if the difference between the two floors is less than this, you'll have to staple the carpet directly to the floor. Cut the carpet underlay back about 25 mm from the edge of the threshold. Then tuck the edge of the carpeting under about 25 mm to cover the area that does not have underlay. Spread the carpet pile apart and staple through both layers of carpet into the floor. ▼

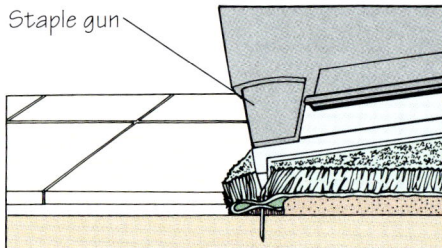

Staple gun

Removing vinyl tiles

A pressing solution

Heat is usually the key to removing vinyl floor tiles. If you need to remove a damaged tile, place a cloth over it and move an iron, turned to a medium setting, across the cloth with slow, even strokes. The heat will soften both the adhesive and the tile, making it possible to prise up the tile with a putty knife. ▼

Shiver your tiles

If heat doesn't help remove a tile, try cold. Place dry ice on the tile (but be careful not to touch the ice directly). Once the tile is cold enough, a smart tap with a hammer should shatter it.

Second-hand tiles

If you want to reuse loose, undamaged floor tiles, you'll have to remove the adhesive clinging to their backs. You can scrape it off with a paint scraper, but it's much easier to soak the tiles in water overnight to soften the adhesive and then remove it with a putty knife.

Repairing vinyl floors

Clear cover

A scrape or heavy scuffing that removes the clear top layer on vinyl flooring can result in the quick deterioration of the layers below. To repair such damage, simply coat it with vinyl seam sealant (sold by flooring outlets). If the flooring has a deeper gouge, replace the tile or the section of sheet vinyl (right).

Bursting bubbles

Water leakage or dampness can cause sheet vinyl to bubble. The repair is easy once you've eliminated the source of the problem and let the floor dry thoroughly. Cut a slit in the centre of the bubble with a utility knife. Then use a plastic tomato sauce or mustard bottle (with a pointed tip) or a glue syringe to squirt vinyl floor adhesive through the slit. Work the adhesive under the bubble with a narrow putty knife or a sliver of wood. Then press the bubble down with a rolling pin, wipe up any excess adhesive, and weight the area until the adhesive sets. ▼

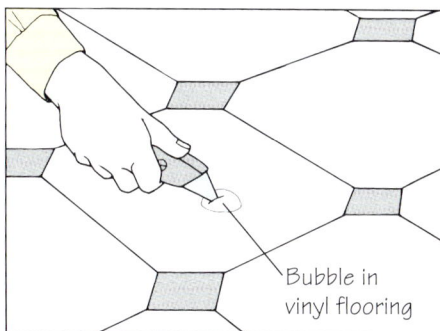

Bubble in vinyl flooring

FLOORING PATCH

To patch a damaged section of sheet vinyl flooring, use a piece left over from the original job or 'stolen' from a hidden place, such as the back of a cupboard or the floor under the refrigerator. The patch should be 25 mm larger all around than the damage. Whenever possible, plan for the patch seams to follow a pattern line in the flooring.

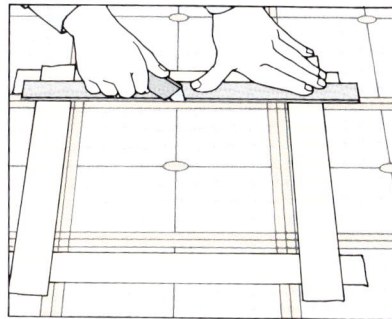

1 Place the patch over the damage, align it with the pattern, and secure it with sticky tape. Use a sharp utility knife guided by a straightedge to cut through the patch and the flooring. Then prise out the damaged material and scrape out all the old adhesive.

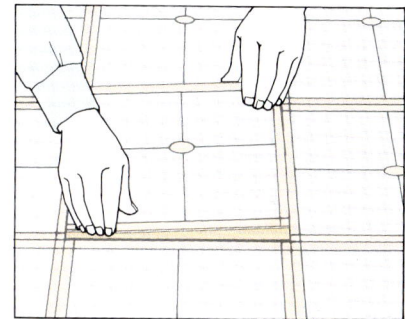

2 Spread vinyl floor adhesive on the back of the patch, fit it into place, and wipe off any excess adhesive with a damp cloth. Weight the patch overnight until the adhesive sets. Then apply vinyl seam sealer to the seams around the patch to bond it to the flooring.

Laying sheet vinyl

Strong-arm flooring

Sheet vinyl covers large areas quickly. But before installing it, you must flatten and trim the rolled material to fit the room. Getting it to stay flat straight off the roll can be daunting. If the weather is warm, spread the sheet outside in the sun to relax it. In winter, try covering the sheet with an electric blanket to warm it and get out the curls.

Nick relief

If you nick or tear vinyl flooring while laying it, disguise the damage with a bathroom sealant in a closely matching colour. Dab a little into the damage and wipe off the excess with a damp cloth.

Procrastinators, this one's for you

To remove floor adhesive from your tools, toss them in the freezer overnight. In the morning you'll be able to chip off the hardened adhesive. Wear goggles to protect your eyes from flying shards.

CERAMIC TILES

Working with tiles

Mixing tiles

By the time you have to replace a tile, you may not be able to find a match. Instead of trying to match existing tiles, remove some extra tiles to form an interesting pattern and replace them with tiles of a contrasting colour or design.

Thinking ahead

For your next tiling project buy half-a-dozen or so extra tiles for future repairs. Wrap them carefully to prevent breakage, and mark the package with the date, the name of the shop they came from and the room to which they belong. Also save some matching grout.

Chipped tile?

You can repair nicks or chips in ceramic tiles with appliance touch-up paint. It dries to a hard, glossy surface, but comes in a limited range of colours.

Marking tiles

During any tiling job you'll have to cut tiles into odd shapes. To mark a line, use a felt-tipped pen or Chinagraph pencil; if you need a precise line, scratch it with a plasterboard screw.

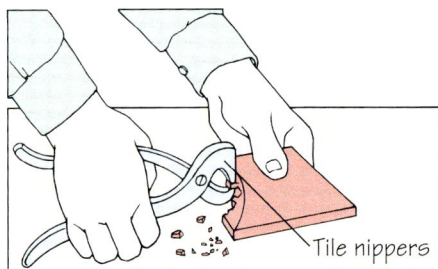
Tile nippers

Nibble a cut ▲

When using tile nippers to make a cut out, start at the edge in the centre of the waste area and work toward the cut line. To avoid ragged edges, keep the jaws parallel to the cut line and place no more than two-thirds of the jaw surface on the tile for each bite. Smooth the edges with 80-grit emery paper.

Life is like that

Poor sealing is a sure way to spoil the look of any tiling job. For professional results, take a tip from painters and reach for the masking tape. Run tape along both sides of your planned line of sealant, apply the sealant, smooth it down and then carefully lift away the tape. You'll get a sealant line with crisp, ruler-straight edges. ▼

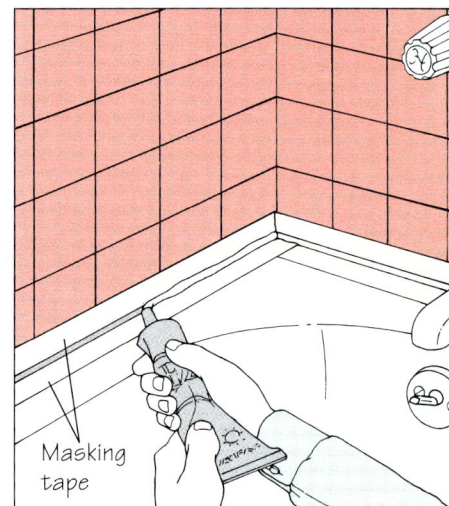
Masking tape

Picking between tiles

When replacing a tile, make sure your new tile is squarely aligned. Round toothpicks make perfect spacers for holding the tile in place while the adhesive sets (see step four, facing page).

Grout match

Matching new grout with existing grout can be tricky. To increase your chance for success, buy a small amount of grout first, mix up a sample batch and let it dry for three days or so. You'll get a much better idea of how the colour will compare to the existing grout.

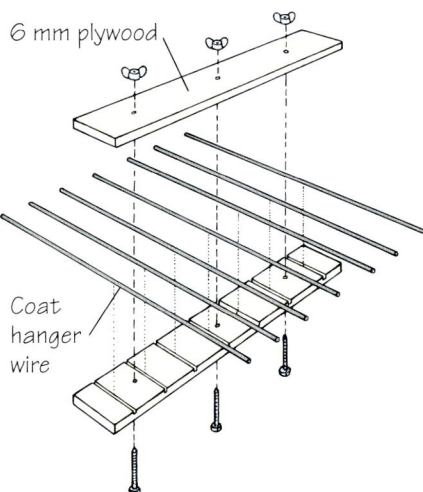
6 mm plywood
Coat hanger wire

◀ Shape shifting

Fitting tiles around irregular projections can be tricky. If you have several to do, make your own contour gauge by sandwiching lengths of coat hanger wire between scraps of 6 mm plywood. Fit the wires into saw kerfs in the bottom piece, spacing the kerfs to suit the degree of accuracy you need. (The more wires you use, the more accurate the tool will be.) Fasten the pieces together with small wing nuts and bolts. To use the gauge, push the ends of its wires against an obstruction until they take on its shape; then move the gauge to the tiles or to paper and trace the cut line.

REPLACING A CERAMIC TILE

Ceramic tiles are durable and stain-resistant, but sooner or later one may crack and need replacement. Fortunately the job isn't that difficult. You'll have to scrape out the surrounding grout, chip out the damaged tile and replace it with a new one, and finally regrout the area around the new tile. If the damaged tile is in a bath or shower surround, the repair is one you shouldn't postpone. A cracked tile allows water to seep behind it, and over time this will damage the plasterboard or other material under the tile. Eventually the moisture will multiply your problems by loosening surrounding tiles. Here's how to get the job done quickly.

1 If the tile is over the bath, use cardboard or an old blanket to protect the bath surface and keep debris out of the drain. Remove any fixture that is covering the tile, such as the spout shown here.

2 Scrape the old grout from around the edges of the damaged tile with a grout saw or a broken hacksaw blade. Work carefully to avoid chipping the edges of the surrounding tiles.

Grout saw

3 Wearing safety goggles, use a sharp cold chisel and a ball-pein hammer to crack the tile in an X-pattern. Tap lightly to avoid damaging other tiles. Prise out the pieces, and chip out the old adhesive.

4 Shape the new tile as needed (facing page). Spread 3 mm of tile adhesive on the back, press it into place and use tape or spacers to hold it. Scrape excess adhesive from joints and wipe clean.

5 When the adhesive cures, press grout into the joints and wipe off any excess with a damp sponge. When the grout is dry use a soft cloth to burnish off any haze from the tile surface.

WINDOWS

Quick fixes

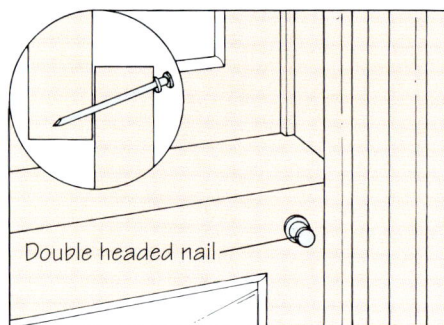

Double headed nail

Nail order ▲

Here's a cost-effective security measure for double-hung windows. Drill a hole through the inner sash and halfway into the outer sash. Then slip a nail into the hole to prevent anyone from pushing the sashes open from the outside. If you angle the hole slightly, the nail won't jiggle out. If you use a double-headed nail, you'll be able to remove it easily.

Lazy guard

Nearly any sliding window or door can get a simple security boost. Cut a dowel or bead to fit flat in the window track. This will prevent the sash from sliding open even if the lock is jemmied. ▼

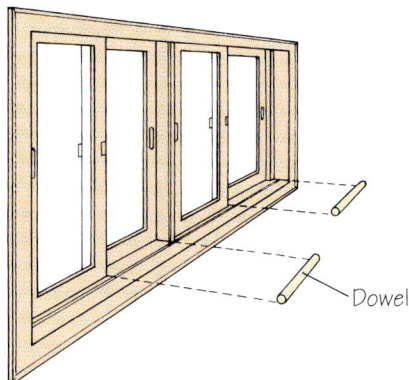

Dowel

Sticking sash?

A window may stick for any number of reasons—including warped or swollen wood or accumulated dirt or paint. Before undertaking major repairs, try lubricating the channels with a little soap, candle wax or silicone spray. ▼

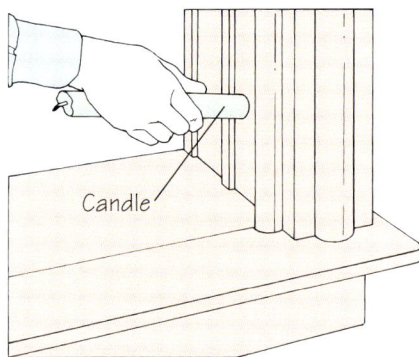

Candle

Stain be gone

Some windows feature vinyl or PVC-clad frames to improve their weather resistance. If you accidentally drip or brush stain or paint onto the frames while working on the surrounding cladding, do not use sandpaper or steel wool to remove it. Instead, dab the stain off with naphtha or mineral turpentine. A slower method, but one that's easier on the vinyl, is to scrub it with a hand cleaner containing lanolin. Before using a cleaning compound, first spot-test it on an unobtrusive portion of the frame.

Removing glass

Upright proposition

Always carry and store a pane of glass, particularly a thin one, in a vertical position. Otherwise, the glass may break under its own weight.

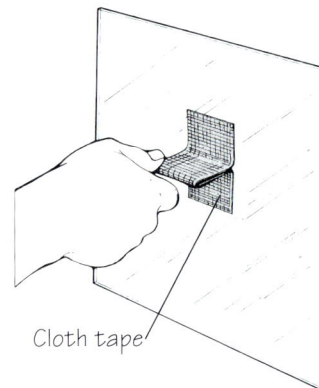

Cloth tape

Handle on a roll ▲

Even a small pane of glass can be unwieldy when you're trying to manoeuvre it into place, so give it a handle. Fold a length of cloth tape into a tab that you can grab. On a large pane use two.

Another glass carrier

To carry a sizable pane of glass safely and easily, slit two short sections of old garden hose and slip them over both the top and bottom edges of the glass.

Slit garden hose

Safety strategies

Most injuries connected with repairing broken windows occur while removing the glass. If you remove the putty first, the glass will be loosened enough for you to prise it from the window. Always wear canvas or leather gloves and goggles when handling broken glass.

Cloth tape

Combine and conquer ▲

Use wide cloth tape to hold together all the pieces of a broken pane while you're removing the putty and sprigs. When you're finished, just lift out the glass or press it out from the back side.

Pull, don't push

When removing broken glass, pull the shards toward you; if they break, any slivers will be directed away from you. Don't forget to wear gloves and goggles.

Installing panes

Don't be a pane killer

When you measure for the new glass, remember that a snug-fitting pane can easily crack when the window frame moves or shrinks. That's why glass should be cut about 3 mm smaller overall than the height and width of the actual opening. Cut the glass yourself (p. 99) or let a glass merchant do it.

Well-prepared rebate

Before installing a new pane, scrape and sand the rebate (the notch in the edge of the sash that the pane fits into). Then give it a coat of primer or oil stain. This will keep the wood from absorbing the oil in the glazing putty.

Pane bed

To cushion the glass, even out irregularities in the wood, and create a weathertight joint, put a bead of putty on the rebate of the sash before setting in the glass. Work the putty in your hands before using to soften it up. If the putty is old, discard it and buy a new tub.

Ear points

Traditional triangular glazier's sprigs are tricky to use. Instead, buy glazier's points with 'ears', which make them easy to press into the window frame with a stiff putty knife. If you have to use regular glazier's sprigs, use the putty that oozes from behind the pane to hold them in place while you tap them in. If you have nothing else to hand, you can use small panel pins instead of proper glazing sprigs. ▼

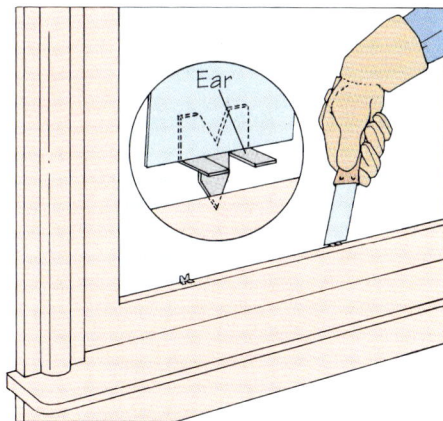

Ear

Roll a rope

Applying the layer of glazing putty around a new pane is much easier if you roll a lump of putty between your hands to form an even rope-like length. Then just press the rope into place along the joint and smooth it. ▼

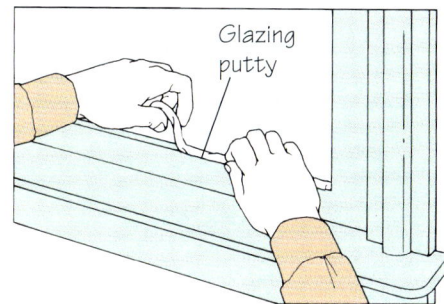

Glazing putty

Nonstick knife

When smoothing glazing putty, dip your putty knife blade in pure turpentine, mineral turpentine or paint thinner now and then. This will keep the putty from sticking to the blade. ▼

Take your time

After installing a new windowpane, wait about a week or so for the putty to cure before painting it. When you do paint, lap the paint just a bit onto the glass to seal the edge of the putty.

DOORS

Easy improvements

A good first impression

The hardwood threshold beneath an exterior door can be a thing of beauty, at least until time and weather take their toll. To restore and protect a weather-worn threshold, first strip or sand off any remaining finish. Then apply a generous coat of boiled linseed oil to the threshold; let it soak in for 30 minutes, and wipe off the excess. Repeat the process about 24 hours later. Let the threshold dry completely; then finish it with two or more coats of marine varnish.

Handing a door

A door can be hung so that it opens either to the right or to the left, depending on personal preference. Make sure, however, that you mount hinges, locks and handles on the correct edges. With lightweight, hollow-core doors, special blocks are included in the construction to accept door furniture. There will be a label on the door edge showing on which side locks must be mounted. ▼

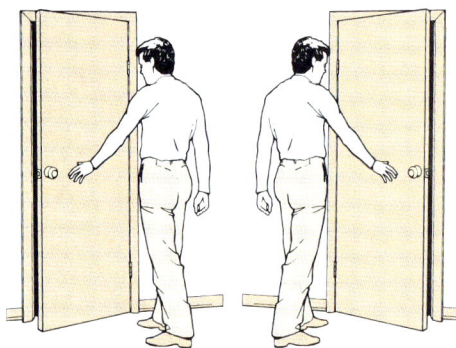

Left-handed door   Right-handed door

Ink a lock

To make sure the latch of a deadlatch lock or lockset aligns with the striker plate, mark the latch with an ink pad (or chalk), then close the door and move the latch against the jamb to make an imprint. Use this to align the plate.

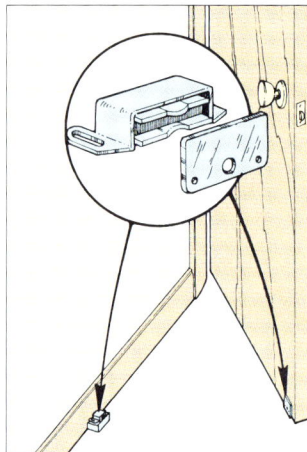

Open-door policy ▲

Bothered by an interior door that slams shut whenever a breeze blows or you walk by it? Screw a magnetic cupboard door catch to the floor, with its striker plate on the back of the door. Make sure the catch is far enough out from the skirting board to allow for the doorknob. If necessary, mount it on a small block of wood to raise it high enough to contact the bottom of the door.

Now you see it

Many people forget to paint or finish the bottom and top edges of a door, and that's a big mistake. Unsealed edges provide access to moisture, which can cause swelling and warping and peeling paint. Coat the edges with an exterior paint or penetrating sealer.

Taming slippery hinges

It's important to mark the position of a butt hinge so that door and jamb match exactly. But it's hard to hold a hinge leaf in place as you mark around it because the pencil tends to follow the grain of the wood and cause the hinge to move. The trick is to use a sharp pencil and press lightly. Another solution is to temporarily screw the hinge in place or stick it down with double-sided tape while you trace around it.

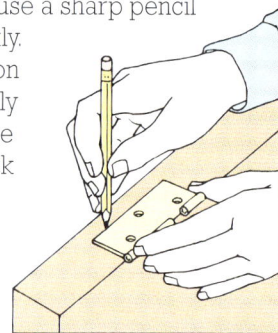

Pop goes the pin

You can remove the pins in loose-pin hinges without damaging the hinge barrel by slipping a nail into the hole at the bottom of the barrel, then driving the nail (and pin) upward with a tap.

Securing the perimeter

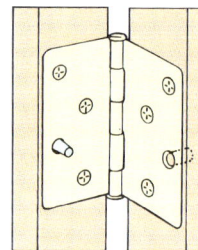

If its hinge pins are exposed, locking an outward opening door offers little security because the pins, and then the door itself, can be removed. To make a break-in less easy, remove two opposite middle screws from a hinge. Run a long screw part of the way into the jamb side of the hinge, and cut off the screw's head with a hacksaw, letting the shank stick out about 6 mm. When you close the door, the shank will fit into the opposite hinge hole, securing the door.

INSTALLING A RIM DEADLOCK

A surface-mounted, or rim, deadlock is just about the strongest door lock available. It's also easier to install than an in-the-door cylindrical deadlock, making it a good choice for anyone without extensive woodworking skills or time. Any locksmith, or well-stocked suburban hardware store, will carry a variety of good-quality rim deadlocks.

1 Cut the outline of the striker plate onto the jamb with a utility knife; then chisel a mortise for the striker plate. Attach the plate, using long screws that penetrate the studs.

2 Tape the paper template that comes with the lock to the door directly opposite the striker plate. Use a nail to mark the centres of the holes you'll be drilling for the lock cylinder and housing screws.

3 Use a hole saw to drill the cylinder hole. (To prevent splintering, drill until the pilot bit pokes through the other side; then finish from the other side.) Drill pilot holes for the housing screws.

4 Mount the lock cylinder and backplate in the hole. The bolts for attaching the cylinder and the connecting bar are notched so that they can easily be cut to fit doors of different thicknesses. Use side-cutting pliers or nippers to cut them, and wear safety goggles to protect your eyes against flying metal pieces.

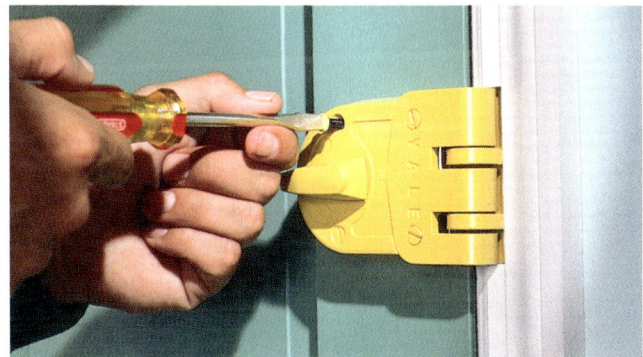

5 Slip the lock into place, and make sure the connecting bar in the cylinder meshes correctly with the lock. Check the fit of the lock by engaging and disengaging the deadlock with the striker plate. If it's in order, drive the housing screws into place. Check the lock's operation carefully, inside and out.

SCREENS AND WINDOW INSULATION

Screen savers

Mosquito block

Even tiny holes can allow squadrons of mosquitoes to zoom through. Touch up small holes in your defensive screen with clear nail polish or shellac.

Screen guard

Any parent knows that screen doors and small children are not the best of friends. Little ones are in and out all day long, and when they can't reach the doorknob they push the screen on the way out. To prevent damage, cover the inside of the screen with a screen guard. Make it from flat aluminium bar, which is easy to bend and shape, and a piece of expanded metal mesh. Both items are readily available from most hardware shops.

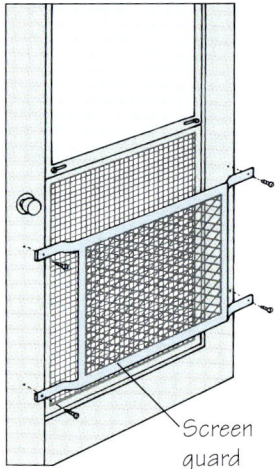

Screen guard

Quick repair

Fix a small puncture in a metal screen with clear sealant and left over screen. Trim around the hole so that the edges are neat and flat. Apply clear silicone sealant to the trimmed edges, and press on a patch slightly larger than the damaged area. Then smooth the sealant and clean up any excess. In a couple of days the sealant will become transparent, making an acceptable temporary repair.

Screen stretcher

The standard way to get insect screening tight on a timber frame is to work from the middle out, switching between the ends and the sides after every four or five staples and pulling the screening taut as you go. But if you have trouble, try this. Start with screening a bit longer than needed. Staple it to one end of the frame, working from the middle out. At the other end, staple the screening to a board held tightly against the edge. Press down on the board to stretch the screening as you staple that end. When stapling the sides, pull taut by hand.

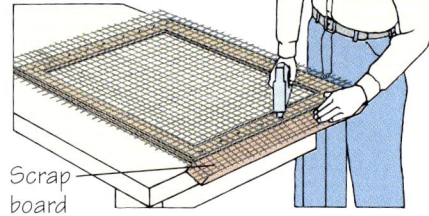

Scrap board

Screen pins

Some outward opening awning and casement windows require interior screens that are easy to remove so that you can fasten or wash the windows. Attach these screens with double-headed nails that slip into holes slightly larger than the nails' diameter. ▼

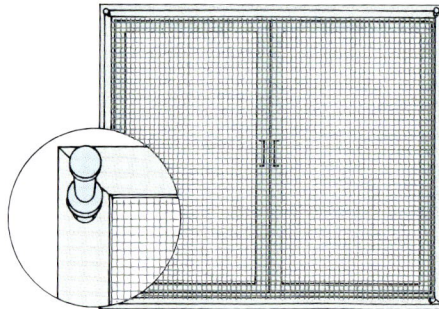

Window insulation

A combination to bet on

By all means replace old windows with double-glazed models. But to upgrade sound older windows, add a 'second window' to the interior. These are available from some glass merchants. They are installed on the interior of the reveals and, by trapping a body of still air between outer and inner windows, help to insulate against heat loss. If the glass panes are more than 80 mm apart they will also help to keep noise out as well.

Remote blind puller

Clear plastic sheeting inside a window is an expedient alternative to other forms of window insulation. But how do you operate a blind behind the plastic? Before installing the plastic, raise the blind all the way and attach clear fishing line to the bottom. Drill a tiny hole in the sill and thread the line through it. ▼

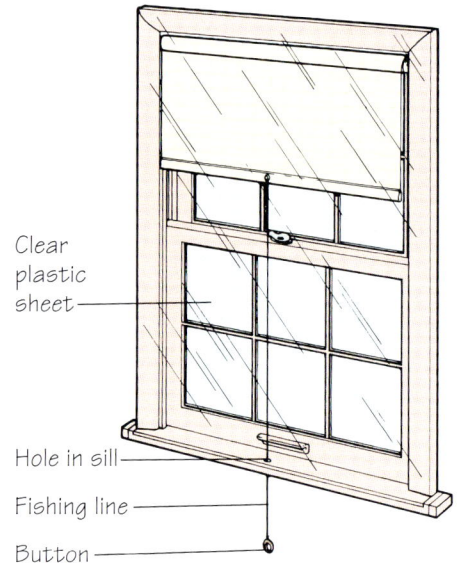

Clear plastic sheet

Hole in sill

Fishing line

Button

REPLACING A SCREEN

On most metal-framed screens the screening is held in place by a spline that fits into a groove. Most have vinyl splines that may need to be replaced—old, stiff vinyl may break if you try to reuse it. To get the right size, take a piece of the old spline to the shop. Also buy an inexpensive tool called a spline roller.

You can choose between fibreglass and aluminium or bronze screening. Fibreglass is not as durable, but it is less expensive and easier to handle. When installing metal screening, it helps to force it into the groove first with the roller before installing the spline. Also, snip the corners of the screen off at an angle to reduce bunching.

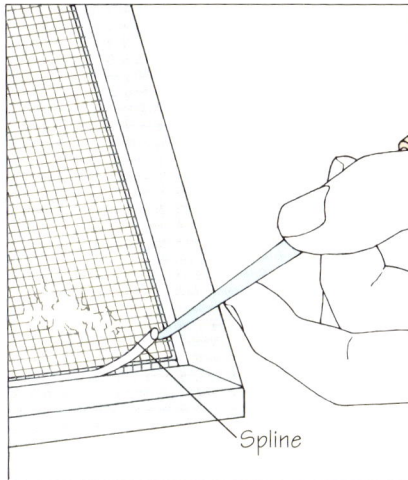

1 Remove the old splines with an awl or a thin screwdriver. Remove splines carefully so that you can reuse them afterwards. Discard the old screen.

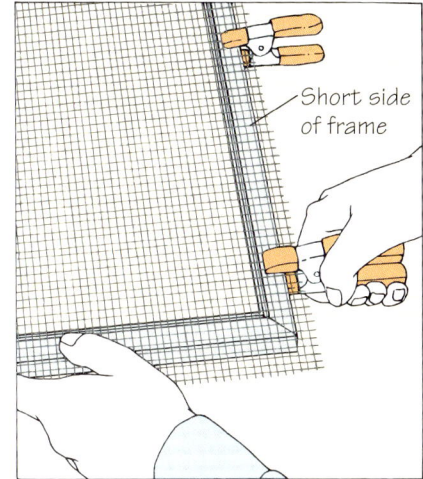

Spline

2 Cut new screening about 25 mm larger than the frame on all sides. Lay it over the frame evenly, and clamp it to one short side of the frame.

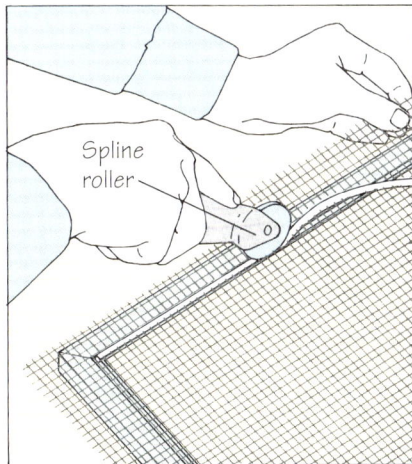

Short side of frame

3 Starting at a corner on the side opposite the clamps, pull the screening taut by hand, and gradually force the new spline into the groove with a spline roller.

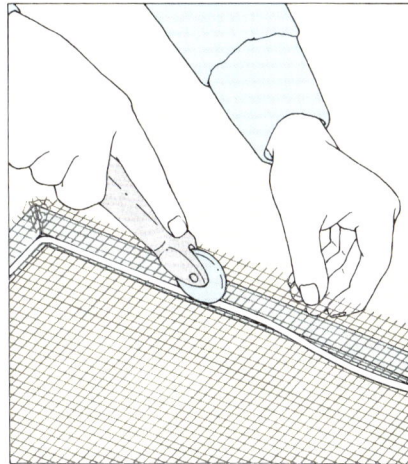

Spline roller

4 Continue the spline around the corner. After finishing all sides, use a screwdriver to push the spline down over the bunched screening at the corners.

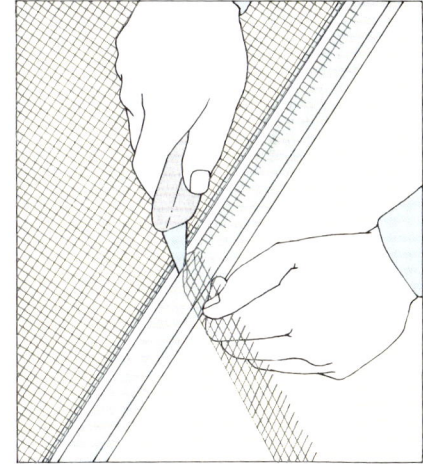

5 Trim off the excess screening around the edges of the groove with a sharp utility knife. You can guide the knife with a straightedge if you wish.

WEATHERPROOFING

Sealing

Timing the job
The best time to seal a joint outdoors is during the spring or autumn. That's when the width of the joint is halfway between its seasonal extremes.

Push or pull?
Even experts disagree about whether it's best to pull or push a caulking gun as you fill a crack. Actually both methods work well, as long as you force the sealant well into the crack. For the pull method, cut the sealant tube spout at a 45° angle, then hold the gun at a 60° angle as you pull it along the crack. For the push method, cut a double angle on the spout and hold the gun at a 45° angle as you push it along the crack. ▼

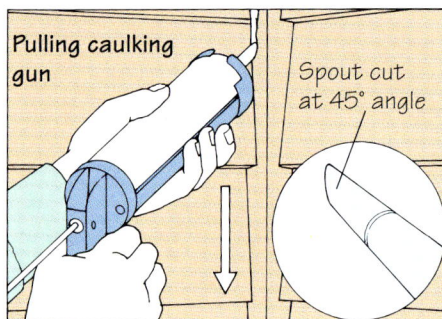

Pulling caulking gun

Spout cut at 45° angle

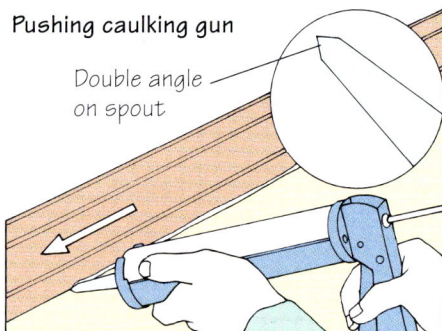

Pushing caulking gun

Double angle on spout

For better sealing
▷ Cut the nozzle opening slightly smaller than the bead you want. Keep the bead between 2 and 10 mm.
▷ To avoid jagged sealant lines, release and resqueeze the gun at a logical break, such as between weatherboards.
▷ Carry a rag to remove build-up on the nozzle, which can mess up the bead.
▷ If you've never applied sealant before, start work on a seldom seen part of the house while you gain experience.

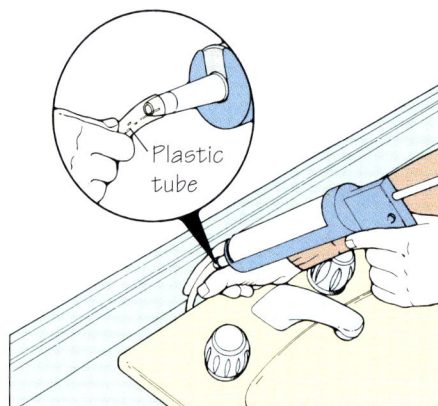

Plastic tube

Reach out to seal ▲
A plastic drinking straw, the sheathing of electrical cable, or a length of plastic tubing makes a handy extension tube for sealing hard-to-reach places. Secure your extender with cloth tape.

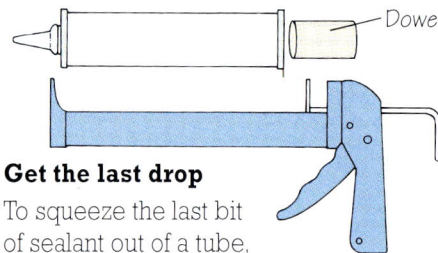

Dowel

Get the last drop
To squeeze the last bit of sealant out of a tube, put a short length of dowel or old broom handle between the caulking gun plunger and the tube.

A lick of advice
Don't smooth sealant with your finger. Some sealants contain harmful chemicals, and some are hard to remove from your skin. Get an inexpensive plastic smoothing tool, or use a plastic spoon or an ice cream or ice-block stick; any of these will do a tidier job than a finger.

Ice cube sealant smoother
To get an ultra-fine, attractive finish on a bead of sealant, smooth it with an ice cube. Use the heat from your hand to melt the cube to the bead shape you want. Then run it over the sealant.

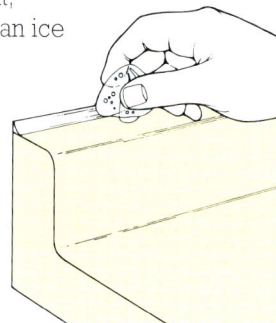

Sealant savers
The hardest part about preserving a partial tube of sealant is remembering—or taking the time—to do it. You can get handy screw-on caps or use one of many simple solutions:
▷ Insert a large galvanised flat-head nail or a small bolt.
▷ Cap the spout with a wire connector (the size normally used for domestic wire).
▷ Skewer the spout with a stopper made from a piece of clothes hanger wire.

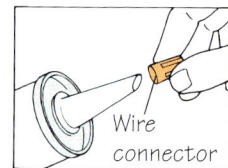

Wire connector

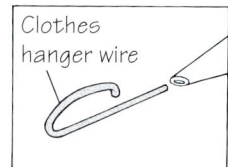

Clothes hanger wire

SEALANT BUYING GUIDE

The sealants here will fill your home's exterior needs and some interior ones as well. Not listed is plain latex sealant, which is suitable only for interior jobs such as filling gaps around trim. When buying a sealant, keep in mind that a standard tube will produce an average-size bead 12 to 15 m long—enough to seal about four windows or doors. If a crack is over 10 mm deep, stuff it with pieces of plastic foam before applying sealant. Besides tubes for caulking guns, sealant is available in smaller squeeze tubes for little jobs. Expanding foam in aerosol cans can be bought for filling extra-large gaps.

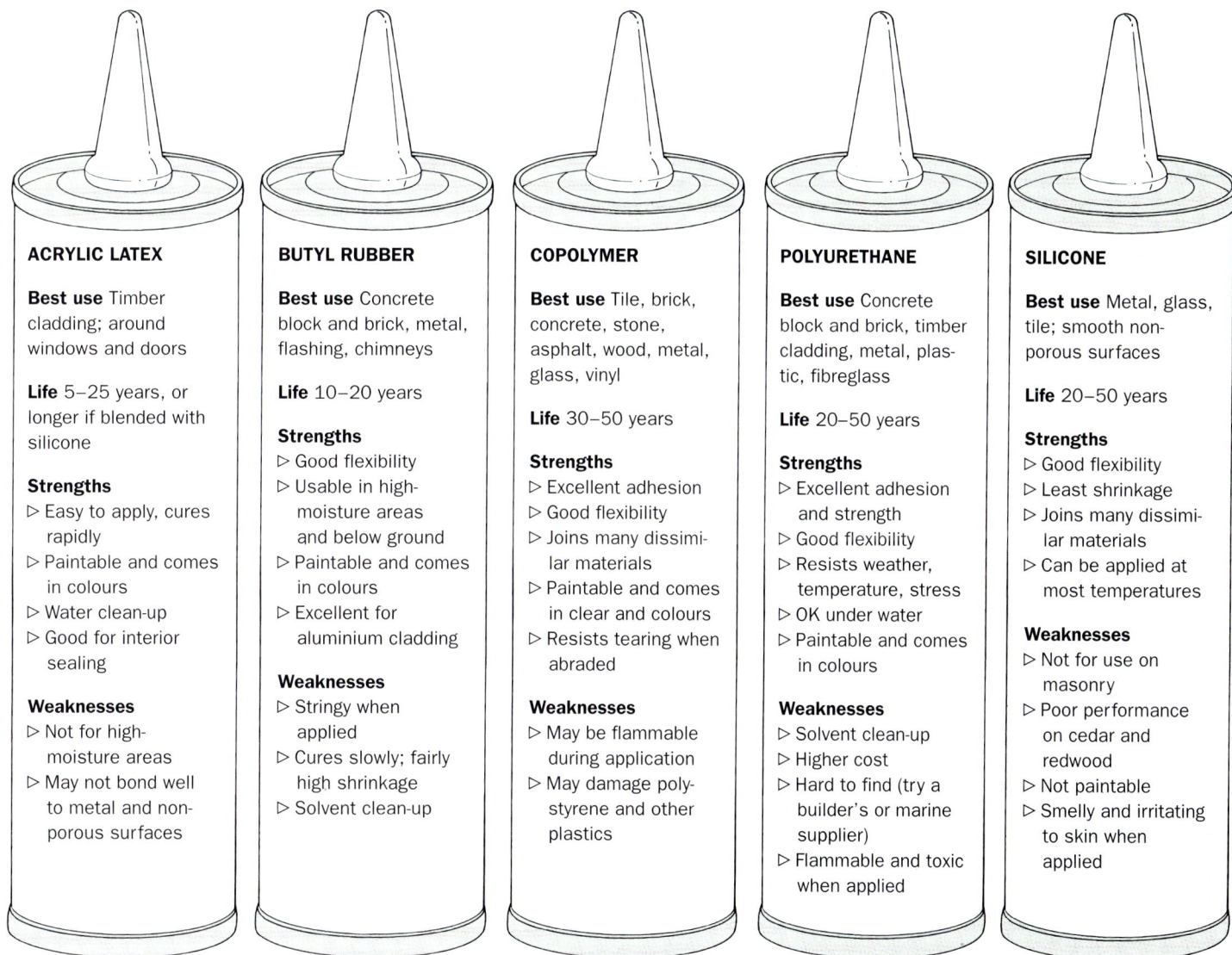

ACRYLIC LATEX

Best use Timber cladding; around windows and doors

Life 5–25 years, or longer if blended with silicone

Strengths
▷ Easy to apply, cures rapidly
▷ Paintable and comes in colours
▷ Water clean-up
▷ Good for interior sealing

Weaknesses
▷ Not for high-moisture areas
▷ May not bond well to metal and non-porous surfaces

BUTYL RUBBER

Best use Concrete block and brick, metal, flashing, chimneys

Life 10–20 years

Strengths
▷ Good flexibility
▷ Usable in high-moisture areas and below ground
▷ Paintable and comes in colours
▷ Excellent for aluminium cladding

Weaknesses
▷ Stringy when applied
▷ Cures slowly; fairly high shrinkage
▷ Solvent clean-up

COPOLYMER

Best use Tile, brick, concrete, stone, asphalt, wood, metal, glass, vinyl

Life 30–50 years

Strengths
▷ Excellent adhesion
▷ Good flexibility
▷ Joins many dissimilar materials
▷ Paintable and comes in clear and colours
▷ Resists tearing when abraded

Weaknesses
▷ May be flammable during application
▷ May damage polystyrene and other plastics

POLYURETHANE

Best use Concrete block and brick, timber cladding, metal, plastic, fibreglass

Life 20–50 years

Strengths
▷ Excellent adhesion and strength
▷ Good flexibility
▷ Resists weather, temperature, stress
▷ OK under water
▷ Paintable and comes in colours

Weaknesses
▷ Solvent clean-up
▷ Higher cost
▷ Hard to find (try a builder's or marine supplier)
▷ Flammable and toxic when applied

SILICONE

Best use Metal, glass, tile; smooth non-porous surfaces

Life 20–50 years

Strengths
▷ Good flexibility
▷ Least shrinkage
▷ Joins many dissimilar materials
▷ Can be applied at most temperatures

Weaknesses
▷ Not for use on masonry
▷ Poor performance on cedar and redwood
▷ Not paintable
▷ Smelly and irritating to skin when applied

WEATHERPROOFING

Weatherstripping

Locating leaks ▲
Cold air that leaks into your home is air that you have to heat. Take a close look around the perimeters of doors and windows. If you see any light, that's where air is coming in. Also run your hand—damp to improve sensitivity—around doors and windows to feel for draughts. Or hold a tissue next to them to see if incoming air causes it to move.

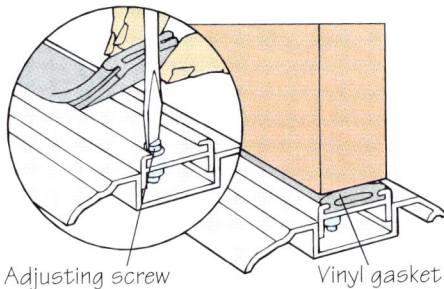

Adjusting screw   Vinyl gasket

At the threshold ▲
Closing the gap at the bottom of a door is an important defence against heat loss. One way is to install a new threshold with a vinyl gasket. An adjustable model—with screws to raise or lower its height—allows you to get it close to an uneven door without having to take the door down and trim it.

Some sticky advice
Self-adhesive weatherstripping doesn't last forever, but it is easy to install and is inconspicuous when used on the inner edges of the frames of doors and casement windows. The best adhesive-backed material to use is EPDM (ethylene propylene diene monomer) rubber weatherstripping. It's more expensive than felt or foam, but it's much more durable and moisture-resistant and provides an excellent seal.

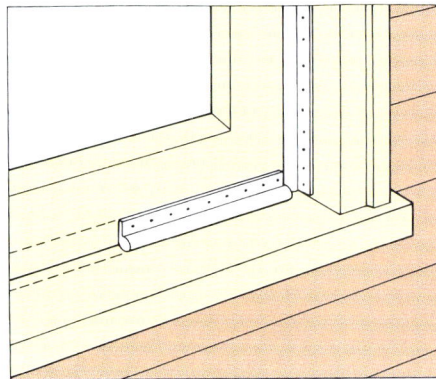

Get with the gasket ▲
An easy, inexpensive way to weatherstrip a window or door is with tubular vinyl gaskets. Nail or staple them on the opening's exterior so that they are not visible inside the house and are hidden from outside view if you have screens or shutters. On a door, attach the pieces to the trim at the sides and the top. On a window, attach the vertical pieces to the trim at the sides and the horizontal pieces to the sashes as shown. Don't worry about putting the gaskets outside; they are very durable and can withstand most temperatures and conditions.

Working with insulation

Safety cover-up
Fibreglass particles may be harmful. When working with fibreglass, wear goggles and a dual-cartridge respirator (p. 65). To keep itchy fibreglass slivers off your skin, wear long pants, a long-sleeved shirt, gloves and a hat. Tuck your sleeves into the cuffs of your gloves for extra protection. If you do get slivers on your skin, don't scratch them. Take a cool or tepid shower; hot water opens the pores, making the itching worse.

Cutting insulation batts
Trimming fibreglass insulation to length is not difficult if you use the squeeze-and-slice method. Place the insulation on a solid timber or plywood surface. Position a length of 100×50 mm timber along the cut line and press it down with your knee; then cut through the fibreglass with a utility knife. It's important to use a sharp new blade to avoid tearing the insulation's bonded facing. ▼

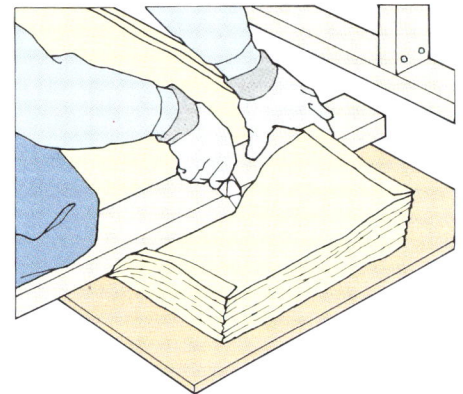

TYPES OF INSULATION

Fibreglass batts and blankets, and loose fill fibreglass and cellulose are by far the most popular forms of domestic insulation, although a number of other materials are available (see below). In cold areas, insulation may require a vapour barrier to be installed on the warm side of the insulation to avoid condensation taking place inside the wall or ceiling cavity.

INSULATION	R-VALUE	THICKNESS	PROPERTIES AND USES
Fibreglass	R1.5–2.0	50–100 mm	Made of glass fibre, held together with a binder. Available as loose fill, blankets and batts, in a range of thicknesses. Economical; easy to install; essentially non-flammable.
Rockwool	R2.0–2.3	75 mm	Made of molten rock. Slightly denser than fibreglass, and a slightly more effective insulator. Available as batts (not in New Zealand) and in granulated form.
Cellulose fibre	R2.6	100 mm	Made from recycled paper waste. Must have fireproofing chemicals added. Available as loose fill, suitable for ceilings (must be coated to stop it blowing around) and walls.
Polystyrene foam (expanded)	R1.3–1.5	50 mm	A polymer. Must contain a fire retardant. Available as panels, boards and beads. Should be protected from fire by being contained by other building materials.
Polystyrene foam (extruded)	R1.7	50 mm	As above, but with a closed-cell construction that does not absorb moisture. Must contain a fire retardant. Can be used in cavity brick construction.
Polyester	R2.0	100 mm	Popular alternative to fibreglass. Available as precut batts, often manufactured with a foil backing. Suitable for most applications.
Polyurethane foam (aged and rigid)	R3.5–4.0	100 mm	Mainly used as sandwich panels in industrial applications. Available in fire-retardant grades, but should be protected by fire-retardant construction. Very effective material.
Reflective foil	R0.4–1.0	Foil	Reflects heat rather than acting as barrier. Works well with other forms of insulation.

RECOMMENDATIONS FOR INSULATION

The R-value of an insulation indicates its resistance to heat loss. Given below are the optimum R values of ceiling insulation recommended for domestic dwellings in winter conditions in various parts of Australia. In New Zealand, houses must satisfy certain minimum levels of energy efficiency, as laid down in the Building Act. Consult the appropriate NZ Standard.

R1.5–2.0	Hot to warm temperate (Bourke, Charleville, Newcastle, Perth, Port Augusta, Roma, Sydney, Wollongong)
R2.0–2.5	Warm temperate, with high temperature range (Cobar, Kalgoorlie, Kingaroy, Mildura, Orbost, Renmark, Whyalla)
R2.5–3.0	Occasional frosts in winter (Albury, Bairnsdale, Geelong, Melbourne, Nowra, Toowoomba, Warrnambool)
R3.0–3.5	Regular cold temperatures, frequent frosts (Ballarat, Condobolin, Griffith, Mudgee, Naracoorte, Tamworth)
R3.5	Cold winters with snow at times (Armidale, Bathurst, Canberra, Cooma, Hobart, Orange, Wagga, Yass)

WEATHERPROOFING

Insulating walls

Check out

You can always check roof insulation by climbing up and taking a look. But how do you know if your house walls are insulated? Here are a couple of tricks:

▷ Remove light switches and power points to see if there's insulation around the fitting. Before probing, however, turn off the power at the meter box.

▷ Find an unobtrusive spot, like a cupboard that backs onto an exterior wall, and cut a small hole in the wall surface with a hole saw.

Installing wall insulation

Most manufacturers of fibreglass batts have products designed for insulating walls. These are slightly stiffer and larger than ceiling batts so that they are held securely when installed between standard 450 and 600 mm wall studs. Make sure that the batts are not pushed in so far that they make contact with exterior brickwork, or dampness may be transferred to the inside. If the insulation is difficult to secure it can be held with thin wires stretched across the studs.

See-through sealer

When installing a plastic vapour barrier over insulation, you have to cut openings for power points and light switches. For a tight seal and fewer air leaks, cut the barrier 6 mm inside the perimeter of each fitting.

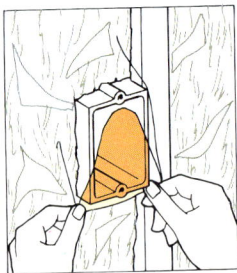

Insulating roofs

Bridge repair

To add insulation to a poorly insulated roof space, run some thinner batts between the joists, parallel to the existing ones. Make sure you route any electrical cables over the top of the insulation: don't sandwich them between the layers. It is not normally advisable to conceal joists under insulation, since this may make access to the roof space hazardous. However, in very cold areas the small risk may be justified. ▼

Tarzan of the attic

You've decided to add more insulation to the roof space. Now, how do you get up there time and again if all you have is a ceiling hatch for access? Secure a stout rope to the rafter directly above the hatch. Then just grab the rope firmly to help pull yourself off your ladder into the roof space. Put a couple of knots in the rope to give yourself a better grip.

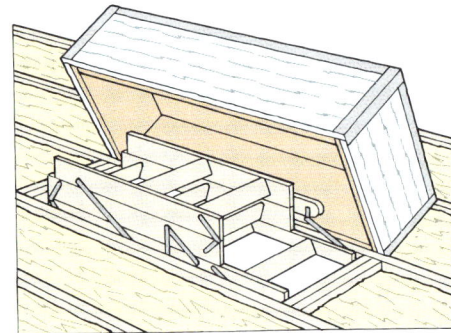

Box block ▲

In particularly cold areas, a ceiling opening, whether a fold-down stair or a simple hatch, could be insulated and weatherstripped to keep heat from leaking from the house. Use self-stick foam or vinyl weatherstrips to seal around the opening's frame. To insulate, build a plywood box that fits around the opening and cover it with foil-faced rigid foam insulation sealed with cloth tape. Hinge the box, or simply lift it aside when you need to access the roof.

Fire hazard to avoid

Take particular care to keep any insulation that you install at least 75 mm away from flues, chimneys (particularly metal chimneys from open fires) and heat-producing electrical fixtures, such as recessed lights, fans and doorbell transformers. To contain loose fill, tack a board or a sheet-metal shield between the joists on each side of a fixture. ▼

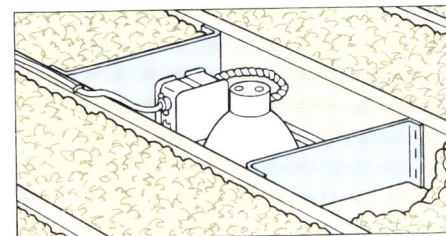

Sun shade

In a hot, sunny region, a shiny foil laminate under the roof helps deflect heat and keep the roof space cooler. Staple the 1200 mm wide fibre-reinforced foil laminate to the bottoms of the rafters, with the shiny side facing down. ▼

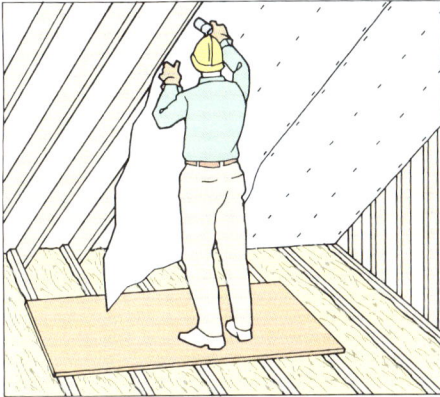

Above crawl spaces

Neat fit

The cross-braced blocking found between deep floor joists in older houses makes it hard to install insulation. To fit batts snugly around the blocking, cut the insulation to create a joint. Then make short lengthwise cuts in the centre of the batt ends as shown. The resulting tabs will fit around the obstruction. ▼

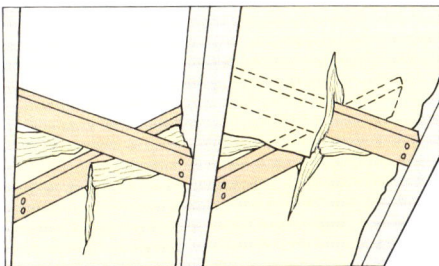

Old hangers never die ▲

Installing insulation in ceilings where the joists are spaced at unusual widths can present a problem—the standard-width batts will not stay in place. An easy solution is to jam wires—slightly longer than the width of the cavity—against the batts. Buy the wires, or cut them from old clothes hangers. Push them in every 600 mm or so, bowing them upward. As an alternative you can lace string or wire across the undersides of the batts.

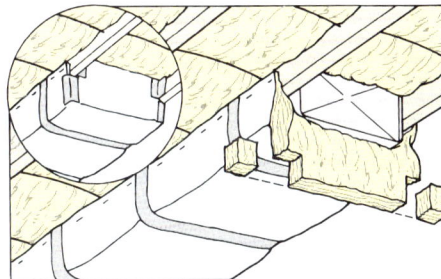

How to wrap a duct ▲

If you want to insulate a duct or piping between floor joists, just cut short sections of insulation, put them across the duct or piping, and staple them to the joists on either side. Put the vapour barrier side (if there is one) out, and seal the seams with tape. When you reach the end, seal the last section as shown.

Moisture barrier

Lay a waterproof membrane on the ground in your sub-floor space to help prevent moisture from damaging the floor insulation and from entering your house. Use sheets of 3 μm polyethylene, extending them several centimetres up the foundation walls and overlapping the edges by at least 200 mm. Use construction adhesive to tack the sheets to the walls and each other. Or secure the edges with cloth tape and weight the seams with bricks. ▼

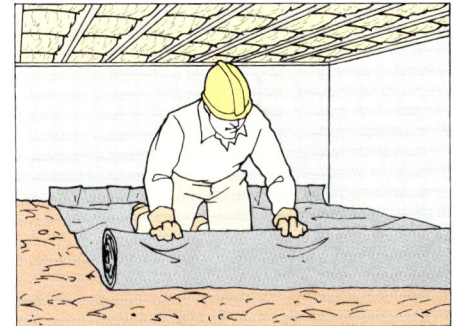

Humid situations

In a very damp area, a foil laminate vapour barrier can provide extra insulation and retard moisture from rising above a sub-floor area. To use it, staple the 1200 mm wide sheets to the joists. Seal the seams with tape. Note, however, that this method should only be used as a last resort, in situations where ventilation cannot be improved. ▼

BASEMENTS AND FOUNDATIONS

Miner's hat trick

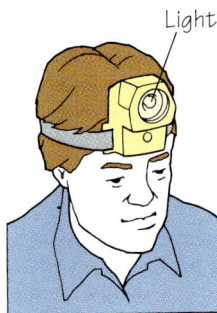

Light

When you have to crawl into the sub-floor space to repair or investigate something, carry a light where it makes the most sense: on your head. It'll leave both hands free. Models with an elastic headband are available from camping (especially caving) equipment shops. For hard-hat versions, try an industrial supplier. These hats are perfect for any job that normally requires a torch.

Check these first

The easiest solution to basement leaks is to keep water away from the sub-floor area. Make sure downpipes direct water away. If you cannot connect directly to a stormwater drain, fit an extension pipe. Also make sure the garden slopes away from the house. Over time the ground around the foundations can sink slightly, creating a mini-moat.

Done in a jiffy

Here are a few simple cures for dampness in basements and sub-floor areas. Make sure all pipes and drains are sealed. Ensure that vents are clean, and have access to the exterior. If there are no vents, have them installed at 2 m intervals. Make sure that no water gathers near walls, and provide sub-surface drainage to keep soil as dry as possible.

Run a test

Having trouble deciding whether basement dampness is due to outside water seeping in, or excess house humidity condensing on the cool walls? Try this simple test. Attach squares of aluminium foil to the walls and floor, sealing all four edges with cloth tape. In a couple of days, remove the foil. If the side against the wall or floor shows beads of moisture, the problem is seepage from outside. But if the moisture shows up only on the foil's outer surface, then it's from interior condensation.

Mirror, mirror, on the ground

At sealing time, don't overlook heat-robbing cracks and gaps between the foundation and the cladding. To save wear and tear on your knees, use an old mirror to see under the cladding. You'll barely have to lean over. ▼

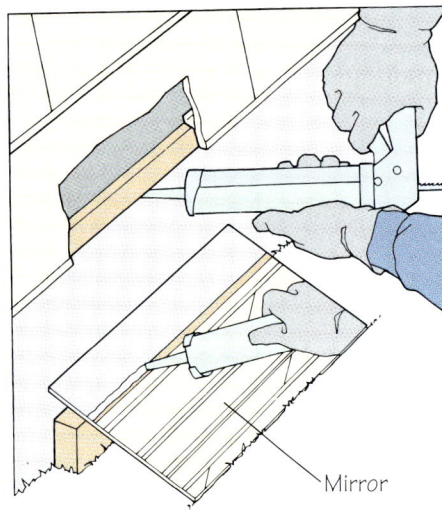

Mirror

Fast furring strips

If you're using masonry nails to install furring strips on masonry basement walls, predrill holes for the nails; the job will be much easier. Start the nails in the furring strips so that they just poke

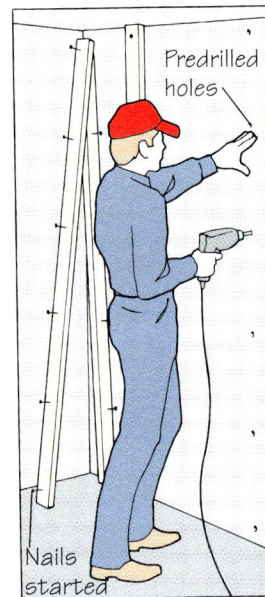

Predrilled holes

Nails started

through the back. Then hold the strip against the wall, and tap the nails to mark their locations on the wall. Drill holes in the masonry with a 3 mm masonry bit; then nail the strips in place. The masonry won't chip and the nails will go straight in.

Save your breath

When drilling into masonry, don't try to blow debris out of the holes. You'll just get a faceful of gritty dust. Instead, use a hand pump or squirt water into them.

Concealing rough walls

Concrete or block foundation walls are not the prettiest surfaces for a basement workshop or rumpus room. If the walls are dry and you don't want to frame and insulate over them, consider stucco in a smooth finish or a decorative texture.

Chill-free concrete floors

Here's how to give a warm covering to a cold concrete floor. Clean the surface, and use a notched trowel to apply a coat of slightly thinned asphalt mastic. Lay down 3 µm polyethylene sheeting, and press flat with a roller. Next, embed pressure-treated 100 × 50 mm timber in rows of mastic. Finally, nail 17 mm exterior plywood to the timber. Now you're ready for underlay and carpet. ▼

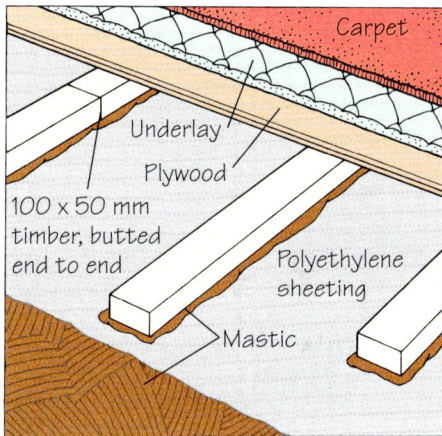

Carpet
Underlay
Plywood
100 x 50 mm timber, butted end to end
Polyethylene sheeting
Mastic

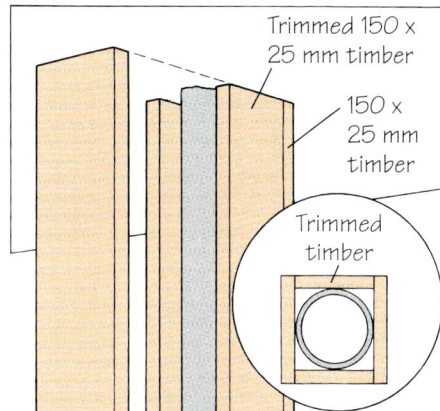

Trimmed 150 × 25 mm timber
150 × 25 mm timber
Trimmed timber

Boxed posts ▲

To hide steel posts, box them in with 150 × 25 mm timber. Trim two lengths so that they're 100 mm wide and join the pieces as shown, packing the bottom edge so it is off the floor. Drill 3 mm holes through the box into the post, and attach the box with self-tapping screws, countersinking the heads. Trim top and bottom with pieces of quad moulding.

Building out basement windows

Small basement windows are good for bringing in light and air, but they need special attention when finishing the interior walls. After the wall framing is in, build a timber box reveal around each, as shown. Make the box's depth equal to the distance between the existing window frame and the new finished wall surface. Secure the box to the framing, and after installing the plasterboard or panelling, trim it with an architrave as you would a standard window. ▼

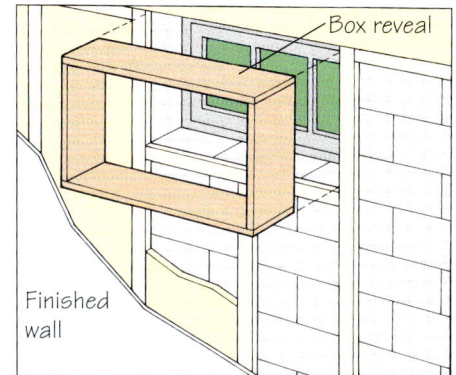

Box reveal
Finished wall

The gold mine below ▶

Here's a way to finish basement walls (provided they are dry) and reap the reward of the extra space. Attach overlapping lengths of 3 µm polyethylene sheets to the full height of the wall with dabs of bitumen. Let them extend about 150 mm onto the floor, where they can be trimmed to fit later. Build a frame against the wall using 100 × 50 mm timber; nail the top to the joists above and secure the bottom to the floor with masonry nails. Drill 38 mm vent holes in the top plate between each stud pair. Insert fibreglass batts, and staple on more polyethylene sheets. Cover with plasterboard, stopping 25 mm short of the floor to prevent moisture from wicking up it. Cover the gap with a skirting.

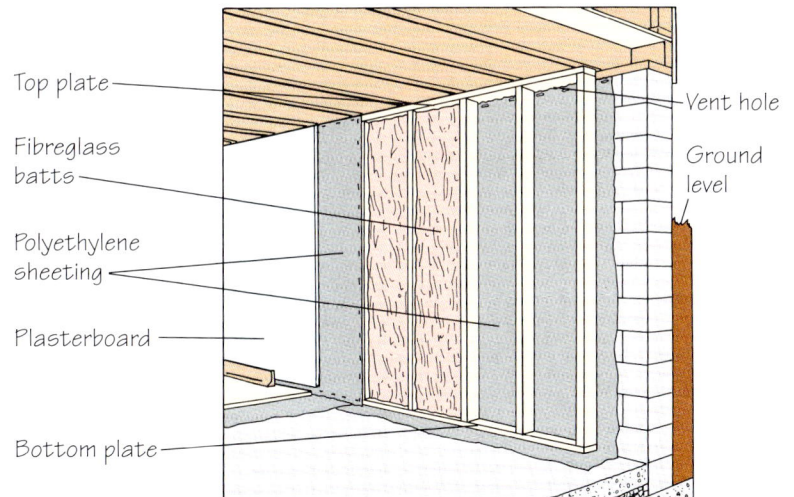

Top plate
Fibreglass batts
Polyethylene sheeting
Plasterboard
Bottom plate
Vent hole
Ground level

CLADDING

Timber cladding

Preventive survey

It's a good idea to walk around your house from time to time with a screwdriver or an awl and probe for areas of rotten wood. Why go looking for trouble? Because the rot will get worse if you ignore it. To repair minor damage, clean away the rotten wood, apply a fungicide and fill the excavation with car body filler. A polyester resin car repair compound adheres well to clean dry wood, and you can smooth, carve or sand it to match adjoining areas.

Closing a split

To repair split weatherboards, prise out the bottom section of the damaged board and insert a shim to hold it out. Apply waterproof glue all along the edge. Then remove the shim, push the section back into place, and nail both the upper and the lower sections. Wipe off the excess glue with a wet cloth.

Lightening up the dark

If your timber cladding has been stained a darker shade than you like, you can lighten it with a pressure washer (available from a hire firm). Use the washer with a solution of either trisodium phosphate or a special cleaning compound sold to go with it. Experiment to find the best amount of cleaner and the correct spraying technique. Wear safety goggles and vinyl gloves.

Handy gauge

When replacing or installing weatherboards, measuring the exposed section of each course is tedious and leaves room for error. Here's a better way. Create a gauge by nailing a cleat to a timber off cut as shown. Then simply hold it up against the bottom edge of the upper course, and rest the next course on the ledge as you nail. ▼

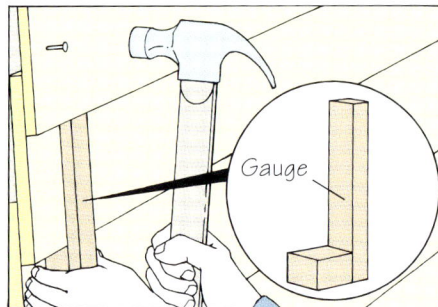

A knotty problem

Knots in weatherboards can present a problem if they are not properly prepared before painting. The resin they contain will eventually bleed through to the surface, causing an unsightly patch. Make sure, therefore, that you seal all knots with a solution of shellac and methylated spirits before the final finish.

Removing vertical weatherboards

If vertical weatherboards need to be removed, you will generally have to remove several to avoid snapping the tongue or the back of the groove from the boards. If the nails are exposed, they can be punched through into the frame, and then four boards can be removed at once, without any damage. If the boards have been secretly nailed, then one board will have to be damaged to expose the first row of nails, and this board may need to be replaced.

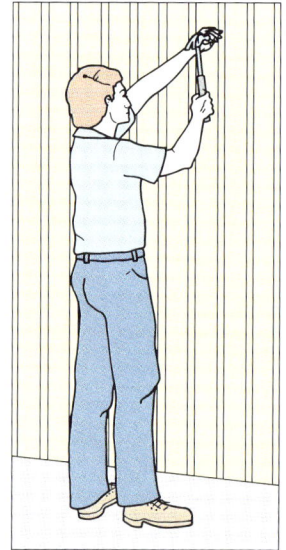

Built to last

When choosing a timber for cladding, it is wise to pick one that is naturally durable, or that has been treated to give it high durability. The timber should also be seasoned to a relatively low moisture content. In Australia, timbers are divided into Durability Classes 1 to 4, with 1 being the most durable. Highly durable to durable timbers include western red cedar, white cypress pine, as well as most of the eucalypt hardwoods from north-eastern Australia and Western Australia. Radiata pine, grown on plantations, is often pressure treated with a chrome-copper-arsenic salt that also makes it highly durable.

REPLACING DAMAGED WEATHERBOARDS

Weatherboards are available in a variety of timbers, profiles and widths. But the steps for replacing damaged sections are the same for all. The bottom edge of each board is usually nailed to the underlying studs every 450 or 600 mm. The top edge is pinched in place by the nailing of the board above. When removing more than one section, work from the top down. Take a damaged board to your timberyard to find the best possible match.

1 If you can see nails, use a nail punch to drive them through the damaged board. Also drive them through on the undamaged board above it to release the damaged piece's top edge.

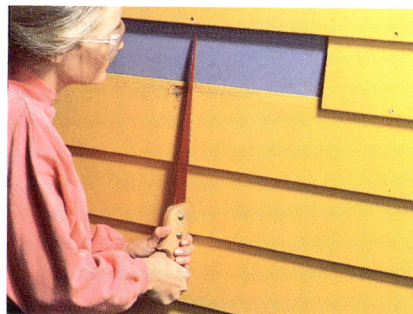

Hacksaw

2 If you can't locate the nails under multiple paint layers, gently pull up the board with a short pinch bar, and slip the blade of a small hacksaw under the board. Feel for the nails and cut them.

3 Cut out the damaged board, using a backsaw or a keyhole saw with the blade reversed. Make sure that the cut is square and that the joints in succeeding courses don't line up.

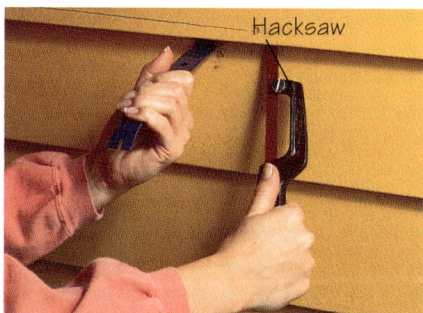

4 Working from the bottom up, install the replacement boards, using galvanised nails. Apply sealant to the joints and where new boards abut window, door or corner trim. Prime and paint.

Dealing with rot

If you find rot in your weatherboards, there is little point in trying to patch the damage, unless it only occurs in one or two small spots. Rot is a type of fungal attack, that ultimately destroys timber. Once the timber has gone soft it is well advanced. It's best to remove the affected weatherboards, or sections of weatherboards, and burn them.

The matching set

Matching a particular weatherboard profile can be difficult. One option is to replace all the boards on one facade with a non-matching profile, and use the good pieces to patch the other sides. The alternative is to find a company that can mill timber to your specifications. Bear in mind, however, that specially milled timber will be expensive.

Don't forget the ends

The part of a board most likely to rot or decay is the end grain. As it dries, it acts like a sponge, soaking up moisture. When replacing boards, therefore, always make sure that the ends get a generous coat of primer or oil stain before they are fixed into place. This way your walls will last much longer.

CLADDING

Brickwork

Mortar quick draw

Use an old sealant tube to fill mortar joints. Push the bottom out by slipping a dowel through the spout. Clean the tube, load it with mortar and replace the bottom. Place it in a caulking gun, after cutting the tip to the right width.

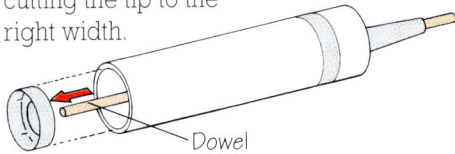

Dowel

Making mortar match

'Age' new mortar joints to match old ones by patting them with a wet tea bag. Or add oxide (from a builder's supplier) to the mortar as you're mixing it. Experiment to get the right shade.

Brick replacement ▲

To replace a damaged brick, chisel out the mortar around it (step 1, facing page), being careful not to chip the surrounding bricks. Then chip the brick apart with a chisel, and pull out all the pieces. Dampen the opening. Spread mortar on the base of the cavity and on the top and ends of a damp new brick, and insert the brick. Add or remove mortar as needed.

New meets old

It's not always possible to get a perfect match when adding new brickwork to old. Here are some simple tricks you can use to minimise the difference.

Plant shrubs or climbing vines where the old work abuts the new, or camouflage the area with a trellis.

Build a small offset into the wall, putting the new bricks on a different plane from the old ones.

Place a window at the juncture of old and new work so that the only visible disparity will be low on the wall.

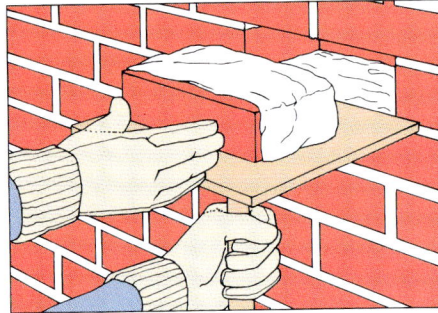

Thumbprint test

When to finish a mortar joint—a process known as tooling, jointing or striking—depends on the mortar mixture and the temperature. The mortar needs to set long enough so that it can take an impression but not so long that it becomes hard. Use the traditional mason's test: mortar is ready for tooling when it will hold a clear thumbprint. ▼

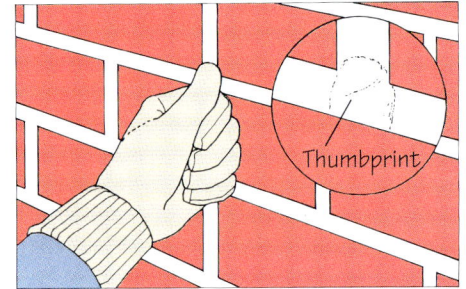

Thumbprint

Getting the right shape

If you need to shape a mortar joint and don't have a special rake or jointing tool (step 3, facing page), improvise your own. Use an ice-cream stick or a 10 mm steel rod, for example, to make the common concave joint. Or carve a scrap of wood or grind an old spoon to the profile that matches joints on the surrounding bricks.

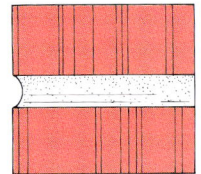

Concave joint

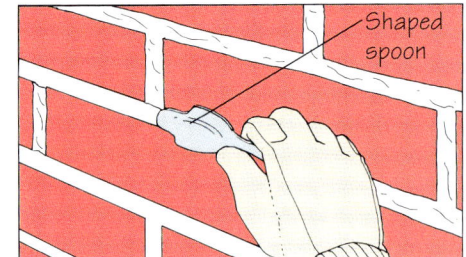

Shaped spoon

Stains

Shady-side solution

Whether you have brick, wood or fibre cement cladding, patches of mould or moss in shaded areas are distressing. Commercial stain removers are available, but you can do a good job with a 50/50 mixture of household bleach and water in a plastic spray bottle. After an hour, flush well with water. Wear goggles and vinyl gloves, and take care not to damage plants. If you'd rather not use bleach, scrub with straight vinegar—it takes elbow grease but works well.

In the first place

The best way to prevent mould from staining timber cladding is to use a stain or paint that contains a fungicide.

Spot removers

Here's how to remove some common stains from bricks and other masonry. Test any cleaner on an inconspicuous spot first. Scrub with a nylon-bristle brush (wire may leave marks). Wear goggles and vinyl gloves when working with solvents or caustic chemicals.
▷ Fresh paint: blot up; then wipe with the solvent recommended for the paint.
▷ Dried paint: scrape off; then remove residue with paint remover as directed.
▷ Rust: mix 500 g oxalic acid crystals in 4.5 litres water and brush on. After three hours, scrub and rinse.
▷ Tar: scrape off, and scrub with scouring powder. Then apply a paste of talc and kerosene, let dry, and scrub again.
▷ Smoke and soot: scrub with scouring powder; rinse well. Apply talc mixed with bleach to stubborn areas.

REPOINTING BRICKS

The most common masonry repair is repointing—replacing damaged mortar joints between bricks. The tools you'll need are a plugging chisel (to clean out the joint), a 1 kg lump hammer, a trowel, a pointing tool (to push mortar in), a wheel rake or jointing iron (to shape the mortar) and a whisk broom. For convenience, use ready-mix mortar. Add colour to match existing mortar, then gradually mix in water until the mortar becomes a uniform stiff paste that you can shape into a ball. Let it stand for 10 minutes; then stir it briefly with a trowel before using. If the mortar becomes too stiff to use, don't add water—mix a new batch. Wear work gloves.

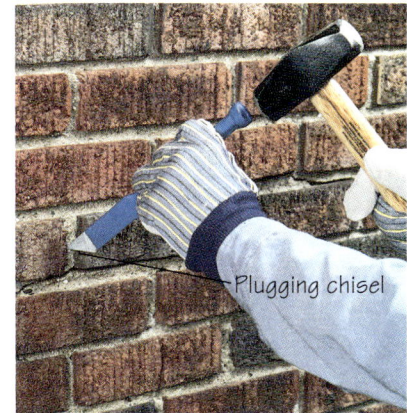

Plugging chisel

1 Wearing safety glasses, chisel out loose and cracked mortar to a depth of 20 mm, or until you reach sound mortar. Be careful not to chip the bricks. Brush away debris, and dampen the bricks with a fine spray of water.

2 Scoop up some mortar onto the back of your trowel, hold it close up to the joint, and push it in, a bit at a time, with the jointing iron. Even quite deep holes can be filled in a single application of mortar.

3 Once the mortar is thumbprint hard, use a jointing tool or wheel rake to smooth the joint to a shape that matches existing mortar joints. Brush away any excess mortar from the face of the bricks as soon as it has stiffened.

CLADDING

Vinyl and aluminium

Helper on a roll

Installing vinyl cladding can be a solo project if you enlist the help of duct or cloth tape. Simply use a piece of tape to hold one end of the cladding panel in place while you install the other end.

Replacing vinyl

Do you need to replace badly damaged vinyl cladding? The chances are that any replacement section you buy won't match your weathered cladding. Instead of using new cladding, replace the damaged section with a section from an inconspicuous part of the house; then put the replacement section in the less noticeable area.

Chalk off

The powdery residue often found on aluminum cladding is called chalking, and it's an intrinsic characteristic of the material. The cladding gradually releases pigment to help prevent dirt from building up. Rain usually washes away chalking. But if it becomes a problem, wash the cladding with a soft rag and a mild, non-abrasive household detergent. Use one-third of a cup of detergent to 4 litres of water. Rinse well.

It's a big job, but...

Spruce up fading aluminium cladding with liquid car wax. First wash the cladding with dishwashing liquid and water, and let it dry. Then use a damp sponge to apply the wax. When it dries, buff it with a towel. Do small sections at a time, and remember that you're after a modest sheen, not a glossy finish.

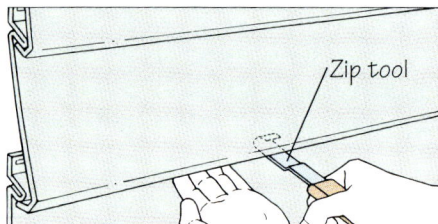

Unzipping vinyl cladding ▲

Vinyl cladding may seem difficult to remove, but it comes off easily with a zip tool (sold by cladding suppliers). Hook the tool under the bottom edge and pull down as you slide along the seam.

Patching vinyl

To fix cracked vinyl cladding, remove the section and glue a piece of scrap cladding to the rear. Prepare the area with PVC cleaner, apply PVC cement, and press the patch in, finished side down.

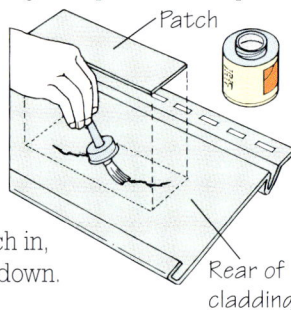

Dent removal

Do you have a large dent in aluminium cladding? Drill a 3 mm hole, insert a self-tapping screw, and pull out the dent. Fill any remaining depression with car body filler; level the filler, let it dry and sand it smooth. Apply metal primer and two coats of a matching spray paint. ▼

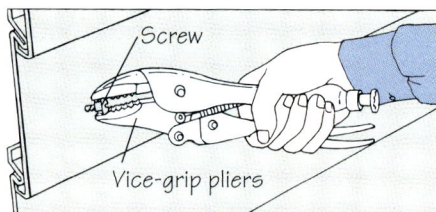

Asbestos cement

Replacing old sheets

When replacing asbestos cement sheets, be sure to observe all the precautions outlined in the box on the far right. Wet the sheets down to minimise dust, lever off cover strips and remove nails. Try to break as few sheets as possible. Wrap old sheets in plastic, seal them, and dispose of them only at an approved site. Check with your local council. Replacement sheets of fibre cement are available in a range of metric sizes, and some minor cutting may be needed to match the older panels.

Replacing cover strips

Many houses built with fibre or asbestos cement sheets have cover strips to seal the sheet joints. These may be made from fibre cement, asbestos cement or timber. If made from asbestos cement, and sound, they need no further attention, other than making sure they are well painted to seal the surface. Timber strips, however, will often rot if they are not kept well painted. Gently prise the old strips off, taking care not to damage the sheets beneath. Replace with new fibre cement or plastic strips.

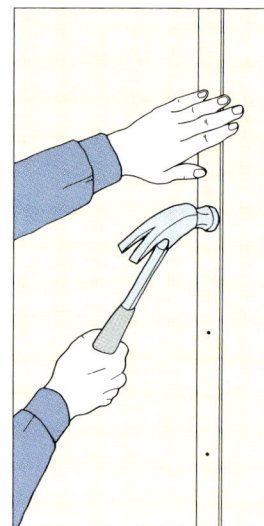

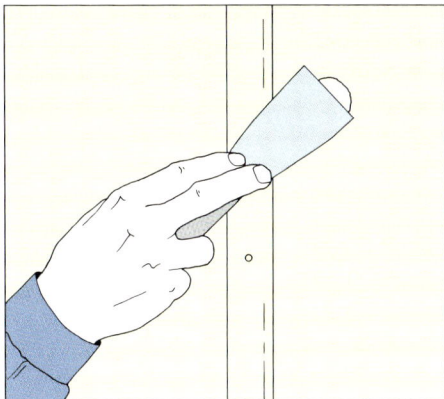

Patching holes ▲

Small holes in asbestos or fibre cement can be patched using commercial external grade fillers, or even fibreglass or car body fillers. These will generally not shrink, and provided the original sheets are sound, with no crumbling edges, the patch should stick well. If, however, the hole corresponds with a crack running through the sheet, patching is probably not worth the effort. The sheets will flex and move about the crack, and the patch will not hold. In this case, you would be better off removing the sheet, and replacing it with a new one.

A new look

If you are thinking about rejuvenating an old asbestos cement clad building, consider the matter carefully. If the cladding is sound it's probably best left alone, apart from repainting. Wash the surface down with a gentle spray of water and a sponge, patch any holes (see above), allow to dry, and repaint. Do not sand. If you would like an alternative finish, but do not want to remove all the old sheets, consider fixing vinyl, aluminium or brick wafer over the top.

Instant bricks

You can completely change the appearance of old asbestos or fibre cement walls by sticking brick wafers to them. Carefully done, the result looks just like real brick. The wafers are cut from actual bricks, and are supplied with an adhesive. If they are standard brick size, mark out your wall to make sure that the spacing is as close to a real brick wall as possible. That is, the brick wafers should be about 230 × 76 mm in size, and mortar joints should be 10 mm wide. Every seven courses should measure 600 mm in height, and every ten bricks should measure 2400 mm in length. Specially cut corner bricks are also available. When the wafers are stuck down, finish by grouting the joints with an appropriate mortar. ▼

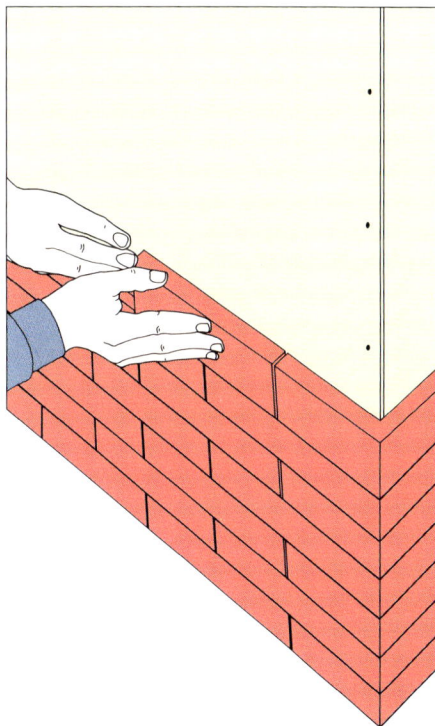

SAFE WORKING WITH FIBRO

Asbestos cement, often called 'fibro', was a popular building material until the early 1980s. At that time, because of concerns about asbestos-related illnesses, the use of the material was gradually discontinued, and asbestos cement was replaced with fibre cement, which contained cellulose fibre instead of asbestos. There are strict guidelines for handling old asbestos cement sheets and other products. Treat as suspect any fibro installed before the mid-1980s, unless you know for a fact that it does not contain asbestos. If you have old asbestos cement at your house:
▷ Leave it alone. As long as it has a sound coat of paint it is safe. If repainting, do not sand first.
▷ Do not use a high pressure water hose, or power tools on asbestos cement products.
▷ If sheets need to be removed, wet the material down first and work in a well-ventilated area.
▷ All asbestos cement waste should be collected on plastic drop sheets, and disposed of in labelled plastic bags, stating that they contain asbestos waste.
▷ When working with asbestos cement wear overalls, and a suitable respirator or face mask.

ROOFS

Gutters

Gutter scoop

Make a handy gutter-cleaning scoop from a rectangular motor oil container. Cut away the bottom portion, and it's just the right size to fit into the gutter. The spout gives you a hand grip. ▼

Keep your hands clean

Are your gutters filled with messy rotten leaves and who knows what? Use a pair of old kitchen tongs and you won't have to touch the stuff. The tongs reach nicely into tight spots, and their pincer action helps you easily grip debris.

Just hanging around ▶

Turn an inexpensive plastic bucket into a handy gutter cleaning aid. Snip the wire handle in half, bend the ends of the wires to form hooks, and hang the bucket on the gutter. Slide the bucket and toss debris into it as you work your way along the length of the gutter.

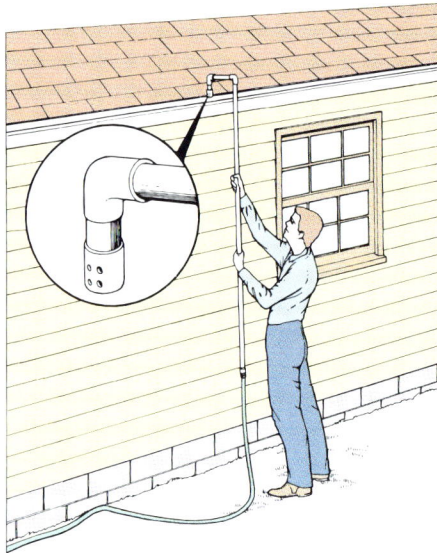

I'm happy down here, thanks ▲

If you're not keen on climbing to clean gutters, this hose extension will let you flush them out while keeping your feet planted firmly on the ground. Make it from 19 mm PVC plastic pipe, two elbows, a garden hose coupler, and a cap. Drill four 2 mm holes in the cap. Glue the parts together with PVC cement.

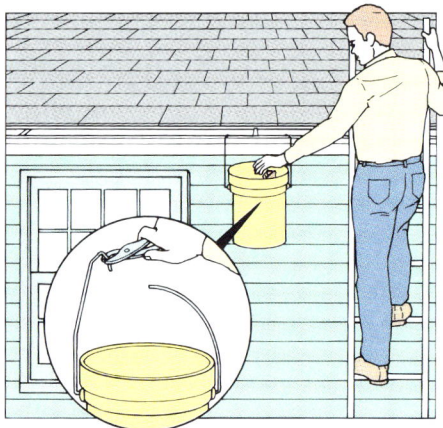

Sign of trouble

A depression in the ground underneath a gutter is a sign that the gutter is dripping water. Look for a sag or leak in the gutter. Check for a clogged downpipe that's causing an overflow.

Give a gutter a lift

A gutter must slope to the downpipe. If it does not, water will sit in it, causing corrosion; and its capacity to cope with run off in big storms will be reduced. If your gutter is sloping the wrong way, remove it and reset the brackets to give a fall of between 1 in 80 and 1 in 150. ▼

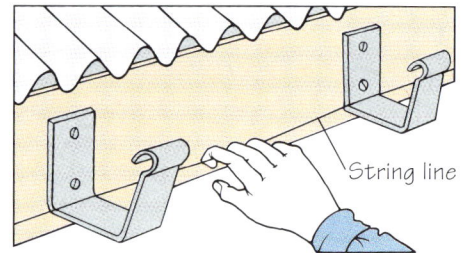

String line

Raise it with a twist

On a gutter that is supported by suspension brackets, straighten a sagging section by twisting the nearest bracket. This will pull the gutter up. ▼

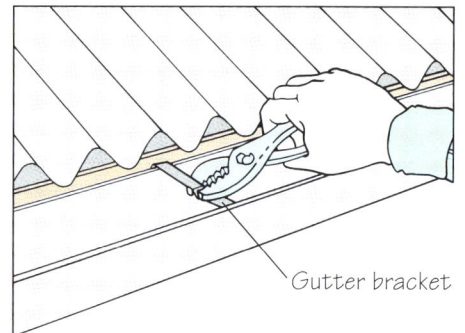

Gutter bracket

Checking and protecting

Keep your distance

Early spring and late autumn are the best times to check your roof for loose or damaged tiles, corroded flashings and cracked sealant. But keep your ladder in the garage. You can often do it from the ground with binoculars.

Does your gutter measure up?

It is generally better to have gutters and downpipes that are too large rather than too small. A gutter with a cross-section of 100 × 50 mm is reckoned to be the minimum necessary to cope with small amounts of debris. Larger gutters would be advisable in areas of high rainfall, or near large trees. Downpipes should measure at least 100 × 50 mm, or be 75 or 80 mm in diameter, and should be no further than 12 m apart. Increase the size to 100 × 75 mm if water is not getting away fast enough.

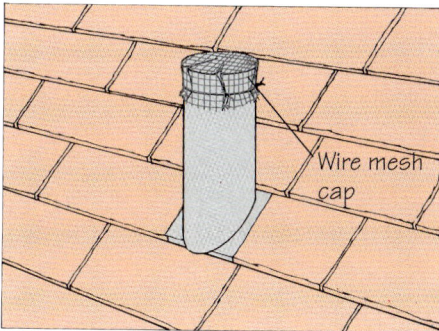

Vent guard ▲

To prevent plumbing vent pipes from becoming clogged with leaves, cover the openings with a piece of 12 mm wire mesh. Secure it with a wire collar or dabs of construction adhesive.

Think like a drip

Don't assume that a leak in the roof is directly over a stain in the ceiling. Water may run along rafters and framing for quite a distance before it finally drops. Next time there's a heavy rain, go into the roof space and look and listen carefully. Once you find the leak, measure to a couple of landmarks—a ridge board, a side wall, or a chimney or vent pipe. Repeat your measurements on the roof, and you'll have a good idea where to look for damage.

No longer out of reach

Downpipes, like gutters, can become choked with debris. The problem is that very often they cannot be cleaned out because the base has been cemented into the stormwater system. If you live in a leafy area it may be wise to have a plumber install a sump at the base of each downpipe. Water from the downpipe will then flow through a grating into the sump, which is, in turn, connected to the stormwater system. Not only will you then have access to the downpipes, should they become choked, but also to the stormwater pipes which can be blocked by tree roots.

CARE UP THERE

Climbing onto a roof is hazardous. Here are some precautions:
▷ Work on a dry, mild, windless day after the dew evaporates.
▷ Use a sturdy extension ladder that reaches at least 1 m above the eaves. The distance between the ladder's feet and the wall should equal one-quarter of the ladder's height. Tie the feet to stakes in the ground. If possible, tie the top as well—to a vent pipe, for example.
▷ Sweep the roof lightly before you start, and keep the work area clear of debris you could slip on, such as slippery leaves.
▷ Wear heavy, soft, rubber-soled shoes and long pants.
▷ Don't go near power lines; their connections are not always insulated. Keep your ladder away too.
▷ Pull up loads with a rope. Don't carry a load up by hand. Use both hands to grip the ladder when you are climbing it.
▷ Place tools and materials where they won't slide off the roof.
▷ Keep other people far away.
▷ For maximum security, wear a safety harness tied tightly to an immovable object on the opposite side of the roof.
▷ Avoid steep roofs (over 30°) and houses over two storeys high.
▷ If you're uncomfortable on a roof, employ a professional.

Metal

Quality at the top

To avoid corrosion, it's best to use one metal throughout a roofing project. If different metals have to be used, it is important to isolate them from direct contact, and to make sure that the 'downhill' metal is more 'noble' than that above it. Otherwise, over time, water will pick up particles from the upper metal, and through galvanic reaction, cause corrosion of the metal lower down. The correct order, from the top of the roof to the bottom of the downpipes, is: zinc (including galvanising), aluminium, iron and steel, lead, copper and stainless steel. This can be further complicated by variations in alloys, so ask manufacturers for their advice.

Tread carefully

Most metal-roofed homes have only light gauge metal. Unless you don't weigh very much, there is a chance that you will bend the sheet down if you walk on it, possibly crimping it permanently. Always walk on the line of fixings, where the roof has maximum support. High-profile sheets do not crimp easily, but stick to the supports anyway.

The patter of raindrops

The sound of gentle rain on a metal roof can be pleasant, but a deluge may be deafening. When putting on a new metal roof, make sure that a fibreglass or similar insulation blanket is installed underneath. Not only will it deaden the sound, but it will also provide good thermal insulation for the house.

Rust never sleeps

Painting can extend the life of a steel roof, but stick to one company's products throughout. Start by removing as much rust as possible with a wire brush. Treat lightly-corroded metal with a rust converter, following the manufacturer's instructions, and then wash the whole area with mineral turpentine. Allow it to dry, and then paint on one coat of galvanised iron primer. When the primer is dry, apply either two coats of water-based acrylic gloss roof paint, or one coat of oil-based undercoat, followed by two coats of roofing enamel. If the roof is used to collect tank water, check that the finishes being used are not toxic.

Got a screw loose?

Wind can badly damage sheet metal roofs if they are not properly fixed down. Check periodically for loose screws, and see if you can re-tighten them. If they still don't seem to be secure, they must be replaced. Insecure screws are often the result of worn or rotten supporting timbers beneath the surface of the roof. If this is the case, the old hole, which should be on top of a corrugation, must be plugged with a dab of silicone sealant, and a new one drilled through the adjacent ridge and into sound wood.

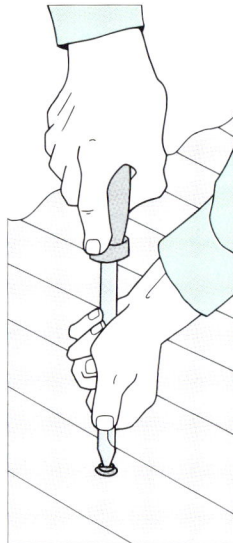

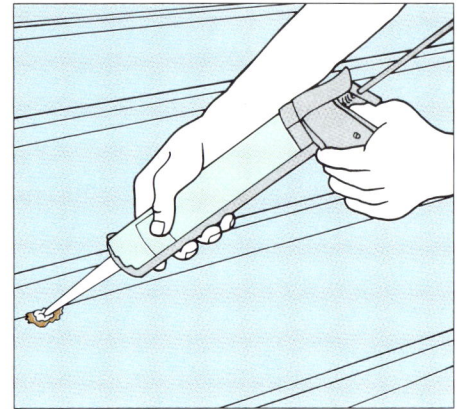

Postponing the inevitable ▲

Small holes in roofing can be patched. If they are due to rusting, however, it is only a matter of time before the roof must be replaced. The easiest way to patch small holes is to use a sealant applied from a cartridge. On metal roofs use a 'neutral cure' sealant; others may release acid which will corrode the roof more quickly. Larger holes can be patched using bitumen and foil bandages, reinforced fibreglass or car body filler, but none is permanent.

Only pure water

If you are collecting drinking water from your roof, it is important that nothing dangerous can enter the supply. Most country homes where rainwater is collected have corrugated steel roofs, and provided they are not painted, and are made of galvanised steel, Zincalume or factory-coloured roofing, are perfectly safe. If the roof needs to be painted it is important that you choose a suitable paint. Some paints are toxic, and will leach chemicals into the water as it flows across the surface. Always check with the paint manufacturer first.

Holes in the roof

If you have to make a hole in your roof for a pipe, flue or vent, make sure you fit a flashing system to seal the edges. These consist of a rubber collar with an aluminium surround that can be bent to suit your roof shape. Cut a hole through the flashing just large enough to fit the pipe and apply a neutral-cure sealant to its underside. Slide the unit down the pipe until it reaches the roof and then shape the flashing by hand, or with a soft mallet, to fit the roof surface. When there are no gaps, rivet or screw the flashing into place.

Flowing uphill

Many metal sheet or decking roofs are installed at a shallow angle, so there is always a danger that rainwater may flow back underneath the sheet ends by surface tension. Manufacturers recommend that the lower ends should be turned down to stop this from happening. If you suspect that water is getting under the edges of your roof, the turn-downs may not be steep enough. Check and increase the bends if necessary. A special tool is available for this job. ▼

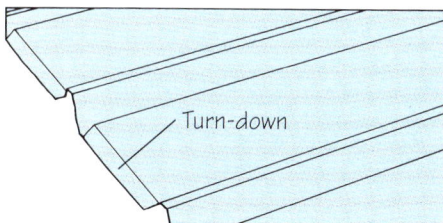

Turn-down

REPLACING SHEET STEEL

The sheet metal material most commonly used for roofing in Australia and New Zealand is corrugated steel. If the roof is old, the steel was almost certainly galvanised, and replacement sheets should be the same, or Zincalume. In the past, galvanised corrugated steel was available only in a limited range of sizes, but now any length is available, the only limiting factor being the size of the truck that carries it.

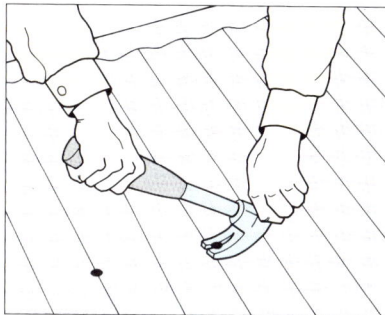

1 Remove old nails and screws from the sheet to be replaced. You may also have to take the fastenings out of the edges of adjoining sheets, since they probably also go through the sheet

2 Lift the bottom of the old sheet out at an angle, and slide it downwards. Wear stout gloves to protect your hands from jagged metal edges. Inspect the roof battens beneath carefully, and replace any that show signs of rot.

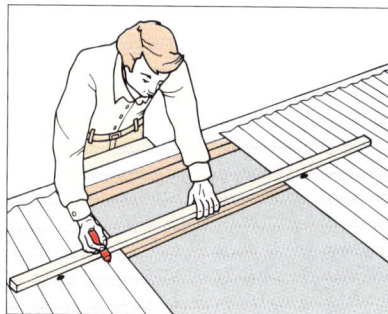

3 Mark the centre lines of battens on surrounding sheets so that you know where to put the screws. Insert the new sheet, and slide it into place so that it exactly replaces the old one.

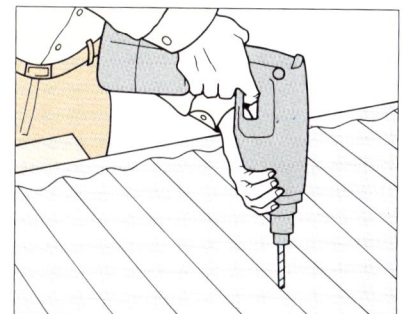

4 Either drill through the new sheet into the batten, or use self-drilling roofing screws. Do not use old screws, as the seals will have perished. Remove metal filings to prevent rust staining.

ROOFS

Slates

New life for old slates

If you are planning to repair your damaged slate roof, try to find a source of good second-hand replacements. New slates are always available, but they will stand out on an old roof. Be prepared to spend some time picking over those on offer to get the best. Give each a gentle tap with your knuckle, and reject any that sound hollow, they are probably delaminating. Also check that the old nail holes are not too large, since that will make them hard to fix into place.

Slipped slates

Slates are nailed to wooden battens and, since most slate roofs are old, the nails rust through, freeing the slates. Because slates overlap one another by a large amount it is not possible to remove those above in order to renail a loose slate to its original batten. Instead, a strip of galvanised iron or lead is nailed to a lower batten, leaving a tail hanging out on the roof. The replacement slate is then slid into place, and the tail of metal bent over its base to hold it in position. *Caution:* think carefully before attempting a slate repair. Slate roofs can be steep, slippery and treacherous. ▼

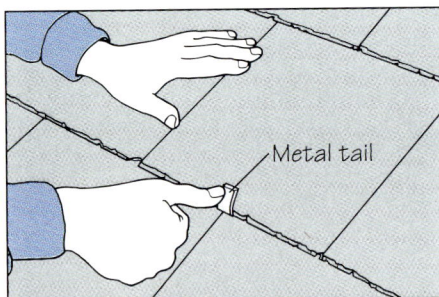

Metal tail

Tiles

Treasure hunt

So many different styles and patterns of terracotta tiles have been used over the years that its often hard to find replacements for those that become damaged. However, most major cities have one or two roof restoration specialists who sell second-hand tiles they retrieve from demolition sites. The same specialists will also stock hard-to-get slates, concrete roofing tiles and perhaps even fibre cement shingles.

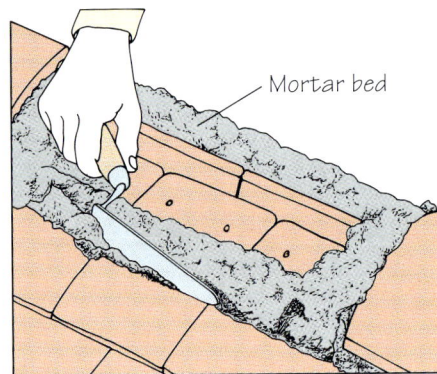

Mortar bed

Pinnacle of peril ▲

The constant expansion and contraction of tiled roofs often dislodges ridge and hip capping tiles from their mortar beds. To repair the damage, carefully chip off the old mortar with a club hammer and cold chisel, and then use a mixture of one and a half parts cement, one part lime and seven parts sand to prepare a new bed. Point the edges with a similar mortar mix, to which a colouring oxide has been added. Experiment with a test batch to match the colour to the tiles. Read the safety instructions on page 165 before attempting this job.

Something to fret about

If you notice that the underside of your terracotta tiles is gradually crumbling away, it is probably due to a condition called fretting. Salt from the atmosphere crystallises under the tile's surface, gradually forcing it off. Upper surfaces are rarely affected, probably because rain keeps them clean Although fretting is most common near the ocean, it can also occur many kilometres inland. Badly fretted tiles will need to be replaced before they fail completely.

Don't be a fool

Tiled roofs can be fragile, and while modern terracotta tiles can withstand some maintenance traffic, older tiles are extremely weak. Many apparently simple repair jobs finish with more tiles being broken than were damaged in the first place. If you must walk on the roof, walk on the strongest part, which is the front edge of each tile. Wear soft-soled shoes, but not thongs or bare feet.

Nearly as good as new

Many home-owners are approached by firms offering to 'reglaze and waterproof' their tiled roofs. Treat such offers with caution. Often, all that is done is to coat the roof with a surface finish which, once applied, must be renewed every five to ten years. If the roof is leaking, the 'reglazing' will only be a temporary solution at best. If, however, you want to return your roof to its original colour and appearance you can apply a coat of paint yourself. Investigate the range of products available, and check their suitability and durability with the manufacturers. Also remember that the roof will have to be thoroughly cleaned first.

Roof cleaning

Roof spring clean

Is your roof starting to look a little bit dingy? The constant fallout of grime and pollution from the air in a city will make any roof look a little bit grubby in time. To give your roof (but not an asbestos cement roof) a spring clean, hire or buy a high-pressure water cleaner. Always work down the roof, otherwise you will squirt water up under tiles or slates into the roof space. Also take care when working on the wet and slippery surface.

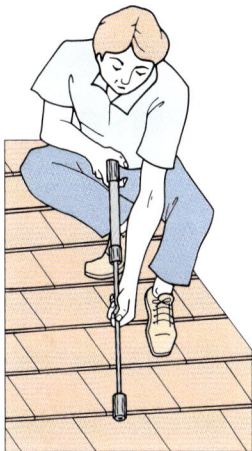

The roof-top garden

Mosses and lichens grow on many roofs, giving them a pleasing patina of age. However, house owners sometimes worry that they may be doing damage. They are not. But if you don't like the look of the growths, you can remove them with either water (see above) or chemicals. For chemical removal, dissolve 2 kg copper sulphate in 45 litres of water. Block the downpipes and fill the gutters with water to prevent the copper solution from attacking the metal. Brush the mixture on, drain the gutters, and leave the chemical for a few days to do its work. The next shower of rain will wash the dead growth off.

REPLACING TILES

Tiles are often damaged by salt attack and storms, and must be replaced. However, tiled roofs are not always easy to work on. They are often much steeper than metal roofs, and old tiles can be quite brittle. An apparently simple repair undertaken by an inexperienced workman may end up causing more damage than it fixes. Carefully assess the risk and complexity of the job before you embark on it. If in doubt, call in a professional.

1 Locate the damaged tile, and support the tiles above it on both sides with small softwood wedges. Then gently raise the tiles above to make sure they are free, and that their interlocking sections are not binding.

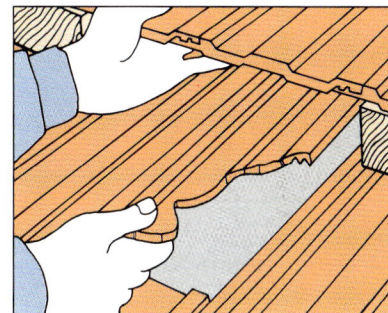

2 Carefully lift and twist the damaged tile to release the interlocking sections from the tiles on either side. If the tiles are nailed or wired, you will need to cut the fixings under the tile with a small hacksaw before you can remove it.

3 Insert the new tile at an angle and engage the interlocking sections on either side. Press the tile firmly into place and make sure it is properly seated. Remove the wooden wedges.

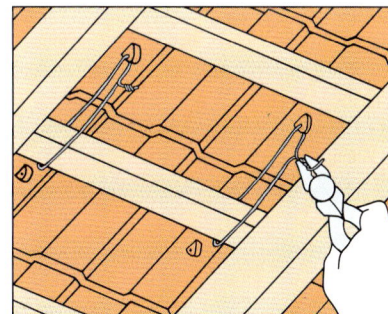

4 Climb into the roof space and examine the repair from beneath. Re-tie any tiles that were previously untied, using new copper ties. At the same time check and replace any rusted ties.

ROOFS

Asbestos cement

A problem material

If your old asbestos cement roof is deteriorating it can be given a new lease of life with a liquid acrylic membrane, which you can apply yourself (see chart below). Follow the manufacturer's instructions, and make sure you clean the surface down thoroughly before starting work. Note that high-pressure water jets must not be used on asbestos cement roofs. If the roof is in poor condition, consider replacing it with metal decking or something similar. Old asbestos cement will probably be harder to dispose of as time goes on.

Softly, like a cat

Asbestos cement roofs are notoriously brittle, and are often criss-crossed with many small cracks. Only walk on such a roof if you absolutely have to, and then stick to the lines of screws that mark the position of structural members beneath. Do not stand on any sheet that has a major crack—it may collapse. ▼

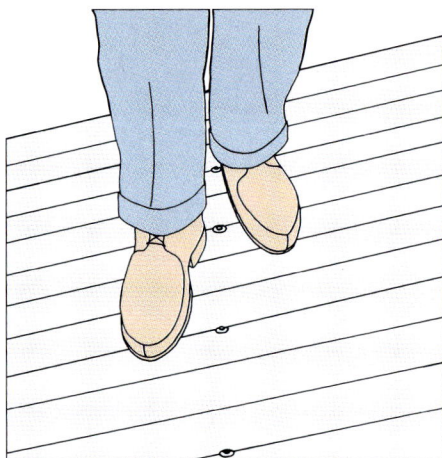

Membranes

An instant roof

Liquid acrylic membranes (see chart below) are probably the easiest roofing material of all for a novice to use on flat roofs. Provided there is a firm, sound base to work on, with care you can produce a roof that will last for 10 years or more. The acrylic, water-based material is applied with a trowel or stiff brush in a series of coats to produce a final, thick, hard-wearing layer. In areas that will be subjected to a lot of traffic, or where there are cracks to bridge, fibreglass or polyester fibre is added to the surface to act as a reinforcement. Follow the manufacturer's instructions with particular care. If the layers are not properly applied, the result will not be satisfactory, and the roof will soon leak.

Track down that drip

When a membrane roof leaks, the actual hole can be hard to find. This is because water, once it penetrates the surface, can travel for long distances between the layers of the roof before it emerges. To track down an elusive leak, search in ever-widening circles, up-hill from the spot where the water is dripping. Look for cracks in seams, holes, bubbles and loose flaps. Examine all flashings (p. 171). Any fixtures that project through the membrane are likely trouble spots.

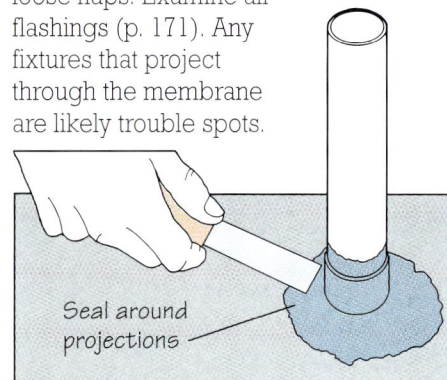

Seal around projections

TYPES OF ROOFING MEMBRANES

The three main types of roofing membranes now in common use are listed below. Each is suited to different applications, and you really need expert advice to choose the best one for any particular situation. Only the liquid-applied membranes can be satisfactorily used by a competent amateur. The other two systems are best left in the hands of an experienced tradesman. Ask for written quotes from a range of suppliers before deciding on which firm to use. Remember that a roof should last for many years, so choose a firm that might be in business when your roof develops problems.

TYPE	DETAILS AND BRANDS
Sheet rolls in one layer	Rubber based, usually supplied in a flexible roll. Edges are solvent welded or heat bonded (EPDM, Butynol, Rhepanol).
Layered sheet rolls	Multi-layer systems, either of the old malthoid type, or these days more commonly based on bitumen or fibreglass layers (Tremco, Ormonoid, Rubberoid).
Liquid-applied	Usually acrylic liquids, reinforced with fibreglass. Applied in layers (Emerclad, Traffiguard).

Not so flash

Leaking flashings—at the junction between the roof and its surrounding surfaces—are a common problem with any type of roof. Membrane roofs, however, are particularly susceptible because they often double as decks, where there are many junctions with walls and doorways that have to be properly and thoroughly sealed. If you have such a roof/deck, make sure that you check the flashings at least once a year, especially in heavy traffic areas where the surface is likely to get scuffed, or where loose edges can be kicked up. Prompt attention will prevent trouble from occurring later on. ▼

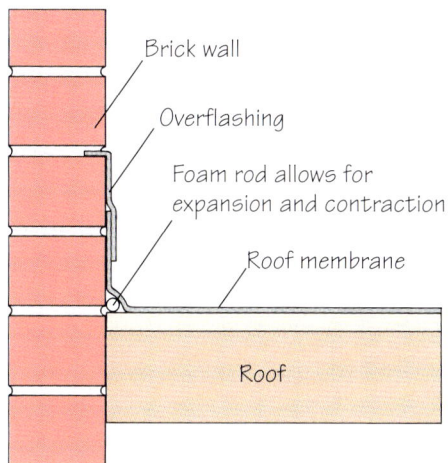

Brick wall

Overflashing

Foam rod allows for expansion and contraction

Roof membrane

Roof

Think again

Membrane roofs are simple and relatively cheap to install, but if yours has reached the end of its useful life, don't just have it replaced with a new one. Instead, consider having a low-pitched, timber-framed steel roof built over the top. Simple to build and completely waterproof, it will outlast any membrane roof by many years.

MEMBRANE REPAIR

Membrane roofs give more trouble than others. The materials used are not very durable, and in time they will crack, split, blister, perish and wear. Small areas of damage can be repaired with a roof-and-gutter sealant, but anything larger will have to be patched. Only attempt simple repairs to old felt and bitumen roofs; other types will need expert attention.

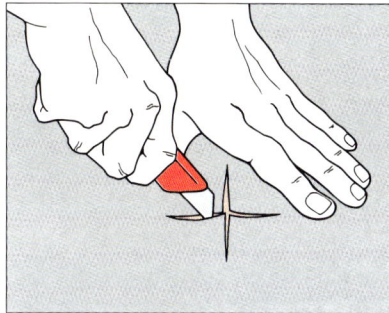

1 First, carefully scrape away any stone chips from the damaged part of the roof, using an old wallpaper or paint scraper. If there is a blister, make a cross-shaped cut through it with a sharp knife and fold the edges back.

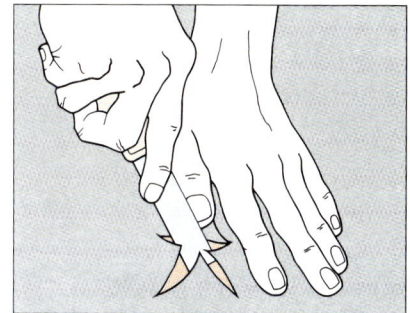

2 When the roof beneath the damage is completely dry, stick down the loose edges with a cold felt adhesive, before patching the entire area with a strip of self-adhesive flashing material. Finally, replace the stone chips.

Insulation safety

Look after yourself

Many roof repairs involve working with insulation materials, sometimes in quite confined spaces. Expert medical opinion seems to vary on whether or not domestic insulation fibres are hazardous. Certainly, some people do report temporary skin and throat irritation. It is therefore wise to always wear gloves, overalls and a face mask when handling insulation to prevent the fibres from reaching your skin or airways.

A real danger

If you discover that your house was originally insulated with asbestos—a white or grey, fluffy fibrous material that was once popular in some areas—call in professional help to deal with it. Do not be tempted to remove or dispose of it by yourself. Asbestos presents a real health problem; its fine, white, hair-like particles being blamed for serious lung diseases and other respiratory complaints. In severe cases, the entire house will have to be enveloped in a large plastic tent to isolated it from the environment while removal takes place.

WORKING WITH PAINT

Mixing it up

Electric stirring

An electric drill mixing attachment is handy for water- and oil-based paints. But don't use the attachment to stir lacquer, epoxy paint, shellac, or any finish that includes 'Do not shake can' on its label. You won't want to do battle with the bubbles that power-mixing stirs up. Instead, stir these paints and finishes by hand; they'll stay fairly free of bubbles.

Spatter shield

Stirring full cans of paint with a drill-driven mixer can splatter paint everywhere. One way to contain the mess is with a large plastic coffee tin lid (one that comes with 500 g or 1 kg tins). Drill a hole in the centre of the lid and slip it onto the mixer shaft before inserting the mixer into the drill. Hold the lid tightly over the paint can while you are mixing.

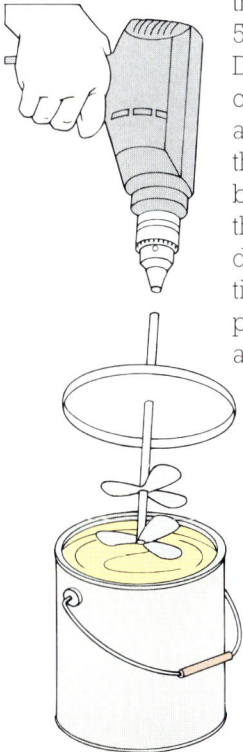

Milk carton mixer

Cut off the top of a clean 1 litre cardboard milk carton and use it as a container for mixing (or just holding) small amounts of paint or stain. The paint won't stick to the wax-coated interior, and the corner of the carton makes a good pouring spout.

Newspaper collar

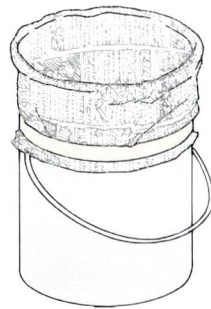

Here's another home-made way to minimise the mess created when stirring a full can of paint. Increase the height of the can by taping some folded sheets of newspaper around it. Any spills will then fall onto the paper and not your workbench.

Home-made mixer

For small jobs you can make your own power mixing attachment by inserting a beater from an old kitchen mixer in your electric drill. This makeshift attachment will work well in 1 litre cans, but the shaft is too short to reach the bottom of 4 litre cans. In order to avoid splattering paint, use a plastic lid as shown at left.

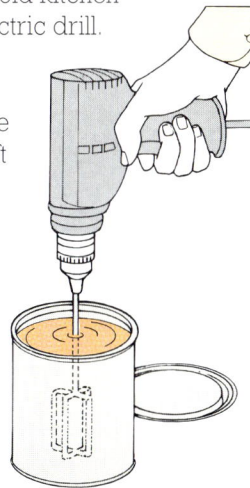

Blending for colour

If the job you're working on requires two or three 4 litre cans of paint, *box,* or mix, the paint from all the cans together to get a consistent colour. To do this, find a clean container and open all of the paint cans. Pour half of the paint from the first can into the extra container. Then pour some paint from the second and third cans into the first can. Move to the extra container and pour in some more paint from the second and third cans. Then pour the contents of all four containers back and forth several times. When the paint is mixed, return it to the original containers and seal the lids tightly. A much quicker alternative is to mix all the paint in a single 20 litre container, if you can find a suitable one.

Holey stirrer!

A paint stirrer is more effective if it has several holes along its length. With each stroke the paint flows back and forth through the holes, allowing for faster, more thorough blending. You can buy a perforated metal stirrer, or make your own wooden one. To make your own, drill small holes in a piece of scrap flat timber, measuring about 38 × 12 mm in size. Be sure to rinse all the paint from the holes to keep them from becoming clogged with dried paint.

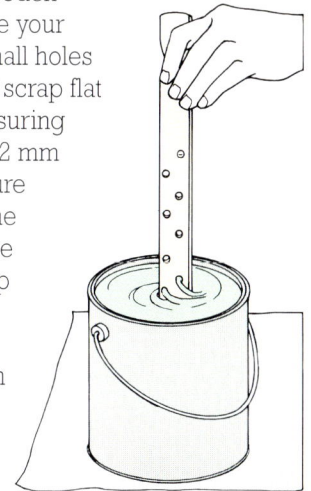

WORKING WITH PAINT

Special remedies

Say 'Cheesecloth'

Strain the lumps from paint by pouring it into an empty can covered with cheesecloth. Hold the cheese-cloth in place around the perimeter of the can with a sturdy rubber band, tape or string.

Screen old paint

Here's another way to deal with lumps in old paint. Use stiff, fine-mesh screening, available at hardware stores. Cut a circle with a diameter 6 mm smaller than the diameter of the paint can. Bend the screen a little so it will fit inside the rim, and drop it onto the surface of the paint. Push the screen slowly to the bottom with a paint stirrer. As the screen travels down, it will carry the lumps of dried paint with it. Even if the brush touches the screen on the bottom of the can, the bristles won't pick up any dried paint.

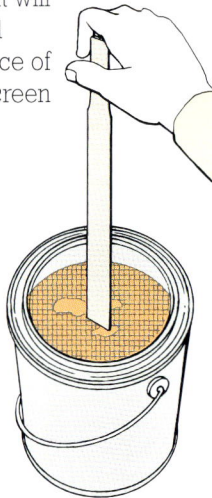

Stocking filter

A clean nylon stocking cut off near the ankle also makes a good paint strainer. Stretch the stocking around the rim of the can and secure it with a rubber band. Dip a brush into the can to force the stocking toe into the paint. The paint rising through the mesh will be finely strained.

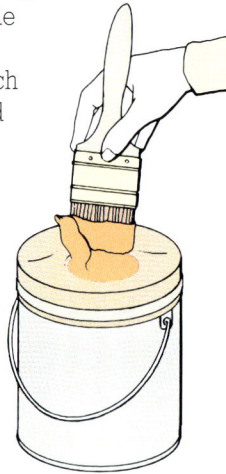

Handling fumes

The fumes of some paints and primers persist even in a well-ventilated room. To reduce the smell, add a few drops of vanilla extract to the paint—up to a tablespoon in 4 litres. The extract won't affect the way the paint performs, and the wet paint won't be so smelly. Note, however, that good ventilation is still required to combat the physical side effects of the noxious solvents.

Paint can handlers

Can holder

One way to keep a work surface clean and to avoid accidental spills is to place your can of paint in an old saucepan. The saucepan catches runs and also provides a convenient brush rest. The handle of the saucepan doesn't collect messy paint drips and makes it easy to carry the can from place to place.

Nail holes

No matter how neat you try to be, paint still tends to accumulate in the lid groove of a paint can, creating puddles of paint that squeeze out when you seal the can. To drain the paint back into the can, use a nail to punch several holes in the groove before you paint. When you reseal the can, the lid will cover the holes and form a tight seal. ▼

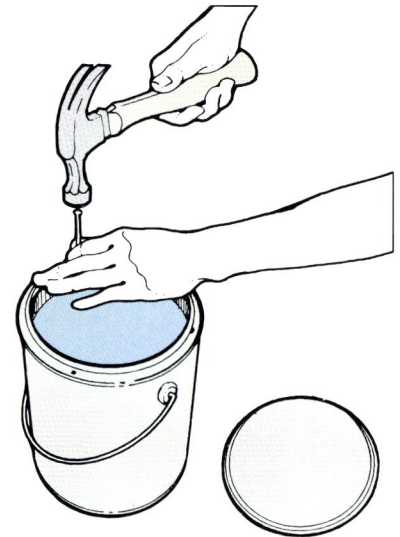

Pour neatly

If you don't have a funnel on hand to help you pour paint neatly, hold a pencil across the opening of the pouring can. The paint will follow the pencil to its end and from there pour neatly into its new container.

Plate catcher

Attaching a sturdy paper plate to the bottom of a paint can makes it easier to keep the floor or other work surface clean. The rim of the plate catches and contains paint runs better than newspaper. Use a little putty or adhesive to make the plate stick to the can. If you do use newspaper under a paint can, put a piece of wax paper between the can and the paper. It will keep the can from sticking to the newspaper.

Brush work

Grip and load

Applying paint successfully begins with a proper grip on the brush. Hold the metal band, or ferrule, between your thumb and fingers. This grip gives you the most control, especially if you switch the brush to your weaker hand. Dip about one-third of the length of the bristles into the paint, and then press the brush lightly against the side of the can. Do not drag the bristles against the rim of the can; that will cause bubbles. Let the paint pool on top of the bristles, but don't overload the brush.

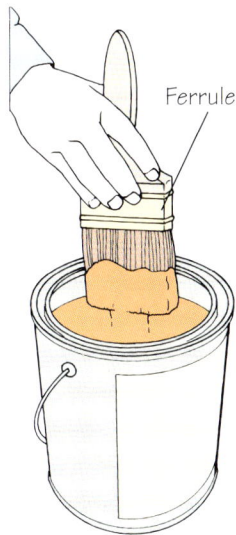

Ferrule

Even strokes

To spread paint evenly with a brush, use a few zigzagging strokes (1) and spread the paint out to cover the gaps (2). To finish an area, raise the brush so that just the tips of the bristles lightly smooth the painted area (3). This is called *laying-off* or *feathering* and removes any unsightly overlapping marks. ▼

1

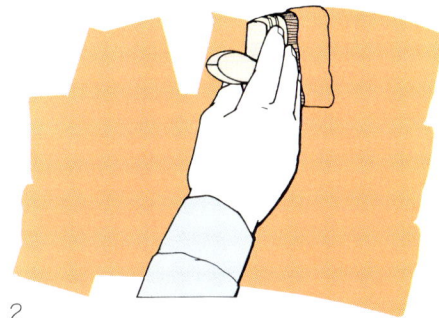

2

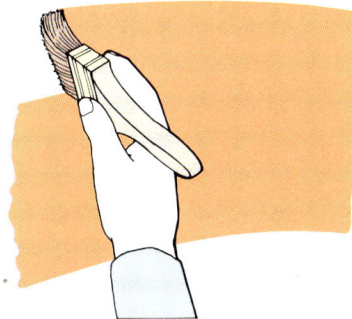

3

Less is better

You'll be less likely to overload a brush if your paint can is only partly filled. The extra free space near the top makes it easier for you to neatly slap the brush against the side of the can to remove the excess paint.

Wire tap

Bend a piece of coat hanger or other heavy wire as shown, and tape it securely to one side of a paint can. Use the wire, instead of the rim of the can, to tap the excess paint from your brush. The wire will keep paint from getting into the lid groove of the can and from dripping down its outside.

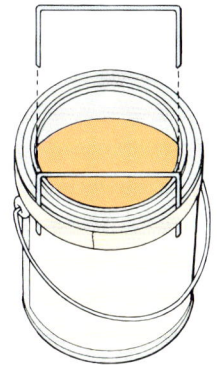

Brush rest

If you'd like an easy way to make a temporary resting place for your brush, just lay an ordinary paint stirrer across the rim of the paint can. Position the stirrer so that it forms a bridge near the middle of the can. That way it will offer a steady support for the wet bristles while the brush handle rests on the (cleaner) rim of the paint can.

BRUSHES

On the job

Make your own disposables

Disposable foam brushes are handy for touch-ups and other small painting jobs. Instead of buying disposable brushes, you can save trips to the paint or hardware store, and some money as well, by making them yourself. You'll need some scrap 19 mm thick foam carpet underlay (often available free from carpet shops) and a bag of spring-type clothes pegs. Cut the foam to size with a utility knife, angling the tip as shown. Snap on a clothes peg handle and you're ready to paint. ▼

Tape protection

Your paintbrush will be easier to clean if you wrap masking tape around the ferrule and the base of the bristles, extending the tape about 12 mm over the bristles. Rather than drying and hardening on the bristles, paint will collect on the tape. When it's time to clean up, remove the tape and clean off any wet paint that remains on the bristles. ▼

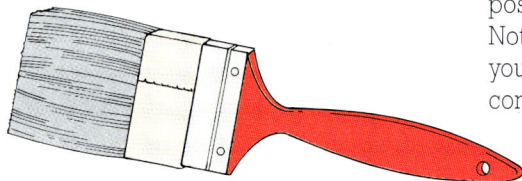

Comb-out

Stray bristles that fall onto a wet paint surface can mar a job. To remove loose bristles before you begin painting, groom the brush. Either use a brush comb bought for the purpose or improvise with a pocket comb or a pet brush.

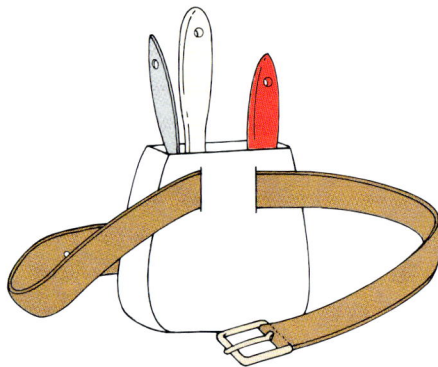

Belted caddy ▲

If you plan to use more than one size of brush during a painting job, you'll want to keep those brushes handy, especially if you are working on a ladder. You can make a reusable brush holder that attaches to an ordinary belt. First, find a clean rectangular plastic container that is wide enough to hold your brushes but narrow enough to keep them upright, such as an economy-size bottle of cooking oil or household cleaner. Cut off the top of the bottle, clean thoroughly, and make two slits in one side to accept the belt. Thread the belt through the loops on your pants and through the slits, positioning the brush caddy on one hip. Not only will you have the brushes at your fingertips, you'll have just one container to clean when the job is done.

Between coats

Freezer wrap

If you are working with oil-based paint and know that you will be using the brushes and rollers the next day, there's no need to clean and scrub your equipment. Just wrap everything in plastic bags or foil and stick the packets in the freezer. The cold temperature will keep the paint from hardening. When you are ready to paint again, thaw the tools for about 45 minutes. You can repeat this procedure for as many coats of paint or varnish as you need. However, if you are using water-based paint, you'll have to wash your tools each night.

Wire hang-up

Here's a way to store your brush during a break. Attach a small wire hook to the neck of the handle by twisting a piece of wire coat hanger around it with pliers. Hang the brush on the edge of the can so that the bristles will stay in the paint and not dry out, but don't let the brush sink too low in the paint or rest on the bottom of the can. ▼

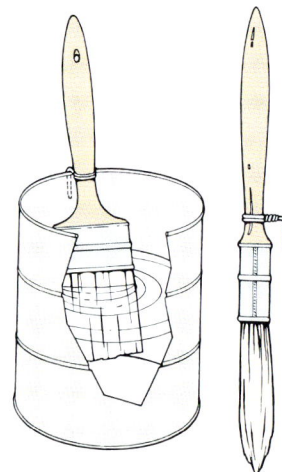

Two coffee tin ideas

A coffee tin with a plastic lid makes a good holder for your brushes while they soak (briefly) in paint solvent or water. Cut slits in the lid, and insert the brush handles in the slits so that the bristles clear the bottom of the tin by about 12 mm. If the tin has no lid, attach a stick to each brush handle with a rubber band. The stick will keep the bristles off the bottom of the tin.

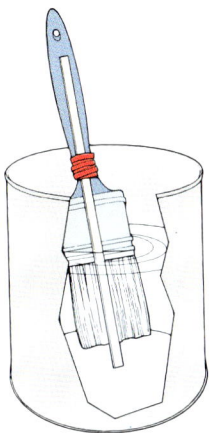

Easy wiper solution

A baby wipe container also makes a great holder. The slit in the top that dispenses the towelettes will hold the handles of most brushes. The bristles should stay about 12 mm above the bottom of the container—to prevent them from bending and to keep them out of the settling paint debris. Don't allow a brush to soak too long. Soaking is not a substitute for thorough cleaning.

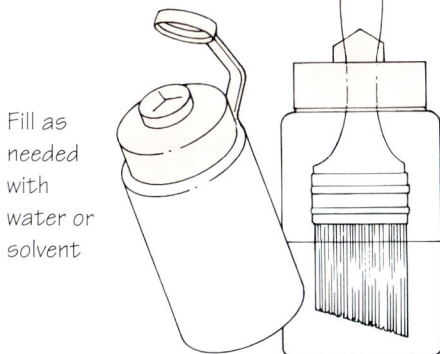

Fill as needed with water or solvent

When the job's over

Newspaper story

Looking for a place to wipe your brush when it's time to clean up? Instead of a piece of scrap wood or cardboard, use a thick wad of old newspapers. Place the bristles between several layers of pages. Then as you remove the brush, squeeze the bristles.

Bristle work

The best way to get a brush clean is to scrub the bristles against wire mesh. You can submerge an old kitchen strainer in a coffee tin filled with water or paint solvent. Another option is to cut a 175 mm diameter circle out of 6 mm wire mesh Bend the material to form a lip around the edge. Place the mesh on the bottom of a 500 g coffee tin and fill it with solvent. The mesh provides a surface for the brush to work against and allows sediment to collect on the bottom.

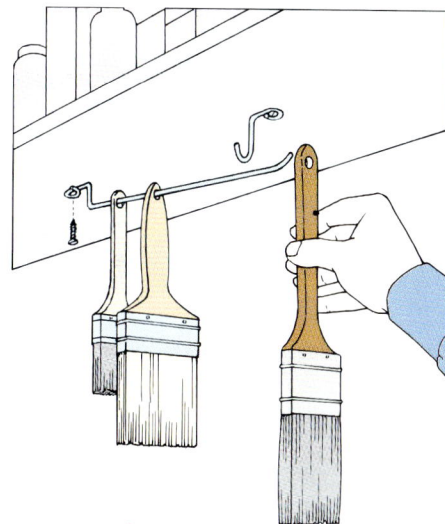

Go for a spin ▶

Remove excess water or solvent from a clean brush by spinning it back and forth between the palms of your hands. To protect yourself and your surroundings from the spraying liquid, hold the brush inside a paper bag.

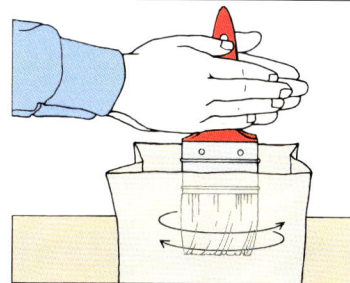

Drying hanger ▲

After cleaning your paintbrushes, hang them up to dry on a three-arm metal towel rail. Or make your own rack out of a wire coat hanger, using a wire cutter and pliers to shape the hanger and fashion the hooks. Mount the hanger with two screws, and provide a drip catcher.

Long-term storage

Store brushes in self-sealing plastic bags. To keep the bristles supple until they are next used, add a teaspoon of vinegar for each brush if water-based paint was used, or a teaspoon of turpentine if oil-based paint was used.

ROLLERS AND SPRAY GUNS

Easy rolling

Bucket brigade

Unless you are working on a ladder, roller trays are not the ideal tool to use for large jobs. They don't hold very much paint and it's easy to step on them accidentally, overturning the contents. Instead of using a roller tray, do what the professionals do, and get the paint directly from a 20 litre bucket. To remove excess paint, run the roller over a roller screen that hooks over the bucket rim. Make one from expanded metal mesh.

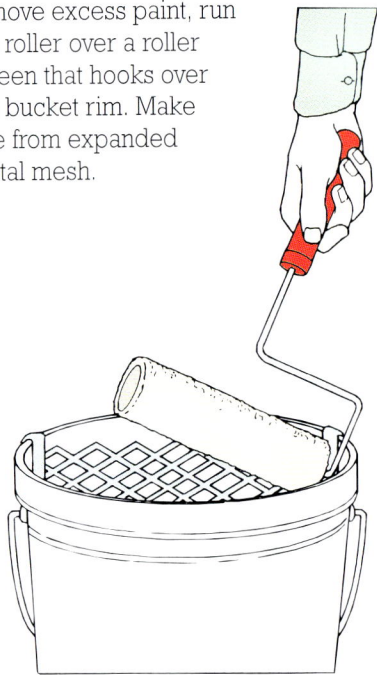

One liner

You can avoid having to clean your roller tray if you first line it with aluminium foil. Overlap all four sides, being careful not to puncture the foil as you fit the corners. When the job is done, return any excess paint to the tin; then peel the foil up carefully and discard it. (For more on discarding paint, see p. 39.)

Another mess manager

Here's how to remove a paint-filled roller cover without getting paint on your hands. Pull a plastic bag over the end of the roller and pull the cover off. Seal the bag and discard it (p. 39).

Clean and dry

Hanger helper

The hook of a wire clothes hanger makes a great tool for squeezing the excess paint from a roller cover. To shape the hanger into a cleaning tool, bend the 'wings' of the hanger so that they can be held together as a handle. Start at one end and pull the hanger hook down the length of the roller several times, turning the roller slightly with each pass.

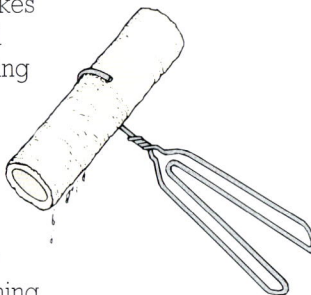

Dangling dryer

Drying a clean roller on its side flattens some of the nap and ruins the cover's smooth rolling action. Instead, tie a small piece of scrap wood to one end of a string and drop it through the opening in the cover. Hang the string where the cover will dangle freely. When it's dry, store it away.

Another hanger trick

This rack helps to keep a roller cover round and paint-brush bristles flat as they dry. To make it, cut near the bottom of a wire hanger at one end; then use pliers to bend the cut sloping wire into a hook for the straight piece. Bend the sides of the hanger closer together so that the straight piece rests on the hook. Slide on your clean roller cover and brushes, and hang them up to dry.

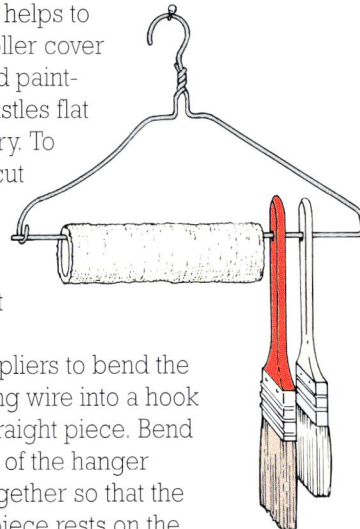

Spray painting

Safe operation

An airless spray gun forces paint out of its nozzle with a lot of pressure—so much so, in fact, that paint can become embedded in the skin. Therefore it is essential to wear long sleeves, gloves, a mask approved for use with a spray gun (not a dust mask) and goggles.

Cleaning up

To clean a spray gun, spray the appropriate solvent through the machine to flush the hoses and the body of the gun. (Collect the solvent in a bucket.) Then remove the nozzle and soak it in solvent to clean the orifice and nozzle tip.

How to handle a spray gun

It's crucial that each spray coat be thin and even. To that end, overlap your strokes a little. Keep your body parallel and your arm perpendicular to the surface. Bend your wrist as you move your arm (insets). This keeps the spray nozzle the same distance—about 200 mm—from the surface during the stroke. Begin moving your arm before you press the trigger, and continue to move after you release it.

Inside corners ▶

To avoid paint build-up in a corner, turn the gun 90° so that the spray fans out horizontally. Then move the gun from the top to the bottom of the corner.

Outside angles ▶

Stand directly facing the edge of an outside corner. Begin at the top and move the gun from side to side, overlapping the strokes as at left. In order to cover both surfaces and the edge, bend your wrist (insets at left).

PAINTING TOOLS

TOOL	USE	WHAT TO LOOK FOR
Brushes	Use 75–100 mm brushes for wide surfaces. Use 38–50 mm brushes for trim and panelled doors. Use 25–78 mm brushes for around glass, etc. For water-based paint, choose nylon or polyester bristles (natural bristles absorb water and lose their shape). For oil-based paints, use natural bristles.	Flagged ends give good paint retention and smooth coating. Tapered bristle body helps paint flow evenly and aids cutting in (see p. 179). Look for fullness and variety of bristle lengths for smooth painting results.
Rollers	Use 175 mm rollers for narrow walls and cladding. Use 300 mm rollers for large walls, wide cladding, masonry, and render. For enamels use blended polyester/wool covers. For water-based paint use synthetic-fibre covers (which won't absorb water).	Construction of roller frame should be sturdy: either professional-quality compression or slip-on type. Avoid types with wing nuts or end caps. Check that the roller cage moves freely.
Paint pads	Use for weatherboards, trim, shingles and timber fences. To store, place fibre side up.	Pads that have fibre applicators are preferable to those made of foam.
Spray guns	Useful on large areas or rough surfaces. Speed and ease of application are main advantages. Need for masking off areas not to be painted a major disadvantage.	Available on hire basis at paint centres or hire outlets. Consult dealer to ensure you match your needs with the spray gun. Make sure the jet and nozzle size is suited to the type of paint being applied.

The right colour

Tried and true

The best way to determine whether a certain colour will suit a room is to hang a large swatch of it on the wall where it is to be and leave it there for 24 hours. Observe how the colour looks as the light changes, under artificial light and at the times when the room is used the most. To make a swatch, either tape a number of paint samples together or coat a thick piece of porous paper or light board with the paint. ▼

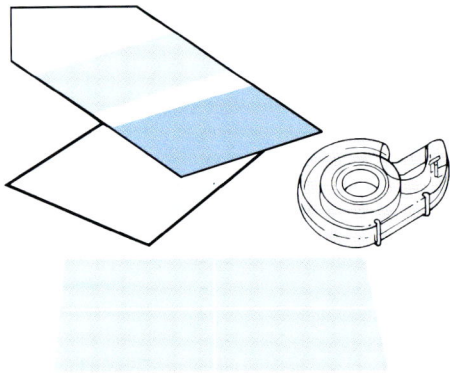

Subdued colours

Bright colours

Dark colours

In the mood ▲

You can use colour to create a mood. Dark colours will absorb light and lend a quiet, intimate feeling to a room. But be careful—too dark a room can end up being depressing. Bright colours are generally exciting; while subdued ones are relaxing and restful.

Lighten up

Before choosing a strong, bold colour for your walls, consider using one a shade or two lighter. You'll find a colour seems to darken and intensify as you spread it across the walls. If you select one that's too strong, you may end up with more colour than you really want.

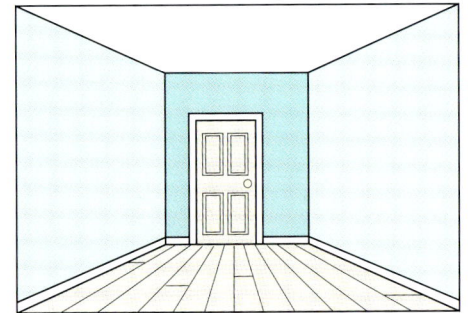

Room make-overs ▲

If you want a long, narrow room to look wider, paint one or both the short walls a bright or dark colour and the other walls a pale colour. If a room is square and lacks a focal point such as a fireplace or large window, paint one wall a rich accent colour such as maroon.

Check the exposure ▶

Rooms that face south, southeast or southwest receive little or no sunshine during the day, making them dark and uninviting. You can lend some cheer to such a room by choosing from a palette of warm colours—yellow, red, orange and brown. Likewise, you can make sunny rooms seem cool with blues, greens, greys and lavenders. But beware of those cool colours if you live in a cold climate. Research shows that people feel colder in rooms with cool colours. If you are committed to off-white, choose either a warm or a cool tint of that neutral colour.

Northwest (noon and afternoon sunlight)

North (well lit all day)

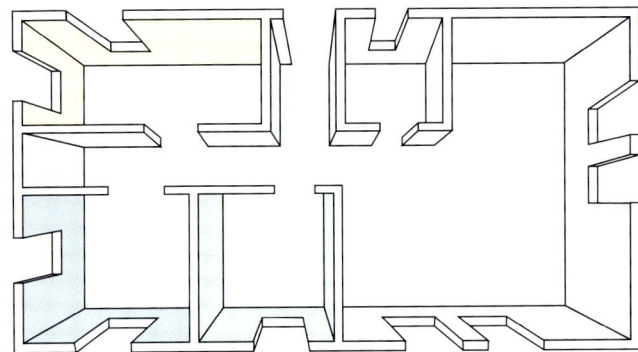

Northeast (some morning and noon sunlight)

West (afternoon sunlight)

East (morning sunlight)

Southwest (some late afternoon sunlight)

Southeast (some morning sunlight)

South (no direct sunlight)

Moving the walls

Colour can also create optical illusions. For example, light colours reflect light and make a small room seem larger. Warm colours seem to advance and 'fill' space, whereas cool colours tend to recede. A white ceiling will seem higher; a dark ceiling will appear lower.

Wheel of colour ▲

While a favourite colour or object often determines the main paint colour for a room, you may wish to consult a colour wheel for a secondary or contrasting colour. The colours that are opposite each other are called *complementary* colours. These hues will enhance each other in a colour scheme. The hues on either side of a given colour are called *related* colours and form the basis for a coordinated look to a room.

What to buy

Nothing but the best

Don't scrimp on the paint and primer or undercoat you buy. You'll get the best results if you buy a premium-quality paint recommended by a reliable paint retailer. Buying a less expensive paint won't really save you money, since it will cover fewer square metres and isn't likely to wear as well as a good paint.

Exact calculation

If your room has an irregular shape or is very large, you may wish to calculate precisely the number of square metres you need to cover. First, measure the length of each wall or section of wall, including any alcoves and other irregular shapes. Add up the figures and multiply by the wall height. Subtract the area of any doors and windows (about 1.8 and 2.1 sq. m each, respectively), and add the ceiling area. (Generally you can use the floor dimensions instead, multiplying length times width.) Finally, multiply that last number by the number of coats you think you're going to need. ▼

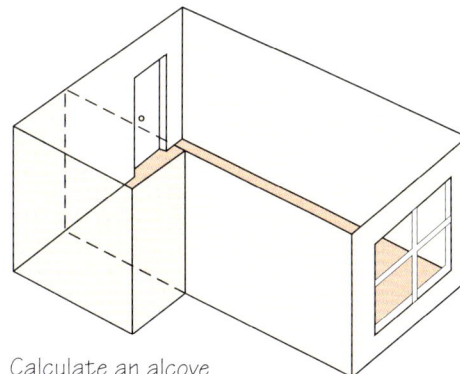

Calculate an alcove
as its own rectangle

Estimating rules

As a rule of thumb, 4 litres of paint provides one coat for four 2.4 m high walls in a 3.6 × 4.5 m room. (You'll need more for rough-textured walls.) Reckon another 2–3 litres for the ceiling.

Free paint

To help prevent yourself from running out of paint in the middle of a job, always buy a little more than you think you'll need, and buy paint in 4 litre, rather than 1 litre tins. You'll spend about the same for a 4 litre tin as you would for two 1 litre tins, and you'll be getting an extra 2 litres of paint for nothing. Save it for touch-ups (p. 189).

Instant blackboard

If you're planning to paint a child's room, a playroom or a kitchen, consider brushing a couple of coats of blackboard paint on a section of plasterboard. Tack on some lengths of painted moulding to frame it. You'll find that this makes a safe place to draw or a convenient message centre. Better still, buy a small sheet of low-density fibreboard and paint and frame that instead.

Washable walls

Would you like to have the finish of an interior flat wall paint and still be able to wash off handprints, dirt and the occasional scuff mark? Most of the large paint manufacturers market a washable paint in flat and low-sheen finishes. Generally, the higher the gloss level, the less you will notice that some areas have been washed often. In high-traffic living areas, such as a family room or a child's bedroom, you can increase the walls' washability by using a semi-gloss paint.

PREPARING A ROOM FOR PAINTING

Removing paint

Say when

If the trim in a room already has three to five coats of old oil-based paint, you can probably add another one or two coats of oil-based paint, but it's not a good idea to apply that many layers of water-based paint. Use a heat gun or chemical stripper to remove the old paint before applying a new coat. And no matter what kind of paint has been used on it, wood trim often looks best if all the built-up paint is removed first.

Caution: before removing paint, check its lead content (see facing page).

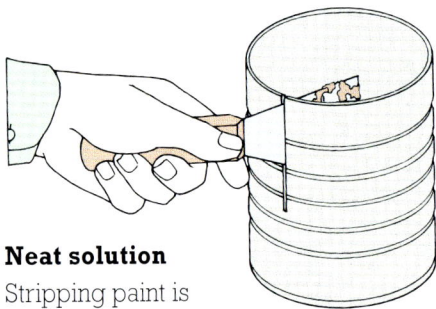

Neat solution

Stripping paint is usually a messy job. Here's a way to contain the blobs of paint and stripper as you clean your putty knife. Use tin snips or a hacksaw to cut a slot in a 500 g coffee tin. The slot should be a little wider than the thickness of the blade of the putty knife, and a little deeper than its width. To clean the blade, insert it into the slot at the handle and pull the knife toward you. The edges of the slot act as a double-edged scraper and catch the residue neatly in the tin. (For more on stripping finishes, see pp. 232–235.)

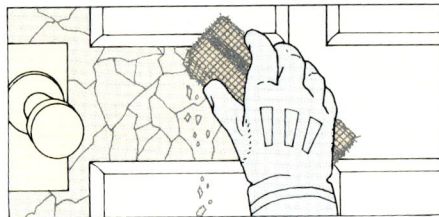

Scraping by ▲

To remove a rough section of built-up paint, try wrapping some metal window screening (not fibreglass) around a piece of scrap wood and using it as you would a sanding block. This improvised scraper removes paint quickly and won't damage the surface.

More preparation steps

Degreasing

Greasy and oily stains show through newly painted surfaces, and could possibly result in adhesion problems later on. Before you paint, check the surfaces for these stains. If the spots are few and small, rub them off with cotton wool balls or a cloth saturated with a solvent such as mineral turpentine or methylated spirits. As you rub, you'll find that paint will come off too, so wear rubber gloves to keep your hands clean.

Crayon and ink marks

Children find it hard to resist the temptation to draw on walls, and unfortunately crayon and ink will show through a fresh coat of paint. To remove crayon marks, put on rubber gloves and rub the areas with a cloth dipped in paint thinner. You can remove ink stains in the same way, using either paint thinner, as for crayon marks, or household bleach.

Wash the walls

Before you get out the paintbrushes, it's a good idea to wash the walls and ceiling thoroughly. Choose a cleaner such as sugar soap that removes grease and grime. Keep water out of electrical outlets by not overwetting the cloth or sponge you are using. ▼

Attack those cracks

Don't rely on paint to hide thin cracks in plaster. You have to take a trip around the room and fill them all first. Open up each crack with an old bottle opener. It is better not to use a putty knife; prising will damage the blade. Reserve your putty knife only for the job of filling cracks. That way you'll find that the knife will last longer.

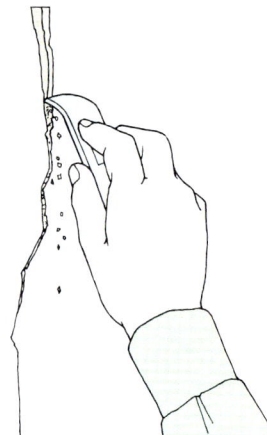

Fill 'er up

Once you have removed all the loose plaster, use a putty knife to fill the cracks with cellulose filling compound. After it dries, sand the area until it is smooth, vacuum it and apply sealer to seal the repair. For more tips on repairing walls, see pp. 129–131.

Safe outlets

When you come to a power point or light switch, carefully paint right up to the edge, using a small angled brush. Alternatively, switch off the main power and loosen the screws holding the fitting in place until you can just get a brush behind the edge of the plate. Do not remove the fitting altogether. You can also get a neat job by sticking masking tape over electrical fittings before painting. But take care when removing it.

Cover-ups

Door protection

An easy way to protect a door from paint is to slip an 'envelope' of polyethylene film over it. To make the cover, staple two large pieces of polyethylene film together on three sides. When you are measuring and cutting the film to size, don't forget to add a few extra centimetres to allow for the doorknob, and to make the cover easy to slip on and off.

LEAD PAINT HAZARDS

Lead is a toxic metal that, if inhaled or ingested, can cause neurological damage, especially in children. It was once a major ingredient in paint, but since the mid-1960s—when new pigment technology allowed manufacturers to lower the lead content considerably—its use has been curtailed, especially in domestic paints. However, even today, some paints—mainly those used for specialised industrial applications—still contain low concentrations of lead, but this fact must be advertised on the label. Generally, the older the paint is, the higher—and more dangerous—the lead levels are likely to be.

Any lead-based paint that is peeling and cracking is hazardous. A greater danger comes from less visible sources: the lead dust that rises when you sand this type of paint, and the lead fumes created by using a heat gun during paint stripping. (Lead-based paint that is intact does not present a danger.) If you notice old, deteriorating paint, or are planning renovation in an area where you may have to deal with an old painted surface, it may be wise to have a paint sample tested for its lead content.

A number of laboratories can test paint samples, and your local Occupational Health and Safety office or Environmental Protection Agency should be able to help with names and addresses.

If a test shows lead in your paint, you may not wish to tackle its removal yourself. Instead, get the job done by a professional decorator.

Before tackling lead removal, read a copy of the *Lead Standard* (from the Australian Government Publishing Service) or, in New Zealand, *Repainting Lead Based Paints* (from any Occupational Safety and Health office).

Roll-down cover ▶

The next time you are doing a lot of painting around the house make yourself this handy plastic drop-sheet. Cut a length of thin builder's plastic slightly longer than the height of your walls. Tape the end of the plastic to a cardboard tube and then roll the plastic onto the tube. When the time comes to use your drop-sheet, run masking tape along the top of the plastic, leaving a sticky edge. Tape the edge to the top of the wall, and then unroll the sheet.

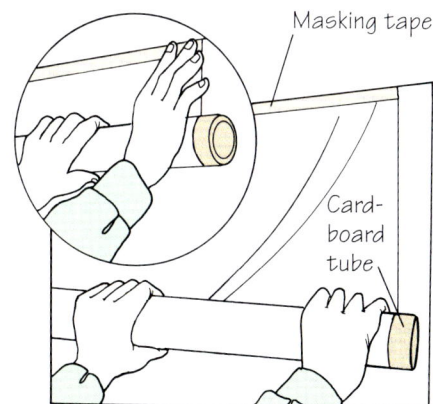

Masking tape

Cardboard tube

PREPARING A ROOM FOR PAINTING

Cover-ups

Drop sheet options

You can never have too many drop sheets. While professionals use heavy canvas ones because they absorb paint spills, provide nonslip footing and won't stick to your feet, most of the rest of us rely on inexpensive plastic drop sheets from the paint shop. To make plastic sheets function more like canvas, cover them with a thick layer of newspaper. And if you need an extra cover, use an old plastic shower curtain.

Go wall-to-wall

Strips of used carpeting can also serve as substitute drop sheets when you're painting or doing messy repairs. The weight of the strips makes them stay in place, and they can be used over and over again. The strips should be about 3 to 5 m long and wide enough so that all four legs of a stepladder will rest on the carpet at one time. Place the strip with its nap side up or down, as you wish. After use, let any wet spots dry; then vacuum the strip if necessary. If you don't have used carpeting on hand, check local carpet retailers and installers; they're usually glad to give away carpet remnants.

Press-on tape

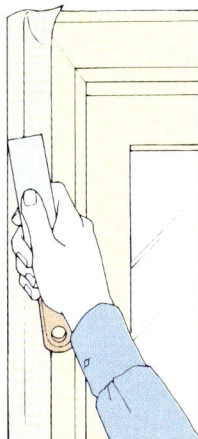

Have you ever peeled away masking tape only to find that paint has seeped underneath it? Masking tape protects a surface only when the seal is perfect. To make sure the tape does its job, press it in place with the flat side of a 50 mm putty knife.

Foiled again

A good way to protect doorknobs, telephone sets, electric switches, taps, handles and other items that you want to keep paint-free is to cover them with aluminium foil. Crimp the foil to fit the shape; it will stay there until you have finished painting. It's also a good idea to keep a couple of plastic sandwich storage bags nearby. Use them as makeshift gloves to protect phones and doorknobs from paint-splattered hands.

◀ **Protection for hardware**

For best results, you should remove all hardware before painting. But if you can't or don't want to do this, you can protect hardware from splatters by applying a thin coating of petroleum jelly. After painting, just wipe the metal clean.

Shoe in

To keep paint off your shoes, slip an old pair of socks over them. The cotton will absorb splatters and save you the work of cleaning up. ▼

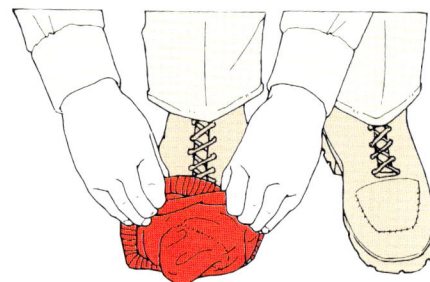

Step-by-step

Work order

Few things are as frustrating as finding you've dripped paint on a newly painted surface. To keep the mess to a minimum, work from the top down. Here's a step-by-step work plan for painting a new room. After the preparation work is done, paint the ceiling. Next seal the walls and the trim. Then give the walls their final coat. Finally, give the trim a final coat, saving the skirting for last.

Primer versus sealer

A primer is used on raw timber or metal as a preparatory layer, prior to the application of subsequent finishing coats. Sealers are available in a number of types, depending on the job in hand. Plasterboard sealers are used to reduce the porosity of a plaster surface. Alkali sealers are used on renders where lime has been used. Bleed sealers deal with water-based stains such as ink, which tend to show through new coats of paint.

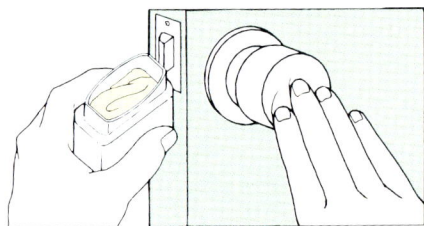

PAINTING WALLS AND CEILINGS

Painting large areas

Cutting in

Use the narrow edge of a brush to edge, or *cut in,* a thin line of paint equal to the width of your paintbrush along the perimeter of the walls and the ceiling. Begin in a corner and put just enough pressure on the brush to flex the bristles. To minimise lap marks, always work from a dry section back into a wet one. If you are working with a non-flat paint, put two people on the job—one cuts in with a brush while the other fills in with a roller. If you are working alone, cut in a section and then fill it in with the roller.

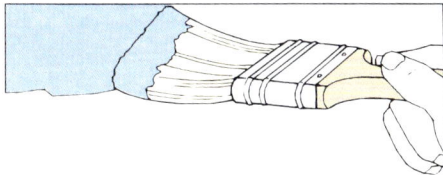

▼

Paint catcher

When you are painting a ceiling, wrap an old face flannel or paper towel around the handle of your brush and secure it with a rubber band. This absorbs the inevitable paint drips and helps keep your hand clean.

Find a stopping place

What should you do if you have to halt a project before you've finished applying a coat of paint—or if you find that you're running low on paint? Try not to stop in the middle of a wall. Instead, finish a wall and then stop. You'll avoid obvious lap marks. And if you have to buy more paint (custom-tinted or not), a slight difference in shade won't be as noticeable.

ROLLING PAINT

After a painstaking job of preparing a room, it's rewarding to see how quickly a roller can cover the walls and ceilings with paint. Begin by saturating a clean roller in the paint, rolling it over the tray ridges or wire grating (see p. 172). Then dip the roller in the paint. (To avoid drips, don't overload the roller.) Spread it on the wall or ceiling as shown.

Paint small sections (1 to 2 sq. m) at a time. Begin painting a ceiling in a corner, and then work across the narrower dimension of the room. Start painting a wall in an upper corner, and work from top to bottom and left to right. If possible work with natural light—you'll find it easier to see any gaps.

1 Apply the paint in zigzag strokes. Use an 'N' or 'M' stroke on walls, as above, and a 'W' pattern on ceilings.

2 Move the roller horizontally to even out the paint, and work back into the wet edge of the previous area.

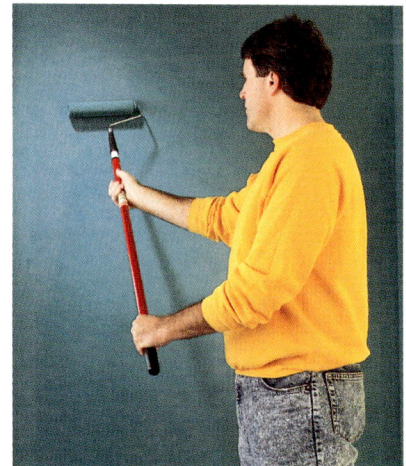

3 To remove roller marks and even out the texture, use light up-and-down strokes. An extension handle on the roller really helps here.

Neat edges

Pane protection

Beginners may wish to cover the edges of the windowpanes to reduce the amount of clean-up that's needed. One way is to mask each pane (p. 184). However, this takes a long time and removing the tape can be a chore, thereby defeating the initial goal. Instead, try rubbing soap or lip balm around the edges of the glass next to the trim. Any paint marks or splatters on the glass will be easy to remove when the paint is dry.

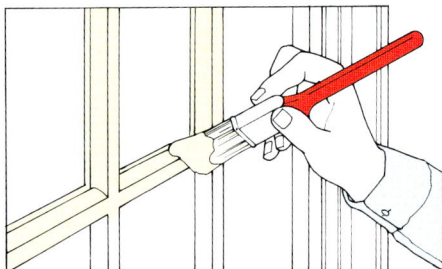

Going steady ▲

If you have a steady hand, you can paint the trim around windowpanes without masking them. You'll find that you have the most control if you use an chisel-edge or cutting-in brush and hold it as you would a pencil. Always work from the glass edge outward. As you do so, be sure to leave a thin paint line on the glass so you will seal the paint to the glass—and keep moisture from invading the paint film, causing the paint to peel. When the paint is dry, scrape off any paint that is beyond the paint line.

Work order

Door stops ▶

When painting a door, begin with all four edges (1). Next, paint the moulding around any glass panes and all wood panels, whether raised or recessed (2). Then paint the door body, beginning at the top and proceeding down the sides (3 and 4). Finish the job by painting the door frame or jambs from top to bottom (5 and 6). As you paint the frame, work from the door toward the outer edges of the frame. For more on door edges, see the facing page.

Mask or remove hardware

Steps for a window

Here's the best sequence of steps for painting a double-hung window. First, pull the top sash three-quarters of the way down and push the bottom sash three-quarters of the way up (below, left). Paint the entire bottom rail (1) and half of each side stile on the top sash (2). Slide both sashes back into place, stopping a few centimetres from their closed positions (below, right). Then finish painting the top sash (3 and 4) and paint the entire bottom sash, working from top to bottom (5 and 6). To finish off, paint the top of the architraves (7), then the sides (8) and finally the bottom (9). ▼

Bottom sash

Top sash

Top sash

Bottom sash

On edges

Connecting colours

When a door connects two rooms that are different colours, what colour should you paint the door edges? Here's the rule of thumb. The latch-side edge should be the same colour as the room that the door opens into. The hinge-side edge, which is visible when the door is open, should be the same colour as the other room.

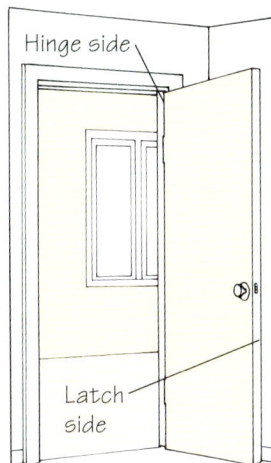

Hinge side

Latch side

The bottom line

If you are not going to remove the door before painting, you can paint the underside with a scrap of carpet. Why bother with an edge that no one will see? Paint helps to seal the end grain, preventing the wood from absorbing moisture and expanding. ▼

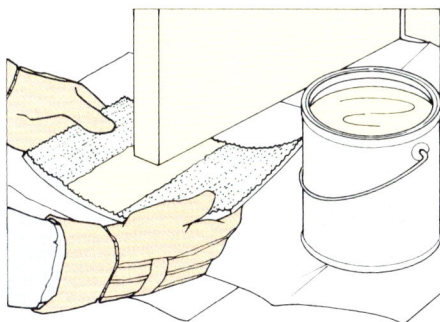

Steps for steps

Painting treads

Here are two ways to paint stairs and still keep foot traffic moving. You can paint every other step, let the paint dry thoroughly, and then paint the rest. Or you can paint half of the width of each step, wait for the paint to dry, and then finish the job.

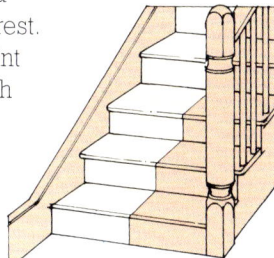

Reaching high places

Painting a stairwell usually involves erecting scaffolding. You can either hire it or make your own. If you hire, ask the dealer to show you how to set it up correctly. If you are going to build your own, begin by analysing the space to determine what combination of trestles, stepladders, extension ladders, and 250 × 50 mm or 300 × 50 mm planks you need. (Three typical situations are shown below.) When you are erecting the platforms, be sure to clamp or nail the planks to their supports, and open or lock any doors that might accidentally knock into the scaffolding. Allow the planks to overhang at least 300 mm on either side. ▼

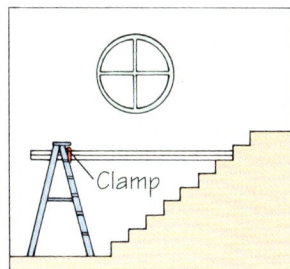

Clamp

Place a trestle so the plank will be level when it is placed on a trestle or ladder step (no higher than the next-to-top one). If the span between supports exceeds 1500 mm, use two planks instead.

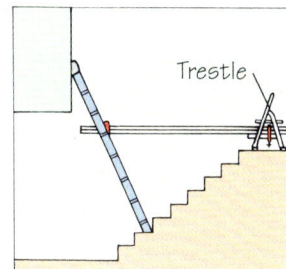

Trestle

When you can't reach the ceiling with the method at left, brace an extension ladder at an angle. Pick a step that allows you to reach the high points easily, and make sure the ladder feet are level.

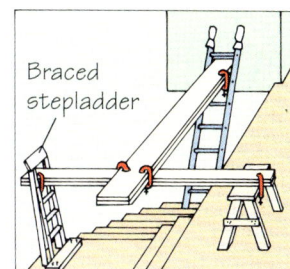

Braced stepladder

If there isn't enough space for a trestle or ladder to open completely, you'll need to brace it in position with a cleat. To make the cleat, nail a board to the landing at the base of the trestle or ladder.

Glove action

Do you have a decorative railing and baluster in need of a coat of paint? Try using a paint glove. It does a great job of reaching the tight spots and crevices of wrought iron work, and it makes short work of thin balusters, whether they're made of wood or metal.

DECORATIVE PAINTING

Stencilling

Make your own stencil

You can easily turn a favourite curtain or upholstery pattern into a stencil. Just copy a length of the original fabric on a photocopier, enlarging or reducing it if desired. Then place a piece of thick polyethylene film (plastic sheet) on top of the photocopy, tape it securely in place, and cut out the design with a craft knife.

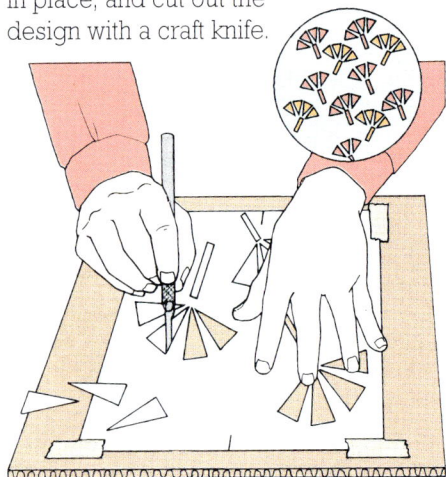

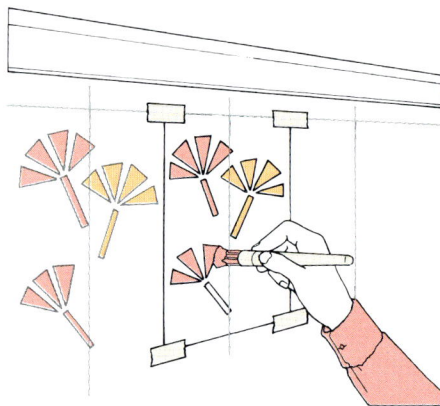

A light load ▲

Successful stencilling begins with loading the brush properly. Dip a stencil brush only about 6 mm into the paint (use a fast-drying water-based or artist's acrylic paint). Next distribute the paint on the bristles by dabbing the tip lightly on a piece of newspaper. The brush will appear dry when it is ready to use. Dab the paint into the stencil openings with short in-and-out strokes, keeping the brush perpendicular to the stencil.

Design ideas

Floor it

Fancy paint effects need not be limited to walls and ceilings; they can be used on floors if a protective coating is added on top. New, non-yellowing, super-hard polyurethanes are ideal for the job; they will protect a painted decoration with a rugged and almost invisible shield.

Ordinary objects

Professional decorative artists use tools other than sponges, rags and brushes. These artists may use a piece of cork, a nail, a bottle top, a broom or even their gloved hands to create a special effect. Here, a piece of cork and a nail are used to simulate a knothole design.

Repeating designs ▶

In any stencilling job, patterns rarely repeat evenly across a surface. Some designs can turn a corner in mid-pattern, but often the design will end awkwardly on a wall. In the latter case, plan to either stretch or overlap it a little on each wall, whichever is easier. To determine how much adjustment is needed, divide the length of the pattern into the distance to be covered on each surface. Then, when you are painting the pattern, work from opposite corners toward the centre of the wall. To make your adjustments less visible, overlap or stretch several repetitions by just a little bit. If you opt to stretch the design, fill in the gaps by hand.

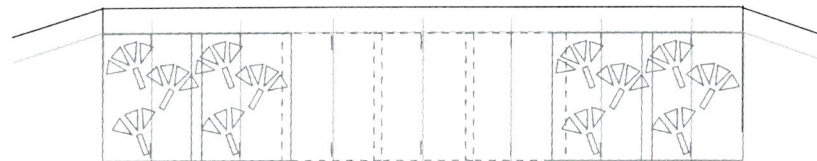

Overlapping stencil pattern

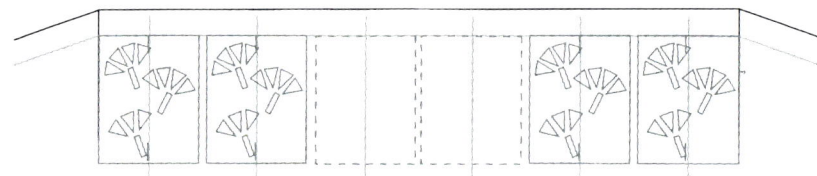

Stretching stencil pattern

TEXTURING TECHNIQUES

Sponging, rag-rolling and stippling techniques add a wonderful dimension of pattern and texture to a routine painting job. All these effects are easy to create.

To prepare a surface for any of the three techniques, apply a base coat and then cover it with a compatible glaze. Use either all water-based or all oil-based products; never apply one over the other.

You can buy glaze that is ready to use (in a limited number of colours), or you can make your own glaze in any colour by simply diluting paint. If you are using water-based paint, mix three parts water with one part paint. For a translucent water-based glaze, make the mix 4:1. If you're working with oil-based paint, begin with equal parts semi-gloss paint and solvent. Try out the glaze and the tool you'll be using on a practice board, thinning the

paint little by little up to a 2:1 ratio. To ensure that the colour and effect will be uniform, mix sufficient glaze to complete the job in hand.

Sponging is an additive technique; you dab the glaze onto a dry base coat. It is the only one of the three techniques shown here that can be carried out with fast-drying water-based paint. Use only natural sponges.

Rag-rolling and stippling are subtractive techniques in which you apply glaze and then partially remove it, and so it is important that the glaze dries more slowly. Fabrics commonly used for rag-rolling are worn cotton bed sheets, gauze, nylon netting and hessian. To see various patterns, use different rags. Stippling brushes, made for the purpose, give the base coat a freckled effect; softer brushes create a mottled look.

1 Sponge on the first colour glaze over a dry (rolled-on) base coat with firm strokes. If you're adding a second colour glaze, be careful not to use too much of the first colour. When a sponge gets filled with glaze, switch to a fresh one.

2 When applying the second colour glaze, you can vary the effect by patting and twisting the sponge. If you're using water-based glaze, clean the sponges with water; if you're applying oil-based glaze, clean them with mineral turpentine.

To stipple a surface, apply an oil-based base coat and let it dry. Apply an oil-based glaze with a pad applicator or wide brush. Press the bristles of a coarse brush into the wet glaze. As the bristles become loaded with paint, clean them with a dry rag.

To rag-roll a surface, prepare the surface as for stippling (above). Then roll a crumpled rag across the wet surface. When the rag becomes saturated, switch to a fresh one.

PAINTING A HOUSE EXTERIOR

Colour scheming

Find coordinates

When choosing the colours, begin by deciding on the main colour. As a rule, it should be a light to medium tone that complements or contains some of the roof colour. For trim choose a light colour, such an off-white or, if you are having your colours tinted, the same colour as the body, but only one-quarter of the colour formula. Next, pick an accent colour for features you would like to stand out, such as the front door and the window shutters. This accent colour is best if it is darker than the main colour, with a moderate contrast (see below). If you are painting the entry steps or a porch, choose a neutral hue that echoes the roof.

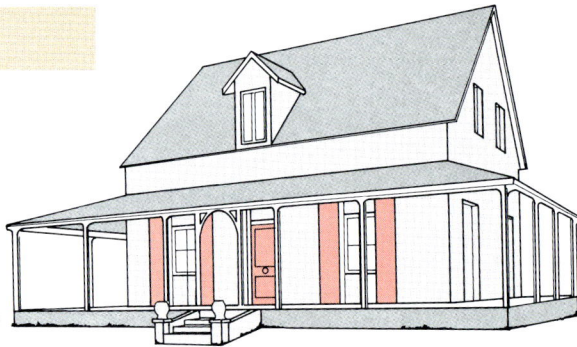

Make a statement ▶

Your choice of an exterior colour scheme can affect the look of your house from the street. Light and warm colours (see pp. 180–181) seem to advance and make a house stand out from its surroundings. Dark and cool colours recede and make a house seem less obtrusive. If your house is small, you can make it seem larger by using an accent that is lighter than the main colour. Stay away from the bold contrast of a light main colour and dark accent colour. The result will probably be a broken up appearance.

Light main colour stands out

Dark main colour recedes

Light accent on darker main colour seems larger

Dark accent on light main colour looks broken up

Time and weather

Choosing sides

Who says you have to paint an entire house at one time? The job will seem much more manageable if you plan to paint just one side a year. If this idea appeals to you, take a trip around your house to determine which side has weathered the most. The north or west side usually receives the most sun; other sides may face prevailing winds and rain. Or if you prefer, begin with the most visible facade. After all, that's what you and passers-by see every day.

A job for two seasons

The best time of year to paint the outside of your house is either in the spring or in the autumn, when air temperatures are neither too hot nor too cold. Not only will you be able to complete the job more comfortably, but the paint will stay wet longer, allowing more time for brushing out. If you live in an area that has a defined wet season, then that time of year is best avoided as well.

Follow the shade

No matter what season it is, schedule the job so that you will be painting in the shade. Direct sunlight makes the paint dry too fast. Fast-drying paint is harder to work with and tends to blister, creating a soft paint surface that is easily damaged. You'll also avoid the eye strain caused by sun glare reflecting from the paint, a problem that occurs especially with light colours.

Getting started

Making an estimate

To determine how much paint you'll need, calculate the size of the area to be painted as you would for an interior (p. 181). If your house has a gable, compute its area by multiplying its width times its height; then divide by two. Keep in mind that exteriors require more paint than interiors. Add about 10 per cent to your total if you have weatherboards, 20 per cent for rough or porous surfaces, 30 per cent for corrugated material, and 50 per cent for a first coat on render or concrete block.

Power washing ▶

As with interior painting, the secret to a successful job is proper preparation. First, check for peeling paint, mould and cracked paint, and make repairs (see chart). Next wash the house with sugar soap, working from the bottom up. You can hire a power washer to remove dirt and blast off any loose or flaking paint. (Wash weatherboards with the power washing nozzle pointed downward—you don't want any water to get between the boards.) If you don't have a lot of dirt and loose paint to remove, or if the surface of your house is render or soft brickwork, then you are probably better off with a garden hose

fitted with a spray nozzle—a power unit could cut through the render. Before washing render, repair any cracks. *Caution:* the pressure from a power washer can be dangerous. Keep the nozzle pointed away from you and others and away from windows; there's enough power to break glass.

COMMON EXTERIOR PAINT PROBLEMS

PROBLEM	CAUSE	CURE
Peeling paint	Paint applied over dirty or mouldy surface	Wash exterior with scrubbing brush and detergent to ensure a dirt-free surface. Remove mould with a mixture of 1 tblsp. dry detergent, 1 litre chlorine bleach and 3 litres warm water. Scrub with a stiff brush. Rinse well with clean water. Remove any loose paint. Prime all bare wood. Use high-quality acrylic paint; it 'breathes' and won't totally trap dampness.
	Moisture coming through substrate, plus poor flashing or sealing around windows and doors	Install adequate flashing at roofs, chimneys and openings, or add sealant where needed.
	No damp-proof course in exterior walls	Have a damp-proof course treatment applied professionally. Most proprietory solutions will not work properly.
Mould	Dirty, moist or warm surfaces support growth of spores (mould is a fungus)	To test 'dirty' spots for mould, wash with 3:1 water and bleach solution. If it's mould, spots will disappear. Or remove with bleach/detergent mixture as for peeling. To prevent mould, each spring apply detergent to house exterior, and hose off; spray nozzle removes dirt that supports mould growth. Or apply a primer and paint with a fungicidal additive.
	Too much shade permits moisture build-up	Trim trees and shrubbery to allow air and sunlight to reach affected area.
	Inadequate venting in eaves, porch ceilings or cladding permits moist conditions	Install vents in areas where mould recurs. Make sure there are no water leaks in the area.
Alligatored or cracked paint	Many coats of paint on an old surface, or paint applied over improperly prepared surface	Sand, scrape or burn off old paint, then repaint.
	Water-based paint applied over gloss oil paint	Sand glossy surface to dull finish. Use proper undercoat under new paint.
	Inferior cladding material	Replace cladding.

PAINTING A HOUSE EXTERIOR

More preparation

Scrape and feather

In order to remove loose paint, use a four-edge blade scraper that has a knob at the blade end. To give the tool some more scraping power, hold on to this knob as you push and pull the blade across the surface—but try not to gouge the wood. Once the loose paint is off, you'll need to smooth out the rough edges of the remaining paint. Start with a coarse grade of abrasive paper and progress to a medium grade, until all the edges are evenly feathered.

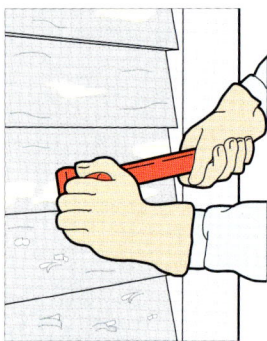

Scaffolding setup ▶

The safest type of scaffolding is a steel pipe system, which is available from hire outlets. It gives you a stable support and a wide, safe work platform (the walkboards hook onto the frame and stay in place). The scaffolding shown here is set up for spray-painting; if you intend to use other tools, you won't need such a wide platform. If the surface around your house is firm and level, rest the scaffolding on casters for easy mobility. Otherwise you'll need to rent adjustable baseplates for the scaffold. Don't try to use pieces of scrap wood to level it.

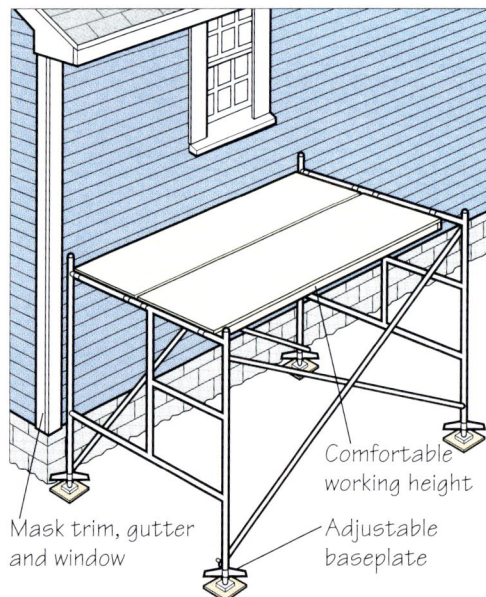

Filling out

After scraping and feathering, you'll still find places where the bare wood is lower than the old bonded paint. Use a putty knife to fill these areas with an exterior grade filler after priming. Let the compound dry, and then sand it smooth.

Of trim and weatherboards

The joints where weatherboards meet the window and door trim are notorious for developing large gaps. These gaps not only look bad, but they also allow air, damp and noise into the house. Scrape out any old sealer, if present, and recaulk the joints with a paintable sealer.

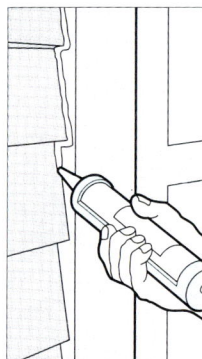

When it's rot

Regularly check timber posts, columns, balusters, and other external woodwork for rotting areas. Repair minor spots with a filler, after applying a timber preservative, and sand smooth. If rot covers large areas then replace timber with a durable species.

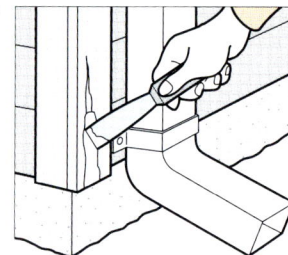

Techniques

Good spray-painting coverage

It's crucial to coat all the edges and surfaces of weatherboards, shingles and other rough textures such as render. Otherwise, moisture will creep into unsealed areas and cause the cladding to fail. If you are spray-painting, choose a windless day (even a 5 to 8 km/h breeze will blow overspray everywhere). Apply three light coats. (1) Spray from below so that the paint coats the underside of each board. (2) Spray at a downward angle and cover the face of each board. (3) Spray straight into the surface. Or, instead of step 3, back-roll or back-brush—go over the wet paint with a roller or brush to force paint into the surface.

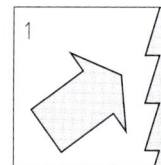

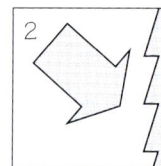

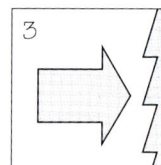

Comfortable working height

Mask trim, gutter and window

Adjustable baseplate

1

2

3

Easier than a brush

If you don't want to spray-paint, try a pad applicator on shingles and weatherboards. The pad reaches under the laps, and the downward motion of the tool pushes the paint into the grooves. To coat the bottom edges of cladding, you can use a brush or narrow roller. ▼

Paint caddy

When you are painting on a scaffold or on a ladder, a brush that's left on top of the paint tin may fall off. What's more, the tin may tip over, creating a huge mess and wasting paint. To avert this trouble, put the paint tin and brush in a bucket, and hang both the bucket and the brush from paint tin hooks. If the bucket is large, you'll also have room for your paint scraper, putty knife, a rag and any other painting tools you need.

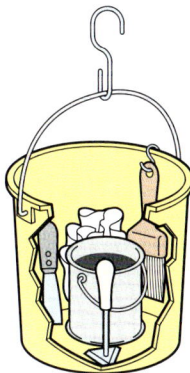

High roller pan

If you want to work with a roller from an extension ladder, here's a handy way to mount a roller tray. Drill two small holes at the top rear of the tray; then form two hooks from wire coat hangers and attach them to the tray. Position the tray on one of the ladder's rungs, and bend the hooks around a higher rung until the tray sits flat. The flanges at the front of the tray will hold it in place.

Order of work

Paint plan

When everything is washed, scraped, sanded, filled and sealed, you're finally ready to begin painting. Begin by priming any spots of bare wood; then paint the cladding (see right). Next do the trim and windows (see p. 186); then move to the doors, along with any posts and balusters. If you intend to paint the entry steps or a porch, do it next. To finish the job, paint the shutters (if there are any) off the windows, and remount them when the paint is dry.

Weatherboards without lap marks

The walls are the most visible part of a painting job, and so it is crucial to avoid lap marks. Work in the shade, and brush from a dry section into a wet one. And instead of working from top to bottom in vertical sections, go all the way across from one natural break to another (see the numbered sequence in the illustration). If there is no natural break, proceed across the entire width of the house, painting only as many courses of cladding in one segment as you can while keeping a wet edge. Work from top to bottom and, if you are right-handed, from left to right. Follow a similar sequence for painting the trim and windows.

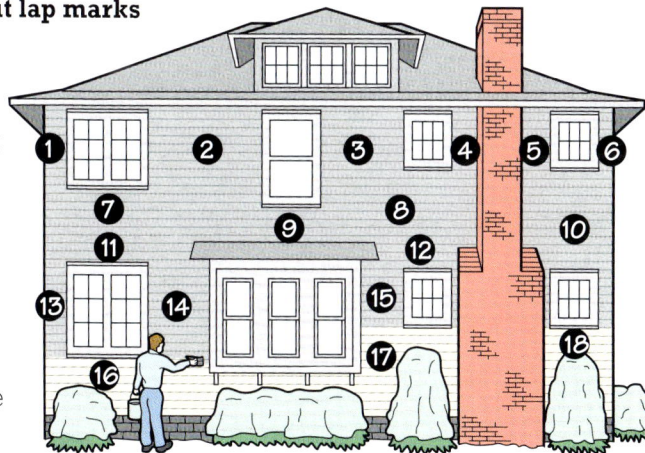

PAINT CLEAN UP AND STORAGE

Flaws and spills

Flaws and spills

Clean line for trim

When painting around trim, keep a flat-bladed screwdriver or putty knife handy, and a cloth dampened with the proper solvent. Then, if you get a bit of paint on the trim, fold the cloth around the tip of the tool and wipe it away. ▼

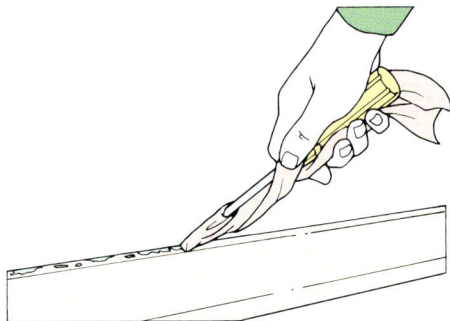

A clean scrape

Here's an easy, accurate way to scrape paint from windows. Place a 100 mm wide filling knife blade against the putty or wood moulding. Slide a razor blade scraper against the knife blade to make a perfect line without damage. ▼

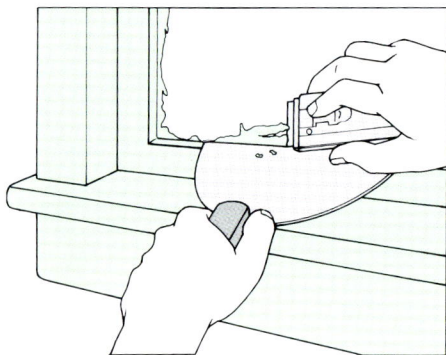

Unmasking

If possible, remove masking tape as soon as the paint is dry enough that it won't run or smear. As you remove the tape, clean away any paint that has seeped under the edges. If, for some reason, you've had to delay this job, soften the adhesive first by blowing hot air on the tape with a small hair dryer.

Handling drips and runs

What should you do if you discover a flaw—a drip, a run, or a stray bristle—when the paint is too dry to brush it out? Don't be tempted to overpaint it; get rid of it. If the paint is hard, either sand or scrape it down. If it is still tacky, hold a piece of masking tape at both ends, press the tape gently over the flaw or bristle, and then pull it straight off. Then, when the paint is hard, sand the area smooth and touch it up with fresh paint.

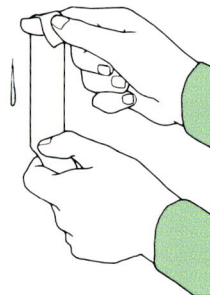

Touch up

Even though paint is dry to the touch, it may not have hardened completely. Because a newly painted surface is still fragile, be careful not to scuff it when you are moving furniture back into the room. Keep a small brush and some extra paint on hand so you can easily repair any marks that you make accidentally.

Wash out

Be sure to wash a water-based paint spill out of clothes while it is still wet; once a stain dries, it is permanent. Your best bet is to wear overalls that completely cover your clothing, including collar and cuffs, or to wear old clothes that you won't mind staining.

Skin treatment

To clean water-based paint from your skin, all you need is some hot soapy water. With oil-based paints you'll need something more. You can rub on some waterless hand cleaner, available at car accessory or hardware shops, or try a little salad oil. (If paint gets in your hair, dip a piece of cotton wool or a tissue in the oil and rub it gently over the painted hair.) You can also use a rag or paper towel soaked in mineral turpentine. If you use mineral turpentine, however, expose your skin to as little as possible, avoid breathing in the fumes and wash well with soap and water afterward.

Wrapping up

Waste not, want not

You can reclaim the mineral turpentine that you've used to clean your painting tools. When you've finished cleaning your tools, put the dirty liquid in a covered coffee tin. Set it aside (away from heat) for a few days to allow the paint to settle to the bottom of the tin. Then pour off the clean liquid and leave the solids in the tin. Save the tin so that you can scrape other paint waste into it. When it is full, discard it as noted on page 39.

Write it down

It's always a good idea to record the brand of paint, as well as the type (such as semigloss or flat) and the names of the colours used for a room. One way to do this is to write the information on a piece of masking tape, and then to stick it to the top edge of a door frame. Then, when it's time to touch up some minor damage, or for a repaint, just hop on a stool and you'll know which tin you're looking for.

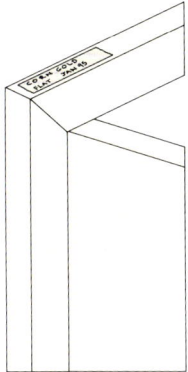

Storing paint

Draw the line

When storing leftover paint, mark a line on the outside of each tin to indicate how much is left in it. Later, you'll be able to tell at a glance if you have enough paint for a job.

Sealing the tin

When you reseal a tin of leftover paint, any paint residue that has collected in the rim can prevent an airtight seal. What's more, it usually squeezes out, making a mess. To minimise the build-up, punch holes in the rim (p. 174) or wipe the rim clean before you close the tin. To improve the seal, stretch a piece of plastic kitchen wrap over the rim. Then tap the lid into place, using light blows on alternate sides of the lid.

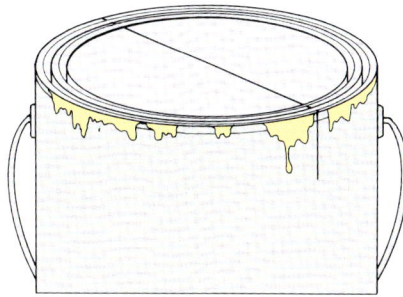

Resealing leftover paint ▲

Have you ever struggled to reseal a tin of leftover paint? Breaking a seal that is coated with dried paint leaves uneven surfaces on both the lid and the rim, making it difficult to seal the tin the next time. So if you need to work from such a tin, mark the exact position of the lid as it sits in the rim—before you open the tin. To do this, draw a line across the lid and the rim at two places. When you replace the lid after using the paint, simply align the marks and press the lid down for a quick and easy seal.

More on leftovers

When you store leftover water-based paint in its original tin, you often get rust and hard flakes in the paint. To avoid this, pour the paint into a plastic bottle or a glass jar with a screw lid. But don't let any paint get on the threads of the lid or you won't be able to reopen it. If you do get paint on the threads, rub a little petroleum jelly on them.

Leftovers yet again

You can also keep leftover paint fresh by pouring it into a resealable plastic bag. Squeeze the air out before you seal the bag; then put the bag into the original paint tin and tap the lid closed.

Waxed paper barrier

Because a large air space will dry up a small amount of paint, you should transfer leftover paint to a smaller container (and a smaller air space) if the original tin is less than half full. Or cut a circle of heavy waxed paper that is the same diameter as the interior of the tin and float it on the paint surface. The waxed paper acts as a barrier, reducing the interaction of the air and the paint.

Avoiding paint skin

Even if a tin of leftover paint is sealed tight, a skin will form on the surface of the paint after a while. Removing the skin before you begin to paint is a messy job at best. To avoid this floating paint skin, store the tin upside down. Then when it's time to open the tin, turn it right side up. The skin will be on the bottom of the tin, leaving the fresh paint on the top.

No oil-based skin

Spreading a thin film of mineral turpentine over the surface of oil-based paint before sealing the tin will keep a skin from forming. To apply the film, put the solvent in a small sprayer. Use very little—only one teaspoonful to a half-empty 4 litre tin of paint. To keep the film intact as you seal and store the tin, take care not to shake or agitate it.

PREPARING TO HANG WALLCOVERINGS

Smart strategies

Cover tests

If there's only one layer of untextured wallpaper on the wall—and it's still adhering tightly—you don't have to remove it before hanging a new one. (More than two layers, however, is more weight than the adhesive is meant to support; the layers are likely to pull away from the wall.) Test the old wallpaper by running your fingertips over it. If you hear a crackling noise, the covering is loose and should be 'removed. You should also check the edges and corners by prising them up with a putty knife. If large sections lift off, continue the removal job.

Covering coverings

If the old wallpaper passes the crackle and corner tests (above), glue any loose areas with PVA glue or wallpaper paste (p. 203). Then wash the surface with detergent or a mild solution of household bleach and water, and apply a primer made for use under wallpapers. Beware, however, if the old layer is vinyl, foil or plastic film. Covering these materials doesn't work very well. You're better off removing them instead.

Mess management

Removing wallpaper is a messy job. Old sheets and bedspreads make first-rate drop cloths. You can either throw them away or use them again. As you work, pick up the bits of stripped paper before they dry. Otherwise they'll make your footing slippery and stick to the drop cloths and your shoes.

Razor's edge

If it's in good condition, plaster is tougher than plasterboard. (Old plaster may be crumbly.) You can reduce the amount of soaking needed on a plaster surface by using a sharp razor scraper to remove wallpaper. The blade will slip easily between the paper and the plaster without damaging the wall.

Don't be stubborn

If a section of wallpaper backing just won't soak off, use a sanding block and 120- or 220-grit paper to sand the edges (only) of the area. Be sure that the backing is dry before you sand. Continue until the transition between the wall and the backing is smooth. Wear a dust mask when sanding.

Soaking solutions

Break it up

To break the surface film on vinyl or painted wallcoverings so the remover can penetrate the covering and soften the paste, use a sanding block fitted with coarse abrasive paper, a wire brush or a scoring tool made for the purpose. Take care not to gouge the wall as you work.

Scoring tool

Spray time ▲

Think twice about hiring a steamer; they work very slowly. Brushing or sponging on chemical remover is also a time-consuming, messy job. You can speed the process up considerably if you put the remover in a pressurised garden sprayer, hold the nozzle a metre or so away, and spray it liberally on the wall. Allow the remover to soak in; the paper should almost fall off the wall. Respray any resistant areas. Before you fill the sprayer, be sure it is free of insecticide residue. When handling chemical removers, wear goggles and gloves.

Adhesive clean up

Use a window squeegee to remove old wet wallpaper paste from plaster walls. Dip it into very hot water, run it across the wall for about a metre, clean the paste from the tool, and repeat the process until all the paste is gone. ▼

Home-made mix

A mixture of 1 part vinegar and 10 parts water makes a good paste softener. To apply it, use a sprayer (pump or pressurised). The smell, while nontoxic, is irritating; so ventilate the room well.

After stripping

Wash and dry

Wash newly stripped walls with clean hot water and a little household bleach (a quarter cup of bleach to 8 litres of water). Then allow the walls to dry thoroughly—usually a few hours, but if the air is humid possibly a few days. Prepare the walls as for paint (pp. 182 –184); make sure the surface is smooth.

Greasy job

Kitchens and bathrooms are usually painted in a gloss paint, which is likely to be coated with a film of grease or soap. Wash these walls with sugar soap. Then seal them with an undercoat suitable for nonporous walls. If the sealant beads up, there's still some grease on the surface; wash the walls again.

Fill in the bumps

You can turn a lightly-textured wall into a surface suitable for wallpaper with a layer of heavy-duty lining paper, hung horizontally. If you choose a suitable pattern, any slight texture that is left will be invisible. Heavily-textured walls are very hard to paper over. If you must do the job, you will probably have to relining the walls with plasterboard first.

Planning the job

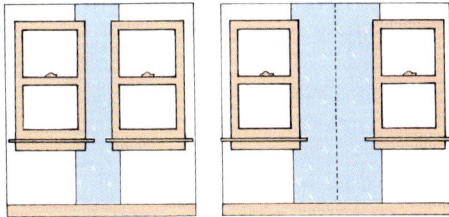

Two window treatments ▲

If you start a project between two windows, consider both the width of the covering and the space between the windows when deciding how to waste as little wallpaper as possible and how to avoid working with narrow strips. In a narrow space you'll probably need to centre the strip (left). In a wider space, try centring the seam (right).

Focal point strategies ▶

If you are hanging a large pattern that would look best centred on a main wall, or if the room has a focal point, such as a fireplace or a window, you'll need to centre the first strip, then work away from one side. Stop the first side when you get to an inconspicuous place for the mismatch. Continue hanging the covering from the other side of the centred strip until it meets at the mismatch spot. As a general rule, try to work away from the major light source in the room. Then any slight overlap where strips join will not cast a shadow.

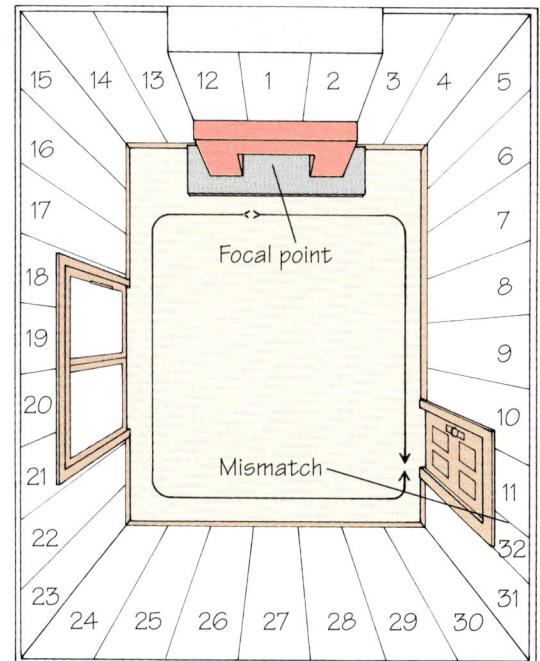

Focal point

Mismatch

HANGING WALLCOVERINGS

Strip tips

Put the top up

Many patterns are almost—but not quite—mirror images top and bottom. If there's a chance that you might accidentally hang your wallpaper upside down, mark an X on the top of the pasted side of each strip as you cut it off the roll. Note that you should do this with identical diamond and striped patterns as well—the shading may vary.

Reverse for one colour

You'll get a more uniform colour with solid-colour, textured (non-matching) coverings if you reverse alternate strips.

Pressure point

When wetting the strips, don't apply too much pressure with the roller or pad applicator—you could remove some of the paste and end up with serious adhesion problems.

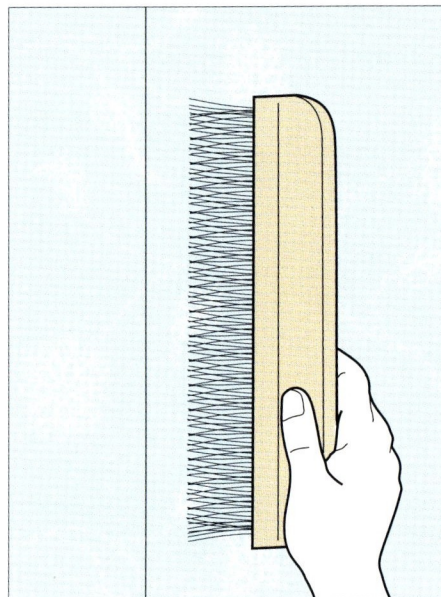

Brushing flock ▲

Never use a seam roller on flocked or other wallpapers with raised patterns. Instead, gently tap the seams with a soft laying brush. That way you won't damage the raised pattern.

All the trimming

When you are trimming wallpaper at the ceiling junction or along skirting boards, always hold a broad knife between the cutting tool and the paper. This ensures a straighter cut and keeps the knife blade from tearing or damaging the paper if your hand slips. ▼

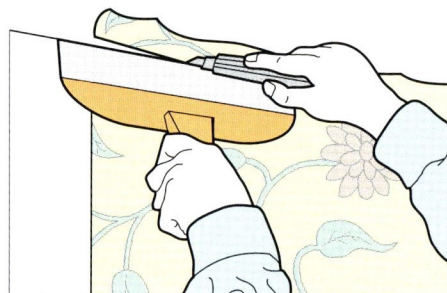

Keep an edge

Keep a sharp blade in your utility knife (and keep the knife away from children). A dull blade makes jagged cuts. To store all those used blades safely, drop them into an empty soft drink can.

Water trays

Go and soak it ▶

You may prefer to use a water tray to wet prepasted papers. If you do, 'backroll' the strip so that the pattern faces in, and then soak the rolled-up paper in clear water to wet the paste. Then proceed with the process of folding the paper.

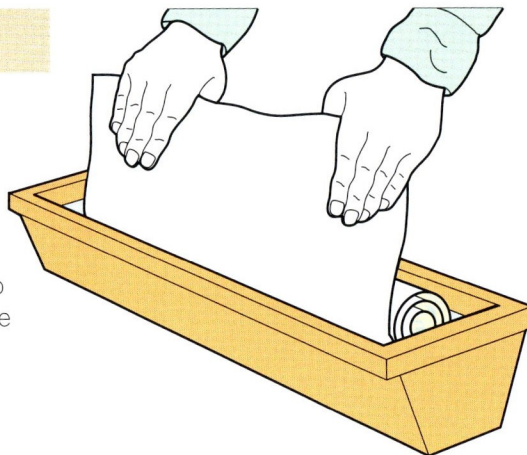

Include the kitchen sink

You may not have to bother with a water tray if you are covering kitchen or bathroom walls. A good-sized kitchen sink or a bathtub will do the job.

One more tray idea

Here's a way to ensure that the strip is submerged uniformly and is thoroughly wet. When you are backrolling the strip, wrap it loosely around a long medium-weight cylinder, such as a length of clean and rust-free metal pipe or a heavy rolling pin.

HOW TO HANG PREPASTED STRIPS

If this is your first wallpapering project, choose a pattern that needs little or no matching. Do a bedroom or a living room—they are easier than kitchens and bathrooms. Start off in a room with no alcoves or recessed windows, so you won't have to cut and match a lot of odd-sized pieces. You will need a ladder, a utility knife and blades, a large flat work surface, sponges, a bucket, a paint roller, clean tepid water, levels, a pencil, a tape measure, scissors, a soft laying brush, a seam roller, an apron with plenty of pockets in it, drop sheets, clean towels and garbage bags.

1 Use a level to strike a plumb line where the first seam will fall. If it is near an inside corner, position it so the strip will extend 5 mm beyond. (It should go 6 to 12 mm beyond an outside corner.)

2 Cut a strip the height of the wall plus 50 mm at the top and at the bottom. Use a roller dipped in tepid water to wet the back of the strip thoroughly, until the paste becomes milky.

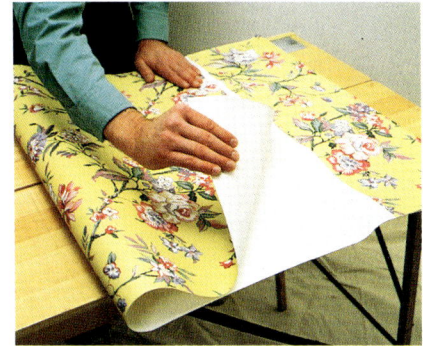

3 Fold, or relax, the strip by turning it pasted side in; make the first fold two-thirds of the sheet, the second, one-third. Roll the folded strip up loosely and let it rest as per maker's instructions.

4 Hang the strip. Begin at the top and align the right or left edge with the plumb line. Release the folds gradually. The strip should overlap both cornice and skirting board by about 50 mm.

5 Flatten the strip against the wall, using the laying brush. Start at the centre of the strip and push out. Any small bubbles that remain will disappear as the strip dries out and shrinks.

6 Hang the next strip (without a plumb line), matching the pattern. After the third strip is hung, lightly roll both sides of the first seam with one pass. Wash off excess paste with a damp sponge.

HANGING WALLCOVERINGS

Paste

Enhancing the paste

Some prepasted coverings adhere better than others. To see how well a prepasted covering will stick to your wall, do a wet test. Wet a 150 mm piece of the pattern, place it on the wall, and let it dry. If you have any doubts about its adhesion, just roll some wallcovering paste activator on the pasted side before hanging it. (The activator looks and applies just like wallpaper paste.)

Mildew stopper

Mildew, ever the enemy in bathrooms and kitchens, can easily find its way to the dried paste beneath wallpaper. When it does, the bond weakens. While the pastes of some coverings have been treated to resist mildew, others have not. If you have chosen one of the latter, you can treat the paste side of the covering with a fungicide as you hang each strip. Before proceeding, test the spray on a patch to be sure that the fungicide won't affect the pattern dyes.

Now you see it

When you are spreading clear paste on wallpaper, it is hard to see if you're coating the surface completely and evenly. If your covering has a background other than white, you can add a few drops of food colouring to the paste to make it more visible. Pour it in drop by drop, just until it has a very light tint. Too much colour will bleed through the paper.

Table talk

Instead of hiring a pasting table, use an old smooth-finished door or a 2400 × 1200 mm sheet of plywood. Choose a sheet with a finished side and no knots.

Less mess

When you are ready to paste, put a drop sheet under the table to catch the inevitable drips. After you've pasted each strip, wipe the table clean (especially the edges). That way you'll keep the pattern side free of paste.

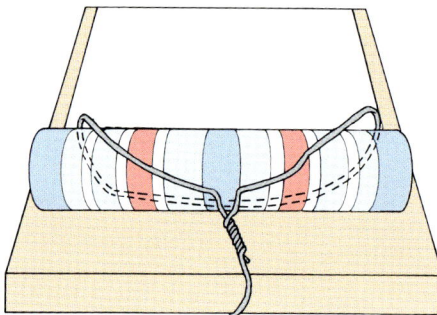

Hanger hold ▲

To keep a strip from rolling up when it's laid out on the pasting table, use this improvised holder. Simply bend a wire coat hanger into the shape shown, fit it over the roll, and secure the hooked end to the edge of the table.

Ceilings

When to do it

If you are papering a small room—such as a bathroom or a guest bedroom—consider covering the ceiling as well as the walls. It'll give the room a feeling of intimacy as well as a finished look.

Choose the direction

When you're covering a ceiling with the same material as the walls, remember that you'll be able to match the ceiling pattern on only one wall. Pick the most prominent wall in the room or, if the room is small, the wall opposite the most frequently used door. In the latter case, the pattern will seem to draw you into the room.

Ceiling strategy

If you plan to cover a ceiling with paper, do so before you do the walls—and be sure to get someone to help you. Cut the strips of covering so that the ends will extend 12 mm down the wall. Then fold the strips accordion-style, and you're ready to go. ▼

Neat edges

1 Overlap 2 New plumb line

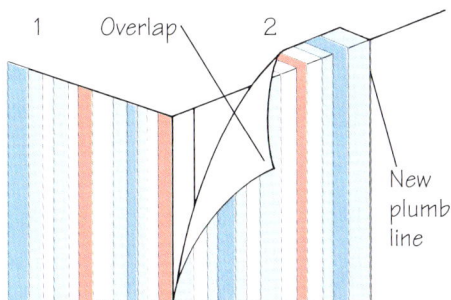

Turn the corner ▲

When covering an inside corner, you must overlap the strips. Never try to bridge a corner with one strip. Measure three spots (top, middle and bottom) from the edge of the last strip to the corner. Use the widest measurement and add 5 mm. Cut the strip to size, knowing that the overlap will vary, and hang it. To finish the corner, strike another plumb line and hang the other cut piece.

Outside wrap

Outside corners are very visible—and seldom plumb; consequently you shouldn't wrap a single strip around the corner. Instead, treat the corner as you would an inside corner, but plan to leave a larger (6–12 mm) overlap. Smooth both strips carefully into place.

Arch comments

If you are not going to cover the underside of an arch, you'll want to leave a crisp edge of wallpaper around the archway. Leave about 25 mm of covering untrimmed. Let the glue dry, and then trim the excess paper with a single-edge razor blade. Dry paper is easier to trim neatly than wet paper.

Odds and ends

Take a recess

Overlap Cut corner

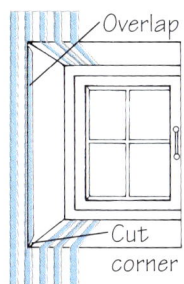

When covering a recessed area (as for a boxed window), start with full-width strips, allowing extra for an overlap on each side of the recess. Snip the corners before smoothing the overlap (above). Cut strips to fit each side and finish the job (below). ▼

Smooth curves ▶

To cover the underside of an arch, follow a method similar to that for recessed areas. When it's time to smooth the overlap around the curve, snip relief cuts at frequent intervals. Cover the overlap with one strip, if possible. Cut the strip slightly narrower than the width of the arch to avoid any peeling edges.

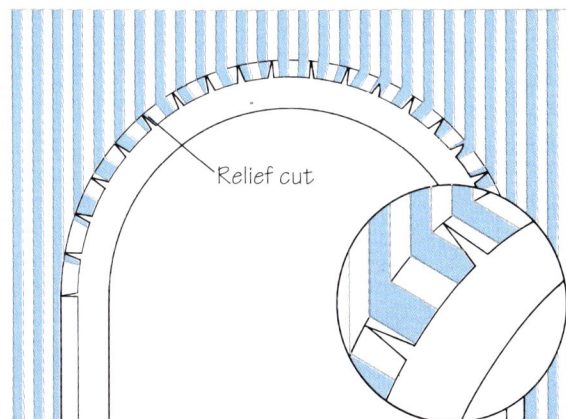

Get behind a radiator

You needn't disconnect and move a radiator or heater to hang wallpaper behind it. First position a full-length strip, smoothing it from the ceiling down to the top of the radiator. Smooth the rest of the strip behind the radiator with a length of wooden dowel or a long ruler. Then crease the trim line into the strip with a dull, long-handled knife. Pull the strip up from behind the radiator and trim along the creased line with scissors. Finally, reposition the bottom of the strip and smooth it down.

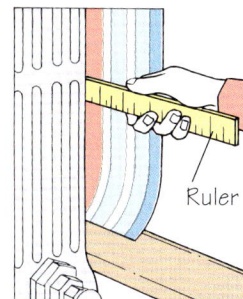

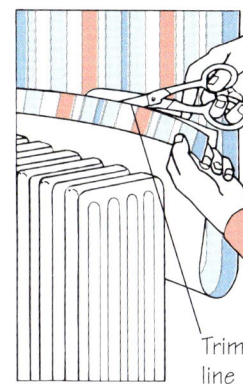

Ruler

Trim line

Relief cut

HANGING WALLCOVERINGS

Borders and accents

More is better

Putting up a border is an easy, inexpensive way to dress up a painted room. But if the room is large, you shouldn't economise too much. As a rule, the larger the room, the more border motifs you'll need. For example, a single border at the ceiling or at the chair rail level tends to make a room look unfinished. Consider adding more borders and accents to unify the room.

Ceiling frame

In a room where the ceiling gets some attention, such as a dining room with a chandelier or a bedroom, put a border on the ceiling. Depending on the size of the ceiling and the effect you want to achieve, you can place the border frame 75 mm—or 600 mm—from the wall.

More frames

Brighten up a boring window or door opening by framing it with a border motif; then add coordinated curtains to complement the look. On a large wall you can create a series of rectangular panels for a formal look. You can also frame a mirror, such as the one on a wall cabinet in a bathroom.

Unexpected places

Looking for ways to accent a room without investing in a border covering? You can hang strips of wallpaper on the rear wall of open or recessed shelving, or you can cover a wastepaper basket. If you're decorating a bathroom, covering the inside of the bathroom cabinet will dress up that typical eyesore.

Ganging together

You can combine several borders of various widths, or cut sections from a border and glue them on both sides of a main border motif to create a decorative stripe around a room.

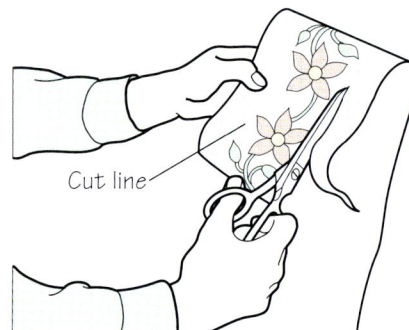

Cut line

Make a stencil effect ▲

To create a stencil effect with a wallpaper border, cut the edging from both sides; then hang the interior motif. It will look very much like a painted design.

Hiding imperfections

Plumb problems

If a room is badly out of plumb, the variations will show around the doors, windows and at the edges of cornices and skirtings. The professionals suggest selecting a random pattern, a floral, or a pattern with a vine motif. It is best to avoid geometrical patterns and stripes because they emphasise irregularities.

Border camouflage

One way to hide an uneven ceiling line is to hang a covering and add a coordinated border. Place the border so that half of it is on the wall and half is on the ceiling. Fold the border over, crease it in half and hang it. At the corners, follow the steps below. This 'half-and-half' approach neatly wraps the room, giving it a finished look. ▼

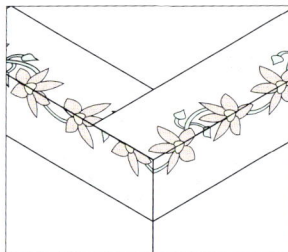

For an inside corner: 1. Butt two border pieces where walls meet, overlapping the ends on the ceiling.

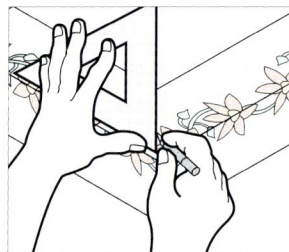

2. Cut a mitre through both layers on the ceiling. Remove the waste and smooth the remaining pieces down.

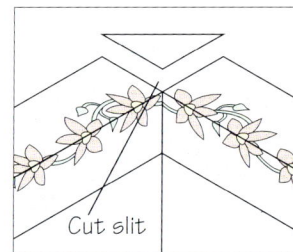

Cut slit

At an outside corner: Slit the ceiling side of one piece and wrap the piece around. Cut a patch to fill the gap.

When things go wrong

Too wet

If a pasted strip becomes too wet, fold it and let it sit a little longer than you normally would. The extra moisture will evaporate. (Don't let it dry too much.)

Too dry

If for some reason you've been delayed and allowed a strip to dry out too much, you may be able to salvage it. Carefully place the dried, folded paper on the table; taking care not to bang it as you do so. Spray a mist of clean water over the strip to relax it. Gently unfold the paper; reapply paste and fold again. ▼

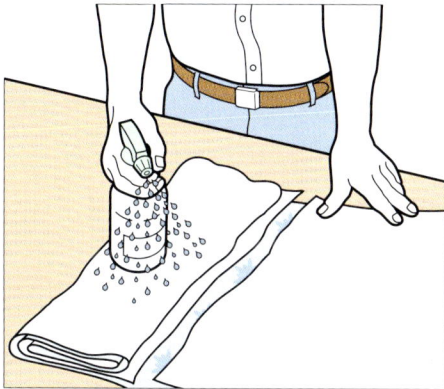

Free advice

While every roll of wallpaper comes with a set of general preparation and hanging instructions, it won't specify the particular needs of the wallpaper you have chosen. If possible, buy your wall paper from a local distributor who employs a trained and experienced consultant. Such a person will be able to advise you if you run into problems.

Making repairs

Mist those curls ▲

You'll have an easier time getting curled-up edges to stay down if you mist the repair area with clean water. With the curl in a relaxed state it will lie in place when the glue is applied.

Tear it up

When a tear occurs, one side has the backing and the other has the pattern. To repair the tear, place the backing side down first and cover it with the pattern side. (Otherwise, the backing will be visible.) Where the two sides meet you will see a small ridge. Gently smooth it down with your fingertip, the eraser end of a pencil or the tip of a toothpick. If the repair area dries as you work, mist it with clean water. ▼

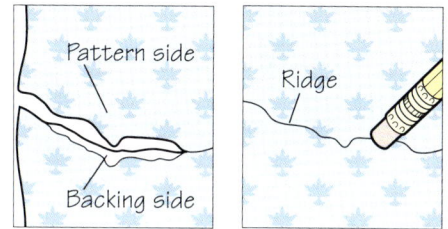

Pattern side
Backing side
Ridge

TROUBLESHOOTING WALLPAPERING PROBLEMS

PROBLEM	CAUSE	REPAIR	PREVENTION
Seams pull apart	Wallpaper shrinks after it is hung	Remove the strips and hang new ones.	Buy high-quality wallpapers; prepare the wall properly; fold according to maker's instructions; overlap seams 1 mm or less. Double-check instructions.
Edges and seams curl when dry	Too much rolling	Apply seam adhesive or vinyl adhesive to edges.	Don't roll seams immediately— wait until several strips have been hung; roll seams just once.
Air bubbles	Overworking the paper	Slit the paper over the bubble and glue down with seam adhesive or vinyl wallpaper adhesive.	Smooth the paper without overworking (small air bubbles that you see when the wallpaper is wet should disappear when it's dry).
Dried paste	Not washing paste off before it dries	Some may be picked off; use a paste remover, or wash paste off with an all-purpose cleaner, or a commercial wall-. paper cleaner available from paper suppliers.	Rinse off excess paste with warm water and clean sponges as you hang each strip; dry with clean towel.

HOME SYSTEMS

ELECTRICAL SAFETY

Rules and regulations

In Australia

There are strict regulations governing electrical wiring and equipment. Firstly, electrical installations must comply with the standards and regulations laid down by the local supplier. Secondly, only licensed electricians are allowed to work on an electrical installation. This includes fixed wiring supplying lights and power points, as well as any accessories connected to the fixed wiring, such as electric cookers, water heaters and switchboards. However, home owners are allowed to replace lamps in light fittings, repair blown fuses, reset circuit breakers and check appliance cords and plugs for damage.

In New Zealand

All electrical installations and equipment are controlled by Act of Parliament. The power connection to the switchboard must be inspected and approved by a registered inspector, while the actual wiring, power outlet and lighting work is certified by the electrician carrying out the work. Electricians must have a current practicing license, and issue a certificate of completion to the home owner on completing any electrical work. Home owners are permitted to carry out minor electrical tasks themselves, such as replacing fuses, resetting circuit breakers, removing and replacing power and lighting outlets and connecting or disconnecting fixed electrical appliances. However, any circuit wiring must be inspected and tested by a registered electrical inspector before it can be connected to the power supply.

Common problems

Colour change

You may have noticed that modern flexible electric cords no longer contain wires bearing the old familiar colours—green (for earth), red (for active) and black (for neutral). The transition to new colours—green/yellow (earth), brown (active) and blue (neutral)—began some years ago, but many cords with the old colour coding are still in use. ▼

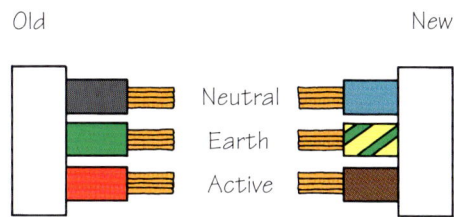

Old   New

Neutral
Earth
Active

Repairing a fuse

To replace a blown fuse, first switch off the main power switch in the switchboard. Pull out the porcelain fuse holders until you find the one in which the wire has been melted. Undo the screws that hold the wire in place, and remove the old melted ends. Note the fuse rating (marked on the front of the fuse holder, in amps) and make sure you use the right thickness of wire. Secure the new piece of wire, replace the fuse holder in its socket, and switch the power back on.

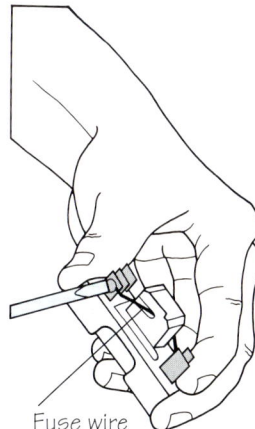

Fuse wire

Resetting a circuit breaker

Some switchboards have circuit breakers instead of the older porcelain fuse holders. If one of these 'trips', cutting off the power, it is a simple matter to switch it back on again. If a circuit breaker keeps tripping (or a fuse keeps blowing) it is a sign that all is not well. It may be that you are overloading the circuit with too many appliances, or that an appliance is faulty. If you cannot identify a faulty appliance (see below), and you are sure the circuit is not overloaded (p. 206), call in an electrician.

No more searching

If you're fed up with hunting for that elusive roll of fuse wire every time there is a problem, consider replacing the old fuse holders with circuit breakers. These are readily available from hardware stores, and simply plug into the socket where the porcelain fuse holder used to go (although some may need to be fitted by an electrician). Now you can restore power with a flick of the wrist.

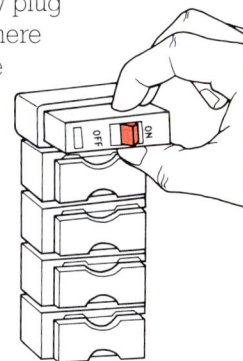

Detective work

If a fuse keeps blowing (or a circuit breaker keeps tripping), try to isolate the problem. Switch off all appliances before putting the main switch (or circuit breaker) back on again. Then switch on all the appliances in turn. If one particular appliance seems to be the problem, have it repaired.

ELECTRICAL SAFETY

Too many appliances

If a fuse or circuit breaker keeps cutting the power off, it may be that you are overloading the electrical circuit concerned. A domestic electric circuit supplying power points is designed to carry a current of 15, 16 or 20 amps, depending on the rating of the fuse or circuit breaker. If you exceed this, the fuse will blow, or the circuit breaker trip. To work out the current being drawn, add up the power ratings (in watts) of all the appliances that are plugged into that circuit (most appliances have their power rating recorded on them somewhere). Divide the total number of watts by 240 (the domestic voltage) and this gives the current consumption in amps.

Avoiding hazards

Leave a sign

Before doing any electrical work, *always* turn off all power at the main switchboard by turning off all circuit breakers, (or removing all fuse holders) and turning off the main switch as well. If you have off-peak hot water, this will have its own switch. Turn it off as well, just to be on the safe side. Once you've turned the power off, tape a prominent sign to the front of the switchboard warning others in the house to leave the power off.

Hoarding the right fuse wire

Always replace a fuse with one of the same amperage. A higher-amperage fuse will allow wires to overheat, which can create a short circuit and start a fire. Do not replace a fuse until you've solved the problem that made it blow in the first place. Keep a supply of fuse wire of the correct amperage near the fuse box; if there is a problem you'll have the right replacement to hand.

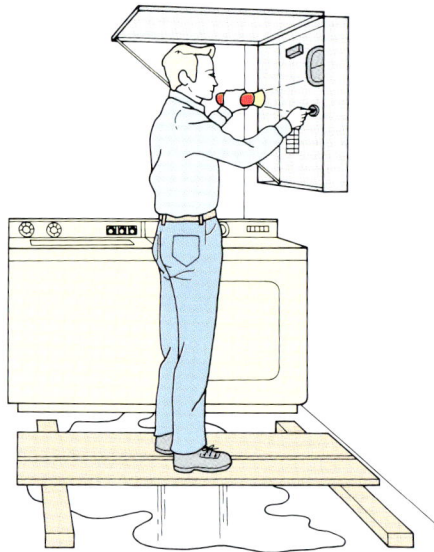

Do away with puddles ▲

Before you turn off the power, don a pair of sturdy shoes with non-conductive rubber soles. Even a dry concrete floor can be a good conductor of electricity. Keep a heavy rubber insulating mat in the vicinity of your switchboard, or stack a few boards nearby where they will remain dry. Stand on the mat or dry boards while at the switchboard. Never do any type of electrical job while standing on a wet floor.

Hand behind your back

When removing a fuse from the switchboard, work with only one hand if possible. Keep the other hand behind your back. If one hand comes into contact with electricity and the other an earth (such as a metal pipe), the electricity may travel from one hand to the other—with your heart in its path.

In an emergency

Seeing sparks

When an appliance gives off sparks, unplug the cord without making contact with the body of the appliance. Or turn the power off at the switchboard. If the sparks come from the cord, plug or wall socket, or if the cord is hot, turn the power off at the switchboard. Call your electricity supplier if the sparks are at the switchboard.

Soaked

Do not touch an appliance that's under water. Making sure you and the plug are dry, pull out the plug without touching anything metal. If an appliance is surrounded by water, turn the power off at the switchboard.

Outdoor power lines

Downed power lines are extremely dangerous. Do not try to move them—not even with a piece of wood. The voltage in these wires is high enough that wood can be a conductor. Do not go near the lines; call the electricity supplier or the fire or police service. If the line falls on a car while you're in it, stay in the car until help arrives.

Helping a shock victim

If you find someone in contact with a live circuit, don't touch him or her. If the switchboard is nearby, turn off the *main* power to the house. If not, use a non-conductive item, such as a wooden chair or non-metallic broom, to separate the person from the live wire. Or carefully loop a sweater or some other piece of clothing around the victim; grasp both ends of the sweater and pull the person away. If the victim does not have a heartbeat, apply cardiopulmonary resuscitation (CPR) if you've been properly trained in the procedure. Check the victim for burns, and if he or she was touching metal, for splinters that may have entered the eyes.

SAFETY DEVICES

There are a number of electrical safety devices available from hardware stores that will make your domestic power supply safer to use, both for members of your family, and for expensive electronic equipment such as computers and fax machines. Safety switches are particularly recommended for use with portable power tools that are operated outdoors with extension leads, often in damp conditions. They also offer protection in bathrooms and kitchens, where electricity and water are found together. In Australia, safety switches are mandatory for power circuits in all new domestic installations.

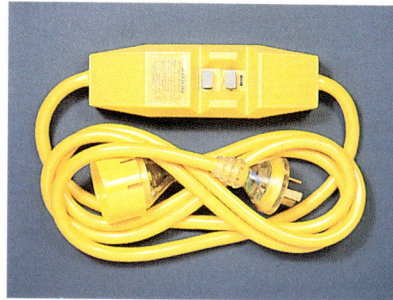

Safety switches cut off the power the instant they detect a hazardous situation. They are available for switchboard installation, as power boards, wall sockets or as part of an extension lead.

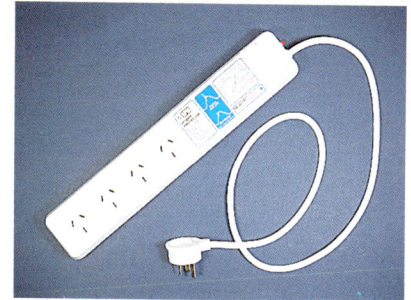

Surge protectors—available to replace standard power outlets, or as plug-in devices—help to prevent overload damage to sensitive electronic equipment, particularly computers.

Power point safety checkers provide a simple, fool-proof way to ensure that your domestic power outlets have been properly wired up. If you detect a fault, call in an electrician.

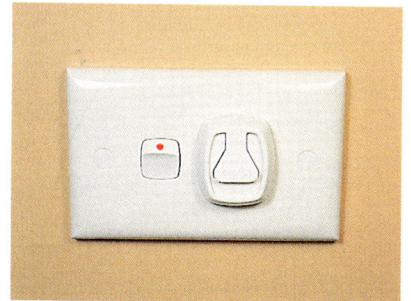

Dummy plugs fit into domestic power outlets to protect the socket from small, prying fingers and metal objects that may be pushed into them by an inquisitive toddler.

PLUMBING BASICS

Before you start

Stay within the law

In most parts of Australia and New Zealand, anyone altering, adding to, or installing water and waste services must have the appropriate qualifications and be licensed to do such work. If you are in doubt, check with your local council or water authority before attempting a job. In the case of a rural property with its own self-contained water supply, you are at liberty to alter pipelines and fixtures to suit your requirements. Always make sure, however, that your alterations comply with all of the relevant health standards, and will not present a health hazard. When in doubt, seek the advice of a local plumber.

Wired pipes

In many older homes the electrical system may be using the water supply pipes to complete the circuit to earth. If you remove any pipes or wiring that carry such an earth path, use a jumper lead prior to cutting or removal so that the earth path is maintained.

Sorting out your pipes

The plumbing in an ordinary domestic dwelling can be divided into two distinct systems: the water supply system and the waste disposal system. Water supply can be further divided into the hot and cold supply. The waste discharged from toilets is called soil, while waste from other outlets—such as the laundry or kitchen—is classified as waste water. There is always a trap under each fixture in the house to prevent any foul air from entering the building. ▶

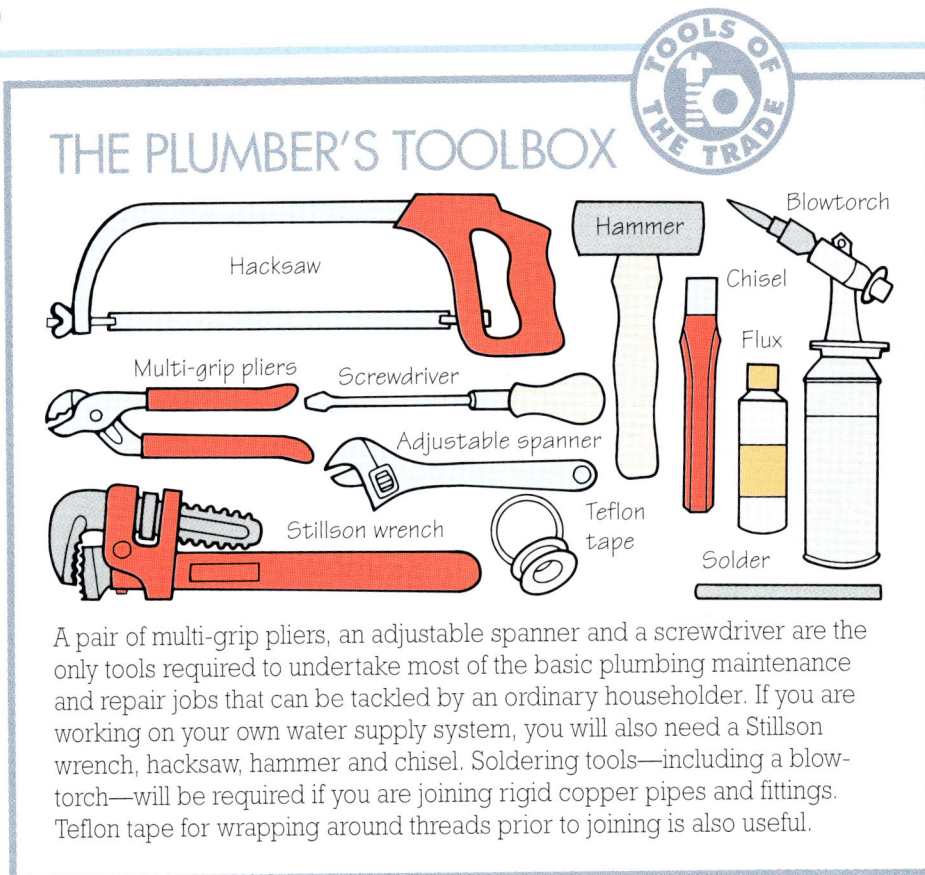

THE PLUMBER'S TOOLBOX

Hacksaw

Hammer

Blowtorch

Chisel

Flux

Multi-grip pliers

Screwdriver

Adjustable spanner

Teflon tape

Solder

Stillson wrench

A pair of multi-grip pliers, an adjustable spanner and a screwdriver are the only tools required to undertake most of the basic plumbing maintenance and repair jobs that can be tackled by an ordinary householder. If you are working on your own water supply system, you will also need a Stillson wrench, hacksaw, hammer and chisel. Soldering tools—including a blowtorch—will be required if you are joining rigid copper pipes and fittings. Teflon tape for wrapping around threads prior to joining is also useful.

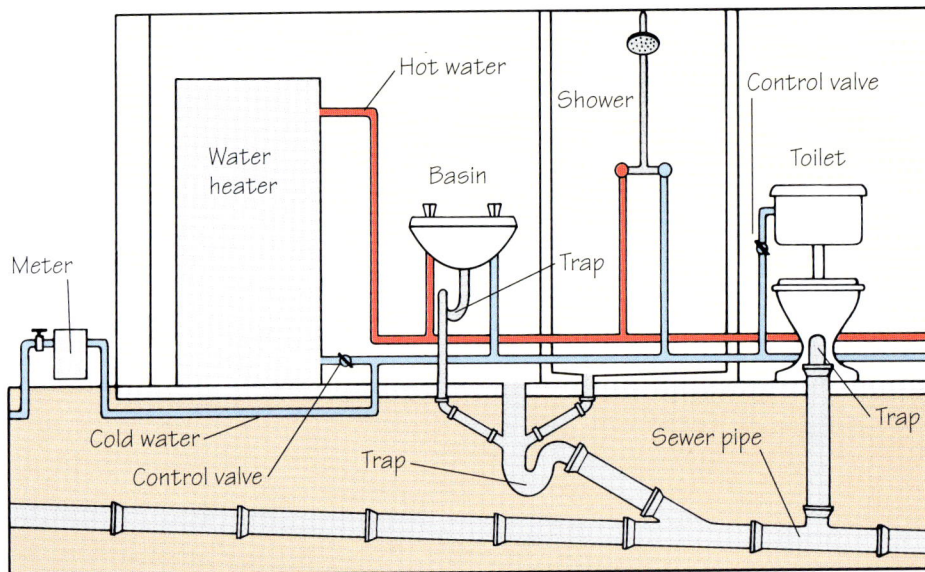

Hot water

Shower

Control valve

Water heater

Basin

Toilet

Meter

Trap

Cold water

Control valve

Trap

Sewer pipe

Trap

PIPES

Plastic pipes

Know your plastics

Three main types of plastics are used in plumbing, and care must be taken not to mix them up since they cannot be joined together in the same system. The three types are as follows.

▷ Unplasticised polyvinyl chloride (uPVC). Commonly used for waste-water systems. A tough, rigid material available in a large range of colours. The straight lengths and fittings used for soil and waste water disposal are coloured cream or light grey.

▷ Polythene. A flexible tube used for rural domestic water supplies and irrigation. Generally supplied in rolls and coloured black for water applications. It cannot be glued, and compression fittings must be used to form joints.

▷ Polybutylene. A light, flexible tubing used for both hot and cold water lines. Fittings are always of the crimp-on or compression type.

Leak control

Repairs to PVC pipes are best left to a licensed plumber. However, small leaks in waste water pipes can be temporarily fixed using some rubber inner tube and a hose clamp. Have the leak properly repaired as soon as possible. ▼

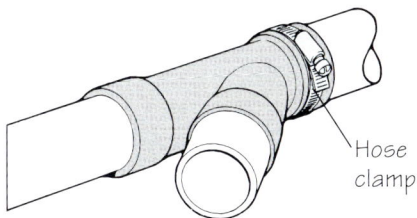

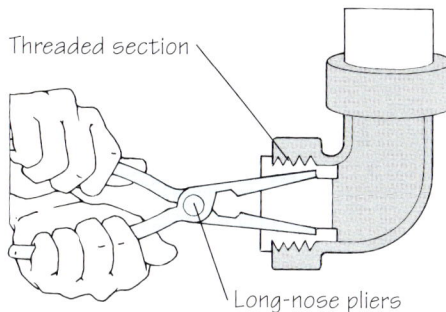

Hose clamp

Get the threads out ▲

Threaded section

Long-nose pliers

Sometimes when you're unscrewing a plastic pipe, the threads stick in the joint and the pipe breaks off. To remove the threaded section, use a gas torch to heat the jaws of a pair of long-nose pliers. Insert the pliers into the threaded section and slowly push the plier handles apart until the hot jaws make grooves in the plastic. Remove the pliers and let the plastic harden; then reinsert the pliers and twist them to unscrew the pipe.

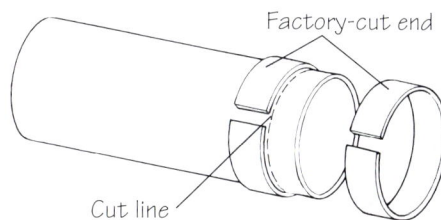

Factory-cut end

Cut line

On the mark ▲

This guide will help you make accurate handsaw cuts in a piece of PVC pipe. Cut a 25 to 40 mm wide length from the factory-cut end of the pipe. Then cut a slit through it so you can slide it onto the pipe being cut. Now you can use the factory-cut end as the guide.

Metal pipes

Know your metals

Copper and stainless steel are used for most water supply pipes because they are corrosion resistant. Copper is the preferred material because it is easy to handle and join, and also because it is capable of withstanding high water temperatures. Some rural buildings still use galvanised iron.

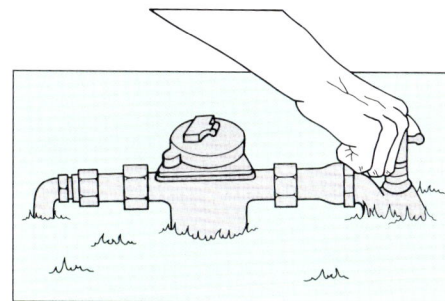

Just be patient ▲

There is really not a lot that an average householder can do if the water supply line starts to leak. Call a plumber, and in the meantime turn off the inlet valve (usually next to the water meter). If the leak is not severe, the supply can be left on while you wait.

Bread stuffing

If every drop of water isn't removed from an existing copper water supply pipe, soldering a joint can be difficult. As the torch heats the water, the water turns to steam and solidifies the solder. To avoid this, push some soft bread into the pipe. The bread will absorb the water. When your soldered joint is finished, turn on the water and the bread will break up and disappear.

PIPES

Frozen solid

To thaw frozen metal water lines (but not any made from plastic), either pour hot water over the affected section, or use a hair dryer adjusted to its maximum setting. Turn off the main supply valve before you try to unfreeze the line, but leave at least one outlet to the affected line open. You can cure a persistent freezing problem by wrapping the exposed supply lines with a length of fibreglass pipe insulation.

Water hammer

A loud noise that can be heard throughout the house every time you turn off a tap is called 'water hammer'. It is usually caused by a valve closing very quickly, loose pipework or a combination of both. Trace as much of the pipework as you can throughout the house, and secure any loose sections with saddles. Wrap tape around the section of pipe underneath each saddle to stop the two from rattling against one another. Unfortunately, much of the pipework is concealed within walls where it is inaccessible. If the problem persists, have a plumber fit a water hammer arrester in the line closest to the valve that's causing the problem.

More noises

Sometimes high water pressure can cause rushing noises in supply lines. This can be cured by having a plumber fit a pressure reduction valve.

JOINING COPPER PIPES

The easiest way to join copper pipes for your own, self-contained water supply system is with capillary joints. Special fittings—such as bends and junctions—are made that fit tightly onto the pipe. Make sure you buy fittings that contain a ring of solder already inside each socket. These only require flux and heat to make a perfect joint. With other types of fittings the solder must be added when the joint is hot, and this calls for more expertise.

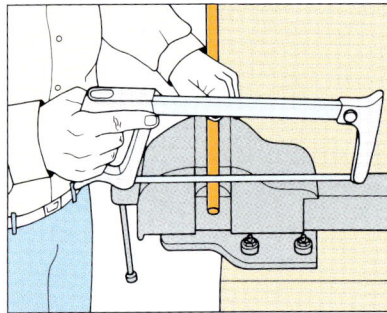

Cut the end of the length of tube to be joined with a fine-toothed hacksaw or pipe cutter, so that it is perfectly square. Use a fine file to remove burrs, and then clean the end of the tube and the fitting socket with steel wool.

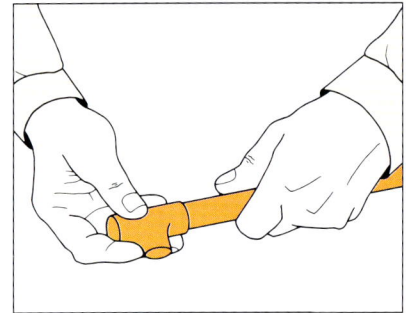

Apply flux to the tube end and the fitting socket, and push the two together as far as they will go. Wipe off excess flux. Capillary joints depend on a very tight fit, so don't do anything to lessen the gap between pipe and fitting.

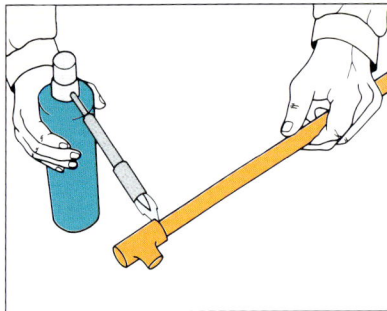

Heat the joint with the flame from a gas torch, moving it all the time so that it plays over the entire joint. Avoid overheating, which will burn the flux and the tin from the solder.

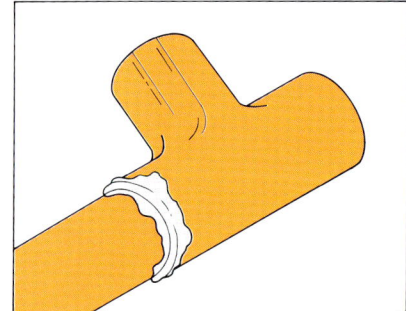

Continue heating the joint until a complete ring of solder appears around the mouth of the fitting. Then remove the flame and allow the joint to cool without disturbance.

FIXTURES

Baths and showers

A sneaky leak

If water seeps out from under your shower base, it may not necessarily be the base itself that is leaking. Water could be escaping from the body of taps situated inside the wall. To check, carefully remove the dress fitting covering the tap and check for leaks beneath. If there is a leak, get a plumber to come and tighten the tap body or replace the sealing ring. Make sure the dress ring is properly fitted afterwards so that water cannot enter the wall. In some cases the problem may not lie with the tap, but with the shower base itself. Check the grouting and renew if necessary. A silicone based liquid is available that can be spread over the entire shower base to seal it against water seepage.

Foam filler

Here's one simple way to solve the problem of loose pipes inside a shower wall. To stop them from moving about, first remove the dress ring from the wall. Tape the pipe into position, and then spray aerosol foam insulation into the wall cavity. Once the foam is dry it should be hard enough to hold the pipe firmly in position.

Warm baths

Before you build in your new bath, consider insulating the space beneath it with fibreglass batts. If the bath is already in position, push the batts into place through the inspection opening.

Laundries

Tap conversion kits

Laundries are normally supplied with hot and cold water outlets. If there are no threaded washing machine taps, don't despair. Your local hardware shop stocks a conversion kit that screws into your existing taps and supplies washing machine connections, while at the same time retaining the taps over the tub.

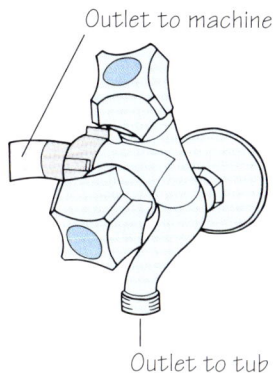

Outlet to machine

Outlet to tub

Kitchens

Dishwasher maintenance

Dishwashers are sometimes connected only to the cold supply, in cases where they have their own built-in hot water system. Always isolate the electrical supply before starting any repair or maintenance. Beside the unit—perhaps in an adjoining cupboard—you will find the unit's water supply isolating valve, and very likely the power point that supplies electricity to the unit as well. Switch both off while working.

Not so clean water

Although you may not have noticed it, the tap that sprays water into your kitchen sink may be fitted with a fine gauze aerator at its end. Unscrew it every so often so that you can give it a thorough clean. You may be unpleasantly surprised by the large quantity of debris you will find trapped there.

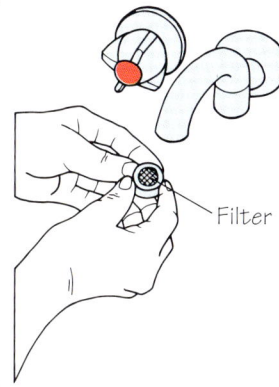

Filter

Don't lose a finger

In-sink waste disposal units will come to a sudden halt if metallic objects are dropped into them. Always disconnect the power before delving into the machine to remove obstructions. When you have finished, press the red overload button you will find at the base of the unit, under the sink bowl. Then restore the power and flush water through to clean the machine out. Don't forget to use plenty of water every time you dispose of any waste down the sink. ▼

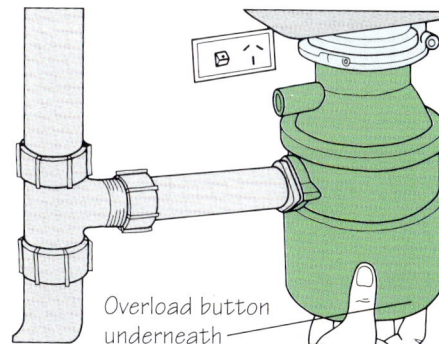

Overload button underneath

TOILETS

Toilet troubles

Hand-bag retriever

You can retrieve an item that your toddler dropped into the toilet without too much fuss. Just slip your hand into a plastic bag for protection. Grasp the item and pull it out of the toilet, then turn the bag inside out. The wet item will be in the bag and your hand will remain dry and clean. ▼

A wise precaution

Every toilet cistern has an isolating control valve beneath it that regulates the water supply. Because it is so rarely used, this valve has a tendency to become very stiff, and may even seize up altogether eventually. To stop this from happening, free up the mechanism by turning the valve tap on and off every so often. Then you can be sure of being able to cut off the water supply without any fuss in an emergency.

Noisy toilet

Most of the noise generated by a toilet suite is due to water rushing into the cistern after the pan has been flushed. You can regulate the flow of water by adjusting the control valve, which you will find situated somewhere on the inlet pipe that carries water to the cistern. If this fails to correct the problem, you can have a plumber fit a special low-noise inlet valve inside the cistern.

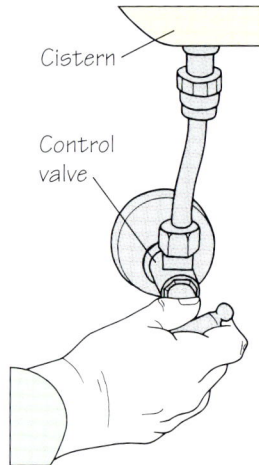

Cistern

Control valve

Saving water

If you want to save water when flushing a toilet try this. Place a clay brick inside the cistern, or fill a plastic bottle with sand or water and position it inside the cistern (making sure, however, that it does not interfere with the ball valve). The bulk of these items will displace water which would normally be used to flush the toilet pan. Experiment with different volumes, so that the flush still removes all wastes.

Doing away with the brick

As an alternative to the brick or bottle idea described above, you can have a dual-flush cistern installed instead. These units provides two flush buttons which release varying amounts of water into the pan, according to the amount of waste to be removed.

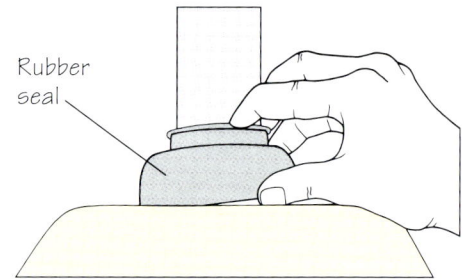

Rubber seal

Leaking toilets ▲

Water from the cistern flows into the toilet pan through a pipe connecting both. This pipe is made watertight, either by an internal rubber seal, or a complete rubber socket. If your pan has a rubber socket, check it every so often for leaks caused by perishing. If the rubber does leak you may be able to replace it without removing the cistern. If not, call in a plumber. A leaking internal seal is harder to fix, and will have to be replaced by a plumber.

Detective work

If your cistern runs continuously, water is probably coming out of the incoming water shut-off valve inside the cistern. This valve, which is actuated by the rising water level, probably needs a new rubber washer. Renew the washer and watch the water level in the cistern. It should be about 25 mm below the top of the overflow pipe when full. ▼

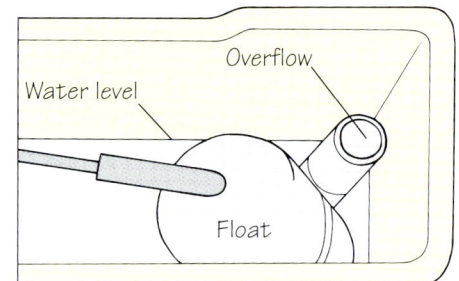

Overflow

Water level

Float

DRAINS AND TRAPS

Unblocking drains

Drainage safety valve

All house drainage systems are fitted with a 'safety valve'. This is an overflow gully, which is placed at some convenient spot in the drainage line. Should there be a blockage, any overflow will run out of the gully, and not inside or underneath the house. The gully usually has a loose grate covering it so that the pipe beneath can be reached easily. It is also higher than the surrounding ground level so that surface water cannot enter it. Make sure you never raise the surrounding ground level—with pavers, for example—above that of the overflow gully. There are heavy fines for householders who allow rainwater to enter the sewer drainage system.

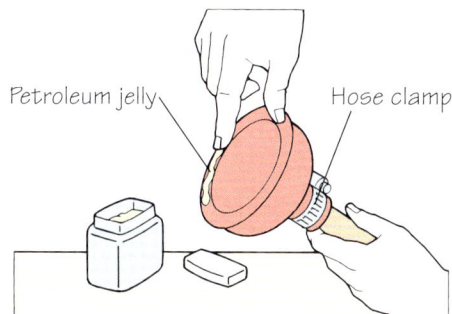

Petroleum jelly   Hose clamp

A better plunger ▲

Your plunger is still the most effective tool for clearing blocked pipes. Fill the fixture concerned with water and move the plunger up and down in a pumping motion. Make it even more efficient with the aid of a little petroleum jelly. Just smear some jelly around the edge of the suction cup. The jelly will create a better seal between the fixture and the cup.

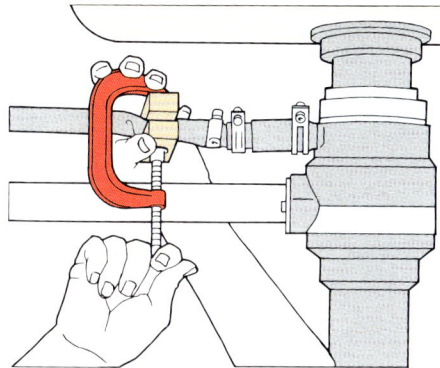

Seal all openings ▲

When unclogging a drain with a plunger, plug or seal the overflow opening in a washbasin or bathtub, or the second drain in a double sink. This allows you to develop the necessary suction and pressure to free the clog. If your dishwasher is connected up to the sink or waste disposal waste line, seal the hose too, by clamping it between two pieces of scrap wood.

Follow the map

Whenever you are carrying out any construction work around the house—even planting trees and shrubs—first obtain a copy of your house's drainage diagram from your local council or water authority. This will show you where all the drainage lines, branches and fixtures are, so that you can avoid damaging them or planting trees too close.

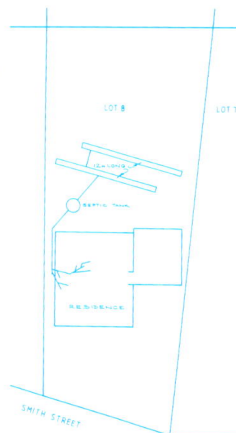

Persistent chokes

If your drains keep on blocking, the problem may be due to tree roots. Don't attempt to remove the roots by yourself, but call in an expert.

Traps

Keeping smells at bay

Every plumbing fixture in the house, such as a sink or toilet, is fitted with a trap. This retains a small amount of water and acts as a seal, stopping unpleasant smells from entering the room. In the case of floor wastes in bathroom floors, this water will slowly evaporate if it is not replenished occasionally. If you plan to leave the house for an extended period, pour a little vegetable oil down the floor waste. This will prevent evaporation. To stop water freezing in traps and toilet pans, add a little salt to the water.

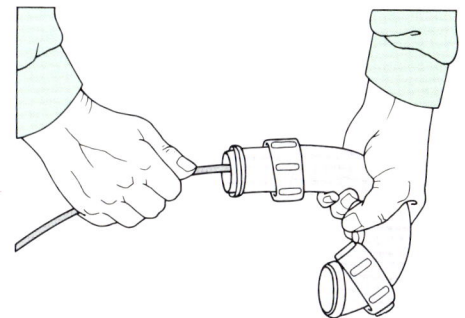

Clearing traps ▲

If a trap becomes blocked, first try clearing it with a plunger. If that doesn't work, remove it altogether and feed a piece of flexible wire through it. This will dislodge the blockage, and the trap can then be replaced.

WATER HEATERS

Routine maintenance

Staving off disaster

Low pressure water heaters are sometimes installed in the house roof space, where they are supplied with water by a cistern with a ball valve. If the heater or the ball valve leaks, water will start coming from the overflow, which usually discharges somewhere under the eaves. Investigate any such overflow straight away. If leaking water corrodes the safety tray that the heater sits in, the house ceiling could be badly damaged.

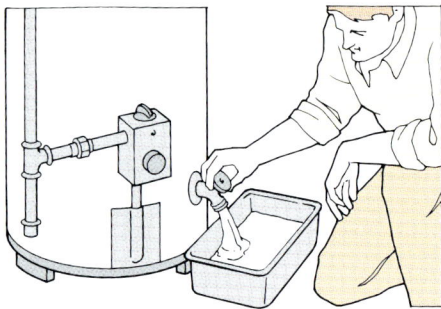

System clean-out ▲

In areas where there is often a lot of sediment in the water supply, sludge can build up in the bottom of the hot water storage cylinder. If you live in such an area, you should flush the hot water tank out every year or so. Turn off the cold supply, switch off the gas or electricity and open a hot water tap somewhere in the house. Now open the drain valve at the bottom of the cylinder and drain the tank until the water runs clear. Before restoring the gas or electricity supply, run the water for a while to make sure all air has been removed from the system.

The quiet performers

Gas hot water heaters work away so quietly and efficiently that their maintenance is often overlooked. Make sure that every so often you check the flue pipe for leaks or blockages, and the combustion chamber for accumulated rust. Also check the pilot light to see that it is clean and free from fluff.

Relieving the pressure

Many domestic hot water systems are at mains pressure—meaning that the hot water storage cylinder is under the same pressure as that in the water mains. To relieve any excess pressure, the cylinder is fitted with a temperature and pressure relief valve. You may have noticed the small lever that is part of this valve on the outside of your hot water system. Operate this lever every six months or so, just to make sure it is still working properly.

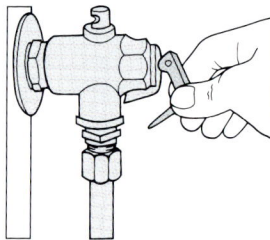

Getting hotter water

Waiting for the hot water

When outlets are a long way from the hot water cylinder, a lot of water will have to be drawn off before any that is hot reaches the tap concerned. There are two ways to overcome this. Either get your plumber to run this 'dead' water back into the hot water cylinder, or have an independent hot water service installed to supply the remote tap.

Losing hot water

Sometimes hot water cylinders are installed with their outlet pipes going directly upwards. This will waste a lot of energy, since the unit will be constantly trying to heat the water in this pipe. You can prevent this waste of energy (and money) by having a plumber install a heat trap in the line.

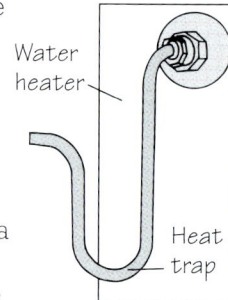

Water heater · Heat trap

Money saver

Hot water pipes are generally inside the house walls, where they are inaccessible. If they are exposed, however, they can be lagged to save energy and money. Use pipe insulation in pre-formed segments, and butt them tightly together, leaving no gaps. Tape all joints firmly with an adhesive PVC tape. Where necessary, cut the pre-formed segments with a sharp knife or scissors to ensure a tight fit around corners and bends. Paint any sections of insulation that are exposed to the weather to stop them from deteriorating. ▼

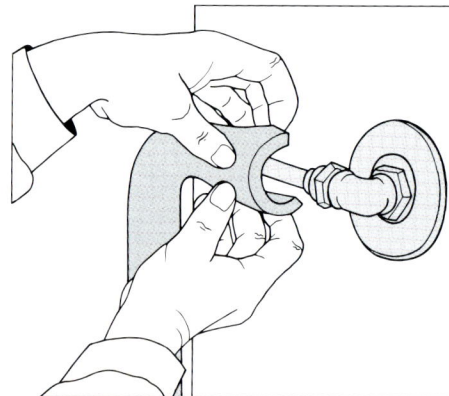

GAS APPLIANCES

Safety first

That sinking feeling

Gas appliances are very safe, irrespective of the type of gas that is used. Remember that natural gas is lighter than air and will collect near the ceiling if it escapes. Liquefied petroleum gas (propane), on the other hand, is heavier than air and will sink to the floor.

If you smell gas

Get out of the house immediately if you think there is a serious gas leak. Call for help from a neighbour's house. This is what you should do if there is a faint smell of leaking gas.
▷ Open all windows and doors.
▷ Extinguish all open flames, including pilot lights.
▷ Do not light a match. Do not smoke.
▷ Do not use the telephone, or switch on lights or electrical appliances. Sparks could ignite the gas.
▷ Call a gasfitter straight away, or phone the gas company from a neighbour's phone. If you cannot reach either, call the fire brigade.

Fresh air

Gas can only burn properly if there is enough oxygen in the air to support combustion. So make sure that any room containing a gas appliance has adequate ventilation (p. 216). Also ensure that each of your gas appliances is fitted with an oxygen depletion device. This sensor sits near the pilot light, and automatically turns the appliance off if the oxygen level in the room drops too low.

Pilot light problems

Unclogging a pilot light

If the pilot light won't burn, the orifice may be blocked. To clean it, turn off the gas at the appliance control valve. Also turn off the electrical supply at the appliance power point. Wait until the unit cools and then remove the access panel and unscrew the bracket holding the pilot assembly. This bracket will also hold the thermocouple, which is a safety device. Dismantle the pilot burner and clean all parts with a cotton swab. Reassemble the unit, restore the gas and power, and check for leaks by applying soapy water. If you suspect any problems call a gasfitter. ▼

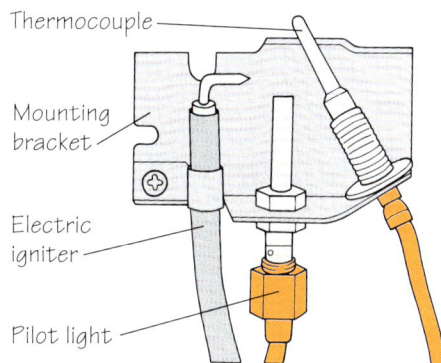

Thermocouple

Mounting bracket

Electric igniter

Pilot light

Finger saver

Want to save your fingers from burns when lighting the pilot light for your water heater or stove? Extend your reach by taping or crimping an alligator clip onto the end of an old telescopic radio or TV aerial.

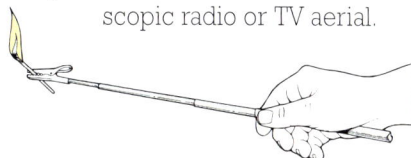

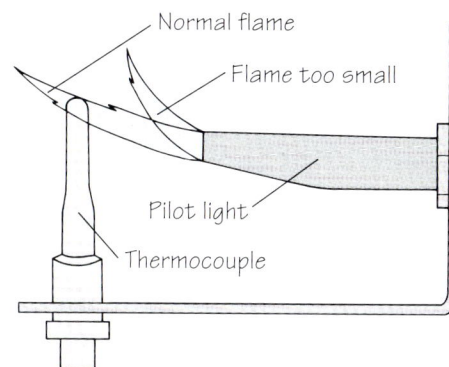

Normal flame

Flame too small

Pilot light

Thermocouple

Not big enough ▲

If your gas burner will not light, but you can still see a pilot light flame, it may be that the flame is too small. The flame has two jobs: it must light the main burner, but it must also energise a device that turns on the gas supply. If the flame is too small, this may not happen. Either clean the assembly yourself, or ask a gasfitter to come and do it for you.

Gas cylinders

How much is left?

To check how much liquid there is left in an LPG cylinder, slowly move your wet hand down the outside surface. You will notice that when you reach the liquid level your hand will feel warmer than it was at the evaporated gas level.

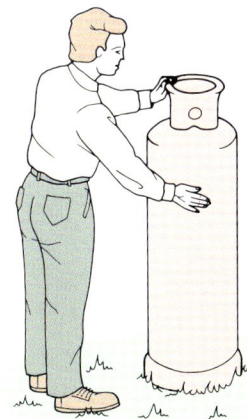

HOME HEATING

Solid fuel stoves

The right stove for the job

Solid fuel stoves can be used for more than simple room heating. Some will also provide domestic hot water, while others can be used for cooking as well. Consider all the options before you buy, to be sure of getting the most appropriate type of stove for your situation. Also make sure that you check with your local council to see if there are any special requirements for stoves that must be met in your area. And last but not least, buy a smoke detector.

Fresh air

Good ventilation is essential in any room that contains a solid fuel stove or open fire. A poorly ventilated room will soon become uncomfortably hot and stuffy if there is not a constant supply of fresh air. On the other hand, you must take care that the usual seating area in the room is not between the stove and the main source of incoming air, otherwise you will find that you are constantly sitting in a draught. Position the stove so that air can reach it from a door or window that is off to one side. ▼

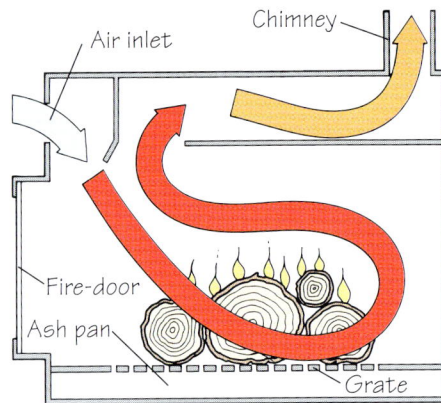

Air from the door will create an annoying draught

A desirable draught ▲

Having trouble lighting your fuel stove for the first time? If you've never used a stove before, it may help to understand the basic principle, which is to create a draught. With the fire-door closed, air enters the stove, flows through it and up the chimney. You can therefore control the rate of burning by adjusting the airflow. A careful examination will show you where the controls for air inlet and exit are situated. If in doubt, get some instructions from the manufacturer.

Air inlet · Chimney · Fire-door · Ash pan · Grate

Only the best will do

Don't use just any old fuel in your solid fuel stove. Some stoves will only work properly with coal or briquettes, while others are designed for burning wood. If you purchase your stove second-hand, make sure you know what fuel it was designed for. In wood-burning stoves use only dry, well seasoned hardwood. New wood will take about six months to dry, and to aid the process you should stack it in a dry place, where air has a chance to circulate. Try to avoid burning pine cones, softwoods, particleboard and any painted or preservative treated (green coloured) timber.

Common stove problems

Fuel stoves are generally trouble-free, and will operate for years with very little maintenance. The most common problems to watch out for are:
▷ Hot surrounds. Make sure the stove is positioned well away from walls, furniture and anything else that may catch fire. Read the manufacturer's instructions regarding correct clearances.
▷ Creosote build-up. This dark, sticky, tar-like substance collects on the inside of the flue or chimney, and it may eventually cause a chimney fire. It is the result of incomplete combustion, the burning of wet or softwood or a smouldering fire. Clean your stove regularly to keep the problem under control.
▷ Excessive smoke. Experimenting with the controls will usually cure smoking. Sometimes it is the result of leaking joints. Check and seal if necessary. ▼

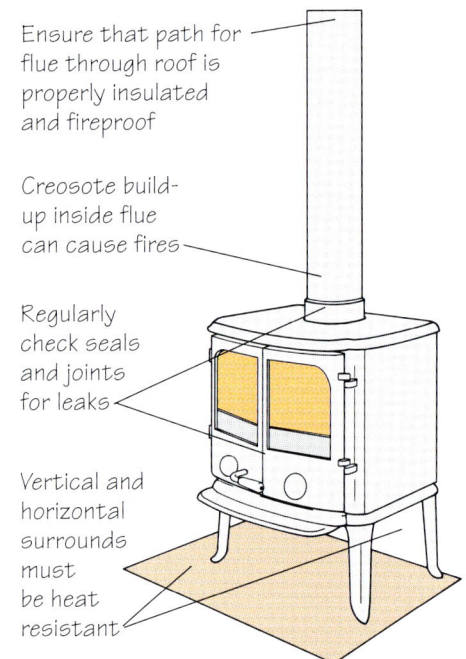

Ensure that path for flue through roof is properly insulated and fireproof

Creosote build-up inside flue can cause fires

Regularly check seals and joints for leaks

Vertical and horizontal surrounds must be heat resistant

Heater wisdom

Making the right choice

Think carefully before buying a new heater. There are three basic types: radiant, fan and convection. If you like to toast your toes, then there is little point in buying a convection heater, which is designed to raise the temperature of an entire room. It may be best to consider a combination—one or two convection heaters for overall heating, a radiator to sit in front of, and a fan heater for quick results on very cold nights or days.

Safety first

Always keep safety in mind with home heaters, especially where children are concerned. Every heater should be properly protected with a stout grill or fence to keep clothes and bodies at a safe distance. With the heater off (or empty) test to see how stable it is. Some heaters are designed to right themselves should they tip over by accident.

All bright and shiny ▶

A large part of the heat generated by any type of radiant heater is reflected by the shiny backing plate. If this reflective surface is tarnished or rusty, much of this heat will be absorbed instead. At the beginning of each winter, remove the protective mesh from the front of the heater and give the reflector a good polish. At the same time, carry out any other routine maintenance—cleaning, checking burners or elements etc.—as advised by the manufacturer.

Electric heaters

Left in the cold

If a fan heater suddenly stops working it's almost certainly because the cutout has tripped, turning off the power. This occurs when the temperature of the heater becomes dangerously high, and the problem will fix itself when the unit cools down. Check for anything blocking the air intake and outlet. Clothes hung over or close to the heater are common culprits. If your heater continues to switch off for no apparent reason, check the interior for dust. Remove any excess with a vacuum cleaner before reassembly and testing. ▼

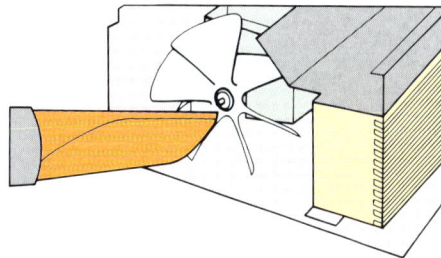

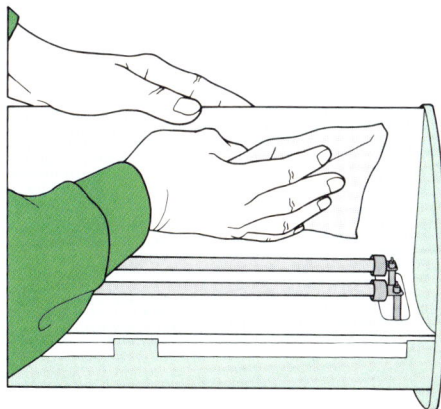

Oil and gas heaters

Just a trim please

Kerosene heaters need little more than a regular cleaning and wick trimming or replacement as required. If your heater starts to smoke or give off excessive fumes it is probably the wick that needs attention. Wick trimmers are available, and some heaters are supplied with one. Use it to remove all excess carbon. If the wick is contaminated or heavily encrusted it must be replaced.

Beware of fumes

Both kerosene and gas heaters give off fumes as they consume their fuel. One of the by-products of combustion is carbon monoxide, which can reach dangerous—even fatal—levels in poorly ventilated rooms. If your heater is not vented to the outside, make sure a door or window is partly open when the heater is on. A feeling of stuffiness or a headache are warning signs of fumes.

Flame check

With a gas heater, it is easy to tell if there is enough oxygen to properly support combustion. Carefully inspect the flame. It should be a well defined blue with a slight orange tip. Yellow tips indicate that the flame is starved of oxygen, and orange streaks are dust particles burning. Modern gas appliances are fitted with oxygen depletion devices (p. 215).

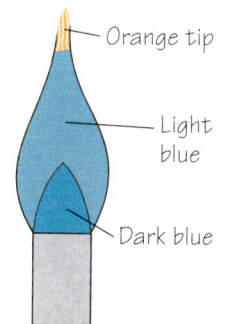

Orange tip

Light blue

Dark blue

HOME HEATING

Heat pumps

Cheap heat

One of the most power-efficient ways of heating your home is with a heat pump, otherwise known as a reverse-cycle air conditioner. When conditions are ideal, one kilowatt of electricity consumed by a heat pump will provide as much heat as three, one-kilowatt electric radiators. However, the effectiveness of a heat pump depends on circumstances. When the temperature outside drops below freezing, it is better to use some other form of heating.

Time to de-ice

Do not switch repeatedly from heat to cool when using a heat pump, or you will damage the compressor. If the room feels too cool, check that the outside coils are not coated with frost. If they are icy, switch to defrost to clear them. Also check the filter for dust and dirt. If it is clogged, remove it and give it a rinse in clean water. Allow the filter to dry thoroughly before you replace it. ▼

Filter pad

CAN YOUR HOUSE BREATHE?

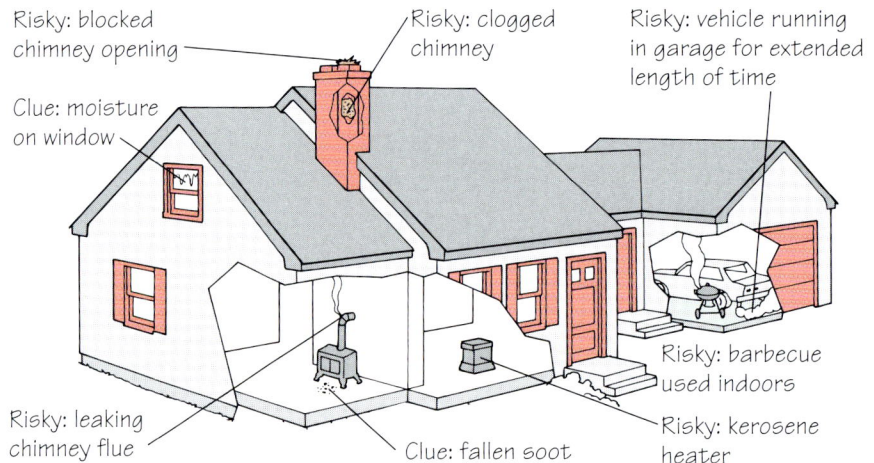

Risky: blocked chimney opening

Risky: clogged chimney

Risky: vehicle running in garage for extended length of time

Clue: moisture on window

Risky: leaking chimney flue

Clue: fallen soot

Risky: barbecue used indoors

Risky: kerosene heater

A house can be made too tight for your good health. Sealing doors, windows and air vents means less fresh air. The air inside the house becomes stale, rooms are stuffy and excessively high humidity starts to show up as moisture on the insides of windows, soot around the fireplace or stoves, and the smell of fumes. Make sure your house can breathe properly by having gas heaters regularly checked and properly vented. Avoid using kerosene heaters, if at all possible, and never heat a room using a cooking oven. Have chimneys and flues cleaned every autumn, in plenty of time before the onset of winter.

Lower heating bills

Divide and conquer

If your house is equipped with central heating you can save considerably on operating costs by zoning rooms into day and evening areas. In that way you will not be heating rooms, such as bedrooms, at times of the day when they are most likely to be empty.

Dress for the weather

The simplest way to reduce home heating (and cooling) bills is to change the way in which you and your family dress. If you wear clothes that are appropriate for the weather outside you will not have to make such drastic alterations to the indoor environment. A change of even a couple of degrees up or down is not really that noticeable, but over a period of a year it will mean a great reduction in your domestic energy consumption.

HOME COOLING

Creating a breeze

Natural ventilation

If the air is cooler outside than in, you can bring the cool air into your house. Because hot air rises, open an upstairs window or, in a single storey house, open doors and windows on opposite sides of the house to encourage a through draught. However, if it's hotter outside, close doors and windows, pull down blinds and draw curtains.

A mechanical breeze

On a very hot, still days or nights, even the simplest of fans can provide a badly needed cooling breeze.

▷ Install vented exhaust fans in hot spots, such as kitchens, where they will draw air away from around the stove and sink.

▷ Ceiling fans in the bedrooms and living areas are especially welcome on sticky, humid nights. Choose a size according to the volume of the room, and place it in the centre of the ceiling. ***Caution:*** do not install ceiling fans in rooms without adequate clearance.

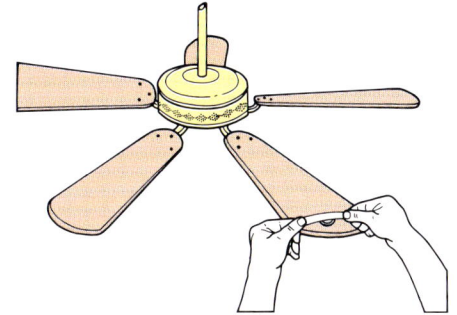

Vibrating ceiling fan ▲

Follow this troubleshooting checklist to discover why a ceiling fan is vibrating—and to stop the annoying vibration.

▷ Clean the blades. Accumulated dirt can throw the fan off balance.

▷ Check for loose screws on the blades.

▷ One or more blades might be warped. Remove the blades, and lay them on a flat surface. They should lie flat. If a blade is warped, replace the entire set. (Blades are usually matched as a set by the manufacturer.)

▷ Examine the blade irons for defects. The irons are set at the factory at a 12° angle. Stack the irons on top of one another. If you find one that doesn't match the others, replace the defective iron.

▷ Check the fan motor. With the blades and irons removed, turn the fan on to the fastest setting. It shouldn't wobble. If it does, send the motor in for repair. Look in your owner's manual for the closest authorised service centre.

▷ If you still haven't found the problem, balance the blades on the reassembled fan by attaching small weights to the tops of the out-of-balance blades. Using washers or coins as weights, temporarily attach them to the blades with tape. Once the blades are balanced, glue the weights in place. For a four-bladed fan, balance two opposite blades at a time.

In the shade

Even if your house is very well insulated, you can still get some benefit from having a deciduous, broad-leaved tree if it's by a window. The tree will keep hot sunlight from entering the window in the summer, and after the leaves fall in autumn, sunlight can pass through and heat the room in the winter. If you're planting trees for future shade, plant them on the north and west sides of the house, where the summer sun is at its hottest. For an immediate way to shade a window, add an awning, porch roof, trellis, or arbour, or install an outside shade or indoor blind. ▼

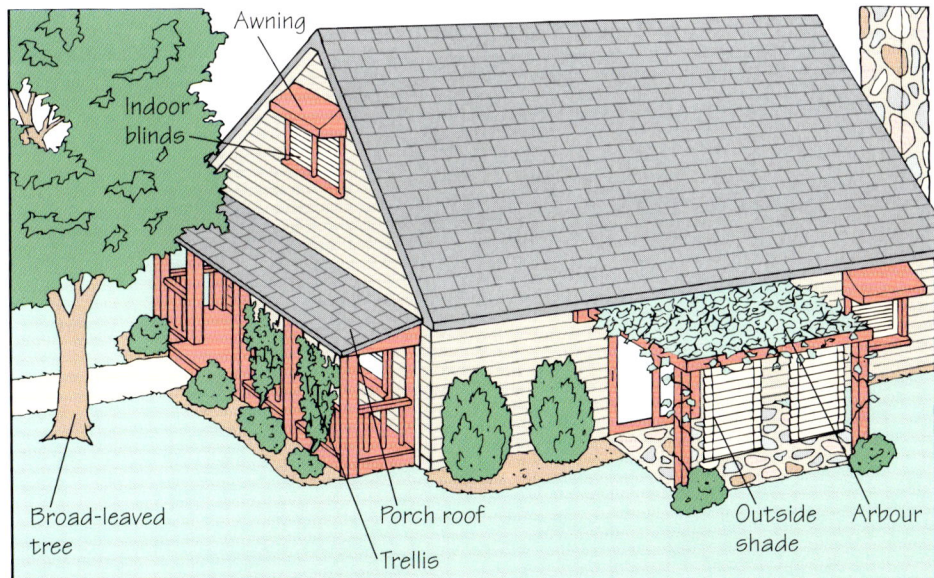

Awning · Indoor blinds · Broad-leaved tree · Porch roof · Trellis · Outside shade · Arbour

HOME COOLING

Evaporative coolers

A cheaper alternative

If you cannot afford the expense of a room air conditioner, consider buying an evaporative cooler instead. In the right conditions—where the air is hot and dry—they can be almost as effective as an air conditioner anyway. Evaporative coolers work by changing liquid water into water vapour. In the process, sensible heat (heat you can feel) is changed into latent or hidden heat. The dry temperature in the room goes down, but the relative humidity goes up. In ideal conditions, an evaporative cooler can provide a 10–15°C difference between inside and outside.

Trouble free operation

Evaporative coolers will remain trouble free, provided they are properly and regularly maintained.
▷ Remove and clean the air filter, as recommended by the manufacturer.
▷ Clean the water tray and remove any slime and dirt.
▷ Check the case and any metal parts for signs of corrosion.
▷ Check plastic parts for signs of deterioration and wear. ▼

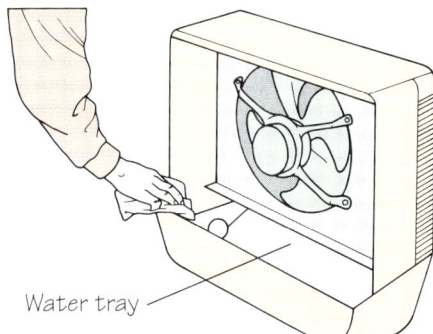

Water tray

Air conditioners

Position, position, position

Because cold air falls, the higher a room air-conditioning unit is placed, the better it can cool a room. Install the unit in the wall that gets the least amount of direct sunlight—usually the southern wall. But if you'd like to place the unit where the sun is normally strongest, consider providing some shade. ▼

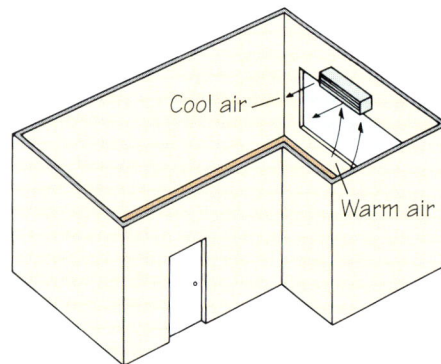

Cool air

Warm air

Cold-weather care

Covering the exterior of a window air conditioner with a sheet of plastic does more than reduce cold draughts on windy winter days. It also serves to keep the condenser coil and fan clean. Make sure you remove the plastic in the spring—before the hot weather comes.

Is it just me?

Does the room feel hotter or cooler than the reading on the thermostat? The thermostat might be affected by strong lights shining on it, a nearby heat-generating appliance, or a breeze from a fan or window. If you can't move the culprit, adjust or move the thermostat.

Regular maintenance

Put paid to rust

An air conditioner should last for about 10 to 15 years, depending on its location and how well you look after it. Check the entire unit at least once a year for any signs of rust, both on the inside and the outside of the casing. This is particularly important in seaside areas, where salt in the air will eventually attack any exposed metal. Treat and repaint any rust patches as soon as they appear.

Filter reminder

However much you use your air conditioner, the filter still requires regular replacement or cleaning. When the unit is in constant use it should be renewed (or cleaned) about once a month. Filters that become clogged with dust may harbour fungi, reduce the air supply or blow out of their frame and allow dust to pass through and collect on the cooling coil. To jog your memory, stick a little label to the casing beside the control switches, showing the date when you last attended to the filter. ▼

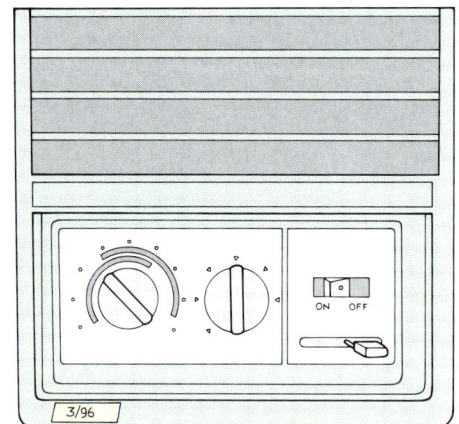

ON OFF

3/96

Common problems

Musty-smelling conditioner

Probably the most commonly heard complaint about air conditioners is that the air 'smells stale'. This can be caused by tobacco smoke, body odour, dirty carpets or furnishings or dampness. If possible, correct the basic problem, otherwise try opening the outside air damper to flush stale air from the room. If the stale smell persists, check the filter (left) and drain holes (far right).

Air not cool enough?

Most air conditioners are capable of maintaining around 10–15°C difference between the inside and outside temperatures. Place a thermometer in the air stream to check. If yours does not, try to increase its efficiency by ensuring good air circulation around the outside coil, and also by shading the coil from the hot afternoon sun. Install a simple awning or some other form of shade.

Bending fins

Bent condenser and evaporator fins in room units can obstruct the efficient flow of air. If you remove the front panel and filter, you can then straighten the fins with a plastic spatula or with a small section cut from a pocket comb. ▼

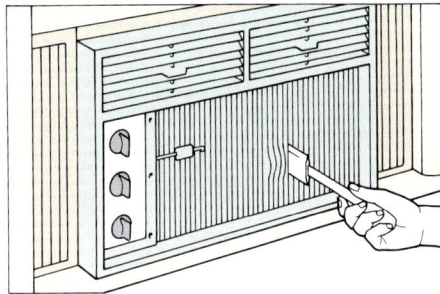

Regular work

It's important to run your air conditioner at regular intervals in order to keep it in good working condition. Make sure it is used at least once every six to eight weeks (if only just for short periods) on the cooling cycle in summer, as well as on the heating cycle in winter.

Blocked drain holes

A clogged drain hole under the barrier between the evaporator and the compressor, or in the channel under the evaporator, may emit a musty smell. To clean the hole, unscrew and remove the front panel. On some models you may have to pull the chassis out a short way. Clean the hole with a bent wire coat hanger, or flush the channel with a large, water-filled kitchen syringe.

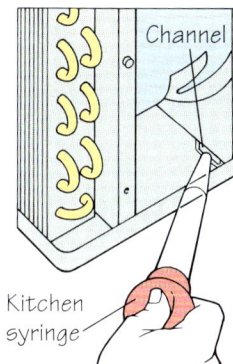

Wire — Drain hole

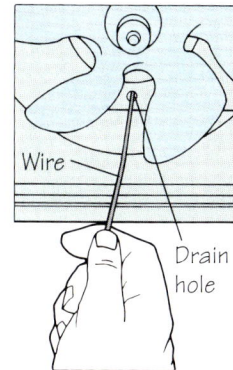

Channel — Kitchen syringe

Too much noise? ▶

The noise created by a window air-conditioner can occur because of several reasons. By following the steps given here, you can soon run your unit with less noise. *Note:* to reach the fan on some models, you have to remove the chassis completely from the housing.

Sash — Shim

1. With the unit running, press your hand on the window sashes. If the noise stops, insert small wooden shims between the sash and the frame. If the glass rattles, re-putty it; as a temporary repair, stick some tape tightly between the edge of the glass and the frame.

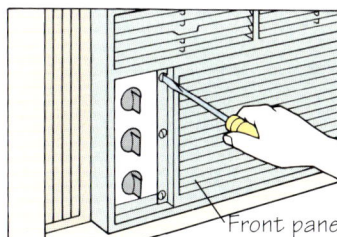

Front panel

2. Press in on the front panel. If the unit's noise ceases, or if the pitch changes, tighten any loose panel fasteners. If the panel won't fit snugly and quietly against the cabinet, secure it to the cabinet with stout cloth tape.

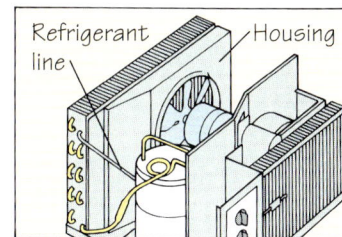

Refrigerant line — Housing

3. Unplug the unit. Slide the chassis partially out of the housing; rest one end on a stool. Spin the fan blades. If a blade hits the cage, bend it slightly for clearance. Jiggle the chassis; if the refrigerant line hits the fan's housing, gently bend it away from the housing.

HOUSEHOLD REPAIRS

REPAIRING FURNITURE

Drawers

No-turn knobs

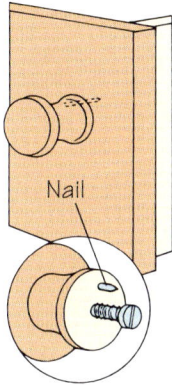

Nail

To anchor a wooden knob on a drawer, drill a hole in the base of the knob. Clip a small nail in half, and insert the lower half in the hole with the point facing out. When you screw the knob on, the point will bite into the wood, keeping the knob from turning.

Dry out a binding drawer

Drawers often stick simply because high humidity has caused the wood to swell. When a drawer sticks, take it out and dry it in a warm place. After a couple of days, test it for fit and sand or plane any areas that stick. Then seal all wood surfaces with a coat of clear polyurethane to retard future moisture absorption.

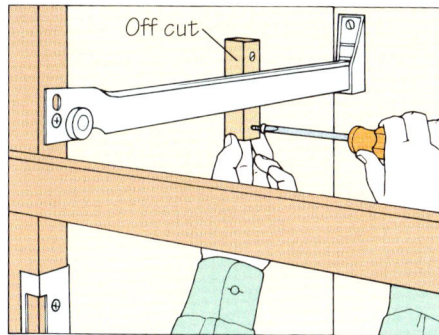

Off cut

Staying on track ▲

On kitchen cabinets, metal drawer slides often bow to the side with use, letting the rollers on the drawer slip out of the track. To fix this, mount a timber off cut on the side of the cabinet to hold the track parallel to the drawer.

Smooth sliding

A quick way to improve the action of a drawer on wooden runners is to remove the drawer and spray the runners with aerosol furniture polish. The wax in the polish will reduce the friction.

Sand and wax

Here's another way to help a wooden drawer slide more smoothly. Lightly sand the bottom edges of the drawer sides and the tops of the runners with 150-grit abrasive paper. Then wax them with the stub of a candle.

Spill preventer

To keep a drawer from pulling out all the way, install a 50 mm nail as a stop on each side about 25 mm in from the back. Drill a 40 mm deep hole that's slightly wider than the nail's diameter. Clip the nail so that it's high enough to catch the top edge of the face frame when the drawer is pulled open. Slip the drawer partway into the cabinet and reach inside to insert the nails.

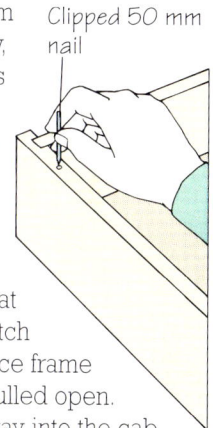

Clipped 50 mm nail

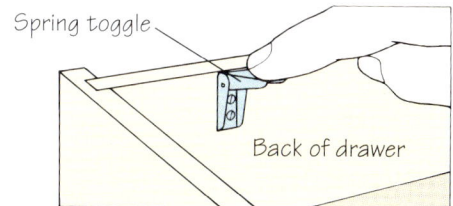

Spring toggle

Back of drawer

Toggle stop ▲

You can also make a drawer stop with the wings of a spring toggle. Drill two holes in one wing and screw it to the inside face of the drawer back with the other wing projecting above the edge. Hold down the top wing to remove the drawer; it will automatically spring back when the drawer is replaced. A pivoting wooden block also makes an efficient drawer stop (p. 56).

Fixing droopy drawers

When a drawer begins to stick and scrape, the drawer's bottom edges and the frame they ride on are often worn. A simple repair is to tap a large drawing pin into the front of the frame just under the drawer's edge on each side. This provides a new minimum-friction sliding surface and raises the drawer to the proper height.

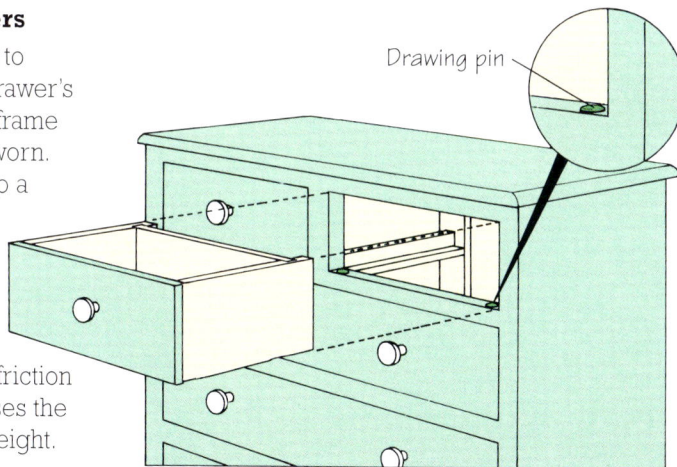

Drawing pin

REPAIRING FURNITURE

Doors

Open-and-shut solution

Sticking cabinet door? To locate the areas that are binding, hold a sheet of carbon paper between the door and the cabinet frame with the carbon side toward the door, then close the door. The carbon will smudge the high spots, showing you where the door needs to be sanded or planed. Move the paper along the edge and repeat as needed. ▼

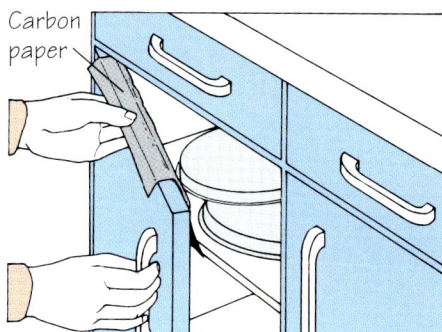

Carbon paper

Door lift

If loose hinges are causing a cabinet door to bind, it is often just a matter of tightening the screws, or if they have pulled loose, replacing them with a thicker gauge. If the hinge is bent, replace it with a more robust one. ▼

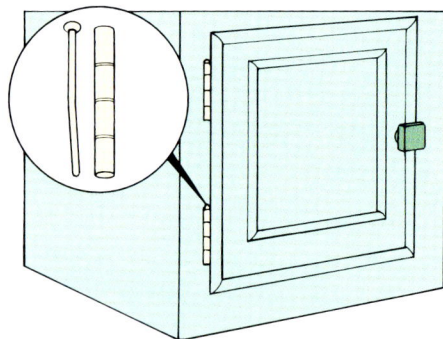

Upholstery

Cardboard strip

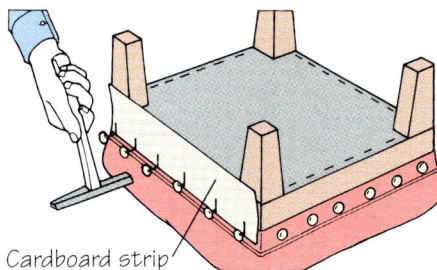

All straight in a row ▲

Getting a row of upholstery tacks straight and evenly spaced is not as easy as it looks. One solution is to pin a dressmaker's tape measure just above the line where the tacks go. Another is to mark the spacing along the edge of a lightweight cardboard strip and press the tacks into it. After driving all the tacks most of the way in, tug on the strip to pull the edge free.

Getting a better hold

Is an old chair frame so peppered with old tack holes that tacks for a new fabric won't hold? Apply a strip or two of muslin to the damaged surface with PVA wood glue and let it dry thoroughly. This will give grip to the surface and let you attach fabric more securely, especially if you use staples instead of tacks.

For future use

Put leftover material from a reupholstery job in a large Manila envelope, and staple it to the bottom of the chair or sofa. Also store extra decorative tacks on the bottom; drive them not quite all the way in. Later, it you need a patch or want to cover an additional small piece, you'll know where the fabric and tacks are.

Torn heavy materials

Sewing a tear in leather, vinyl or certain heavy fabrics may do more harm than good. Try gluing on a patch instead. Use a razor blade to cut a neat circle or square around the rip, and glue a backing of similar material behind the hole. Then trace the hole on paper and use it as a pattern to cut a patch to glue to the backing. Cut the patch from an inside or underside area of the upholstery if necessary.

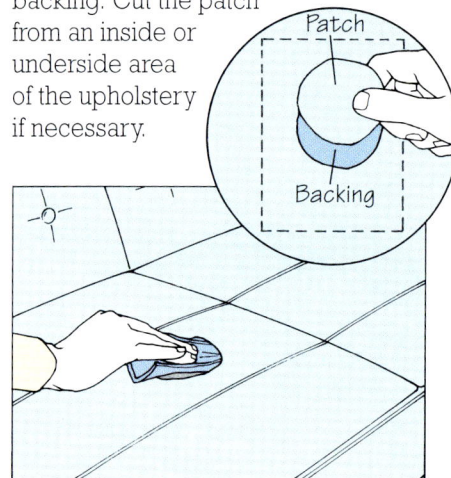

Patch

Backing

Chairs

The old-fashioned way

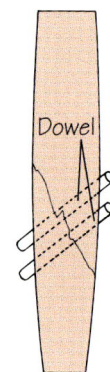

Dowel

Broken chair leg, rung or stretcher? If the parts still fit snugly, fix it with dowels. Glue and clamp the parts together. Then, after the glue dries, remove the clamp and drill angled holes for dowels through both parts. Insert the dowels, glue them in place, and trim them. (For more dowel use tips, see p. 79.)

Spring action

To replace a broken spindle in a chair back that's difficult to take apart, cut off the top tenon of the new spindle. Drill a hole in the top of the spindle, and insert a small spring and a dowel. Then glue the tenon you cut off into the hole in the top of the chair back, and drill a matching hole in it. Apply glue to both ends of the spindle, and set it in place. As you do, press the dowel down and let it pop into the top hole. ▼

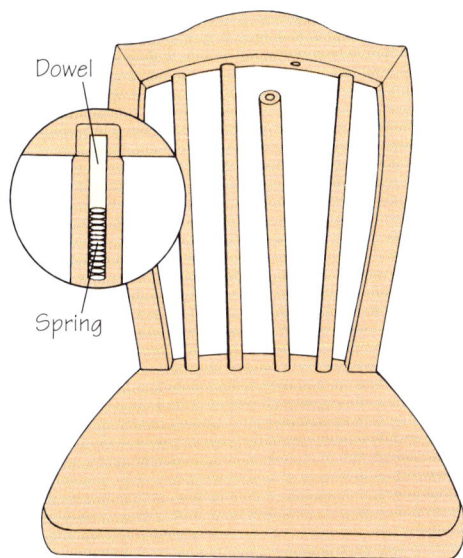

Dowel

Spring

Raising cane

To take the sag out of a cane chair seat, soak it well with hot soapy water, rinse it, and let it air-dry. The cane will shrink, and as it does so, pull taut.

Leg problems

Get a leg up

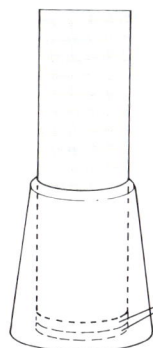

To build up a tubular metal table leg on an uneven floor, put furniture leg tips on all four legs, adding washers inside the tip of the leg you want to lengthen.

Washers

Even keel

T-nut

Nut

Coach bolt

Caster cup

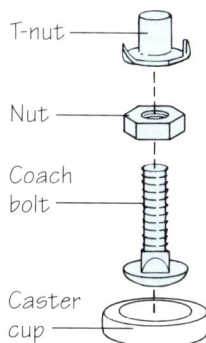

Uneven legs got a piece of furniture wobbling? Put this easy-to-make furniture leveller on all four corners. For each leveller, use a coach bolt with a mating T-nut and ordinary nut. Drill a hole and tap the T-nut over it; then screw in the bolt with the nut on it. After you level the piece, tighten the nut against the T-nut to keep the bolt from moving. Put a caster cup under each leveller to protect the floor. ▼

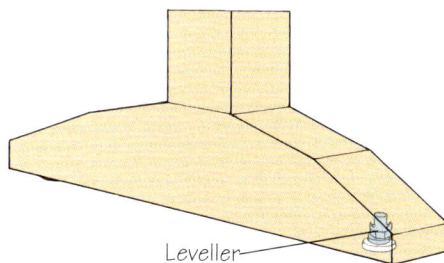

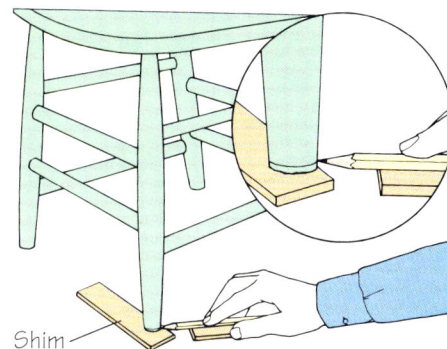

Leveller

Shim

Cure for the wobbles ▲

If a chair or table wobbles because one leg is shorter than the others, put the piece on a flat surface and shim the short leg until the wobble stops. Then mark around each leg with a pencil held flat on a thin wood block slightly higher than the shim. Finally, trim the legs with a small handsaw; they will all be exactly the same length.

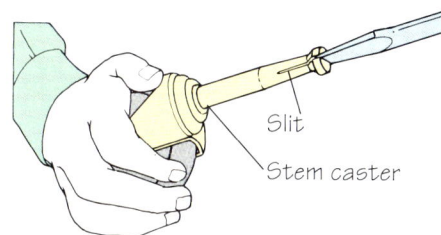

Slit

Stem caster

Faster casters ▲

To keep stem casters from falling out of loose sockets, wrap the stem with steel wool. For a more permanent solution, cut a slit in the top of the stem with a hacksaw. Then spread the slit with a screwdriver just enough so that the caster will not drop out.

REPAIRING FURNITURE

Taking it apart

Avoid a jigsaw puzzle

When you take a chair to pieces for regluing, it's often difficult to tell one leg or rung from the other. Before starting, put masking tape labels with numbers or letters and alignment marks on each joint. Then putting the chair back together will be only a matter of matching markings. You can peel the tape off without damaging the finish.

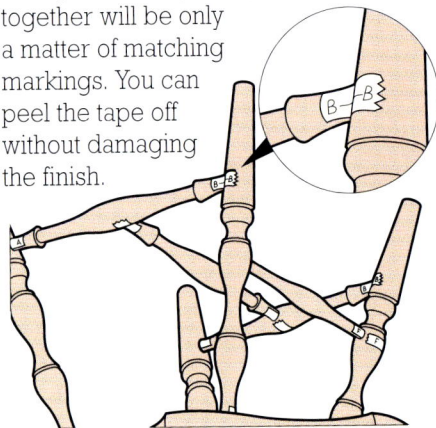

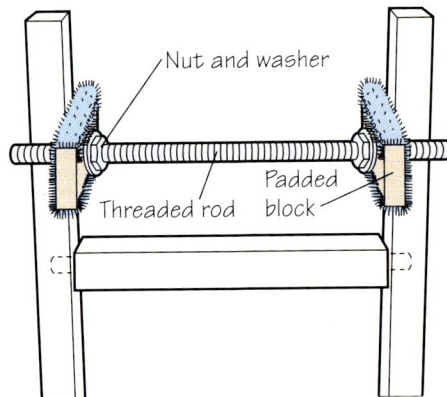

Irresistible force ▲

Here's a simple device for opening stubborn chair joints. All it consists of is a threaded rod (with two nuts and two washers) going through two blocks of wood padded with carpet. Use it to apply outward pressure slowly and evenly to the joints to force them open. To do this, just alternately tighten the nuts on either side a little bit at a time.

Nut and washer

Threaded rod

Padded block

Old cabinetmaker's trick

After taking apart a piece of furniture for regluing, dab or brush hot vinegar on the joints to loosen and remove the old glue. It usually works in minutes, but loosening a thick layer of glue could take up to an hour. The vinegar won't harm any finish, leaving only a white film that you can easily wipe off.

Ream it out

To sand off the old glue in a round mortise, use abrasive paper wrapped around a wood dowel. Use a thin chisel to remove built-up glue from the bottom of the mortise.

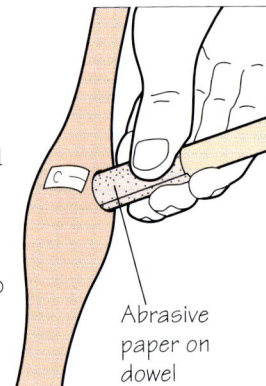

Abrasive paper on dowel

Don't break a leg ▶

When removing the spreaders or rungs on a chair, it's easy to accidentally break one of the chair's legs. To avoid this, support the chair so that the leg rests lightly on a carpeted surface. Then tap straight down on the leg with a rubber mallet. This will loosen the bond and let you pull the spreader or rung out without damaging it or the leg.

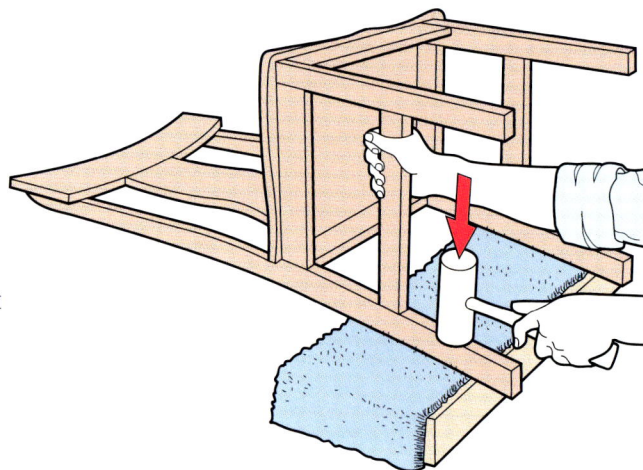

Putting it together

Four commandments

Here are some basic rules for reassembling or repairing furniture.
▷ Don't use nails, L-brackets or mending plates. Use glue and, if necessary, dowels or splines. Use screws only where they were used before.
▷ Remove all the old glue so that the new glue can attach to the wood fibres.
▷ Use the right glue—usually white PVA wood glue. Avoid epoxy; future disassembly is nearly impossible.
▷ Always clamp the parts of a glued joint together until the glue dries—an unclamped joint is a lost cause.

Loose joints 3

If a rectangular tenon is too small, glue thin pieces of veneer to all four sides. When the glue dries, use a utility knife or abrasive paper to fit the enlarged tenon into the mortise.

Loose joints 4

Glue and wrap strips of a thin porous or absorbent fabric (cheesecloth, panty hose or cotton sheeting) around a loose tenon. Use as many layers as you need, and soak each with glue. Let the glue harden; then sand the tenon to fit and glue it in. Trim any excess material with a utility knife.

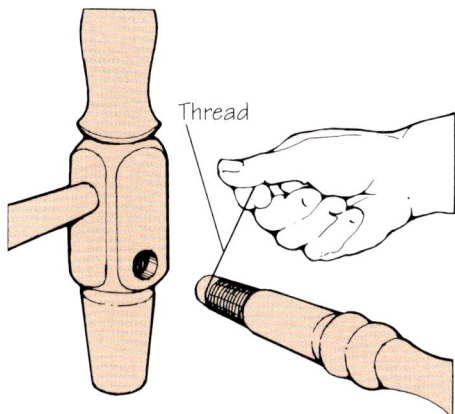

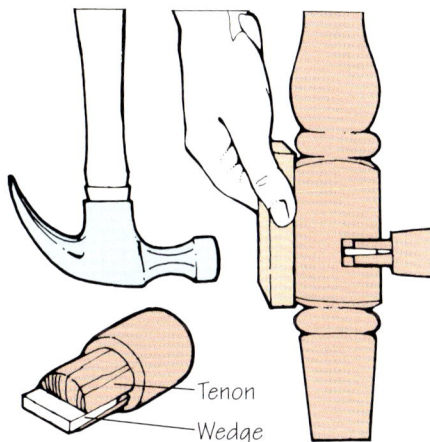

Loose joints 1 ▲

If a furniture joint you are regluing is only slightly loose, you may be able to rely on the glue itself to bridge the gap. If it is so loose it's wobbly, however, here is one trick to try. Coat the tenon with glue, and wrap it tightly with cotton thread. After the thread dries, glue the tenon into the mortise.

Loose joints 2

If a round tenon is too small for a hole, glue a thin wood shaving around it before gluing it in the mortise. The advantage of this filler is that you get a joint that's all wood. Make sure the shaving is the same thickness all around so that the tenon remains centred in the mortise.

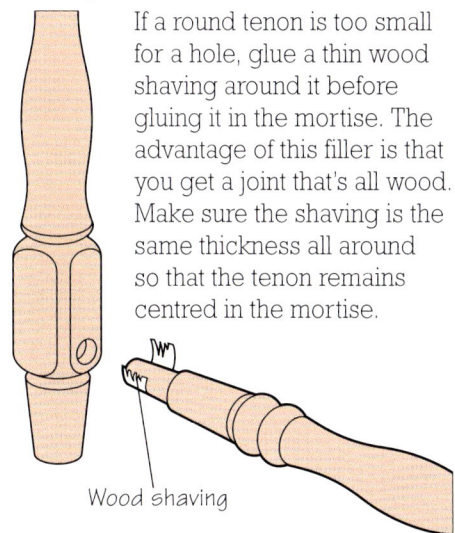

For a really loose joint ▲

Make a slot in the tenon, cutting at a right angle to the grain on the end of the tenon. Cut a wedge that will be driven tightly into the new slot when the joint is reassembled. Experiment to get the wedge the right length. Don't make it too thick because it may split the rung. Put glue on the wedge and the slot as well as on the rung and in the mortise before reassembling and clamping.

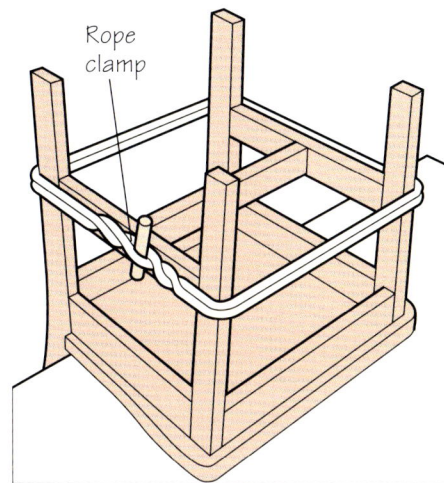

Quick chair clamp ▲

If you don't have bar clamps, the easiest way to secure chair legs while the glue is drying is to wrap two turns of rope around the legs. Then insert a stick between the turns and tighten the rope like a tourniquet. You can also use elastic cords to hold the legs (p. 86).

Old but still practical

If you need to glue a valuable antique, use animal glue. It dries hard and strong but can be softened and removed with alcohol so that you can easily correct a mistake. Animal glue pellets are still available from specialist suppliers, although they may be hard to find.

Another use for animal glue

Because animal glue sets slowly, it's good when you have a complicated assembly and have to arrange several clamps, or to fit together a lot of chair rungs and legs. Animal glue takes three or four hours to set versus twenty minutes to one hour for white PVA wood glue and construction adhesive.

FIXING FURNITURE SURFACES

Scratches

Nuts to scratches

You can actually hide a fine scratch on furniture by rubbing it with the meat of a pecan or other oily nut, or with a little peanut butter. But if that sounds a bit too nutty or smelly, there are alternatives. It's actually the oil in the nut that's doing the job, and olive or vegetable oil will work even better—without the danger of further damaging the finish by rubbing too hard. Rub the oil in well with your thumb, and polish the surface with a clean soft rag.

Coffee to the rescue

For a brew that will obscure scratches on a dark furniture finish, mix one teaspoon of instant coffee in one tablespoon of water or vegetable oil. Don't use this on shellac or a valuable antique.

More home scratch removers

Several other common household items can hide small scratches on finished wood. Here are some to try (test them in an inconspicuous spot first):
▷ Iodine works on mahogany and other reddish finishes.
▷ Liquid and paste shoe polish come in shades that match wood finishes.
▷ Felt-tip markers in brown, red and yellowish hues let you match a range of wood tones, although some may require two or more markers.
▷ Crayons in similar colours also work if warmed slightly first to soften them.

Basic scratch removal

Simply applying paste wax and buffing will often eliminate fine scratches. For more pronounced marks, sand with the grain using some superfine wet-or-dry abrasive paper lubricated with baby oil. To even up the shine and get a satin finish, rub the area with superfine steel wool, also lubricated with oil. For a higher shine, wax and buff. But don't wet-sand older veneer pieces; they often have tiny high spots where the finish will wear off.

Wear and tear

Marker magic

Worn finish on a chair arm or table edge can be fixed with timber markers, available from specialist wood-finishing suppliers, that seal and refinish the surface. Wipe the area with mineral turpentine and rub it over with superfine abrasive paper. Then draw over it with a marker of the appropriate colour. Feather out the repair by rubbing it gently with your finger. Repeat several times to build up the new finish. ▼

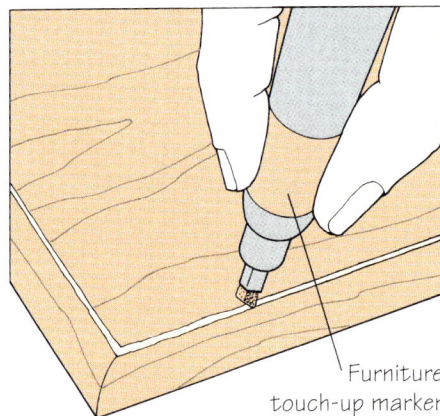

Furniture touch-up marker

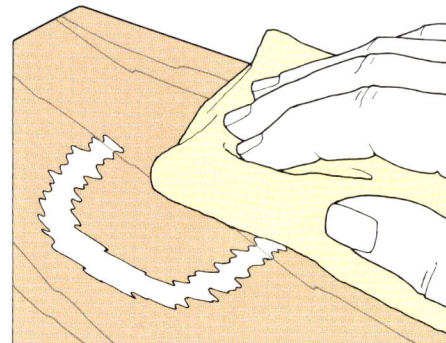

White rings ▲

A white ring left by a wet drink container will often disappear if you just wipe up the moisture and wait a couple of hours. If the ring persists, try passing a hair dryer set on low heat back and forth over it; keeping the nozzle at least 300 mm away and letting the wood get warm but not hot. If a trace still remains, rub it firmly with olive or vegetable oil; then buff vigorously with your palm to create friction. Wipe clean.

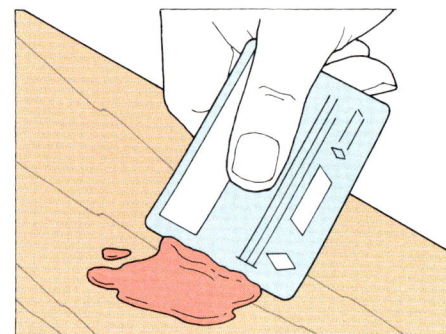

Spilled nail polish ▲

Don't wipe it up! The solvents in nail polish soften most finishes, and wiping may take off the finish. Instead, let the polish dry completely; then gently scrape it off with a credit card. Wax the surface, using superfine steel wool.

Pearly and plaque-free

To brighten a dulled lacquer or varnish finish, mix a little non-gel toothpaste with water and rub it on with a cloth. If necessary, blend in a pinch of baking soda to make it more abrasive.

Scorched surface

To remove a surface burn, rub it with a paste made of fine fireplace ash and lemon juice. Then wipe the area clean, and touch it up with the same kind of finish that is already on the surface. To determine the finish type, see p. 232.

Burn marks

To treat burns that go into the wood, mask closely around the area with tape, and scrape out the charred wood using a craft knife with a rounded blade. If necessary, stain the bare wood to match the finish. Mix equal parts of clear nail polish and acetone-based nail polish remover; apply it one thin coat at a time until you fill the hole, letting each coat dry before applying the next. Sand the surface with extra-fine paper, and then remove the tape. If a burn goes through a veneer, patch the veneer (p. 231). ▼

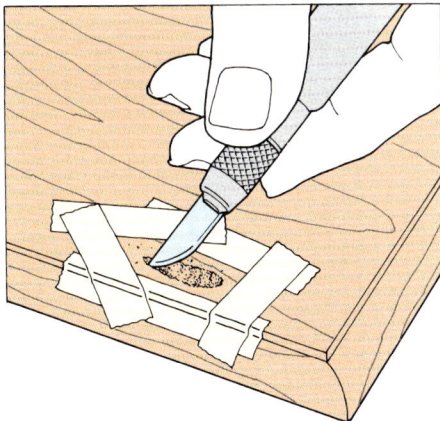

Deeper damage

Soft fill

To hide nicks and gouges on a table leg or cabinet side, use a wax (or putty) furniture filler stick and dark furniture wax (both available from specialist wood-finishing suppliers). First clean the area with mineral turpentine. Fill the larger gouges with filler from a stick matching the lightest shade of the wood. Smooth the filler with a small piece of wood and buff lightly with superfine steel wool. Then use the dark wax to fill the small scratches and even up the colour. The repairs are not durable enough to withstand hard use, so don't try this on a table top—the first time you write on it you'll poke your pen into the filler. ▼

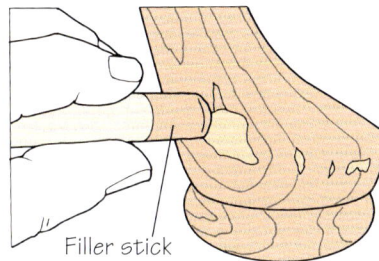

Filler stick

Hard fill ▲

A more solid way to fill deep scars on furniture is with a shellac stick. Get one that closely matches the colour of the finish. To apply it, use a special curved burn-in knife (or a grapefruit knife) heated on a smokeless heat source such as a spirit burner. Reheating the knife often, press it against the stick and melt shellac into the hole a little at a time to fill it just above surface level. Use the hot knife to smooth the shellac. After the patch cools, carefully sand it level with superfine wet-or-dry paper and a little baby oil. Remove any excess shellac with alcohol. This procedure takes skill; practise on worthless furniture first.

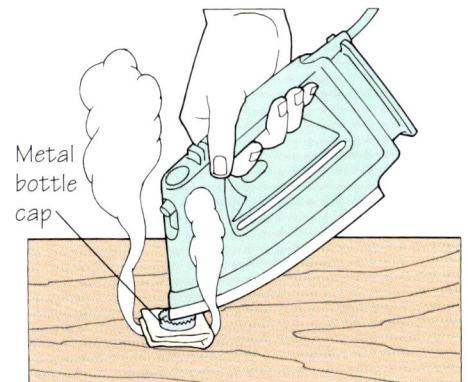

Burn-in knife

Shellac stick

Iron away dents ▶

A surface dent can often be removed by swelling the compressed fibres back to their normal size. Prick the finish in the dent several times with a fine pin so that moisture can penetrate into the wood. Then cover the dent with a pad of wet cloth, put a metal bottle cap on top to spread the heat, and apply an iron on a high setting for a few minutes. Be careful not to scorch the finish. Afterwards, fill the pinholes with a thin coat of varnish.

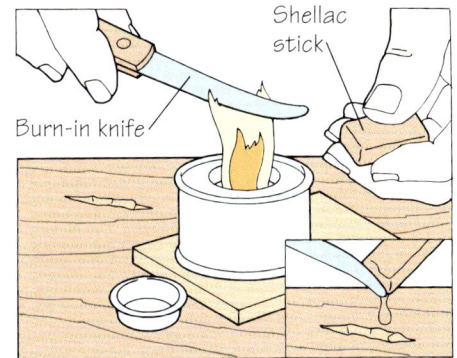

Metal bottle cap

FIXING FURNITURE SURFACES

Veneer

Don't take a sip

Regluing old, brittle delaminated veneer is tricky. Try this. Cut a length of plastic drinking straw and press it to flatten it somewhat. Fold it in half and fill one end with woodworking glue, dripping the glue in from above very slowly in tiny drops (this requires patience). Slip the filled half under the veneer and gently blow in the glue. Wipe off any excess, cover the area with waxed paper and a wood block, and clamp overnight. ▼

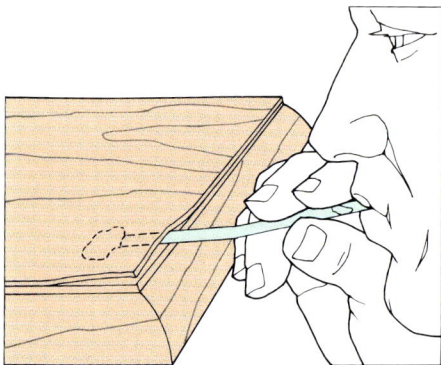

Older means easier

Flattening blistered or peeled veneer on an older piece is often easy because heat and moisture will soften the animal glue commonly used to bond veneer before the 1940s. Lay a damp towel over the area and carefully heat it with an iron set on *Low*. Then press the veneer flat with a rolling pin and clamp it or weight it down overnight. One caveat: don't wet and heat a shellac finish unless you plan to refinish the piece. To test for shellac, dab some alcohol on a hidden area; if the finish is shellac, it will dissolve, cloud or become sticky.

Just a sliver ▶

A blister in veneer usually results when the veneer swells up and becomes too large to fit its original area. Use a sharp craft or utility knife to cut a thin sliver (1 mm wide) from the centre of the blister. Cut with the grain for the length of the blister, tapering the cut's ends. Work woodworking glue under the veneer with a straw (see hint at left), clamp or weight the area, and let it dry.

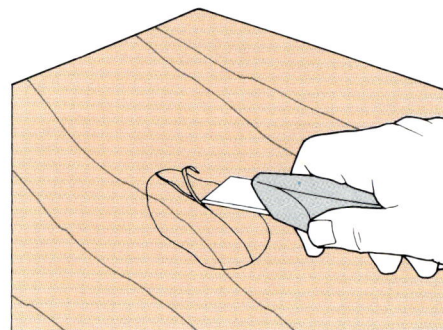

Plastic laminate

Cure for a peeling worktop

When laminate comes loose, it's usually along an edge. To reattach a loose edge, spread contact cement on the base surface under the laminate. Then coat the bottom of the laminate by pressing it down briefly on the base and pulling it away. Prop up the laminate with toothpicks until the adhesive is almost dry (a few minutes less than the recommended drying time). Then press it in place and roll with a rolling pin. ▼

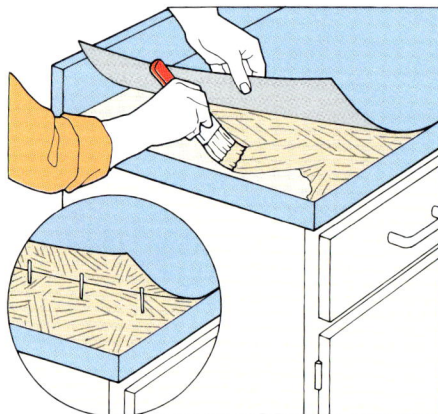

Frying pan burn the counter?

Rubbing toothpaste on the laminate may remove a slight surface discolouration, but a deeper burn can't be removed. Instead, cut out the affected area and put in a heatproof insert. Kits with mounting hardware are available in several sizes. Alternatively, set in a wood-block cutting board, or perhaps a marble pastry slab. ▼

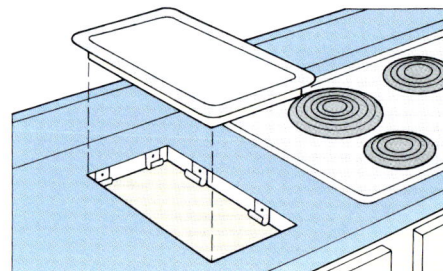

Hot separation

To remove plastic laminate from a surface, heat one edge with an iron or a paint heat gun to soften the adhesive. Slide a putty knife under that edge to lift the laminate. Then work your way along the length of the piece, heating and pulling the laminate free as you go.

PATCHING VENEER

Replacing small, chipped or damaged sections of veneer is easy, but requires careful fitting. Buy a piece of veneer from a local supplier, or a veneer specialist. To glue it use contact cement, sold at hardware shops.

Replacing a large area of veneer, such as an entire chest top, is also simple. But for large areas, use a gel-type contact cement, which is easier to spread. Also available are wide, ready-glued strips of popular timber veneers which can be applied with an iron. Let the new veneer's edges overhang on all sides, and trim them with a utility knife after mounting. Don't stain a large section of veneer until after you mount it.

1 Use a utility knife to remove the damaged veneer and to straighten the edges of the cut-out section. When possible, cut with the grain to hide the joint. Scrape or sand off any old glue.

2 Sand the new veneer smooth, and test stains on it until you get a good match. If the new veneer is thicker than the original, sand it down on the back to the proper thickness.

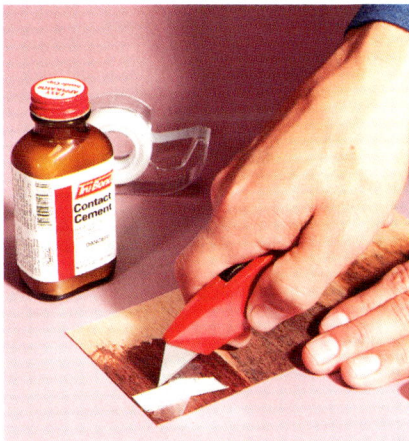

3 Outline the missing area on paper by rubbing with the side of a pencil lead. Cut out the paper, and use it as a template to cut an exact copy of the area from the new veneer.

4 Test-fit the patch, and trim it if necessary. Carefully apply a layer of contact cement to the back of the patch and to the base wood, and let it dry. Then press the patch into place.

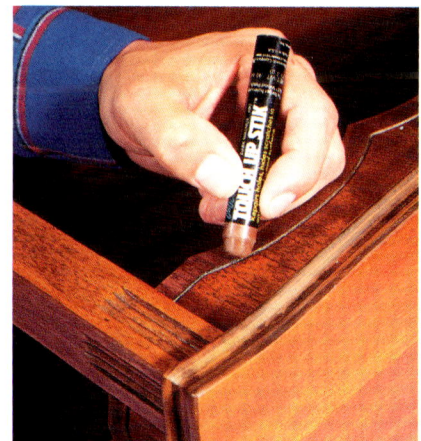

5 Finish the patch with oil or varnish to match. Then hide the joint using a furniture touch-up putty stick in a matching colour. Use the touch-up stick last because finish won't adhere to the putty.

STRIPPING FURNITURE

Before you strip

Clean up your act

Sometimes all that's needed to make that grimy garage-sale bargain look like new is a good cleaning. Mix equal parts of boiled linseed oil and mineral turpentine. Warm the mixture slightly in the top of an old double boiler, and rub it on with cheesecloth, sacking or superfine steel wool, depending on how dirty the surface is. After removing the bulk of the dirt, buff with a soft cloth.

Quick new finish

If all that's wrong with a finish is some rings, hazing, alligatoring or general dinginess, restore it with furniture refinisher. Sold in restoration or wood craft shops, refinisher melts and rejuvenates the finish without destroying its patina as stripper does. Just brush it on, wait the recommended time, then rub with fine steel wool. You get a reworked finish that's lighter in colour than the old one, with scratches and dirt removed. Refinisher won't change a piece's basic colour, rescue a thin, flaky finish or repair deep stains and gouges. Experiment on an unimportant piece first. ▼

Cheaper quick finish

You can sometimes rejuvenate an old, but otherwise solid finish with the solvent that softens it. Work out what that solvent is (see below), brush it on, let it stand until most of it has evaporated and then rework the finish with fine steel wool. It takes more elbow grease than a commercial refinishing product, but it costs a lot less. Always test a hidden area first, and be prepared to strip and refinish the piece if this doesn't work.

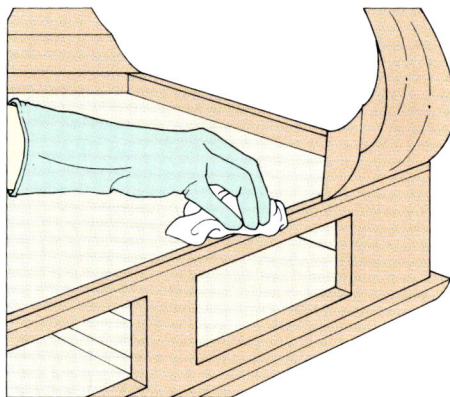

What finish is it? ▲

Clear finishes are difficult to tell apart, but it's important to know what you're working on. Finishes with a low sheen and very little surface thickness are likely to be penetrating oil finishes. To identify other types of finish, moisten a rag with methylated spirits and vigorously rub an unseen spot. If the finish softens, it's shellac. If it doesn't, try the test using lacquer thinner. If the finish softens, it's a lacquer-base finish. If neither product affects the finish, it's probably a varnish. You'll find a list of finishes and their solvents on page 236.

Tips on stripping

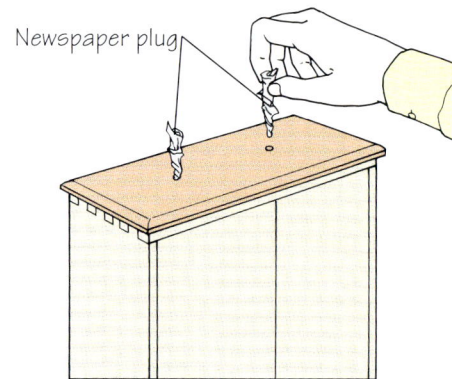

Newspaper plug

Plug up first ▲

After removing the hardware to prepare a piece for stripping, fill key and screw holes with twisted bits of newspaper before applying the stripper. The paper will keep the holes from getting clogged with stripper sludge, which is difficult to remove after it dries and hardens.

Bits and pieces

Take the tedium out of stripping hinges, knobs and other hardware. Fill an old coffee tin with enough stripper to cover a couple of pieces; then tie a string to them and lower them into the tin. Cap the tin with the plastic lid, leaving the string hanging out. After the required time, pull the pieces out and clean them. You can use the stripper several times.

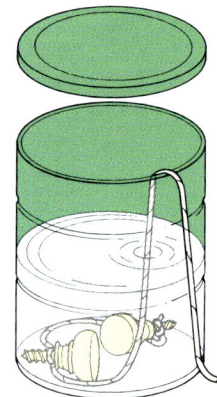

Maybe don't do it yourself

Before stripping a piece, particularly one that's not valuable or that you plan to paint, look into having it dip-stripped. It may not cost much more than buying do-it-yourself chemical stripper. But make sure the dip-stripping is not done in a strongly alkaline bath; it's damaging to joints and veneer, and for that reason it has a bad reputation.

No drip

The best way to avoid having stripper run off vertical surfaces is to use semi-paste stripper, or to keep turning the piece so that the surface being stripped is horizontal. But if you need to keep liquid stripper from running, sprinkle it with some whiting (available from paint suppliers). On open-grain woods, however, sawdust is a better choice because whiting can plug pores and show through a light-coloured stain.

Recycle those tuna tins

Put a shallow tin under each chair or table leg to catch stripper drippings. You'll not only control the mess but you can save the drippings and reuse any that are still clear for a second coat. ▼

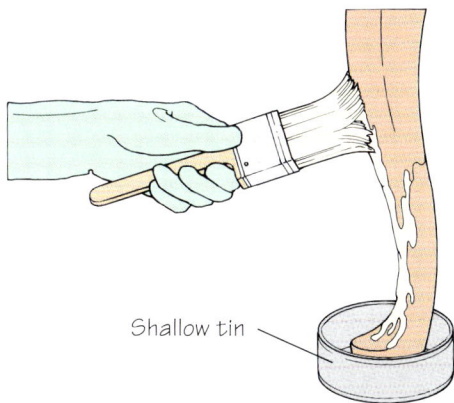

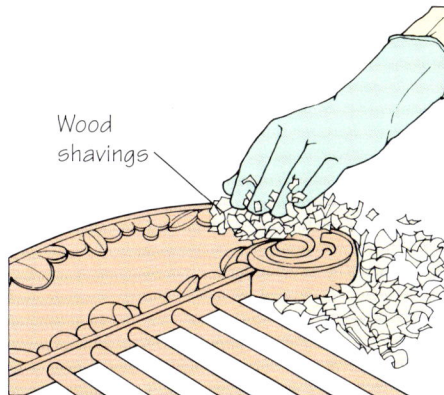

Shallow tin

Wood shavings

Waste not ▲

Wood shavings from a planer or jointer are good for scrubbing loosened finish out of carvings and other finely detailed areas, and as an added benefit they absorb the sludge. If you don't have enough shavings from your own work-shop, ask a local woodworker or cabi-netmaker if they can let you have some. Sawdust will also do the job, but not as well as shavings.

Absorb the mess

On a messy stripping job, the sludge will be easier to remove if you add a material that soaks up some of the soft-ened finish. Sawdust works well, and so does cat litter.

Stripper helper

If you're removing a heavy coat of paint, cover the stripper with some plastic—a garbage bag or an old dry-cleaner bag. The plastic keeps the stripper from evaporating so that it works for longer.

SAFETY FIRST

STRIPPING RISKS

If a product is strong enough to remove paint, you don't want to breathe it into your lungs or get it on your skin or in your eyes. But some strippers require more precaution than others. This is especially true of ones containing methylene chloride. Methylene chloride is fast acting, but it is flammable and a skin and eye irritant. Inhaling high levels of it causes dizziness and headaches and reduces the body's ability to absorb oxygen. Long-term repeated exposure is associated with cancer in laboratory ani-mals. Avoid methylene chloride if someone in your family is preg-nant, has heart or lung problems or is sensitive to chemical fumes.

The wisest course is to use a water-based stripper whenever possible. It takes hours to work and raises the wood grain, but is much less noxious. Even so, take care when working with any paint remover. Wear long sleeves and pants, goggles, solvent-resistant gloves and a respirator with an organic-vapour filter. Work in a well-ventilated area—outdoors when possible. Consider using a heat gun to remove a heavy build-up of old paint.

Dispose of the old finish and leftover stripper safely (p. 39).

STRIPPING FURNITURE

Stripping tools

Scratch prevention

Rounded corner

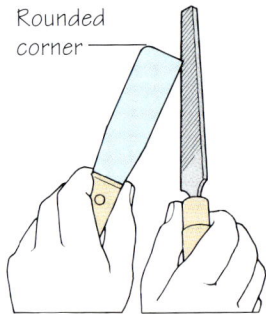

Prepare a putty knife for removing finish by gently rounding the corners with a file. Remove burrs from the edge with fine abrasive paper.

No more messy putty knife

Lightly coat your putty knife with non-stick cooking spray, and the stripper and old paint won't adhere to it.

New use for old tools

With its flat, flexible blade, an old plastic kitchen egg slice makes a great scraper for removing stripper. Hold the slice upside down and push it along as shown for clean operation. ▼

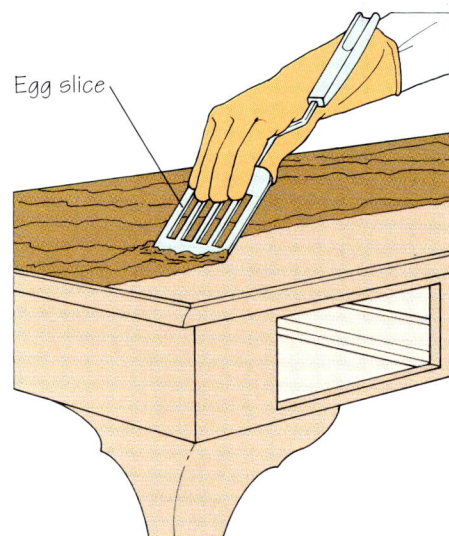

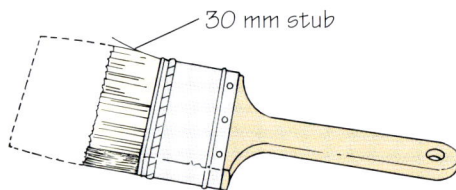

Egg slice

30 mm stub

Short brush ▲

An old paintbrush is a good tool for removing softened finish in hard-to-reach areas. Just trim the bristles to a stiff stump about 30 mm long. Dip the brush in water (for water-based stripper) or mineral turpentine (for solvent-based) and use it to remove the old finish from carvings, turnings and grooves.

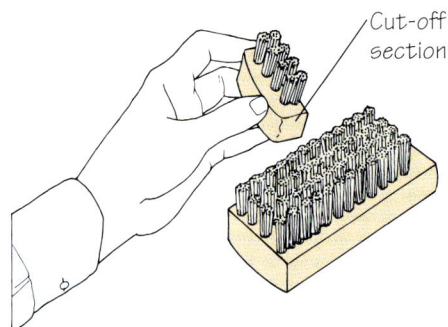

Cut-off section

The little brush that can ▲

To reach into curves and crevices when stripping furniture, cut two rows of bristles from a stiff-bristle scrubbing brush. Use the cut-off piece to work stripper into the areas and later to rub off the loosened finish.

No-mess scoop

Here's a way to remove loosened finish with less mess. Cut an aluminium pie dish in half, using heavy scissors, and put the halves to work as scooper-scrapers. The dish is rigid enough to scrape up the old paint and hold it too.

Snappy solutions

To remove softened finish on turned legs, twist a piece of hessian or old panty hose and move it back and forth across the surface as you would a shoeshining cloth. On fine

Hessian rag

turnings and grooves in furniture legs, remove the sludge with coarse twine or with medium-grade steel wool wrapped around a string. If you need to get old finish out of a really tight groove, use unwaxed dental floss.

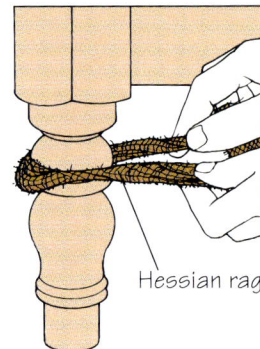

Save that old fishing pole

Bamboo is a good material for making tools that remove stripper sludge. You can quickly cut it with a utility knife to whatever shape you need, and it's soft enough not to mar most timbers.

Other ways to strip

Press it off

Remove a heavy build-up of varnish or other clear finish with an old steam iron. Put several layers of damp cheesecloth over the surface to absorb the finish, and press with the iron on a *Medium* steam setting. Often this will remove most of the finish, leaving only a thin layer to be removed with stripper or with the appropriate solvent.

REMOVING AN OLD FINISH

Before starting, remove all hardware from the piece and put cardboard or thick layers of newspaper under it. Apply stripper with an old paintbrush that you can dispose of when finished. To avoid rust spots, don't use steel wool with water-based stripper.

Caution: when working with stripper, wear an organic-vapour respirator and protective gloves, goggles and clothing. Handle stripper containing methylene chloride with special care (see box, p. 233).

1 Brush on a heavy coat of stripper in one direction; back-and-forth strokes reduce the stripper's potency. Let it work for the specified time. If solvent-based stripper starts to dry, apply a little more.

2 Rub lightly with a plastic pot cleaner or medium steel wool to loosen the finish. Then use a wide, flexible putty knife to remove finish on flat surfaces. If needed, apply another coat of stripper.

3 Remove finish along edges and corners with a brass-bristle brush—the type sold for cleaning pots. It works better than a toothbrush and won't damage the wood the way that steel will.

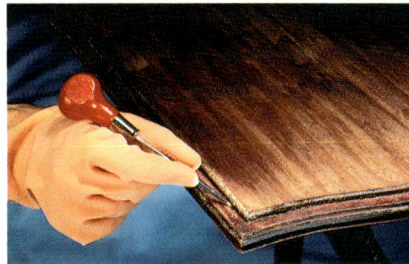

4 Clean finish out of narrow grooves and creases with an awl or a sliver of bamboo. Use light strokes to avoid damaging the wood. For more intricate areas, see the hints on the facing page.

5 Wash the entire area to remove any residue of the stripper. Use mineral turpentine to remove remains of solvent-based stripper, and plain water to remove the remains of water-based stripper.

It's not just for ovens

Use oven cleaner to strip paint and varnish. It's cheaper than stripper, sprays on, and doesn't sag much on vertical surfaces. But use it only on non-valuable pieces you plan to paint, because it darkens the wood. Neutralise the stripped surface with vinegar, wash it with water, and let it dry thoroughly before painting. Wear gloves and goggles.

Out of the ashes

You can strip the finish from hardware with this home brew: 250 g of wood fireplace ashes mixed with 9 litres of water. This mild caustic solution will loosen paint on hardware that is soaked in it overnight. Even though the solution is mild, be sure to wear rubber gloves when putting hands into the bucket.

Sour milk

Does the paint on an old piece resist every stripper you try? It may be milk paint from last century. If so, household ammonia will take it off. On the other hand, if the milk paint is in good condition, the piece is probably more valuable with the paint on than it would be stripped and refinished.

VARNISHING AND STAINING FURNITURE

Before varnishing

Quick preview

Want to know what a wood surface will look like with a clear varnish finish? Just dampen a rag with mineral turpentine and wipe it on an area. If you like the effect, go ahead and varnish the wood; it will look almost the same as the wet wood. If you don't like the look, then stain before varnishing.

Mineral turpentine wiped on

Bleach solution

Banish black water marks ▲

Black water marks on stripped table tops disappear like magic when you apply oxalic acid (sold in hardware stores). Wearing protective gloves and goggles, make a solution with boiling water as directed, and brush it carefully just on the stain. When the stain is gone, neutralise the surface with distilled white vinegar, assessing any colour differences while the wood is wet. Touch up overly light areas with stain.

Bleach it off

After you strip wood, you sometimes find that the old stain has penetrated so deeply that it won't come out. Ordinary chlorine bleach will often lighten the stain. Apply a generous coat, and give the piece a few days to dry. Neutralise the bleach with a white vinegar wash. Bleach will also remove many types of spots from stripped surfaces.

Staining wood

Instant patina

Getting new wood to match the old on repaired furniture is tricky. On light-coloured pieces, experiment with a pale amber stain before applying the final finish. Try to find a hue that approximates the effect of aging, so the new wood will finish the same as the old.

COMMON FINISHES FOR FURNITURE

For best results, apply a finish following label directions and observe any precautions about safe handling or flammability. Lacquer, polyurethane and most varnishes come in satin, semigloss and glossy finishes.

FINISH	SOLVENT	CHARACTERISTICS	HOW TO APPLY
Penetrating oil	Mineral turpentine	Soaks into wood fibres for natural-looking finish. Tung oil is most durable type.	Wipe or brush on, let stand for 30 min. or so, then rub vigorously. Apply two or more coats.
Shellac (white or orange)	Methylated spirits	Thin, lustrous clear or amber surface film. Wears well, but is easily marred by spills.	Brush on three to eight thin coats. Easy to spot-repair. Also use to seal wood for other finishes.
Lacquer	Lacquer thinner	Thin, hard film. Very good spill and wear resistance. Used on commercial furniture.	Spray on with professional equipment; brush on slow-to-dry type. Don't use over other finishes.
Acrylic varnish	Water (before the varnish dries)	Thin, hard film with no amber tones. Moderate resistance to wear and spills.	Spray or brush on two or three thin coats.
Oil-based varnish	Mineral turpentine	Hard warm-toned film. Moderate to good resistance to wear and spills.	Brush on two or three coats. Easy to recoat but hard to spot-repair. Sand between coats.
Polyurethane	Mineral turpentine	Very hard warm-toned film. Excellent resistance to wear and spills. Looks plastic.	Brush on two coats. Hard to spot-repair. Recoat within specified time. Don't use over shellac.

Cure for blotchiness

New softwoods, such as pine, Western red cedar and oregon, are notorious for absorbing stain unevenly with very blotchy results. The same is true for dark stain on some hardwoods. To prevent this, before staining the wood, seal it with a thin coat of shellac (one part shellac to five parts methylated spirits). Let it dry for 30 minutes; then sand with very fine paper. If using a spirit-based stain, apply it quickly and sparingly, or the alcohol will liquefy the shellac.

Tidy stain applicator

Here's an efficient way to apply stain. Use a hacksaw to cut an ordinary thick-nap paint roller into three equal sections. Hold a roller piece in your hand to wipe on stain. The roller absorbs more stain than a brush and applies it more evenly than a cloth. After the stain soaks in, wipe off the excess with a cloth.

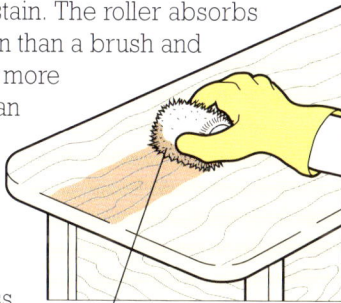

Paint-roller section

Mix-and-match stains

Need a wood stain to match an existing piece? Any colour stain can usually be mixed with any others of the same brand and type. Pick the stain that comes closest to the colour you want. Then work out what tone is missing and add some stain in which that tone predominates. Adding mahogany or rosewood boosts red tones. Maple heightens orange, oak yellow and walnut brown. Test your mix on a hidden spot.

A NATURAL FINISH

Before staining and varnishing a piece, make sure the surface is clear of traces of stripper or old finish. Sand it smooth, and repair any defects. Filling the surface before varnishing (steps 2 and 3) is optional but is often done to close the large pores on open-grain timbers and produce a smooth finish. Use a neutral-colour paste wood filler, thinned as directed. Add a tinting colour or stain to make it match your stain colour. Test the stain and filler colours on an unobtrusive spot. For accurate results, sand, stain, fill and varnish the test patch. Work in a well-ventilated space; wear a respirator. (For tips on using filler, see p. 90; for selecting a brush, p. 92.)

1 Stain the surface in one operation. Work quickly. In general, water- or mineral turpentine-based stains are easier to use that spirit-based ones.

2 On open-grain wood, apply a generous wet coat of wood filler and brush in thoroughly (left). Let it dry until dull and flat (right) but not rock hard.

3 Wipe off the excess filler with hessian, going across the grain. Rubbing with the grain tends to pull the filler out. Let the surface dry overnight.

4 Sand lightly with very fine paper and wipe with a tack cloth. Apply three coats of varnish; sand and wipe again between coats.

PAINTING AND ANTIQUING FURNITURE

Painting furniture

Smooth finish

To get an extremely smooth paint finish, work in a dust-free area and give the paint a chance to flow out, losing its brush marks. Here are some tips.

▷ Apply two coats of enamel undercoat, sanding between coats.
▷ Use an oil-based paint with a slow drying time (about 24 hours).
▷ Use a paint additive to increase penetration and drying time.
▷ Strain paint (even fresh paint) through a filter, and thin it by up to 10 per cent.
▷ Paint surfaces horizontally when possible—if necessary, turn a piece on its side. Lay a door flat.
▷ Use a good natural-bristle brush.
▷ Put on a thin coat of paint, applying three or four coats.
▷ Paint the surface across the grain first. Then make light, full-length strokes with the grain, using just the tip of the brush.
▷ Sand thoroughly with fine paper and wipe with a tack cloth between coats.

Disposable mini-applicators

For small touch-ups and tiny tight corners, apply the paint with a cotton bud. You'll get neat, accurate results, and you can throw the applicator away when you've finished. For hard-to-reach spots, use a pipe cleaner. Simply bend it in half and twist its ends together as shown, forming a loop of the size you need.

Pipe cleaner

Map pin helper

The next time you paint a cabinet, press a few map pins into service. Put one on a cabinet door lip to keep the door and frame from touching while the paint dries. Also use pins as temporary drawer and door pulls. The holes will be covered later by the knobs.

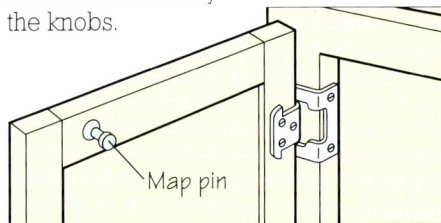

Map pin

Antiquing

Home-made finish

Antiquing can magically transform an old, shabby (or unpainted) piece of furniture, and you don't need a kit to do it. Just give the piece a base coat of satin or semigloss enamel, and let it dry for at least a day. Then make a transparent glaze by mixing clear timber sealer or thinned varnish with a dark tinting colour. Apply the glaze and then wipe it off, leaving flat surfaces lighter than grooves and recesses in order to simulate natural wear. Experiment on timber off cuts first to be sure of the results. ▼

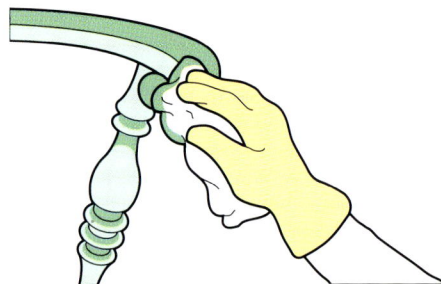

Feigning the ravages of time

Before antiquing a new piece, you may want to 'distress' it. Round corners and edges slightly by sanding or filing. Dent edges with a ball-pein hammer, and mark flat surfaces with a bunch of keys. Make worm holes and irregular scratches with a sharp awl. But don't go overboard; a little damage goes a long way. It helps to examine naturally worn pieces. Sand the distressed areas afterwards.

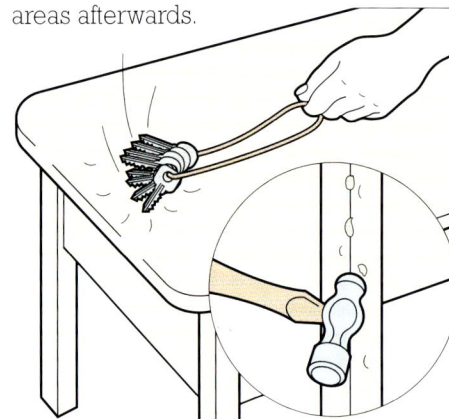

Age spots

To mimic worn areas on a piece you're making look old, use a small stick to apply paint stripper to the base coat in little irregular patches. Wipe the stripper off gently when the paint has the look you want—ranging from a simple crackling effect to total removal of the paint. Neutralise the stripper with water or solvent as directed, and let it dry thoroughly before applying the glaze.

Cracking paint on purpose

Try this to create areas of crackled paint in your imitation antique finish. Before applying a base coat of oil-based paint, brush on some PVA wood glue thinned with water and let it dry thoroughly.

238 / Household Repairs

Old at heart

Before painting a piece you're antiquing, stain the wood a dark brown. When you remove paint to simulate wear, the wood underneath will look old and dark.

Other fake finishes

Fine freckles

One way to heighten the effect of glazing is to splatter fly specks of very dark colour on the surface after wiping off the glaze. Make some of the glazing solution deeper in colour, dip a toothbrush into it, and flick it over the surface. The effect varies depending on how close you hold the brush to the surface and how quickly you move it. ▼

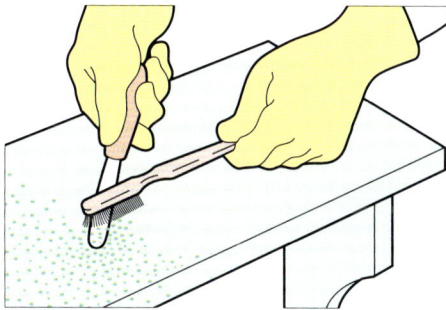

Fake wood grain

You can simulate wood grain with the glazing process used for antiquing. Apply a base paint that matches the lightest tones in the wood you're imitating and a glaze that matches the darkest. Create grain by wiping the glaze lightly with steel wool, and then a dry brush, in a wavy pattern. Or you can drag a feather or piece of carpet across the surface, or use graining tools from a paint supplier or restoration centre.

AN ENAMEL FINISH

You don't have to strip furniture in order to paint it. But for paint to adhere, the surface must be free of grease and dirt, and any gloss must be dulled by sanding. If the piece was painted before the early 1980s, the paint may contain lead; wear a face mask when working with old finishes. Either oil- or water-based gloss finishes will provide a tough finish if you apply at least two coats over undercoat. Oil-based enamels have a wet look when dry (see 'Smooth finish', facing page); water-based finishes are more satiny. Wear a dust mask when sanding, and a respirator when painting.

1 Wipe the surface with mineral turpentine on a rag. Sand off the shine with medium-grade paper. If the surface is still rough, sand again with fine paper.

2 To fill nicks and gouges, apply wood filler with a putty knife. Let it dry as directed; then sand smooth. Wipe the surface clean with a tack cloth.

3 Prepare the surface with an oil-based undercoat, which brushes on easily, dries quickly and provides the best surface for an oil-based enamel.

4 Apply two or three coats of enamel. Let each dry thoroughly; if finish is glossy, sand with very fine-grade paper and wipe with tack cloth between coats.

SPRAY-PAINTING FURNITURE

Spraying techniques

Spray booth

Want to spray-paint a piece of furniture but afraid of the mess? Use a large cardboard appliance packaging box as a spray booth. A local shop may be happy to give you one they have discarded.

Turn and paint

It's easier to paint a chair if you turn it upside down and spray the legs and rungs first, spraying their insides before their outsides. Then turn it right side up and spray the back and seat. This works with a small table as well. ▼

Spray inside first

Corners first and last

When spray-painting the outside of a piece of furniture, spray the corners first, aiming directly at each corner and coating both sides of it evenly. But when spraying the inside of a cabinet, it's best not to spray into the corners. Instead, just spray straight onto the flat surfaces, doing the back first, then each side.

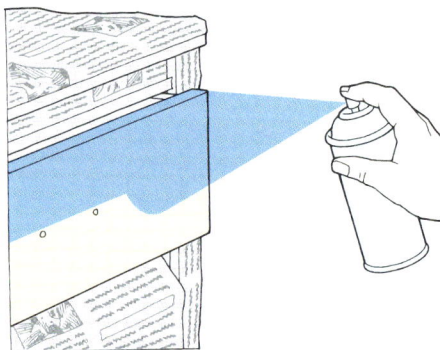

Just a crack ▲

To spray a drawer front, leave it in the cabinet. Mask the cabinet, and the inside of the drawer; then pull the drawer out about 10 mm. Paint will then cover the drawer edges without much getting inside. After the drawer dries, remove it to paint the cabinet case.

Get an angle on it

With open-weave material, such as cane, you'll get a finer, more even finish if you hold the spray can at about a 45° angle above the material. On wicker, spray first from one side at a 45° angle, then from the other side, to penetrate the weave as much as possible. ▼

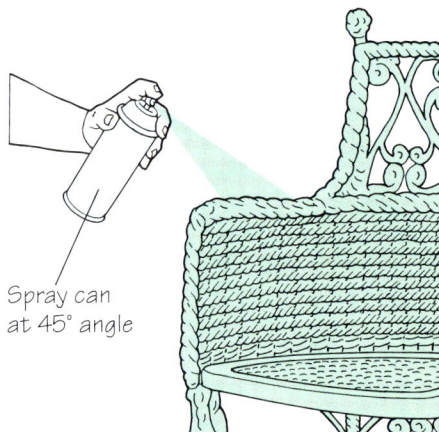

Spray can at 45° angle

Not the way you think

When spray-painting a flat surface, such as a table top, begin on the side nearest you and work toward the opposite side. This may seem a little strange, but when you spray a flat surface you hold the can at a slight angle, causing it to send some overspray ahead of it. By starting nearby, you cover up that overspray as you progress across the surface. If you work in the opposite direction, the overspray would leave a pebbly texture on the areas you had already painted.

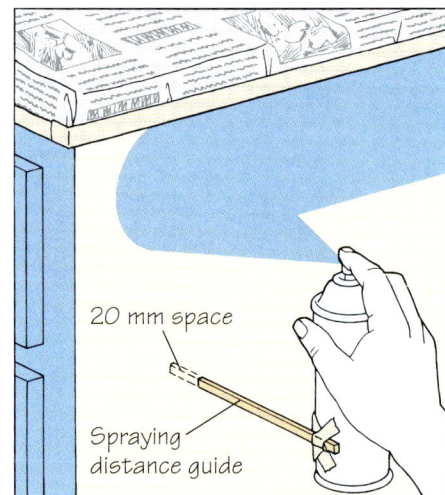

20 mm space

Spraying distance guide

Keeping your distance ▲

For an even finish, you need to keep a spray can the same distance from the surface the entire time you are spraying. After you work out the best distance for spraying with a can, tape a stick to the can as a guide. Make the stick about 20 mm shorter than the distance so that you won't scrape it across the paint.

Clean lines

If you want to leave some parts of a piece of furniture unpainted, use masking tape and sheets of newspaper to protect the areas. For a clean line along a tape edge, direct the spray so that it is blowing over the tape rather than towards the tape edge.

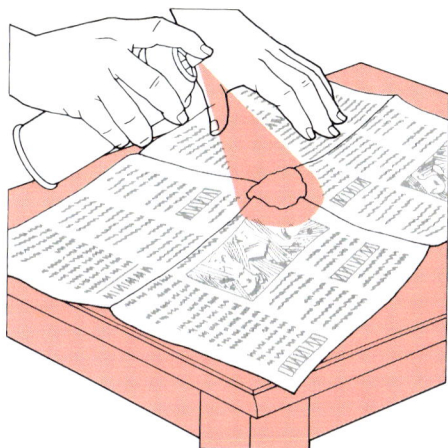

Instant feathering ▲

To touch up a small spot, try this. Fold a newspaper in quarters, and then unfold it and cut a hole in the centre the size of the spot to be touched up. Place the newspaper over the spot, with the folds in the paper peaked up slightly. Then make several quick passes over the hole with the spray can. If you move quickly it prevents paint build-up, and the raised paper at the folds lets the paint feather out around the spot to blend in with the rest of the surface. Perfect your technique on off cuts before working on good furniture.

For better spraying

Elusive last drops

No paint comes out of the spray can but you can still feel paint sloshing around inside? The paint pick-up tube may be on the side of the can opposite the direction you are spraying. Twist the nozzle a half turn and try again.

Paint pick-up tube

Cleaner spraying

To keep your airless spray painter from dripping on your clothes and the floor, make a drip-cloth out of an old towel and wrap it around the sprayer just below the nozzle. The cloth will catch drips and make cleaning up easier. ▼

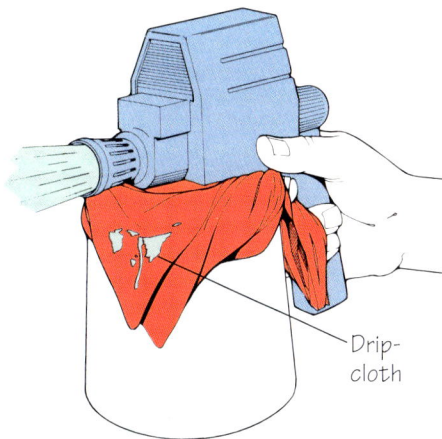

Drip-cloth

Sure shot

To clear a clogged nozzle on an aerosol paint can, remove the nozzle and put it on the end of the spray tube on a can of penetrating lubricant. Fire a shot of lubricant through the nozzle. ▼

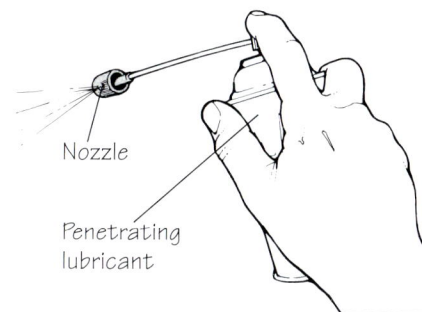

Nozzle

Penetrating lubricant

More cures for clogging

If the nozzle of an aerosol paint can is clogged and you don't have penetrating lubricant, don't give up; try these tips.
▷ Soak the nozzle in lacquer thinner or mineral turpentine overnight.
▷ Save the nozzles of discarded spray cans to use as instant replacements for clogged ones. Store them in a small jar filled with solvent.

Preventing clogs

There is a simple way to keep a spray-paint can nozzle from becoming clogged in the first place. After spraying, turn the can upside down and press the button briefly. It will emit a short blast of pure propellant, which will clear the nozzle of paint.

APPLIANCE REPAIR TIPS

Parts protocols

Parts on ice

Keep track of small parts while making repairs. As you disassemble an item, put the parts into prenumbered compartments of a plastic ice cube tray. Reverse the procedure for reassembly. An egg carton works as well. ▼

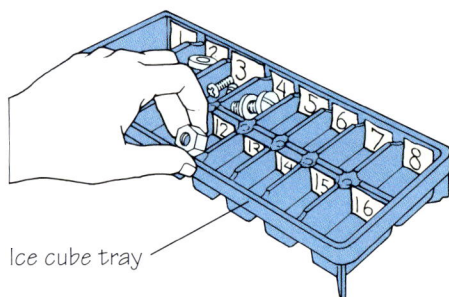

Ice cube tray

All in a row

Sticky tape can also keep parts in the right order. Staple a strip of cloth tape, adhesive side up, to your bench top, and as you take the parts off, stick them to the tape in sequence.

Parts saver

While waiting for new parts to arrive, don't leave small parts and screws just lying around. Put them in resealable plastic sandwich bags so that you won't lose them.

Grease bag

Here's another use for those resealable plastic bags. They can keep your hands from getting dirty when you have to grease bearings or other parts. Just put some grease into a bag, add the parts, seal the bag, and work them around in the grease until they are coated.

Metal paint tray

Parts washer ▲

Use a metal paint tray to wash small parts. Fill the deep end with solvent and soak the parts in it. Then use the upper end as a work area for brushing and wiping the parts after they've soaked.

Oops!

Dropped a part and can't find it? Turn off the lights and close the blinds. Then turn on a torch, hold it close to the floor, and rotate it in a circle. Like a searchlight, the beam raking across the floor causes a small object to cast a large shadow, making it much easier to find.

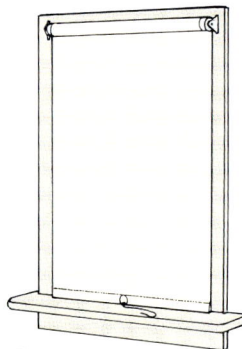

Sources of cheap parts

Need some small—but difficult to find and expensive—part for one of your appliances? Try the thrift shops run by local charitable agencies, such as the Smith Family or Red Cross. They sometimes have old appliances from which you can salvage parts, and the cost is always very reasonable.

Electrical fixes

Won't wiggle off

When joining two or more electrical wires, don't just twist the ends together and cover them with a strip of insulating tape. Always use a proper connector—which can be bought in the electrical section of your local hardware shop—to make a safe junction.

Vital spray

Keep a spray can of electrical contact cleaner handy for appliance repairs. A quick burst of this non-conductive cleaner is often all you need to cure a sticky switch or 'noisy' volume control. The cleaner is often sold by car parts suppliers as well as most electronics hobby shops, where it is sometimes labelled 'switch cleaner'. ▼

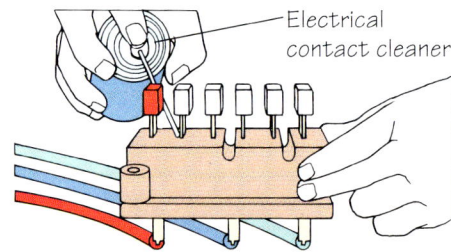

Electrical contact cleaner

USING A MULTIMETER

A multimeter is a battery-operated tester that can tell you whether an electrical part, such as a power cord, switch, or heating element is working or defective. It may look complex, but most tests are simple. For accuracy and ease of use, select a digital model that automatically senses and sets the range you are testing.

The most common test is for electrical continuity. A continuity test can locate short or open (interrupted) circuits. You can also test for resistance to electricity's flow, which occurs in heating elements and other parts. Both tests are made using the ohms (Ω) scales. A reading of zero or near zero (less than .05 ohms) signals a complete circuit. The circuit is incomplete when the reading is infinite resistance—infinity (∞) on an analog (non-digital) meter or a flashing number or other indicator (check the manual) on a digital meter.

The meter's DC volts settings lets you measure a battery's voltage or a low-voltage system such as a doorbell. The AC volts settings can be used to measure the house electricity supply, but it's safest not to do this.

To set up a multimeter, insert the red lead into the appropriate positive (+) jack and the black lead into the negative (–) jack. You may need to 'zero' an analog meter by touching the two probes together and then turning the adjustment knob until the needle is over zero.

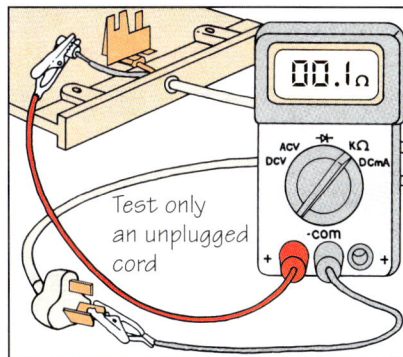

Check a power cord one wire at a time. Set the meter for ohms (Ω). Touch one probe to a disconnected lead, the other to each angled plug prong in turn. A zero or very low reading on only one prong shows continuity. There's an open circuit if both prongs show infinite resistance, a possible short if both read zero, or near it.

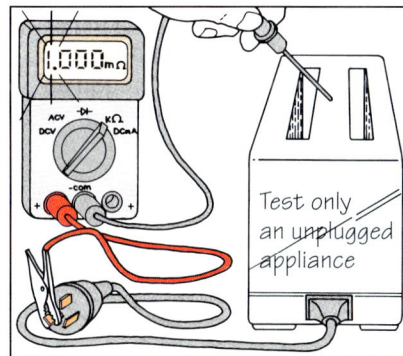

To test a cooker element for resistance, set the meter for ohms (Ω). Touch the probes to the element's two terminals. The reading should be between 20 and 100 ohms. If it's much higher, the element is defective and may have an open circuit. If lower, it may have a short. Test also for an earth fault (below, left).

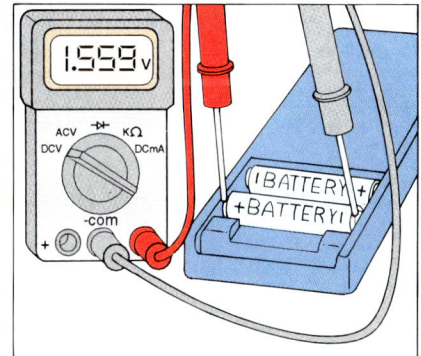

Always check a repaired appliance for an earth fault—a dangerous current leakage. Set the meter for ohms (Ω). Touch one probe to a metal part on the body and the other to each angled plug prong in turn. The meter should show infinite resistance on both. The straight earth prong should read zero or near zero.

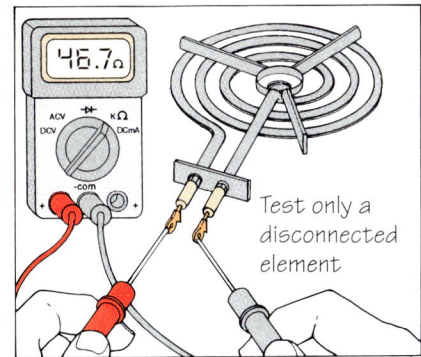

For greatest accuracy, test a battery's voltage while it's powering a device. Select a DC volts setting slightly higher than the battery's rating, and touch the probes to the battery's terminals (red to + and black to –). If the DC volts scale reading is much below the battery's rating, replace or recharge the battery.

APPLIANCE REPAIR TIPS

Gaining access

Nameplate cover-up

Have you taken out every visible screw from a small appliance and it still won't open? Look for screws hidden under the manufacturer's nameplate. Remove the plate's mounting screws, or if the plate is glued on, carefully prise it off with a screwdriver. Stick-on labels or decorations may also conceal recessed screws. Rub your fingers over them to find the screws. If you feel one, lift a corner of the label and peel it back. ▼

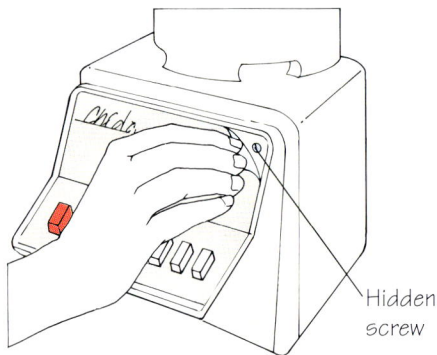

Hidden screw

Secret screws

Sometimes an access screw is hiding under a plastic plug set flush with the surface of an appliance's housing. Insert the tip of a small screwdriver into the seam around the plug to prise it out.

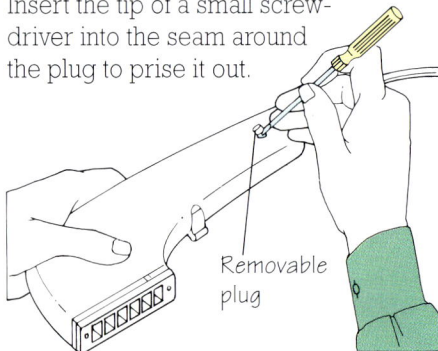

Removable plug

Underfoot screws

Also look for screws hiding inside an appliance's feet, especially rubber or plastic feet that fit into holes on the housing. Often you can pop them out with your fingers or a small screwdriver. ▼

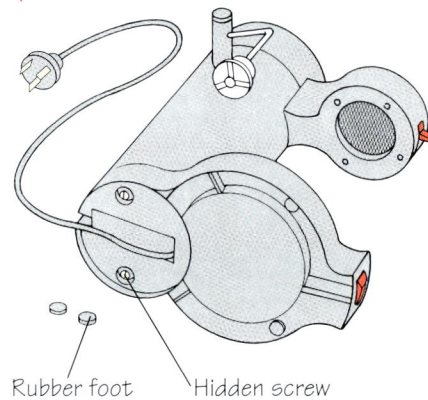

Rubber foot   Hidden screw

Interlocked

No signs of a screw? The moulded plastic housings on some small appliances are held together by interlocking posts and holes. Look for the tops of posts projecting from one part through another. Prise open a nearby seam to pop the posts out of the holes. ▼

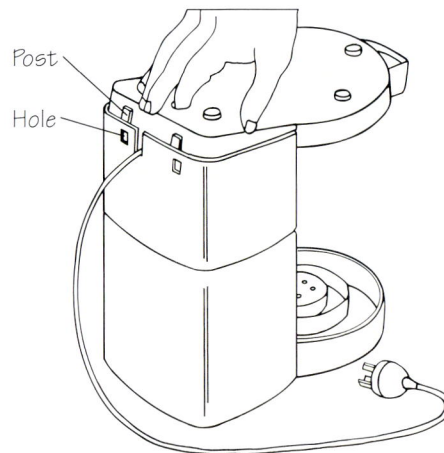

Post

Hole

Tough to crack open

Tabs and notches just under the seam often hold small appliance housings together. Pressing down on the tab side of the seam will usually free the tab from the notch. If necessary, slip the tip of a small screwdriver into the seam and gently prise the pieces apart. If there are several tabs, work your way around the seam, opening one tab at a time. ▼

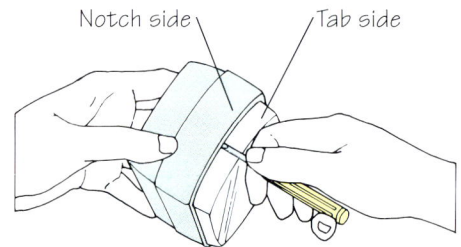

Notch side   Tab side

Taking things apart

Left-handed parts

When disassembling appliances with moving parts, remember that nuts and bolts on rotating components may have left-hand threads. If a part doesn't loosen when turned in the normal anticlockwise direction, try turning it clockwise instead. Forcing it the wrong way will strip the threads.

Back off a minute

If you are having trouble getting a screw to go back into an item, don't force it in. Instead, stop and very lightly turn the screw anticlockwise until you hear a click or feel the screw drop slightly. Gently turning a screw in the wrong direction like this is often the easiest way to literally get it back in the groove. After that, it should go in easily.

Paper clip to the rescue

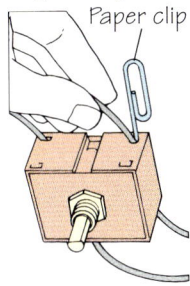

Paper clip

Switches often have self-locking terminals that clamp onto a wire when it is inserted. To free a wire from this type of terminal, just insert a straightened paper clip and pull the wire out.

Push, don't pull

Don't pull off a spade-type terminal; you're likely to damage the wire. Push it off with a screwdriver instead. ▼

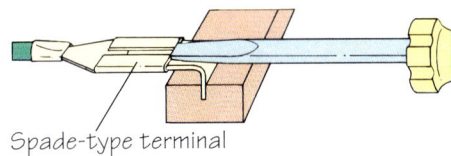

Spade-type terminal

Small appliances

Save your sole

Have you got an iron with a dirty soleplate? As long as it's not aluminium and doesn't have a non-stick coating, you can revive it. Mix two tablespoons of salt with enough water to form a paste. Unplug the iron and rub the paste over the soleplate with crumpled newspaper; wipe clean with a damp paper towel. ▼

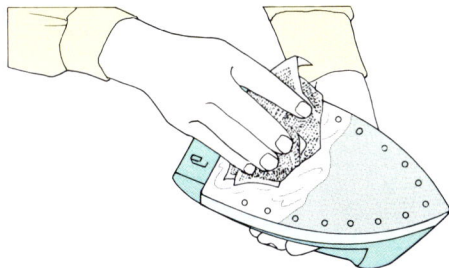

SAFE APPLIANCE REPAIRS

Do not attempt any appliance repairs—particularly electrical repairs—unless you know exactly what you are doing. A botched repair may cost you not only money but, far more seriously, may cause a fire or even a death as the result of an electric shock. If you have any doubts at all about your ability to do the job, call in an expert. After any repair, however competent you are, always test the appliance for an earth fault (a current leakage, as when a bare wire touches a metal housing). With a large appliance, it's easiest to use a multimeter (p. 243). But you can test a more portable appliance using a test light with alligator clip leads. Before plugging in the appliance, connect one lead of the test light to a bare metal spot on the appliance and the other lead to a reliable earth—such as a metal cold-water pipe, for example. With the appliance still unplugged, turn its on-off switch to *On*. Then plug it in. If the test light glows, the appliance has an earth fault and is dangerous. Pull out the plug—do not turn it off using the on-off switch.

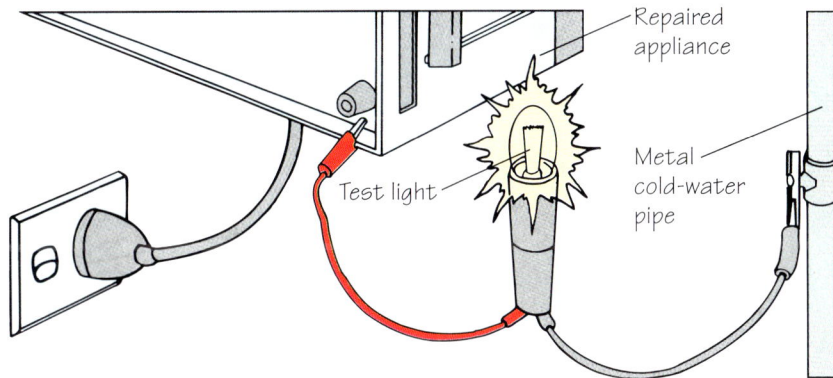

Repaired appliance

Test light

Metal cold-water pipe

Don't slam it against the wall

Is the persistant whirring of an electric clock driving you to distraction? Try turning it upside down for a few hours. If that doesn't fix the problem, unplug it and put it in a slightly warm oven (under 60°C) for an hour. Either action will help to redistribute the lubricant in the clock, making it quieter.

No greasy shower

After you oil the centre bearings on a portable domestic fan, put a large paper bag over it and then turn it on for a few minutes. Any oil that the fan throws off will hit the bag, instead of being flung around the room.

REFRIGERATORS AND FREEZERS

Refrigerator problems

What's the buzz?

Is there an annoying 'buzz' from your refrigerator while the motor is operating? It's probably the condenser coil vibrating against the wall behind, or against its mounting brackets. Try moving the fridge out from the wall a bit, and check for loose mountings.

In from the cold

It's tempting to put a freezer—or an old extra refrigerator—in the garage or out on the veranda. But don't unless the space is heated. A freezer or refrigerator can't keep food safely cold when the surrounding temperature drops too low. As the air temperature drops, the compressor will kick on less often and will actually stop running below about 4°C, letting the food spoil.

Light leaks

To see if a refrigerator door gasket is forming a tight seal, put a 150 watt outdoor floodlight in the compartment and shine it toward one side at a time with the cord coming out near the opposite side. With the door closed and the kitchen lights off, look for light leaks. ▼

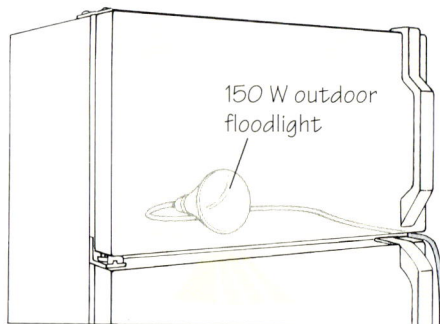

150 W outdoor floodlight

Gasket repair

You can often fix a single small crack in the gasket around a refrigerator door with silicone sealant. Roll the gasket open (see step 1, facing page) and apply the sealant to the inside of the gasket, being careful not to apply too much. Make sure that the sealant cannot come into contact with any food.

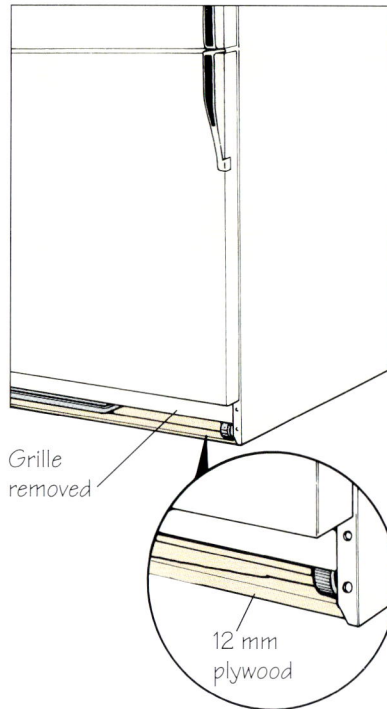

Grille removed

12 mm plywood

Open and shut ▲

Are your children always leaving the refrigerator door slightly ajar? Put a piece of 12 mm plywood under the front legs. The board won't show behind the grille, and the tilt is too small to be noticeable but still enough to shut the door. However, don't do this if you have an automatic ice maker, which requires the unit to be perfectly level.

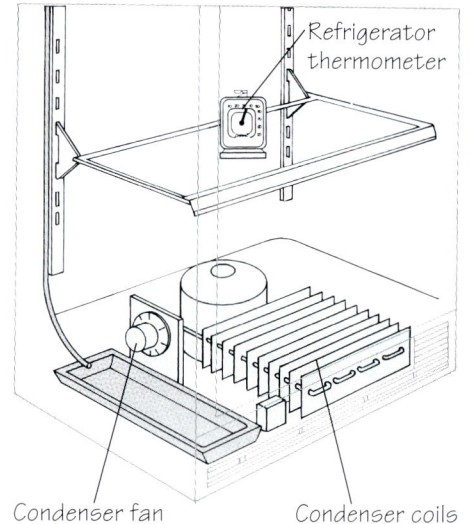

Refrigerator thermometer

Condenser fan   Condenser coils

Fridge under the weather ▲

Food not keeping well in your refrigerator? Put a refrigerator thermometer in the centre of the food compartment and leave it overnight. It should read between 1°C and 4°C. If you can't maintain this temperature by adjusting the refrigerator's thermostat, check for clogged condenser coils under the refrigerator or on the back of the unit. Also look for an obstructed or defective condenser fan underneath.

Another use for ice cream

To check a freezer's temperature, put a refrigerator thermometer on top of a carton of ice cream or frozen food and leave it for a day. Look for a reading of around −18°C. Actually ice cream alone can tell you if a freezer is at the right temperature. If the ice cream is firmly solid without being brick hard, the temperature is about right.

Slippery ice cubes

Do ice cubes stick to the tray of your automatic ice maker? Take out the tray, and wash and dry it well. Then lightly coat the inside with non-stick cooking spray, and wipe off any excess. The cubes will slide out easily, and there will be no strange taste. It lasts longer than vinegar, which is often recommended as a solution to this problem.

Frosty tubes

If there's frost on one of the tubes running into your fridge's compressor, it probably melts regularly, leaving a messy puddle. The solution is to cover the tube with a foam sleeve or wraparound insulation, sold by suppliers of air-conditioning parts. The tube is the suction line coming from the evaporator coils inside the unit; its location may vary from unit to unit. ▼

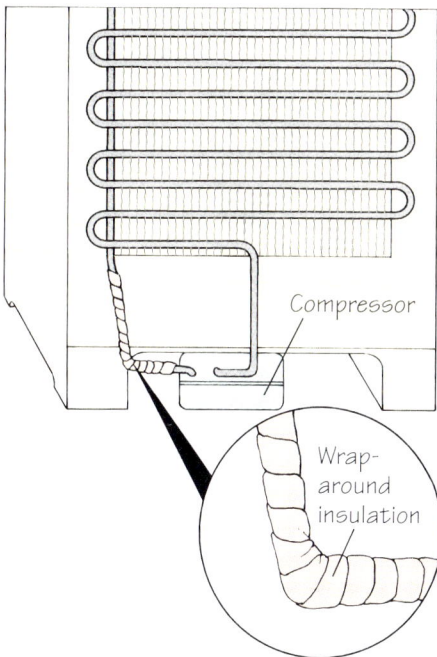

Compressor

Wrap-around insulation

NEW DOOR SEAL

A damaged refrigerator door seal wastes energy. Replacing one is easy. Order the seal ahead of time. Your local appliance store may not stock one for your model refrigerator, but they can probably order one in. Most seals are held by a retainer strip and screws, although some simply slip under a retainer and others are held only by screws. When installing a new gasket, don't overtighten the screws; that may crack the plastic door liner. Do the screws up slightly, then close the door. Gently twist the door if necessary to conform it to the cabinet; then tighten the screws finally.

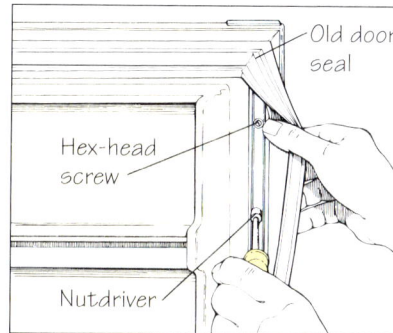

Old door seal

Hex-head screw

Nutdriver

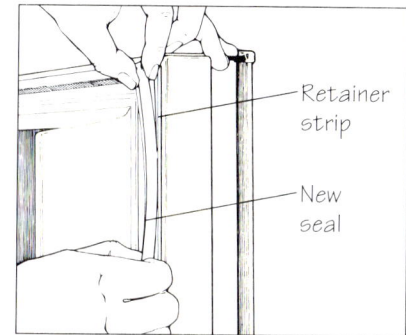

Retainer strip

New seal

1 Roll the seal back and use a nutdriver to loosen—but not remove—the screws. Slip the seal from under the retainer. Before installing the new seal, inspect it. If it is crimped, soak it in hot tap water for a few minutes.

2 Position the new seal over the retainer corners at the door top. On each side, start at one corner and slide the seal under the retainer. Carefully tighten the screws at each side's centre, then the corners, then in between.

Preventing emergencies

Safety light

A tripped circuit breaker could turn the food in your freezer into a spoiled mess before you discover it. If your freezer does not have a clearly visible 'on' light, put a low-wattage night-light in the same power point as the freezer. You'll see immediately when the power is off.

Avoiding a meltdown

If your area suffers frequent power blackouts, keep your freezer full, packing empty spaces with packets of picnic-cooler artificial ice or plastic bottles of frozen water. If there's a prolonged blackout, 15 kg of dry ice will keep an average 270 litre freezer cold enough for about three days. For dry ice, check the Yellow Pages. Wear heavy gloves when handling it, and put newspaper between it and your food.

DISHWASHERS AND STOVES

Dishwashers

Rusty rack repair

Is the plastic coating peeling off the racks in your dishwasher? Cover them with pieces of flexible clear plastic tubing. For most racks, tubing with an outside diameter of 6 mm and an inside diameter of 3 mm works well. Cut it into 6 mm lengths and slip them over the rusted rack ends. ▼

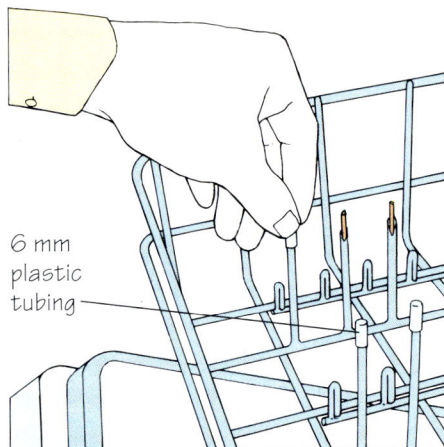

6 mm plastic tubing

Another rack saver

You can also touch up a rusty dishwasher rack with paint, but don't use just any paint because it might come off on your dishes. There is a special paint that's made just for coating damaged areas on dishwasher racks. It is heat-resistant, has a rubberised finish, and is safe to use around dishes. It comes in standard rack colours, in small bottles with a brush in the cap. You can buy it from appliance parts suppliers.

Rusty machine

Iron in the water is the usual cause of blotchy yellow or brown stains in a dishwasher. To remove the stains, let the empty machine fill, add half a cup of citric acid crystals, and run it through a cycle. For a permanent solution, put an iron filter on your water supply.

Turned to stone

To remove the chalky mineral deposits known as lime from your dishwasher's interior, let the empty machine fill, put in a cup of white vinegar, and run it through a cycle. Then add detergent and run it through another cycle. But don't do it too often; vinegar is an acid, and excessive use of it could damage the enamel in time.

Not-so-hot water

To dissolve detergent and get dishes clean, the hot water in your dishwasher should ideally be at 60° C. Test the water in the sink next to the dishwasher. Run it until it's as hot as it will become, catch some in a cup, and insert a thermometer. If it's not hot enough, try insulating the hot-water pipes between the water heater and the dishwasher. As a last resort, raise the water-heater setting, but it's best to avoid this if you have young children in the house.

Black marks

If your dishes have mysterious black smears, it may be the result of metal, especially aluminium utensils, rubbing against them. Separate pots and dishes when you load the dishwasher. Also, don't put in throw-away aluminium pans. The thin aluminium coating breaks down under the heat and marks dishes.

Gas stoves

Clean jets

If the jet on a gas burner becomes clogged, clean it with a straight pin or a pipe cleaner. Don't use a toothpick; its tip might break and stay in the hole. ▼

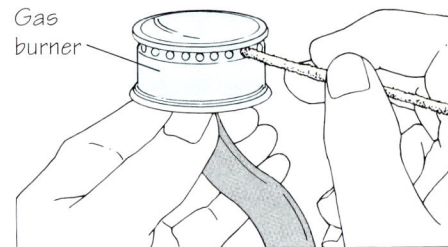

Gas burner

Microwave ovens

Banish smells

Keep the inside of your microwave clean with warm water and a mild detergent. No special cleaners are necessary, and don't use abrasive creams or powders or scouring pads. If the oven develops a smell, put several teaspoons of lemon juice into a cup of water and boil it in the oven for five minutes or so.

The age of plastic

Be sure to follow your oven manufacturer's advice about the use of metal containers for microwave cookery. It is generally best to avoid any metal cookware (including foil containers, or any with metal trim) since they reflect the microwaves, resulting in uneven cooking. In some circumstances metal in a microwave can also cause arcing, which may damage the oven.

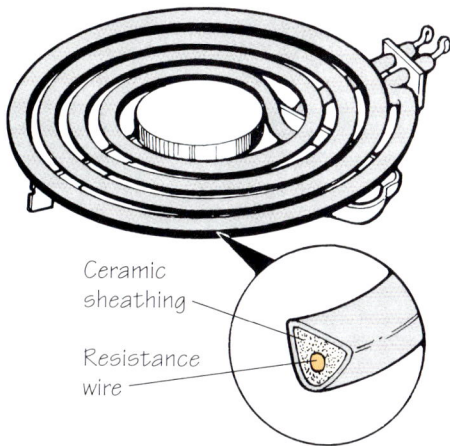

Ceramic
sheathing

Resistance
wire

Hot spot ▲

If a stove top element develops a spot that glows brighter than the rest of the coil, the ceramic insulation sheathing has broken down, exposing the nichrome resistance wire inside. The element may continue working for a while, but it's best to replace it at once. The hot spot could damage your cookware.

Too hot for comfort

Covering the floor of your electric oven with aluminium foil to catch drips may sound like a good idea, but don't do it. Foil reflects and intensifies heat, which can cause the element to burn out prematurely. Don't cover a rack with foil either. This traps heat in the bottom of the oven and keeps it from reaching the heat sensor near the top. The overheating in the bottom could damage not only the element but the oven lining and the oven-door glass as well. It can also considerably alter cooking times.

STOVE ELEMENTS

Replacing a burned-out stove top element on an electric stove is a job that can be expensive to have done, but takes only a few minutes to do yourself, provided your stove has plug-in elements. Any element that is held in place by screws should be replaced only by a qualified serviceman. Buy a new replacement element direct from the manufacturer, or from an appliance parts specialist. Take the old element in with you, and also make a note of the make and model number of your stove in case you need it.

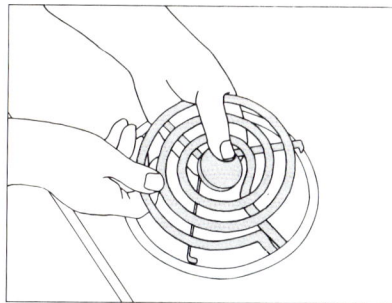

1 Before starting, make sure that the stove is switched off. Gently raise the end of the element opposite the connector and pull it out. If it has not been removed before it may be a bit stiff.

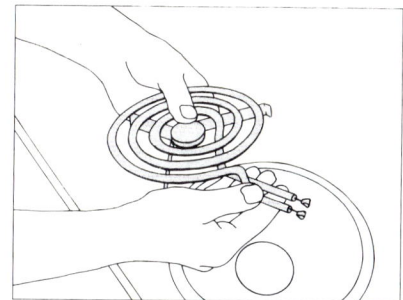

2 Examine the ends of the element. If they are corroded, the connector will also need replacing, a job for an expert. Otherwise, buy a new element and reverse the order of removal to insert it.

Hidden fuse ▶

If the elements, timer and lights on your electric stove won't work, you've probably blown the fuse. If you still have your owner's manual, check it for the fuse location. It's often under the stove top, probably inside a protective housing. If it's not, look elsewhere, perhaps under the fluorescent light cover, in the top of the storage drawer or above the control panel. If it's an ordinary ceramic fuse holder, replace the wire with more of the correct rating. If the fuse blows again, have the stove checked.

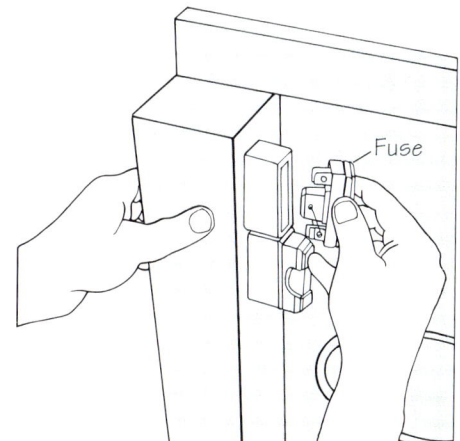

Fuse

WASHING MACHINES AND DRYERS

Washing machines

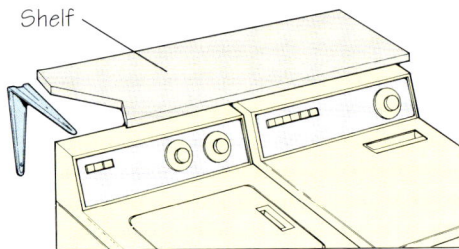

Shelf

Bridging the gap ▲

Are you always dropping or spilling things into the no-man's-land behind your washer and dryer? There's no way to eliminate the gap; the machines must sit away from the wall because of the washer hoses and the dryer vent. An easy solution is to cover the space with a shelf mounted on brackets. As an added bonus it'll give you a place to put detergent packets, bottles of bleach and other laundry clutter.

Lint trap

To avoid plugging drains with lint from the washer, secure an old panty hose foot to the end of the drain hose with a strong rubber band. When the washer drains, the foot will collect the lint in the wash water. Turn the foot inside out to clean it after every wash. ▼

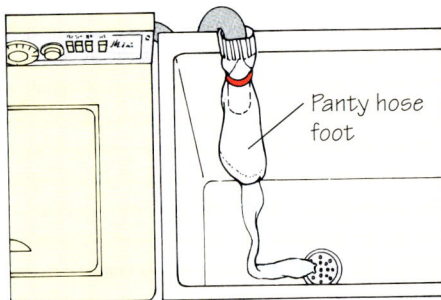

Panty hose foot

Fabric snagger

Is there something in your washing machine that's catching on your clothes? Rub an old panty hose over the agitator and the tub surface. Smooth any rough spots with very fine abrasive paper.

Car tool to the rescue

If you can't remove the cap holding your washing machine agitator, try turning it with a car oil filter spanner. This tool has a flexible strap that can be adjusted to fit a round object snugly. ▼

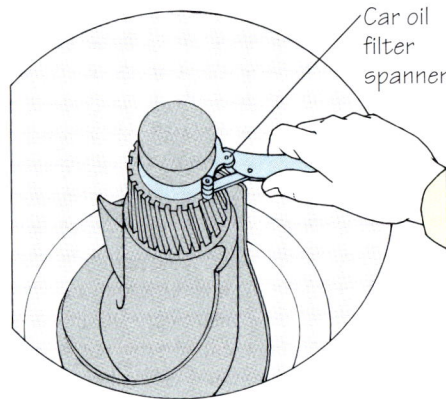

Car oil filter spanner

Avoid the flood ▶

Replace your washing machine hoses if they are starting to look worn and perished. A burst pipe in the middle of wash can create a minor flood in the laundry. Measure the old hoses and buy only good quality replacements, complete with fittings, from an appliance parts specialist. Hoses are usually marked hot and cold. Make sure that you connect the correct tap to its appropriate inlet at the back of the machine. Do not have the hoses too tight or you will place strain on the mixer valve.

Dryers

Bulb burnout

If the light bulb in your electric dryer (or oven) keeps burning out, make sure that you're using an appliance light bulb. Ordinary bulbs can't withstand the heat.

No heat?

If your dryer drum turns, but the air doesn't seem to be heating up, the thermostat may have cut out. Let the machine cool down for a while and then try it again. If the air still won't heat, the thermostat may need to be replaced. Call in a service expert.

Keep hot air safely flowing

If you are installing a vinyl duct for a dryer, use only an approved, non-flammable duct, and avoid any dips that may collect water and lint, thereby blocking airflow and creating a fire hazard. Keep the duct under 6 m long. Use aluminium if you need a longer duct.

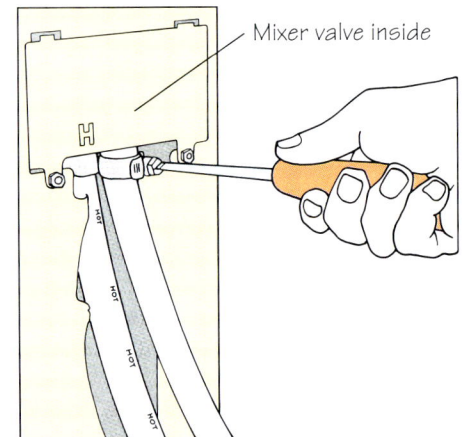

Mixer valve inside

ELECTRONIC EQUIPMENT

Split personality

Fed up with all those arguments about which channel to watch? Why not install a second TV in the rumpus room or one of the children's bedrooms? Provided the incoming signal is not too weak in your area, you can divide it between the two sets without any appreciable loss of quality, and without having to climb on the roof or fiddle with the aerial. Buy a splitter from an electronics hobby shop and fit it as directed. If the signal in your area is weak, or if the picture on the original set deteriorates, you can get a splitter with a built-in amplifier. ▼

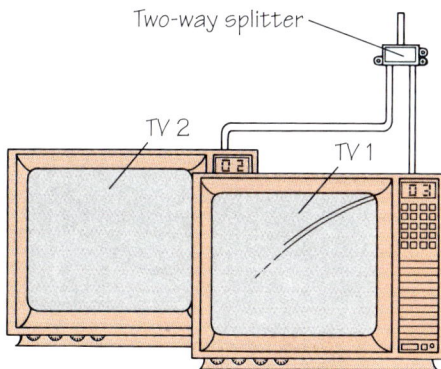

High-pass filter

Get the picture

Poor television reception in fringe areas can usually be improved with an aerial amplifier. Although not difficult to install, the most effective amplifiers are designed to be attached to the aerial mast, as close as possible to the top. In this position very little of the already weak incoming signal is lost. However, if you don't wish to climb onto the roof, try out one of the indoor amplifiers, which can be installed close to the TV receiver.

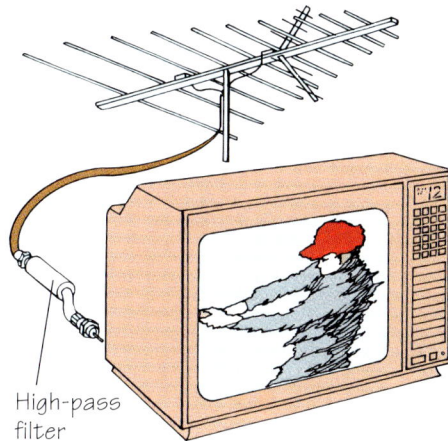

Two-way splitter

TV 2

TV 1

Ham problem ▲

If your TV develops wavering lines occasionally for no apparent reason, the cause may be an amateur (ham) radio operator, especially if it happens on VHF channels and not on UHF ones. In order to correct the problem, install a high-pass filter—sold at electronics hobby shops—between the TV and its aerial wire. Get a filter for either a coaxial cable or a flat twin-lead aerial wire, depending on your setup.

Is everybody happy?

When family arguments over which TV channel to watch spread to the VCR, don't go out and buy a new machine to restore domestic harmony. There are cheaper solutions available at your local electronics store. Either buy a video combiner, which will enable you to direct the video signal to up to four televisions in the house, or a video signal transmitter. This latter device plugs into your VCR and transmits sound and picture, without connecting wires, so that they can be received by any number of TVs within a radius of about 10 m.

Follow my leader

If you move into a new area and want to know what sort of TV aerial you need to buy, just go outside and take a look. It's unlikely that you will be able to get away with anything less than that which your neighbours have installed.

Master zapper

When all the space on your coffee table is taken up by remote controls, it's time to buy a universal unit. Various models are available that can take the place of up to six existing controllers.

Don't use shampoo

Confused about how to clean VCR heads? The safest and easiest way is with a videocassette cleaning cartridge. Use the 'wet' type that requires you to place a few drops of cleaning solution on the tape; it's less abrasive than the 'dry' type. You run it through the machine like a normal cassette, and it takes about 30 seconds to do the job. How often? After 40 to 50 hours of use. That's every month if you watch five films a week; every six months if you average one film a week.

Cool it

In theory, it is not a good idea to put a VCR on top of a television because heat from the TV could damage the VCR. But if there's no other convenient spot for the VCR, cut four small spacers from 6 mm plywood, paint them flat black, and put one under each VCR leg. They'll be practically invisible.

ELECTRONIC EQUIPMENT

Hi-fi equipment

The art of concealment

Transform that jungle of wires behind your TV, VCR or stereo into a neat, attractive cable. Just clip the plugs from a coiled telephone cord and wrap the coils around the wires. The cords are not expensive and come in a variety of colours and lengths. Electronics and car parts outlets also carry plastic tubes especially designed for organising wire clutter.

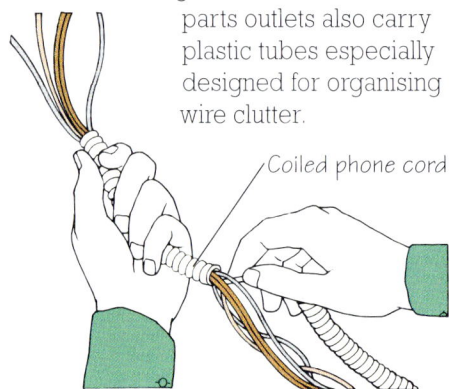

Coiled phone cord

Underfoot wiring

To run speaker cable from one side of a room to another, or from room to room, drill small holes and run it across the underside of the floor. Keep the cable away from electrical wires, and secure it with insulated staples to joists and bearers. Always try to keep speaker cables as short as possible.

Two for the price of one

You can make your existing television aerial double as FM radio aerial as well. Simply use a splitter (see p. 251) to divide the incoming signal into two, and then run one cable to the television and one to the radio. However, this may not work very well in areas where the signal is particularly weak.

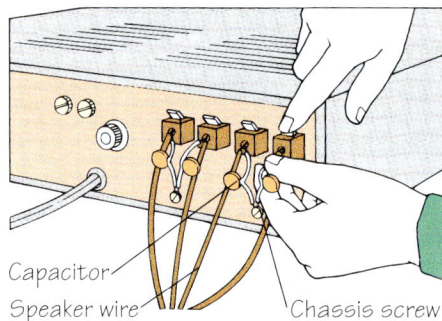

Capacitor
Speaker wire
Chassis screw

Get off the line ▲

If your stereo picks up someone's CB radio, install capacitors on the speaker outlets. Get four 0.01–0.3 microfarad (mfd) disc capacitors at an electronics store. There are usually four outlets, two for each speaker. With your stereo unplugged, insert one capacitor wire into each outlet along with the speaker wire lead. Attach the capacitor's other wire to a chassis screw to earth it.

Torn speaker

To fix a ripped speaker cone—for a while, at least—take it out of the cabinet and cut a patch from a paper coffee filter. Coat one side of the patch liberally with rubber cement. Holding the back of the cone with one hand, gently apply the patch to the front and rub lightly to smooth it. Let the cement dry before reinstalling the cone.

You can fix a simple tear using the cement alone.

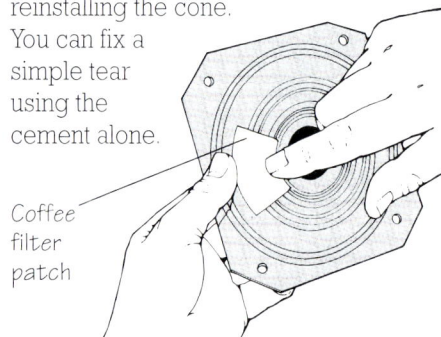

Coffee filter patch

Record and tape care

Record clean up

Fed up with your favourite old vinyl records sounding as if they are being played through a storm of static? Try giving them a wash to remove all that accumulated dirt and dust. Use clean, lukewarm water, to which has been added a little wetting agent—a mild detergent, available from most photographic stores. With a tissue or soft cloth, apply liberal quantities of water (avoiding the label), rinse thoroughly under cold water, and then prop the record up on edge and allow it to dry away from any heat.

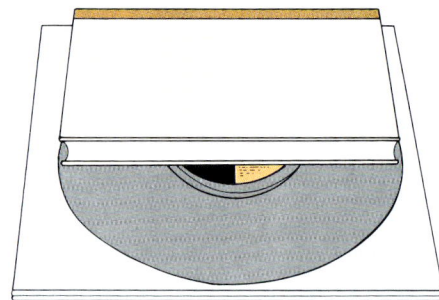

Warped performance ▲

A vinyl record can sometimes become so warped that the player arm is not able to keep the stylus in its grooves. Although it is generally impossible to make a record perfectly flat again, you can sometimes take some of the warp out, so that it is at least playable enough to tape. Take the record out of its sleeve and place it between two sheets of heavy glass, large enough to cover the entire record surface. Weight the top sheet, and leave the record in a cool place for at least a couple of weeks.

Save a cassette ▲

Has a favourite, irreplaceable audio cassette tape snapped apart? Fix it with a splicing kit from an electronics store. The kit should have a trimming instrument, splicing tape, a splicing block and instructions. If either end of the tape is inside the cassette and the cassette case can't be unscrewed, get an empty cassette case too. Then carefully prise apart the old case, transfer the tape to the new case, splice the broken ends, and screw the new case shut.

Nothing is forever

Recordings on tape do not last forever, even if unplayed. Within a year or so—depending on local conditions—the recording will begin to deteriorate. If you have a valuable old recording, perhaps of a deceased family member or friend, run it through your tape player at regular intervals, and transfer it to a new tape every five years or so.

CD clean up

Even though CDs are very durable, still treat them with great care. The best way to clean a CD is with a soft, lint-free cloth, wiped gently from the centre to the edge. Do not use any of the cleaning solutions intended for vinyl records.

Computers

Computer wrap

If you have to move a computer any distance, pack it into the original cartons, if possible. Otherwise pack it as snugly as you can in other cartons, using crumpled paper on all sides to cushion the units. Never wrap a computer in plastic. Condensation can form on the inside of the plastic and damage the computer.

Rodent care

Is your mouse pointer moving jerkily across the screen? It may be that the mouse needs a clean. Turn it over and you will see that the ball that controls the pointer's motion is trapped inside the body of the mouse by a plastic disc. Finger pressure in the direction of the arrows will rotate the disc, releasing the ball. Clean the inside of the cavity with a soft brush to remove all fluff, and then reassemble the mouse. ▼

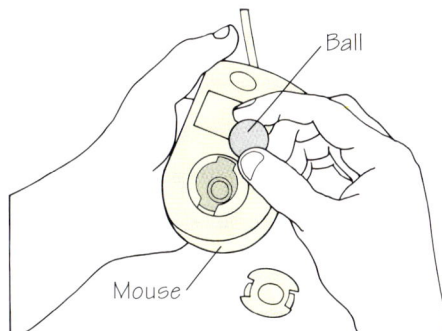

Ball

Mouse

Down with dust

Dust is the great enemy of computers; a speck in the wrong place can lose you large amounts of data. Always keep your computer, keyboard and disks covered when they are not in use. Plastic covers are available from computer retailers.

Always back up

Moving a personal computer can be a tricky business, especially because you risk losing any valuable information stored in it. Even if it's handled carefully, a computer hard disk can be damaged by being jarred in a moving van or truck. To lessen the chances of losing data, copy whatever is stored on your hard drive onto back up disks and carry them separately to the new location. 'Head parking' programs are also available that move the read/write heads off the hard disk, lessening the chances of damage during transport. Consult your local computer supplier.

Telephones

Room to move

If your phone cord is too short you don't have to have to call the phone company to fix the problem. Extension cords of various lengths are sold in most electronics hobby shops. Simply plug one end into the wall socket and the phone into the other. Make sure the cord packet carries a notice showing it has telecommunications authority approval.

Double your pleasure

More than one phone can be plugged into an outlet, using a double adaptor, available from electronics shops. Make sure it has an approval sticker.

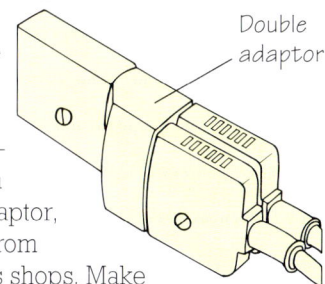

Double adaptor

CHAPTER 9

BACKYARD AND GARDEN

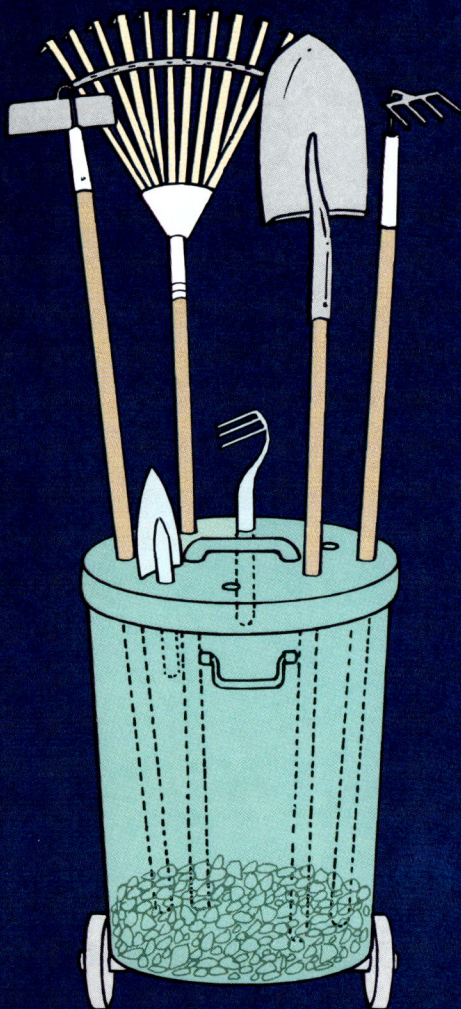

PLANTING A GARDEN

Breaking ground

Making a bed the easy way

Why not take a break from digging and let a cover crop prepare your new garden bed? Cover crops—which can be a mixture of tick beans, lupins, mustard, Algerian oats and rycorn—are planted in autumn and left to grow during winter. By spring the crop is ready to dig into the soil. As it rots, the vegetation will enrich the bed, while its roots will have already loosened the soil. Do not leave the plants too long or they will become woody, and will be slow to break down.

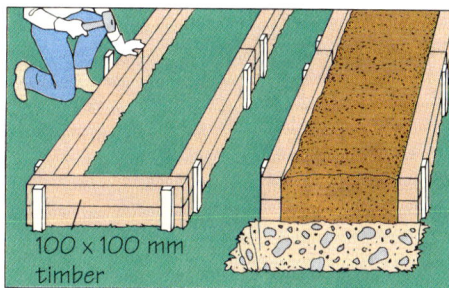

100 x 100 mm timber

On the rocks ▲

If you'd like to have a lush garden on a rocky, sandy or other otherwise inhospitable site, build a raised bed. A bed can be as long as you like, but it must be fairly narrow—about 1.2 m across. That way you can work on it from both sides without stepping on the soil, which would compact it and ruin the aeration. To build a bed, first install a suitable edging, such as 100 × 100 mm treated pine, or perhaps some old railway sleepers if your local garden supply centre carries them. Fill the bed with a generous layer of compost-rich topsoil. The drainage will be good and the plants will develop healthy root systems.

Setting things straight ▲

To establish straight rows in a garden, fill two plastic bottles with water and set one at each end of the row. Then stretch a string line between them and move them from row to row. It is easier than driving stakes in for the string.

Seedlings

Greenhouses from the take-away

You can start seeds in the folding plastic food containers that you find at many fast-food outlets. Wash the container and half fill it with a lightly moistened seed-starting mix. Place the seeds and close the lid, securing it with a rubber band. The clear lid allows light to pass through, holds moisture in, and lets you keep track of progress. ▼

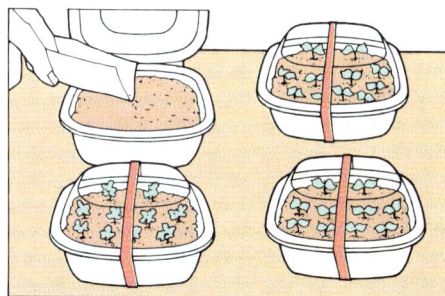

New life for yoghurt containers

Small plastic yoghurt containers make handy mini-pots for starting seeds indoors. Punch drainage holes in the bottoms of the cups. For easy carrying, place the cups on a tray. Fill them with soil, place them on a sunny windowsill, and they're ready for your seeds. ▼

All-weather ID

This inexpensive plant label will always remain readable. Cut a tag from an old disposable aluminium-foil pie pan. Place the tag on a soft surface, such as a towel, and use a ballpoint pen to inscribe the plant name on it. Attach the tag to a stake next to the seedling. The imprint will last indefinitely.

Quick cover

On chilly spring nights, protect seedlings from frost (and set the stage for an extra-early harvest of flowers or vegetables) with a simple tent-like structure. To build it, you need only construct a frame of PVC pipe and cover it with woven plastic shade material or with the polyethylene sheeting pictured here. This light, sturdy greenhouse can be moved from spot to spot as the need arises, and it is easy to store at the end of the season.

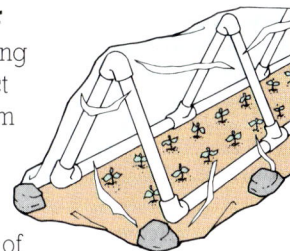

PLANTING A GARDEN

Edgings and trainers

Shake it

A bundle of treated pine pieces makes an edging around your garden beds that's attractive, inexpensive and practical too. Set the pieces in an overlapped alternating pattern, driving them into the ground with a protective block of wood and a mallet. ▼

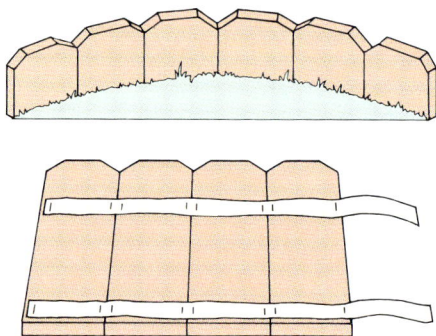

Stay flexible ▲

If you have a curved or elaborately shaped garden bed that needs a decorative edging, join a number of timber edging planks together by stapling to their backs a couple of heavy-duty plastic strips. If it is a large bed, assemble about 2 m of edging at a time, leaving a short length of extra plastic at the end of each section. Dig a shallow trench to take the edging, position the sections, level them and then staple them together. Refill the trench with soil.

Tongue-and-grooving ▶

You can also use 150 × 25 mm treated pine or cedar tongue-and-groove planks, available from some timberyards, as an edging. To make the planks easier to drive in, cut the bottom edges at a 45° angle. The length of the stakes should equal the depth of the roots that you're containing, plus 70 mm for the above-ground section and a bit extra for the length of the 45° cut. Use a mallet and protective block of wood to drive the tongue sections into the grooves.

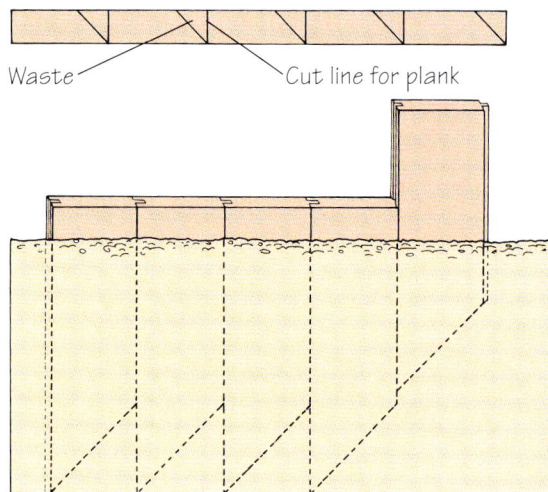

Waste — Cut line for plank

Movable trellis

Would you like to brighten the side of your house with a vine *and* retain easy access to the wall behind it for painting and repairs? Make a movable trellis out of a section of concrete reinforcing wire or galvanised fencing, and hang it on hooks screwed into the cladding. When it's time to work on the house, gently unhook the trellis and rest it on a support such as the stakes shown here. ▼

Lampshade support

The metal frame of an old lampshade makes a great freestanding support for top-heavy plants such as peonies. Collect various sizes for plants both large and small.

Making compost

It's in the bag

Rather than fussing with bins and heaps, why not do all your composting in a bag? First fill a heavy-duty garbage bag with garden waste, such as grass clippings and leaves, and organic kitchen scraps. Add about a shovelful of soil and one-quarter of a cup of a high-nitrogen fertiliser. Moisten the mixture thoroughly. Seal the bag and leave it in a sunny place; roll it over twice a week, taking care not to tear the bag. In two months (or less), the wastes will have turned to soil-enriching humus.

Blending in

An easy way to speed up the composting process is to put your collection of fruit and vegetable peelings, eggshells and other easily biodegradable scraps in a blender along with a cup of water. (Don't use meat or dairy scraps, as they tend to attract animals.) Purée the scraps and pour the mixture on the compost heap. The mush will decompose quickly—usually in a few weeks. To minimise the mess, collect the scraps in a small plastic bag and purée them every few days.

Small wonder

If you have a compact garden and don't need a lot of compost, you can use a household plastic laundry basket as a compost bin. Choose one that's an attractive colour and has perforations on the sides. A removable hinged lid will make it easy to add to the pile.

Vegetable gardening

Slinging melons

To make room for more eatables in a small garden, train melon vines on a trellis. As the fruit grows heavy, hold it with a sling made from a rag or a nylon stocking. Tie the ends in a knot or fasten them with a safety pin.

Instant shade

Lettuce thrives in the spring, but once summer comes, the home-grown leaves start to taste bitter. To extend the growing season, build a portable shade structure. Connect eight lengths of PVC pipe with four three-way fittings, and cover the frame with a woven plastic shade cloth, available at garden supply centres. The cloth keeps plants cool as it filters the sunlight. At season's end, fold the cloth and take the frame apart. ▼

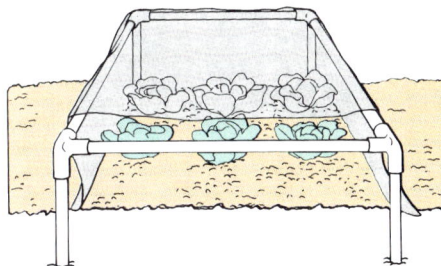

Lettuce water

If you water leafy greens in the evening and then pick them the next morning, they'll be crisp and full of flavour.

A LEAD-FREE HARVEST

While the hazard of lead paint is well known (see p. 183), the dangers from soil contaminated with lead are not. Lead may be found in soil around older homes that were weatherproofed with lead-based paint, or are located near a busy street where the exhaust from leaded petrol has made its way into the soil. Lead was also added to some insecticides used on farms a generation ago.

Home-grown greens and root vegetables readily absorb lead, concentrate it in their tissues, and then pass it on to consumers.

While very little research on lead in soils has been carried out in Australia and New Zealand, environmental authorities have agreed that levels of 300 mg of lead per kg of soil call for 'investigation', and levels of 1000 mg/kg call for 'action'. However, testing for lead is difficult, so anyone interested may find it impossible to have soil samples analysed

Fortunately there's an easy and inexpensive remedy: compost. Research conducted in the USA has found that adding compost to mildly contaminated topsoil at a rate of 25 per cent of the volume reduces the lead vegetables take in by as much as 60 per cent.

LANDSCAPING

Working with bulbs

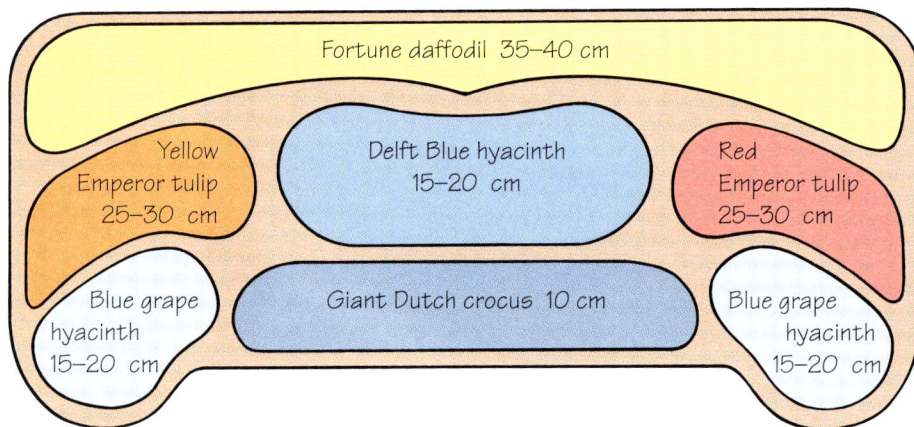

Fortune daffodil 35–40 cm

Yellow Emperor tulip 25–30 cm

Delft Blue hyacinth 15–20 cm

Red Emperor tulip 25–30 cm

Blue grape hyacinth 15–20 cm

Giant Dutch crocus 10 cm

Blue grape hyacinth 15–20 cm

WHAT TO PLANT AND WHERE IN A SMALL GARDEN

This 2.4 × 1.2 m garden is filled with reliable and popular springtime bulbs, chosen and placed with the varying heights of the plants, the mix of colours and different blooming times in mind. Look for strong, healthy bulbs—the larger the better. They should feel firm when squeezed (gently), and they should be free of nicks, soft spots and decay. A light surface mould, which can develop when the bulb is stored, is common and does no harm. Prepare the soil first by loosening it and adding organic material; then work some general bulb food into the soil. Plant the bulbs, pointed end up, randomly (not in rows) at the depth and spacing called for in the chart.

Bulbs

	Fortune daffodil	Delft Blue hyacinth	Giant Dutch crocus	Yellow Emperor tulip	Red Emperor tulip	Blue grape hyacinth
Number of bulbs	40	20	40	15	15	40
Spacing	15 cm	15 cm	7 cm	15 cm	15 cm	7 cm
Depth	15 cm	15 cm	7 cm	15 cm	15 cm	7 cm

Grand plans

A mower-friendly lawn

Mowing will be faster and easier if you eliminate the grass peninsulas and islands that require a lot of turning manoeuvres with the mower, and add to the trimming time. Use your mower to draw a new perimeter that you can mow without a stop. Fill the areas outside the line with mulch, ground cover and shrubbery. You may want to spray the unwanted grass to kill it first.

The acid test

When planning a new garden it helps to know the soil's pH. (This is a measure of its acidity. Pure water has a pH of 7; acid solutions have a pH less than 7; and basic ones a pH greater than 7.) This helps in the choice of plants, and will prevent unnecessary losses later on. Easy-to-use kits for measuring pH are available from nurseries and garden centres. Take soil samples from various parts of the garden, follow the instructions in the kit, and match the resulting colours against the chart provided.

A visual trick

Give a small garden the illusion of greater space by 'forcing the perspective', a technique known to architects. Just angle the plantings toward each other as they extend to the rear of the landscape.

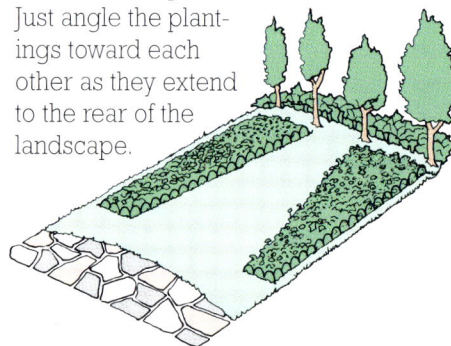

FOUNDATION PLANTINGS

When you are devising a planting scheme, try several different combinations on paper first. Using 3 mm graph paper, make a scaled master plan of your house, letting each square equal 25 cm. Include any existing trees and other landmarks. Use removable (and perhaps colour-coded) stickers to help you mark the plan.

Pull attention away from the driveway. Avoid placing plants along the edges.

Draw the eye to the entry. Low-growing plants lead visitors to the front door.

Highlight the front door with taller plants or vines. ***Caution:*** some vines damage timber and bricks over time. Ask a local nursery to help you choose.

Plant shrubs 1 to 2 m away from the house foundations to help prevent the build-up of dampness there. Limit the number of tall shrubs as they may provide hiding places for a burglar.

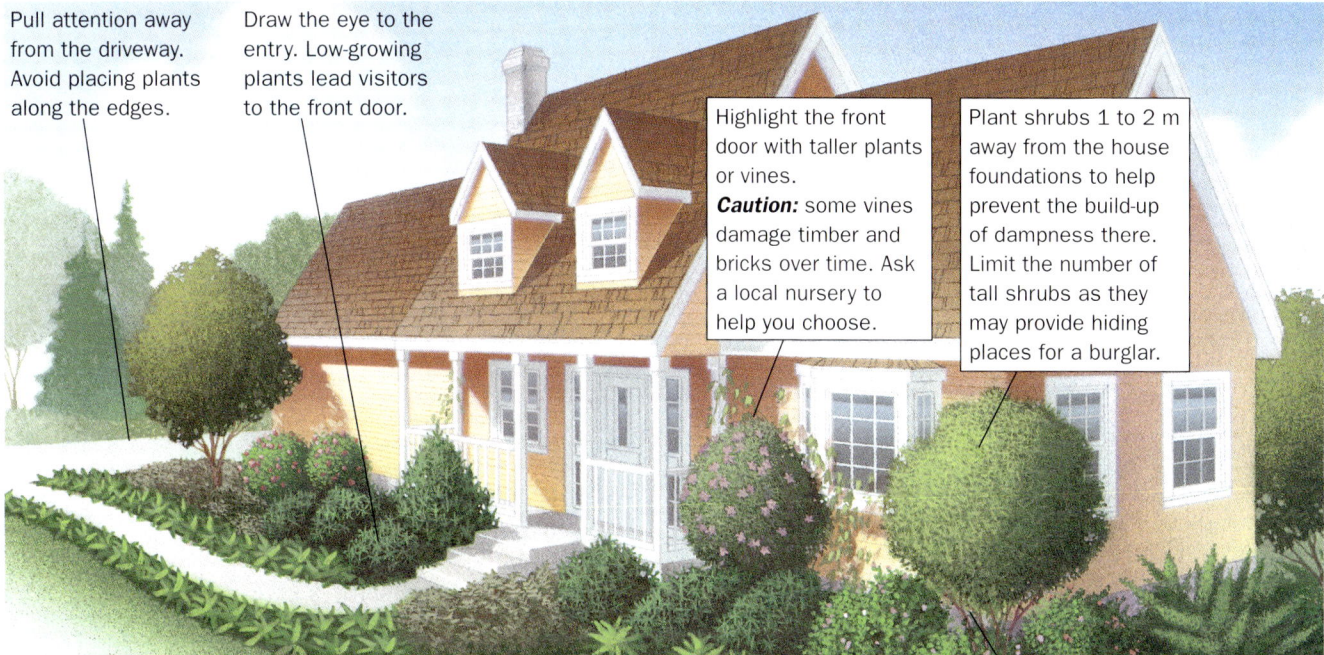

Choose plants with interesting branches that, when leafless, will enhance the winter landscape, such as the red-twigged dogwood and the winged euonymous.

Vary plant types. Mix deciduous and coniferous shrubs with ground covers, vines, and flowers to give a sense of texture and interest.

Use colours wisely. Place colourful flowers and plants where you want people to look. Colours should complement each other and those of your house.

Wrap plantings around a corner to tie the side to the front garden. Use a tall shrub to soften a corner's hard edge.

Hide large, unattractive features, such as an exposed foundation, air conditioner or meter box, with full shrubs.

LANDSCAPING

The basic plan

Where do I start?

Feeling daunted by the prospect of landscaping a new garden? Don't be. Tackle the job step by step, and try not to be in too much of a hurry. Flick through all the books and magazines that are available, and walk around nurseries and leafy suburbs to get ideas. Don't be afraid to copy a feature exactly, provided it can be accommodated in your garden. Spend a lot of time in the garden itself, at various times of the day, visualising the changes you could make.

Making do

Try not to plan a garden that is simply not suited to your situation and circumstances. Some local conditions can be changed to a certain extent, but it's important to recognise basic limitations from the outset, and to plan with them in mind. Consider all of these factors.
▷ Climate. Find out about local rainfall, temperature, sunshine and wind. How do they vary with the seasons?
▷ Microclimate. Are there local conditions that affect just your garden—trees that act as a windbreak, for example?
▷ Soil type. Do you have loam, clay or sand? Have the soil's pH measured to see if it is acid or alkaline (p. 258).
▷ Drainage. Are there boggy areas? Can the drainage be improved?
▷ Existing features. Are there any trees and shrubs you would like to keep? Rocky outcrops, streams and natural ponds are all great landscaping assets.
▷ The house. Where must paths and drives run? Where are the best views? Don't forget the question of privacy.

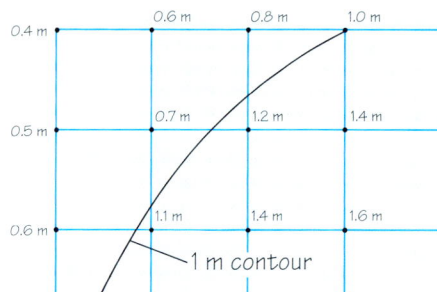

Contour map ▲

In order to plan your new garden properly you will need a contour map of the site. To prepare one, peg the site out in a grid system, with the pegs 2 m apart. Make up a calibrated rod, with a horizontal sighting device that you can slide up and down it. Starting at the lowest peg, measure the relative height of every other peg in turn. You will now be able to guess with reasonable accuracy where the contour lines should run.

Measure, measure, measure

It's a simple matter to accurately measure the position of all the features on your land. First establish a long base line, say between two survey pegs down one boundary. To fix the position of a tree, for example, measure down from each end of the base line to find two points on either side of the tree that are roughly equidistant from it. Measure from these points to the tree and transfer the measurements to your plan.

Getting it all down on paper

Your final base plan should include contour lines, together with the positions of all major features. Make sure you also show the location of power lines, and underground services such as water, sewage and phone lines. Now—using sheets of tracing paper—you are ready to experiment with various layouts. ▼

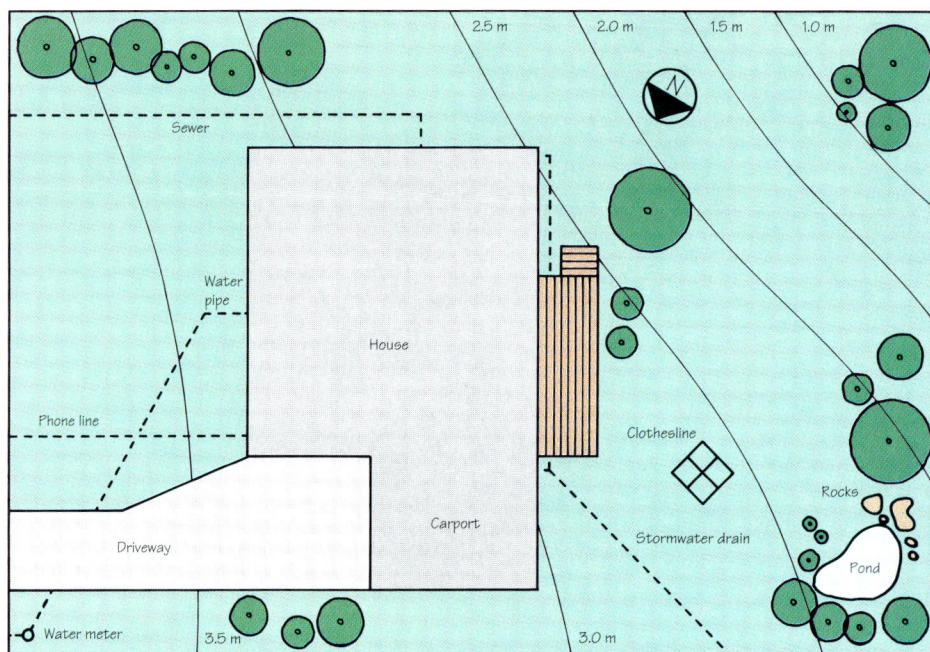

Novel ideas

Formal vegetables

The vegetable patch doesn't have to be the least decorative element in your garden. With a little planning it can become an attractive feature. Draw out a combination of rectangles, squares and circles on graph paper first, later transferring the plan to the garden with string lines. Plant English box, boxleaf honeysuckle, lavender or rosemary to define borders, and fill the areas between with colourful vegetables, such as rainbow chard, red mignonette lettuce, red cabbage and an assortment of peppers. ▼

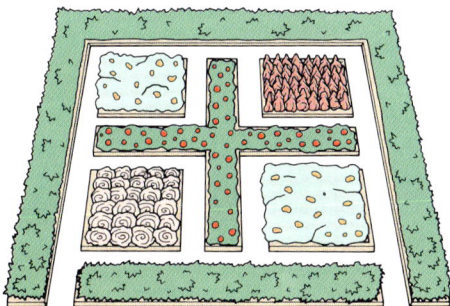

Rural charm

Try this novel alternative to that tired old bed of straggly plants—a wildflower meadow. Dig the area over thoroughly and remove all weeds, particularly sorrel and couch grass. It may even be necessary to spray repeatedly with a herbicide containing glyphosate to do the job properly. Remove large clods with a rake, and then sow with one of the wildflower seed mixtures available from nurseries or mail order seed suppliers. Keep the area well watered until the seeds germinate.

A pleasant surprise ▲

Consider adding a touch of whimsy and interest to your garden with one or two statues. Choose the correct size and number of pieces, depending on the size and nature of your garden. It's generally best to err on the side of restraint. Begin your search in garden centres, country junk stores or even city antique centres. Remember, that you don't have to buy a pristine, new statue. A battered subject, artistically entwined with a creeper, will impart an intriguing air of antiquity. Take particular care with the placing, perhaps aiming to pleasantly surprise an unwary visitor.

Difficult situations

Shady retreat

Don't be put off by the prospect of gardening in the shade. There are many plants that will thrive in shady spots, even under dense trees. First build up the soil depth by some 20–25 cm by adding organic matter, but not around trunks. Remove fibrous roots. Plant clivea, plectranthus, ferns, hellebores, lily-of-the-valley and Solomon's seal.

Trim those trees

Another option for shady spots is to increase the amount of light reaching the ground under trees. Thin out overhead branches. It is possible to selectively remove about one-third of a tree's branches without losing its shape and character. Never, however, lop all the branches to one height. This makes the tree look unsightly, and generally results in the tree putting on extra growth to compensate for the losses.

Gardening on concrete

Unit or inner-city dwellers, faced with concrete gardens, can still find scope for their green thumbs in a 'no-dig' garden. Build low walls from loose bricks or sleepers to define the edges of the proposed garden bed. Then put down a thick layer of newspapers, followed by a layer of kitchen vegetable scraps or seaweed. Now put down some lucerne hay or pea mulch (from a produce store) and on top of that some manure or blood and bone, then some more hay or mulch. Finally, add about 10 cm of fully broken-down compost, and your no-dig bed is ready for vegetables, or a selection of flowering annuals and bulbs. ▼

HANDLING WEEDS, INSECTS AND ANIMALS

Weed attack

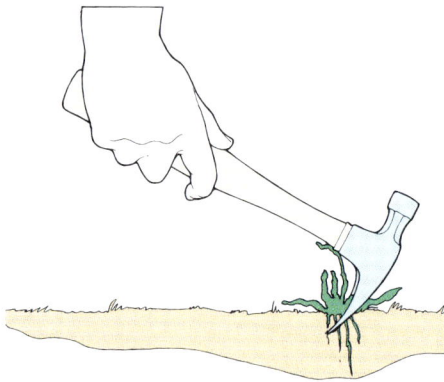

Hammer those weeds ▲

You can use a long-handled weeding fork, called a fishtail weeder, to rid your lawn of dandelions and other weeds. But if you don't have one on hand, root out the pests with the claw of an old hammer and then pull them up, root and all. The deeper you can grasp the root, the better.

Customising a hoe

To turn a regular hoe into a precision instrument, file a notch into the side of its blade. With this sharpened V you can delicately snip weeds off at their base, even in the most hard-to-reach corners.

When to weed

Timing can be a great help in your war against the weeds. Wait for a hot, sunny day; then hoe the weeds (without seed heads) in the morning and leave them lying on the surface of the soil. The sun will wither the weeds and in time transform them into beneficial organic mulch.

Weeds in concrete

You can use boiling-hot water to kill weeds that sprout through concrete joints—without endangering yourself or the wildlife. Boil water in a kettle and pour it into the cracks, and watch the weeds wilt. If you have a lot of weeds, use a large saucepan, but be careful not to splash the hot water on yourself.

Pest preventives

Gardening helpers

▷ Landscape your garden with species of plants that are naturally insect- and disease-resistant. Ask at your nursery or garden centre about varieties that will do well in your local area.
▷ Select grass seed that has been inoculated with beneficial fungi called endophytes to protect your lawn against the most troublesome grass-eating insects and increase drought tolerance.
▷ Reduce soil-borne diseases by varying your flower and vegetable plantings. Rotate the crops, changing the type of plant and its location each year.
▷ Keep your landscape free of weeds, dead leaves and rubbish—these provide a refuge and breeding place for insect pests and plant diseases.

Possum deterrent

Possums have become so used to human company that no suburban garden is safe from them, and they can cause considerable damage. Large trees can be protected by placing a smooth, 60 cm wide metal collar around the trunk. This will cause the possum to slip every time it tries to climb the tree. Another option is to hang outdoor lighting, which can be left on all night, from trees or bushes that are under attack. This can help when buds are forming— a particular possum favourite—on trees such as magnolias. As a last resort, an approved electric fence can be set up around flower beds—particularly roses—at a height that will prevent possums from entering the area.

Safe stoppers

Slug it out ▲

Slugs love beer. Just put a bottle of beer that's two-thirds empty in the ground with the neck slightly exposed. They'll crawl in for a sip and drown. Another tactic is to edge a slug's favourite area—moist, shady gardens— with coarsely crushed eggshells.

ATTRACTING THE GARDENER'S FRIENDS

While many gardeners strive to rid their gardens of insect and animal pests, others go to great lengths to entice visitors from the animal kingdom to their gardens. Below is a sample of who is invited, how they are encouraged to come, and why.

ANIMAL TYPE	SHELTER AND ENVIRONMENT	FOOD AND WATER	BENEFITS TO GARDEN
Birds of all types	Build nesting boxes, leave dead trees in place for nests; offer protective shelter of many trees and bushes; provide sources of dripping water.	Plant berry-laden bushes, fruiting vines and trees that produce nuts and berries; set out bird feeders with seeds, suet, peanut butter and cornmeal balls; provide small pools of water.	Eat insects; provide nature-watching opportunities.
Butterflies	Leave areas of tall grasses; encourage wildflowers; install windbreak in warm sunny spot; provide large flat rock for sunning; keep birdbaths and bird feeders at a distance; plant solid-colour purple, mauve, white and yellow (no red) flowering plants.	When weeding, allow milkweed to remain in the garden for caterpillars to munch on; plant spring-blooming, nectar-producing plants, such as lilacs, peonies and lavender; plant autumn blooming plants such as sedum; and provide small puddles of water.	Offer nature-watching opportunities; enhance beauty of the garden.
Earthworms	Create soil rich in organic matter; refrain from using pesticides; loosen the soil before adding live, shop-bought worms.	Mix organic matter into soil; add a layer of mulch to keep soil moist.	Burrow constantly into soil, tilling and aerating it; ingest organic waste and deposit humus-rich castings in soil.

Easy wasp control

The smell of vinegar attracts wasps. To cure a wasp problem, put 5 cm of vinegar in a long-necked bottle. They'll crawl in and won't be able to crawl out.

Soap story

Insecticidal soaps provide effective protection against many kinds of insects, including aphids, mites and whiteflies, and don't harm wildlife, children or pets. Use a commercial brand or make your own by mixing one to three teaspoons of a mild dishwashing liquid into 4 litres of water. Test on a few leaves and wait 48 hours, as some plants are sensitive. If there's no ill effect, spray the plants well (wetting both the tops and bottoms of the leaves) once every two to three days for a period of two weeks.

Oily spray

Mixing vegetable oil and non-detergent liquid soap makes another effective, inexpensive and non-toxic spray that is fatal to aphids, spider mites, scale, mealybugs and some caterpillars. Mix one cup cooking oil with one tablespoon liquid soap; then dilute it, using one teaspoon oil-soap mixture for each cup of water. Spray the leaves as for soap spray, but only when air temperatures are below 30°C. If it's hotter than that, the oil can damage some foliage. The spray is effective against eggs as well as adult insects.

Insect allies

Some insects are on your side. Dragonflies and spiders eat thousands of irritating insects, including mosquitoes and flies, and consume great numbers of garden pests, such as aphids. ▼

EASIER GARDENING

Lifesavers

Latex liners

Your gardening gloves protect you from thorns, but they don't help much against the cold. To increase their insulation value, slip your hands first into a pair of lightweight latex gloves. These will keep your hands warm and dry, and you'll hardly know they are there.

Petroleum jelly 'glove'

When close work—fine pruning or weeding or some late transplanting—forces you to work without gloves in cold weather, you can keep the chill out of your fingers by rubbing your hands with petroleum jelly. It'll also make cleaning up quicker and easier.

Knee protectors

Much of a gardener's work is done on the hands and knees, and that can cause joints to ache. To combat the problem, make a kneepad out of a piece of Styrofoam or other rigid foam insulation about 50 cm square and 2.5 cm thick. Wrap the pad in a plastic garbage bag. The foam not only serves as a cushion, it also insulates against cold, and keeps out dampness from the soil. ▼

Child's play

Another device that can save you from the discomfort of squatting or kneeling is your child's tricycle. Turn it around so that you are riding it backward and you'll find yourself at exactly the right level to get your fingers down into the dirt. And when you've finished weeding or planting one patch, you can push yourself along to the next one.

Circle gardens

A further way to minimise bending and kneeling is to confine your most work-intensive garden beds to small-diameter circles, say 60 or 90 cm wide. You'll be able to reach the entire garden without a lot of effort and do most of the work sitting down in the same spot.

Friendlier tools

A blister-proof rake

Does leaf raking leave your hands raw with blisters? The cure for that is to pad the handle with a length of 20 mm foam rubber tubing, available from hardware shops. Coat the rake's handle with contact cement, cut the tubing to length, and slip it on.

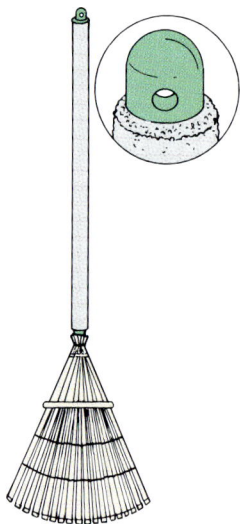

Tall tools

Be good to your back by standing up while weeding and planting bulbs. All you'll need are a few tools with long handles, which are available from most large garden supply shops.

A back-saving sledge ▶

Heaving a heavy weight into a wheelbarrow or garden cart can strain your back badly. The next time you need to move a big rock, tree or shrub, make a simple sledge out of a scrap piece of 6 mm plywood. Drill a pair of holes in one end of the plywood and attach a loop of rope. Roll your load onto the sledge and pull. You'll find that it will slide easily across the lawn without damaging the grass—or your back.

Softer stepping

To cushion your foot as you dig, slip a piece of old garden hose over the shoulder of the shovel where you step on it.

SEEDING AND FEEDING YOUR LAWN

Better spreading

Sowing in the wind

Even a moderate breeze scatters seed as it drops out of the spreader, and that means gaps in your new lawn. Try mixing the seed with barely damp clean sand. The weight of the sand will help shield the seeds from the wind and enable them to fall straight down.

Crisscross coverage

It is crucial to spread seed and fertiliser evenly. Try setting the spreader application rate at half of what is recommended on the package, and then make twice as many passes. Work back and forth across the whole lawn from left to right; then turn and repeat the process at a right angle to the first passes. This is a bit more work, but you'll eliminate gaps and surpluses in your spreading. ▼

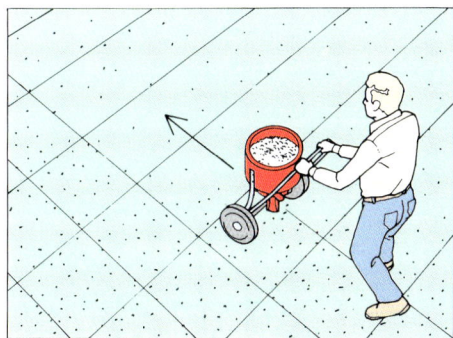

Flour power

It's often hard to tell which areas have been covered with fertiliser or seed. Mixing some kitchen flour with the ingredients before you spread them will mark what you've covered without harming the lawn or the wildlife, and it disappears with the first rain.

Nourishing thoughts

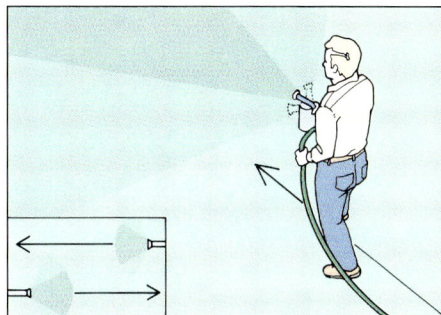

Spray as you walk ▲

Spraying a liquid fertiliser greatly reduces the likelihood of fertiliser burn. All you have to do to avoid burning your grass is to wet the lawn before you spray, or water it immediately afterward. To apply the fertiliser, connect a sprayer to a garden hose. Walk in a straight line fairly slowly and move the spray nozzle back and forth.

Turfing a lawn

Turf versus seed

Turfing a lawn provides an 'instant' living carpet that is ready for (minimal) traffic in a couple of weeks. It is not surprising, then, that turf is expensive. If you do the job yourself, expect to pay a lot more per square metre than for seed. Hiring a professional to do it will increase the cost even more. Whether you choose to lay turf or plant seed, you'll need to prepare the soil well. For turf, you should also rake it carefully—that way the roots can get a good grip.

A quick pickup

Pause in your passes with the spreader for a moment, and the machine applies a fertiliser overdose that kills the grass below. To quickly remove the spill before it does any harm, use a workshop vacuum cleaner. If it's grass seed you spilled, empty the cleaner first; then you can retrieve the wasted seed.

Aerating shoes

An easy way to aerate your lawn is to strap on a pair of aerating sandals, available from most large gardening supply shops. The special 'shoes' have thin spikes that poke holes into the soil as you walk. The holes loosen the soil, making it more water-retentive and more receptive to fertiliser feedings. ▼

Rolling out the carpet

Turf is delivered in strips that are rolled and stacked. As you roll out your new lawn, stagger the ends of the strips, the way you would for bricklaying. In addition, make sure that the edges of each strip butt tightly against the previously laid strip. A snug fit will minimise any gaps in the lawn and will keep the strips from drying out too quickly.

Make a stand

If you stand on a board or piece of plywood as you lay the strips, you won't disturb the soil you've worked so hard to prepare.

LAWN CARE AND MAINTENANCE

Mowing

Recycle those clippings

You'll reduce your lawn's need for fertilisers and save yourself some raking and carrying if you switch to a mulching mower, a rotary-blade machine that shreds clippings and returns them to the lawn. Left to decompose in place, clippings can reduce fertiliser needs by 25 per cent annually. What's more, you'll be doing your part to reduce the burden on local landfills.

Working against gravity

Cutting the grass on a slope or bank can be a dangerous business—one slip and your foot may end up in the mower. Mowing across the slope, rather than up and down, minimises the danger. And to be extra-safe, why not put on a pair of cleated golf or sports shoes first?

Push a reel mower

Reel mowers are back and are cutting the grass cleanly. Today's versions look like the mowers of ages past but in fact are much improved. New models are lighter, self-sharpening and more manoeuvrable. And unlike their noisy powered rotary counterparts, which bruise the grass as they cut, reel mowers cut grass blades cleanly. But because you have to push this quiet cutter around, you'll be happier with one if your lawn is under 200 sq. m, and at least fairly level.

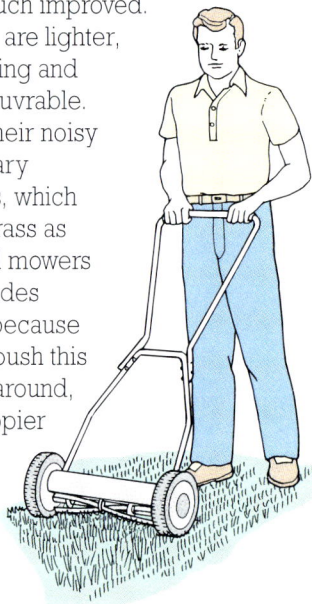

That blade is blunt

If the grass develops a greyish brown cast a day or two after mowing, it's a signal that your mower blade needs sharpening. Look closely and you'll find that the tips of the grass blades have been shredded rather than neatly sliced. Those ragged ends not only look bad, they provide easy entry for grass diseases. For hints on sharpening tools, see page 273.

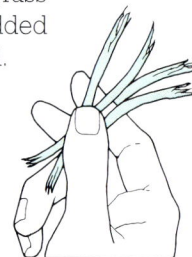

Patching

Four-legged culprit

Patching can occur for several reasons, but by far the most common is a female dog urinating on the grass. If your dog is a likely culprit, have a bucket of water at the ready and when you see the dog in the act quickly drench the area. The water will dilute the highly nitrogenous liquid so that it won't cause any harm.

Coffee tin spreader

Don't use a regular spreader when it's time to reseed bare spots. It throws seed everywhere, with only a fraction landing on target. For precision seeding, you can fashion a spot seeder from an empty 500 g coffee tin and a pair of plastic lids. Into one lid drill holes large enough to let grass seed pass; snap this in place when reseeding. Keep the other, unpierced lid snapped over the tin's base. When the job is finished, reverse the lids and you'll seal in the unused seed for safe storage.

Set the height ▶

Mowing by the calendar won't help your lawn; it doesn't care how many days it's been since the last cut. You'll work less and have a healthier lawn if you let the grass do the scheduling. Set the lawn mower to the correct height for your grass: 1–2 cm for couch and bent, and 3–4 cm for Kentucky bluegrass, perennial rye and tall fescue. Then cut often enough so that you never remove more than one-third of the grass blades. Taking more will weaken the root system.

Correct mowing height, with healthy root growth

Closer mowing height, with shallow roots that need more food and water

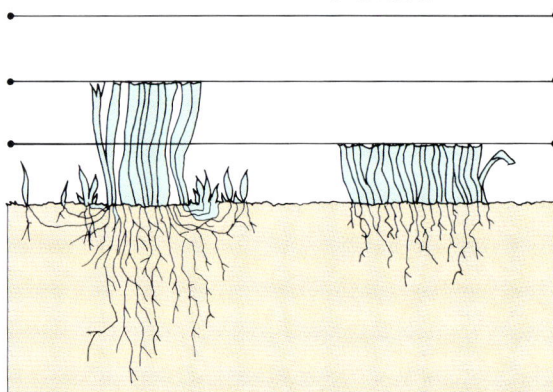

Guides for watering

Watering and your soil ▶

Turf guides recommend giving a lawn 2.5 cm of water with each irrigation—no matter what type of soil you have. What does vary with the soil texture is the frequency of irrigation. Use the chart at right to find out how often to irrigate and how deeply 2.5 cm of water will penetrate. If you don't know what kind of soil you have, do the test below.

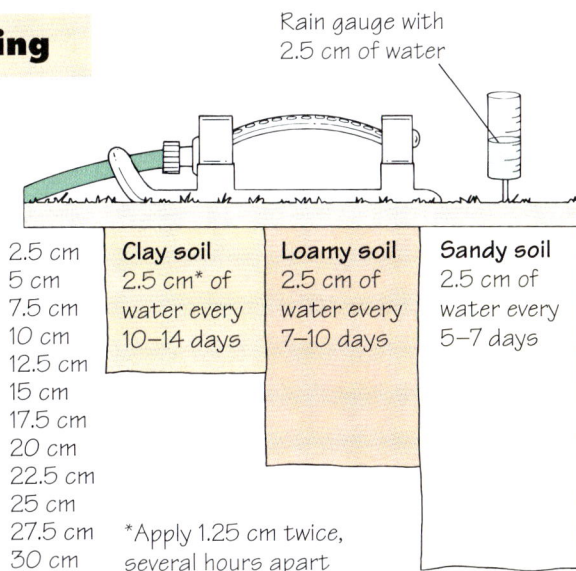

Rain gauge with 2.5 cm of water

	Clay soil	Loamy soil	Sandy soil
2.5 cm 5 cm 7.5 cm 10 cm 12.5 cm 15 cm 17.5 cm 20 cm 22.5 cm 25 cm 27.5 cm 30 cm	2.5 cm* of water every 10–14 days	2.5 cm of water every 7–10 days	2.5 cm of water every 5–7 days

*Apply 1.25 cm twice, several hours apart

The squeeze test

To determine your soil's texture, use a trowel to extract several small samples from the turf's root zone (7.5 to 10 cm below the surface). Shake these up together in a paper bag, extract a table-spoonful, and squeeze it in your fist. If it makes a ball that stands up to a poke, the soil is clay. A ball that cracks with a poke or two is loam; a ball that crumbles easily is sand. Use the chart above and the test below to determine if you have watered your type of soil deeply enough.

Dig deep

An old screwdriver makes a good tool for double-checking the effectiveness of your lawn watering. After you've finished sprinkling, push the tool through the turf. It will penetrate wet soil easily and will register resistance when it encounters the dry zone below.

Waste not

On a sunny, breezy day, as much as half of your sprinkler's droplets may evaporate before they reach the ground. But nothing could be simpler than reducing this kind of waste. All you have to do is switch your watering to early morning hours, when the air is still and the sunlight less intense.

Sprinklers and hoses

Testing a sprinkler

How fast does your sprinkler sprinkle? Surrounding it with empty tins will give you the answer. Run the sprinkler for exactly one hour, and then measure the depth of the water in each tin. This test will let you determine not only the sprinkler's average output, but also if there are any gaps in its sprinkling pattern.

The hose for the job

A perforated hose is a precise way of delivering water just where the garden needs it—but not if the hose is too long. With an old G-clamp or spring clip, though, you can shorten the hose to match the length of the bed or lawn. ▼

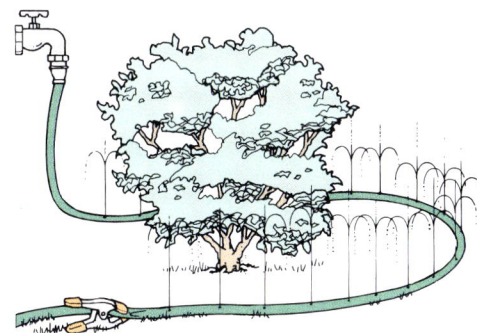

Cutting out those cut corners

A hose tends to cut the corners as it follows you around the garden, and in the process it may flatten prized flowers or vegetables. To protect your plantings (and reduce the wear on your hose), install permanent guards at the outer corners of each garden bed. Drive a series of stout wooden stakes into the ground at the appropriate points, and then drop short lengths of PVC pipe over them.

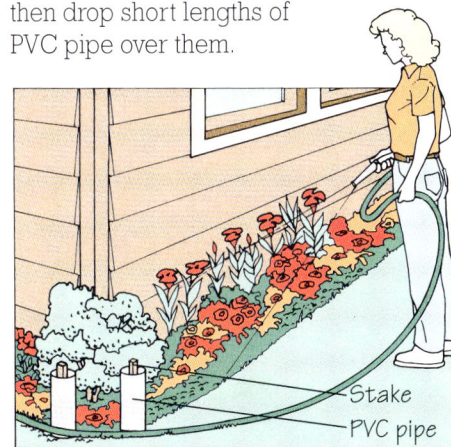

Stake
PVC pipe

TREES AND SHRUBS

Good buys

Weather beaters ▶
A couple of rows of dense, tall-growing evergreen trees set between your house and the prevailing winter wind can help reduce your heating bills. Because trees provide shelter for a distance five times their height, you can set them well away from the house. To create a dead air space, and add a further layer of protection, plant more compact evergreen shrubs 1.5 to 2 m from the foundation.

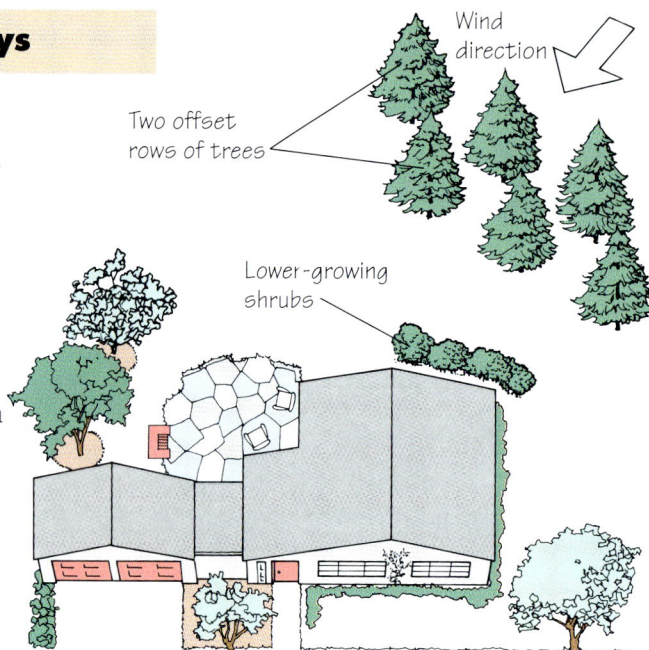

Wind direction

Two offset rows of trees

Lower-growing shrubs

Symptoms of good health
Clues to vigorous plants are ample new growth and unblemished leaves. Avoid plants with signs of severely damaged (cracked or dry) roots.

No bargains
Some plants found on the discount shelves in nurseries and other plant suppliers can turn into very large trees, quite unsuitable for any suburban garden. A bargain today could become a costly problem tomorrow, with bills for root and falling branch damage, as well as for the tree's removal. Also avoid buying plants that have outgrown their pots. Although they may look healthy enough, they are generally stressed and may never recover their full vigour and thrive as one that was not potbound.

Protective measures

Tender staking
Letting the wind sway a newly planted tree strengthens the trunk. You'll be doing your transplants a favour if you keep the stakes low and the support loose— just tight enough to keep the tree from toppling.

Keep it protected
Bark protects trees from infection and disease, so avoid chaining bicycles or other potentially damaging items to a tree. Nailing or wiring signs, such as a garage sale notice, to a trunk or branch may also cut or bruise the bark; instead, try using cotton string to hang signs.

A bumper crop
Rabbits and mice often like to gnaw the bark of young trees. You can ward off these pests with sleeves made from flexible, perforated plastic drainpipe. Cut 10 cm diameter pipe into 60 cm lengths, slit each piece down one side, and gently slip one around the base of each sapling. The pipes protect the trees, and the perforations allow air to flow through to the covered bark.

Stripping a circle
Keeping the soil around young trees and shrubs clear of grass and weeds increases the amounts of water, air and nutrients that reach the roots and keeps the trunks from being damaged when you use a power trimmer on the lawn. Here's how to dig out a circular patch. Loop a rope around the trunk and around your spade. Adjust the loop so that when pulled outward, the spade reaches the desired radius. Move around the plant, digging as you go.

PLANTING A TREE OR SHRUB

Before you buy a young specimen, imagine the size and shape of the mature plant. Review your landscaping goals (pp. 258–259): will it grow fast, give shade, add colour?

If necessary, check on buried cables and pipes (p. 278) before you dig the planting hole. Be sure that the ball rests at the same depth as its previous planting. (Look for the old soil-stain ring on the bark.) Don't dig a hole that is much too deep and then backfill it. The weight of the tree will probably sink the root ball below ground level.

Improve the soil if needed (below), but don't overdo it. In addition, resist the urge to fertilise. Research shows that rich soil in the planting hole doesn't help a plant. The roots tend to ignore the outlying soil and grow in circles in the richer soil. This will then stunt the plant's growth.

1 Dig a hole the same depth as the plant's root ball and 60 to 120 cm wider. Make the sides vertical and roughen them. Loosen the soil in the base of the hole if it is hard.

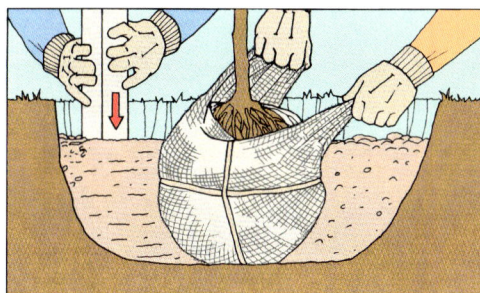

2 Test the soil from the hole (p. 267). If it is sandy or dense clay, mix in an equal amount of organic matter, such as compost. Fill the planting hole three-quarters full, and tamp it down with a piece of wood. Loosen and pull back the hessian (remove plastic root control bag completely).

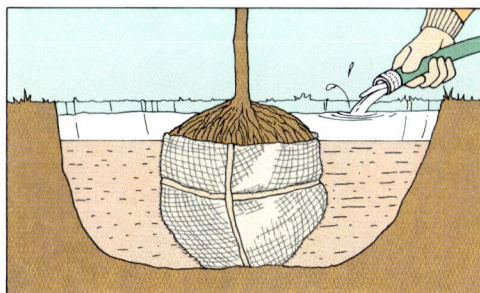

3 Irrigate the planting hole thoroughly with water from a hose. This will settle the soil and remove air pockets. When the water has soaked in, continue filling the hole with soil.

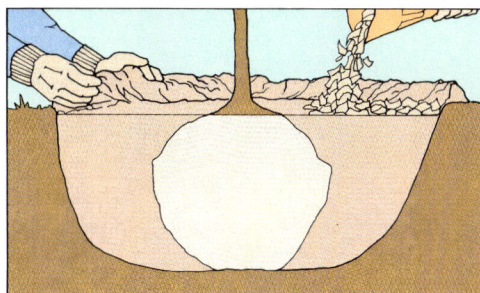

4 Use some extra soil to build a shallow moisture-retaining 'saucer'. Then add a 7 cm layer of mulch, being careful to keep it away from the trunk. Once again, water the tree thoroughly.

TREES AND SHRUBS

Pruning

When to prune?

The best time to prune most flowering shrubs is right after they have finished blooming. An earlier trimming removes buds that provide that year's show, while a late pruning may interfere with the production of buds necessary for the next year's blossoms. An exception is shrubs that bloom repeatedly through-out the growing season, such as hybrid tea roses. Prune them in early spring.

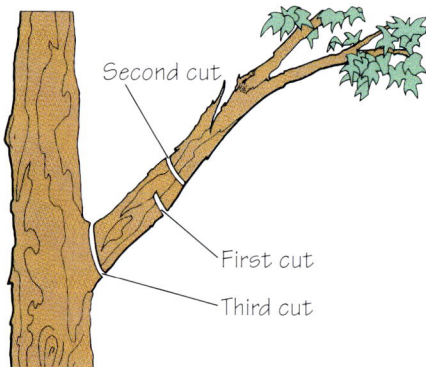

Treatment for a neglected shrub ▶

When you are bringing an overgrown shrub back under control, remember the three Ds: remove all dead, diseased or damaged branches. Next remove the weaker of each pair of crossing branches—branches that rub against each other. Finally, thin the bush by removing several of its oldest branches at their base. Be sure while you are doing this, though, to leave behind a framework of healthy younger branches to fill in as replacements.

Second cut

First cut

Third cut

Removing a storm-damaged limb ▲

If you just saw a cracked or splintered limb off at its base, it's liable to tear a strip of bark off the trunk when it drops —and that means you've done more harm than good. To avoid this mishap, use only a sharp bow saw or pruning saw and cut in three steps. First undercut the limb 30 cm away from the trunk—cut up from the bottom no more than halfway through the limb. Remove the branch with a second cut a few centimetres far-ther out along the limb and down from the top. Remove the remaining stub in one cut from top to bottom, just outside the 'collar' (see chart, facing page).

Scissor-type pruner

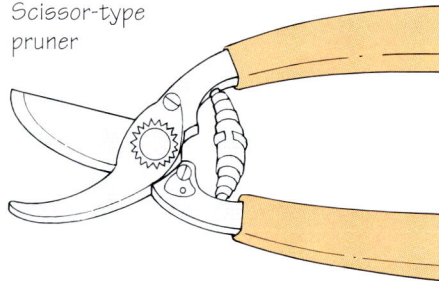

Blade-and-anvil pruner

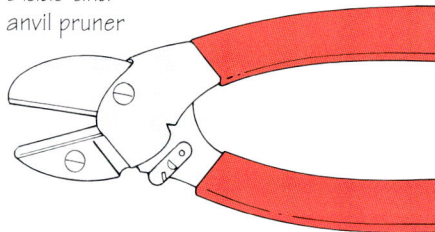

The kindest cut ▲

You'll make the cleanest, easiest cuts with scissor-type pruners—in which the blades slip past each other with a scissor-like action. Blade-and-anvil pruners are less expensive, but they require more strength to use and they crush as they cut, leaving a ragged wound that's an invitation to disease.

Pocket holder

A long-handled pruner is a handy tool for trimming high branches, except that it takes three hands to use one properly. Create an extra hand by putting on a carpenter's apron and resting the end of the pruner's pole in one of the pockets. This leaves one hand free to steady the pole and one to pull the line. ▼

Watering wisdom

Home-made drip irrigator

One of the best ways to make sure that a shrub or tree gets enough water is through drip irrigation. You can fashion a cheap dripper by punching a nail hole into a plastic bucket about 2 cm up from the bucket's base. (This will keep enough water in the bucket so it won't blow away later on.) Set the bucket next to the shrub and fill it with a hose. The water will drain out gradually, soaking the soil close to the plant's roots.

Water-saving tips

If you live in a dry area there are a number of ways you can limit water usage and still keep the garden looking fresh, green and healthy.
▷ Add plenty of compost or other types of organic material to dry, sandy soils.
▷ Spread mulch around plants, but keep it well away from trunks and stems.
▷ Add water crystals to the potting mix of plants to be kept in containers.
▷ Reduce the lawn area and replace with ground-covering plants.
▷ Buy automatic tap timers for use with drippers and soaker hoses.

THE CHANGING WISDOM ABOUT TREE AND SHRUB CARE

Scientific research has revolutionised tree and shrub care over the past decade. What was gospel when you planted your trees is probably considered nonsense now that they are finally big enough to prune.

	THE OLD-FASHIONED WAY	CURRENT WISDOM
Pruning	When removing a branch in the past, you always cut it off flush with the tree's (or shrub's) trunk.	Modern arborists make the cut just beyond the thickened 'collar' of bark and wood that surrounds a branch's base. This promotes faster healing with less danger of decay.
	Traditionalists advised painting pruning wounds with shellac or asphalt to protect the area against decay.	Today arborists know that trees naturally seal off wounds by forming chemical boundaries around them, and that any artificial coating promotes decay by keeping the wound's surface moist.
Feeding the root system	Conventional wisdom used to hold that each tree's root system was the mirror image of its branches. To fertilise a tree, you had to inject the food at least 45 cm into the ground and work no farther out than the 'drip line' (the circle that marks the outer limit of the branches' reach).	Experts now believe that even large trees spread most of their roots through the top 30 to 40 cm of soil, and that 60 per cent of the fine 'feeder' roots lie outside the shadow of its branches. It's best to feed at the rate recommended on the product label, but concentrate the food outside the drip line and simply sprinkle it over the surface and water in.

ROSE BUSHES

Generally, bare-root roses are planted in the winter time, but pot-grown roses can be planted at any time of the year.

Dig a hole twice as wide as the root system, leaving a mound in the centre of the hole to support the roots. Position the bud union (where the top joins the rootstock) level with the soil surface if yours is a mild climate, or 2.5 to 5 cm below ground if winters are severe.

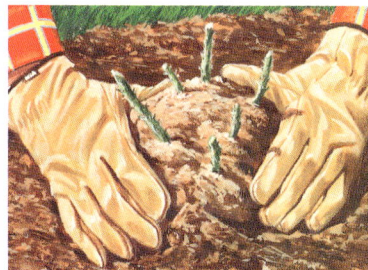

Add soil around the plant and over the canes, gently firming it with your hands. Water the surrounding area well. Do not give the plant any fertiliser until new growth has well and truly started.

GARDENING TOOLS

Improvisations

Protecting the lawn

The job of clearing twigs, stones and other non-leaf debris from a lawn is easier if you use a steel rake with inflexible tines rather than a flexible leaf rake. To prevent the sharp rigid teeth from digging into the lawn, drive cotton reels over the rake's two outside teeth. You'll find that the rake will ride smoothly as it cleans up the lawn.

Digging measure

Mark commonly used depths on the handles of your digging tools. That way you can gauge just how deep you've gone without interrupting your digging. For more on post hole diggers, see p. 277.

Tape marks depth

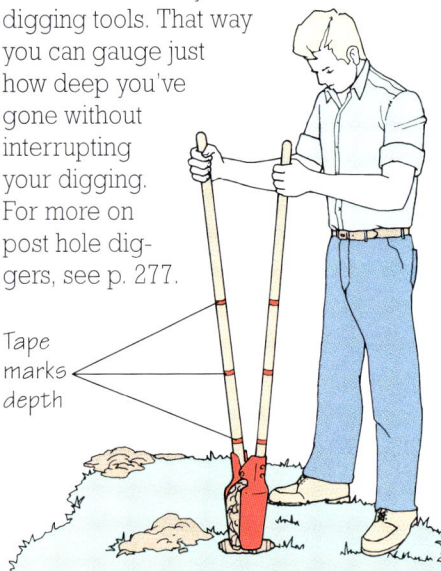

Back saver

Here's a job for an old D-handled garden tool that you don't use anymore (or better yet a broken one). Saw off the business end if necessary, and sharpen the wooden handle to a point. You will then have a digging tool for planting seeds and bulbs.

Step on it

To increase the amount of pressure you can put on a digging tool, such as a fork or a spade, have a short length of angle iron welded to the shoulder of the tool. It will also be kinder to your foot.

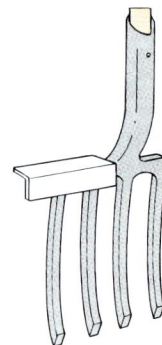

Wheelbarrow extender ▶

Your wheelbarrow will hold more leaves if you add a lightweight frame to it. To make this extension, staple chicken wire to lengths of 25 × 25 mm timber. Don't make the frame so high that loading the leaves will be difficult. When it's time to rake the leaves, hold the frame in place with elastic tie-downs while you fill and empty the barrow.

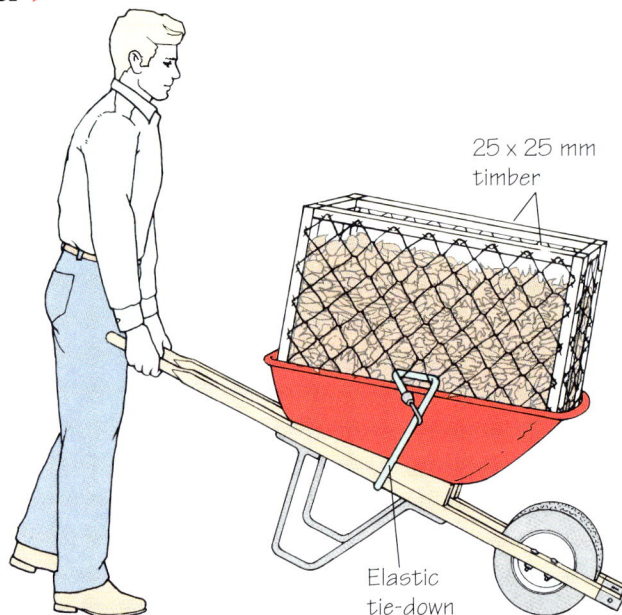

25 × 25 mm timber

Elastic tie-down

Tool tips

Dirty business

Tools last far longer if you clean and oil them after every use. This is very important for digging tools, whose protective coatings wear away from use. Scrape off the dirt with an old putty knife (hang one on a nail where you store your tools). To oil tools, always keep a bucket of oil-soaked sand. Clean the tool, then drive into the sand.

Bright IDea

Small tools are easy to lose in the garden, but not if you paint at least part of the handle a bright colour (other than brown or green). As a bonus, if someone borrows one of these personalised tools, you'll be more likely to get it back.

Tool caddy

If you have an old unused golf bag, give it a new life as a carrier for your gardening tools. Store long-handled tools where you formerly kept your woods and irons, and keep your work gloves and small tools in the zipper pockets. If the bag has a trolley attachment, use it to wheel your tools around the garden.

Rubbish bin stand

Here's another clever way to store long-handled tools. Make a holder out of a large rubbish bin, preferably one with built-in wheels so that you can cart your tools around the garden. First use a spade bit to drill holes in the lid to accept the tool handles. Then drill a few small holes in the bottom of the bin for drainage. To help hold the tools in place, add some coarse gravel to the bottom.

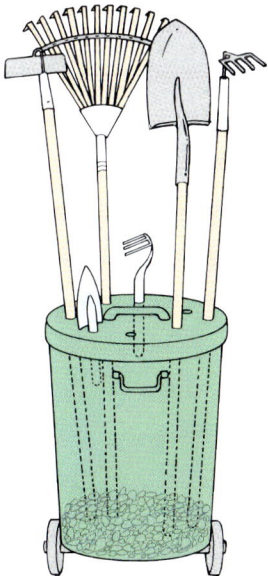

KEEP TOOLS SHARP

For rough sharpening jobs, use a bastard (coarse) or a second-cut (medium) file to re-establish the bevel. To create a sharp digging or cutting edge, use a smooth (fine) file or a sharpening stone. Depending on the garden tool, use a toe-to-heel stroke, a straight stroke or a sweeping motion. Always clamp the tool firmly in a vice. For more on files and sharpening techniques, see pp. 20 and 22–23.

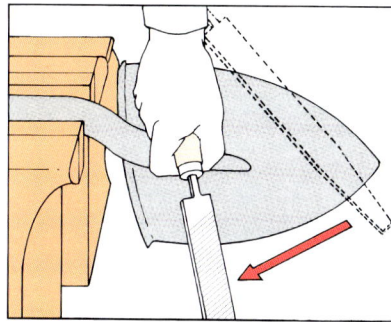

Sharpen a spade by holding the toe of the file on the bevel at a 45° angle. Push the file diagonally in one direction, ending the stroke at the heel of the file. Work from the centre out on one side; repeat on the other side.

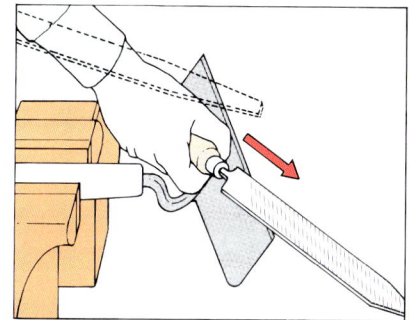

Hoes are bevelled on the outside surface of their blades. Hold the file as for the spade, but begin with the toe at the near end. Push the file diagonally away from you, ending the stroke near the heel.

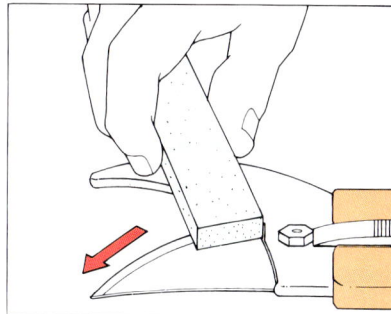

Renew the cutting blades of pruning shears or secateurs with a small flat stone. Place the stone on the bevel at the edge of the blade, and rub the cutting edge with sweeping strokes.

Give hedge clippers a fine cutting edge with a smooth single-cut file. Hold the file perpendicular to the cutting edge. Use straight pulling strokes without any side-to-side movement.

OUTDOOR POWER TOOLS

Mowers

Sharpen and balance a blade

Before sharpening a single rotary blade, disconnect the spark plug wire and remove the blade, following the manual's instructions. Put the blade in a vice and sharpen both ends equally. Use a bastard file and a toe-to-heel stroke (p. 273) to restore the original bevel, usually a 30° angle. Don't try to file out deep nicks, as you'll remove too much metal and unbalance the blade. As you work, check the blade's balance occasionally by hanging it on a nail driven into the workshop wall. If one side persists in dropping lower, resharpen that end to remove more metal. ▼

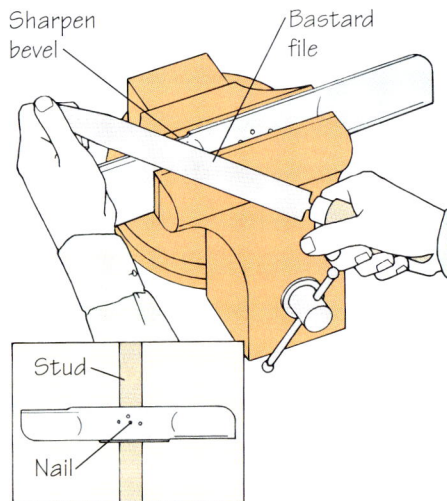

Sharpen bevel

Bastard file

Stud

Nail

Don't cut the cord

You'll be less likely to mow over the cord of an electric mower if you wrap a spiral of colourful tape down the length of the cord. It'll be more visible as it snakes around the lawn. Or use a bright orange exterior extension cord.

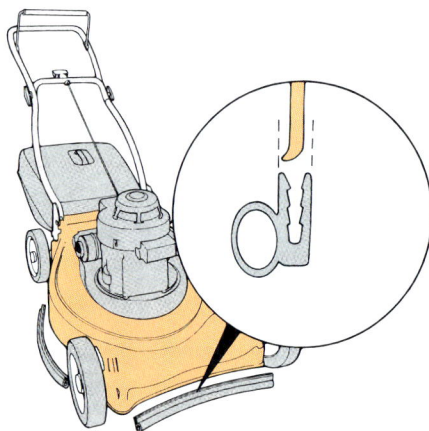

A bumper for trees ▲

If grass grows right up to your trees, there's a danger that your mower could bang into the trunks and damage their bark. As a safeguard, slip a pair of inexpensive plastic car door edge guards onto the edges of your mower. The bark of your trees will stay healthy.

Preparing for storage

If you are planning to be away from home for any length of time, make sure you prepare your mower properly for storage. Run the mower until all the fuel is out of the system, and change the oil. Remove the spark plug and squirt a little oil into the hole. To distribute the oil within the hole, pull the starter cord a couple of times. Replace the plug and put the mower away.

Running on empty

Using up the remaining fuel prior to storage can take a long time if the mower tank isn't nearly empty. To solve the problem, you can use a plastic pipe to siphon off most of the fuel. What little is left will be used up quickly.

Put a guard up

Grass cutting with a side catcher will be safer if you install a rubber guard at the back of your mower as a protection against flying rock fragments. Cut the guard from a narrow piece of 3 mm thick rubber, and blind-rivet it to the top edge of the mower body. The rubber guard will give with the contours of the lawn and won't hinder the manoeuvrability of the mower. ▼

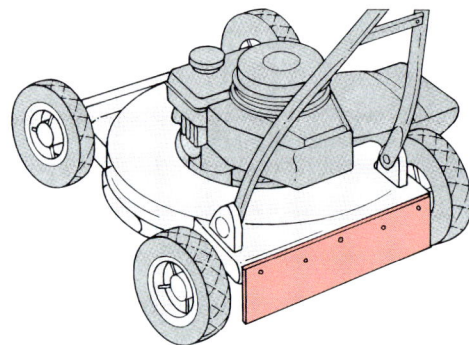

Easy rider clean up

An easy way to clean off the grass that builds up around the blade of a ride-on mower is to flush it out with water. Just attach a sprinkler ring to a hose and slide it under the mower. Turn on the water and wash the clippings away.

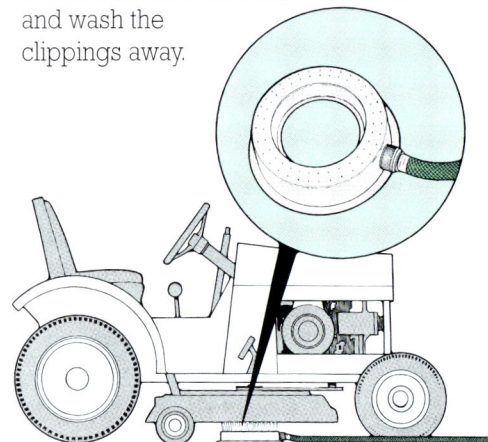

Line-trimmers

Some buying tips

When shopping for a line-trimmer you will need to decide between an electric or petrol-driven model. Electric models are ideal for average to small gardens, being lightweight and easy to start. But in a large garden the long extension cord is hard to drag around, and it will keep getting tangled in obstructions. In these circumstances, a petrol-driven machine is preferable. Choose—from the many models available—one that is the right size and weight for your build. Check for excessive vibration, and also that the starting cord is easy to pull.

Preventing plant damage

Never use line-trimmers and brushcutters around the trunks and stems of trees or bushes. The whirling cord will ringbark even quite large plants, killing or badly damaging them. Instead, stay at least 10 cm away, and hand weed the last little bit later on. ▼

Chain saws

Out of chips

A chain saw needs sharpening when it starts to produce sawdust rather than chips. A resharpened chain saw runs faster and is smoother. It's safer, too, since you don't have to press down so hard when cutting.

Mixing two-stroke fuel

Chain saws run on a mixture of petrol and oil, but the exact ratio varies with different makes, so check the tool's manual before proceeding. Never mix and store fuel in a plastic container. Instead, buy one of the metal cans sold at hardware stores for mower fuel.

Shake it up

Don't forget to shake a chain saw for at least one minute before you use it. This redistributes the oil in the tank.

Starter-rope savers

The starter rope of a chain saw can fray and break too quickly for one of three reasons. First, you may be pulling the rope at an angle, causing it to rub against the saw's housing. Be sure to pull the rope straight. Second, you may be using a replacement rope that is too short for the saw, or made of the wrong material. The rope must be the same length as the original and made of nylon, not cotton. Finally, the saw may be suffering from engine problems. An engine that's hard to start forces repeated use of the rope, wearing it out more quickly. Check for a tired spark plug, incorrect fuel mixture, dirty air filter or failing ignition.

SAFETY FIRST

HOW TO BE CAREFUL

▷ Before a cleaning or repair job, turn off the motor, remove the ignition key (if there is one) and disconnect the spark plug wire, securing it away from the plug.
▷ Store petrol in a red petrol tins away from the house, flames or sparks and children.

Lawn mowers

▷ Wear leather shoes and long trousers, even in hot weather.
▷ Keep away from moving parts.
▷ If you leave a mower, turn it off.
▷ Before mowing, clear away all obstructions.
▷ Know where the kerbs are.

Chain saws

▷ If possible, fit an older chain saw with a bar tip guard and an anti-kickback chain.
▷ Wear hearing protection, a face shield, non-slip, steel-toed shoes and stout gloves (to lower the danger of accidental cuts).
▷ Brace the saw on the ground or on a log when starting it.
▷ Stand uphill from the work.
▷ Maintain secure footing. Grasp the saw with both hands. Never hold it more than chest high.
▷ Turn the saw off if you have to walk with it.
▷ Let a professional do a job that requires any climbing.
For more on tool safety, see p. 24.

SETTING POSTS

Down-to-earth advice

Burial services

Before you dig any post holes, remember to call your local water, electricity, gas, cable TV and telephone service suppliers. They will be able to tell you if any pipes, wires or other services cross the line of your proposed fence. Once you know where any pipes or wires are located, dig at least 1 m (or the distance specified by the service supplier) away from them. That way you won't cut service to your house or neighbourhood and end up with an expensive repair bill—or worse, injure yourself.

Natural hazards

If you encounter a root that's too large to remove with a spade or post hole digger, use a pruning saw or axe. But make sure you're not killing a tree by severing a main root, and also that it's not a power line or drain (see above), before you chop away.

Work on one cylinder

Sometimes loose soil caves in as fast as you can dig it out, leaving you with a crater rather than a cylindrical hole. If that happens, wedge in a heavy-duty cardboard tube—used on building construction sites when pouring wide concrete columns, and available from concrete formwork suppliers—to shore up the loose edges. Dig inside the tube, and gradually work it down as the hole gets deeper. Once the post is ready to be set in position, the tube will also hold the concrete or dirt fill.

Ready, get set

Add a second level ▶

If you are setting many posts, consider buying a tool that has two levels mounted at a 90° angle to each other. When it's time to plumb a post, have someone hold the post in place while you place the tool against it. Adjust the post's position as necessary, and secure it with braces as shown.

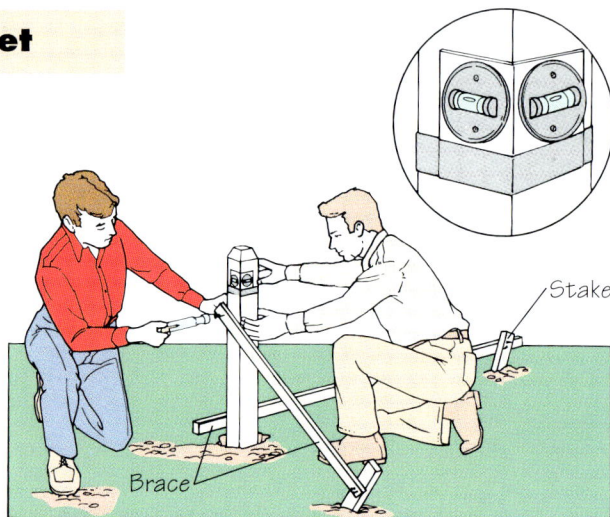

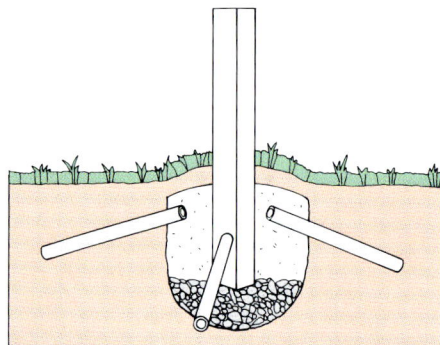

Stake

Brace

Rock-solid post anchor ▲

Gate posts, clotheslines, flagpoles and handrail posts all need firmly anchored footings. You can do this without a mass of concrete. After digging the hole for the concrete footing, drive three or four lengths of old pipe or angle iron, each 1.5 to 2 m long, at an angle into the surrounding soil. Let their ends protrude into the hole so they will become embedded in the concrete when you pour it. This added reinforcement will prevent the footing from shifting under stress.

Nail holder

Another way to reinforce a post in its footing is to drive nails into the post before you set it in place. The nails provide a gripping surface for the concrete when it is poured into the hole. For best results, use 150 mm flat-head nails. Stagger the nails on each side and down the post, driving them about halfway into the wood. ▼

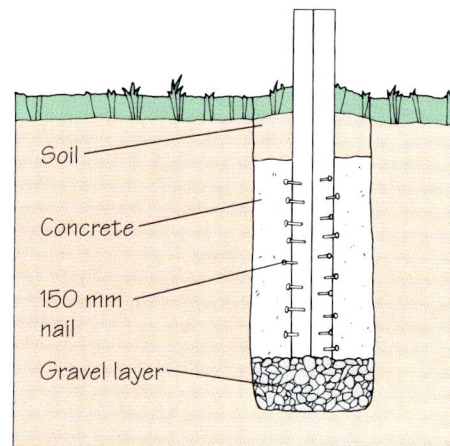

Soil

Concrete

150 mm nail

Gravel layer

TOOLS FOR POST HOLES

Digging a deep cylindrical hole calls for an arsenal of tools that can help you handle rocks and soil without fear. The tools shown on this page will help you dig the post holes for fences as well as the excavations for concrete pier footings. (To avoid the growing network of underground pipes and wires, see the facing page.)

Clamshell digger. You can use this digger in all types of soil. Simply plunge its open jaws into the hole, spread the handles to make the jaws bite the dirt, lift it out and push the handles back together to release the dirt. Loosen rock-filled or clay soil by stabbing with it. The deeper you dig, the less you'll be able to move the jaws.

Hand auger. The twisting motion used to power this tool works well in reasonably soft ground, but not in rocky soil. The cutting teeth can churn soil up into the space between the jaws, but they are powerless against rocks.

Power auger. This petrol powered tool (usually hired) is ideal when you need to dig many holes in stone-free soil. (It isn't so useful in rocky ground.) The corkscrew auger, varying in diameter from 10 to 25 cm pulls itself into the ground and spins the dirt onto the surface. However, the tool is heavy and its weight can be hard on your back, especially in clay soil. Use one only if you're strong enough, or have someone to help you. The larger models can only be used by two people.

Trenching shovel. This type of shovel has a narrow curved blade that will flare the bottoms of holes for concrete footings. A smaller one can be used to finish the bottoms of holes dug by other means.

Heavy-duty crowbar. This is an essential tool for working in heavy clay or rocky soils. It dislodges large rocks, breaks up rocky ledges and loosens up clay. One that is 1.5 m long and weighs around 10 kg can tackle most jobs.

BUILDING AND REPAIRING FENCES

Picket fences

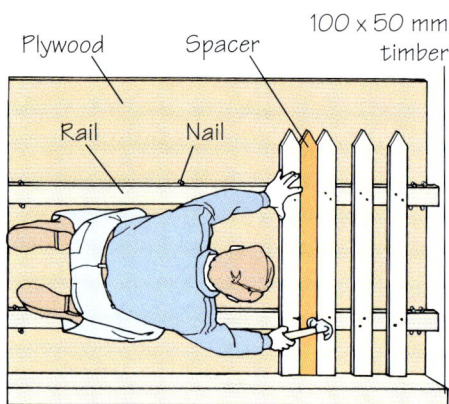

Plywood   Spacer   100 x 50 mm timber

Rail   Nail

Spaced out ▲

Spacing the pickets evenly on their rails can be a major task. An easy way to do this is to make a spacing guide with a 2400 x 1200 mm sheet of plywood and a 2400 mm length of 100 x 50 mm timber. Nail the timber to the bottom of the plywood; this will align the ends of the pickets evenly. Next drive nails into the plywood at intervals to hold the rails in position. To assemble the pieces, lay the pickets next to one another and nail every other one. (The intermediate, unnailed pickets act as spacers.) Remove the spacers, check for square and continue to the end.

Design your own

If you'd like to try your hand at designing your own picket fence, use more than one picket style and vary the spacing between the pickets. Begin with a pencil and paper, and experiment with various repeating patterns. Once you've settled on a pattern, make a spacing jig (as shown above) to help you place the pickets accurately on the rails.

Removable fence sections ▶

Building a fence with light, removable sections makes a lot of sense. It lets you open the space for a party or ball game, move large objects in and out of the house and run the mower between the fence posts instead of having to trim beneath the pickets. To make fence sections removable, support the rails on joist hangers instead of fastening them permanently to the posts. Purchase joist hangers sized to hold 100 x 50 mm timber (available from a builder's supplier). You'll need four for each fence section. Position the hangers where the rails are to align, and fasten them to the posts with screws. To assemble the fence, rest the rails in the hangers.

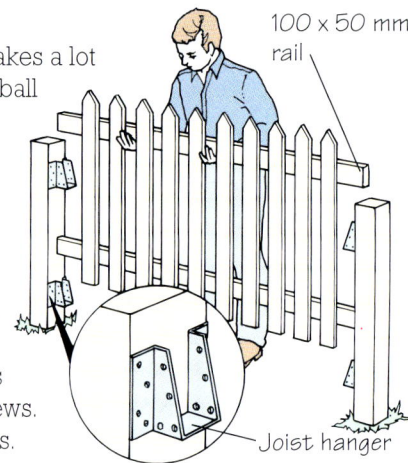

100 x 50 mm rail

Joist hanger

Working with boards

Spacer block   Post   Upper rail

Jig

◀ Nailing jig

When fastening fence boards, use a jig to get them in perfect alignment and at the correct height. The jig shown here is made of a board with two spacer blocks; one block rests on top of the upper rail while the other marks the top of the fence. Starting at a post, position the first board with the jig next to it. Nail the board to the top rail, and then repeat with the next board and the next. When you reach the second post, check that the gap between it and the last board is uniform at both top and bottom. Then go back and nail all the boards in the section to the bottom rail.

◀ Cutting scallops

You can give a board fence a decorative finished look with the help of a strip of 6 mm hardboard. Here's how. For each post-to-post section, tack one nail to each post just at the top of the boards, and tack a third nail in the middle of the fence section 150 mm down from the other nails. Bend the hardboard strip between these nails and trace a smooth curve. Cut out the curve with a power jig saw, finishing the end of the cut by hand with a coping saw. Smooth the cut edges of the boards with either a rasp or a Surform tool.

FENCE REPAIR

Before you tackle any single repair, inspect the entire fence. If one post has a severe lean to it, give the others a firm shake to see if they're wobbly too. If one picket is rotten, probe others with an old screwdriver to see if they're spongy as well. If most of the framework seems solid, go ahead and perform the repairs and maintenance shown here. But if the framework is falling apart, or if half the posts are rotten, consider building a new fence.

Realign a sagging gate

L-bracket   Coach bolt

Turnbuckle

Support blocks

Push a sagging gate post back into place and reconnect it to the horizontal members with two L-brackets and screws. If the gate itself is sagging, tighten the hinge screws. If they no longer grip, replace them with longer screws or fill the holes and refasten the hinges (p. 14). Next, raise the gate on support blocks; open a turnbuckle fully and install it diagonally with coach bolts. Depending on the turnbuckle, tighten it with a crowbar or a spanner. Finally, resecure any loose pickets with some galvanised screws.

Replace a post

Pull at angle

Push down

100 x 50 mm lever nailed to post

Block

Pull out the nails that secure the fence sections on each side of the vertical post. Swing the sections about 1 m out of the way, propping the ends on scrap boards.

Prise the old post out of the ground while a helper pulls it at an angle to keep it from slipping back into the hole. Position the new post; then reposition the two fence sections and nail them into place. Brace the post to hold it plumb, and pour in the concrete. (For more on setting posts, see p. 276.)

BUILDING AND RESTORING DECKS

Planning

Outdoor room

A deck is an outdoor living room, and as such it needs a sense of enclosure. You can achieve this with a simple perimeter railing or by edging it with a few low benches or planters.

Caution: for safety's sake, put a slatted railing around any deck raised 1 m or more above ground level.

On the beams

When building a deck, don't try to make do with bearers and joists that are too small. Undersized supports, while they may meet the local building code, also make a deck feel soft underfoot since they bounce rather than staying rigid. It's worth the extra cost to increase the dimension of the supports. You'll end up with a deck that is sturdier and safer.

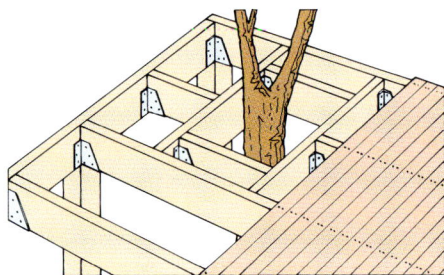

Built-in tree ▲

If you want to design a deck around a tree, plan to box the tree in with short joists. These short lengths will compensate for the interruption in the joist system. Be sure that the box is large enough to let the tree grow. If children are going to be playing on the deck, build a small fence around the tree opening as a safety measure.

Building

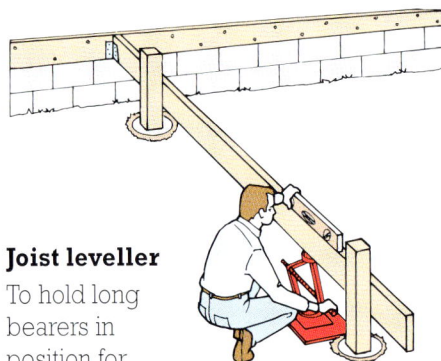

Joist leveller

To hold long bearers in position for levelling, secure one end of the timber and support the body of the piece with the help of a car jack. Adjust the jack to level the piece as necessary; then secure or support the other end at just the right position. You'll find that the jack is a strong and helpful partner.

Do your level best

Before you cut posts to their final height, tack-nail the bearers in position, using a level as you go. Then, with the bearers in place, check your work by placing a spirit level on a straight length of timber that's been laid diagonally across the deck. Repeat in the opposite direction. Adjust the position of the bearers as needed, and then cut the posts.

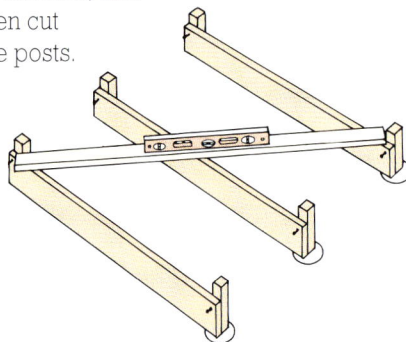

Erosion barrier

Before you build your deck, decide if rainwater seeping through the boards will erode the soil. This is likely to happen if the ground slopes. If you decide that erosion could be a problem, all you need to do to keep the soil in place is to cover it with a generous layer of gravel before you build the deck.

Spaced-out boards

It's easy to space deck boards evenly. Just drive 3 mm diameter nails into several timber off cuts. Push the nails down between adjacent deck boards, and then fasten the boards into place. ▼

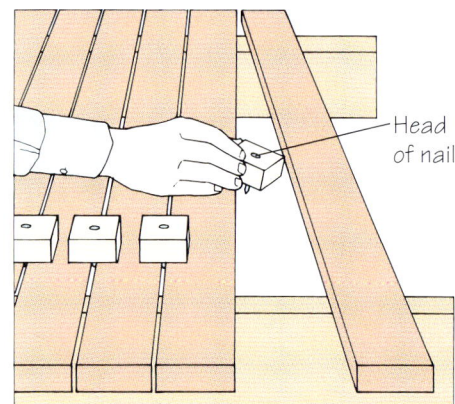

Head
of nail

Fasten-ating problem

While nails are usually used in deck building, they may not the best fastener to use with softer timbers. The hammer blows needed to drive them flush dent the surface, marring the project. A better choice might be galvanised self-drilling screws. As you seat these screws with a power driver, they countersink themselves. The spiral threads won't allow the screws to back out (as nails tend to over a period of time).

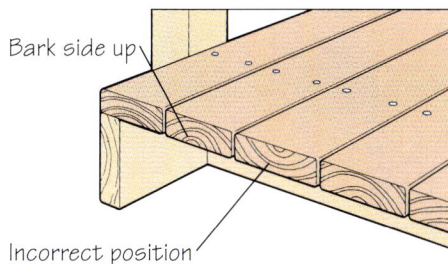

Bark side up

Incorrect position

Direction of the board ▲

When placing a deck board, follow this rule: bark side up. To tell which is the bark side, check the annual growth rings on the end of the board; the convex side is the bark side. Putting this side facing up (and the concave side down) means that it'll be less likely to *cup,* or warp, and you'll also avoid *feathering,* or splitting along the annual rings, which results in long spear-like splinters. Put the bark side down only if that side has bad knots or splits.

Drive it straight

You can straighten a crooked deck board as you nail or screw it down by wedging it into position. First, screw a timber off cut to the top of the joist closest to the end of the problem board. Hammer a wedge between the end of the off cut and the board until the board is properly spaced, and then nail or screw the board to the joist. Repeat at other joists as necessary. ▼

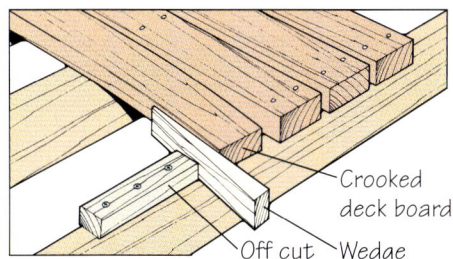

Crooked deck board

Off cut   Wedge

Movable deck umbrella

A deck umbrella is more useful if you can move it around as needed. To help you get it in the right spot, mount pairs of galvanised plumbing pipe straps on the deck posts or railing in key places. (The straps should be slightly wider than the umbrella pole.) Then just slip the umbrella pole through the straps, until the pole rests on the deck. ▼

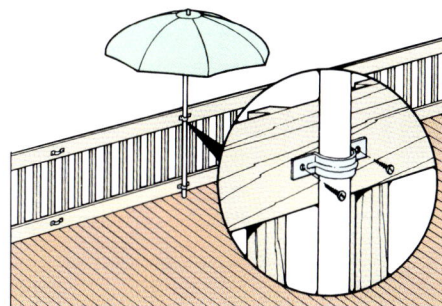

Finishing up

True grit

Don't slip on wet deck steps. If you intend to paint them, mix one part fine clean white sand with four parts paint. If not, glue down non-slip strips with an exterior construction adhesive. Either way, the gritty texture will provide grip.

Wait to paint

If you use a pressure-treated wood to build your deck, be prepared to wait a for few months before painting it. The pressure-treating process saturates the wood with chemicals and usually leaves it too wet to accept paint or stain well. If you have to cut the timber during construction, make sure that you brush some preservative on the raw ends.

Instant weathering

If you are replacing a portion of a deck, you can give it an 'instant' weathered appearance. Apply a solution of one cup of baking soda and 4 litres of water to the new portion, allow it to dry and rinse it off. When the area is dry, apply a water sealant. The sealant forms a moisture barrier beneath the surface of the wood, allowing the deck to continue to weather gradually.

Spray-on sealers

Choose a windless day to spray on a wood sealer. Using a pump garden sprayer, you can apply the sealer between the deck boards without any trouble. To clean a water-based sealer from the sprayer, spray water until it is clear. (For an oil-based sealer, soak the sprayer parts in solvent.)

Restoratives

Waterproof test

Over time, moisture takes a toll on a deck. An easy way to tell if you need to reseal your deck is to pour a glass of water on it. If the water beads up, the deck is waterproof. But if the surface absorbs the water quickly and turns a darker colour, it's time to reseal.

Speedy deck cleaners

Deck oils and finishes do a good job of bringing your deck back to life, but if the deck is very dirty, you may have to do some heavy scrubbing. If so, consider renting a high-pressure washer; it will make the job easier.

MASONRY AND CONCRETE

Mortarless helpers

Trade secrets

The great secret of successful paving is a firm, flat base. Whatever the surface is that you are going to pave over, make sure that it has been properly compacted, and will not subside later. When the foundations are satisfactory, spend as much time as necessary making the sand bed absolutely flat and smooth. Then it will just be a matter of laying the pavers down, one after another ▼

Neat edges

When laying the edging for a path with parallel sides, take care to keep the sides evenly spaced; it will make life easier when you smooth and level the base and lay the pavers or concrete.

A day's work

Lay down and level only as much sand as you can cover with pavers in one day, and then throw a cover over the sand pile. Uncovered sand is guaranteed to be disturbed by wind, rain, children or a some local cat who thinks its found the world's biggest litter box.

Dry idea

Before you sweep sand between newly laid bricks or pavers, be sure it's dry. Wet sand will bridge the gaps rather than fill them. To make sure the gaps are filled completely, wait a few days and then sweep sand into the gaps a second time. This is important because the sand helps bind the paving together, and also fills any spaces where dirt might enter and provide support for weeds.

Paver saver ▲

The best way to lock pavers into their sand bed is to use a hired plate compactor, but be careful with this heavy machine. Don't let it sit in one place too long, or the pavers could settle unevenly or crack. Some specialists place sheets of plywood on the pavers and run the compactor over them; the plywood distributes the weight of the machine.

Stone paths

Interlocking retaining walls ▶

Want an easier way to build a retaining wall? Try a system of interlocking blocks. Block styles vary among makers, and interlocking methods differ as well. Here, fibreglass pins fit into holes in the blocks. While they are heavy (up to 40 kg each) and expensive, the blocks will last almost forever and don't require mortar to hold them in place, or a concrete footing. The only other materials you'll need are sand or gravel, and some landscaping fabric (available from hardware shops).

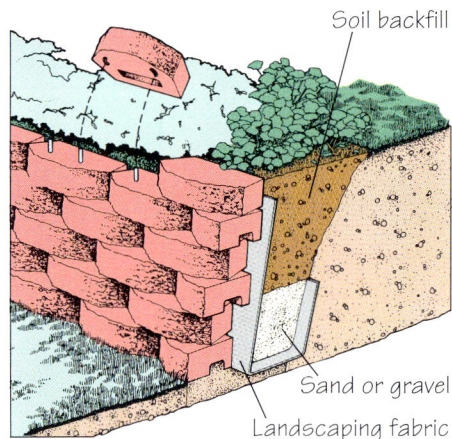

Soil backfill

Sand or gravel

Landscaping fabric

Make sand stay put

If your flagstone path has fairly wide joints, you may find that the sand tends to wash away. If you get around to resetting the stones, set them in sand as before, but change your approach to the joints. Mix a little dry cement with the sand and pack the mixture firmly between the stones. Then, to set the filler, sprinkle the joints with a little water. The sand will stay put.

Put the design on paper ▲

Working with flagstones is like solving a giant jigsaw puzzle. Some stones fit together without cutting, but others need to be cut to fit. An easy way to find the best candidate to fill any given space is to make a template out of brown paper. Just lay the paper over the space and fold back the edges until it fits (don't forget to leave room for the sand joints). Take the template over to your stockpile of stones and choose one that's closest to your needs. Mark any cut lines. Place the stone on sand, and score along the cut lines with a bolster and a club hammer. Strike the stone firmly to split it.

Stepping-stone walks

Before you dig any holes for a stepping-stone path, place the stones on top of the grass and space them so that the strides between the stones are comfortable. Take a couple of practice walks. When the placement looks and feels right, sprinkle flour over the path. Then lift the stones out of the way and use the outlines to dig holes for the stones.

Pattern making

If you'd like a path that has a random pattern but isn't as irregular as the one at left, here is a plan that uses stone pavers that have been uniformly cut into three sizes, measuring 60 × 60 cm, 45 × 45 cm and 60 × 45 cm. Numerous other such patterns are possible. ▼

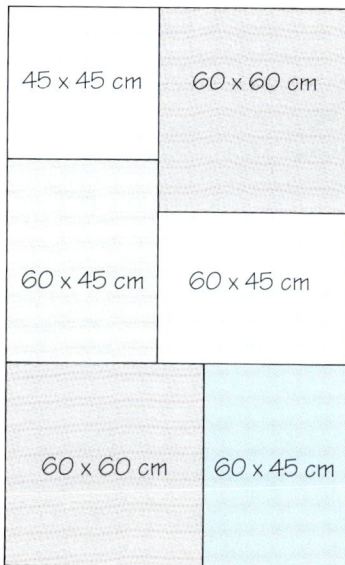

45 × 45 cm	60 × 60 cm
60 × 45 cm	60 × 45 cm
60 × 60 cm	60 × 45 cm

Some concrete secrets

Using leftovers

Almost every concrete pour leaves you with leftover concrete. If you plan ahead, you can make some extra patio blocks or small concrete slabs that you can put to good use. Before you pour, build some extra forms from scrap timber (45 cm or thereabouts is a useful length), oil them lightly, and place them on heavy polyurethane sheets. When you've finished your paving job, pour the leftover concrete into the forms.

Concrete connection

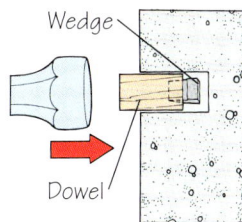

Wedge

Dowel

To securely mount a screw, hook or nail in a solid concrete surface, create a firm base for the fastener.

First drive a steel tool-handle wedge partway into the end of a length of dowel, and then use a masonry bit to bore a hole in the concrete the same diameter as the dowel. Drive the dowel into the hole, wedge end first. As you hammer it in, the wedge will expand the dowel, creating a supertight fit.

Flagstone fake

The next time you pour a concrete path or patio, you might want to try a decorative finish for it, such as the flagstone effect shown here. While the smoothed concrete is still wet, use a brick jointing tool to carve the outlines of joints between the simulated flagstones. For best results, plan your design ahead of time and work quickly (you don't want the concrete to set too soon). Go over the surface again with a trowel, and then use an old paintbrush to remove particles of concrete and smooth the edges of the design.

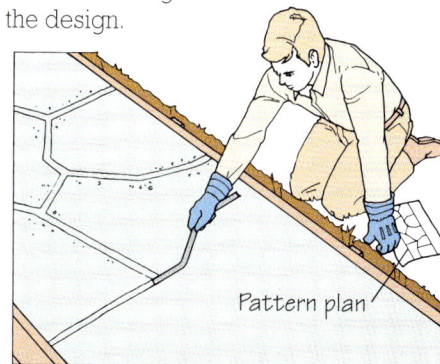

Pattern plan

REPAIRING MASONRY AND CONCRETE

Patios, paths and steps

Concrete shock absorber

Hammering a chisel to remove loose material from a crack in concrete can make your hands and arms tingle. Reduce this excessive shock by punching a hole into a sponge-rubber ball and pushing the drill or chisel through it. When you hammer the tool, hold on to the sponge rubber. You won't feel the vibrations as much. (*Note:* don't forget to wear eye protection for this job.) ▼

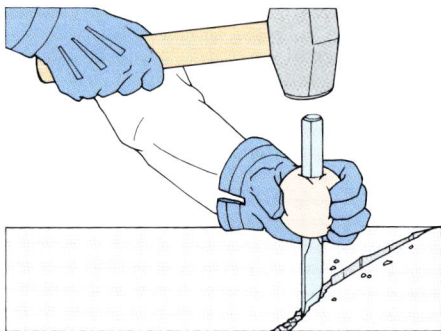

Hold your chips

When chipping away at concrete, keep the pieces from scattering all over the place, including into your face. Push the chisel through a square of fly screen. Wear safety goggles, just in case.

Crack filler

When filling a crack in a concrete path or drive, make sure that you clean out all loose material first, and then undercut the edges with a hammer and chisel to provide a grip for the filler. Brush the enlarged crack with a PVA bonding agent, and also mix PVA with the sand, cement and water mix that you use to pack into the crack to repair it.

Railing against the weather

Moisture seeping into the space between a wrought-iron railing and its concrete base encourages rust to form below the surface. To prevent that from happening, use copolymer sealant (see p. 151) to fill any gaps between the iron and the concrete.

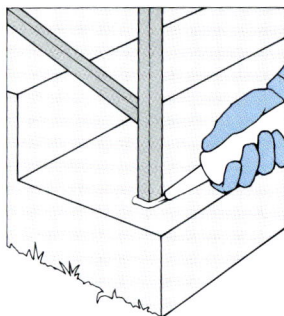

Paver puller

Over a period of years, some individual bricks or pavers in your sand-base patio or path may need relevelling. But how do you get the tight-fitting brick or paver out? Make two pullers like the ones shown here from coat hanger wire. Slip the pullers down both sides of the offending paver, turn them a quarter turn, and pull up the paver. For larger paving blocks, make four pullers and get a second person to help you. ▼

No more moss

Moss thrives in warm, damp climates, growing almost everywhere. Not only is it unsightly, it makes concrete and brick steps, patios and paths dangerously slippery. To get rid of moss, mix one part household bleach with three parts water in a plastic watering can. Apply it to the mossy surface, and then scrub with a stiff-bristled brush.

Driveway cures

Fresh stain

Cover a fresh oil or grease spot on your paved or concreted driveway with baking soda or cat litter. If you use litter, grind it with a brick until the litter is a fine powder (there's no need to bear down hard). Let the soda or litter stay there for a day or so; then sweep the area clean.

Stubborn spots

If the baking soda or cat litter treatment (above) won't budge an oil or grease stain from a concrete driveway, saturate the spot with carburettor cleaner. Or use a commercial degreaser.

Push grooming

The next time you clean your driveway, try taping a garden hose to the handle of a push broom. The nozzle will direct water in front of the broom as you push it over the surface.

Layout and staking tips

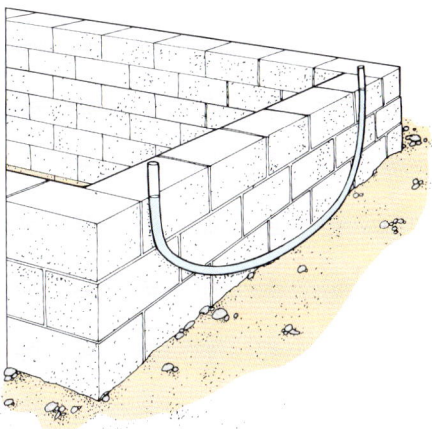

Long level line ▲

Use this simple tool to maintain a level line over a long distance. Almost fill a length of 12 mm diameter clear plastic tubing with water. The water will seek identical levels at each end, giving you an accurate levelling device for laying out projects such as decks and fences.

Don't split the stakes

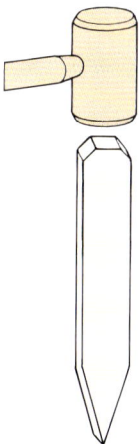

When wood stakes split, it's usually because you've struck them on the corners, instead of in the centre, when driving them into place. To solve this problem, simply take the time, when making the stakes, to cut off the upper corners. Then you'll have no choice but to hit each stake in the centre, and it will go into the ground with minimal splitting.

Lighting up

Dimmer views

If you have a dimmer switch installed on your exterior spotlights or floodlights, you'll be able to produce diffused light at the touch of a dial, creating just the right mood for a party on your patio or in the garden. Be sure, however, that it is a heavy-duty dimmer, one designed for exterior use. To avoid the annoying hum that many dimmers cause, choose one with a filter. Have the dimmer installed by a qualified electrician.

Sand in your socket

If the lamp socket of a garden light is corroded, you can clean it out with the type of emery board used for finger-nails. First, shut off the electric power at the meter box and then remove the light globe to gain access to the socket. Brush out any grit, and then rub the contacts clean with the emery board.

TYPES OF OUTDOOR LIGHTING

Light can be used many ways: to set the stage for an outdoor party, add a dramatic touch to a garden or improve the security of your home. Here's a brief sampler.

TYPE	TECHNIQUE	COMMON USES
Backlighting	Places a light fixture behind an object.	To silhouette a shape and cast shadows beyond it.
Contour lighting	Focuses two or three beams at different angles around an object. (To deepen the contrast of light and shadows, make one light more intense.)	To draw attention to trees, statues, fountains and other items with sculptural interest.
Cross-lighting	Mounts two beams of equal intensity on opposite sides of its target.	To make an object or area prominent.
Diffused light	Sets several non-directional lights, on posts and in the ground.	To soften the contrast between light and shadow and set a mood.
Downlighting	Directs light from a tree or roof to a specific area.	To outline paths and driveways or to increase security around the house, often with a movement sensor.
Grazing	Brushes light beams across a surface.	To emphasise the texture of plants, vines, rock gardens and stucco.
Moonlighting	Beams light from a high place such as a tree or roof.	To enlarge the area of diffused light, as for a large outdoor party.
Uplighting	Directs (usually) one light beam upwards from the ground.	To draw attention to bushes or trees.

GARDEN IMPROVEMENTS

Furnishing the outdoors

A movable feast

If you'd like an easy way to move your outdoor table around the garden, just install a pair of large casters at the bottom of the legs at one end of the table (100 mm or larger wheels negotiate a lawn well). Then when it's time to follow the shade, mow or rake under the table, or make room for other activities, just lift one end and go.

Metal protector

Outdoor furniture with metal feet usually comes with protective plastic or rubber tips. Over time, the metal cuts through the tips and starts to rust and scratch the deck. To lengthen the life of these plastic protectors, fit a metal washer inside the bottom of each one.

Lawn chair repairs

To clean dirty aluminium frames, use extra-fine (No. 000) steel wool and a little kerosene. If the aluminium is pitted, rub the areas with aluminium cleaner. Finally, protect the frames by spraying them with clear acrylic finish.

Cloth control ▶

Wind wreaks havoc at a picnic—napkins and paper plates fly away and the tablecloth yearns to set sail. To anchor a cloth to the table, glue spring-type clothes pegs to the underside of the table with epoxy adhesive. You'll need about eight for an average table. Space them around the table, and tape them in place until the adhesive dries.

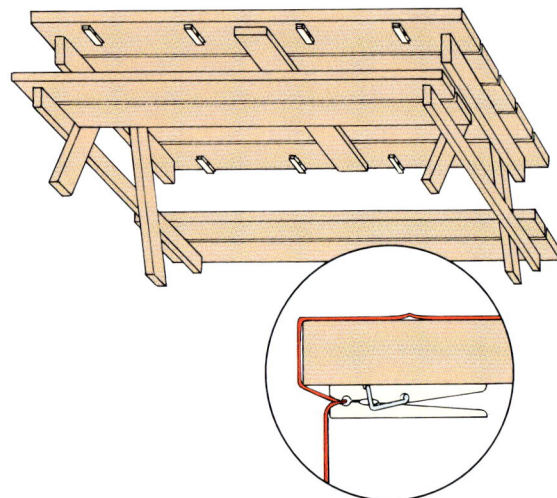

Lawn chair revival

Don't throw away a perfectly good lawn chair just because the fabric covering is torn or ruined. Replace the covering with cedar or some other durable timber. Cut 12 mm thick slats and fasten them to the frame with pop rivets. You'll have to drill holes in the slats, and possibly the chair, to accept the rivets. ▼

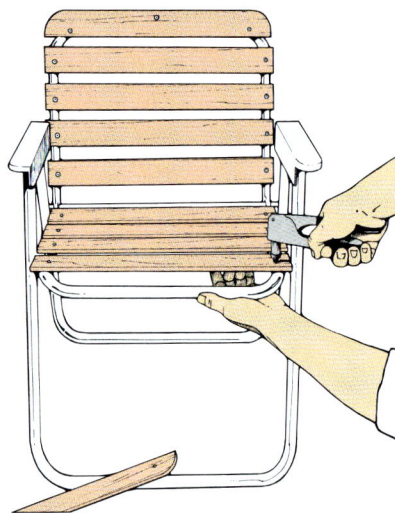

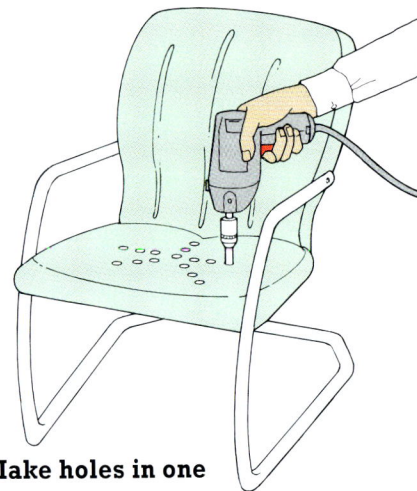

Make holes in one

The water that pools in the contoured seats of metal lawn chairs invites rust. A solution is to drill several drainage holes in the seat. Be sure to file the edges of the holes. Then paint the chair (and the edges of the holes) with rust-preventive paint. Drilling holes also works for plastic chairs—but instead of controlling rust, it just helps the plastic dry faster.

For the children

Bolt alert

Protruding bolt ends on play structures are dangerous. You should either cut off the protruding ends with a hacksaw (filing down any rough edges) or cover them with cap nuts.

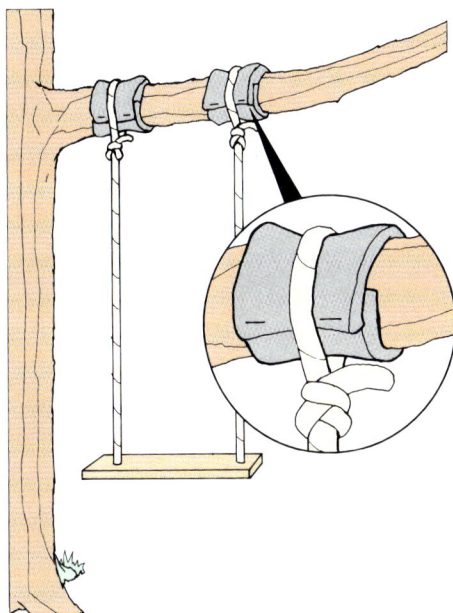

Branch saver ▲

A tree swing is fun for the children, but not so healthy for the tree branch. The sawing action of the rope cuts the cambium layer just under the bark, killing the branch. To prevent damage, make a protective sleeve out of tough rubber, such as an old car tyre or plastic material. Tack it to the tree with staples, and tie the rope around the sleeve.

Swing easy ▲

Chains on a child's swing can cut into small fingers. To make the chains softer to hold, thread lengths of foam insulation tube onto them, or slit lengths of garden hose and snap them into place.

Bird foiler

To keep birds from leaving droppings on a swing seat, attach a corner bracket near each end of the top rail of the play set. Run an old broom handle (or a long dowel) between the brackets and attach it to them, using a long nail in each end. Whenever a bird tries to land on the play set, the broom handle will rotate, sweeping away any possibility of the bird perching there. You should have no further problem with bird droppings. ▼

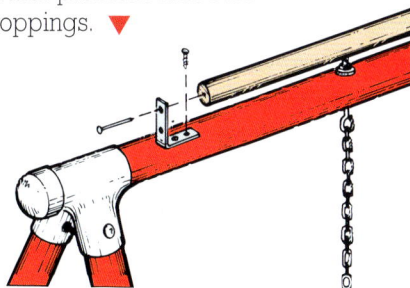

PLAY SET RULES

A play set, whether it's home-made or store-bought, can be a safety hazard. Lay a 25 cm layer of cushioning material under the play set: sand, pea gravel or an organic material such as shredded bark. Don't rely on grass. It will soon wear away, and dirt is as hard as bitumen. Clean or replenish the cushioning material as needed. Once the set is up, inspect it periodically for loose and broken parts, the damage caused by use and exposure to weather.

The safest play sets will have the features listed below.
▷ Handholds will be placed at strategic points and be easy for small hands to grasp.
▷ The slope of a slide will be no more than 30°, with a level section at the end to slow a child's exit speed.
▷ Side guards at the top of the slide will be fastened securely.
▷ Swings will be spaced 60 cm apart, with the seats being at least 80 cm from the frame.
▷ Any platform that is more than 80 cm in the air will be protected with a solid or slatted enclosure at least 100 cm high. The slats will be tightly spaced.
▷ Corners and edges will be rounded to prevent injuries.
▷ Hardware will be recessed or covered (see hint at top left).

GARDEN IMPROVEMENTS

For the birds

Slide-out feeder

If you want to attract birds to a hanging feeder near a second-storey window, you'll need to hang the feeder a metre or so out from the house and still be able to reach it easily. Mount a cord-operated curtain rod on a length of timber, and hang the feeder from one of the movable eyes. Then nail the timber to a beam under an eaves and add a supporting bracket. With a pull of the string, you'll be able to fill the feeder and slide it out so the birds can see it.

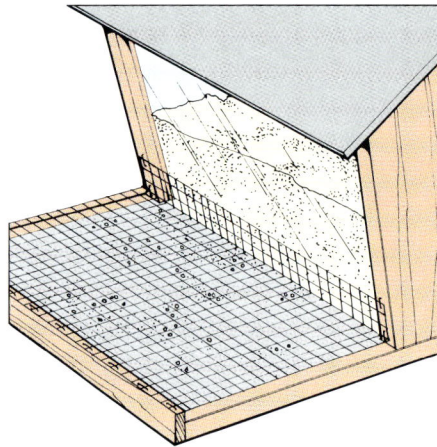

Keeping seed in its place ▲

When birds search through a feeder for the perfect morsel, a lot of rejected seed ends up on the ground. Add a lip to the edge of the feeder's tray, and stretch a piece of fine wire mesh over the tray with enough clearance for the seeds to spread out under the wire. Staple the wire to the lip and the frame of the feeder. The birds will be able to eat, but they won't be able to scratch vigorously among the seeds.

Letter boxes

Painting boxes

If you'd like to dress up your galvanised metal letter box with a coat of paint, it'll stick better if you first wash the exterior with some vinegar. (The mild acid removes much of the oiliness from the surface and gives it some 'tooth' to hold the paint.) To paint the box, apply a coat of a primer specially formulated for use with galvanised metal, and follow with a coat of paint (any kind).

Two-door opener

You can avoid stepping into the street to retrieve the mail from your outdoor letter box if you build one with a door at both ends. It'll let you avoid passing cars and trucks, as well as the inevitable roadside mud and puddles. ▼

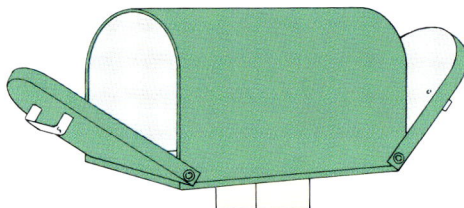

Clothes lines

Laundry basket hang-up

Here's a simple slide-in shelf that will support your laundry basket at waist height on a 100×100 mm post. Just cut a notch in a 400×300 mm piece of 19 or 21 mm plywood, fasten a slot made of 100×50 mm blocks to the post, and slide the shelf into the slot. To hold the basket in place, add a top bracket (locate the position of the bracket by measuring the depth of your basket). You'll have to tip the basket to fit it under the top bracket.

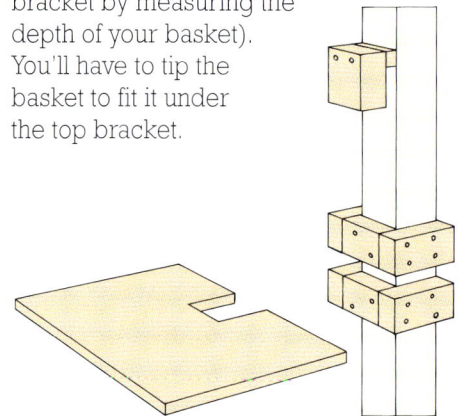

Clothes peg storage

If you want a sheltered home for your clothes pegs, build a covered box with a hinged lid out of 19 or 21 mm plywood. Drill holes in the bottom and ends for drainage, and attach the box to a post.

That certain glow

You'll never run into your clothes line at night if you sponge some luminous paint down the length of the wires. Once the paint dries, it'll glow in the dark.

SEASONAL JOBS

Firewood

Splitting wood

For strenuous bending and lifting activities, such as splitting wood, wear a wide leather weightlifter's belt. Its support reduces fatigue and helps to prevent lower back pain. You can find these belts in most sporting equipment shops.

This end up

You'll split a log more easily if you hit into its true top end. How can you tell which end should be up? Check the diameter at each end of the log. The smaller end is almost always the top.

Tyre holder ▲

Here's an easy way to hold logs for splitting. Stack a couple of old car tyres and set the logs (one at a time) in the opening. As a bonus, the tyres will keep the split halves from falling, and will also protect the axe blade if it falls short.

On the chopping block

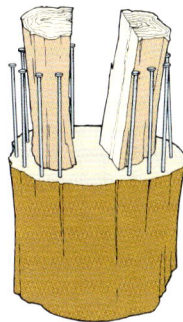

Prevent your chopped wood from falling to the ground each time it's split. Drive some 250 mm long nails around the edge of the chopping block, leaving an opening at the front and back so that your axe is clear. The nails act like a fence to catch the pieces and save you from a lot of bending over.

Handle saver

If you split a lot of wood, you've probably missed the mark enough times to damage the axe handle. A good way to prevent this is to tape a 150 mm piece of rubber hose to the underside of the handle, next to the head. This will triple the life of the handle and take the sting out of the misses.

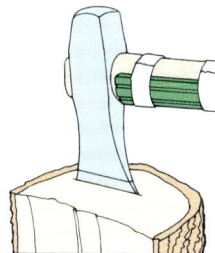

Beware of the log pile

Log piles are often a hazard, providing attractive homes for insects, spiders, snakes, rats and mice. If possible, keep the pile well away from the house and try to keep the stack only one log deep, so that there are fewer hiding places among the timber. Always keep a pair of stout gloves handy near the stack to protect, not only against bites and stings, but also against splinters. Do not store firewood inside, where termites might escape into the house structure.

Outdoor furniture

Only once a year

Outdoor furniture—tables, chairs and barbecues—blends into the background to such an extent that its proper maintenance is often overlooked. Set a weekend aside every autumn to check for worn finishes, rotting wood and rusting metal. A regular coat of paint, preservative or oil can lengthen the life of an expensive item by several years.

Snow and ice

Good brooming

If your driveway or footpath is covered with only light snow, try sweeping the powdery stuff away instead of lifting it off with a shovel. It will save wear and tear on your back. And if you're apt to encounter patches of ice, screw a scrap of angle iron to the top of the broom head; you'll be able to flip the broom over and scrape at the ice.

Friendly ice removal

The next time you clear an icy path, try using a garden fertiliser containing urea, instead of salt or a chemical de-icing compound. That way you won't ruin the soil or harm or kill nearby shrubs and trees. Another strategy is to try covering the ice with a layer of sand, sawdust or cat litter.

POOLS AND PONDS

Swimming pools

Not such hard work

Are you put off the prospect of installing a swimming pool by the thought of all the maintenance involved? Don't be. The water in a modern pool will remain healthy, clean and sparkling with a minimum of fuss. A few minutes attention each day is all that is required—an investment of time that amounts to no more than about one hour a week.

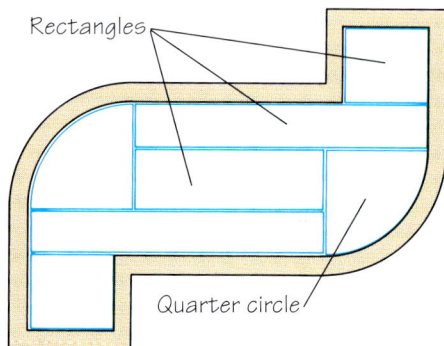

Rectangles

Quarter circle

How much water? ▲

If you have ever puzzled about how to work out the approximate capacity of your swimming pool in litres, so that you can add the correct quantities of chemicals, here's how to do it (using centimetres in all calculations). For rectangular pools, multiply length by width by average depth, and divide by 1000. For circular pools, multiply the diameter by the diameter by the average depth by 0.8, and then divide by 1000. For oval pools, multiply greatest width by greatest length by the average depth by 0.8, and then divide by 1000. Break odd-shaped pools down into a series of simple geometric shapes, calculate the volume of each, and add all together.

Pool repairs

Tell-tail stain

Suspect that there's a leak in your pool but can't pinpoint it? Try this method. Buy an ordinary washing blue bag and lower it into the water attached to a piece of string, near where you think the leak may be. Provided that the pool is undisturbed, the blueing will flow towards the leak. If you don't find the leak at your first try, move the bag to a series of other locations until you do.

Underwater repair

You don't have to empty your swimming pool to repair a small tear in the liner. Provided the damage is not more than about 1 cm long you can patch it underwater, using a kit available from pool suppliers. Make sure the sand backing under the liner has not been disturbed, and cut a circular patch from the material supplied. Apply adhesive to the back of the patch only and press it over the hole. Weight the patch with a bag full of sand until the adhesive has set. ▼

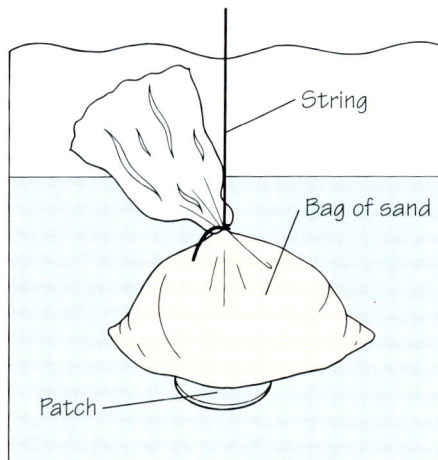

String

Bag of sand

Patch

Pool afloat

Don't be tempted to drain your concrete pool for repainting, without first getting some expert advice. An empty pool can float on top of water in the ground beneath it, pushing up as much as a metre in extreme cases. To prevent this, pressure under the pool has to be relieved as the water inside is removed. This is best done by an experienced operator.

Swimming pool safety

Do your duty

Never become complacent about pool safety. You may not have children, and find it difficult to see why you should have to pay for expensive fencing. But try explaining that to the parents next door after a drowning tragedy. Always obey local council regulations on pool fencing, and if there are none, make sure the pool is completely enclosed by a fence 1.2 m high, free of hand and foot holds. Gates must be self-closing and self-latching, and the release catch must be out of reach of young children. Over 90 per cent of backyard drownings involve children under five years of age.

Handle with care

Swimming pool chemicals, particularly those that contain chlorine, should always be treated as dangerous. If mixed with a number of common household products—such as soaps and detergents, vinegar and other acids, paints and solvents, oils and greases—they can become highly flammable and even explode. Keep chemicals separate and away from water and fire; wear gloves and avoid contact with skin and clothing.

Garden ponds

Basic guidelines

It can be hard to decide on the position, size and shape of a garden pond. In the first place, use a length of rope to mark out the general shape you have in mind, and then walk around it to assess its impact on the rest of the garden. Leave the rope down for a few days while you think about it. Here are some general guidelines to consider when planning a new garden pond.

▷ Choose a sunny, open site, within easy reach of a hose.

▷ If you fill an existing depression in the garden it will create the most natural-looking informal pond.

▷ Informal ponds look best in large gardens because you need an extensive sheet of water for the best effect.

▷ Formal, geometrically-shaped ponds look best in small gardens.

▷ Place your pool so that its longest axis runs away from the spot where it is most likely to be viewed. Seen across its smallest axis the pond will tend to look insignificant.

▷ Try not to place ponds under trees, where roots may cause damage, or falling leaves will be a nuisance. ▼

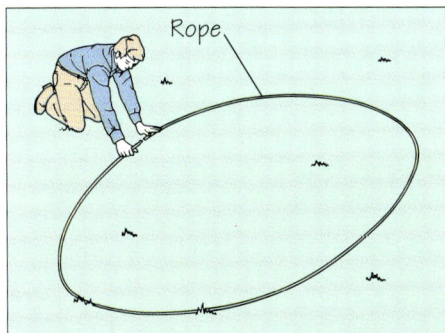

Rope

Small is beautiful ▲

A garden pond doesn't have to be an elaborate affair. In a small courtyard particularly, a suitable container, such as an old stone trough, will make an attractive miniature water garden. Sit the container on a firm rock base, which can be partly filled with earth and turned into a simple rockery.

Long-lasting liners

The water in a garden pond is usually contained in a concrete, fibreglass or vinyl liner. Concrete will last longest, provided it is properly constructed. Poorly-built concrete ponds will soon crack. Fibreglass, firmly supported, is also good for many years. Good quality vinyl liners last for 10 years or more, depending on how they are treated and how much sunlight they receive.

Concrete preparations

New concrete is toxic to fish, since it makes the water extremely alkaline. Before stocking a new concrete pond, either coat it with a special paint intended for this situation, or keep the pond full of water for six months and then empty and rinse it before you start to introduce plants and fish.

The silver lining

If you intend keeping fish in your vinyl-lined garden pond, make sure that you buy the appropriate liner. The liners that are usually used for swimming pools are toxic to fish, so most manufacturers produce at least one type specially for use in garden ponds.

Keep it simple

You can have pond liners cut to shape, but it's probably cheaper and easier to buy a standard length and cut it yourself. Since lengths of liner are generally either square or rectangular, avoid complex shapes for your pond that may lead to wastage and unnecessary expense. Calculate the amount you need carefully before putting in your order. To assess the extra length and width that will be needed to follow the curves of the hole you have excavated, use a length of builder's plastic as a guide. ▼

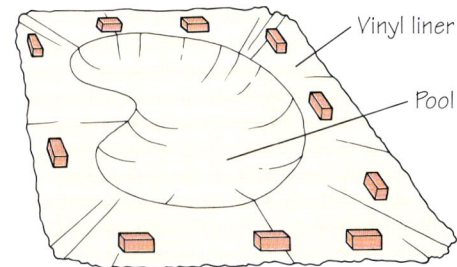

Vinyl liner

Pool

Not fit for fishes

Fish do not like the chlorine present in most town tapwater. When filling, or topping-up a pond, let the water stand for a week or so before using it. As an alternative, use one of the chemical water treatment additives available from aquarium suppliers and many pet shops, and follow the manufacturer's instructions carefully.

CAR AND GARAGE

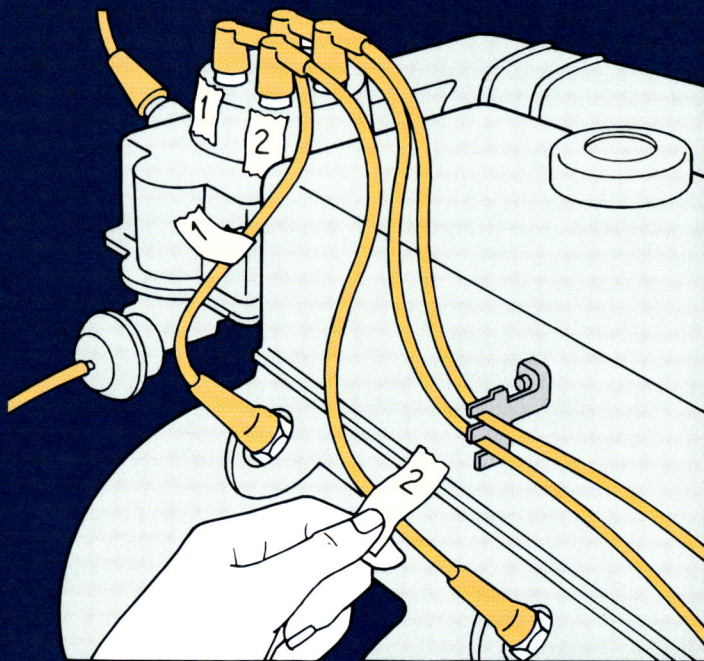

TOOLS AND EQUIPMENT

Handling tools

Rubbery spanner

If you start threading a spark plug, bolt or nut in a spot that's hard to reach, it's likely you'll scrape your knuckles. To keep your skin intact, get things going with a short length of rubber fuel line, car vacuum hose or garden hose. The hose should fit snugly over the bolt, nut or spark plug insulator. Slip the hose into the tight area, and twist it to start threading on the part. If you need a grip for twisting, insert the blade of a short screwdriver into the open end of the hose and turn the driver's handle. Finish the job with a universal socket and extension on a ratchet handle.

To the point

When removing a stubborn six-sided nut or bolt, don't be tempted to use the wrong tool, such as pliers or a spanner that 'almost fits'. It can round off the points on the nut without removing it—and then you'll have to take a hacksaw to it (p. 96). Instead, spray a penetrating oil on the nut and let it soak for a while. Then pick a spanner that fits tightly; a six-point spanner is best, otherwise a universal ring-type spanner may be used as an alternative if the right size is unavailable. Shifting spanners are best used only on four-sided nuts and bolts.

Painful extremes

Spanners and other tools carelessly stored can either stick to your fingers in freezing weather, or burn you on a hot summer's day. Always store hand tools where they will not be exposed to any extremes of temperature.

Garage equipment

Seat relief

It's tiring to squat or kneel while you work on the brakes or suspension. Give your knees a rest by making a combination seat and tool caddy. Bolt together two pairs of 75 × 25 mm wooden strips with one side of a sturdy plastic crate or wooden box sandwiched between them. At each corner, attach casters to the bottom strips. As long as you aren't on the heavy side, you can sit on the crate, roll into position and remove and store tools and parts inside the crate all at once.

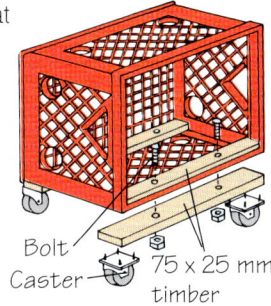

Bolt
Caster
75 × 25 mm timber

Cheap creep

A mechanic's creeper is ideal for any jobs that need to be done under the car, but they can be expensive to buy. A cheaper alternative is a scrap of smooth vinyl flooring. Lay this under the car and you'll find that you can easily slip and slide into the right working position.

SAFETY FIRST

FIRE CONTROL

It's a good idea to keep a fire extinguisher rated for oil, petrol and electrical fires around the garage and in your car. Store a compact extinguisher in your glove compartment, or mount it within easy reach of the driver's seat. Under the seat is one ideal spot. Oil-rated fire extinguishers and their mounting brackets are available from car accessory shops.

A fire extinguisher, however, will not help much if it's very windy. You can try to smother a small fire with a heavy tarpaulin or blanket. But if the fire is not controllable don't risk injury; simply get away from it immediately and call the fire brigade. The fire can travel to the fuel tank and may cause an explosion.

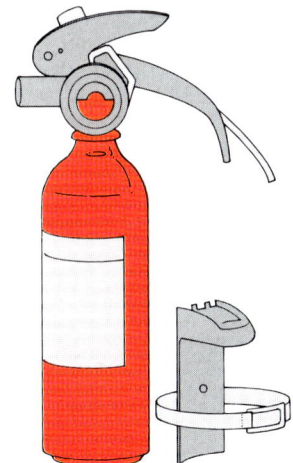

CHANGING THE ENGINE OIL AND OIL FILTER

Engine oil

Leak lookout

Leaking fluids are often the first sign of car trouble. Check under your car at least once a week for leaks. To identify them, spread a length of white paper under the car, secure the corners with heavy weights, and leave it overnight. The colour and location of the leak will identify it. Clear water near the front seats is usually harmless condensation from an air conditioner. Green or yellowish liquid with a sweet smell under the engine or radiator is anti-freeze. Red or brown fluid with a strong odour under the engine is power steering fluid; under the transmission, it's transmission fluid. Brown or black slippery liquid under the engine is motor oil. An oily fluid near the wheels or the rear of the engine could be brake fluid. A colourless or nearly colourless watery liquid under the engine compartment could be leakage from the washer reservoir—the location varies from car to car. Repair leaks, and check the appropriate fluid reservoirs for low levels.

Squint saver

Your oil dipstick can be easier to read. Just drill small holes through the dipstick (provided it's not made of spring steel) at the 'Full' and 'Add' marks. Make sure you clean off any metal filings afterwards.

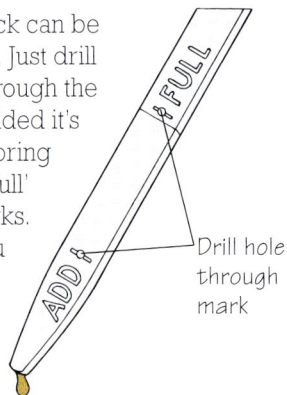

FULL

ADD

Drill hole through mark

Safety first ▶

If you have to work under your car, jack it up and lower the frame or axles onto steel axle stands (check your owner's manual for location of jacking points). Never work under a car supported only by a jack, no matter how sturdy it seems. Be sure to set the road brake, put the transmission into *Park*—or first gear for a manual transmission—and chock the wheels that remain on the ground. Chocks are available at car accessory stores. Always wear safety goggles when working under a car.

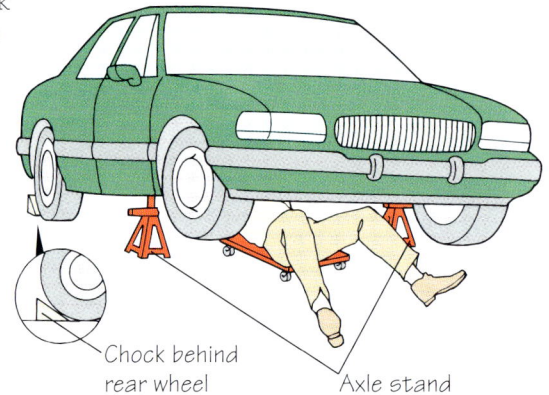

Chock behind rear wheel

Axle stand

Keep it pure oil

Be sure to remove the plastic lock ring that sometimes clings to the neck of an oil container after you remove its cap. If the ring falls into the engine while you're pouring in oil, it can cause big problems. If you use a funnel, make sure you first wipe off any debris.

Lock ring

When to change

Oil change periods vary enormously between the different makes and models of cars. Always be guided by the advice given in your owner's manual. Detergents in oil make it turn black, so colour is no indication of an oil's life. Arduous operating conditions—many short trips or dusty roads—usually require more frequent oil changes.

Rubbish to the rescue

If you don't have a sump oil drainer, use a clean plastic container instead, and guide the oil into it with a funnel. Check the engine oil capacity first to ensure that your container is large enough.

Diversionary tactics

If the sump plug on your engine is angled in such a way that oil comes out awkwardly, try this: make a funnel by cutting the bottom from a plastic milk or bleach bottle. After you've loosened the plug, position the funnel so that the oil will run into your container. Once the funnel is in place, remove the plug. ▼

Engine

Bottle

Chassis rail

DISPOSING OF CAR WASTES

The rules for disposing of used automotive materials vary from one location to another, depending on the local laws. Always check product labels for disposal suggestions and call your local council or state environmental protection agency for their disposal recommendations.

Treat all vehicle fluids—including antifreeze, coolant, windscreen wiper fluid, brake and clutch fluid, transmission fluid, power steering fluid, battery acid, car paint, oil, diesel and petrol—as hazardous wastes. Before buying engine oil check to see whether or not the seller will accept and correctly dispose of the used oil if you return it. The same rules apply to old car batteries.

If you save money by buying cheap batteries, engine oil and other car fluids from department stores without disposal facilities, then you will have to find your own proper method of getting rid of them.

Never simply tip car wastes down the drain, where they will end up polluting waterways and beaches. Often your local tip will have an area set aside for some car wastes, such as old tyres, batteries and discarded oil. Otherwise you may have to make a trip to the nearest hazardous waste dump—ring your council for advice.

In some areas there are occasional hazardous waste collection days, although you will have to arrange for storage in the meantime.

Oil filters

Slippery business

Can't get a grip on a slippery oil filter? Fold a strip of sandpaper in half lengthwise with the grit side out. Place the sandpaper between the filter and the special oil filter wrench. With the sandpaper grit gripping the wrench and the filter, the wrench will no longer slip.

Homely solution

If you have a small car with a cramped engine compartment and don't have a specialised filter wrench on hand, try one of those rubber sheet jar openers to remove the oil filter. You probably have an opener of this type in the kitchen.

Piercing problem

Sometimes an old oil filter can't be budged with any wrench. If this happens to you, use a hammer to drive a large screwdriver right through the filter, about 50 mm from the engine block. Then turn the filter anticlockwise, using the screwdriver handle as a lever. Once it has been unstuck, remove the screwdriver and spin the filter off. To catch the oil that will leak out, keep a tray handy under the filter.

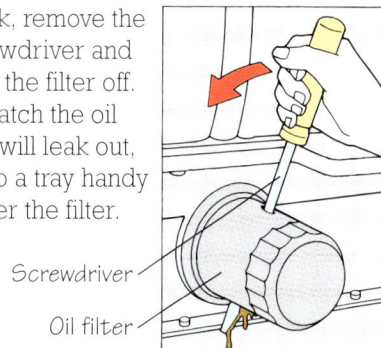

Screwdriver

Oil filter

Keep it clean

Here's one way to eliminate oil spills and mess when you're removing the oil filter: after loosening the filter, place a plastic bag around it. Once you've removed the filter, you can simply let it drop into the bag without any oily mess coming into contact with your hands.

Fill 'er up!

When you first start the engine after changing the oil, it takes a few seconds for the oil pump to move the new lubricant through the engine. If the filter screws on vertically or at an angle, you can speed up the oil flow by filling the new filter with fresh oil before you screw it into place. Don't try this on a horizontally mounted filter or one mounted upside down; the oil will spill out.

TUNE-UP

Spark plugs

Heads up!

While working on the engine you can accidentally bang your head against the latch under your car's bonnet. To avoid this painful situation (and a large lump), cushion the blow by cutting a slot in an old tennis ball and slipping the ball over the latch to cover it.

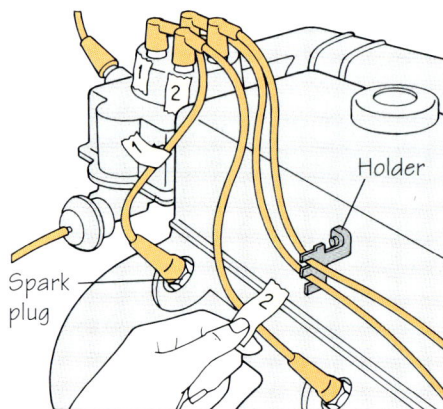

Every spark has its place ▲

You should always reconnect a spark plug wire to the correct spark plug, or the engine will misfire. To avoid a mix-up, remove one wire and plug at a time and replace them before going on to the next one. If you need to remove all the plugs at once, read your owner's manual to determine the spark plug's numbering order, and then wrap masking tape flags around each plug lead with the correct number clearly marked on each. When refitting the leads, treat them gently, always follow the same route, and place them in the same clips and holders that they were in originally. It often helps to make a simple sketch of the wiring layout before starting work.

Flip-flop stop ▶

When using a plug socket spanner fitted with a universal joint to install a spark plug, the joint may be too floppy to reach its target. Try supporting it with a few turns of sturdy tape, such as duct tape or automotive electrical tape. The joint will still remain flexible enough to twist and turn.

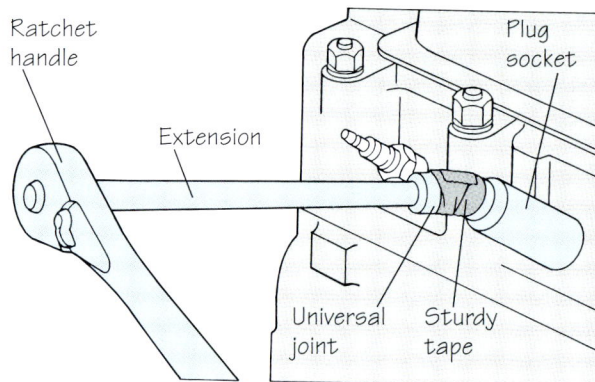

Gap facts

Spark plugs are not always gapped correctly as they come out of the box or when they are removed from the engine. Before installing a plug, check the gap against the specifications for your car, using a feeler gauge. To adjust the gap, bend the side electrode on the plug with the gapping tool on the gauge, or tap the plug lightly on a hard flat surface. Never bend the electrode with pliers; you could damage it. ▼

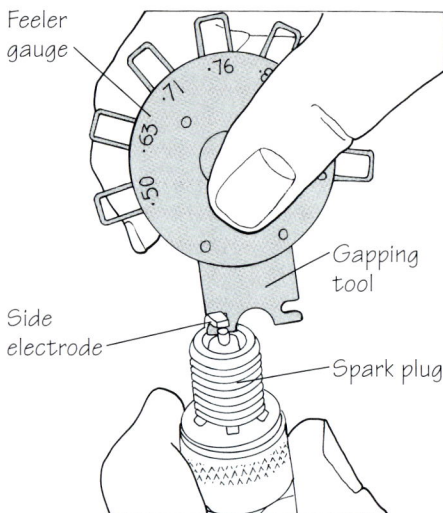

Head ache

A cylinder head can be damaged if you strip its threads while installing or removing a spark plug. To prevent damage to the head, let the engine cool down before removing a plug. Before installing a new plug, check that the threads are clean and dry. It will make removal easier later on. To avoid cross-threading (when the plug goes in crookedly), turn the plug by hand until you feel it seat; then tighten it to the car maker's specifications.

Other tune-up hints

Timing is everything

If your car has an engine with a timing mark, you'll be able to see the mark better if you highlight it with white chalk or typist's correction fluid. Or put a piece of light-coloured tape on each side of the correct timing mark, spacing the pieces about 2 or 3 mm apart. When the engine is running, the dark line between the pieces of tape will be even easier to see than a paint or chalk mark.

Filter fixes

A clogged air filter can cause an engine to run poorly or stall. To see if the filter is clogged, remove it and shine a light or flashlight through it. For a rectangular filter, place the light against one side. If the light barely shows through, the filter is dirty. Replace it. If you don't have a new filter on hand, reuse the old filter by banging it sharply on the ground, thus removing some of the dirt. Put in a new filter as soon as possible.

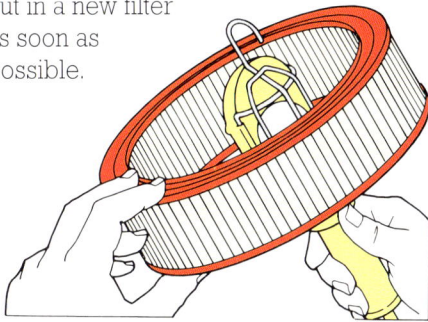

Plugged on purpose

For some tune-up procedures, you have to remove and plug a vacuum hose. (Clamping the hose won't give complete blockage.) Instead of using tape to plug the end, which doesn't always provide an airtight seal, try a golf tee. The tee's tapered shape makes a perfect plug. ▼

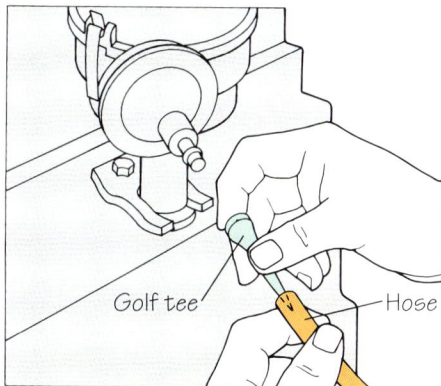

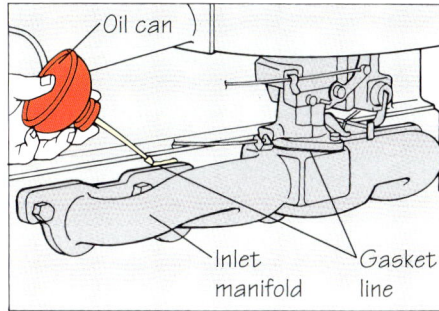

Golf tee   Hose

Oil can

Inlet manifold   Gasket line

Leaky manifold ▲

Does your car idle roughly without a sign of the standard problems? There could be a leak in the inlet manifold. Try squirting some motor oil along the gasket lines. If there is a leak, the oil will momentarily plug the hole and the idle speed will change. When the oil is sucked through the leak, the rough idle will resume. Try tightening the retaining nuts or bolts to the manufacturer's specifications, using a torque wrench. If that doesn't work, replace the gasket.

PCV leak

If you don't find the reason for a stumbling engine and leaking noises after checking all the vacuum lines, try the PCV (positive crankcase ventilation) line. There may be a crack close to the bottom of the line, where it's exposed to high temperatures.

Wake-up call

Has the starter in an older car given up? You may be able to knock some sense into it if the solenoid clicks but the starter won't turn over. This can be a sign that a worn brush is wedged sideways. A sharp blow on the starter housing with a wooden or rubber mallet may dislodge it. But have the starter repaired as soon as possible.

Fuel injection

Cold start

Traded in your carburettor-equipped car for a new one with electronic fuel injection? Just remember not to floor or pump the accelerator pedal before turning the key to start a cold engine, as you might once have done with your old car.

Hot tempered

Trying to restart a hot fuel-injection engine on a hot day can leave you hotter than the motor. If the engine will crank but not start, you probably have a vapour lock. Here's the solution: turn the ignition key on and off for about three seconds without cranking the engine. After several on-and-off cycles, try starting the engine without pressing the accelerator pedal; if that fails, press the pedal down about 25 mm.

Leaky injector

On an engine with multi-port fuel injection (one injector for each cylinder), air leaks can occur around the O-rings on the fuel injectors. If you can reach them with your fingers try to rock each injector body side to side, then fore and aft. Any movement will be very slight, but if there is a change in idle speed, the O-ring seal is leaking. You can obtain replacement O-rings from a car accessories shop. Take care not to touch the spark plug leads.

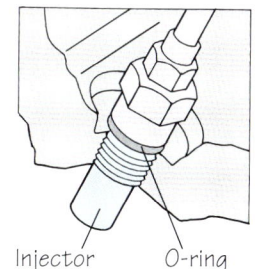

Injector   O-ring

COOLING AND EXHAUST SYSTEMS

Coolant and radiator

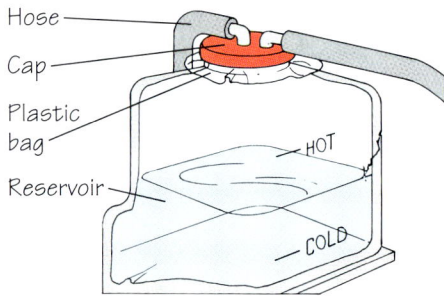

Hose
Cap
Plastic bag
Reservoir
HOT
COLD

It's in the bag ▲

If the motor is not installed at its base, you can temporarily repair a leaking plastic coolant reservoir (or windscreen washer reservoir). Place a clean sturdy plastic freezer bag inside the tank. Fill the tank to the proper level; then replace the cap and trim off any excess bag, if necessary. Have the reservoir re-placed or repaired as soon as possible.

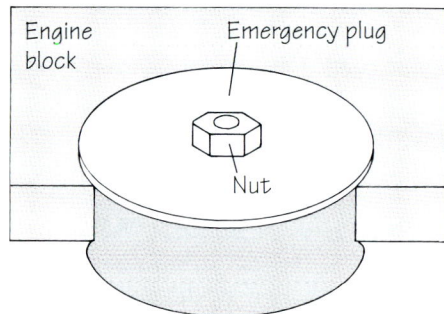

Engine block
Emergency plug
Nut

Plug it! ▲

Metal welch plugs can loosen or cor-rode and leak. If the leak is severe you may be able to buy an emergency replacement made from rubber. To fit it, drain and save the engine coolant, hit the damaged plug with a punch and prise it out. Fit the rubber plug and have it replaced as soon as possible.

A pinch in time

You may be able to make a temporary quick-and-dirty fix if a radiator tube springs a leak. Wait until the radiator and coolant cool down, or put on a pair of heavy gloves. Then use pliers to bend away the fins near the damaged tube and to pinch the leaking tube closed on both sides of the leak. This will cause more damage than the original leak, but it could keep the car going long enough to get you as far as a car mechanic. ▼

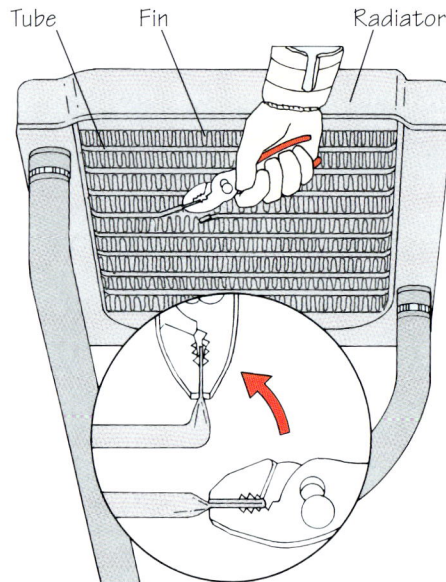

Tube   Fin   Radiator

Sweet poison alert!

Antifreeze is very poisonous, but its sweet taste can be alluring to small children and household pets. Always keep it in a securely closed container, well out of the reach of tiny fingers. Clean up or hose away any spills—no matter how small they are. Drained antifreeze/coolant mixes should be gathered in a suitable container and disposed of properly (p. 295).

Hoses

A hose in time

A burst coolant hose usually means a stranded car. To avoid breakdowns on the road, many manufacturers recom-mend that you replace all the coolant hoses, such as the radiator, heater and bypass hoses, every four years or 60 000 km, whichever comes first.

Hot tip

If you must repair a hose leak around hot engine parts, you can protect your hands from burns by wearing kitchen oven mitts. Of course you can't do much fine work with the mitts on. It's better to let the engine cool down if possible.

Hose taming

If a stiff radiator hose is difficult to install, soak it in hot water for a few minutes to make it more pliable.

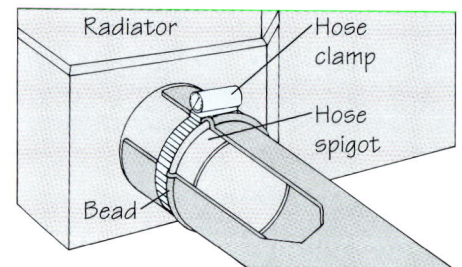

Radiator   Hose clamp
Hose spigot
Bead

Clamp cramps ▲

When installing a hose clamp, make sure it's positioned between the radiator and the bead on the hose spigot. The clamp should be snug against the bead. If the clamp is on the wrong side of the bead, the hose can leak. If the clamp is too far from the bead, pressure and sediment can build up in the void.

Belts

Chirp, chirp, chirp

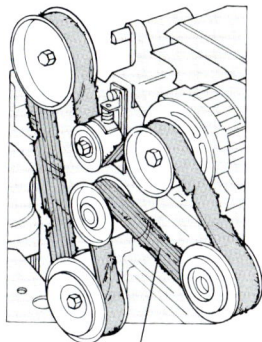
Worn serpentine belt

Does your car make a chirping noise? You don't have a nest of birds under the bonnet, but you do have a drive belt that needs some urgent attention. The chirping may be caused by a belt that is cracked, frayed, glazed (has a shiny look), loose or oil-soaked. Replace the faulty belt with a new one as soon as possible

Stifle that scream

If you hear squealing noises when you start your car engine, or when you turn the steering wheel to its limits, a drive belt might be slipping. Check for a loose belt when the engine is cold and switched off. First consult your owner's manual to see how much free-play is permitted, and then press your finger firmly against the middle of the belt. With many modern V- and serpentine belts correct tension is vitally important for the correct running of the engine. If your manual recommends that you have the tension adjusted by a garage then do so.

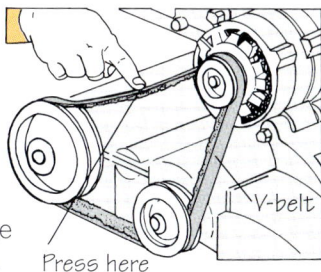
V-belt
Press here

EXHAUST DRAG

The sound of a dragging exhaust pipe or muffler calls for immediate action. Don't keep driving. The offending pipe or muffler could wedge itself under your car, or it could break free and end up in the path of another vehicle. If the muffler or exhaust pipe is dragging because of a broken hanger, you can temporarily rehang it until it is properly repaired. Wear thick gloves or use rags to protect your hands while touching the hot metal.

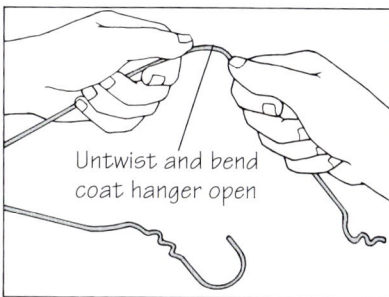
Glove   Rag   Broken hanger

1 Drive carefully up onto a kerb so that one side of the car is raised. Never work under any vehicle that's supported by a jack. Take a look at the situation. Remember that the exhaust will be hot.

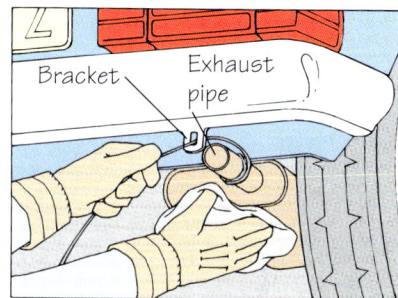
Untwist and bend coat hanger open

2 You can use heavy wire, such as a straightened coat hanger, to temporarily support the muffler or exhaust pipe. Look for one of these in your car, or at a nearby business or house.

Bracket   Exhaust pipe

3 Wrap the wire support around the end of the exhaust pipe. Slip the support through a bracket while lifting up the pipe; then twist the ends of the wire support together.

Alignment check

Misaligned pulleys are often responsible for belt noise, erratic operation of belt-driven accessories, belts jumping off pulleys and uneven belt wear. With the engine running, look at the pulleys from the side of the engine compartment. If you can see a pulley wobbling, it's misaligned and needs adjustment.

Don't trust your eyes

Here's another way to check for pulley alignment, as long as there is adequate space in front of the belts and at least two outer pulleys are in line. With the engine off and cold, place a straight-edge across the pulley faces. If it won't rest on the faces and there's more than a hairline gap, the pulleys are not aligned.

TRANSMISSION, STEERING AND SUSPENSION

The transmission

Fluid check

Good automatic-transmission fluid should be translucent and odourless. If it's cloudy or opaque and smells burnt, the fluid is in bad condition. To check the condition of the fluid, pull out the transmission dipstick and let a little fluid drip onto a paper towel. After a few minutes, good fluid will form an even red, pink or tan circle. Burnt fluid will form a bull's-eye that's darker in the centre than at the edges.

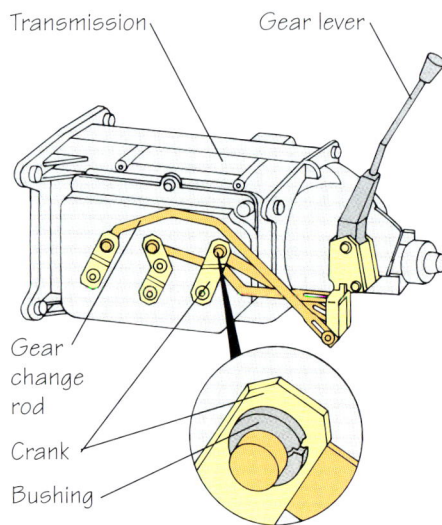

Transmission   Gear lever

Gear change rod

Crank

Bushing

Loose link ▲

A loose gear linkage can make a manual transmission difficult to change; it can even make the transmission jump out of gear. A practical do-it-yourselfer can test the linkage by getting under the car and wiggling the gear change rods back and forth. If there's play at the ends of the rods near the cranks, check for worn bushings and replace them.

Magic mushroom

When you remove the oil pan from an automatic transmission to replace the fluid and filter, don't be surprised if you find a loose mushroom-shaped plug in it. The plug keeps debris out of the transmission during factory assembly and is knocked into the transmission at the last minute. Just toss it out.

Steering and suspension

Stop and go

If the power assistance on your steering seems to stop and start as you turn the wheel around a corner, look for a loose or worn V-belt (p. 299) on the power steering pump. If you find one, adjust or replace it. A slipping belt cannot supply constant hydraulic assistance.

Shimmy solution

Steering-wheel shimmy that increases with speed is usually caused by an out-of-balance front wheel. But before the wheels are balanced, check the inside of the wheel rims. An accumulation of grease from a nearby fitting, dried mud and even snow and ice can throw the wheel out of balance. The shimmying may subside if you just clean the wheel.

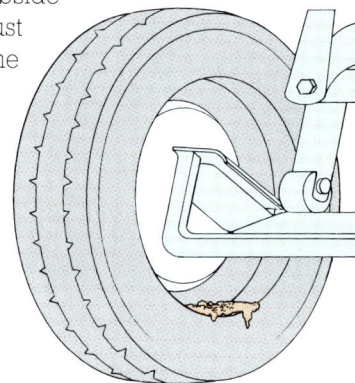

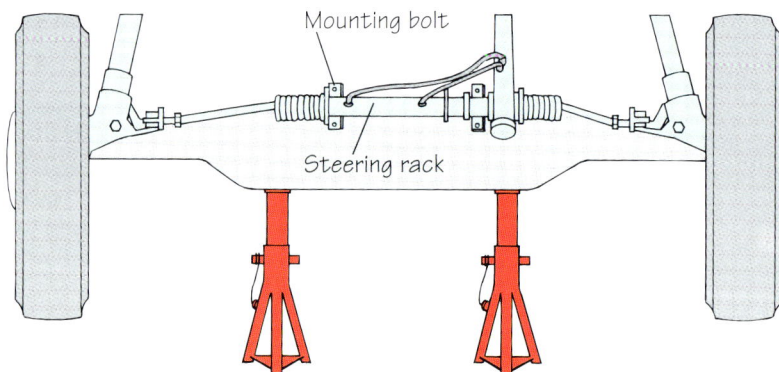

Mounting bolt

Steering rack

Lost control ▲

Erratic steering may indicate loose parts in the steering linkage. To check for excess play, wiggle the steering wheel while a helper watches the front tyres. There should be less than 10 mm of steering-wheel play before the tyres move. If there is too much play, check for loose steering-rack mounting bolts. Place the car on axle stands and chock the rear wheels (p. 294). Then move the front wheels while watching the steering rack; the rack shouldn't move. If it does, tighten the bolts.

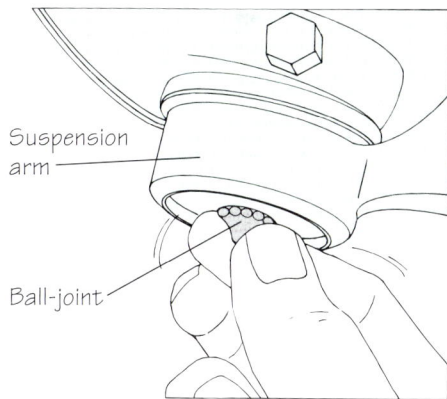

Suspension arm
Ball-joint

Ball-joint wear ▲

When you replace a ball-joint, check the suspension arm it's mounted in for excess wear. Insert the new ball-joint into its housing; then try to wiggle it from side to side. If it can wiggle, you'll have to replace the suspension arm too.

Fitting grabber

You can remove a broken grease fitting by tapping a rectangular concrete cut nail into the remaining portion of the fitting. Then twist the nail with pliers. It's painless, effective and can be performed right on the vehicle. ▼

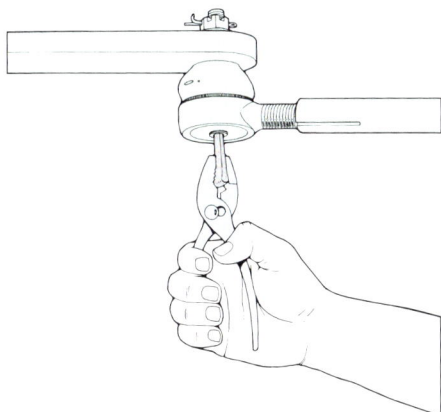

Strutting out

MacPherson struts, used at the front of many front-wheel-drive cars, can be bent if the car hits a kerb or a deep pothole. Check for a bent strut under the bonnet by loosening the nut on the strut rod in the centre of the strut tower. Rotate the strut rod exactly 360°. If the top of the tyre moves in and out, the strut is bent and should be replaced. ▼

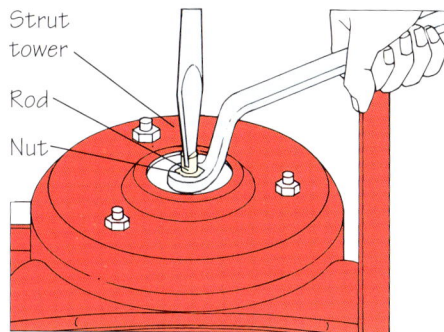

Strut tower
Rod
Nut

Nothing to boot about

A car owner needs to add one more check to the maintenance list when it comes to a front-wheel-drive vehicle with constant velocity (CV) joints. If you look under the front of your car, you'll see a pair of accordion-ribbed rubber boots by each front wheel. The CV joints are housed inside these boots and are packed with grease. A CV joint will last for years as long as the boot remains sealed. The boot itself may split from fatigue, especially in cold-weather areas. Rocks and potholes can also cause damage. Inspect the boots every three months. Look for grease outside the boot or sprayed onto the surrounding components. The sooner you have a damaged boot replaced, the better your chances are of keeping the mechanic's repair bill down.

Down in the valley

Here's another way to spot CV joint boot failure: the first place that a boot usually cracks is in the valley of the ribs' Vs. To get a clear view for inspection, have a helper turn the steering wheel all the way to one side and back.

Noisy warning

A clicking or clunking noise from the drive shaft as you turn or accelerate is a late warning that the CV joint is on the road to certain failure. The noise indicates a lack of grease in the boot and contamination from road grit. Get the car repaired as soon as possible.

Snappy service

The mounting nut on a shock absorber often rusts on tight. When it's time to replace the shock absorber, the nut may be difficult to remove. If you can snap off the mounting stud, you can remove the old shock absorber. Place a socket spanner with a long extension over the stud and nut. Then rock the stud back and forth until it breaks. The rubber bushings will protect the chassis. ▼

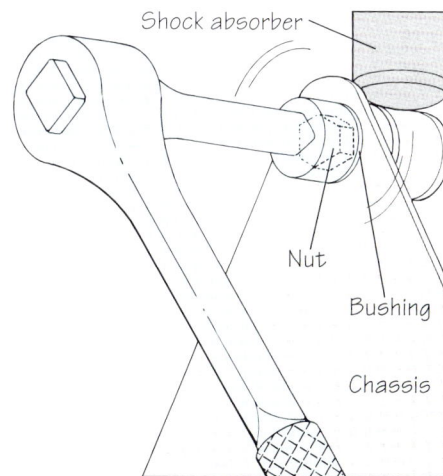

Shock absorber
Nut
Bushing
Chassis

TYRES

The valve

Leak detector

A slow leak may be caused by a faulty valve. To check the valve, remove the cap and wet the end of the valve with a solution of soapy water. If bubbles appear, the valve is leaking. Deflate the tyre fully; then unscrew and replace the valve core. If that doesn't work, have the whole valve replaced.

Cap extractor

Some valve caps are buried deep within fancy hub caps. You can remove them by using the cap from a felt-tip marker or highlighter. Push the marker cap over the valve cap until it sticks; then unscrew both caps.

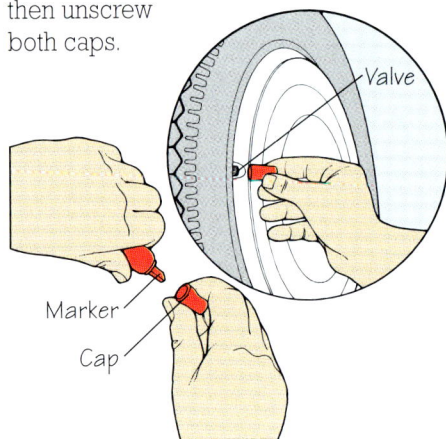

Valve

Marker

Cap

Cap this

Extender valve caps, from accessory stores, make pressure checking easier. They are longer, have a dot on the end, and contain a spring loaded valve through which air can be added without removing the cap. Another type has a line around it which disappears when air pressure drops.

The treads

Front

Full-size spare tyre

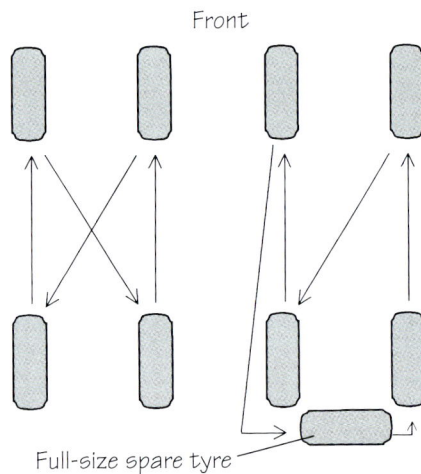

Rotation notation ▲

Some car manufacturers recommend rotating tyres from wheel to wheel periodically to equalise tread wear. However, other manufacturers do not recommend this practice, so check your owner's manual first. Rotate your tyres as shown above (including the spare if it is full-sized and not a space-saver) Rotation is often recommended every 10 000 km. A good time to do it is every other oil change. So you'll know the previous position of the tyres, use a dab of nail polish to make identification marks.

Don't just look

Improper tyre inflation and worn treads can cause an accident. Don't rely on visual inspection alone to check the inflation of a radial tyre. The radial sidewalls normally bulge where the tyre meets the road, making it difficult to determine when they're bulging too much. Use an accurate pressure gauge at least once a month.

Depth perception

When tyre tread depth wears down to 1.5 mm or less, replace the tyre. In this almost bald condition, the tread can no longer channel away rainwater and skids can result. Try one of the following ways to measure tread depth. Use a tread-depth gauge sold in car accessory shops, or insert a 10 cent coin, head down, into the tread. If you can see the top of the Queen's hair, the tread's too low. Or look for the wear bars cast into the tyres; when the tread's low, they are revealed as gaps in the tread.

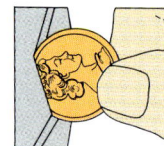

Reading treads

The wear patterns on your car's tyres show a lot about the car's suspension, how well you maintain the tyres and your driving habits. ▼

A worn centre points to an over-inflated tyre.

Wear along both edges tells you that the tyre was underinflated.

Feathered tread edges indicate incorrect wheel alignment or too-hard driving.

A single worn spot shows that you've skidded with the car's brakes locked.

A scalloped, or cupped, wear pattern means that the wheel is unbalanced, suspension or steering parts are worn, or the wheel bearings are faulty.

CHANGING A TYRE

Tyre changing is a basic skill every driver should have—not only in case of a flat, but in order to rotate the wheels periodically (see facing page). The best time to practise tyre changing is during free time in your garage or driveway, not alongside an isolated road in the rain.

Make sure you keep a spare tyre, jack, jack handle or screwdriver, wheel brace, rubber mallet, wheel chocks and tyre pressure gauge in the boot. Before using a spare tyre, check its air pressure. If it's low, do not use it; have the car towed.

Park on firm level ground and turn off the engine. Apply the hand brake, and put the transmission into park (or a manual transmission into reverse). Make sure everyone is out of the car before you start changing the tyre. If the ground is soft, put a stout piece of timber under the jack to keep it from sinking into the ground. If necessary, place a reflective triangle between you and oncoming traffic. The triangle should be at least 50 paces away in a built-up area, and 150 or more in a derestricted zone. After changing the tyre, don't forget to remove the chocks and return your tools and equipment to the boot.

If your spare tyre is a 'temporary' type or space-saver, observe the precautions set out in your owner's manual, which are generally to drive no faster than 80 km/h and no farther than about 80 to 100 km.

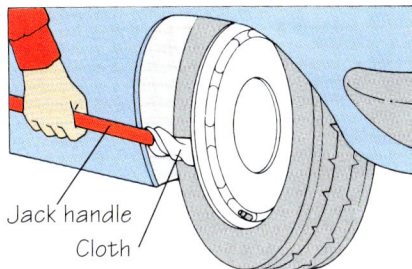

Jack handle
Cloth

1 Remove the hub cap with the jack handle or a screwdriver wrapped in a cloth. Some hub caps have special locks. Check your owner's manual if the hub cap can't be prised off.

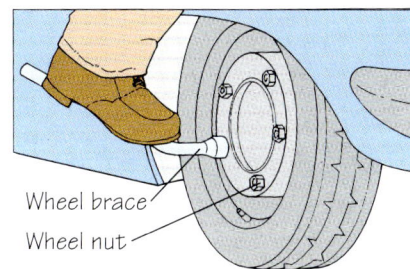

Wheel brace
Wheel nut

2 Loosen the nuts two or three turns. If one won't budge, set the brace horizontally and push down on its handle with your foot. Most nuts are loosened in an anticlockwise direction. With an old car, check your owner's manual first.

3 Chock the wheels and then raise the car until the tyre is just off the ground. Lower it a few millimetres and just loosen the wheel nuts. Finish jacking up the car until the tyre is about 100 mm off the ground. Remove the jack handle.

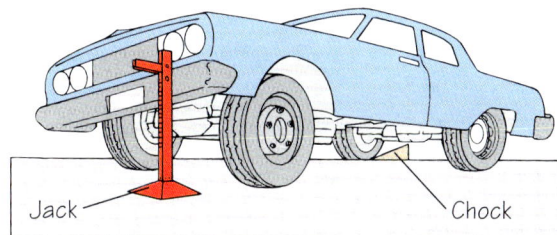

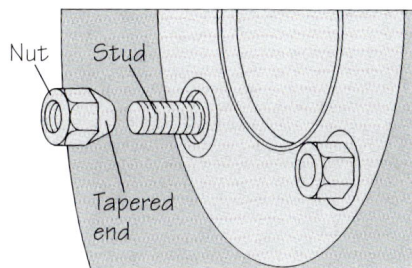

Jack
Chock

Nut Stud
Tapered end

4 Remove the wheel nuts, and pull off the tyre. Mount the spare tyre on the studs. Press against the wheel, and thread on the nuts by hand, starting at the bottom. The tapered part of the wheel nuts should face the wheel.

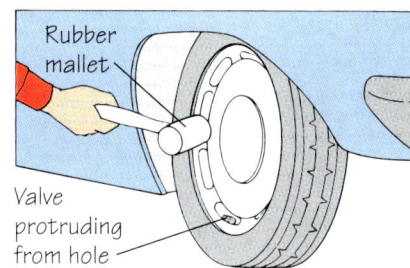

Rubber mallet
Valve protruding from hole

5 Lower the car until the wheel is taking a fair amount of the car's weight and then tighten the wheel nuts in a crisscross pattern (see p. 304). Lower the car completely and refit the hub cap so that the tyre valve fits through its access hole.

WHEELS AND BRAKES

Getting wheels on or off

Four-nut pattern

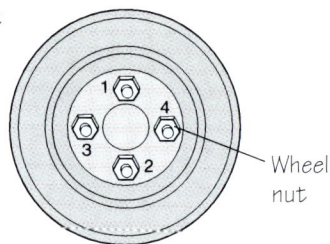

Five-nut pattern

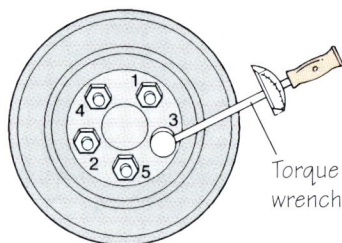

Wheel nut

Torque wrench

Nut cracker ▲

Always tighten the wheel nuts in a criss-cross pattern—not in a circle. Overly tight wheel nuts can crack the wheel or warp disc brake rotors. Some cars require the wheel nuts to be tightened to a specific torque. Check the owner's manual, and if necessary buy an inexpensive torque wrench and follow the recommended tightening sequence. Usually the correct torque will be reached in three stages.

Not too tight

Most mechanics and tyre service centres tighten wheel nuts with an air-powered spanner, sometimes called a 'rattle gun'. Although it is quick and effective, it often tightens nuts so that they cannot be removed with your car's wheel brace. When your tyres are being rotated or changed, ask the service manager to check the wheel nuts' torque, or to fit the nuts by hand.

Brace spinner

Cross-type wheel braces work well, but can raise blisters on the palms of your hands if you are changing several tyres in quick succession. To spin the brace easily, and without damage to your hands, make a spinner from a 200 mm length of PVC pipe that is at least 40 mm in diameter. Cement a cap to one end. When you use the wheel brace, slide the pipe over the socket opposite the one you'll be using and spin away. ▼

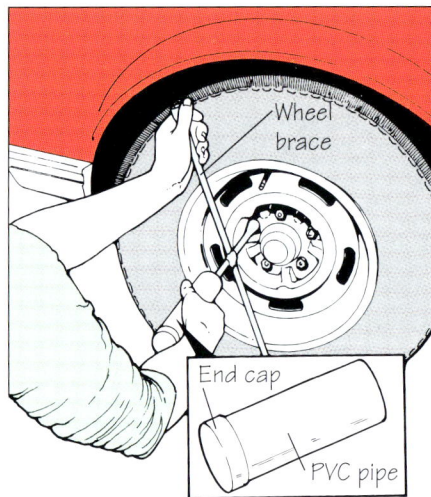

Wheel brace

End cap

PVC pipe

Bust it loose!

On older cars, a wheel may not come loose even though all the wheel nuts or bolts have been removed. It may be that it is being held in place by rust or alloy corrosion. To free it, mount the car on axle stands, refit the wheel nuts until they are finger tight, and then strike the wheel rim firmly with a large rubber mallet. If one wheel is stuck in this fashion, check the other three as soon as possible. To discover this problem by the roadside would be inconvenient.

Rust and rattles

Rust alert

If you mount new tyres on old wheel rims, make sure they are rust-free. Rust at the hub can weaken the wheel. If it's on the rim, rust can cause slow air leaks from tubeless tyres. Remove all rust with a wire brush; apply a rust-arresting fluid and when it dries, rust-resistant paint.

Easy off

The next time the wheels are off the car, wire brush the studs and wheel nuts and apply spray penetrating oil. To avoid getting spray on the brake surfaces and other components, aim it at the studs from the side. To be absolutely sure the studs won't corrode, coat them with a little oil before replacing the nuts.

Rattle traps

Hubcaps (wheel covers) can sometimes be the cause of annoying rattles. To isolate the culprit, remove one hubcap at a time and go for a short test drive. Then try these cures:
▷ Look for a pebble or loose wheel nut rattling around inside the hubcap, and remove (or refit) it.
▷ If a loose emblem is rattling, tighten it, glue it down with epoxy, or remove it.
▷ Many devices are used to hold hubcaps in place. Some have steel spring

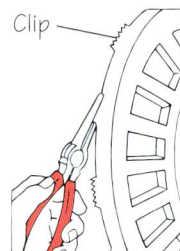

Clip

clips that become deformed and no longer hold the hubcap in place at all points. If necessary, carefully reshape the clip using pliers.

Brakes

Braking awareness

Quite a few cars on the road have brake problems. If you notice any of the following conditions seek professional advice—don't wait for an accident.

▷ Rhythmical vibrations felt through the pedal under light braking may indicate that brake rotors are warped or brake drums are out-of-round.

▷ Pulsations under hard braking or on wet slippery surfaces could be due to anti-lock braking (ABS). This may be normal, but have it checked if in doubt.

▷ Pay attention to the brake warning light on the instrument panel. If it stays lit after the engine is started, the brakes could be unsafe.

▷ Brakes that pull the car to one side, grab suddenly, drag or lock up prematurely are dangerous. The brakes should be checked for hydraulic fluid leaking onto the brakes, sticking disc brake callipers or wheel cylinder problems.

▷ An occasional squeak or squeal from disc brakes when braking lightly is OK, but any loud screeching, grinding or shuddering may mean worn-out brake pads or brake shoes.

▷ Noise can come from pad noisemakers. These emit a metallic sound when pads are near the end of their life.

▷ Changes in the feel of the brake pedal may also indicate trouble. A pedal that is high or difficult to press down could be a sign of a power brake problem. A too-soft pedal that goes nearly to the floor may be caused by poorly adjusted drum brakes or a serious brake failure. A spongy-feeling pedal often indicates air trapped in the brake system.

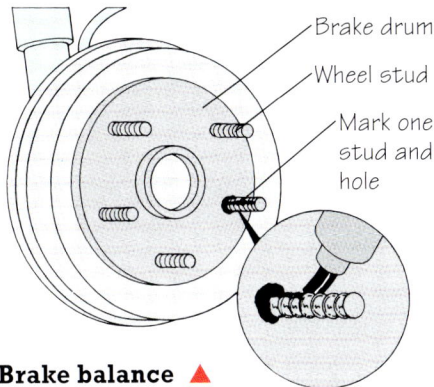

Brake balance ▲

If you remove a drum to do work on a drum brake, be sure that you reinstall it in its original position. As a guide, mark one stud and the hole it goes through with chalk, paint or a felt-tip marker before you remove the drum.

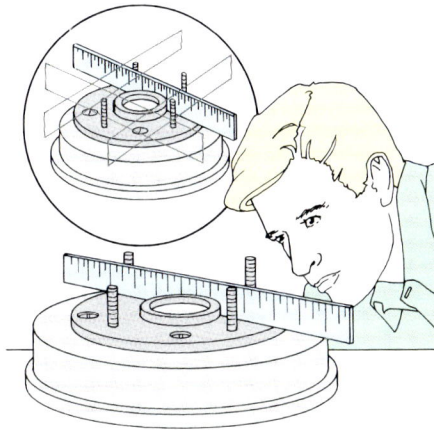

Wheel wobble ▲

Vibration can be caused by a warped brake drum. To check the drum, jack up the car and chock it securely. Spin the wheel to see if it wobbles in and out. If it does, remove the wheel and brake drum. Lay a straightedge across the drum's mounting surface in all directions. If you can see daylight under the straightedge, replace the drum.

Hang it up

When you remove a brake calliper to do work on a disc brake, don't let it hang by the rubber brake hose. Use a length of coat hanger or other heavy wire to hang the calliper from the suspension. This will ensure a secure resting place for the calliper where it won't get knocked about, which can cause damage to the hose. ▼

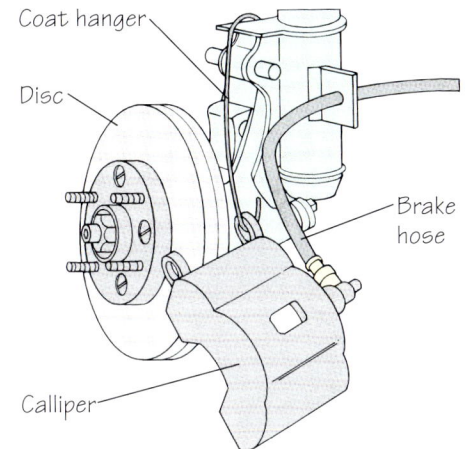

Taking up the slack

The adjustment for most handbrake cables is beneath the lever itself. Stretched cables should generally be replaced, although adjusters can sometimes be bought at accessory shops. Check with your registration authority on the legality of adjusters before fitting one; they may be illegal in your area. ▼

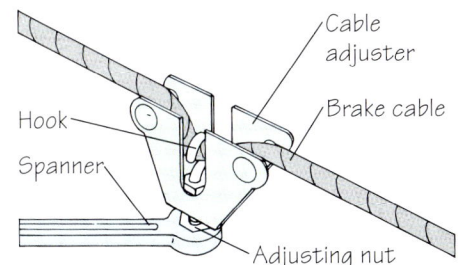

ELECTRICAL SYSTEM

The battery

Shocking caution

When disconnecting battery cables, always start with the negative cable. If you start with the positive cable (on the post marked POS or +) and your spanner accidentally touches another metal part, the battery will be short-circuited, sparks will fly and you may receive a shock. In addition, the spanner may weld itself to the metal part. ▼

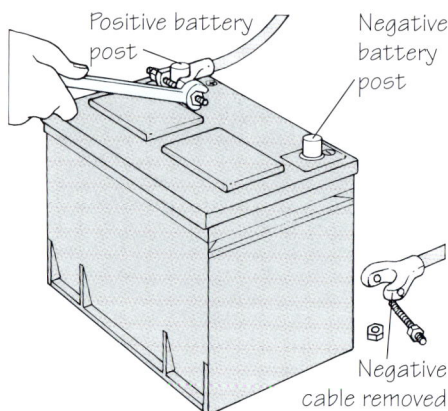

Positive battery post

Negative battery post

Negative cable removed

Charger checks

A totally flat battery, one that won't even raise a glimmer from the lights, may have to be sent to an auto electrician before it will accept a charge. Before connecting a charger always check the owner's manual. With some car computers the battery must be disconnected before a charger is attached.

A swipe in time

Dirt and grit on a battery can form a path for a slow electrical drain, especially in damp weather. Whenever you check the oil, clean off the top and sides of the battery with a damp cloth.

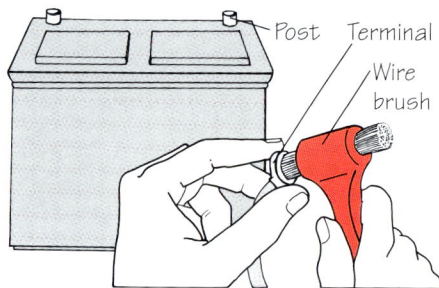

Post   Terminal

Wire brush

Terminal care ▲

Boiling water poured gently over corroded battery terminals will remove corrosion. Then thoroughly rinse all areas of the car touched by the hot water and corrosion mixture. Wipe the terminals clean when the leads are disconnected, or use a wire brush if necessary. Special battery terminal tools are cheap and effective. Apply a thin smear of petroleum jelly to slow the onset of fresh corrosion.

Secret vents

A maintenance-free battery has an extra electrolyte inside, so it may take years of water evaporation to affect the battery's output. When that time comes, however, a flat sealed-top battery will have to be replaced. But if your model has disguised vent caps, you may be able to extend the battery's life. Try prising the vent caps off carefully with an old screwdriver, without breaking or cracking them. If you can accomplish this feat, you can replenish the water in the battery.

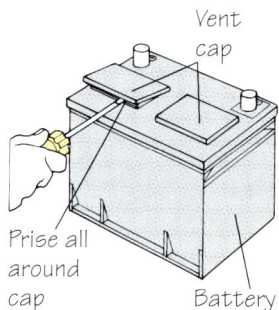

Vent cap

Prise all around cap

Battery

Too tall, too small

Battery dimensions and specifications may vary dramatically. Before replacing a battery you will need to know its capacity (look at the 'Specifications' page in your owner's manual), the type of terminals to match the leads on your car and the battery's dimensions. It is also worth noting the method used to attach the battery to the car—an over-the-top clamp or a side clip. Measure its length, width and height, and take this information with you when shopping.

Electrical connections

Disconnected

Most electrical problems are caused by loose, corroded or faulty connectors. If you trace a fault to a particular connector, open it and check the prongs to see if they're loose or damaged. If they seem to be alright, spray the prongs with some aerosol electrical switch contact cleaner; then reconnect the halves. You can find the cleaner in most large electronics hobby shops. If the problem persists, try replacing the connectors to see if that cures it.

The right stuff

If you have to open an electrical connector, you may find that it has a special grease inside to help keep out moisture, retard corrosion and dissipate heat. In most cases, it's silicone dielectric grease (check the service manual for the car, or call the parts department of your car dealer). Use only the correct grease if you have to replace it. Never apply ordinary automotive grease.

Lights

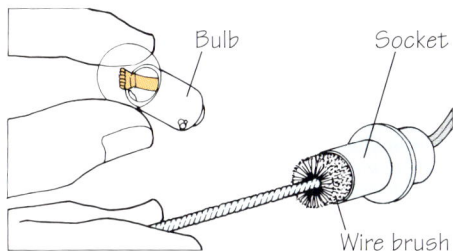

Bulb | Socket | Wire brush

Can't be too clean ▲

If a light refuses to work it doesn't necessarily mean that the bulb is no good. Corrosion in the socket can prevent electricity from reaching the bulb. Use a wire brush to clean out the socket.

Sticky fingers

When handling a quartz halogen bulb, keep your fingers off its glass. These bulbs burn so hot that the oil on your fingers will crack the glass. If you do accidentally touch the glass, clean it with a dab of alcohol.

Drain plug

If you need to keep the car door open for a long time and you can't switch off the interior light independently, wedge a tennis ball between the door edge and the light switch. It will keep the light off and reduce battery drain. If you don't have an old ball, cut a triangular wedge of scrap wood and pad it with rags.

Door edge

Tennis ball | Interior light switch

A NEW AERIAL

Replacing a car radio aerial is a common 30-minute repair that most people can do themselves. But yanking all the old wiring out without noting the way the cable is routed through the body panels can turn the job into a couple of hours of unamusing labour.

Before routing the new cable through the car, make sure it's long enough to reach the aerial location. Marking the cable path with string lets you compare the lengths of the cables. Pull the cables and string through the path carefully, tugging them gently as they clear various tight spots.

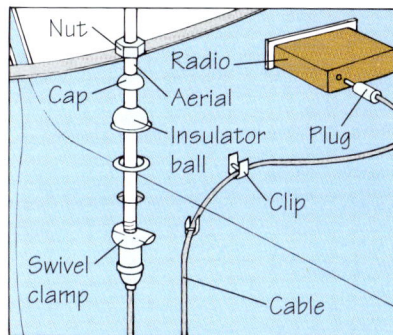

Nut | Radio | Cap | Aerial | Insulator ball | Plug | Clip | Swivel clamp | Cable

1 Unplug the old cable from the radio jack. Tape a length of sturdy string to the cable plug. Free the cable from any clips or brackets. Remove the nut at the aerial; slide other parts off.

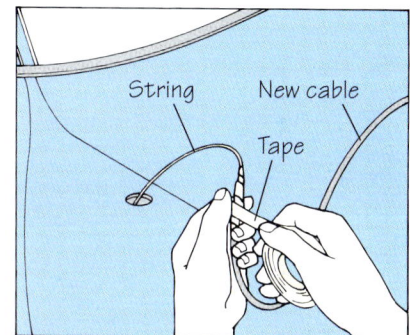

String | New cable | Tape

2 Push a screwdriver through the hole down one side of the clamp; pull the aerial and old cable out. Tape new cable to string end; pull it through. Plug in the new cable; attach the new aerial.

Aim to please ▶

After having your headlights aimed by a professional, park the car at the entrance to your garage. Mark the outline of the patterns made by both the high and the low beams on the back wall of the garage. Also mark the position of the front wheels on the garage floor. If the headlights go out of alignment, use these marks to check and re-aim them. To adjust a headlight, remove any trim to reach the adjustment screw above the light.

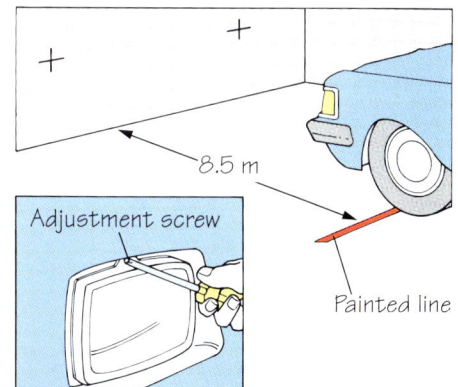

8.5 m

Adjustment screw

Painted line

FUEL SYSTEM

Petrol in the car

Your car's Breathalyzer

In some areas, petrol blended with alcohol is becoming available. In rare cases a car's engine may stumble if the blend contains more than 10 per cent alcohol. If in doubt, the alcohol content can be estimated. Tape a photocopy of a metric rule to a glass jar. Pour in 5 cm of water. Very slowly add the same amount of fuel without mixing it with the water; the fuel will float above the heavier water. Seal the jar with a lid, and shake it. The alcohol will separate from the fuel and mix with the water. Let the jar stand for five minutes; then check the new levels. If the volume of the water (on the bottom) has increased by more than 10 per cent (above 6 cm), there is too much alcohol in the fuel. Switch to another brand of petrol. ▼

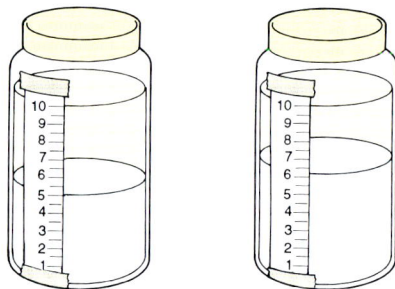

Cap keeper

Ever driven off leaving the fuel tank's cap behind? If the cap is made from steel, use two-pack epoxy to glue a magnet inside the fuel filler flap. Attach the cap to the magnet when filling up.

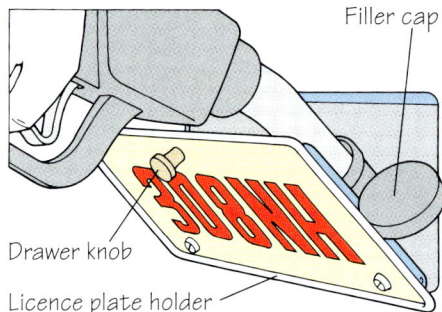

Filler cap

Drawer knob

Licence plate holder

Filler flap ▲

Some cars have their fuel filler hidden behind a hinged, spring-loaded number plate holder. To make it easier to open the holder, drill a hole through the plate and install a small drawer knob. Once you remove the fuel cap, wedge it behind the holder to keep it open while you insert the filler nozzle.

Saving fuel

Most drivers are familiar with the tried and tested ideas for saving fuel—don't accelerate or brake too hard and avoid high speed running. Here are a few more useful tips:

▷ Check tyre pressures often. Every 14 kilopascals below the recommended pressure increases fuel consumption by more than one per cent. The lower the pressure, the worse the effect.
▷ Keep a record of your car's fuel consumption. Any sudden increase could indicate time for a tune-up, that the wheels need realigning or that the brakes need adjustment.
▷ Don't let the engine 'warm up'. It uses less fuel to re-start an engine than it does to let it idle for 30 minutes.
▷ Any unnecessary weight in the boot uses extra fuel.
▷ Only use a roof rack as a last resort. Its effect on fuel consumption is drastic.

Leak stopper

You can temporarily plug a small fuel tank leak with bubble gum! Chew the gum until all the sugar is gone, then press it into the leak (after cleaning off any dirt first). The petrol will harden it into an epoxy-like mass that should hold until you reach a garage.

Don't choke on it!

If the engine of an older car often stalls immediately after starting, the choke may be opening too much. If your car has a specified opening gap (not an angled gap) between the choke plate and the carburettor barrel, you can use a drill bit that is the same size as the gap (a 9 mm bit for a 9 mm gap) to check the opening. While the engine is cold, remove the air cleaner cover, start the engine, and the instant the choke opens, insert the bit. It should slide in and out with a light drag. To avoid dropping the bit into the carburettor, stick a piece of masking tape around its end. If the bit is a loose fit, have the choke adjusted. Because the choke opens quickly, don't hold the bit in place to retest; the result will be inaccurate. ▼

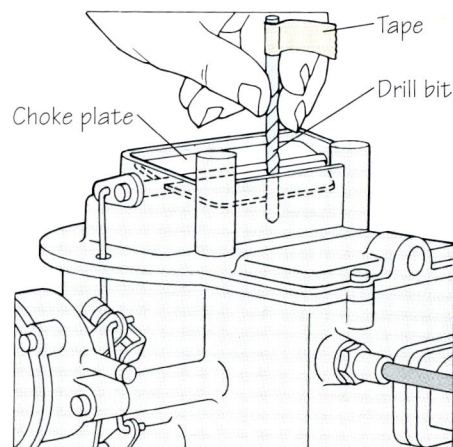

Tape

Drill bit

Choke plate

PAINT TOUCH-UP

Applying paint

Rust arrester

After scraping or sanding rust from a chip or scratch, apply a rust converter. This product transforms rust into an impervious black coating that prevents further rusting under the paint. Follow the instructions on the label to apply two thin coats. Let the converter dry for 48 hours before applying paint.

To prime or not

Acrylic automotive paints may require an undercoat of a solvent-base primer or sealer. Lacquer and enamel paints don't. Check paint labels carefully for primer recommendations.

Fill 'er up

It may take several coats of touch-up paint to fill a chip up to the original paint surface. Dab on the coats with a small artist's brush, a cotton swab or the torn end of a paper match. Allow each dab to dry before applying the next layer.

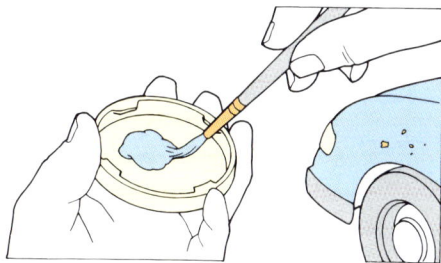

Spray away ▲

Want to touch up a small chip or two but the matching colour of touch-up paint is available only in an aerosol can? Shake the can well. Spray some paint into a jar lid or paper cup; apply it with a brush.

PAINT PROBLEMS

Before using a primer or paint, do a test in a hidden spot, such as under the bumper. When painting, always work in a well-lighted area. Here are a few problems encountered with spray paints and ways to deal with them:

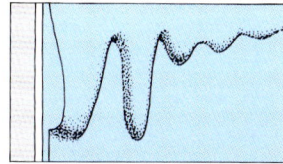

Drips and runs occur when paint is sprayed on too thickly. Let the paint dry completely; then smooth the area with wet-and-dry paper (200 grit first, then 600). Clean the area and repaint it.

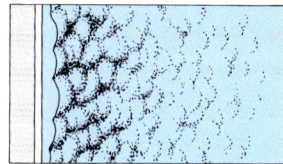

Orange peel, as the name implies, resembles the rough skin of the citrus fruit. It's caused by spraying too thin a coat, or by paint that's improperly mixed (not enough solvent). Rub with wet-and-dry paper, clean and repaint the area when dry.

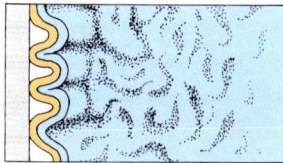

Wrinkling or lifting occurs when paint is applied over an incompatible primer. Rub right back down to the bare metal, and start the job again, using a compatible primer and paint. When in doubt, read the instructions on the paint container carefully.

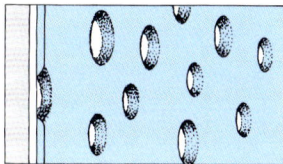

When silicone or wax isn't completely removed, small spots, called fish eyes, let the old surface show through. Wipe off the wet paint with thinner. Clean the area with alcohol or a precleaning solvent, and start the whole job over again.

Mask task ▶

When painting small areas with an aerosol spray paint, use this trick to avoid the problem of masking off the surrounding surface. Cut a 2.5 cm hole in a piece of stiff card measuring at least 25 × 15 cm. Hold the card about 15 cm from the area to be painted and start spraying through the hole, using a circular motion to 'feather' the edges. Don't spray for too long— short bursts are better than long ones.

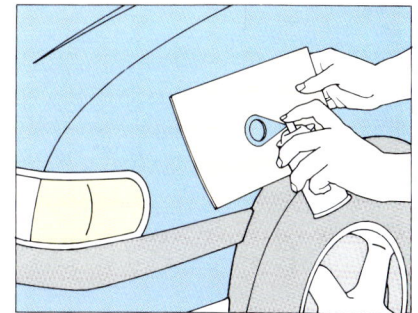

KEEPING UP APPEARANCES

Car cleaning

Foaming seat

You can give your vinyl car upholstery a fresh clean look by scrubbing it with foaming household cleaner. Or use a mixture of 30 ml liquid dishwashing detergent in 1 litre hot water.

Hair of the dog

Instead of pouring leftover stale beer down the drain (or worse yet, down your throat), you can use it to clean off the leather upholstery in your car. Just don't do this on the road; a police officer may misinterpret the odour.

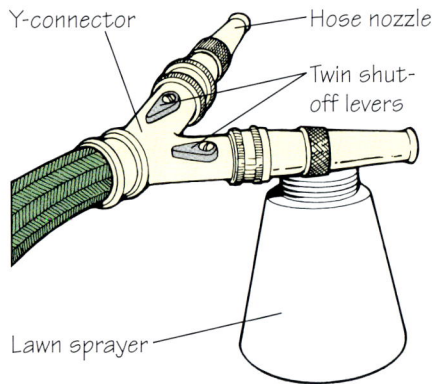

Y-connector — Hose nozzle — Twin shut-off levers — Lawn sprayer

Double-barrelled ▲

For convenient car washing, attach a Y-connector with double shutoff valves to your garden hose. Screw a hose nozzle onto one side of the Y and a lawn sprayer holding concentrated liquid car soap to the other side. With this double-barrelled setup, you can switch from soapy water for washing to clear water for rinsing with the turn of a lever.

Bug off

Here's a remedy for removing dead insects from your car. Spray the car with a mixture of half a cup baking soda and two cups warm water. Wait two minutes; then respray the car and sponge off the insects. The baking soda neutralises acid in the insects, making them easy to remove, but it won't damage the paint.

Sapped

Remove dried tree sap from your car by following these steps. Carefully break off lumps of sap, using a plastic kitchen spatula to avoid scratching the paint. Soak a soft cloth in a mixture of laundry detergent and hot water. Wearing heavy plastic or rubber gloves, rub the sap residue with the cloth as hard as you can. Continue rubbing and breaking off lumps until the sap disappears; then rinse with cold water. When the surface is dry, treat the area with a mild cutting compound, then polish the entire car.

Off, damned sticker!

To remove stickers from metal or glass heat them with a hair dryer until the glue loosens, then carefully peel them off. If they won't peel, try heating them with a hair dryer and then prise them off using a putty knife with its blade covered by duct tape. After removing a sticker get rid of any remaining adhesive by rubbing it with your thumb. If it doesn't come off try petrol or nail polish remover (but not on paintwork).

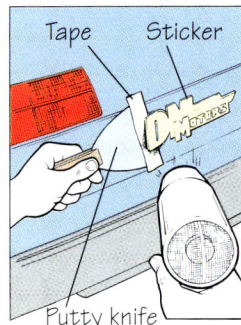

Tape — Sticker — Putty knife

Cheap scrubbers

A small scrap of a deep-pile carpet makes a good car scrubber. An unused dust-mop head is also handy—just stick your hand into the pocket and scrub.

Hot wheels ▲

Your brakes can heat parts of the wheel to 150°C or more. Never apply a cleaner to such a hot wheel. The chemicals contained in these cleaners can do damage at high temperatures. Cool off the wheel with a garden hose before applying a cleaning solution.

White-washed

For the reappearance of the whitewalls hidden under the dirt on your tyres, tackle the dirt with a soapy, non-metallic pot-scrubbing pad from the kitchen.

A repelling thought

Apply a thin coat of one of those clear plastic-protecting-and-enhancing sprays to alloy wheels to help keep road salt, insects, grease, dirt and other debris from staining them.

Stubby to the rescue!

To remove dried polish from the seams and crevices on your car, trim the bristles on a paintbrush so they are 20 mm long, then brush away the deposits.

The windscreen

Clogged washer

Does your car's windscreen washer refuse to pump, even though the washer tank is filled with fluid? Open the bonnet, switch on the ignition, and have a helper operate the washer control knob. Listen for the sound of the washer motor. If it is whirring, check the hoses and joints all the way from the tank to the bonnet to make sure they haven't sprung a leak. If no leaks are evident, clean the nozzles with a piece of fine fuse wire, or a fine sewing needle. Push the eye of the needle into a cork to make it easier to use as a tool. ▼

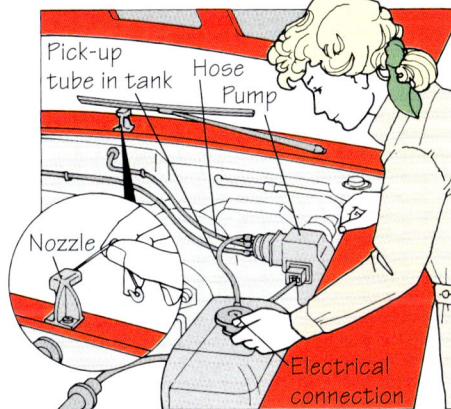

Pick-up tube in tank
Hose
Pump
Nozzle
Electrical connection

More solutions

To remove nongreasy dirt from a windscreen, spray it with a mixture of one part vinegar and three parts water. For a really grimy or hazy windscreen, use a mixture of half a cup ammonia and 4 litres water. Because hazy glass can be caused by vapours from vinyl, wash vinyl surfaces using a proprietory vinyl cleaner. Dry, and apply a vinyl dressing to prevent the build-up of haze again.

WIPER WOES

The rubber blades on windscreen wipers wear out quickly because of dirt, and because they harden in the sun. Replace them before every rainy season. If they are still not working, look below for the solution.

Straighten a bent arm with the wiper at mid-stroke. Using two pairs of pliers, carefully twist the arm until it's parallel to the glass. If the tip is bent, remove the assembly to straighten it.

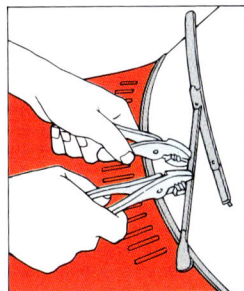

Water beads indicate a build-up of grease, wax, oil or grime. Try increasingly stronger cleaning solvents. Cover the car when it's parked outdoors to protect it from air pollution.

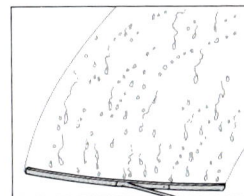

Smearing is a sign of a dirty windscreen or wiper, a worn blade or a poor mix of washer solution. Clean the wipers and windscreen, and replace the solution; if this fails, replace the blade.

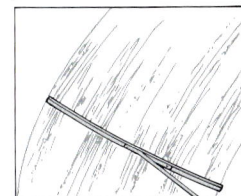

Smearing in only one direction often occurs when the blades are the wrong size or when they harden due to hot weather or old age. Replace them with new blades.

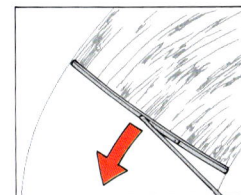

Chattering is caused by a bent wiper arm or a frozen blade on a cold day. Straighten the arm (see above left), thaw out or replace the blade, or replace the wiper arm and blade.

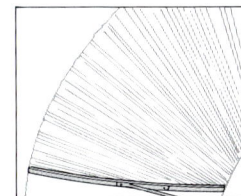

Fog eraser

If the windscreen fogs up, make sure that air is being directed onto the inside of the glass through the ventilation slots. If it isn't, the fan or air-conditioner could be faulty. Until you fix the problem, smear a small amount of dishwashing liquid over the inside of the screen.

Glass repair

A small scratch out of the line-of-sight on a windscreen can sometimes be removed by using jeweller's rouge on a polishing pad attached to an electric drill. Several passes may be needed. All damage *within* the line-of-sight should be referred to a windscreen specialist.

STORAGE AND SECURITY

Everything in its place

Valuable papers

Keep a large envelope in the glove box or another safe place to hold receipts for repair work and replacement parts. If warranty work is needed, you'll have any needed proofs of purchase or service handy. Write the due dates for tune-ups, oil changes and tyre rotation on the outside of the envelope.

Pocket protector

Attach a pocket-type shoe storage bag to the back of a car seat with extra-strong Velcro tape to keep all maps, cans, bottles, tissues and small toys semi-organised—especially on long trips.

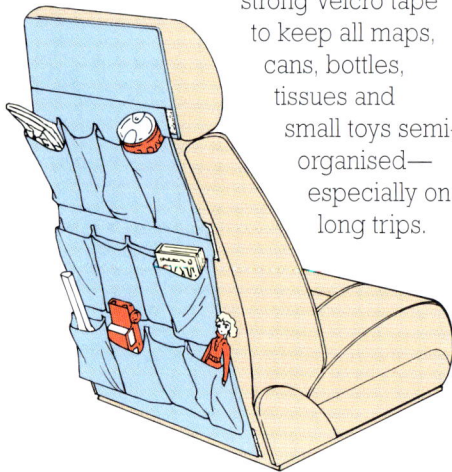

Mat tact

Does your floor mat refuse to stay in one spot, or do the corners flip up all the time and get in the way of your feet? Use Velcro tape at each corner of the mat to keep it and the corners in place.

Visor advisory

Here's another way to put Velcro tape to use. Apply it to a annoying drooping sun visor to hold it up out of the way.

Containment policy

Be prepared for an emergency. Wrap tools and road warning signs in an old rug, and secure the bundle in the boot with a rope or an elastic cord. The rug keeps the items together and prevents them from rattling around, and it comes in handy if you have to crawl under the car. The rope or cord stops the bundle from rolling about.

Carpet capers

Carpet remnants are useful for lining the boot of your car. They can protect your luggage and stop the boot's contents from rattling about. If you want to line the tray of a utility, make sure you use indoor/outdoor carpet.

Kneepads

Storing and retrieving items from the tray of a utility can be hard on the knees. To protect them, pad the top of the tailgate with indoor/outdoor carpet. Attach a sheet of hardboard to the tailgate with self-tapping stainless steel screws; then glue the carpet to the hardboard with construction adhesive. ▼

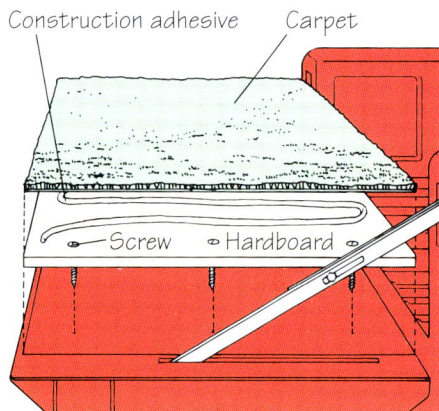

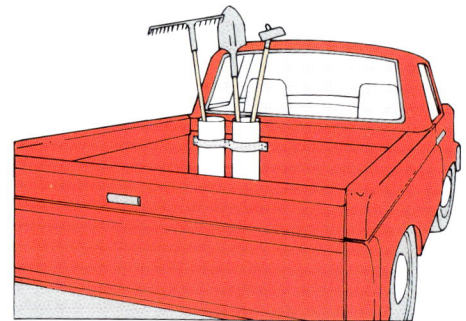

Construction adhesive   Carpet

Screw   Hardboard

Tool caddy ▲

You can carry tools such as rakes and shovels upright in the back of a utility by making holders from 1 m lengths of 150 mm diameter PVC pipe. Secure the pipe to the inside of the utility tray with galvanised pipe straps and stainless steel self-tapping screws. You can attach several pipes, but make sure that your view from the driver's seat won't be restricted and that items don't protrude beyond the tray.

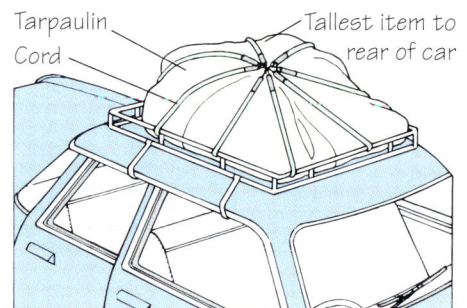

Tarpaulin   Tallest item to
Cord   rear of car

Beat the wind ▲

Planning to carry a load on a roof rack for a long trip? Spread a large tarpaulin over the rack; then load it, with the tallest items to the rear of the car. Wrap the tarpaulin over the items, and secure the bundle with octopus elastic cords. The streamlined shape will help fuel consumption, and the tarpaulin will provide protection from the weather.

Roof padding

If you need to carry items on your car's roof-top without a rack, you can protect the paint by placing a scrap of carpet underlay beneath the cargo.

Aiming devices

You can more easily line up a trailer or caravan's hitch with the tow bar's ball using these simple tips:
▷ On a car: mount a rear view mirror on the trailer so that it faces to the car, and adjust it so that you can see the hitch and the ball from the driver's seat.
▷ On a utility: place a strip of brightly coloured vinyl tape over the top of the tailgate, directly above the hitch, and a second piece on the trailer above its hitch. Keep the two pieces of tape aligned as you back up to the trailer.

Keys and locks

Backup key

A copy key, made from a flat stock key can be cut to suit many cars. Have one made by a locksmith and keep it in your wallet or purse. If the car's regular key is lost, you have a spare to hand.

Magnetic attraction

Another handy method for storing a spare car key is a magnetic holder that can be bought from most car accessory shops. Have a spare key cut and place it in the holder. Then put the holder in some convenient spot under the car. You will have to find an area of bare metal, free from underbody sealer.

Stuck in the boot

Boot lock cylinders often become jammed, in some cases because of an unsuccessful theft attempt. Less damage is caused if a locksmith replaces the barrel, but it may not always be possible to find one in an emergency. If you must get at your prized possessions inside the boot urgently, drill through the keyhole with a large bit (such as 12 mm), and insert a thin screwdriver to release the latching mechanism. However, before doing anything drastic, try removing the rear seat squab to see if you can gain access to the boot that way.

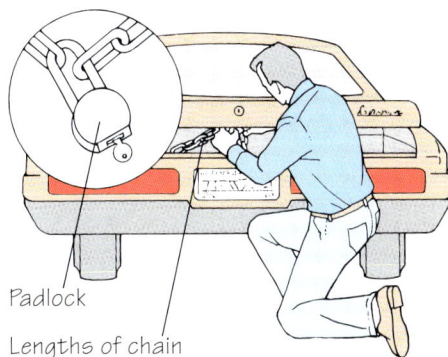

Padlock

Lengths of chain

Linked ▲

Thieves can easily pop your boot open with a crowbar. Take this step to foil them. Bolt a few links of chain inside the boot lid, and anchor a second length to the boot floor; then connect the free ends of the two chains with a padlock. The chains should be just long enough to let you fit your hands inside to open or close the lock, but not long enough to allow luggage or valuables to be removed. Cover the chains with pieces of rubber hose to keep them from rattling or damaging items stored in the boot.

Fair exchange

As an insurance against lost keys, give duplicates to your partner, even if he or she rarely drives your car. This way, if your key becomes worn and refuses to work, you can always have a new one cut from your partner's less-used copy.

Needle-nose pliers

When a key breaks off in a lock it is sometimes possible to extract it using a pair of needles. Insert them at an angle in the end of a cork, pushing them through until their tips almost touch. Using your improvised 'pliers' it may be possible to grip the broken key end.

Jammed latch

A door that bounces back open after you swing it closed may have a jammed latch. Inside the U-shaped opening in the side of the door is a rotating latch with a pair of prongs. If it's flipped to the closed position, the door won't shut. To unjam the latch, pull, lift or push the exterior handle as if to open the door. If the latch doesn't rotate to the open position, hold the handle open and move the latch downwards with your finger (take care) or a screwdriver. ▼

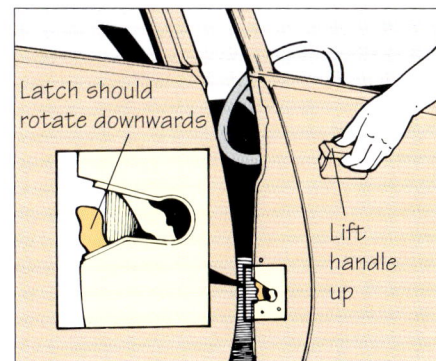

Latch should rotate downwards

Lift handle up

WEATHER EXTREMES

Heat and dust

The brush off

No matter how new or well-sealed the car, a thin patina of dust will be spread over its interior after a visit to the bush and some gravel road driving. Wiping it off the dashboard, centre console and door trim may be easy enough with a cloth treated with some car plastic and upholstery dressing, but getting rid of dust from crevices can be annoying. For this job, buy a natural bristle basting brush from a kitchenware shop, and knead a little lanolin into its bristles. The brush can now be worked into the tiniest crevices, and will collect dust on the way. Buff with a clean cloth afterwards for an enduring shine. ▼

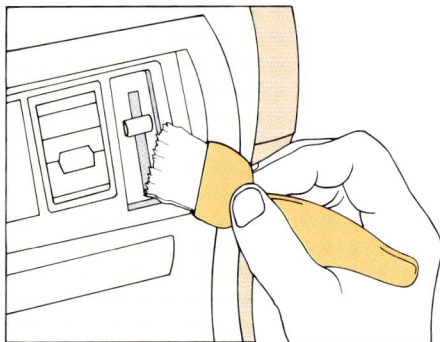

Open and shut case

Heat, dust and cold can all cause a car's locks and latches to seize up, and rubber door seals to perish and become stuck. As a matter of course, every time the car is serviced, check the operation of all of the car's doors and locks, and follow the recommendations in the owner's manual regarding the lubrication of locks (some car makers recommend it, but others do not).

Taking a dim view

On some cars, heat causes the lighter, volatile parts of interior plastics, such as dashboards and other components, to evaporate. These form a thin smear on the inside of a car's windows. To remove this irritating and tenacious film, use some cloudy ammonia and a constantly refreshed clean cloth. Particularly stubborn deposits may be shifted with mild nail polish remover. Take care not to spill either chemical, and work only in a well ventilated area with all of the car's doors open. Buff the glass clean after you have finished.

Sunburn protection for cars

The harsh ultraviolet (UV) component of sunlight causes damage and splitting to exposed parts of the plastic dashboards of some older cars. However, protection for gentle human skin can also work for cars. A non-allergenic SPF 15+ suncream will block out the UV rays and protect the plastic. Try a small amount on an inconspicuous area first to make sure there is no reaction between the suncream and the plastic.

In the hot seat

The interior temperature of a car that has been parked in the summer sun for a while can exceed 70°C. Don't immediately get into a vehicle that may have reached this temperature. Instead, open all the doors to allow hot air to escape. Then, open all the windows. Make sure the car is in neutral or park, and start the engine. Reach inside and start the air conditioner with the fan full on. Wait for a few moments until hot air has purged from the system before getting into a more comfortable interior.

Good for the circulation

If your car can be parked securely in direct sunshine with all of its windows open 5 to 10 mm, it will generally remain cooler than if the windows are all shut. So that fresh air can enter the stationary car to replace the hot air flowing out of the open windows, make sure the car's ventilation system is switched to *Fresh Air* and not *Recirculate*. ▼

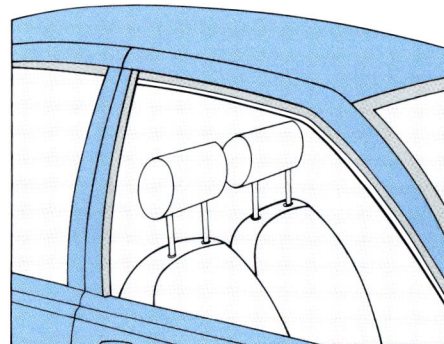

Ouch!

Don't leave tools or equipment out in extremes of weather for any length of time. It is amazing how quickly metals can become too hot or too cold to touch.

Wheel cooler

Buy a cheap steering wheel cover from a car accessory shop and cut it in half. When parking in direct sunshine, place the half-cover on the top part of your car's steering wheel. This is a quick and easy way of keeping the wheel cool.

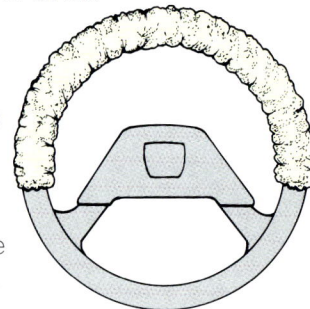

Outback motoring

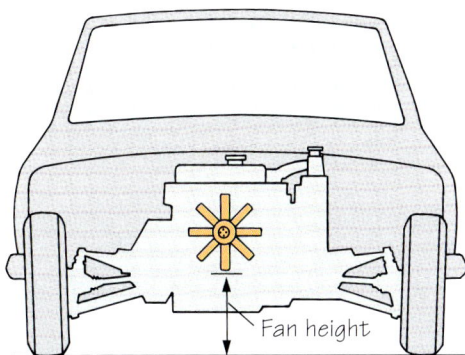

Fan height

That sinking feeling ▲

If fording a stream where a substantial portion of an older car's cooling fan is likely to become submerged, remove the fan belt for the crossing to prevent the fan from splashing water onto the distributor, which may cause the car to stall. Measure the height of the fan above the ground, and the depth of the water first. Cars with electric fans or thermostatic fan clutches do not need to have their fan belts removed. It is unwise to remove a serpentine fan belt, as it may be difficult to replace.

Plastic protection ▶

Another precaution that will help prevent an older car from stalling during a water crossing is a plastic bag placed over the distributor. The bag should be large and loose fitting, and can be held in place with a stout rubber band. Remove it after completing the water crossing. Also remove the car's carpets or mats before a crossing and place them on the back seat out of harm's way.

Temporary fan belt

If your fan belt has broken, and is lost, a temporary one can be made from panty hose or stockings. If using stockings, first tie them top-to-toe with a single reef knot to make one long nylon cord. The two important pulleys are the engine crankshaft (usually the bottom) and the water pump and cooling fan (usually attached to the engine). Ignore all other pulleys, such as those operating the alternator and air conditioning. Starting with the top pulley, wind the nylon repeatedly over the two pulleys, until there is enough left to pull very tight and tie in a reef knot. Keep engine speed low and remember that, without the alternator, the car may travel as little as two hours in daylight; less at night. ▼

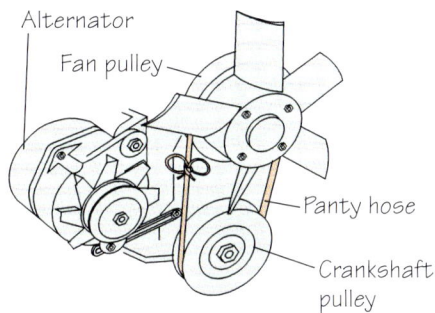

Alternator

Fan pulley

Panty hose

Crankshaft pulley

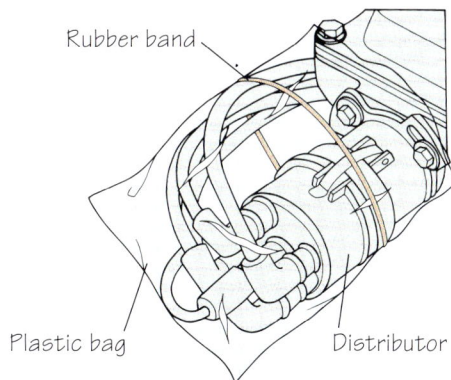

Rubber band

Plastic bag

Distributor

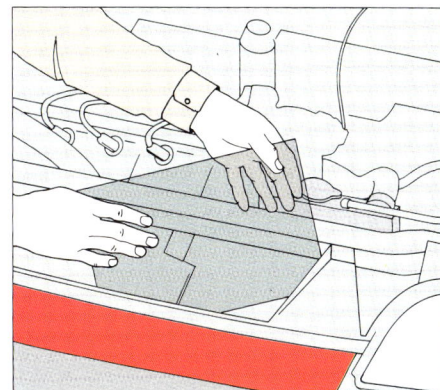

Insect screen ▲

Driving in the bush at night will expose your car to many flying insects. These can eventually block the radiator. To combat this problem, cut a piece of metal flywire so that it fits in front of the radiator, but behind the car's grille. Check it regularly. If it becomes covered in insects it will impede the flow of fresh air and the engine could overheat.

Water into wine

Carry emergency radiator water in the plastic bladder of a used up wine cask. The variety with a twist tap may be more secure than one of those that you have to press. Don't overfill the bladder, and it will conform to the odd shapes in an out-of-the-way corner of your car's boot. Also don't load anything on top of the bladder or it may burst.

Disposable mats

Cheap and disposable paper floor mats—similar to those often used by the service departments of car dealerships—can be made from old wrapping paper. They are ideal for use in areas where mud or sand may be brought into the car on boots and shoes.

WEATHER EXTREMES

Hot tips

Saving fuel in summer

The aerodynamics of the modern car have been designed so the car slips through the air best when the windows are closed. If the choice is driving with the windows closed and the air conditioning switched on, or the windows open and the air conditioner switched off to save fuel, then closed windows wins. At country touring speeds most cars will use more fuel with the windows open and the air conditioning switched off, than they would if the windows were closed and the car's interior made more comfortable by its air conditioning.

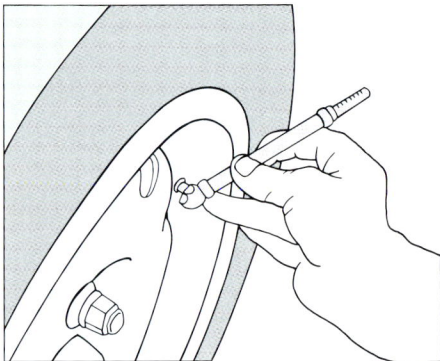

Keeping up the pressure ▲

Check tyre pressures when the tyres are cold—never when they're hot. On summer country roads at a touring speed of around 100 km/h, tyre temperatures can easily exceed 100°C. If you check the pressure of tyres when they are hot then they will appear too high. If you let them down to the correct level when hot, they will be dangerously low when the tyre has had a chance to cool down.

Preparing for the cold

Anti-freeze, anti-boil

Using anti-freeze in a car's cooling system isn't only beneficial in cold country areas. Modern cars need anti-freeze at all times to prevent corrosion inside the engine. Also, anti-freeze is anti-boil as well. Correctly used it will reduce the likelihood of an engine overheating when the outside temperature soars.

Thinning for the cold

Have your car serviced before heading for the snowfields, or very cold country, to make sure the battery and starter motor are in tip-top condition. Mention the destination to the service manager and, if recommended, drain and refill with a lighter grade of oil for cold temperature operation.

Jumper leads

The right jumper leads

Don't grab the first set of jumper leads you see, especially if they're cheap. Budget priced leads often prove to be useless when they're needed most—in an emergency. A good set will have thick, high quality copper or copper-plated clamps; thick cables; and be as long as possible. Car batteries are often on opposite sides in different makes, so the leads have to be able to reach across at least one car's width. Buy leads that are at least 4 or 5 m long.

Lighten up

Lighter-viscosity motor oils (5W30 or 10W30) make a car easier to start in cold weather than heavier-weight oils such as 10W40. Check your owner's manual to see if lightweight oils are recommended for your car. If so, switch to one when cold weather threatens.

Heat cure

A car's battery produces much less power when the temperature is close to zero. If you're leaving your car in an outdoor carpark for a week, or even a weekend, while skiing, remove the battery and keep it indoors. A battery carry strap—available from a car accessory shop—clips over the battery terminals and makes it easy to lift. Replace the battery just before you intend leaving. Be sure to connect the earth strap first when reinstalling the battery.

Avoid tangles

To keep jumper cables from getting tangled, lay them side by side and wrap cloth tape around the pair in at least three or four places. But don't tape them together within 1 m of either end. ▼

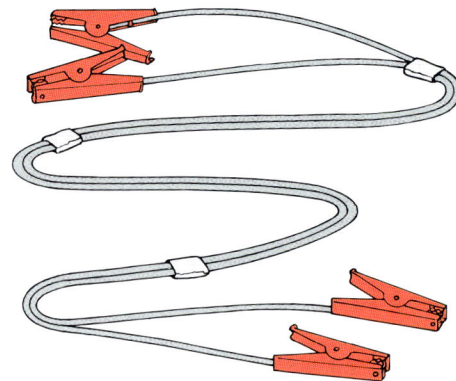

Snow and ice

Traction aid

Keep six or so heavy-duty vinyl floor mats in the boot in case you get stuck in snow or mud. Place them rough side up under the drive wheels. Align them end to end to make two rows of a high-traction surface, at least a metre or more long.

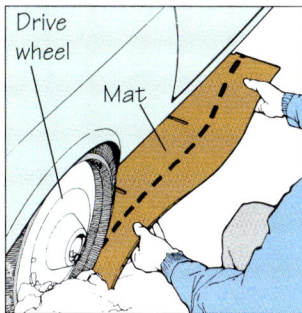

Labour saver

Instead of scraping snow and ice from the windscreen on a winter morning, try one of the following. The night before, cover the windscreen with a heavy-duty plastic garbage bag that's been cut open along its edges. Close the doors on the edges of the plastic sheet to keep it from blowing away. Or cover the windscreen with a piece of old carpet (pile side up) that's been cut to fit. In the morning, sweep off any snow, peel off your cover, and drive away. ▼

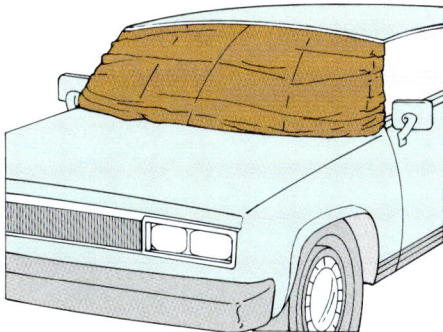

Chilled out

Door locks can freeze overnight in cold areas. Here's what you can do to prevent or cure the problem.
▷ Cover the locks with tape before going through a car wash.
▷ Keep lock cylinders lubricated by squirting in a lock lubricant, penetrating oil, or cigarette lighter fluid, unless the owner's manual advises against this.
▷ Place a drinking straw into the key slot and exhale into it until the lock thaws.
▷ Heat the key with a lighter or matches, then slowly work it into the frozen lock. Be sure to wear thick gloves so you don't burn your fingers. ▼

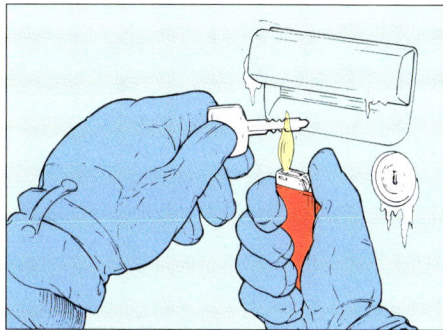

Emergency scraper

If you're caught without an ice scraper in your car, you can use a plastic credit card to remove all but the thickest ice build up. Just be careful that you don't damage the card's black magnetic strip.

Gritty aid

If travelling in areas prone to slippery mud or fresh snow and ice, carry a couple of bags of cat litter and sand in the boot. The extra weight will aid traction and, if the car does become bogged, the cat litter and sand spread in front of the driving wheels may get you going.

Car heater

Finding the heat

On a cold day, it often seems that the car takes too long to heat up. To see if the heater is working, stick a meat thermometer into an interior heater vent. With the engine warmed up, the heater set on *Hot*, and the selector on *Vent*, the thermometer should read about 90°C.

Faulty thermostat

To isolate a faulty thermostat, warm up the engine with the radiator cap removed. Stick a meat thermometer into the coolant. If it reads at least 80°C and the upper radiator hose is hot to the touch, the thermostat is OK. If not, replace the thermostat.
Caution: never remove the radiator cap from a hot engine!

Hot hands

With the heater on, carefully touch both heater hoses (they could be hot). If they're not hot, have a mechanic check the water control valve or heater core.

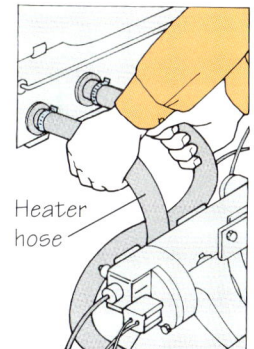

Final test

Check each selector setting (*Vent, Floor, Demist,* etc.) inside the car. If air isn't flowing to the correct outlet, or if the airflow changes speed or location as you accelerate, have a mechanic look for vacuum-control or linkage problems.

GARAGE

Keep out the elements

Seal it up

Keep cold air, rodents and debris out of your garage, and save on energy bills to boot, by installing weatherstripping on the garage door. You can buy vinyl weatherstripping designed specifically for closing gaps around all the edges. If only the bottom of the door needs sealing, try using a garden hose to do the job. Cut a length of hose that's as long as the door, slit it lengthwise, fit it around the bottom of the door, and nail or staple it into place.

Even it out

If your garage floor is uneven, you can still create a good seal between the bottom of the garage door and the floor. Simply tack 20 mm sponge pipe insulation to the bottom

Sponge pipe insulation

of the door, with the slit facing down. Keep the insulation out of sight when the door is closed by setting it back 12 mm from the door's front edge. But remember that a well-sealed garage means an even greater danger of carbon monoxide build-up. Never run an engine inside a closed garage.

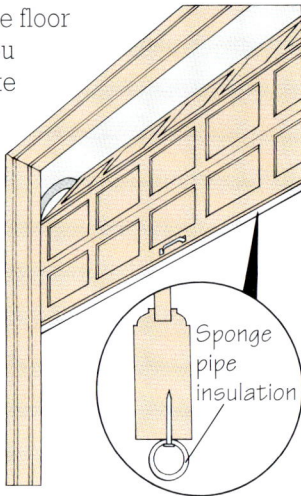

Moisture barrier

Do you have a panelled wood garage door? Protect its vulnerable bottom section from moisture by running paintable caulking along the joint where the bottom horizontal rail joins the panels. ▼

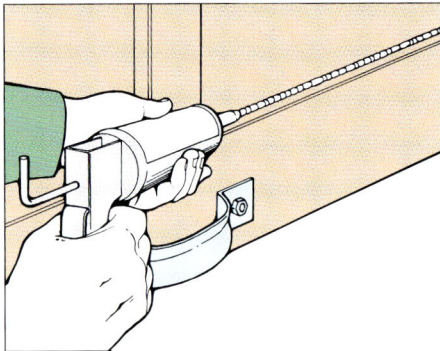

Melt control

If you live in a cold climate, or on an unsealed road, you know what a mess snow, ice and mud create. Confine the mess to the area beneath the car by gluing rubber garage door seals to the floor with construction adhesive. Most of the garage floor will stay clean, while water will be channelled to the driveway and mud can be hosed away. ▼

Garage door bottom seal

K48 096

Parking

Things that go bump

Judging how far is far enough when parking your car in the garage is often tricky. Save your car and the garage wall from damage by hanging a tennis ball, or a sponge rubber ball, from the ceiling to use as your guide. To install it, park your car exactly where you want it. Then mount a screw eye in the ceiling, positioned so that when the ball hangs, it touches the windscreen on the driver's side. No more guesswork!

Front and centre

Have you parked your car only to find you could barely get out because of lack of space on the side? End the frustration by applying a strip of reflective tape the width of your car to the back wall of the garage. You'll centre your car with ease.

You can only hope

Keep lawn mowers, bicycles and other equipment out of the way by painting white lines on the garage floor, outlining a space for each item. As long as all the family members return the items to their designated spots, you won't have to get out of the car to move them before you can park in the garage.

Door protection

Avoid damaging your car door when you open it by attaching a piece of carpet to the wall where the door makes contact. Pieces of foam rubber insulation or padding also work well to prevent dents and chipped paint.

Door-to-door barrier

Parking one car next to another in a two-car garage often leads to damaged doors on both cars. Avoid scratches and dents altogether by creating a cushioned barrier. Buy several lengths of straight radiator hose and a thin wooden dowel. Put the length of dowel through the hose, and secure a screw eye on each end of the dowel so that the hose is securely attached to the wood. Suspend the barrier from the ceiling with rope tied to each screw eye. Hang it so that it meets the car doors just below the handles. ▼

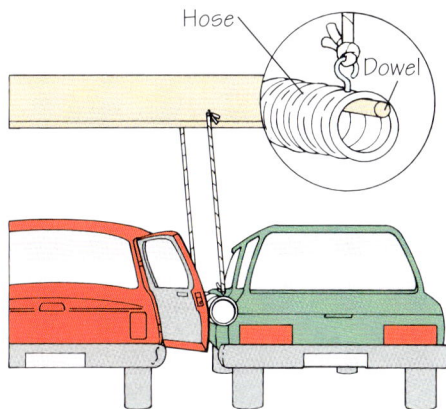

Mirror, mirror in the corner

Before you get out of your car at night, you can quickly and easily check to see if all its lights are functioning. Install a mirror at an inside front corner and another one in a back corner of the garage. Be sure that the two mirrors are positioned so that when you are sitting behind the steering wheel and looking in the side or rear-view mirror, you can see the headlights in the front mirror and the tail lights in the back one.

Garage doors

Garage door opener safety

Mark your calendar with reminders to periodically inspect your automatic garage door opener. Follow the owner's manual, and keep in mind the following:
▷ Every month check the safety features for proper operation. Check that the manual disconnect works properly.
▷ Every three months adjust the open and closed settings, if necessary. Check that the door opens and closes properly.
▷ Every six months see that the door and door hardware operate smoothly. Lubricate if necessary. Check the tension on the chain/cable or the opener.
▷ Every 12 months tighten all the nuts and bolts. Check the fasteners on the garage door and the door opener.

Add a button

Consider installing two buttons instead of one when you put in an automatic garage door opener. Place one by the door to the house and the other inside the garage, right by the garage door. When you need to take something out of the garage, there will be no need to race to beat the closing door.

Clamp it

When working on a manual garage door, set it at a comfortable height by securing a G-clamp or locking pliers on the door track. This is safer than propping the door with a chair or other object.

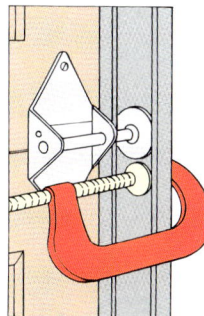

Spring safety

Roll-up garage doors use tightly coiled springs. If one snaps, it can injure you and damage property. Install a safety cable through the centre of each spring. The cable will not interfere with the action of the door or springs, and it will prevent a broken spring from whipping around. Hardware stores will stock suitable cable as a repair kit for one-piece garage door locks. *Note:* this does not apply to doors with torsion springs; they should be worked on by experts. ▼

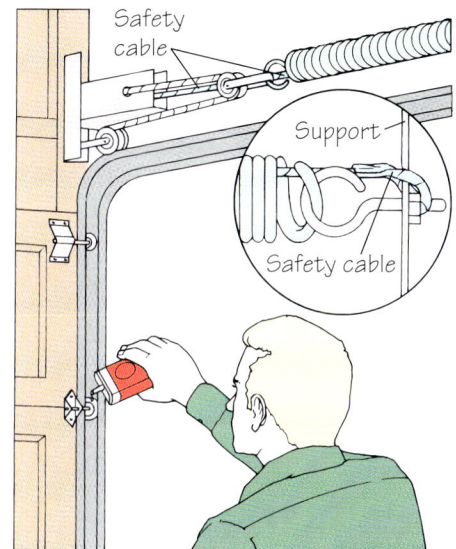

Keep on rolling ▲

Doors move sluggishly because of inadequate lubrication in the roller bearings. Periodically apply a thin film of lightweight oil to the rollers and hinges. Go easy, though; too much oil will collect dirt. Keep the tracks clean by wiping them occasionally with a cloth dampened with oil.

CHAPTER 11

MORE HINTS

CURTAINS AND BLINDS

Hang it up

Easier curtain hanging

You needn't have an extra hand to install curtain rods without trouble. Simply use masking tape to hold the brackets in place while you work. Not only will you free up your hands for marking, drilling and attaching the brackets, you'll minimise arm strain as well.

Wrong way up

Is your window rounded or oddly shaped at the top? If so, try mounting your blind upside down. To do this, install the brackets at the base of the window and attach a small pulley at the top. To raise and lower the blind, secure a cord to the edge of the blind and run it through the pulley.

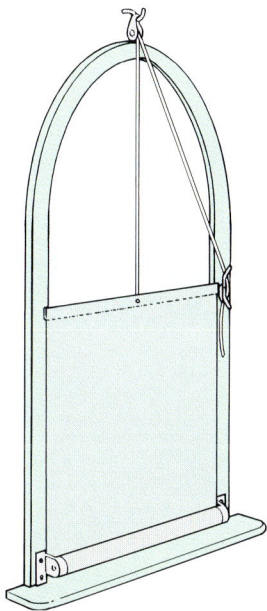

Just like new

Quick patch

Small tear on a blind? Fix it before it grows any larger. Stick a piece of masking tape on the back and coat the front with clear nail polish.

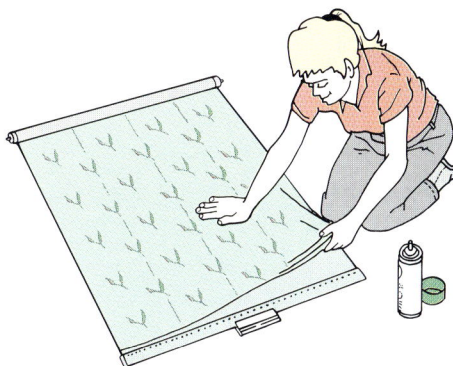

A new life for blinds ▲

Instead of discarding worn blinds, give them a face-lift. Choose a fabric to complement your decor, and cut it to fit the blind. Apply a thin coat of rubber cement or spray-on adhesive to the blind; then attach the fabric. Carefully smooth the fabric to eliminate air bubbles, which could cause wrinkling when the blind is rolled up.

Hidden talent

If the bottom of a blind is badly stained or worn, don't throw it out. Turn the blind upside down and attach the damaged end to the roller. First, unroll the blind and take out the staples holding it to the roller. Then remove the pull and slat at the bottom, open the hem, and staple that end to the roller; make sure the blind's long edges are at a perfect right angle to the roller. Sew a new hem for the slat, and reattach the pull. ▼

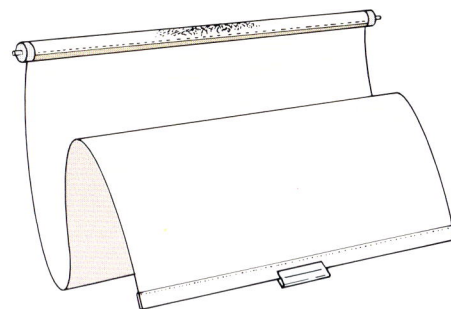

Blind renewal

Replace a frayed Venetian blind lifting cord without taking down the blind by using the old cord to pull the new one into place. Remove the buckle on the lifting cord, and clip off the cord a few centimetres above the loop. Tape the ends of the new cord to the cut ends. Then open the bottom of the blind and pull on the knotted ends of the old cord to draw the attached new pieces through the blind. ▼

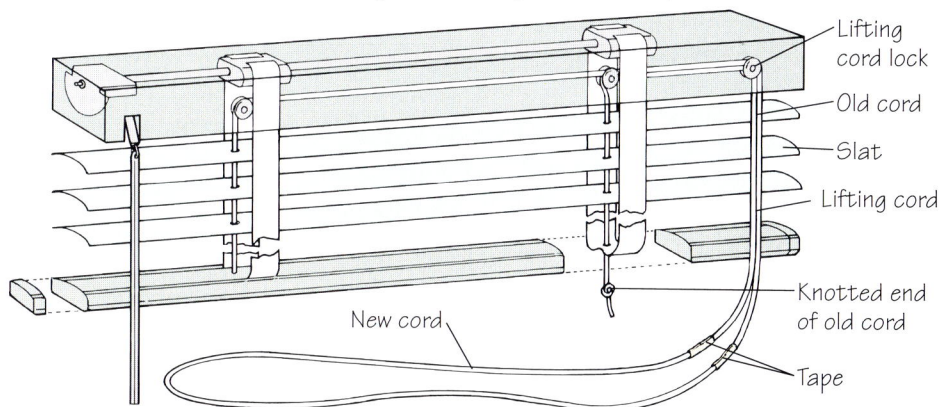

Lifting cord lock
Old cord
Slat
Lifting cord
Knotted end of old cord
New cord
Tape

PICTURE FRAMES

Making the frame

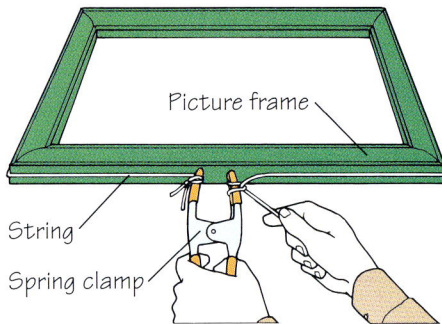

A picture-perfect clamp ▲

You can hold picture-frame joints together until the glue sets by using only a spring clamp and some string. Cut a piece of string to fit around the perimeter of the frame. Tie one end of the string to a jaw of the clamp, and run it around the frame. Then squeeze the clamp open and tie the other end of the string to its other jaw. Release the clamp to pull the string taut around the frame.

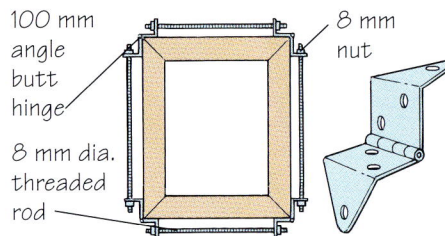

Handy hinge clamp ▲

For larger frames, make a clamp from four threaded rods and four angle butt hinges. Drill holes for the rods at the ends of the hinge leaves; then bend each leaf 90°. Push the rods through the holes in the hinges, forming a square larger than the frame, and screw a nut onto each rod end. Twirl the nuts to tighten the clamp around the frame.

Quick finish

To tint and protect raw wooden picture frames easily and inexpensively, use a coat of brown paste shoe polish. Give the paste a few minutes to soak into the wood, wipe off any excess, and then buff the surface with a soft, lint-free cloth.

Faster framing

Most people secure the artwork and glass within a picture frame with panel pins, but it's easier to use glazier's points. Push the points into a softwood frame with an old screwdriver or stiff-bladed putty knife; in hardwood, tap them into position with a hammer.

Wiring the frame

Wiring like a professional

Make your own picture hanger with a length of 1 mm stranded wire, two eye hooks, and two 10 mm long pieces of copper tubing. Attach the eye hooks to the picture frame. Slip the pieces of tubing onto the wire; then thread the wire through the eye hooks and loop it around them. To keep the ends of the wire from unravelling, slide the pieces of tubing over them and crimp the tubing down over the wire with pliers. ▼

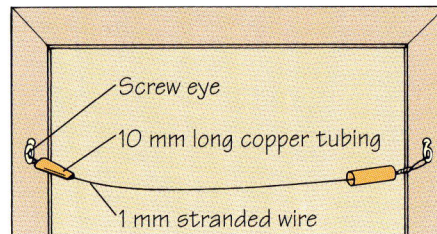

Go fishing

Super-strong nylon fishing line (monofilament) is practically invisible, making it a good material to use when hanging pictures from picture rails.

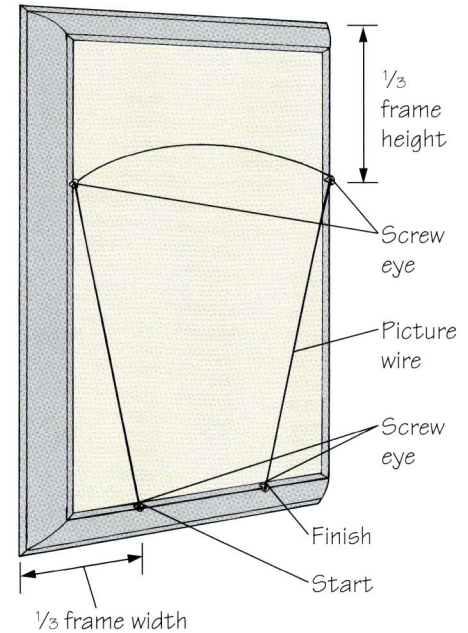

Recipe for stress ▲

A heavy load can cause the joints of a large wooden picture frame to separate. To prevent this, arrange the picture wire to support the frame at the bottom. Attach screw eyes to the frame as shown; then fasten one end of a length of braided picture-hanging wire to one of the bottom screw eyes. Thread the wire through the two side screw eyes, and fasten it to the other bottom screw eye. Pull the wire taut before fastening it to the last screw eye.

PICTURE HANGING

Hanging the picture

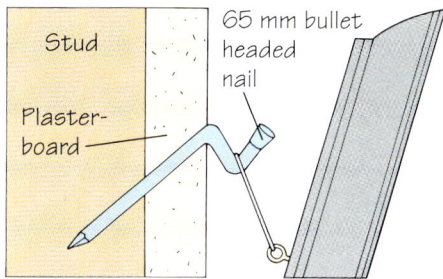

Stud

Plaster-board

65 mm bullet headed nail

Quick hanger ▲

To make an inexpensive picture hanger, grasp the shank of a 65 mm bullet headed nail in the jaws of a vice; then, using round-nose pliers, bend the nail to the shape shown. To start the nail into the wall, tap its head lightly with a hammer; then use a nail punch positioned at the bend to drive the nail home.

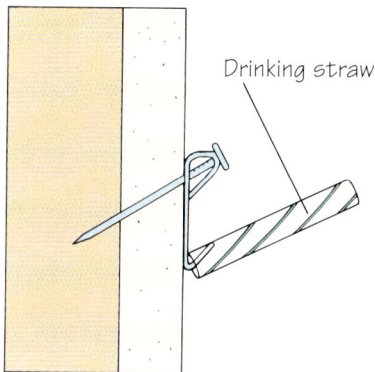

Drinking straw

In good position ▲

Slip a section of drinking straw over a picture-hanger hook to help position the picture wire over it. Remove the straw once the picture is in place.

A dent marks the spot

Avoid hit-or-miss. With this handy tool made from a wire coat hanger, you can create a small indentation in the wall, showing you exactly where to mount your picture. Cut a 250 mm piece of wire from a hanger, and file one end to a point. Using pliers, bend the wire as shown, forming a hook at the pointed end and a finger-sized loop at the other end. To use the tool, insert the pointed end under the picture wire or other hanger. Position the picture on the wall, holding it by the looped end of the tool, and gently push the point into the wall to mark the spot.

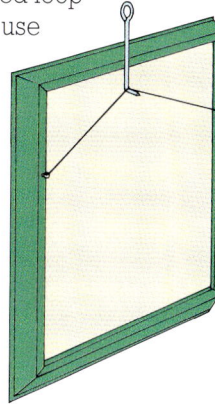

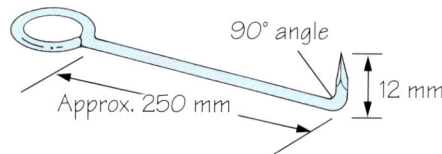

90° angle

Approx. 250 mm

12 mm

Wallpaper cover-up

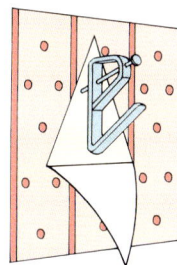

Don't damage your wallpaper with picture-hanger holes. Instead, install the hanger underneath the wallpaper. Slit a tab in the wallpaper where you want to install the hanger; moisten the area, and very carefully peel down the tab. When it's time to re-arrange your pictures, disguise the hole by gluing the tab back into place.

Keeping it straight

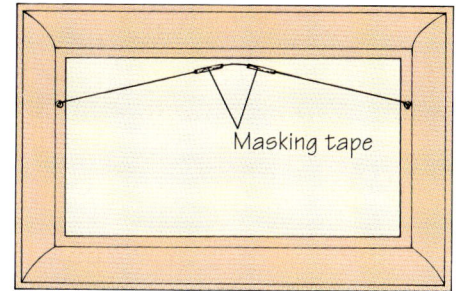

Masking tape

No-slip picture ▲

Keep your pictures from sliding around on the wall by wrapping bits of masking tape around the picture wire on both sides of the wall hanger or hook.

Sticky trick

Another way to keep a picture straight is to use a drawing pin gripper on the lower corners of the frame. Push the pins through short pieces of masking tape from the sticky side, and attach them to the frame. The pins' points will hold the frame in place without penetrating the surface of the wall. ▼

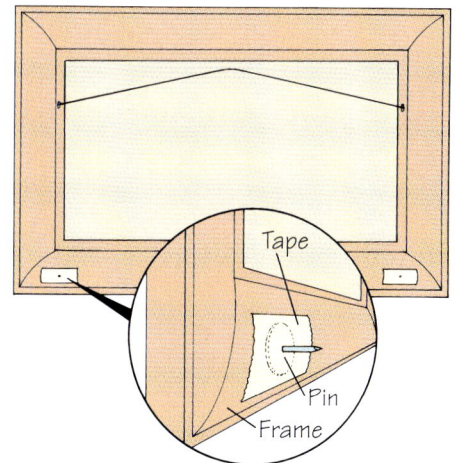

Tape

Pin

Frame

CHILDPROOFING YOUR HOME

Household menaces

Cures for the common cord

Pulling on a dangling power cord can result in a benchtop appliance falling and causing an injury, and playing with a long window-blind cord can result in the child's pulling the blind off the wall or in accidental strangulation. Keep cords out of reach of children by rewiring plugs to remove excess length, raising cords on wall hooks, or tying up their excess length. ▼

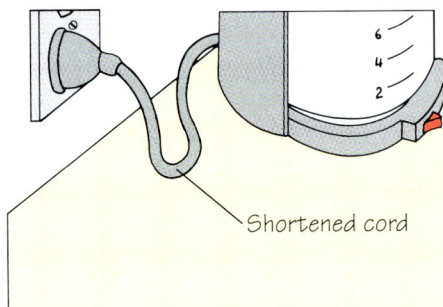

Shortened cord

Prop it up

It's easy to catch little fingers under the lid of a piano keyboard or a chest. To avoid this, glue blocks made from cork to the edge of the lid; on some pianos you can use small suction cups to hold the lid either open or closed. ▼

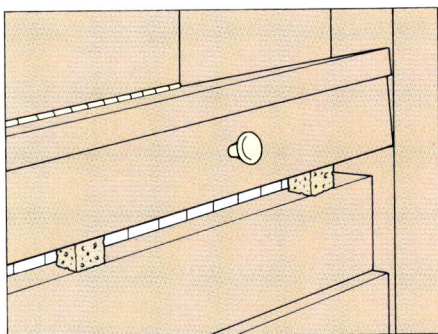

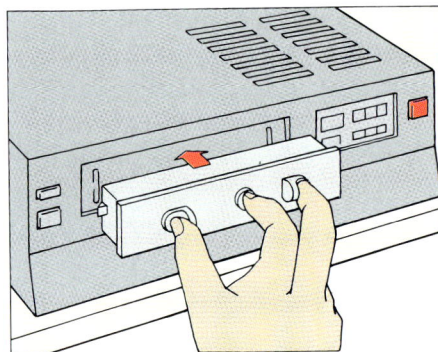

Open wide ▲

Children are fascinated by the way VCRs seem to swallow up videotapes. Keep your machine from 'eating' other items by either placing the VCR out of reach, or by putting a protective cover over the slot. To make your own cover, build a box out of 6 mm plywood and fit it over the entire unit.

Windows and doors

Door ajar

Keep a room off-limits to children but still allow for ventilation by installing a hook with a spring clip near the top of the door. Be sure to screw the eye as close to the edge of the door as possible. When it's latched, children won't be able to enter, but the door will stay slightly ajar.

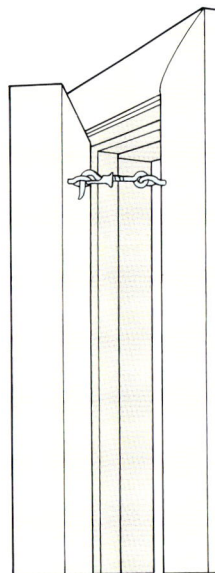

Finger saver

Keep your toddler's fingers from getting caught in a door with a simple removable doorstop made from 25 mm quarter round moulding and a 150 mm length of coat hanger wire. Drive one end of the wire into the end of the moulding, and bend the other end to form a hook. Slide the wire over the top door hinge, making sure the moulding is positioned between the leaves of the hinge. ▼

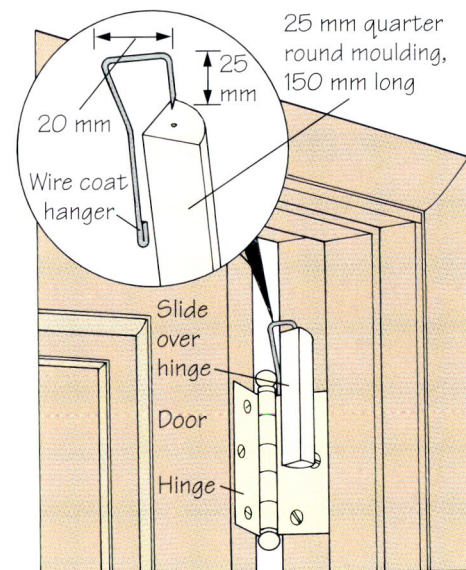

25 mm quarter round moulding, 150 mm long

25 mm

20 mm

Wire coat hanger

Slide over hinge

Door

Hinge

Window safety

A child can fall out of a window in the twinkling of an eye. To avoid such a tragedy, install window locks, which can secure windows in the partly open position. If you don't have locks, open only the tops of double-hung windows; drill a hole through both sashes, and insert a long nail into the hole, locking both windows together. Don't rely on a screen to keep a child in; the slightest pressure can cause it to pop out.

Seeing spots

To a child in motion, a closed sliding glass door or picture window can easily seem to be open space. Prevent tragic accidents by attaching colourful stickers to the glass at the child's eye level.

Stair safety

All fenced in

Because children can squeeze through even tiny openings, make sure deck rails and stairway balusters are child-proofed. An easy solution is to attach heavy-duty plastic garden mesh to the inside of the railings. Fasten the mesh to the railings with 12 mm staples, or tie it into place with strong string. ▼

Safe stairs

With crawlers and toddlers in the house, a safety gate is essential at the top and bottom of every staircase. Select one-piece gates, or the type with sliding sections—a child's head can easily get caught within the bars of an accordion-type gate.

Garage

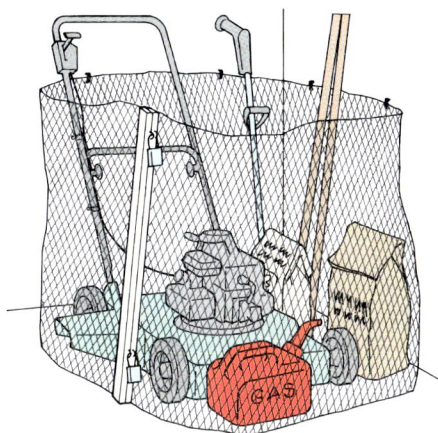

Out of reach ▲

The typical garage is full of dangerous tools and toxic substances. Enclose these items in a childproof enclosure made by attaching standard-width chicken wire to the walls. Staple timber to the sharp cut ends. Install screw eyes in the wood to accept two padlocks.

Open sesame

Make sure that your garage door opening switches and remote control devices are out of a child's reach. And if your automatic garage door is old, replace it with a newer model that reverses if it touches anything while closing.

SAFE AT HOME

A child's natural curiosity can lead to dangerous situations. Keep your child safe and prevent accidents by following some basic rules and using your common sense.

▷ Never leave a child unattended in the bathroom or kitchen.

▷ Install safety plugs in all unused power points.

▷ Store household cleaners and other chemicals in a locked box or cupboard.

▷ Remove the doors from any discarded appliance, regardless of where it is stored.

▷ Place a thick, soft rug underneath your baby's cot in case the baby climbs out and falls.

▷ Don't bathe an infant in the sink when the dishwasher is running—hot water could back up into the sink and scald the child.

▷ When cooking, turn pot handles away from the edge of the stove.

▷ Prevent a child from closing and locking a door by draping a thick towel over the top of the door.

▷ Keep house plants out of reach by hanging them from the ceiling.

▷ Every six months, re-evaluate your home; look for new, reachable dangers.

▷ Talk to your children about household dangers and the importance of keeping safe.

CHILDPROOFING YOUR HOME

Kitchen safety

Keeping company in the kitchen ▶

Kitchens pose many hazards; reduce the risk of accidents by installing a stove guard or by removing the control knobs when the stove is not in use. But always remember that it's never a good idea to leave a child alone in the kitchen. Toddling children soon learn they can reach forbidden delights, such as a cook-top, by pushing a chair into the desired position and climbing onto it. In such a case, even the best stove guard won't prevent a nasty accident.

Locks and latches ▲

Toddlers love to explore and investigate every corner. To protect your appliances and cabinets from your children, and the children from your appliances and cabinet contents, install childproof latches or locks wherever necessary.

Sit tight

Small children can easily slip about on polished wood or plastic high-chair seats, ending up with their heads under the tray. A rubber mat firmly secured to the seat keeps baby in place.

Temporary solution

All children are insatiably curious, especially when they get the chance to explore a new environment. When visiting a house that may not be childproof, temporarily 'lock' accessible cabinets with heavy-duty string or thick rubber bands. Simply loop the string around the cabinet handles and knot it tightly; make sure it's secure enough to keep the child from pulling the door open and squeezing a hand inside. ▼

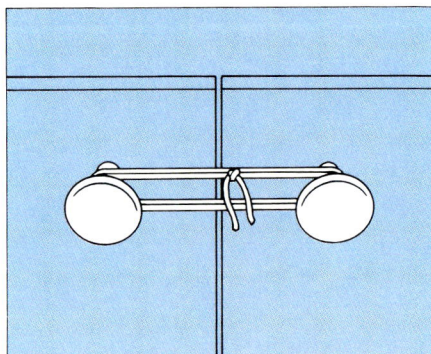

Anchored down

Any child who bounces on the open door of a freestanding stove or dishwasher risks tipping the appliance over onto him- or herself and becoming the victim of a serious accident. Prevent this by anchoring the appliance firmly to the wall or floor with brackets.

A safer bath

Nonslip grip

Water and soap residue can make baths very slippery. Reduce the risk of falls by installing adhesive, nonslip strips to the bottom of the bathtub and shower tray. To ensure a tight seal between the strips and the bottom of the bath or shower, make sure that the surface is clean before putting them in place. Nonslip rubber mats are also a satisfactory solution, and easier to keep clean.

No more bumps

Many accidents are the result of falling against one of the water taps in the bathtub. Protect your child from bumps by placing a protective cover over the spout or spouts. You can make your own covers from a length of pliable rubber hosing (available from most hardware shops). Select a size of hose that fits securely over the spout. This same precaution will help to prevent painful burns from taps heated up by the passage of scalding water.

No burns here

Temperatures that seem comfortable to adults can seriously burn children's sensitive skin. Have your plumber adjust the thermostat on your hot water unit to a lower setting, thereby lessening the chances of an accidental burn.

Running hot and cold

You can safeguard against burns while bathing even without changing the setting on your hot water unit. Simply fill the bath partway with cold water, then top it off with hot. But always remember to run a little cold afterwards to cool the spout down. And of course never leave a child unattended in the bathroom.

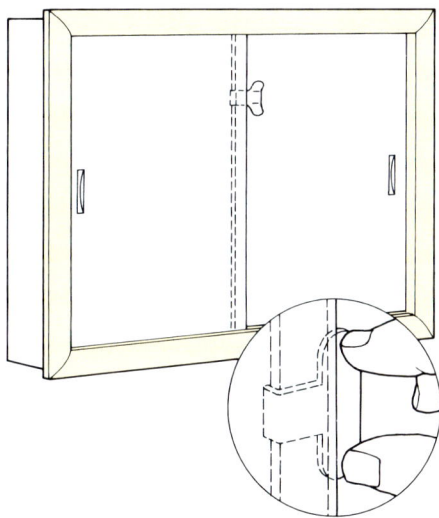

Bathroom cabinet safety ▲

Keep that bathroom cabinet securely locked—even if you think it is out of reach. Children quickly become adept at climbing, and the typical bathroom cabinet is full of potential hazards, such as razor blades, medications, cleaners, scissors and tweezers.

In the nursery

Pets begone ▶

If a safety gate isn't enough to keep a curious pet out of the baby's room, replace the traditional solid door with a screen door. A screen will keep pets out and allow you to hear if the child cries, or to peek in without disturbing the baby. Remember, pets should not be left unattended with newborn babies.

Child's play

Unlidded bins and boxes are the safest containers for toy storage—you won't have to worry about children pinching their fingers or getting trapped inside. But if your toy box must have a lid, drill several holes in the walls of the box to allow ventilation should a child get caught inside. (For more ideas on storing toys and sports equipment, see pp. 122–123.)

Say no to plastic

To reduce the risk of suffocation, use a mattress protector instead of a plastic bag for the cot's mattress cover. Make certain that the protector is securely fastened to the mattress. Don't keep a pillow in the cot, and be sure that any toys left there are unbreakable, and too big to fit into the baby's mouth.

On the move

A bouncing toddler can 'walk' a lightweight cot across the floor—and close to something that may be unsafe. Prevent this by securing the cot to the wall with a pair of heavy-duty hook-and-eye fasteners screwed into the wall studs. Use this same trick to keep a wooden high chair firmly in place. ▼

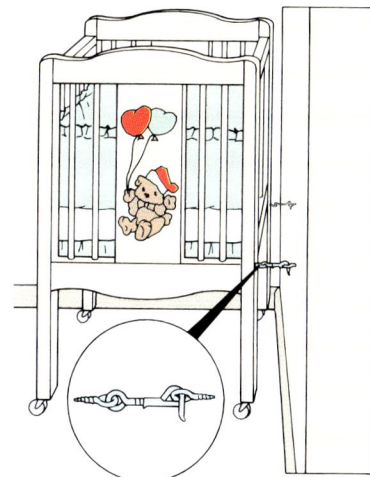

DISASTERPROOFING YOUR HOME

Bushfires

To stay or to leave?

It is often difficult to decide whether or not you should stay with your house when a major fire threatens. If not ordered to evacuate, you must make your own decision. Consider the following.
▷ Has your house and surrounding land been well prepared (p. 329)?
▷ Do you have the basic clothing and equipment needed to fight the fire?
▷ Are you physically and mentally prepared for the coming struggle?
If you do decide to stay, evacuate children, the sick, the elderly and animals well before the fire arrives; secure valuable papers and possessions, and notify the local emergency services.

When the fire arrives

Remain outside—properly dressed—for as long as possible as the bushfire advances on your house, so that you can extinguish falling embers and prevent spot-fires from starting. If you have an emergency plan (see below, right) then everybody will know what to do. Before the fire-front arrives, and the heat becomes unbearable, retreat indoors.
▷ Close all doors and windows.
▷ Remove curtains and blinds and hang wet woollen blankets up in their place.
▷ Block door bottoms with wet towels.
▷ Place containers of water and wet towels in each room (including the roof space) to deal with spot-fires.
▷ Constantly patrol the house interior.
▷ Keep a watch on the progress of the fire through a small, protected window.

A wall of water

If you live in a bushfire prone area, consider installing a sprinkler system as an added form of protection. In order for the system to be effective you must have your own water supply (at least 20 000 litres in a swimming pool, tank or dam) and a self-contained, portable pump. A simple garden system will do, but use metal fittings. Install spray nozzles to cover land to the north and west of the house, as well as along gutters and the edges of verandas and decks. ▼

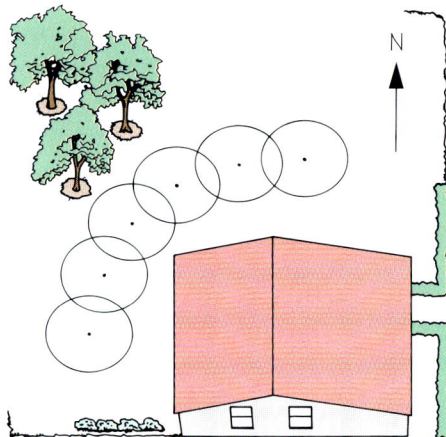

Your personal survival kit

Everybody who stays to help protect your home against a fire must be properly dressed and equipped. An inadequately dressed firefighter risks injury, severe burns and even death. Cover as much of your body as possible, including your head, with hard-to-burn clothing and a hat. Particularly suitable are a boiler suit, heavy cotton jeans, or a long-sleeved pure wool jumper and loose-fitting wool trousers. A woollen balaclava will protect most of your face. Stout boots and heavy gloves are essential.

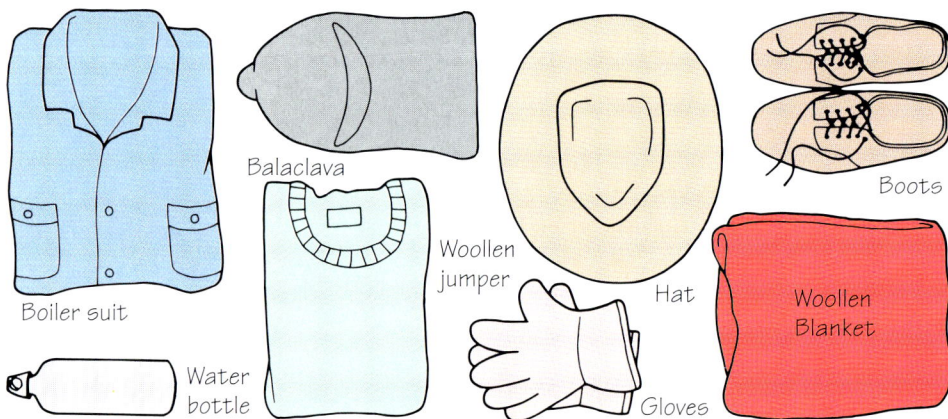

Boiler suit
Balaclava
Woollen jumper
Hat
Boots
Woollen Blanket
Water bottle
Gloves

The family fire drill

The best way to be certain that you are ready for a bushfire emergency is to develop a family fire drill, and to practice it regularly. Draw up lists of jobs that must be done each summer, as a matter of course, and those that must be done when a fire threatens. Appoint an overall controller, and allocate specific tasks to individuals. Make sure that provision has been made for the possibility of one or more people being away when a crisis looms. Keep a store of emergency clothing on hand at all times, and don't forget to plan for pets, stock and vehicles.

PREPARING FOR THE WORST

Thorough preparation of the house and its surrounding grounds at the start of each summer—and then at regular intervals throughout the bushfire season—is essential if you want to maximise your chances of surviving a fire without any major damage. Every house presents its own particular set of problems, but all of the points detailed below should be looked at carefully.

Many houses are lost to fire for the same reasons. During the bushfire season, and especially when fire threatens, pay particular attention to the following areas.

▷ The roof, where sparks and embers can blow in under tiles and set fire to roof timbers. Seal around vents, bargeboards, fascias and skylights. Consider installing metal roofing, if you don't already have it.

▷ The underfloor area, especially if building timber, firewood and other flammable materials are stored there. If it is at all possible, close the area off so that sparks and embers cannot be blown in.

▷ Cracks and crevices, particularly around windows, doors, vents and in the corners of decks and verandas. Embers can either gather there, or worse still, find entry to the interior of the house.

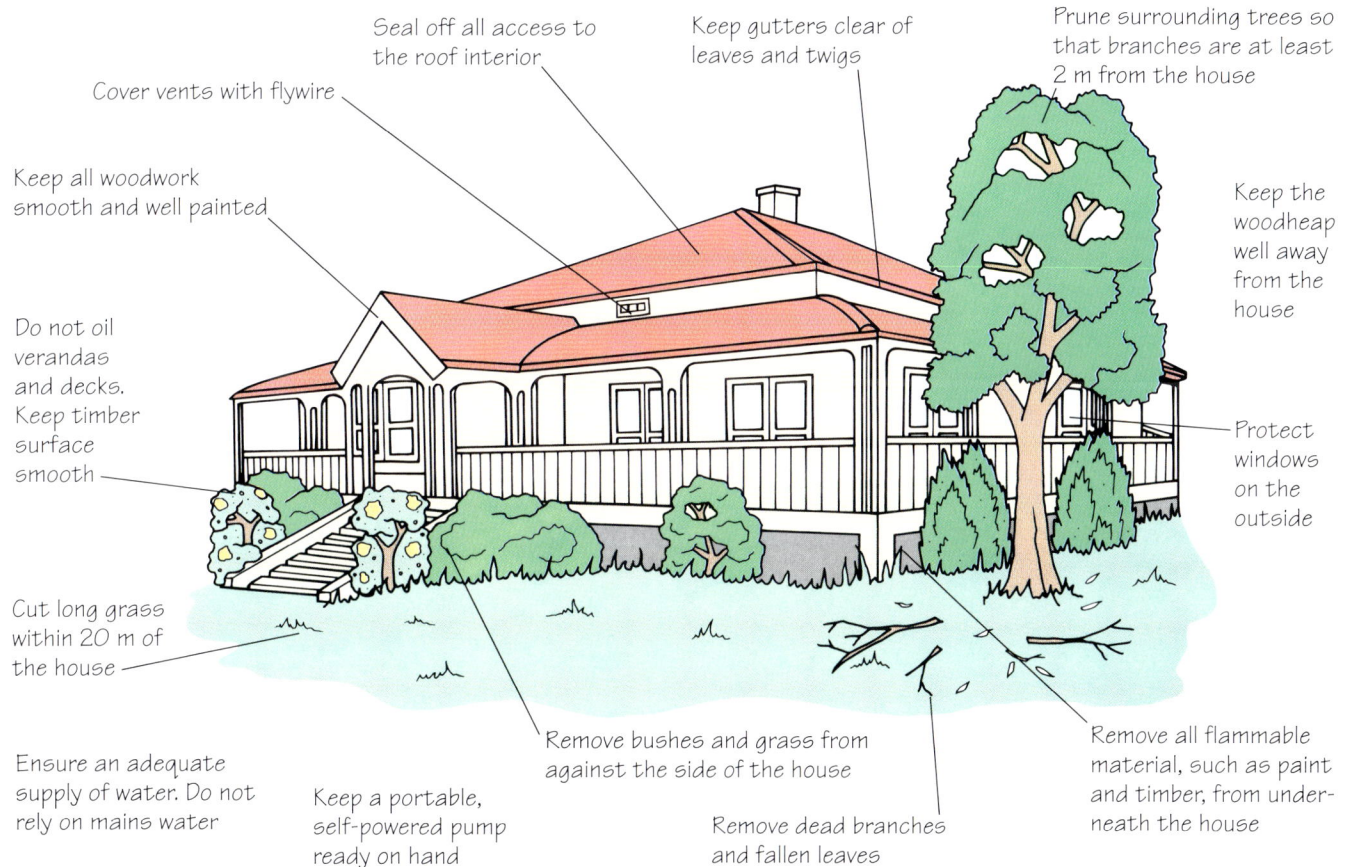

Seal off all access to the roof interior

Cover vents with flywire

Keep all woodwork smooth and well painted

Do not oil verandas and decks. Keep timber surface smooth

Cut long grass within 20 m of the house

Ensure an adequate supply of water. Do not rely on mains water

Keep a portable, self-powered pump ready on hand

Keep gutters clear of leaves and twigs

Prune surrounding trees so that branches are at least 2 m from the house

Keep the woodheap well away from the house

Protect windows on the outside

Remove bushes and grass from against the side of the house

Remove dead branches and fallen leaves

Remove all flammable material, such as paint and timber, from underneath the house

DISASTERPROOFING YOUR HOME

Stay alert

Don't relax when the main fire has passed your house. Go outside as soon as possible, and deal with any spot-fires. Hose the house down, being particularly careful to inspect the roof space and the underfloor area. You will have to remain vigilant for at least three or four hours, since sparks and cinders will continue to fall.

Fire damage

Don't despair

Major fire damage to your house may seem like the end of the world, but all is not lost. Depending on circumstances, concrete footings, brickwork, structural steel and even structural timber (if the depth of char is less than 2 mm) may all be reusable. If in doubt, consult a building surveyor or structural engineer.

Still standing

If brick walls in a fire-damaged building still appear to be sound, upright, and show no signs of movement if pushed, then they are probably alright. It is the mortar joints that are the most vulnerable part of a brick wall. Check to see if the mortar is crumbly or badly cracked. If it is sound, simply clean the walls down with a nylon brush and cleaning soap to remove smoke stains.

Storms

A bolt from the blue

A direct lightning strike can completely destroy your household electrical and electronic equipment. When you hear a storm approaching, disconnect all electrical appliances, particularly computers, modems and faxes. Also disconnect external aerial and power leads to television and radio sets. Try not to use the telephone, although if you absolutely have to, keep calls brief and don't touch metal, brick or concrete. If you live in a lightning-prone area, consider installing a surge protection device to shield vulnerable equipment. ▼

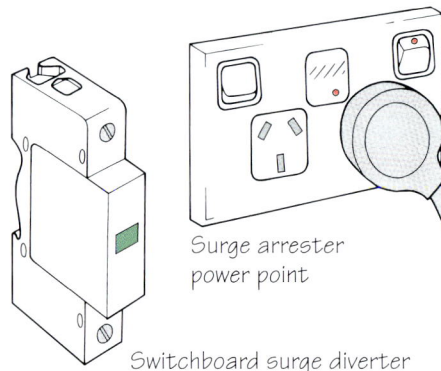

Surge arrester
power point

Switchboard surge diverter

Keep your head down

You can work out how far away an electrical storm is by counting the number of seconds between the lightning flash and the following thunderclap. When you know the time in seconds, divide it by three, and the result is the approximate distance in kilometres. If you are outside, and an electrical storm approaches closer than about 3 km, seek shelter indoors urgently (never under or near a tree).

Floods

When it's time to leave

If you must evacuate your home in the face of a flood, take these precautions. Stack as much furniture as possible well clear of the floor. Empty freezers and fridges and leave the doors open so they won't float. Switch off all services. Place a sandbag in the toilet bowl to prevent sewage from flowing back into the house. Move the car to high ground.

Flood damage

A long, slow process

Don't try to hurry repairs after a flood. Wait until everything is thoroughly dry, a process that may take months. Begin these tasks when the water goes down.
▷Remove everything wet from the house, including floor coverings, furniture, clothing and bedding.
▷Drain and start drying and cleaning the house as soon as possible. Pay particular attention to the underfloor area, wall cavities and other water traps. It may be necessary to take up floorboards and to cut inspection holes in walls so that mud can be flushed out.
▷Leave windows and doors open as wide as possible to speed drying. ▼

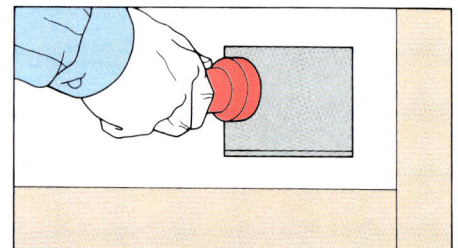

Slow drying ▲

Concrete floors dry very slowly after a thorough soaking. The interior can remain damp for weeks, so it is important not to try and re-lay floor coverings too soon. To check if concrete is dry, cut about one square metre of polythene sheet and tape all four sides to the floor. Cover it with a blanket and leave it for 24 hours. If condensation forms underneath, the floor is still too damp. Remove the polythene and leave the floor for a few more days before trying again.

First aid for carpets

The chances of a carpet surviving a flood are greatly increased if it is properly and promptly treated.
▷ Take the carpet up as soon as the water recedes, and hose off any mud.
▷ Try to dry the carpet as soon as possible to stop the backing from becoming irreparably damaged.
▷ Carefully stretch and tension the carpet as it dries, to try and help it retain its original shape.
If your efforts seem to have been successful, have the carpet professionally cleaned before it is relaid. It may also need to be treated with a fungicide.

THINKING AHEAD

When disaster strikes—a severe storm, an earthquake or a flood—you must deal with situations as they arise, trying your best to avoid personal injury and severe damage to your property. There are, however, a number of sensible precautions you can take beforehand that can minimise the impact of a catastrophe. If you live in an area that is prone to natural disasters, read and act on the following suggestions.

In an earthquake zone
▷ Regularly check chimneys, roofs and walls for stability.
▷ Make sure the house is firmly bolted to its foundations.
▷ Secure all household appliances that are connected to water, gas and electricity lines so that they cannot move.
▷ Store breakables, heavy objects and flammable or hazardous chemicals on the bottom shelves of cupboards.
▷ Attach tall, heavy furniture to a wall so it cannot topple over.
▷ Secure wall-mounted mirrors and heavy pictures, especially over beds.
▷ Fit stout latches to cupboard doors so that they will stay closed.
▷ Know where the safe areas are in each room—under desks, beds etc.

In a flood-prone area
▷ Know your area's flood history.
▷ Find out about the local evacuation plan (if there is one).
▷ Identify valuable or personal items and store them so that they can easily be removed to a place of safety.
▷ Know where the nearest high ground is, and the safest way to get there.

In a storm-prone area
▷ Keep the structure of your house—particularly its roof, guttering and downpipes—in good condition.
▷ Trim surrounding trees so that branches are well clear of the house.
▷ Clear away any loose roofing sheets and other potential missiles.
▷ Know your local community disaster plan.
▷ Know where the nearest high ground is, and the safest way to get there.

An all-purpose emergency kit
▷ A portable radio, with a fresh set of spare batteries.
▷ A torch, fuel lamp (with spare fuel), candles and matches.
▷ Water containers, tinned food, a tin opener and cooking equipment.
▷ A set of spare clothes.
▷ A first aid kit and a supply of medicines for anyone that needs them.
▷ Stout, waterproof plastic bags with tape to seal them.
▷ The telephone numbers of local emergency services.

ELIMINATING HOUSEHOLD SMELLS

Musty smells

Book freshener

To rid books of musty smells, store them for a few days in a paper bag filled with crumpled newspaper. The newspaper will absorb the smell. Repeat several times with fresh newspaper until the smell is completely gone.

Sweet linen

Freshen stored linen by placing an unwrapped bar of scented bath soap in among it. Replace the soap with a fresh bar every few months. An added bonus: after a few months the soap will be dry, making it last longer in the bath.

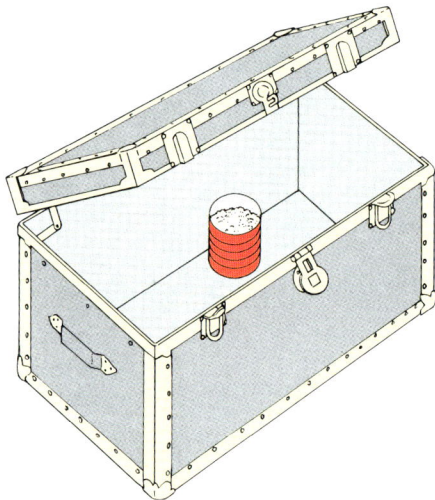

The cat's meow ▲

Here's a terrific way to deodorise a musty trunk. Simply pour some cat litter into a large uncovered coffee tin, place it in the trunk, and close the lid. The next day the smell will be gone, and you may remove the tin.

Household smells

Bin there, done that

Cat litter can also be used to eliminate rubbish smells. Sprinkle it in the bottom of rubbish bins to keep them smelling fresh. Change the litter every week or whenever the bins get damp.

The persistent smell of mothballs

The smell of mothballs can linger in an enclosed space for months. Restore a fresh scent by scrubbing every part of the space with a mixture of equal parts white vinegar or lemon juice and rubbing alcohol. Repeat the procedure if the smell remains.

Whole-house deodorant

Chase out the stagnant air of winter with the fresh scent of spring. Open doors and windows on opposite sides of the house, so that there is a through-breeze, and then place flowers or a deodorant in the path of the incoming air. If you are unable to create a natural breeze, try using a fan or air conditioner instead.

Simple solution

Banish bathroom smells by lighting a match or candle in the room. Allow it to burn for a few seconds, then put it out and leave it in a dish for five minutes.

Fresh scent

For a unique air freshener, spray a bit of your favourite perfume or cologne onto a light bulb. The heat from the light bulb will release the aroma of the perfume, sending your favourite scent wafting through the room. ▼

Pet smells

A concrete answer

Concrete absorbs smells, and a urine-soaked concrete floor has a terrible smell that can permeate the entire house. To deodorise it, scrub the floor with a solution of half white vinegar and half water. Or put undiluted methylated spirits in a spray bottle and spray the floor thoroughly.

A strong solution

Severe urine stains may require the application of a commercial pet smell remover (available from supermarkets and pet shops). If a slight smell remains even after this treatment, apply two coats of shellac to the problem area.

PETS

The great outdoors

The run-around ▶

If you chain your dog to a stake in the garden, you know that it soon becomes tangled. Prevent this by building a pivoting tether. Remove and discard the wheel from a plate-type ball-bearing caster by cutting through the axle. Sink a 100 × 100 mm post firmly into the ground, and screw the plate to the top of it. Make a pivoting arm by drilling a hole the size of the caster's old axle through one end of a 500 mm strip of 75 × 25 mm hardwood. Position the arm on the caster plate; slide a bolt through the plate and the arm, and secure it with a nut. Attach a stout screw eye to the opposite end of the arm, and hook the dog's chain to it.

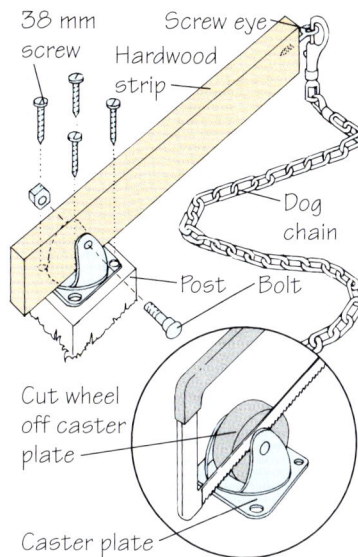

38 mm screw
Screw eye
Hardwood strip
Dog chain
Post   Bolt
Cut wheel off caster plate
Caster plate

No-tip dish

To protect your pet's outdoor water supply from accidental spills, serve up the water in an aluminium ring-type cake tin. Keep the tin in place by placing it over a wooden stake that's been firmly driven into the ground.

Wood stake
Ring-type cake tin

Have pet, will travel

Make car travel less traumatic for yourself and for your pet by securing the pet carrier or cage with an elastic strap so that it won't slide around. Twist the strap around the handle of a carrier or through the wires on a cage, and hook the ends of the cord to the sides of the car or to the seat-belt mechanism.

Protecting house plants

Keep off

Stop your and other cats from using potted plants as a litter box by burying a few mothballs in the soil.

Plant protection

This wire mesh shield lets water into the soil but keeps animals out. Make a paper pattern the same diameter as the pot, and tape the pattern to a piece of wire mesh. Using wire cutters, cut out the shield; then cut a straight line to the centre, and cut out a circle 2 cm larger than the plant's stem. Coat the cut edges with clear nail polish, and slip the shield into place.

12 mm wire mesh

Washing your pet

Bath time

Don't be tempted to wash your dog too often. A dog's skin is covered by a layer of grease, which helps to regulated its temperature. Washing removes this layer, and it is not fully replaced for about six weeks. For the same reason, a freshly washed dog should not be allowed outside for several hours on cold days. As a general rule, bathe dogs that live indoors every month or so; those that live outside only need to be washed three or four times a year.

Slip-sliding away

The slipping and sliding that usually accompanies bath time can frighten even phlegmatic dogs. Ease your pet's nervousness by providing a secure nonskid surface to stand on. When bathing your pet in a sink, cut a hole for the drain in a foam-backed place mat and position the mat foam side up for your pet to stand on. When bathing your pet in a bathtub, put down a non-slip rubber bath mat.

Drain strainer

Prevent blockages when bathing a pet by covering the drain with an inverted tea strainer or a nylon kitchen scourer. Either will keep pet hair out of the drain.

Dog dry-cleaner

Need to give your dog a wash but can't get it near the tub? Try a dry bath. Rub cornmeal into your pet's fur, then brush it out. If your pet needs a deodorant, follow with a baking soda rub.

CONTAINER GARDENING

Pots and repotting

Stand up straight

Does your flowerpot wobble when you put it down? Here's how to make flowerpots, planters and boxes sit flat without scratching or slipping. Apply four evenly spaced dabs of silicone sealant to the bottom. Before the sealant dries completely, turn the pot right side up and place it on a sheet of waxed paper. Once the sealant cures, the container will have four stable, level feet. ▼

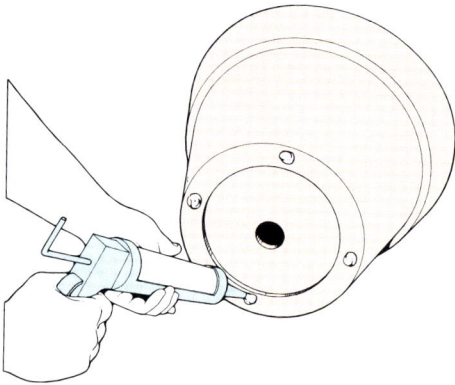

Room to grow

Repotting a plant is easy when you take advantage of the old pot. First, layer some potting mix in the bottom of the new pot. Place the old pot inside the new one, and pour potting mix in around it, gently tamping the mix with your fingers. Then remove the smaller pot and it'll leave a well that's the perfect size for your plant's root ball.

Full of holes ▶

If your flowerpot has holes, you may want to think twice before you automatically spread a layer of gravel beneath the soil. The last few centimetres or so of soil in the bottom of a pot remain saturated with water, whether there's a gravel base or not. Because saturated soil lacks oxygen, roots won't grow into this area, and by adding gravel you reduce the growing area available to the plant roots. On pots without drainage holes, however, continue to add the gravel layer to collect excess water that has no way of draining out.

20 cm deep pots

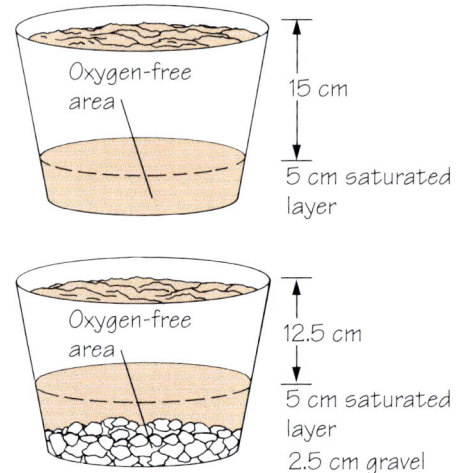

Oxygen-free area — 15 cm
5 cm saturated layer

Oxygen-free area — 12.5 cm
5 cm saturated layer
2.5 cm gravel

Keeping plants healthy

Too rich for me

Plants thrive in good soil. For a good, rich soil that drains well, try this recipe. Combine equal amounts of loam, compost or peat moss, and perlite or coarse sand. Then stir in two teaspoons of superphosphate, three teaspoons of horticultural lime, and two teaspoons of all-purpose granular fertiliser for every 4 litres of soil. Your plants will love it.

A fungus among us

Combat fungus on house plants with this baking soda solution. First, trim off any badly infected leaves. Mix one tablespoon of baking soda into 4 litres of water; use a spray bottle to apply the mixture on the remaining leaves. Repeat this procedure every few days until all signs of the fungus are gone.

The brush-off

Recycle a soft toothbrush by using it to remove scale insects from leaves. Dampen the brush in a solution of soapy water, or an appropriate pesticide, and gently scrub away the insects. Check the plant weekly, and repeat as necessary. If you find a toothbrush too cumbersome, use a soapless facial cleansing sponge (available in the cosmetics section of the chemist). ▼

FRESHLY CUT FLOWERS

Stem treatment

Hardy harvest

Minimise moisture loss when cutting flowers by harvesting them on a cloudy day or early in the morning. Be sure to make clean cuts, using pruning shears or a sharp knife; don't break or tear the stems. To prolong the life of the freshly cut blooms, plunge the stems directly into tepid water after cutting.

Daffodil know-how

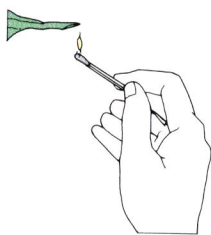

Newly cut daffodils secrete a milky substance that creates a seal when it mixes with water, preventing the stems from absorbing moisture. To avoid this, singe daffodils by briefly passing the cut end of the flower through the flame of a match. Repeat every time you recut the stems.

Kind cuts ▲

Freshly cut flowers need water to survive. Encourage your flowers to drink up by recutting their stems every few days. When recutting green stems, first carefully cut a 5 cm slit running from the base of the stem up. Next, cut the bottom of the stem at a 45°angle. If possible, cut stems under water to eliminate air bubbles that could get trapped in the stem and block water intake. Let the flowers stand in deep water in a cool place for several hours before arranging them.

No wilting here

Some flowers, including hollyhock, black-eyed Susan, gerbera, dogwood and butterfly bush, will wilt unless you boil their stems before arranging them. As the hot water rises upward, it forces air down and out of the stems, eliminating the airlocks that prevent water from reaching the flower heads and foliage. Protect the blooms by securing a plastic bag securely around the flowers with a twist-tie. Carefully holding the flowers diagonally, place the stems in the boiling water for approximately 20 seconds. Then plunge the stems into a bucket of tepid water and leave them for several hours before arranging.

5 cm boiling water

Half fill bucket with tepid water

Whittling away wood

On woody plants, carefully scrape the bark from the last 5 cm of the stem with a sharp knife or florist's scissors; then slit and recut as described at left.

There's life at the bottom

Before arranging flowers, strip off all the lower leaves. If they are submerged in water, they'll rot and produce a gas that hastens wilting. If the flowers are tall, trim off the uppermost buds (which are unlikely to flower) to allow the others a greater share of water which will increase their chances of blossoming. ▼

Water treatment

Straight up, no ice

If you've ever created an arrangement of cut tulips, you know that they tend to droop soon after cutting. Keep them standing straight by adding a few drops of vodka to the water.

Home brews

The best way to preserve cut flowers is to use a commercial preservative. But if you don't have any, mix two teaspoons of medicinal-type mouthwash into 4 litres of water—it'll be more effective than the old-fashioned options of aspirin or sugar. A can of a clear soft drink mixed with 4 litres of water can also help (because of the acid in the drink).

BARBECUES

Home-made barbecues

Quick & easy cooking

Do you have everything you need for the picnic—except the barbecue? Don't despair; you can build a temporary barbecue quickly and easily. Simply stack concrete blocks in a U-shape around a concrete slab or a bare patch of ground. Make the structure about 40 cm high (two layers of standard-size blocks). Top it with a grille and you're ready to cook. ▼

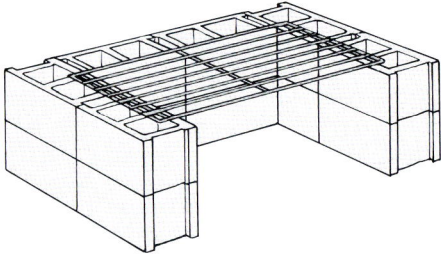

Just rolling along

When your guests can't come to the barbecue, bring the barbecue to them instead with this unique mobile cooker. Transform an old (paint-free) metal-bed wheelbarrow by placing an oven rack across the top. ▼

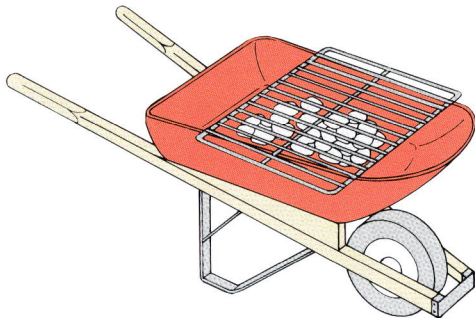

Charcoal fire-lighters

Carton starter

You can make a disposable charcoal starter by loading briquettes into an empty 1 litre waxed milk or fruit juice carton. To start the fire, just light the carton. Or as an alternative, fill a paper shopping bag with charcoal and kindling. Staple it shut and you have a one-step, no-mess fire starter.

Cleaning the barbecue

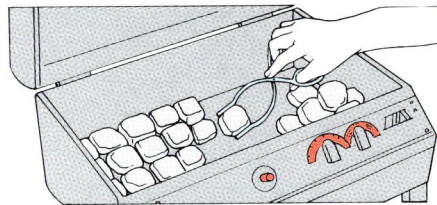

Burnt out ▲

Yes, even permanent briquettes in a gas barbecue need to be cleaned—but here's an easy way to do it. Simply turn the briquettes so that the greasy side is face down. Then light the barbecue, set the temperature on high, and close the cover. Let it burn for 20 minutes and your briquettes will be as good as new.

A safe start

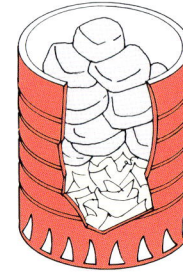

A 1 kg coffee tin will serve as a reusable charcoal starter. Using a punch-type can opener, cut a series of openings all around the bottom edge of the tin. Then remove the entire` base with a standard can opener, and place the tin securely in your barbecue—be sure it doesn't wobble. Put a small wad of paper and scraps of dry wood in the tin; then fill it to the top with charcoal. Light the paper through the triangular openings at the bottom. Once the briquettes are burning, lift the tin off with tongs (it'll be red-hot) and spread out the briquettes.

Leave it for the morning

The worst part of a barbecue is the clean up. Make it easier by removing the cooled grille from your barbecue and dropping it in the grass, cooking side down. Let it sit there overnight, and in the morning wipe away the dew (and grease) with damp paper towels.

Overnight soak

For really tough baked-on grease, put your dirty grille inside a heavy-duty plastic rubbish bag. Mix a solution of half a cup liquid dishwashing detergent and 4 litres water. Pour the mixture over the grille and seal the bag with a twist tie. Let it sit overnight. The next day, use a stiff brush to remove the residue. Rinse the grille thoroughly.

FIREPLACES

A good fire

Getting started ▶

The best way to lay a fire is to create a pyramid out of the logs. For the base of the pyramid, use one large log and one medium-sized log, keeping the smaller one in the front. Stuff a generous quantity of newspaper, twigs and kindling into the gap between the two logs, and top off the pyramid with a small log. Always start a fire from the bottom by lighting the paper and kindling at both ends. Keep the fire going by replacing the logs as needed. As the rear log burns, use a poker to carefully roll the front log to the rear and then put in a new front log. Add other logs as required.

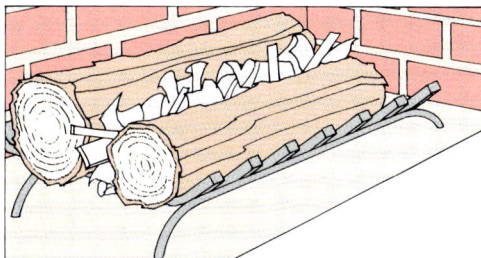

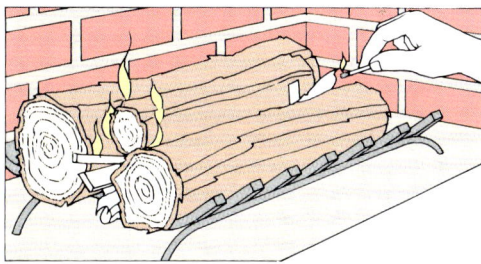

A newsworthy start ▲

If you have trouble lighting wood fires, try this fail-safe fire starter. Beginning at an outside edge, tear a section of newspaper into strips, stopping just short of the fold. Tightly wedge the paper underneath the logs, add kindling, and then carefully light the ends of the strips.

Ash sifter

Fires burn longer when you separate the coals from the ashes. To do this, cut a piece of metal mesh (available from most hardware stores) and fit it over the grate. The openings in the mesh will let the fine ashes fall through, and at the same time hold the glowing coals up closer to the flames. ▼

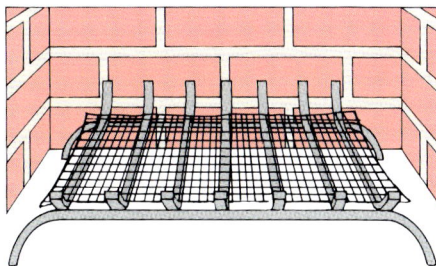

Open up

Fires need oxygen in order to burn, and often the only air supply is the warm air from the house. To stop heated air from rushing up the chimney, feed your fire fresh air from a window left open just a crack—only about 2.5 to 3 cm. If you pick a window on the windy side of the house, you may strengthen the fireplace's updraft and reduce smoking.

In the end

Because embers can smoulder even when there are no flames, you should be certain that the blaze is completely extinguished. Don't pour water on the flames; this can cause heavy smoking and a cloud of ash. Instead, put out the flames with baking soda, sand or dirt. It's also wise to keep some baking soda close by in case the fire gets out of hand and needs to be smothered.

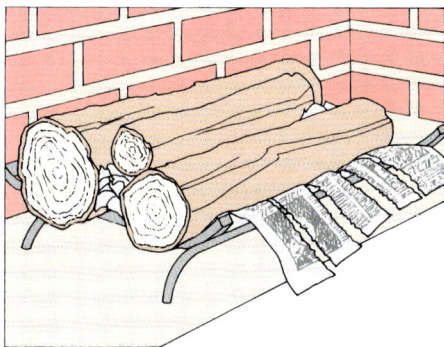

Glass doors

Recycle those ashes

It sounds strange, but smoke stains can be removed from the glass doors in combustion stoves with ashes. Just dip a damp cloth into cooled ashes and rub away the stains.

Unsmoked glass

If the smoke stains on your glass combustion stove doors refuse to come off with ashes, as described above, use a foam-type aerosol oven cleaner. Simply spray on the foam, let it sit for the time recommended on the can, and wipe it off, following the manufacturer's instructions. Your doors will sparkle.

CHRISTMAS DECORATIONS AND WRAPPINGS

Ornaments and lights

Pretty blocks

Create your own colourful Christmas tree ornaments by covering small cardboard boxes with scraps of fabric or wallpaper. Tie a ribbon around them to create a package. You can wrap scraps of wood as well. ▼

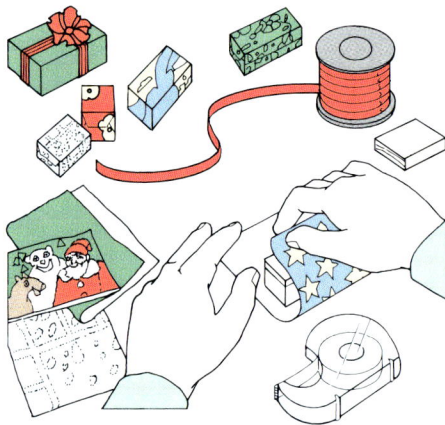

Needle in a haystack

Always make sure that you check your Christmas lights carefully before you drape them round the tree. The faulty bulb that stops the entire string from working can be almost impossible to find once concealed by leaves and branches. When buying lights, try to find a set that is not going to be completely disabled by one faulty globe.

Light fixtures

Having trouble securing lights where you want them on the tree? Tie them to the branches with green pipe cleaners.

Tending the tree

Tree test

To make sure that the Christmas tree you are buying is fresh, look at it carefully, smell it and handle it. A fresh tree will have a good green colour and a pleasant fragrance. If you lift the tree a few centimetres off the ground and bang the stump down, the needles shouldn't fall off in substantial numbers. As a final test, hold a branch about 15 cm from its tip between your thumb and forefinger and pull your hand toward you, allowing the branch to slip between your fingers. If the needles adhere to the branch, the tree is fresh; if they fall off, it's not.

Drink up

To fire-retard your tree and keep its needles green, mix a solution of 8 litres hot water, two cups corn syrup, quarter cup liquid bleach, two pinches Epsom salts and half a teaspoon borax. Saw several centimetres off the bottom of the trunk, and let the tree stand overnight in a bucket filled with this mixture. Use this mixture in the tree stand, too.

It rings a bell

Nothing attracts a child's attention like a Christmas tree. To warn you of little hands reaching for the colourful ornaments, tie a number of small bells to the lower branches of the tree.

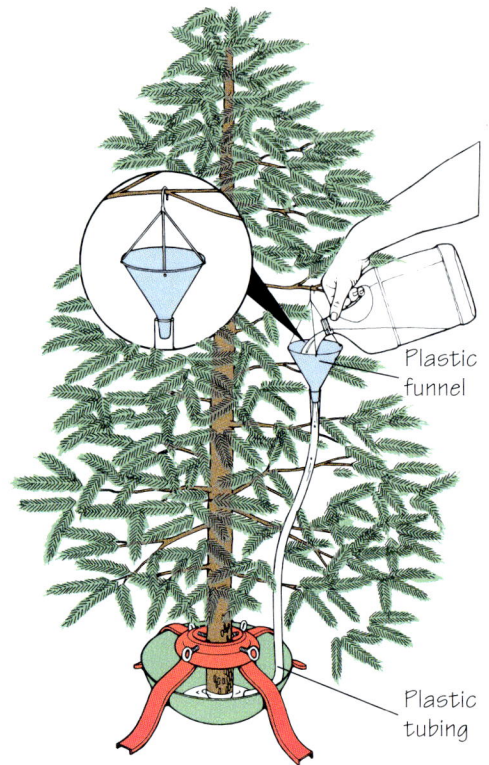

Plastic funnel

Plastic tubing

No more aching back ▲

Make this simple watering device and you'll never again have to squirm underneath the branches of a Christmas tree. You'll need a medium-sized plastic funnel, a length of plastic tubing, and some straight wire. Punch three holes along the top rim of the funnel, thread a length of wire through each hole, and twist the wires together to form a hook at the top; hang it from a branch of the tree. Force the tubing over the small end of the funnel, and put the free end of the tube in the water trough of the tree stand. Next time the tree needs water, just use the funnel.

Stand tall ▶

Keep your tree straight and tall with this sturdy stand. Drill four equidistant holes around the rim of a 20 litre plastic bucket. Partly fill the bucket with sand and move it into place. Soak the sand with water, tamp it down, and add more sand, leaving the holes exposed. Trim the lowest branches off the tree, and use a saw to cut an X into the bottom surface of the trunk. Insert the trunk into the sand, and stabilise the tree with four lengths of fishing line. Tie each line to a sturdy branch; then pass the lines through the holes in the bucket and tie them securely.

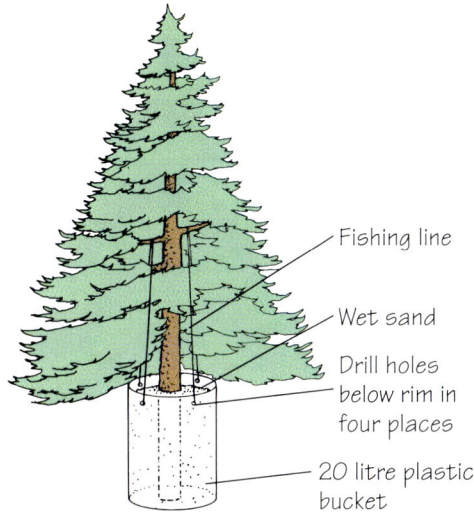

Fishing line

Wet sand

Drill holes below rim in four places

20 litre plastic bucket

In the bag

Don't drag your dried-out Christmas tree through the house, leaving behind a trail of needles. Instead, take it apart one branch at a time. Using a pair of pruning shears, cut the branches into little pieces and drop them straight into a plastic garbage bag. When you've finished, all you'll have to carry is the bare tree trunk and a garbage bag. ▼

Faster fakes

If you're putting up a reusable artificial tree, here's a way to make the job a little bit easier. Dip the ends of the branches into some petroleum jelly before inserting them into the frame.

Gift wrapping

Wrapping-paper resources

If you want an economical alternative to traditional wrapping paper, try scraps of unused wallpaper, especially the shiny, metallic kind. Or use aluminium foil and brightly coloured ribbons.

Emergency wrapping

When you run out of wrapping paper on Christmas Eve and have a couple of items left to wrap, don't despair. Black and white newspaper, tied with red ribbon or gold cord, makes a parcel that is more than acceptable.

CHRISTMAS TREE CARE

The fresh scent of a real pine tree puts people in the Christmas spirit; but a tree can be a serious fire hazard if it is used carelessly or allowed to dry out. Here are some tips for keeping a tree fresh and safe for several weeks.

▷ If you are storing your tree for a few days before decorating it, keep it inside in a cool area, away from the sun and wind.

▷ Help your tree retain moisture during storage by making a straight cut across the trunk, 3 cm from the bottom. Stand the tree in a bucket of water, so that the water covers the cut.

▷ Before putting the tree in place, make another cut across the trunk, 3 cm above the first.

▷ Use a stand that holds at least 4 litres of water, and check the level daily to ensure that it remains above the top cut.

▷ Place the tree away from electrical appliances, candles and other sources of heat and flame.

▷ Don't use combustible decorations on the tree.

▷ Check all wires and connections; don't use lights with frayed cords; never use lighted candles.

▷ Always turn all the tree lights off before you go to sleep, and before leaving your home.

SPORTS EQUIPMENT

Out in the wild

Here's a hot tip

A broken and frayed bootlace end can be frustrating on a walk because it is difficult to thread through the lace holes. Here's a simple solution to the problem. Using a match or a lighter, melt a scrap of nylon rope. Let the drippings land on the frayed lace end; then use a twig or a toothpick to shape the end. ▼

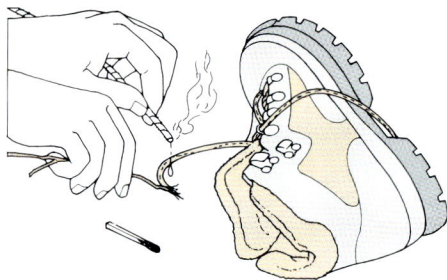

Handy oil

Usually the lantern or camp-stove pump plunger needs a bit of oil just at a time when there is none to be found. At a pinch, you can use a drop of salad or cooking oil as a substitute.

High and dry

Keep your vital topographical and bush-walking maps from becoming water damaged and worn by having them laminated at an office services centre or instant printery. First cut the maps up into convenient sections that will fit into your jacket or backpack pocket. This will save folds, which are always the first places that tear on a frequently used map. Erasable track notes and bearings can be written on laminated maps with a Chinagraph or wax marker.

Bright and shiny ▲

Soot accumulates quickly on campfire cookware. Keep your pots and pans bright and shiny by placing them in disposable aluminium pie dishes when cooking. When these aluminium shields become black with soot, toss them out.

Light my fire

As a precaution, always carry a candle stub in the bottom of your waterproof matchbox. With its help, you'll be able to light a fire—even with damp kindling.

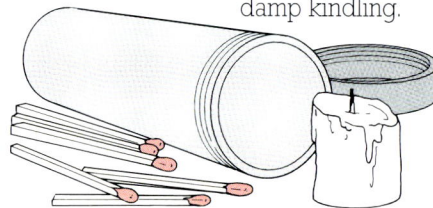

Be prepared

Never go on a bushwalking trip without your own instant, all-purpose repair kit. Contents will vary; here are some ideas.
▷ A tube of instant (Supa) glue.
▷ A tube of contact cement, invaluable for boot and shoe repairs.
▷ A couple of needles and some strong thread or twine.
▷ Lengths of string and nylon cord.
▷ A ripstop nylon repair kit.
▷ A vinyl repair kit (for air beds).

Inflation devices

A lazy solution

It is hard work inflating footballs and other such items by hand. If you have an air compressor, harness its power. To adapt the compressor, fit a car tyre valve extender onto an inflator needle and attach the two with silicone sealant.

Rapid inflator

If you don't have an air compressor around the house, you can still create your own easy inflation system, using a vacuum cleaner. Buy a plastic pipe reducer to fit the air valve on the inflatable item, and use it to connect the vacuum cleaner exhaust port to the valve.

Fishing equipment

Don't throw it out ▲

The next time a ballpoint pen runs out of ink, recycle it by removing the spring and ink tube and using the barrel to carry split shot whenever you go fishing. The pen makes a great dispenser—whenever you need a sinker, simply unscrew the barrel and let the shot roll out one by one. Clip the pen to your pocket for easy access.

Get a grip

Hard-to-detach fishing rod sections will be easier to pull apart if you provide yourself with a good grip. Here's how. Buy two pieces of rubber surgical tubing (available at chemists), cut them lengthwise, and place one on each side of the ferrule.

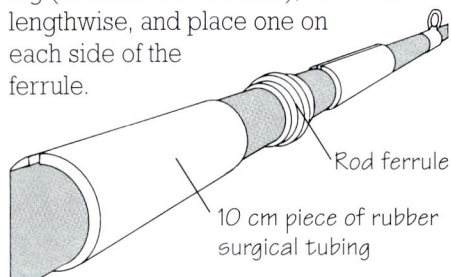

Rod ferrule

10 cm piece of rubber surgical tubing

Just a teaspoon

Turn an old teaspoon into a spinner by breaking the bowl off the handle. Drill a hole into one end of the bowl, and wire a swivel onto it. Use it to enhance another lure, or drill a hole in the other end, attach a hook to it, and use it by itself. Don't throw away the handle; use it to make a minnow by drilling four small holes along its length and attaching a swivel to the hole at one end, a single hook in the hole at the other end, and double hooks in the other two holes. ▼

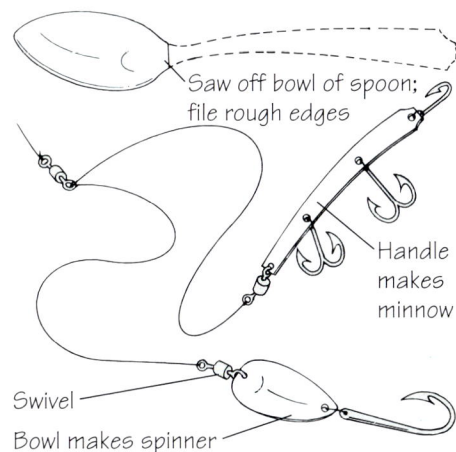

Saw off bowl of spoon; file rough edges

Handle makes minnow

Swivel

Bowl makes spinner

SKI REPAIRS

As most skiers know, scratches and gouges impair the manoeuvrability of skis. You can easily repair a small gouge in the plastic base of a downhill ski by using a proprietory filler (from a ski or outdoors shop) and a soldering iron or propane torch. However, if your skis have deep gouges that penetrate the core, have them fixed at a ski repair centre by an expert.

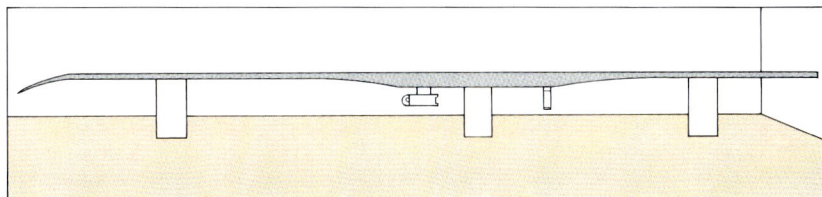

1 Support the damaged ski on wood blocks placed on a flat surface. For extra support, butt the tail of the ski against a wall. If you have a workbench, you can clamp the ski in a vice, but be sure to protect the ski from scratches by placing pieces of cardboard or wood between the jaws of the vice and the ski.

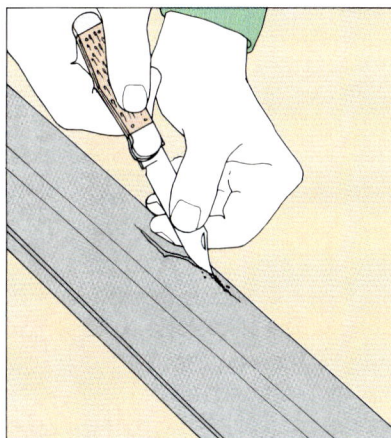

2 Using a knife or an old screwdriver, remove all traces of wax and dirt from the gouge. Then very carefully heat the area around the gouge by passing a soft torch flame over it or by holding a soldering iron close to the area.

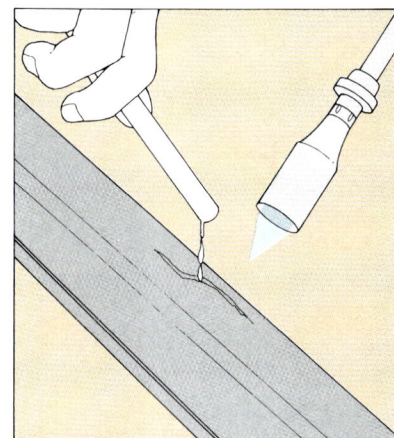

3 Once the plastic around the gouge is soft, use a torch or soldering iron to melt the candle of filler. Fill the gouge with candle drippings while keeping the whole area warm. Slightly overfill the gouge. Let the material cool and harden and then use a flexible putty knife to scrape the patch flush with the base.

BOATS

Canoe corner

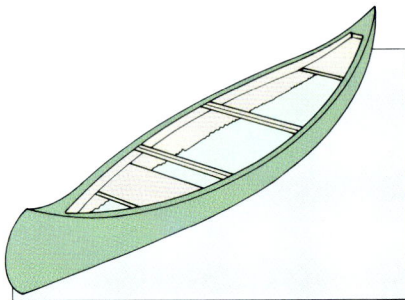

Noises off ▲

Glue scraps of carpeting to the bottoms of coolers and tackle boxes to prevent them from knocking around in the bottom of a canoe (or other boat)—and to keep the noise from alerting fish and wildlife to your presence. Even better, pad the entire canoe bottom with outdoor carpeting. Keep the carpet clean by hosing off any dirt and hanging it from a tree limb or clothesline to dry.

Quiet, please!

Pad the gunwales with short lengths of foam rubber piping and your paddles won't bang on them when you stroke. With the piping slit along one side, installation is simple—just cut the foam to the required length and press it into place on the gunwales.

It's time to slim down

Paddles that have thick blades can be clumsy. To keep them slicing through the water, sand the edges of the blades to a thickness of about 3 mm; use a portable electric sander for best results. Varnish all sanded areas to keep the paddle from becoming waterlogged.

Trailer tricks

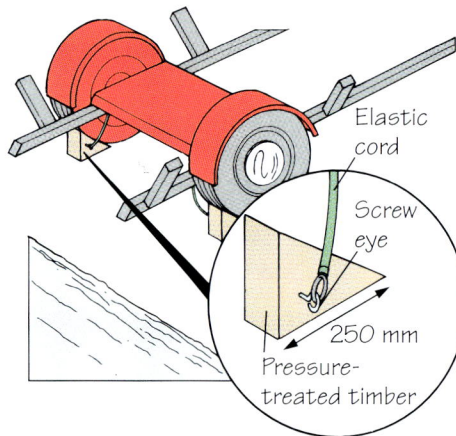

Elastic cord

Screw eye

250 mm

Pressure-treated timber

Take them with you

Save time and aggravation at the launching ramp with these attachable chocks. Cut a 25 cm triangle from a piece of 200 × 100 mm pressure-treated timber. Attach a screw eye to one side, and connect an elastic strap to the eye. When you are ready to load your boat onto its trailer, place a chock behind each rear wheel and hook the straps to the undercarriage of the trailer. Load your boat and drive away; the chocks will follow. Once you're out of the way of the other boat-owners, you can stop and detach the chocks. But keep them fastened to the trailer with the elastic cords so that they'll be ready for the next time.

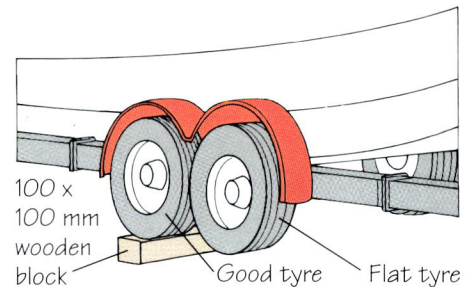

100 × 100 mm wooden block   Good tyre   Flat tyre

On the road ▲

At a pinch, a 100 × 100 mm wooden block makes a good temporary jack for a boat trailer that has a double axle (four tyres). Simply loosen the wheel nuts on the flat tyre; then ride the good tyre up onto the block. Place chocks behind the wheels on the other side of the trailer to prevent it from rolling. The flat tyre will now be high enough for you to remove.

Put a leash on it

A couple of 2.5 cm wide nylon dog leads will keep a boat from bobbing up and down during transit. Using an eyebolt, attach a tie-down with hooks on the ends to the front of the trailer. Slip the handle loops of the leads over the cleats on the bow of the boat. Clip the lead hooks to the free tie-down hook. Keep the winch strap attached as usual.

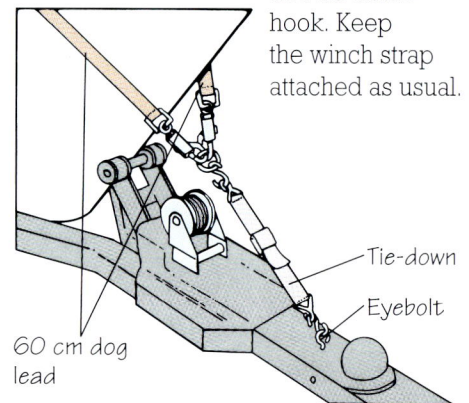

60 cm dog lead

Tie-down

Eyebolt

Add it yourself

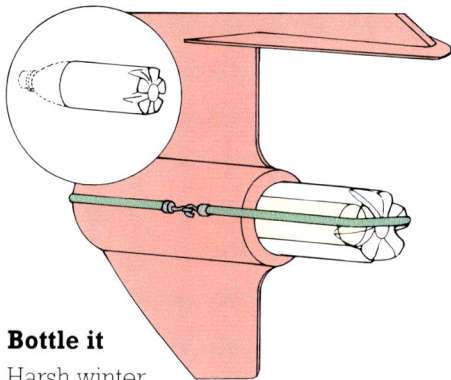

Bottle it

Harsh winter weather can wreak havoc with exposed metal parts. While the propeller is usually stored away separately, the propeller shaft is left out in the cold. Protect it from corrosion with this cover made from a 2 litre plastic soft drink bottle. Using a sharp knife, cut off the neck of the bottle. Lightly grease the exposed propeller shaft, then slide on the bottle; hold it in place with an elastic cord.

All aboard

If your boat has a recessed fishing rod holder mounted on the stern, you can

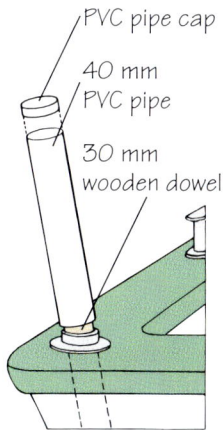

PVC pipe cap

40 mm PVC pipe

30 mm wooden dowel

use it to rig a removable hand-hold to help guests coming aboard. Cut a suitable length from a wooden dowel and slide it inside an equal length of PVC pipe. Top off the assembly with a PVC pipe cap.

Not a puddle in sight

Rain can easily pool in a full-length boat cover, making the cover hard to remove without tipping at least some of the water into the boat. Encourage the rain to run off by propping up the cover with this home-made support. Cap both ends of a wooden dowel with the rubber tips from a discarded pair of crutches. Place the support vertically where the water usually accumulates. ▼

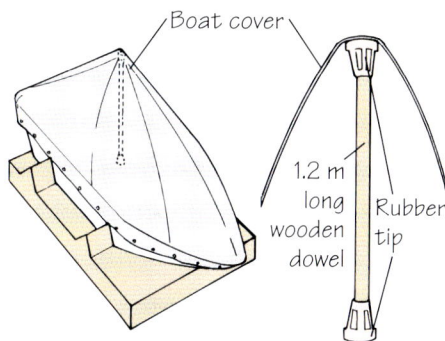

Boat cover

1.2 m long wooden dowel

Rubber tip

Anchors away

On a small- to medium-sized boat, the last metre of anchor chain (or even the anchor itself) can bang against the bow as you haul it up—sometimes damaging the boat. Warn yourself that the anchor is close to the surface by tying a piece of brightly coloured tape to the line a few metres above the spot where the chain begins.

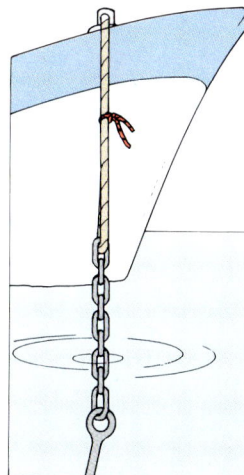

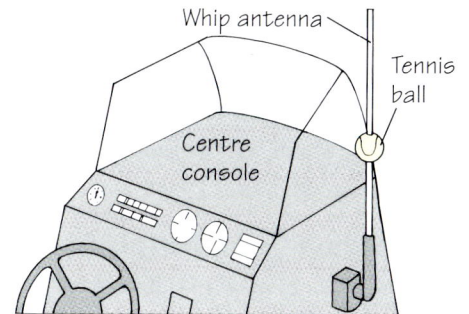

Whip antenna

Tennis ball

Centre console

Follow the bouncing ball ▲

The tall whip antenna required for a loran unit or CB radio is often attached to a boat's centre console, where it can slap against the windscreen during rough weather. Protect both the antenna and any surfaces it may damage by installing a buffer. Just drill a hole that's slightly smaller than the diameter of the antenna through a tennis ball and slide the ball down onto the antenna.

Easy maintenance

Regular care pays

One good tug on a dirty or rusty clip holding down a boat cover or canvas top may end up tearing the material instead of opening the clip. Prevent this problem by smearing the clips with a thin coat of petroleum jelly two or three times each year.

More absorbent than ever

It's nearly impossible to prevent oil from leaking into the engine trays, and every boat-owner knows what a mess that can be to clean up. Make life easier by spreading an opened disposable nappy in each tray. The nappy will absorb the spills, making clean up simple.

Special delivery

The space behind the kickboard and underneath the base of a kitchen cabinet provides a safe haven for all kinds of insects because it's difficult to reach. Deliver a dose of insecticide to the residents by drilling a 10 mm hole through either the kickboard or the cabinet floor. After spraying, plug the hole with a dowel button or length of dowel. ▼

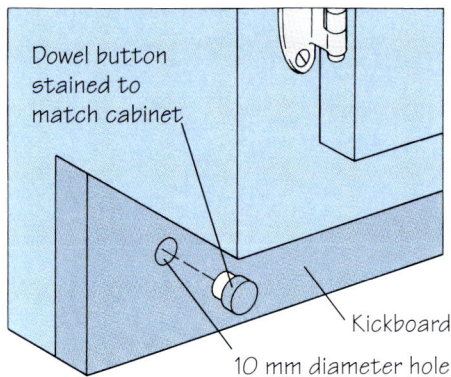

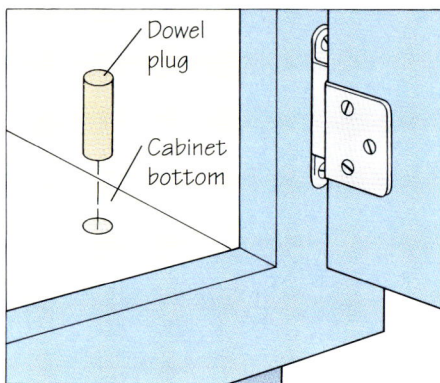

Dowel button stained to match cabinet

Kickboard

10 mm diameter hole

Dowel plug

Cabinet bottom

The great survivors

To keep cockroaches under control you must deprive them of food and shelter. Make sure that anything edible is put away, and wipe down food preparation surfaces carefully before going to bed at night. Wring out dirty sponges and dishcloths; seal rubbish in plastic bags and put it in the dustbin. Block off all nooks and crannies, paying particular attention to any gaps where water and drainage pipes puncture the walls.

Don't give up

Ants are among the most persistent of all household pests. The best solution is to cut off access to the foods that they like, but this is not always easy. Wipe down work surfaces and cupboard shelves thoroughly, and leave a few bay leaves scattered about. If the ants keep coming back, try a commercial bait. Even with these, however, it may take a year to get rid of the problem entirely.

Unwelcome tenants

Possums in the roof can be a noisy—not to say destructive—nuisance, and once happily installed they can be difficult to remove. If you live in an area where possums are common, try to discourage them by spraying with a repellent such as thiram, or a solution of quassia chips. Buy 60 g of quassia chips (the wood of a tropical American tree) from a local chemist and boil them in 10 litres of water for about 15 minutes. Spray the solution on buds and foliage that might attract the possums.

Under siege

Once possums are in your roof they will have to be evicted. Block up all ways into the roof space, leaving open only the one that the possums generally use. Wait one night until the possums have left the roof to feed—you may have to actually watch them go—and then cover up the final exit. But don't expect the possums to give up easily. They will return, night after night, looking for a way back in. Only then will you find out if you have discovered all possible entrances.

Behind bars

As a last resort, persistent possums can be caught. First of all, consult your local council or the National Parks and Wildlife Service for their advice, and also for any regulations governing the capture and transport of native animals. Hire a box trap from your local vet, or the council, and bait it with fruit. Release the captured animal several kilometres away—or as advised by the National Parks and Wildlife Service—but expect it to return. In New Zealand, unlike Australia, possums are a declared pest, and can be exterminated.

No more fun and games

When you go away the mice will play, so before closing up your caravan or holiday home for the winter, put out some home-made mouse-repelling sachets. Make small bags out of scraps of fabric, and fill them with crushed, dried peppermint leaves. Tie the bags securely and toss a few under beds, in cupboards and wardrobes, inside the stove and in the dishwasher.

MOVING HEAVY OBJECTS

Damage control

Glass handles

When moving heavy mirrors or panes of glass, cover the edges with pieces of foam rubber tubing. Slit the pieces of tubing lengthways so that they slide easily over the edges. The tubing will protect your hands from injury and the floors and walls from gouges.

Magic carpet ride

Don't take a chance of hurting yourself or your polished floor when moving heavy objects. Instead, slide carpet scraps, pile side down, under them. The rough backing keeps the objects from slipping, while the pile glides easily over the floor. In addition to making the move easier, the carpet will prevent the objects from scratching the floor.

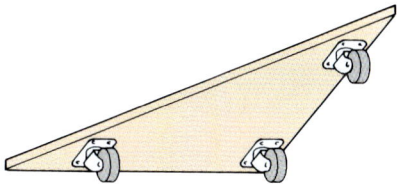

On the move ▲

Moving your sofa (or any other heavy and awkward, four-legged piece of furniture) will be easy if you slip a small three-wheeled furniture trolley under each leg. Make your own from pieces of 12 mm plywood or timber and three standard furniture casters.

Freewheeling

To keep heavy or unwieldy objects from falling and breaking during transport, wheel them around on a skateboard. You'll save your arm and back muscles.

Wide loads

Hand trolleys are good for moving things around, but the lip just isn't deep enough to handle large objects. Remedy this by adding an extension made of 50 mm diameter PVC pipe. With a hacksaw, cut narrow slots into the pipe—the slots should fit snugly onto the trolley lip, but if they're too tight, widen them slightly with a file. For added strength, glue the pipes together. Attach the assembly to the trolley with a few taps of a rubber mallet; the extension pulls right off when not in use.

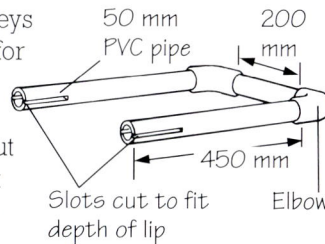

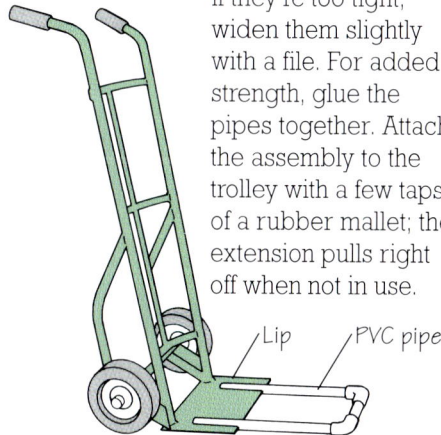

50 mm PVC pipe — 200 mm — 450 mm — Elbow
Slots cut to fit depth of lip

Lip — PVC pipe

Protect soft floors

Casters and trolley wheels can easily damage soft timber flooring during a move. Instead of rolling the wheels directly over the floor, safeguard it by rolling them over strips of a thin, hard material (such as 6 mm thick hardboard or 3 mm thick rigid acrylic plastic).

SAFETY FIRST

LOOK AFTER YOUR BACK

Whenever you have to lift a heavy load, prevent back injury by following these steps.

▷ Position yourself as close to the load as possible.

▷ Always flex your knees; never bend forward from your waist.

▷ When leaning forward while lifting, keep your back perfectly flat; never arch it.

▷ When pushing heavy objects, bend your knees, keep your back flat, and power the push with your legs.

▷ If you need to turn while lifting or pushing, move your feet; don't twist your back.

▷ Never try to move a really heavy load by yourself—get help. A two-person lift is half the strain.

HOUSEHOLD MOVING

Before the move

Moving checklist

Moving day is difficult at best, with all the last-minute details to take care of. Remove some of the stress and worry by completing the following tasks in the weeks preceding the move.

▷ If necessary, have your major appliances serviced. If you plan to drive to your new home, have your car serviced as well. If you are having your car moved by truck, make sure that the petrol tank is nearly empty.

▷ Empty all storage containers of flammable materials, such as petrol, kerosene and propane.

▷ Drain petrol and oil from your lawn mower and all other power equipment.

▷ Drain water from all garden hoses.

▷ Dispose of flammable and caustic items such as matches, cleaning fluids, bleach, drain cleaners and acids.

Mapping out the territory

Draw up a plan of your new home on graph paper to a scale of 1:20. Indicate where you want to put each piece of furniture and other large items, such as fridges. This will save you from having to move heavy pieces twice. ▼

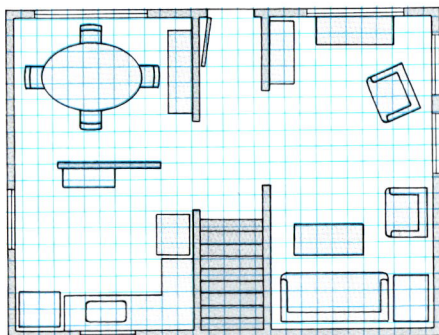

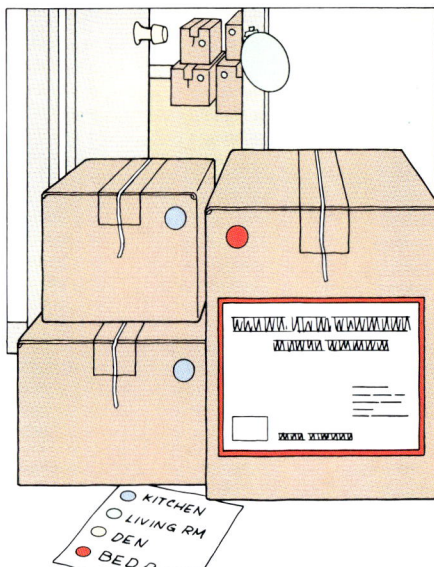

Moving by colours ▲

By assigning a colour to each room of your new house, you can eliminate much of the disorganisation on arrival day. Here's how. As you pack up the contents of your old home, colour-code the boxes to the new rooms, using brightly coloured stickers or markers. On moving day, attach a colour-coded balloon to each room's door frame to show the movers where to put the boxes.

Easy unpacking

Before packing up everything, select a dressing table drawer to contain any linen, clothes and towels you'll need for the first night in your new home. Then, when you're exhausted at the end of the move, you won't have to conduct a frantic search for these necessities.

Boxes

As flat as a pancake

You can buy packing boxes from many major moving companies or truck rental firms. But you can save money by using your own. Start collecting boxes from grocery and liquor stores a few months before the move. Rather than keeping the empty boxes open and letting them take up a lot of space, flatten them for easy storage by slitting open the bottom tape and collapsing the sides. Before filling the boxes, reseal the bottoms with strong packing tape.

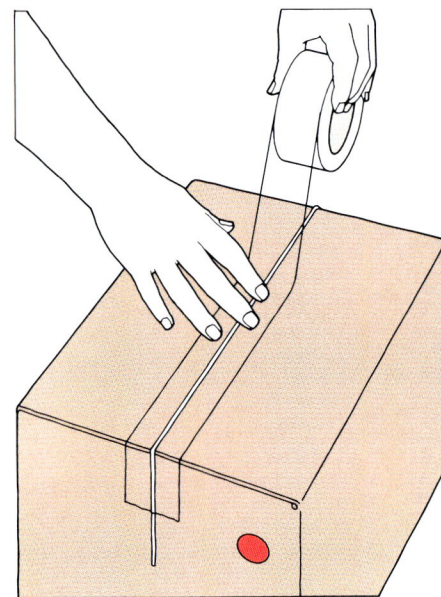

Quick opening ▲

Before taping boxes closed, first run a length of tough string along the seam. Place the tape over the string, leaving a few centimetres of the string hanging off the end. When it's time to unpack, pull on the string to slit open the tape.

Protective padding

Bright spots ▲

Small items can easily disappear in the mounds of crumpled paper generated during unpacking. Keep little treasures safe by wrapping them in pieces of brightly coloured tissue paper. They'll be easy to spot, and you won't accidentally throw them out.

Out of the linen cupboard

Save space by cushioning breakable items with towels, face cloths, sheets, pillowcases and tablecloths. You'll also save money on paper, and you won't need to pack your linen separately.

Dishes and glasses

On the edge

Believe it or not, the best way to pack plates is on edge, rather than flat. Wrap the plates in bubble wrap (if you are using newspaper, place each dish in a plastic bag to save washing-up time later), and arrange them on their edges inside a sturdy carton. For the safest ride, layer 5 cm of folded paper between the plates and 8 cm of paper on the bottom of the carton.

All stuffed up

Because of the dividers, liquor cartons are ideal for transporting cups and glasses—ask a local liquor store to save you some discarded boxes. But if you don't have any of these boxes on hand, you can still safely transport glasses and cups. Stuff your glasses and cups with crumpled paper before wrapping them in bubble wrap. Then nestle the wrapped pieces in the spaces between your other dishes. Don't nest unwrapped glasses—they will bump together and break or chip.

Odds and ends

The bases are loaded

When packing table lamps, wrap the bases in paper or bubble wrap and alternate them end for end. Pack the shades separately, but don't wrap them in newspaper; the print can cause stains. Instead, use bubble wrap or pieces of plain, unprinted paper.

Artful packing ▶

Small pieces of art can be placed between blankets or pillows for safe transport—don't use newspaper for padding because it can stain. Or use a collapsed cardboard box; slide in the item and seal the edges. Large valuable artworks should be padded, wrapped and crated by a professional.

Like clockwork

Before sending your grandfather clock off on a trip, take these steps to ensure a safe arrival. Remove the weights, pendulum and finials, and pack them separately. Keep the hammers and weight chains from moving around by securing them to the case of the clock with strong cord or tape. For long-distance moves, consult an expert—the works may need to be protected against damage.

X marks the spot

Tape an X across each mirror with masking tape before wrapping it in paper or bubble wrap; if there's an accident, the tape will hold the shards in place. Small mirrors can be put on edge and packed in sturdy boxes, but large mirrors need to be shipped in special cartons that your mover can provide.

Packing in the knowledge

Pack books on edge in small cartons, alternating the directions of the bindings. Pack the cartons so that they weigh less than 20 kg each.

HOUSEHOLD MOVING

Large appliances

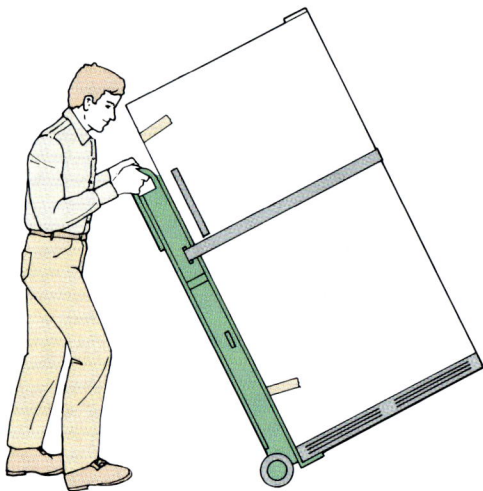

Upstanding appliances ▲

When transporting a refrigerator or an upright freezer, make sure the unit stays upright throughout the move. If it is put on its side, the fluid will flow out of the compressor and you'll have to let the unit stand upright for 24 hours before you can start it again without causing damage. To help you keep a unit upright while moving it, hire a special heavy-duty trolley.

Clean machine

Before moving your refrigerator, thoroughly wash and dry the inside and let it air out for at least 24 hours. On moving day, toss in a sock filled with charcoal briquettes, freshly ground coffee or baking soda to absorb moisture and smells. Tightly knot the neck of the sock so that its contents don't spill. Finally, seal the door shut with masking tape.

A different beat

Keep the drum inside your washing machine from banging around in its cabinet by stuffing towels between the drum and the housing.

Bulky beds

Restrain yourself

The day of the big move, don't forget to tie sofa bed mechanisms firmly in place before transporting them to their new location. You don't want them opening up unexpectedly while in transit. ▼

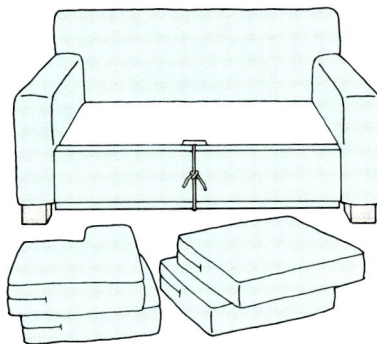

Down the drain

Water beds should always be drained before they're moved. You can hasten the process by weighting down the valve so that it's the lowest point on the mattress. ▼

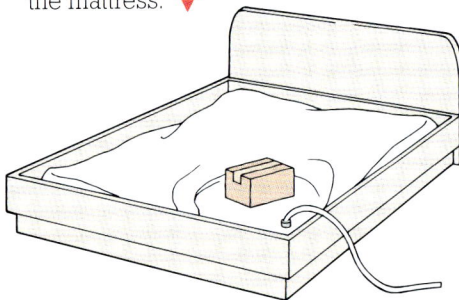

Electronics

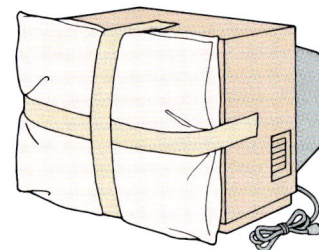

Unplugged ▲

Transporting a warm television set can cause severe internal damage. To make sure yours is at room temperature, disconnect it the day before you move. Also, to protect the screen while moving, tape a pillow over it.

No news here

Whenever possible, pack electronic equipment and small appliances in their original cartons. If you no longer have the original foam padding blocks, cushion the units with bubble wrap or crumpled paper. Don't use shredded newspaper; it can get into the machines and cause internal damage. (For hints on moving a computer, see p. 253.)

Plant relocation

Keep them happy

Pack plants in cardboard boxes that are at least 2 cm higher than the tallest plant. To keep the boxes strong and dry, line them with plastic rubbish bags, and wrap terracotta pots with aluminium foil. Group plants of similar size, and stuff the spaces between them with bubble wrap or loose packing material.

LOADING A TRUCK

If you have a lot of muscle power at your disposal, you may want to hire a truck and do your own moving. Begin by parking the truck as close as possible to your home. Pull out the truck's loading ramp and place it on the highest front step, if possible. Then, following the guidelines shown below, load the truck one-quarter full at a time, packing everything solidly from floor to ceiling. Tie in each quarter with rope, and fill any spaces with small cartons. Be sure to pack the truck snugly to make the best use of the space and to prevent damage to your belongings.

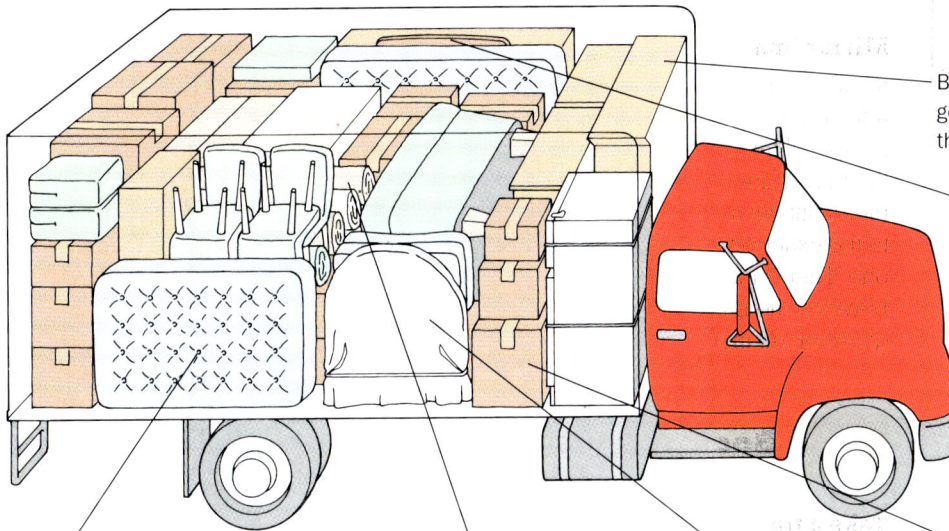

Bring in the largest items first—generally large appliances and then furniture.

Keep mirrors upright, and tie them in place or wedge them between a mattress and box spring. Never lay a mirror flat.

Position long items, such as mattresses and box springs, table tops and sofas, along the sides of the truck and turn them on their edges.

Roll up rugs and place them lengthwise in the centre.

Fit odd-shaped items along the sides or on top of other items.

Put heavy cartons at the bottom and lighter cartons on top. Stack heavy cartons on top of each other only if they are of nearly equal strength and weight.

Sleeves for leaves

Protect delicate foliage from crushing during transit with funnel-shaped plant sleeves. Make your own by rolling lightweight cardboard into a funnel and securing it with tape.

In your new home

In hot water

Upon arriving at your new home, turn on the hot water service so that you will be able to have a badly needed shower by the time you have finished unloading the truck. This will also give you a chance to call a plumber in time should there prove to be any problems.

Lighten up

The first items you should unpack (before it gets dark) are the lamps and other portable light fixtures. Place them around the house, plug them in, and turn them on as needed. If there is nothing to put them on, set them directly on the floor. You'll have light for unpacking, and you'll find out if any fuses are blown or circuit breakers tripped.

MISCELLANEOUS HINTS

Keys

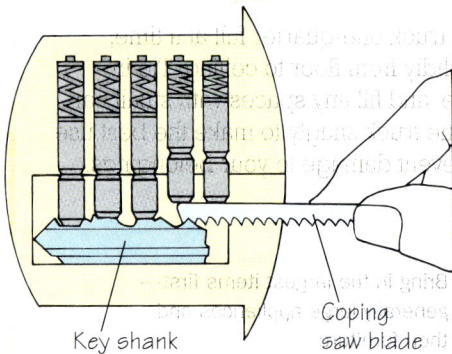

Key shank

Coping saw blade

Key broken in lock ▲

If a key breaks off in a lock, try this. Use a coping saw blade to push up the tumbler pins and grasp the broken key shank. Then, very carefully, slowly pull it out. Don't tug at the key shank, or you may damage the lock. If this doesn't work, call a professional locksmith.

Connect the dots

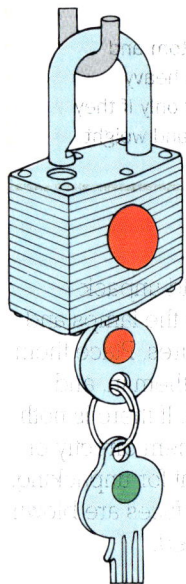

If you carry a lot of keys, it can be tricky to remember which one goes in what lock. Colour-coding your keys and locks will enable you to see at a glance which is the proper key. Simply place a colourful sticker on a key and a matching sticker on the corresponding lock.

Mirror repair

It's all done with mirrors

Want to disguise damaged silver on an old mirror? Simply scrape off any peeling or discoloured silver, and then tape a piece of shiny aluminium foil over the spot on the back of the mirror.

Mirror image

Resilvering an antique, bevel-edged mirror can be expensive. Instead, scrape all the old silver off the back of the mirror and have your local glass merchant cut a new, inexpensive mirror to the exact size and shape of the old one. Then sandwich the new mirror between the backing and the clear glass remaining from the old mirror.

Book repair

Take a tip

To reattach a loose book page, cut a 10 mm strip of tissue paper the length of the page and fold it in half lengthwise. Coat the back of the tissue paper with white PVA wood glue. With the crease toward the spine, place one half of the

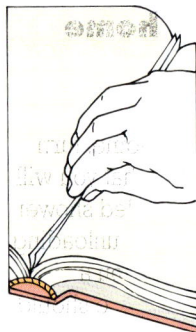

strip on the loose page and the other half on the following page. Push the strip into the spine and line up the pages' outer edges. Place some waxed paper across the strip, close the book, and let the glue dry.

All wet and soggy

Dry out a waterlogged book by placing it in a frost-free freezer for several hours. The freezer will draw the moisture from the book and separate the pages.

Scissors

Bent out of shape ▲

Don't discard a pair of scissors if one of the blades is bent out of shape. Instead, place the blade in a vice between three, evenly-spaced blocks of wood. Tighten the vice slightly. This technique works with bent knives as well.

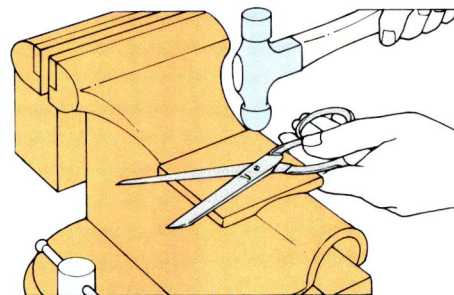

Wiggly scissors ▲

Loose scissors blades? If the pivot is a rivet, or if tightening the pivot screw doesn't help, place the pivot head on a metal surface and hit the other end firmly with a ball-pein hammer.

Cutlery

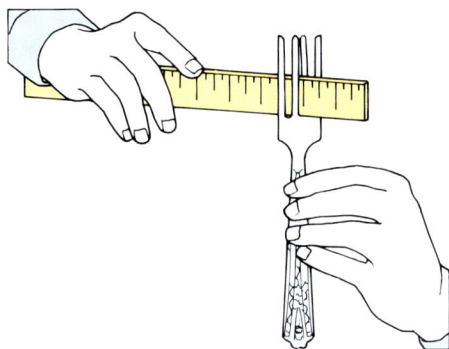

Pointing every which way ▲

Don't discard a fork simply because the tines are bent—straighten them. If the tines of the fork are bent toward each other, insert a cheap wooden ruler between them and force them apart. If they are bent outwards, line a vice with soft cloth and gently tighten it to clamp and realign the tines.

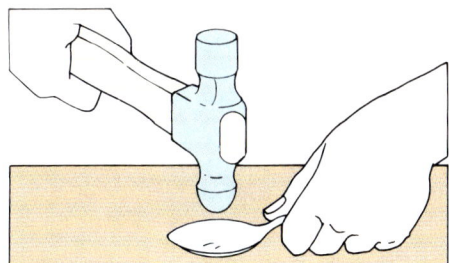

Lumps and bumps ▲

When a spoon gets dented, it usually bulges inward. To fix it, place the spoon on a wooden surface and gently tap it with a ball-pein hammer.

Crockery

A clean fix

Before repairing a piece of crockery, make sure it is clean by soaking it in a solution of half a cup household bleach and 2 litres water, washing it and letting it dry. To fill the crack, use epoxy, either alone or mixed with whiting or kaolin powder and a pigment (all sold by art supply stores). Fill the crack slightly higher than the surface, and smooth with a fine abrasive after the glue hardens.

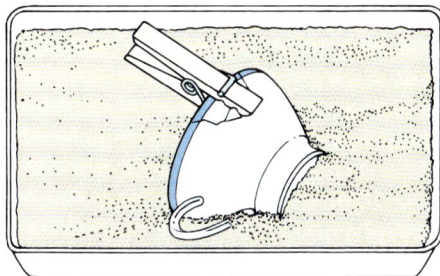

Like a day at the beach ▲

To repair a plate, cup or even a figurine, bury the largest piece in a container of sand with the broken surface just protruding. Make sure the broken surface is horizontal so the other piece balances on it. If the piece won't balance, hold it in place with a prop, or with a simple clamp such as a clothes peg.

Sticky choice

Mend valuable china (or glassware) with a water-soluble adhesive, such as white polyvinyl acetate (PVA) glue, which lets you take a piece apart and fix it again. Use water-resistant epoxy to repair everyday pieces, but keep in mind that once it hardens you can't dissolve it.

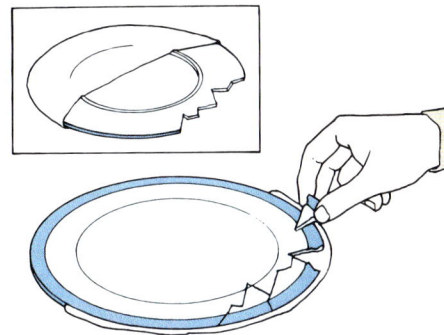

A way with wax ▲

Piecing the parts of a broken plate together is easier if you use a mould. To make one, heat paraffin wax until it softens, then pack it over the bottom of the unbroken side of the plate. After the wax has set, carefully arrange the mould under the broken side and fit the broken pieces in it. Glue only one or two pieces at a time.

Under pressure

To clamp the pieces of a mended plate together while the glue sets, drive six nails in a circle slightly larger than the perimeter of the plate. Lay the plate face down between the nails, and stretch rubber bands over it. ▼

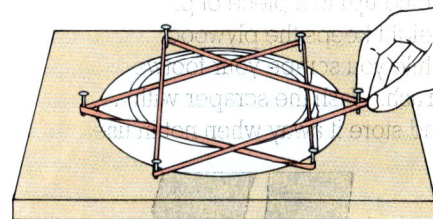

Timing is everything

To remove excess epoxy, wait until it begins to set, then slip a sharp knife point under it and peel it off. If you try too soon you'll smear the glue; too late and you won't be able to remove it.

MISCELLANEOUS HINTS

Boot cleaning aids

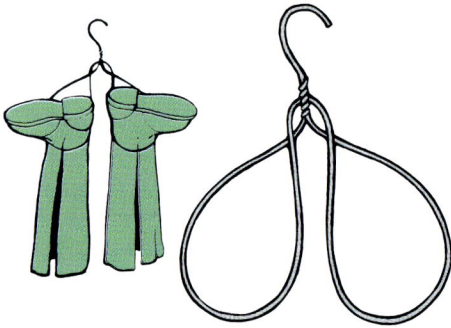

Kick up your heels ▲

Use a coat hanger to speed drying of rubber boots and other footwear. Bend the hanger to create two loops. Slide the boots through the loops, sole side up, and slip the assembly over a hook or nail. Hanging the boots this way helps them retain their shape and speeds drying by allowing plenty of air circulation.

The brush-off

Although this boot and shoe scraper is portable, it won't move around when you use it. Using screws, attach a large, stiff-bristled scrubbing brush (bristles facing up) to a piece of plywood. Your weight keeps the plywood in place while you scrape your footwear on the brush. Wash the scraper with a hose, and store it away when not in use. ▼

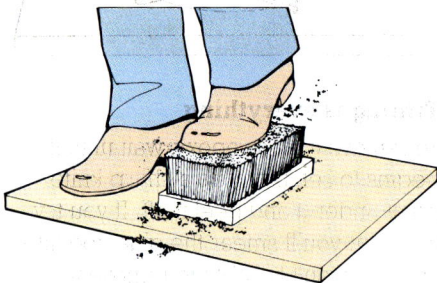

No more mud

Tired of scraping mud off your boots—or worse yet, off your floors? Prevent mud from coming into the house by providing a convenient boot scraper. Pick a location near the back door where there is no danger of someone running into it in the dark. Fill a 30 × 30 cm hole with concrete, and sink a spade 15 cm deep into it. When the concrete dries, you'll have a permanent boot scraper—complete with a handle you can hold on to for balance.

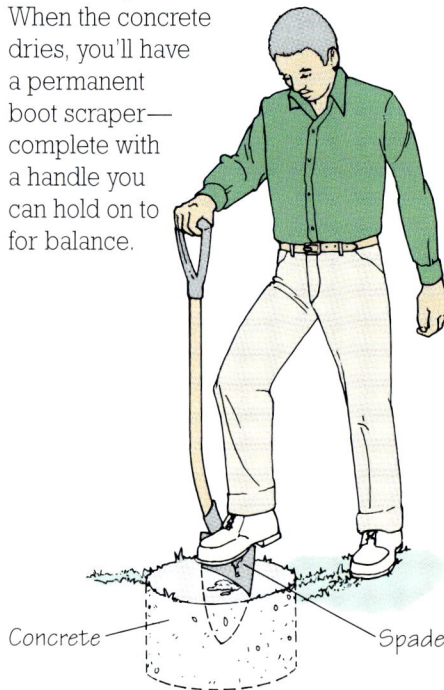

Concrete   Spade

Chains and zippers

Tiny tangles

If a knot develops in a fine chain, don't try to pull it out; you may just tangle it further. Instead, spread the chain on a piece of waxed paper and place a drop of baby oil on the knot; use a couple of straight pins to slowly pick out the knot.

Easy gliding

Have a zipper that's hard to move? Keep it sliding easily by rubbing it with either soap, paraffin wax or pencil lead.

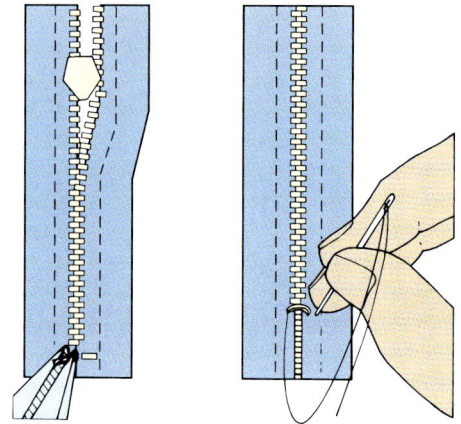

Restoring the zip ▲

If a zipper slider comes loose, prise off the bottom stop of the zipper with a pair of needle-nosed pliers. Then move the slider to the bottom and carefully thread the loose track through the slider. Pull the slider up the tracks, and create a new stop by sewing several stitches at the bottom of the zipper.

Spectacles

Fog lifter

Coat both sides of your spectacle lenses with a thin film of soap suds, let them dry, then polish them with a soft, lint-free cloth. The transparent coating left behind won't impair your vision, but it will keep your glasses from fogging up.

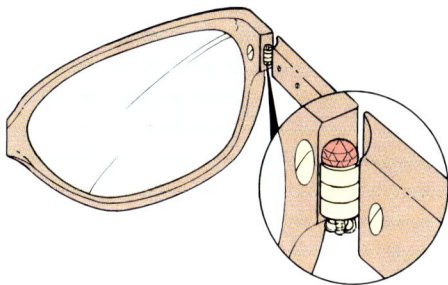

Where did it go? ▲

If you lose the screw that holds one of the side arms to your spectacles, here's a temporary repair. Insert a stud-type earring into the hinge.

No loose screws here

Do the screws keep working loose in your spectacle frames? Coat the threads with clear nail polish. When it dries, the screws should stay in place.

A better bath

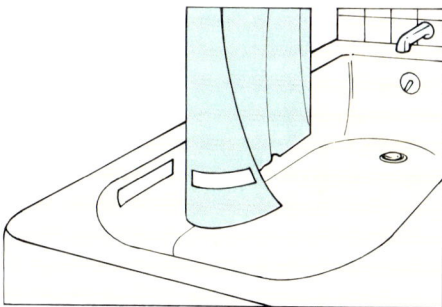

Curtain call ▲

Don't let the curtain attack you next time you enter the shower—keep it in place with Velcro tape. After cleaning the bath or recess, simply attach the tape to both the side of the tub or recess and the bottom of the curtain. Before turning on the water, secure the curtain to the tape.

No more non-slip tape

A 30 minute soak in laundry prewash makes it much easier to scrape off strips of non-slip bathtub tape. Use a single-edge razor blade for scraping, holding it flat against the bath. Finally, remove any excess adhesive by spraying it with aerosol lubricant/penetrating oil, and scrubbing with a towelling rag.

Candle wax

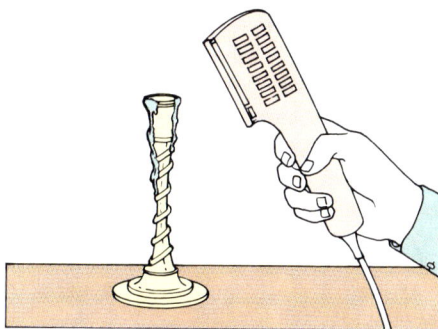

Hot melt ▲

It's difficult to prevent candle wax from dripping and hardening on candlesticks, but clean up can be easy. Remelt dripped wax with a hair dryer set on high heat; work on a small area at a time and wipe off the wax as it softens. After cleaning the candlesticks, mist them with a vegetable cooking-oil spray to make future wax removal easier.

Cool candlesticks

Another way of removing wax from candlesticks is to place them in the freezer for about an hour; the wax should then peel off easily.

Sticky situations

Rejuvenate your tape

Age and weather conditions can dry up masking or electrical tape. Revive the adhesive by popping the tape in the microwave oven, set it on high and leave for about a minute.

Saving postage

Often, when the weather gets warm, the glue on the back of postage stamps melts enough for them to stick together. When this happens, don't throw them out. Instead, place the stuck-together postage stamps in the freezer until they become unstuck.

Photo finish

Heat and humidity often cause photographs to stick together. If your photos were taken within the last 10 years, it's probably safe to soak them apart. Place the photos in a shallow pan filled with tepid water. Every few minutes carefully try to separate them, but if there's even the slightest resistance, continue soaking. Change the water as often as necessary to keep it lukewarm. After separating the photos, dry them by hanging them from a clothesline with spring clothes pegs. ▼

RECYCLING DIRECTORY

Part of the human condition is to accumulate possessions, ending up with lots of leftover and used-up bits and pieces that are going to 'come in handy one day'. And so we're faced with the problem of what to do with all those 'useful' odds and ends, without being wasteful or cluttering up the environment.

Many of the hints in this book show how to make good use of discarded items or leftover scraps of materials, such as carpeting. Following is a guide to such hints, arranged alphabetically by material. If you have a batch of old clothes pegs, tins, unmatched socks or hangers, check the appropriate entries for suggestions on using them. Each entry gives the use, page number and tip title. And just to brighten things up, you'll find a handful of new tips scattered throughout. To find other tips or suggestions, check the index.

A

Ashes
▶ To remove furniture surface burn, p. 229, 'Scorched surface'
▶ To remove smoke stains from fireplace doors, p. 337, 'Recycle those ashes'

B

Baby wipe container
▶ To hold paintbrush during project, p. 177, 'Easy wiper solution'

Bag
▶ Paper bag as dust catcher during drilling, p. 10, 'Wall hang-ups'
▶ Paper bag for removal of excess oil from a fan, p. 245, 'No greasy shower'
▶ Paper bag to contain mess when removing excess water or thinner from a brush, p. 171, 'Go for a spin'
▶ Plastic bag as glove to protect doorknobs, telephone etc., when painting, p. 178, 'Foiled again'
▶ Plastic bag filled with sand or water to exert pressure when gluing together irregular shapes, p. 87, 'Bag it'
▶ Plastic bag for storing and dispensing putty, p. 40, 'Airless container'
▶ Plastic bag to avoid spills when removing car oil filter, p. 295, 'Keep it clean'
▶ Plastic bag to catch sawdust from a table saw, p. 30, 'Collecting dust'
▶ Plastic bag to cover windscreen overnight in winter, p. 317, 'Labour saver'
▶ Plastic bag tô dispose of Christmas tree, p. 339, 'In the bag'
▶ Plastic bag to grease bearings or other parts, p. 242, 'Grease bag'
▶ Plastic bag to keep clamp from sticking, p. 89, 'No sticky clamps here'
▶ Plastic bag to line a workshop vacuum cleaner, p. 63, 'Easy-empty cleaner'
▶ Plastic bag to remove a paint-filled roller, p. 178, 'Another mess manager'
▶ Plastic bag to repair a coolant or windscreen washer reservoir, p. 298, 'It's in the bag'
▶ Plastic bag to retrieve items fallen into toilet, p. 212, 'Hand-bag retriever'
▶ Plastic bag to store leftover paint, p. 195, 'Leftovers again'
▶ Plastic bag with magnet, to pick up spilled washers, nuts or nails, p. 62, 'Magnetic bagger'
▶ Plastic bag to protect distributor from water, p. 315, 'Plastic protection'
▶ Plastic garbage bag as apron, p. 64, 'Instant aprons'

Baking tray
▶ As storage shelf in workshop, p. 56, 'Serving up hardware'

Ball
▶ As buffer on boat antenna, p. 343, 'Follow the bouncing ball'
▶ As chisel cover, p. 20, 'Guard duty'
▶ As guide when parking car in garage, p. 318, 'Things that go bump'
▶ To convert hammer into a mallet, p. 15, 'Cushion the blow'
▶ To cover car bonnet latch to protect person from injury when working on car engine, p. 296, 'Heads up!'
▶ To cover ends of saw fence, p. 31, 'Bumpers for fence guides'
▶ To hold curved pieces in mitre box, p. 84, 'No more bouncing ball'
▶ To keep interior light off when car door is open for extended periods, p. 307, 'Drain plug'
▶ To reduce shock when hammering chisel or star drill, p. 284, 'Concrete shock absorber'

Basket
▶ Large basket to catch sawdust, p. 30, 'Collecting dust'
▶ Laundry basket as substitute for toy box, p. 122, 'A tisket, a tasket'
▶ Plastic basket as equipment holder on ladder, p. 44, 'Basket case'

Baster
▶ To clean drain hole of air conditioner, p. 221, 'Blocked drain holes'

▶ To transfer solvents from one container to another, p. 90, 'Out of the kitchen'

Bath mat

▶ To protect bench top, p. 53, 'Mat top'

Beater

▶ As paint mixer attachment for electric drill, p. 173, 'Home-made mixer'

Belt

▶ As substitute for tool-honing strop, p. 22, 'Home-made strop'
▶ To hold tools on shelf, p. 58, 'Tool belt'
▶ To store a ladder, p. 45, 'Buckle up'
▶ To store a rug, p. 124, 'Flying carpet'
▶ To tie a ladder, p. 45, 'Keep it closed'

Bicycle handlebar grip

▶ For rubbing steel wool in a corner or groove, p. 40, 'For tight spots'

Bicycle tube

▶ To increase torque with hand-screw clamp, p. 36, 'Turning point'

Binder clip

▶ To hang work gloves, p. 64, 'Rubber gloves hanger'

Blue bag

▶ To find leak in swimming pool liner, p. 290, 'Tell-tale stain'

Bottle opener

▶ To help mend cracks in walls when painting, p. 182, 'Attack those cracks'

Bottle or jug (plastic)

▶ Four litre bottle as drip irrigator, p. 271, 'Home-made drip irrigator'

▶ Four litre bottle as nail bin, p. 60, 'Neat nail organisers'
▶ Milk or bleach bottle as funnel for used engine oil, p. 294, 'Diversionary tactics'
▶ Motor oil container as a gutter-cleaning scoop, p. 164, 'Gutter scoop'
▶ Oil container for workshop storage, p. 60, 'Great cheap parts bins'

'A bottle of brushes.' Clean paint-brushes simply and effectively in a large plastic bottle. Just cut a hole in the side of a 4 litre bottle, pour in mineral turpentine or water—according to the type of paint—and insert the brushes. The handle makes it easy to carry. ▼

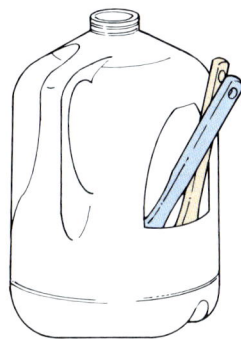

▶ One litre plastic bottle as drill holder, p. 11, 'Drill holder'
▶ Rectangular plastic container as brush holder on belt, p. 170, 'Belted caddy'
▶ Squeeze bottle as refillable glue dispenser, p. 38, 'Economical refills'
▶ Squeeze bottle to apply adhesive to vinyl floor, p. 141, 'Bursting bubbles'
▶ Two litre bottle as scoop, p. 62, 'Nuts and bolts scoop'
▶ Two litre plastic bottle as string dispenser, p. 59, 'String out'

▶ Two litre plastic bottle to protect boat propeller from corrosion in winter, p. 343, 'Bottle it'

'Convenient bag dispenser.' Plastic grocery bags come in handy, but storing them can be a nuisance. Try this quick and simple method for easy dispensing. Using a utility knife or shears, cut off the top and bottom of a 2 litre plastic drink bottle, leaving a 75 mm wide opening at the top. Mount the bottle, top down, on a wall or cupboard door with small screws and washers. Stuff the bags into the bottle, and pull them out as they are needed.

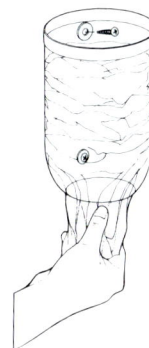

Box

▶ Bread box to hold tools, p. 46, 'Handy storage'
▶ Cardboard box for cleaner spray-painting jobs, p. 240, 'Spray booth'
▶ Cardboard box to shelter saw blade while cleaning, p. 29, 'Oven cleaner'
▶ Detergent box as home-made manual file, p. 41, 'Handy manuals'
▶ 'Disk storage.' The plastic boxes made to hold 5¼ inch computer diskettes are perfect for organising 130 mm sanding discs. Use the dividers to sort and label different grits, coatings and backings.

Brick

'Handy holder.' An ordinary building brick makes a convenient no-spill organiser for holding small parts and tools. For the greatest capacity, select a brick with 10 holes. Glue a piece of cardboard to the bottom to protect the surface it sits on and to keep the items from falling through when the brick is moved. ▼

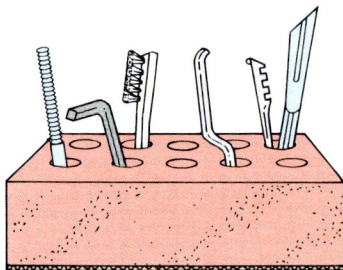

▶ To decrease volume of water in cistern, p. 212, 'Saving water'

Broom handle
▶ To hold a bucket on a ladder, p. 45, 'Bucket holder'
▶ To keep birds off swing set, p. 287, 'Bird foiler'

Broom straw
▶ To extend the reach of an oil can, p. 41, 'Straw applicator'

Brush
▶ Pet brush, to remove loose paintbrush bristles, p. 176, 'Comb-out'

Bubble gum
▶ To temporarily plug a petrol tank leak, p. 308, 'Leak stopper'

Bubble wrap
▶ To line toolbox, p. 46, 'Tool cushion'

Bucket
▶ To avert paint spills when on ladder or scaffold, p. 193, 'Paint caddy'
▶ To hold extension cord, p. 42, 'Cord keeper'
▶ To soak saw blades for cleaning, p. 29, 'Soaking pan'

C

Cake container
▶ As a toy box, p. 122, 'A tisket, a tasket'
▶ To store circular saw blades, p. 29, 'Capping saw teeth'

Candle
▶ To help light a campfire, p. 340, 'Light my fire'
▶ To help wood drawer slide smoothly, p. 223, 'Sand and wax'

Carbon paper
▶ To fix a sticking cabinet door, p. 224, 'Open-and-shut solution'

Cardboard
▶ To confine spray of aerosol paint when touching up car, p. 309, 'Mask task'
▶ To hold screws when disassembling an item, p. 14, 'Keeping track'
▶ To line up upholstery tacks straight and even, p. 224, 'All straight in a row'

Cardboard drum
▶ To store tall items in a wardrobe, p. 118, 'Quick sorts'

Cardboard tube
▶ As extension for vacuum cleaner crevice tool, p. 63, 'Long reach'
▶ To organise moulding, pipe, dowels etc., p. 61, 'Stand-up storage'

Cards
▶ Playing cards for help with sanding curved surface, p. 82, 'A crooked pack'

Carpenter's apron
▶ To help manage a long-handled lopper when pruning, p. 270, 'Pocket holder'

Carpet

'Shake, rattle, and roll no more.' A remnant of foam-backed carpet makes an effective, inexpensive typewriter pad. Place a square, foam side down, beneath the typewriter and it will stay firmly and quietly in place. ▼

▶ As overnight windscreen cover during winter, p. 317, 'Labour saver'
▶ As pad on workbench, p. 82, 'Padded workbench'
▶ As substitute drop cloth, p. 184, 'Go wall-to-wall'
▶ For comfort when standing on concrete floor, p. 49, 'Foot ease'

► On ladder rung, to clean shoe soles, p. 45, 'Shoe cleaner'
► Power tool storage idea, p. 58, 'Power tower'
► To apply contact cement, p. 38, 'Carpet scrap applicator'
► To finish furniture, p. 239, 'Fake wood grain'
► To line car boot, p. 312, 'Carpet capers'
► To line tool box, p. 46, 'Tool cushion'
► To move heavy objects more easily, p. 345, 'Magic carpet ride'
► To pad a sawhorse, p. 54, 'Soft saddle'
► To pad tray of a utility truck for knee protection, p. 312, 'Kneepads'
► To paint underside of door, p. 187, 'The bottom line'
► To prevent items from noisily knocking about in canoe, p. 342, 'Noises off'
► To protect bench top, p. 53, 'Mat top'
► To protect car door from damage in garage, p. 318, 'Door protection'
► To scrub car, p. 310, 'Cheap scrubbers'

Carpet underlay

► With clothes pegs, to use as foam paintbrush, p. 176, 'Make your own disposables'

Caulking tube

► To fill mortar joints, p. 160, 'Mortar quick draw'

Chain

► To draw circles when making layouts, p. 34, 'Circle chain'
► To increase clothes storage, p. 119, 'Put 'em in chains'
► To store toys, p. 122, 'Chain gang'

Chest handles

► To hang tools, p. 58, 'Handle holder'

Clamshell container

► To start seeds, p. 255, 'Greenhouses from the take-away'

Clipboard

'Clip it.' An old clipboard needn't be tossed out. Take the spring clip and screw it to your workbench. It can hold notes or assembly instructions securely in place. An oiled rag held in place by the clip will quickly and easily coat small metal parts. Or secure a piece of steel wool in the clip and periodically draw your soldering iron tip across it to keep it clean. ▼

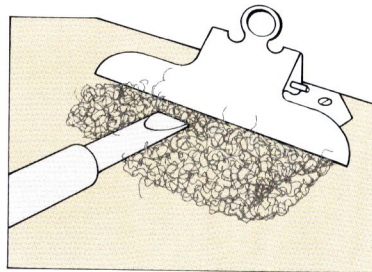

► To store sheet abrasives, p. 25, 'Put it away'
► When sanding small parts, p. 83, 'Against the grit'

Clothes peg

► As a gauge, p. 70, 'Clothes peg on the line'
► To anchor cloth to picnic table, p. 286, 'Cloth control'

► To keep power cords out of the way, p. 51, 'Cord hangers'
► With carpet pad, as substitute for foam paintbrush, p. 176, 'Make your own disposables'

Comb

► To remove loose paintbrush bristles, p. 176, 'Comb-out'

Cork

► For bit storage, p. 11, 'Put a cork on it'
► To build a bulletin board, p. 108, 'Bulletin board'
► To childproof piano or chest, p. 324, 'Prop it up'
► To protect chisels, p. 20, 'Guard duty'

Corkscrew

► To remove plasterboard, p. 137, 'Corkscrew handle'

Cotton bud

► To apply paint when refinishing furniture, p. 238, 'Disposable mini-applicators'
► To mend chipped paint on a car, p. 315, 'Fill 'er up'

Crate

► As combination stool and tool caddy, p. 293, 'Seat relief'

Credit card

► As ice scraper substitute, p. 317, 'Emergency scraper'
► To remove dried nail polish from wood furniture, p. 228, 'Spilled nail polish'

RECYCLING DIRECTORY

Crutches
▶ To keep rain from pooling on boat cover, p. 343, 'Not a puddle in sight'

Curtain rod
▶ As a handy measuring tool, p. 33, 'Sliding track'
▶ As a large compass, p. 71, 'Adjustable rod'
▶ To hang bird feeder, p. 296, 'Slide-out feeder'

Dish rack
▶ For storing tools and supplies, p. 56, 'Recycled dish rack'

Door
▶ As a pasting table, p. 200, 'Table talk'

Door handle
▶ For drawer pull, p. 56, 'Stronger pull'

Drawer knob
▶ To open licence plate holder easily when filling a car's petrol tank, p. 308, 'Filler flap'

Drawing pin
▶ To keep picture hanging straight on wall, p. 323, 'Sticky trick'

Dresser drawer
▶ For under-bed storage, p. 105, 'Recycled drawers'

Earring
▶ Stud earring used to temporarily fix spectacles, p. 353, 'Where did it go?'

Edge guard from car door
▶ To cover lawn mower edges, p. 274, 'A bumper for trees'

Egg carton
▶ To keep small parts in order when repairing appliance, p. 242, 'Parts on ice'

Elastic cord

'No-tip rubbish bins.' If you are having difficulty keeping rubbish bins from tipping or blowing over, try securing them with elastic cords. For each bin, you will need two 9 mm screw eyes and a 80 cm hook-ended elastic cord, available at hardware stores. ▼

▶ As a substitute for web clamp, p. 86, 'You don't have to jump for the cords'
▶ To secure chair legs while the glue dries, p. 227, 'Quick chair clamp'

Electrical box
▶ To store small items, p. 60, 'Ready-made storage modules'

Electrical cable sheathing
▶ For sealing hard-to-reach places, p. 150, 'Reach out to seal'

Film canister cap
▶ To cover G-clamp jaws, p. 36, 'Recycled film caps'
▶ With rubber ball, to hold curved pieces in mitre box, p. 84, 'No more bouncing ball'

Floor mat
▶ To provide a non-skid surface when a car is stuck in snow or mud, p. 317, 'Traction aid'

Flywire
▶ As a sander for paint build-up, p. 182, 'Scraping by'
▶ As a screen to prevent insects from clogging a car's radiator, p. 315, 'Insect screen'
▶ For safety when breaking concrete, p. 284, 'Hold your chips'
▶ To protect light bulb, p. 51, 'Prevent popping lights'
▶ To remove lumps from old paint, p. 174, 'Screen old paint'
▶ With laundry detergent cap, as a wire brush, p. 47, 'The brush-off'

Foam rubber
▶ For router bit storage, p. 27, 'Protect those bits'

'Snug fit.' Keep the contents of your socket wrench case neat and organised by cutting a piece of 6 mm thick foam rubber to fit inside the lid and gluing it in place. When the lid is closed, the sockets will stay put. ▼

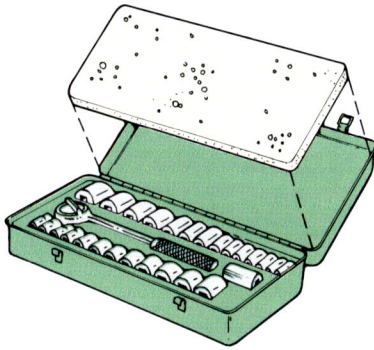

Foil box
▶ Cutting strip from foil or plastic wrap box attached to workbench, to cut tape and cords, p. 53, 'Handy cutter'

Fuel line
▶ For easier threading of a spark plug or nut, p. 293, 'Rubbery spanner'

G

Gloves
▶ Leather gloves to cover plier jaws, p. 19, 'Padded jaws'
▶ Work gloves as pads for ladder ends, p. 44, 'Padded ends'

Golf bag
▶ As a carrier for gardening tools, p. 281, 'Tool caddy'

Golf shoes
▶ As a safety measure when mowing lawn, p. 266, 'Working against gravity'

Golf tee
▶ To plug a vacuum hose for car engine tune-up procedures, p. 397, 'Plugged on purpose'

Guitar plectrum
▶ To apply putty, p. 90, 'For all those guitarists'

H

Hacksaw blade
▶ For gluing large areas, p. 88, 'Spreading the glue'
▶ On the edge of a workbench, p. 53, 'Handy cutter'
▶ To cut sandpaper, p. 80, 'Hack it up'

Hairpin

'Well-groomed wires.' Old-fashioned hairpins and bobby pins are terrific for routing thin loudspeaker or telephone wire along skirting boards, rafters and moulding. Clip off the ends so they slide into the cracks while holding the wire.

Hammer
▶ Using claw to pull up weeds, p. 262, 'Hammer those weeds'

Hammock
▶ For storage, p. 125, 'Hanging around'

Hanger, coat
▶ As substitute for contour gauge, p. 142, 'Shape shifting'
▶ As tissue holder, p. 59, 'Quick wipes'
▶ For drying paintbrushes, p. 177, 'Drying hanger'
▶ In a doorstop, p. 324, 'Finger saver'
▶ To clean drain hole of air conditioner, p. 221, 'Blocked drain holes'
▶ To create winter storage rack, p. 103, 'Winter wear storage'
▶ To hold a paintbrush during a break in the job, p. 176, 'Wire hang-up'
▶ To hold insulation in place, p. 155, 'Old hangers never die'
▶ To hold wallpaper strip, p. 200, 'Hanger hold'
▶ To mount a roller tray, p. 193, 'High roller pan'
▶ To mount pictures precisely, p. 323, 'A dent marks the spot'
▶ To preserve sealant, p. 150, 'Sealant savers'
▶ To remove paint from brush, p. 175, 'Wire tap', and p. 178, 'Hanger helper'
▶ To remove patio bricks or pavers, p. 284, 'Paver puller'
▶ To rest a hot soldering iron, p. 97, 'Resting place'
▶ To speed drying of footwear, p. 352, 'Kick up your heels'
▶ To support a brake calliper when doing engine repairs, p. 305, 'Hang it up'
▶ To temporarily support a dragging exhaust pipe or muffler, p. 299, 'Exhaust drag'

RECYCLING DIRECTORY

▶ To unclog a plumbing trap, p. 213, 'Clearing traps'
▶ When drying paint rollers, p. 178, 'Another hanger trick'

Hanger clips

▶ As substitute for spring clamp, p. 86, 'Spring clamp look-alikes'

Hessian

▶ For texturing when painting, p. 189, 'Texturing Techniques'
▶ To remove softened finish on furniture, p. 234, 'Snappy solutions'

Hook and eye

▶ To keep ladder closed, p. 45, 'Keep it closed'

Hose

'Spring renewal.' Give new life to a worn-out garden hose. Wrap a piece of hose around a newly planted sapling. Staple the ends together around a support stake.

▶ As protective cover on water tap, p. 326, 'No more bumps'
▶ For easier threading of a spark plug or nut, p. 293, 'Rubbery spanner'
▶ For help when sanding curved indentations, p. 82, 'Matching curves'
▶ On shovel, to cushion feet, p. 264, 'Softer stepping'

▶ To carry glass safely and easily, p. 144, 'Another glass carrier'
▶ To cover circular saw, p. 29, 'Capping saw teeth'
▶ To cover level, p. 35, 'Bubble cover'
▶ To keep a rope from fraying, p. 42, 'Rope saver'
▶ To keep power cords out of the way, p. 51, 'Cord hangers'
▶ To make child's swing chain easier to hold, p. 287, 'Swing easy'
▶ To protect axe handle, p. 289, 'Handle saver'
▶ To store saw, p. 21, 'Great cover-ups'
▶ Vent hose, to create a cushioned barrier in garage, p. 319, 'Door-to-door barrier'

I

Ice cream or ice-block stick

▶ To smooth sealant, p. 150, 'A lick of advice'
▶ To shape a mortar joint, p. 160, 'Getting the right shape'
▶ With sandpaper, to sand hard-to-reach places, p. 82, 'Not just a nail file'

Ice cube tray

▶ To keep small parts in order when repairing appliance, p. 242, 'Parts on ice'

Inner tube

▶ To cover circular saw, p. 29, 'Capping saw teeth'
▶ To pad car roof when carrying large items, p. 313, 'Roof padding'

Insulation

▶ Foam insulation to elevate small projects while you finish them, p. 93, 'It's a hold-up'
▶ Foam insulation to make chains on child's swing softer to hold, p. 287, 'Swing easy'
▶ Foam insulation to protect car door from damage in garage, p. 318, 'Door protection'
▶ Pipe insulation for moving mirrors or glass panes, p. 345, 'Glass handles'
▶ Pipe insulation to pad a rake handle, p. 264, 'A blister-proof rake'
▶ Pipe insulation to protect gunwales, p. 342, 'Quiet, please!'
▶ Pipe insulation to seal the bottom of a garage door, p. 318, 'Even it out'
▶ Rigid foam insulation as knee cushion, p. 272, 'Knee protectors'

J

Jar opener

▶ As oil-filter wrench substitute, p. 295, 'Homely solution'

Jumper cable

▶ Battery clips from jumper cable as substitute for spring clamp, p. 86, 'Spring clamp look-alikes'

K

Key ring

▶ To childproof a toolbox, p. 46, 'Keyless lockup'
▶ To childproof electric plugs, p. 24, 'A plug for safety'

Knife holder strip

▶ To hold tools, p. 58, 'Holding power'

L

Ladle, gravy

▶ To transfer liquid stain, p. 90, 'Out of the kitchen'

Lamp

'A well-lit paint job.' If you're painting a room that is not naturally lit by the sun, it is difficult to be accurate. Put an old table lamp to use. Rather than using a shade, wrap aluminium foil around the wire support to form a reflector. You will be able to concentrate the light right where it is needed.

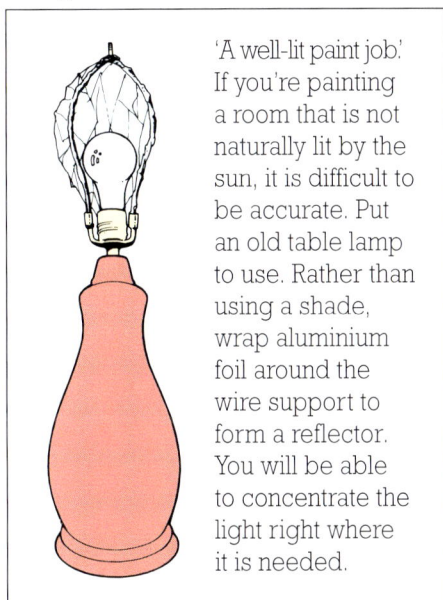

Lampshade frame

▶ To support plants in garden, p. 256, 'Lampshade support'

Laundry detergent cap

▶ With window screen, as a wire brush, p. 47, 'The brush-off'

Lid

▶ Jar lid to hold a squirt of aerosol paint when touching up small chips on car, p. 309, 'Spray away'
▶ Plastic coffee tin lid for mixing paint, p. 173, 'Spatter shield'
▶ Plastic coffee tin lid to catch dust when drilling overhead, p. 10, 'Another dust catcher'

Lunch box

▶ As tool holder, p. 46, 'Handy storage'

M

Map pin

▶ As temporary drawer or door pull, and when painting a cabinet, p. 238, 'Map pin helper'

Marble

▶ As a level, p. 35, 'Marble-ous level'

Matchbox

▶ To sharpen craft knife, p. 41, 'Matchbox sharpener'
▶ To transport a razor blade, p. 41, 'Sharp storage ideas'

Milk or fruit juice carton

▶ To collect draining car engine oil, p. 294, 'Rubbish to the rescue'
▶ To mix paint, p. 173, 'Milk carton mixer'
▶ To start fire in barbecue, p. 336, 'Carton starter'

Money

▶ For taking measurements, p. 32, 'One for the money'

Muslin

▶ To help furniture hold tacks, p. 224, 'Getting a better hold'

N

Nappy

▶ As tack rag, p. 92, 'Make it tacky'

Needle

▶ To clear clogged windscreen washer nozzle on a car, p. 311, 'Clogged washer'

Newspaper

▶ For clean lines when spray-painting, p. 241, 'Clean lines'
▶ For texturing when spray-painting, p. 241, 'Instant feathering'
▶ To fill up key and screw holes when preparing to strip furniture, p. 232, 'Plug up first'
▶ To minimise the mess when stirring a full can of paint, p. 173, 'Newspaper collar'

Nylon netting

▶ For texturing when painting, p. 189, 'Texturing Techniques'

O

Oven rack

▶ Mounted over a wheelbarrow, as a mobile barbecue, p. 336, 'Just rolling along'

RECYCLING DIRECTORY

P

Packing
▶ Rigid foam packing to store razor blades, p. 41, 'Sharp storage ideas'

Paddle
▶ As towel rail, p. 111, 'Paddle bar'

Pan or tin
▶ Aluminium foil pie pan for garden ID tag, p. 255, 'All-weather ID'
▶ Aluminium foil pie pan to keep campfire cookware clean, p. 340, 'Bright and shiny'
▶ Aluminium or plastic pan to make a rack for wet shoes, p. 103, 'Moisture control'
▶ Baking tin as shelf, p. 56, 'Serving up hardware'
▶ Oven pan for cleaning circular saw blades, p. 29, 'Soaking pan'
▶ Ring-type cake tin as outdoor water dish for pet, p. 333, 'No-tip dish'
▶ Standard cake tray or pan as revolving storage shelf, p. 60, 'Workbench catchall'

Panty hose or nylon stockings
▶ To apply finish to wood, p. 92, 'Absorbent stockings'
▶ To check surface smoothness when sanding, p. 83, 'Snagging stockings'
▶ To collect lint from washing machine drain hose, p. 250, 'Lint trap'
▶ To extend life of workshop vacuum cleaner filter, p. 63, 'Thrifty timesaver'
▶ To find rough spot in washing machine interior, p. 250, 'Fabric snagger'
▶ To hold fruit on the vine, p. 257, 'Slinging melons'

▶ To make an emergency fan belt for a car engine, p. 315, 'Temporary fan belt'
▶ To make mouse-repelling sachets, p. 344, 'No more fun and games'
▶ To remove softened finish on furniture, p. 234, 'Snappy solutions'
▶ To strain lumpy paint, p. 174, 'Stocking filter'
▶ To tighten loose furniture joints, p. 227, 'Loose joints 4'

Paper clip
▶ To free a wire from a self-locking electrical terminal, p. 245, 'Paper clip to the rescue'

Pastry brush
To remove dust from a car interior, p. 314, 'The brush off'

Pen
▶ Ballpoint pen, as a dispenser for split shot, p. 340, 'Don't throw it out'
▶ Clip from pen to hold pair of glasses in pocket, p. 64, 'No more broken glasses'

Pencil sharpener
▶ To chamfer ends of dowels, p. 79, 'To the point'

Pegboard
▶ As a trammel substitute, p. 34, 'Pegboard circle'

Phone book
▶ As a disposable work surface for small finishing jobs, p. 93, 'Bring out the Yellow Pages'
▶ To muffle noise when hammering indoors, p. 15, 'Directory assistance'

Pie container
▶ To cover circular saw blade, p. 29, 'Capping saw teeth'

Pie dish or tray
▶ Aluminium, as scraper to remove loosened furniture finish, p. 234, 'No-mess scoop'
▶ For rot-free outdoor chair legs, p. 93, 'Leg rests'

Pill container
▶ For dispensing thin wire solder, p. 97, 'Dispensing solder'

Pin
▶ To clean clogged gas burner on stove, p. 248, 'Clean jets'

Pipe
▶ Copper pipe to mend a burned or stained carpet, p. 140, 'Pile plugs'
▶ Plastic pipe as plant guard in garden, p. 267, 'Cutting out those cut corners'
▶ Plastic pipe as power tool holder, p. 11, 'Drill holder'
▶ Plastic pipe to carry tools in the back of a utility, p. 312, 'Tool caddy'
▶ Plastic pipe to divide apron pockets, p. 46, 'Pockets for tools'
▶ Plastic pipe to extend lip of hand trolley, p. 345, 'Wide loads'
▶ Plastic pipe to hold a bucket on a ladder, p. 45, 'Bucket holder'
▶ Plastic pipe to hold hammer, p. 17, 'Hammer hold'
▶ Plastic pipe to organise moulding, pipe, dowels etc., p. 61, 'Stand-up storage'
▶ Plastic pipe to protect bark of young trees, p. 268, 'A bumper crop'
▶ Plastic pipe to store sanding belt, p. 25, 'Put it away'

Pizza cutter

'Easy slice.' An old sash window that's been painted shut will open easily with the help of a pizza cutter. Run it back and forth in the grooves. Because the blade rolls along instead of being pulled like a knife, it won't cut into the wood.

Plastic wrap box

▶ Attaching strip from plastic wrap or foil box to cut tape, p. 52, 'Handy cutter'

Pliers

▶ As a torch stand, p. 43, 'Prop it up'

Plywood

▶ As a pasting table when hanging wallcoverings, p. 194, 'Table talk'
▶ As a sledge when doing garden work, p. 264, 'A back-saving sledge'
▶ To keep refrigerator door closed, p. 246, 'Open and shut'
▶ To stand on while turfing a lawn, p. 265, 'Make a stand'

Polystyrene

▶ Polystyrene as a kneeling pad, p. 139, 'Save your knees'
▶ To hold small tools, p. 58, 'Small tool organiser'
▶ To protect plane's cutting edge, p. 20, 'Plane rest'
▶ To store saw, p. 21, 'Great cover-ups'

R

Rag

▶ To apply a textured finish to a painted wall or surface, p. 189, 'Texturing Techniques'
▶ To clean up paint spills on trim, p. 194, 'Clean line for trim'
▶ To keep ladder from scratching surface, p. 44, 'Padded ends'

Razor blade

▶ As a scraper to remove paint from window glass, p. 194, 'A clean scrape'
▶ As a scraper to remove old wall-covering from a plaster wall, p. 196, 'Razor's edge'

Record album cover

▶ To cover circular saw, p. 29, 'Capping saw teeth'

Report cover spine

▶ To store saw blades, p. 21, 'Great cover-ups'

Rolling pin

▶ When wetting wallcovering, p. 192, 'One more tray idea'

Rubbish bin

▶ To store long-handled yard tools, p. 273, 'Rubbish bin stand'

S

Safety pin

▶ To clear clogged windscreen washer nozzle, p. 311, 'Clogged washer'

Salt and pepper shakers

'Shake it on.' Salt and pepper shakers are perfect for holding powdered abrasives like pumice and rottenstone. Application is neat and easy to control. ▼

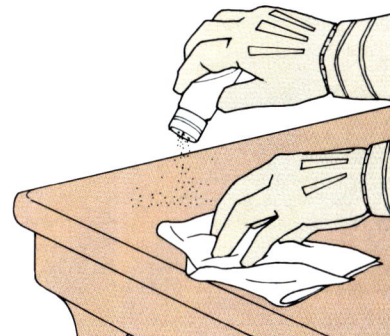

Saucepan

▶ As paint catcher, p. 174, 'Can holder'

Shade or blind

▶ As a substitute for wardrobe doors, p. 119, 'In the shade'
▶ To protect workbench, p. 52, 'Roll-on protection'

Sheet

▶ Bed sheet for texturing when painting, p. 189, 'Texturing techniques'
▶ Bed sheet to tighten loose furniture joints, p. 227, 'Loose joints 4'

Shoe bag

▶ To organise items in car, p. 312, 'Pocket protector'

Shoe sole

▶ To clean sanding belt, p. 25, 'Prolonged life'

RECYCLING DIRECTORY

Shower curtain or liner
▶ As drop sheet when painting, p. 184, 'Drop sheet options'

Shower curtain ring
▶ To store nuts and washers on a pegboard wall, p. 60, 'Nut rings'

Silverware pouch
▶ To store drill bits, chisels and files, p. 46, 'Tool roll-up'

Sink mat
▶ As safety measure on high-chair seat, p. 326, 'Sit tight'

Skateboard
▶ To move heavy objects, p. 345, 'Freewheeling'

Sock

'Sock it to me.' Keep your safety glasses and goggles free from dust and scratches by storing them in a sock.

▶ As ladder pads, p. 44, 'Padded ends'
▶ To collect lint from washing machine drain hose, p. 250, 'Lint trap'
▶ To protect shoes when painting, p. 184, 'Shoe in'

Spade
▶ As a boot scraper in concrete, p. 352, 'No more mud'

Spatula
▶ Plastic spatula to remove furniture stripper, p. 234, 'New use for old tools'

Sponge
▶ To make disposable paintbrushes, p. 176 'Make your own disposables'

Spool
▶ Electrical wire spool to store Christmas lights, p. 124, 'Reel 'em in'
▶ Wooden spool to protect lawn when raking, p. 272, 'Protecting the lawn'

Spoon
▶ Plastic spoon to smooth sealant, p. 150, 'A lick of advice'
▶ To make a spinner for fishing, p. 341, 'Just a teaspoon'
▶ To fashion a mortar joint, p. 160, 'Getting the right shape'

Squeegee
▶ To remove old wet wallcovering paste from plaster walls, p. 197, 'Adhesive clean up'

Steering wheel grip
▶ As a steering wheel heat protector, p. 314, 'Wheel cooler'

Strainer
▶ Food strainer, with coffee tin, to clean paintbrush, p.177, 'Bristle work'
▶ Tea strainer to catch hair in drain when bathing pet, p. 333, 'Drain strainer'

Straw
▶ Drinking straw for measuring, p. 33, 'Dip straw'
▶ For sealing hard-to-reach places, p. 150, 'Reach out to seal'

▶ To position picture wire, p. 323, 'In good position'
▶ To reglue delaminated veneer, p. 230, 'Don't take a sip'
▶ To remove glue, p. 89, 'Sip it up'
▶ To thaw a frozen car lock, p. 317, 'Chilled out'

Suede brush
▶ To clean sanding belt, p. 25, 'Prolonged life'

Suncream
▶ To protect car dashboard and plastic from ultraviolet light, p. 314, 'Sunburn protection for cars'

Swim float
▶ To pad car roof when carrying items, p. 313, 'Roof padding'

T

Tape dispenser
▶ As solder holder and dispenser, p. 97, 'Dispensing solder'

Tape measure
▶ As a portable ruler, p. 32, 'For good measure'

Telephone cord
▶ To organise hanging wires, p. 252, 'The art of concealment'

Tin
▶ Coffee tin as seed spreader, p. 266, 'Coffee tin spreader'
▶ Coffee tin for paint-stripping mess, p. 182, 'Neat solution'

▶ Coffee tin for soaking paintbrush, p. 177, 'Two coffee tin ideas'
▶ Coffee tin to soak hardware in stripper, p. 232, 'Bits and pieces'
▶ Coffee tin with kitchen strainer to clean paintbrush, p. 177, 'Bristle work'
▶ Empty tins to test lawn sprinkler, p. 267, 'Testing a sprinkler'
▶ Small tins as pocket dividers to convert nail pouch into tool carrier, p. 46, 'Pockets for tools'
▶ Soft drink can for mixing epoxy, p. 38, 'Cool it'
▶ Soft drink can to store used razor blades, p. 198, 'Keep an edge'
▶ Tuna or cat food tin to help in cleaning a soldering iron, p. 97, 'A clean tip'
▶ Tuna tin to catch drippings when stripping chair and table legs, p. 233, 'Recycle those tuna tins'

Tissue paper
▶ To keep small items safe when moving, p. 347, 'Bright spots'

Toilet paper holder
▶ As workshop tape dispenser, p. 59, 'All-in-one tape dispenser'

Tongs
▶ To remove muck from gutters, p.164, 'Keep your hands clean'

Toothbrush
▶ As tool when finishing furniture, p. 239, 'Fine freckles'
▶ To apply stain or finish in hard-to-reach places, p. 92, 'Miniature brush'
▶ To remove scale insects from plant leaves, p. 334, 'The brush-off'

Toothbrush holder
▶ To store glass cutter, p. 98, 'Wheel protection'

Towel rail
▶ As rail to aid balance on ladder, p. 45, 'Rail steady'

Trailer stoplight
▶ For workshop signal, p. 49, 'Home alone'

Tray
▶ For workshop storage, p. 56, 'Serving up hardware'

Tricycle
▶ For gardening, p. 264, 'Child's play'

Tubing
▶ Clear plastic tubing for levelling during construction, p. 285, 'Long level line'
▶ Thin tubing for sealing hard-to-reach places, p. 150, 'Reach out to seal'

Tyre
▶ As storage device, p. 61, 'Retreads'
▶ To hold logs while splitting them, p. 289, 'Tyre holder'

Tyre tread gauge
▶ For woodworking measurements, p. 68, 'Rubber gauge'

U

Utensil tray
▶ For storage, p. 20, 'Tray organiser'

V

Veneer
▶ Veneer scraps to enlarge a wood tenon, p. 227, 'Loose joints 3'

Vinyl flooring
▶ As makeshift car mechanic's creeper, p. 293, 'Cheap creep'

W

Wastebasket
▶ For storage, p. 118, 'Quick sorts'

Wine cask bladder
▶ As a store for emergency car radiator water, p. 315, 'Water into wine'

Wire
▶ To clear clogged windscreen washer nozzle, p. 311, 'Clogged washer'
▶ To remove blockages from plumbing traps, p. 213, 'Clearing traps'

Wire shelving
▶ For wet shoe storage, p. 103, 'Moisture control'

Wood shaving
▶ As a joint filler, p. 227, 'Loose joints 2'

Y

Yoghurt containers
▶ As trays for starting seeds indoors, p. 255, 'New life for yoghurt containers'

INDEX

BACK TO BASICS FEATURES

INDEX

INDEX

INDEX

HEALTHY HOME FEATURES

▶ Disposal of compounds with solvents, p. 39, 'Disposing of Hazardous Waste'

▶ Disposal of hazardous waste from car, p. 295, 'Disposing of Car Waste'

▶ Lead in garden soil, p. 257, 'A Lead-Free Harvest'

▶ Lead in paint dust and fumes, p. 183, 'Lead Paint Hazards'

▶ Weathertight house and the build up of carbon monoxide, p. 218, 'Can Your House Breathe?'

I

INDEX

INDEX

INDEX

PVC pipe *(contd)*
  as hand trolley extension, 345
  as hose extension, 164
  as power tool holder, 11
  as spanner holder, 304
  as spool holder, 124
  for stand-up storage, 61
  as tool caddy, 312

Q

Quick-connect terminals, 245
Quick-Grip bar clamps, 37

R

Racks and rails
  in bathrooms, 110–111
  bike, 123
  furniture, 125
  golf, 123
  in kitchens, 108, 109
  in laundries, 112
  over-the-car-bonnet, 124, 125
  shoe, 103
Radial arm saws
  controlling blade depth of, 77
  ripping with, 77
  safety with, 31
Radiators
  car, 298
  reflectors for, 217
Rain gutters, 61
Rakes, blister-proofing of, 264
Random-orbit sanders, 25
Ranges, cooking, 248–249
Rasps, 20, 25
Razor blades, 41
Rebates, 145
Rebating router bits, 27
Recordings, magnetic tape, 253
Records, vinyl, 252
Recycling
  directory of, 354–365
  of labels, 60
Reel mowers, 266

Refinishers, 232
Reflective foil insulation, 153
Reflective tape, 47
Reflectors, 217
Refrigerators, 246–247
Regulations, electrical, 205
Regulations, plumbing, 208
Remote control units, 251
Repointing of bricks, 161
Respirators, 65
Retaining walls, 282
Retractable extension cords, 51
Retreads, 61
Rings, nut, 60
Ripping, 30
Ripping hammers, 17
Ripsaws, 21
Rockwool insulation, loose-fill, 153
Rods, wardrobe, 119
Roller blinds. *See* Window blinds.
Roller pans, on ladders, 193
Rollers, paint
  application of paint with, 185
  care for, 178
  selection of, 179
Roofs, 164–171
  asbestos cement, 170
  cleaning of, 169
  corrugated steel, 166–167
  gutters on, 164
  inspection of, 165
  insulation of, 171
  membrane, 170–171
  mosses and lichens on, 169
  repair and replacement of, 164–171
  safety on, 165
  sheet metal, 166–167
  slate, 168
  tile, 168–169
  vent guards on, 165
Ropes
  for attics, 154
  carrying plywood with, 67
  as chair clamps, 227
  fraying of, 42
  positioning sheet laminate with, 101
Rose bushes, 271

Rottenstone, 363
Rounding-over router bits, 27
Router bits, 26–27
  cleaning of, 27
  combining of, 78
  pilot guides for, 27
  sharpening of, 22
  storage of, 27
Routers, routing
  buying of, 27
  direction of cut with, 78
  housing jigs for, 78
  setting up of, 26
  storage of, 59
  tables for, 26
  troubleshooting for, 78
  use of, 78
Rubber bands, 86
Rubber gloves, 64
Rubber mallets, 17
Rubbish bins, no tip, 358
Rules, rulers, 32
  drafter's, 71
  oversize, 32
  See also Measurers, measuring.
Rust
  of bolts and nuts, 96
  on cladding, 161
  on clamps, 36
  dehumidifiers for, 49
  under paint, 309
  prevention of, 36, 47
  on roofs, 166, 167
  in wheels, 304
Rust converters, 309
Rust removers, 39
R-value, 153

S

Sabre saws. *See* Jig saws.
Safety
  antifreeze and, 298
  asbestos and, 171
  asbestos cement and, 163
  avoiding accidents, 24
  back injuries, 345
  in bathrooms, 326–327, 353

Safety *(contd)*
  carbon monoxide buildup and, 217, 218
  car waste disposal and, 295
  Christmas trees and, 339
  clothing and, 64–65, 328
  dummy plugs and, 207
  during disasters, 328–331
  electrical safety devices, 207
  electrical systems and, 51, 205–207, 245
  fibreglass and, 152
  finishing hazards, 91
  fire control and, 293
  fireplaces and, 337
  fire prevention and, 51, 55, 154
  first-aid kits, 59
  flammable liquids and, 91
  furniture repair and, 233
  garage doors and, 319
  gas smells and, 215
  glass and, 144–145
  hazardous wastes and, 39, 55, 91, 194, 295
  hot water and, 327
  ladders and, 44–45
  lead-base paint and, 183
  lead-contaminated soil and, 257
  in lifting heavy objects, 345
  in lighting pilot lights, 215
  in mowing, 266
  outdoor power tools and, 275
  play sets and, 287
  power tools and, 24, 275
  protective equipment, 65
  red markers and, 31
  roofs and, 165
  safety switches and, 207
  shock prevention, 51, 245
  in stripping furniture, 233
  surge protectors and, 207
  swimming pools and, 290
  table saws and, 31
  in working under car, 294
  See also Childproofing; Disasterproofing
Safety First features. *See box on facing page.*
Safety glass, 98
Safety goggles, 65, 98, 141, 145

SAFETY FIRST FEATURES

▶ Appliance repair and test to prevent shock, p. 245, 'Safe Appliance Repairs'

▶ Asbestos cement hazards, p. 163, 'Safe Working With Fibro'

▶ Child accident prevention, p. 325, 'Safe at Home'

▶ Children's outdoor swing and slide set hazards, p. 287, 'Play Set Rules'

▶ Christmas tree dangers, p. 339, 'Christmas Tree Care'

▶ Electrical risks in the workshop, p. 51, 'Avoid Shock'

▶ Finishing compounds for wood and their hazards, p. 91, 'About Finishes'

▶ Fire extinguisher selection for garage and car, p. 293, 'Fire Control'

▶ Fire prevention in the workshop, p. 55, 'Fighting Fire'

▶ First-aid kit for the workshop, p. 59, 'First-Aid Kits'

▶ Furniture stripping compounds and their hazards, p. 233, 'Stripping Risks'

▶ Lifting heavy loads, p. 345, 'Protect Your Back'

▶ Outdoor power tool precautions, p. 275, 'How to Be Careful'

▶ Power tool precautions, p. 24, 'Avoiding Accidents'

▶ Roof repair precautions, p. 165, 'Care Up There'

▶ Safety work gear selection, p. 65, 'Protective Equipment'

▶ Table saw precautions, p. 31, 'Power Saws'

INDEX

T

INDEX

TOOLS OF THE TRADE FEATURES

▶ Brushes for applying finish, p. 92, 'Choosing the Right Brush'

▶ Clamps for holding jobs together, p. 37, 'User-Friendly Clamps'

▶ Electric drill for everyday jobs, p. 11, 'Buying a Drill'

▶ Hammers to match the task, p. 17, 'Hammers'

▶ Handsaw types, p. 21, 'The Right Saw'

▶ Jig saw and common blade types, p. 29, 'Jig Saws'

▶ Plumbing tools, p. 208, 'The Plumber's Toolbox'

▶ Post hole digging tools, p. 277, 'Tools for Post Holes'

▶ Router and basic bits for it, p. 27, 'Buyer's Guide'

▶ Screwdrivers and the various types of tips, p. 13, 'Screwdrivers'

▶ Stud-locating devices, p. 135, 'Stud Finders'

▶ Vacuum cleaner for workshop clean up, p. 63, 'A Workshop Cleaner'

INDEX

XYZ

Acknowledgments

*The editors wish to thank the
following organisations for the
assistance they provided:*

American Plywood Association
Atlas Van Lines, Inc.
Carol Cable Company
DAP, Inc.
Emergency Management
    Australia
Emperor Clock Company
Food and Drug Administration
Gem Electric Manufacturing
    Company, Inc.
GE Wiring Devices
Hardwood Plywood & Veneer
    Association
Hoover (Australia) Pty Ltd
HPM Industries Pty Ltd
National Association of Canoe
    Liveries & Outfitters, Inc.
National Glass Association
National Paint & Coatings
    Association
Nodak Farm & Home
North American Insulation
    Manufacturers Association
NSW Technical and Further
    Education Commission
Protector Safety Pty Ltd
Ridgeway Clocks
Rubbermaid Incorporated
Sligh Furniture Co.
Tahran Paint and Decorating
    Center
WAP International